Additional Praise for *Breaking the Heart of the World:*

"Dismiss the idea that yet another book on the League fight might be redundant. Cooper places the struggle in the widest possible context and in the process makes a major contribution to our understanding of the sometimes troubling nature of American political culture. He also provides a needed lesson for the current generation of historians, namely that insight and judiciousness are not mutually exclusive qualities."

– William C. Widenor, author of *Henry Cabot Lodge and the Search for an American Foreign Policy*

"John Milton Cooper, Jr. has produced a masterpiece of meticulous scholarship and incisive argumentation. Never before has the debate on American participation in the League of Nations been so thoroughly analyzed on the basis of such extensive research. And never before have the implications of Woodrow Wilson's ultimate failure been so intelligently – and so regretfully – explored."

– Niall Ferguson, author of *The Pity of War: Explaining World War I*

"The story of Woodrow Wilson's shattered dream of a new world order has never been told before with such sympathy, rigor, and panache. We are all indebted to Cooper for his masterly narrative of the collision between the President who first led this country into war in this century and those at home who defeated him in its aftermath. It is a tragic story, the story of a fall from a great height, for after it, Wilson was in every respect a broken man. A sobering account of a moment which could have gone the other way."

– Jay Winter, *Columbia University*

BREAKING THE HEART OF THE WORLD

Woodrow Wilson and the Fight for the League of Nations

JOHN MILTON COOPER, JR.
University of Wisconsin, Madison

CAMBRIDGE UNIVERSITY PRESS

PUBLISHED BY THE PRESS SYNDICATE OF THE UNIVERSITY OF CAMBRIDGE
The Pitt Building, Trumpington Street, Cambridge, United Kingdom

CAMBRIDGE UNIVERSITY PRESS
The Edinburgh Building, Cambridge, CB2 2RU, UK
40 West 20th Street, New York, NY 10011–4211, USA
10 Stamford Road, Oakleigh, VIC 3166, Australia
Ruiz de Alarcón 13, 28014 Madrid, Spain
Dock House, The Waterfront, Cape Town 8001, South Africa

http://www.cambridge.org

First published 2001

Printed in the United States of America

Typeface Sabon 10/12 pt.   *System* QuarkXPress®   [GH]

A catalogue record for this book is available from the British Library.

Library of Congress Cataloging in Publication Data

Cooper, John Milton.
  Breaking the heart of the world : Woodrow Wilson and the fight for the League of
  Nations / John Milton Cooper, Jr.
      p. cm.
    Includes bibliographical references and index.
    ISBN 0-521-80786-7
      1. United States – Foreign relations – 1913–1921. 2. Wilson, Woodrow, 1856–
  1924. 3. League of Nations – History. 4. Wilson, Woodrow, 1856–1924 – Health.
  5. World War, 1914–1918 – Peace. I. Title.

E768.C66 2001
973.91′3 – dc21

                                                                    2001025489

ISBN   0 521 80786 7   hardback

In Memoriam

Arthur Stanley Link, 1920–1998
Margaret Douglas Link, 1918–1996

Contents

Acknowledgments

As lonely as they complain of being, all authors incur many debts along the way of writing their books. Scholars in general and historians in particular take on especially large burdens of indebtedness, which they can only repay with thanks. Such repayment affords them a moment of pure pleasure, which I wish to enjoy now.

Librarians and archivists from one corner of the country to the other have aided me in searching for and finding material. The list of manuscript collections consulted gives some indication where these indispensable helpmeets are located. Special thanks should go to that great institution in my home state and hometown, the State Historical Society of Wisconsin, which has proved itself again for me the best place of all for research in American history. Several people gave me special help that greatly expedited my research, namely, Allen Bond, Elizabeth Cooper Doyle, Glen Gendzel, Christopher Leahy, and Erez Manela.

Fellow writers and scholars most generously shared their gifts and knowledge with me by reading the manuscript of this work and by offering advice and criticism from which I have profited greatly. They are John Morton Blum, Elizabeth Cooper Doyle, Anthony Gaughan, Robert Kraig, Thomas Sutula, and John Thompson. Cambridge University Press enlisted the services of several accomplished historians who likewise shared their knowledge and insight to my great profit. Lloyd Ambrosius, Frank Ninkovich, and especially Thomas Knock produced commentaries and suggestions that helped me immensely.

Others have contributed to this enterprise in different ways. At Cambridge University Press, Frank Smith has lived up to his reputation as a model editor and fount of encouragement, while Alia Winters has dealt with the innumerable necessities of putting a book together. G&H Soho, Inc., especially Mary Jo Rhodes and Christina Viera, did a marvelous job of turning the manuscript into a book. My family, and particularly my wife Judith, have kept my spirits up and my priorities straight over more years of this enterprise than we care to remember. Finally, on a sad note, two people who gave so much to me and so much to all scholars who work in this era are no longer here to receive my profound thanks. The dedication is a small token of the appreciation and gratitude that I feel for them.

Introduction: The League Fight

"The League fight" was the name that contemporaries gave to the events of 1919 and 1920, and this name has stuck to them ever since. The name appears to have originated with the central protagonist in the conflict. In September 1919, as he toured the country giving speeches to plead for membership in the League of Nations, President Woodrow Wilson called the conflict "this great fight for the League of Nations." Others soon shortened Wilson's phrase to "the League fight."[1]

Up to a point, this name aptly characterizes what happened in the United States at the end of World War I. These events had all the ingredients of a fight except actual physical blows. They swept passionately committed people into opposing camps. The leading antagonists were men, and some women, who were hardened veterans of earlier political battles. They often proclaimed themselves to be "fighters," and they were convinced that the stakes in this combat were both figuratively and literally mortal. Moreover, the League fight occurred at the end of the most destructive war in human history up to that time. As a result, more than three quarters of a century after the event, the heat and din of the fight can still be felt and heard.

Yet, apt though the name may be, to call these events a fight does not comprehend their scope and character. For one thing, its passions and antagonisms never obscured the grandeur of the fundamental issue. The quality of thought and expression that went into its debates were almost always high. Indeed, they were usually far more elevated than in almost any political debate in the United States since the Civil War. For American foreign policy, this conflict elicited a breadth and depth of discussion that had not arisen before and that remain unmatched since. Given the ferocity of the fight, it is astonishing how few appeals there

1. Woodrow Wilson speech at San Diego, Sept. 19, 1919, in Arthur S. Link, ed., *The Papers of Woodrow Wilson* (Princeton, N.J., 1990), LXII, 382.

I

were to fears, hatreds, and prejudices. Dwelling on the combative aspect also obscures two of the most important features of the League fight. One was the large area of agreement that existed among the principal antagonists. The other was the virtual unanimity of basic assumptions and values that embraced even the most bitterly opposed participants. Several times this conflict could have ended in a compromise settlement that would have partially satisfied most of the main contenders and pleased the great majority of the American people.

Furthermore, the League fight would almost certainly have resolved itself into some such compromise but for the actions of a single person. As everyone then and later recognized, that person was Woodrow Wilson. His overweening role in World War I and its aftermath has always been beyond dispute. Winston Churchill gave a classic expression of the assessment of Wilson's role when he wrote in the early 1920s:

> It seems no exaggeration to pronounce that the action of the United States with its repercussions on the history of the world depended, during the awful period of Armageddon, upon the workings of this man's mind and spirit to the exclusion of almost every other factor; and that he played a part in the fate of nations incomparably more direct and personal than any other man.[2]

Churchill was writing about the war itself and American intervention in 1917, but his judgment holds equally true for the League fight. Other factors besides Wilson's thought and emotions also shaped the course of events in 1919 and 1920, as they had done earlier. Still, when other influences and actions have received due consideration, two incontrovertible facts remain. First, the League fight would not have taken the form that it did without Wilson. His plans and strategies set the terms and laid out the arena of the conflict. Second, the League fight would not have ended as it did without Wilson. At almost any stage he could have brokered a settlement that would have resolved the conflict differently.

There is an additional reason why appreciating this single person's critical role is essential to an understanding of the League fight. To Churchill's appreciation of "this man's mind and spirit" must be added another element – his body. Wilson's physical condition played an inescapably crucial role in the course of events. Midway through the League fight, at the beginning of October 1919, he suffered a severe cerebrovascular accident – better known in popular parlance as a "stroke." The devastating impact of that stroke on Wilson himself and on the League fight are incontrovertible. The president's incapacity

2. Winston S. Churchill, *The World Crisis* (London, 1923), III, 229.

removed him from physical contact with all but a handful of other participants for the rest of the conflict. It left him unable to deal with the situation at all for more than a month after the stroke. This was just at the time when the sides in the League fight were positioning themselves for their first showdown. Even after he began to recover somewhat, the effects of the illness left him incapable of exercising sound judgment about what he and his supporters should do. But the role played by Wilson's physical condition also needs to be viewed from a broader perspective. The kind of stroke that he suffered does not occur as a bolt out of the blue. Such strokes cast lengthy premonitory shadows on their victims' health and behavior. Wilson's actions particularly during the three months before the stroke likewise need to be judged at least partly in light of his impending physiological catastrophe.

The crucial role played by one person's physical condition in such a momentous struggle reflects on more than just that person's character, gifts, and shortcomings. This aspect of the League fight speaks to both the structure of the American system of government and the larger stakes of this conflict. The president collapsed at a critical juncture in the history of the United States and the world. More than the League fight occupied America in 1919 and 1920. Truly terrible events also exploded during these months, in the form of nasty domestic turmoil over labor and race relations, economic readjustment, and free speech and rights of dissent. After Wilson's stroke, those other pressing concerns received even less attention and action from him than his sporadic interventions in the foreign policy controversy. The impact of these troubles illustrated the overreliance of twentieth-century American politics and government on the office of the president and its occupant. Most pointedly, Wilson's collapse furnished the clearest case that has yet occurred of what the Constitution defines as presidential "inability." This episode glaringly exposed the inadequacy of the Constitution's original provision for dealing with presidential incapacity. Wilson either should have stepped down – preferably voluntarily, perhaps provisionally – or should have been removed from office through the intercession of sympathetic colleagues. Why neither of those solutions prevailed forms an important dimension of the League fight.[3]

The centrality of Wilson and his health to this conflict points to its largest dimension of all. As nearly everyone recognized at the time, the League fight was about much more than American membership in the

3. Since Wilson's time, the Twenty-fifth Amendment has been adopted to deal with presidential incapacity. There is considerable disagreement about the adequacy of this amendment to deal with cases of presidential disability.

new international organization set up by the president and the peace negotiators in Paris at the beginning of 1919. The participants all knew that they were caught in a great historical moment. Their words and deeds would profoundly affect the fate of generations to come. Their decisions would touch the peoples of the whole world. This perception of truly momentous stakes guided the actions of all the principal contenders in the League fight. This perception led Wilson to formulate the strategy that made him and eventually his illness play such a critical role. A different leader with different perceptions might well have guided matters in other directions and caused less political damage through the accidents of health. Other participants – opponents, critics, and supporters of the Wilsonian approach – likewise acted from a comparable perception of the earthshaking risks and opportunities that surrounded their conduct. Not everyone saw those stakes in the same way, but none of the major actors ever forgot the high seriousness of their words and deeds.

The fundamental issue in the League fight involved primarily American foreign policy: What should be its values and aims, its scope and direction, and its conduct and control? A secondary but equally significant issue involved how the future role of the United States would affect world politics.

On the first point – American foreign policy – the contenders appealed to two prevailing sentiments. One was Americans' virtually unanimous belief in their country's uniquely virtuous and democratic character. The other was vigilant regard for such national interests as security, prosperity, and sovereignty. Few participants in the League fight strayed outside these bounds of common assumptions. On rare occasions, more idealistic spokespersons might verge on an almost sacrificial vision of American service in the cause of peace, freedom, and justice. The advocates of League membership, self-styled "internationalists," held no monopoly on such idealism. Some of their most fervent opponents, who were often tagged as "isolationists," painted equally glowing pictures of world uplift.

Other critics and opponents of the League sometimes expressed hardbitten suspicion toward human motives and skepticism about amelioration of the human condition, but those expressions almost never sprang from deeply held regard for what later came to be called "realism." Anything verging on that attitude was usually momentary and tactical. Dour reflections about ignoble aims always referred to other nations, in Europe and Asia – never to the United States of America. The disagreement over values and goals really revolved around the proper mixture of idealism and self-interest. All sides in the League fight insisted that their positions would promote both ends.

The fight over the scope and direction of foreign policy ranged across a broad spectrum of opinion. At one end, League enthusiasts wanted to make common cause with other nations to create a new international community. In the middle were people who either more guardedly accepted or grudgingly acquiesced in League membership. At the other end stood those who demanded outright rejection and insisted on the largest possible freedom of national action. The opposite poles of thought on this question produced nearly all of the most eloquent arguments. For the internationalists the premier exponent was Wilson himself. For the isolationists, who preferred to call themselves "Irreconcilables," the finest spokesperson was Senator William E. Borah of Idaho. But the bulk of the participants and the main body of debate occupied the middle ground. There, the concern was how to reconcile this projected leap into more committed international involvement with practical regard for sovereignty and caution.

The isolationists appealed to hallowed tradition, especially George Washington's warning against "permanent alliances" and Thomas Jefferson's ban on "entangling alliances." Curiously, however, they attracted only a small minority to their way of thinking. Insistence on an unimpaired Monroe Doctrine also drew broad support and figured centrally in the debates and maneuvers. Yet it remains striking that large majorities of Americans in 1919 and 1920 were willing to take some steps away from the hallowed policy of avoiding international commitments outside the Western Hemisphere. The importance of isolationism lay less in its immediate impact than in its future influence. The League fight elicited more thoughtful, well-rounded expressions of isolationist views than had come before. These debates afforded such resourceful speakers as Borah and his senatorial colleague Hiram Johnson of California an opportunity to make isolationism a major strand of their subsequent careers. Equally important, the League fight occasioned the cultivation of promising future constituencies for isolationist policies. That was especially true among ethnic groups that were alienated by the treatment accorded their homelands and among liberals who were disillusioned by what they perceived as betrayals of international idealism. These constituencies figured to some extent in the League fight, but they would play much larger roles in the massive isolationist upsurge of the 1930s.

In the League fight itself, the main contention was over how best to conduct American foreign policy and who should control that conduct. This aspect assumed by far the greatest immediate importance, and this was what branded the whole affair with its inescapable character as a fight. This struggle over conduct and control had three interlocking dimensions. Those dimensions were, in ascending order of significance: first, formal and constitutional; second, partisan and factional; third, personal, strategic, and ideological.

The first dimension formed the skeleton of the conflict. The framers of the Constitution had laid out a field for unending contention when they separated powers between the executive and the legislative branches and, by both enumeration and implication, gave both branches a role in foreign policy. The League fight occurred at a particularly painful juncture in this struggle. During the two preceding decades, many developments had expanded the role and powers of the executive. That expansion of executive power had stemmed from three factors. One was the set of international commitments that flowed from the Spanish-American War. The second was the diplomatic activism of Republican presidents Theodore Roosevelt and William Howard Taft, as well as that of the Democrat Wilson. Finally and foremost came the departures of World War I. At the same time, succeeding Congresses and the Senate in particular had resisted that expansion of executive power by varied means. Those means of resistance included debate and criticism, obstruction of initiatives and reduction of appropriations, and, in the case of treaty making, limitations through amendments and reservations.

In those circumstances, it seems unlikely that even the gentlest, most collegial, and least partisan approach would have guaranteed harmonious relations between the Capitol and the White House over the momentous issues that arose at the end of World War I. As matters transpired, just the opposite approach prevailed. The initial fault lay largely, though not entirely, with President Wilson. During the first part of the League fight, he radically asserted the executive prerogative in foreign affairs. He declined to take counsel with legislative leaders and refused to include anyone from Capitol Hill among the American negotiators at Paris. Wilson compounded the problem by likewise avoiding counsel with noncongressional leaders of either party. Why he chose to pursue such an approach and how that choice affected the course of events are intriguing, critical questions.

Yet, as in other great controversies in American history, the formal and constitutional dimension provided only the skeleton, not the muscle and blood of the events. What moved and shook the struggle between the two ends of Pennsylvania Avenue was its best noted and most frequently deplored feature – partisanship. Because American two-party politics are essentially adversarial, some degree of clash over these big issues was probably unavoidable. Still, conditions at the end of World War I made the situation particularly sour. Bitterly fought midterm elections in November 1918 had given the United States divided government by awarding majorities in both houses of Congress to Wilson's Republican opponents. That circumstance boded ill for cooperation over peacemaking and League membership. Whether a more conciliatory approach on the president's part might have dampened rancor and helped to build bridges of bipartisanship poses another critical question.

It took two sides to fail to cooperate, and the Republicans have earned their share of criticism as well. Then and later, their behavior drew special scorn as an example of allegedly seeking selfish advantage at the expense of nobler goals. That scorn was undeserved at the time and remains misplaced in retrospect. To blame the Republicans, or the Democrats, in 1919 and 1920 for behaving like partisans is like blaming the weather for the way the League fight unfolded. Moreover, such blame misinterprets the true meaning of the parties' respective interests. Naturally, as committed political professionals, Democratic and Republican leaders sought to make hay out of the League fight. Likewise, as human beings with strong personalities, they could not avoid being swayed by personal feelings about each other. Ill will ran high on both sides. Nearly every leading Republican cordially despised Wilson, while the president regarded most of them with anger and contempt. Nor did good fellowship extend broadly within the respective parties. Both of them were suffering from wrenching factional divisions over domestic issues.

Those circumstances did not plumb the depths of this partisan dimension of the conflict over the conduct and control of foreign policy. The champions of both parties' main positions spun grand designs for the role of the United States in world politics, and the terms of League membership played a critical part in those designs. During the preceding three years Wilson had wrought the considerable feat of weaning the Democrats away from their previous isolationist leanings. He had instilled instead an acceptance of international activism based on transcendence and reform of traditional power politics. At the same time, leading Republicans – such as ex-presidents Roosevelt and Taft, former secretaries of state Elihu Root and Philander C. Knox, and Senator Henry Cabot Lodge – had been working to extend and refine their party's earlier thrust toward greater international activism within the framework of traditional power politics. Persistent isolationist sentiment showed that neither of these approaches commanded unanimous support within its own camp, but these competing approaches to international activism, Wilsonian and Republican, formed the grounds of contention between the two biggest sides in the League fight. Herein lay the deepest aspect of the partisan conflict. Democrats and Republicans

alike believed that they were contending for the soul of American foreign policy.

More than that, these partisans in 1919 and 1920 believed that they
were contending over the future course of world politics. This was the
other deep-delving issue in the League fight. For most of the participants, concern about world politics was secondary to the contention
over American foreign policy. But this concern remained intimately
intertwined with that conflict, and it was fought with equal fervor. All
participants feared and wished to prevent a repetition of what they
called "Armageddon" – the huge, hideous global conflict that had just
ended. Between and within the main contending camps, and among the
isolationists as well, many disagreed about whether and when there
might be another world war, but only a few denied that one could
happen.

Instead, nearly everyone presented ideas for ridding the world of the
risk of another global conflagration. Wilson and League advocates con-
tended that safety for America and the world could come only through
wholehearted participation in an organization that would strive to
defuse international tensions, foster mediation and arbitration of disputes, promote arms reduction, and, as a last resort, be empowered to
enforce collective security procedures. The majority of Republicans likewise welcomed procedures to dampen conflicts and stressed the development of international law, but they did not welcome arms reduction
and viewed collective security with a jaundiced eye. For them, the road
to national and global safety lay through continued exercise of the
greatest possible American sovereign power. Some of those Republicans
also conceded that such sovereign power should be exercised within
international consultative arrangements and perhaps also within carefully limited security commitments to a few other nations. Some isolationists denounced any effort to prevent a future world war as a snare
and a delusion, but other isolationists maintained that the path to peace
lay through a luminous American example of the avoidance of militarism, excessive armaments, and any form of international power politics. In short, nearly all the participants believed that they were also
contending for the soul of the world.

This global issue invested the League fight with its greatest momentousness at the time, and it continues to lend poignancy to the event
eight decades afterward. This issue was what Wilson invoked when he
challenged Americans to build a new world order by joining the League
of Nations. "Shall we or any other free people hesitate to accept this
great duty?" asked the president when he presented the Treaty of Ver-

sailles to the Senate in July 1919. "Dare we reject it and break the heart of the world?"[4]

Eventually, both of those things did happen. The United States did reject League membership. The heart of the world did break with another, more terrible world war exactly twenty years later. Did the one thing cause the other? Would Wilson's design have saved the world from that second deluge of death and destruction? Would Wilson's design have spared the world a further half century of upheaval, bloodshed, and threatened global annihilation? Could Wilson and his adversaries have found a satisfactory approach to salvation through compromise? Would they have tried to reach a meeting of their minds if the president had not become incapacitated or if others had acted in different ways? What reverberations and legacies did this great debate and controversy leave for those who came afterward? These questions still haunt the League fight, and they deserve to be answered as well as they can be answered.

4. Woodrow Wilson address to Senate, July 10, 1919, in Link, ed., *Papers of Wilson*, LXI, 434.

tion between those great nations which sincerely desire peace and have no thought themselves of committing aggressions."[3]

That bare statement constituted all that Roosevelt or anyone else said about a peace-enforcing league of nations until the outbreak of World War I. The war itself and the glaring failure of earlier peace projects to prevent it spawned fresh and urgent interest in international enforcement on both sides of the Atlantic. Starting in September 1914, in a series of magazine articles, Roosevelt argued that "surely the time ought to be ripe for the nations to consider a great world agreement among the civilized military powers *to back righteousness by force.* Such an agreement would establish an efficient world league for the peace of righteousness." During the next two months, he urged that the "great civilized nations which do possess force . . . combine by solemn agreement in a great World League for the Peace of Righteousness," and he demanded that the United States must "become one of the joint guarantors of world peace under such a plan."[4]

These ideas soon attracted other Republican advocates. In June 1915, Roosevelt's closest friend, Henry Cabot Lodge, became the second prominent American advocate of international enforcement. In a commencement address at Union College in Schenectady, New York, the dapper, aristocratic senator from Massachusetts likened armed force in international relations to fire in human life. Lodge maintained that this presently "unchained" entity must be controlled rather than abolished. Such control must come through "substitution of the force of the community" for the force of individual nations. "The great nations must be so united," Lodge maintained, "as to be able to say to any single country, you must not go to war, and they can only say that effectively when the country desiring war knows that the force which the united nations place behind peace is irresistible." Lodge had coined the name of a future peacekeeping world body.[5]

Even before Lodge spoke out, other Republicans had also warmed to the idea of international enforcement. Starting in January 1915, a group

3. Theodore Roosevelt, Nobel Prize address, May 5, 1910, in Hermann Hagedorn, ed., *The Works of Theodore Roosevelt* [National Edition], XVI, 308–309.

4. Roosevelt, "The Belgian Tragedy," *Outlook*, Sept. 23, 1914, in ibid., XVIII, 27, 29–30; "How to Strive for World Peace" *New York Times*, Oct. 18, 1914, ibid., 53; "An International Posse Comitatus," *New York Times*, Nov. 8, 1914, ibid., 83.

5. Lodge, "Force and Peace," speech of June 9, 1915, in Henry Cabot Lodge, *War Addresses, 1915–1917* (Boston, 1917), 32–35, 40–41.

of lawyers, editors, and professors met regularly in New York to found a national group that would draw up plans for an international peace-keeping organization and lobby for its creation. They enlisted several public figures in their movement, including the president of Harvard University, A. Lawrence Lowell, and their biggest catch was ex-President William Howard Taft. This group held its founding convention at Philadelphia on June 17, 1915, where they adopted a platform that called for "a league of nations" in which member states would pledge to settle disputes peacefully and "jointly use forthwith both their economic and military forces against any one of their number that goes to war." They named their organization the League to Enforce Peace, and they elected Taft their president. Usually known thereafter by its initials, the "LEP" quickly became the strongest advocate of the league idea and later of membership in the League of Nations.[6]

In addressing the LEP convention, Taft struck the same notes as Roosevelt and Lodge had done. "We do not think the ultimate resort to force can be safely omitted from any effective League of Peace," he declared. Taft proposed likewise "only to include the more powerful nations," and he rejected any "demand for equal representation of the many smaller powers." Taft also injected a newfound note of urgency. The sinking of the *Lusitania* just six weeks earlier, on May 7, 1915, had raised the danger of the United States' being drawn into the world war. In response, Taft challenged America's traditional isolation from world politics outside the Western Hemisphere. "We have got to depart from the traditional policy of this country," he avowed. The world war had shown that Americans must "step forward and assume certain obligations in the interest of the world . . . [because] we are likely to be drawn in ourselves."[7]

Both the political pedigrees and the arguments of its advocates had guaranteed that the league idea would rouse opposition. The first response came from the likeliest quarter of all. Speaking in New York just two days after the LEP meeting, William Jennings Bryan denounced its program as "a policy of 'fighting the devil with fire.'" Americans would be repudiating the hallowed American policies of Washington and Jefferson and the Monroe Doctrine in order to make "ourselves partners with other nations in the waging of war." Joining other nations in such a

---

6. League to Enforce Peace, "Warrant from History," June 17, 1915, quoted in Ruhl J. Bartlett, *The League to Enforce Peace* (Chapel Hill, N.C., 1944), 40–41. On the inception and founding of the LEP, see ibid., 25–47.

7. *League to Enforce Peace, American Branch: Independence Hall Conference held . . . (June 17th) 1915* (New York, [1916]), 15–16, 18–19.

league, Bryan had charged, "by the terms of which we let them declare war for us and bind ourselves to furnish our quota of men and money . . . would not be an ascent to a higher plane; it would in itself be a descent and would impair our influence and jeopardize our moral prestige." Americans would do far better to "remain true to the ideals of the fathers and . . . be content with the glory that can be achieved by a republic," eschewing "empire" and "military glory" in order "to rely upon the uplifting power of that which is pure and good and noble."[8]

Everything about Bryan made him the perfect opponent of the league idea as it had thus far developed. For nearly twenty years, as the Democratic party's three-time presidential nominee and ideological conscience, he had opposed earlier Republican foreign policies. He had especially abhorred Roosevelt's and Taft's great power activism, which he saw as thinly disguised imperialism. That opposition had made him one of only two first-rank American political figures with widely known foreign policy views; the other was his opposite and nemesis, Roosevelt. Also, by the time that he spoke out against the LEP, Bryan had shown that he could back his words with deeds, even at the cost of personal sacrifice. Less than two weeks earlier, he had resigned his post as secretary of state in protest against what he had seen as Wilson's willingness to risk war with Germany in response to the sinking of the *Lusitania*.[9]

Not everyone who shared Bryan's approach to foreign policy rejected international enforcement. Throughout 1915 and 1916, a number of pacific-minded Democrats, third-party Progressives, and Republicans – including senators Robert M. La Follette of Wisconsin and George W. Norris of Nebraska – had spoken favorably about novel methods to require nations to settle disputes peacefully. Conversely, not all devotees of Republican-style great power activism liked the league idea. Both Lodge's son-in-law, Representative Augustus Peabody Gardner of Massachusetts, and Roosevelt's earlier imperialist cohort, Albert J. Beveridge, scorned the league idea as a chimerical peace project that might endanger sovereign control over such essential matters as immigration or territorial integrity. Even the erstwhile progenitor of the league idea now repudiated his brainchild. In August 1915, in a magazine article about American foreign policy toward the world war, Roosevelt had warned,

8. Bryan speech, June 19, 1915, in *The Commoner*, XV (July 1915), 9.
9. On Bryan's foreign policy, see Kendrick A. Clements, *William Jennings Bryan: Missionary Isolationist* (Knoxville, Tenn., 1982); and on his denunciation of the LEP, see John Milton Cooper, Jr., *The Vanity of Power: American Isolationism and the First World War, 1914–1917* (Westport, Conn., 1969), 54–59.

"Even the proposal for a world peace of righteousness, based on force being put back of righteousness, is inopportune at this time." Not until Americans were "prepared to make our words good . . . and willing to back up our deeds" would they be entitled "to move for the establishment of a world agreement to secure the peace of justice." Until then, the United States "would excite merely derision if it propositioned at this moment the creation of a 'World League for Peace.'"[10]

Roosevelt did not dismiss the league idea altogether – only what he regarded as its untimely presentation by Taft and the LEP. In part, his reaction had stemmed from his break with Taft in 1912, first to oppose him for renomination by the Republicans and then to bolt and run as head of the new Progressive, or "Bull Moose," party. Bad blood still ran hot between the two ex-presidents. But Roosevelt's stand was also consistent with his earlier opposition to Taft's foreign policy, especially the effort to extend the scope of international arbitration. It might be tempting to interpret Roosevelt's turnabout as an assertion of "realism" in the face of suspected utopian tendencies among league advocates. In the same magazine article, he scorned "childish make-believe" and the "spirit of grandiloquent and elocutionary disregard of facts." Yet, as many observers then and later recognized, Roosevelt was no cold-eyed realist. He was an international moralist and national idealist. In that article he also praised the warring peoples of Europe for "showing splendid and heroic qualities," and he lauded all those in history who had fought "successful wars for righteousness."[11]

One person remained conspicuously silent amid these first largely (though not simply) partisan debates over the league idea. That was President Wilson. The accidents of politics had given the Democrats a leader who had not shared the party's earlier Bryanite leanings in foreign policy. This prim, polished, long-jawed former professor and president of Princeton University not only looked different from the image that the Democrats had projected since 1896 under Bryan – he was different. In both domestic and foreign affairs, he had embraced lines of thinking that bore a strong resemblance to Roosevelt's, especially in his enthusiastic endorsement of Republican-style great power activism at the turn of the twentieth century. Back then Wilson had echoed Roo-

10. Roosevelt, "Peace Insurance by Preparedness against War," *Metropolitan* (Aug. 1915), in Hagedorn, ed., *Roosevelt Works*, XVIII, 298–299. On other early espousals and rejections of the league idea, see Cooper, *Vanity of Power*, 37, 59–60, 121–122.

11. Roosevelt, "Peace Insurance," in Hagedorn, ed., *Roosevelt Works*, XVIII, 299, 304, 311, 314.

seveltian preaching on how strenuous engagement in world politics would ennoble politics and society at home. Since then, however, Wilson had gotten himself into rhetorical harmony with the Democrats' more pacific approach to foreign affairs, and until the sinking of the *Lusitania* he had gotten along comfortably with Bryan as his secretary of state. Still, in view of what had gone before, an espousal by Wilson of the league idea might have been expected.[12]

Just when Wilson came to believe in international enforcement is not known. A decade later, his brother-in-law and closest friend, Stockton Axson, recalled that shortly after the outbreak of World War I the president had privately laid down four principles for the reform of international relations – no more conquests, equality of rights among great and small nations, no more private manufacture of munitions, and "an association of nations, all bound together for the protection of the integrity of each, so that any one nation breaking this bond must bring upon herself war; that is to say, punishment, automatically." Also, in December 1914 Wilson drafted a plan for nonaggression, arbitration arms reduction, and avoidance of war in the Western Hemisphere. This "Pan-American Pact" never came to fruition, but it was noteworthy that its first clause read: "That the contracting parties to this solemn covenant and agreement hereby join in a common and mutual guarantee to one another of undisturbed and undisputed territorial integrity of the complete political independence under republican forms of government." This marked Wilson's first use of the word "covenant," and the words of this clause offered an uncanny prefiguration of Article X, the collective security provision of the Covenant of the League of Nations.[13]

Preoccupied as he was with both the trials of diplomacy with the warring nations and his struggle with Bryan for control of the Democratic party, Wilson did not choose to speak out on the league idea for

12. On Wilson's earlier foreign policy thinking, see John Milton Cooper, Jr., *The Warrior and the Priest: Woodrow Wilson and Theodore Roosevelt* (Cambridge, Mass., 1983), 60–61, 119–120; and Thomas J. Knock, *To End All Wars: Woodrow Wilson and the Quest for a New World Order* (New York, 1992), esp. 3–30.

13. Ray Stannard Baker interview with Stockton Axson, Feb. 8, 10, 11, 1925, Ray Stannard Baker Papers, Library of Congress, Box 99; Wilson, "A Draft of a Pan-American Treaty," [Dec. 16, 1914], in Link, ed., *Papers of Wilson*, XXXI, 471–473. On this draft, see entry, Dec. 16, 1914, Edward M. House Diary, ibid., 469–470. Doubts about when Wilson first privately espoused the league idea are raised in Knock, *To End All Wars*, 99. Based upon a close examination of Axson's papers, Knock argues that Wilson probably made this utterance in February 1915. See ibid., 288, n. 12.

over a year. He finally broke his silence in a speech to the LEP on May 27, 1916. Echoing Taft, he called for a departure from traditional isolation. "The interests of all nations are our own also," he declared – even those of "the nations of Europe and Asia." But Wilson departed from earlier advocates of enforcement with his pointed advocacy of reform of international relations. He called for such changes as open diplomacy among nations, the right of all peoples to choose their own sovereignty, equal rights for all nations, and freedom from aggression. To institute those rights, he affirmed that "the United States is willing to become a partner in any feasible association of nations formed in order to realize these objects and make them secure against violation." Wilson looked forward to the time "when coercion shall be summoned not to the service of political ambition or selfish hostility, but to the service of a common order, a common justice, and a common peace."[14]

Wilson soon both hedged and clarified this new stand. In a Memorial Day address, the president harked back to Jefferson's ban on entangling alliances and avowed:

> I shall never myself consent to an entangling alliance. But I would gladly assent to a disentangling alliance – an alliance which would disentangle the peoples of the world from those combinations in which they seek their own separate and private interests and unite the people of the world upon a basis of common right and justice.

He also personally wrote into the Democrats' 1916 platform commitments to uphold the international principles of sovereign choice, territorial integrity, equality, and freedom from aggression, and he included a pledge that "it is the duty of the United States to join with the other nations of the world in any feasible association . . . to prevent any war begun either contrary to treaty covenants or without warning and frank submission of the provocation and causes to the opinion of mankind." Wilson had unfurled his colors as a league man.[15]

During the 1916 campaign both parties and their candidates largely avoided the question. The Republican platform endorsed "pacific settlement of international disputes and . . . the establishment of a world court," but the Republican platform committee scrapped the draft of a plank endorsing the LEP program. Reportedly, the person who demanded that the endorsement be dropped was Senator Lodge. Up to

---

14. Wilson speech to LEP, May 27, 1916, in Link, ed, *Papers of Wilson*, XXXVII, 113–116.
15. Wilson address, May 30, 1916, ibid., 126; Wilson draft of platform [ca. June 10, 1916), ibid., 195–196.

then Lodge had continued to say kind words about the league idea, and he had shared the speakers' platform with Wilson before the LEP on May 27. A major about-face was in the works. Still, the Republican nominee, former Supreme Court Justice Charles Evans Hughes, called for "the development of international organization" that would be backed by "the preventive power of a common purpose . . . [and] some practical guarantee of international order." Hughes likewise affirmed that "there is no national isolation in the world of the Twentieth Century." Thereafter, the league idea figured in the campaign mainly in occasional references by Wilson.[16]

Things changed dramatically once the election was over and the president knew that he had won a second term. For the first time in international affairs, Wilson demonstrated the extraordinary boldness that had been the hallmark of his political career at home. In December 1916 and January 1917 he mounted a campaign to end the war and establish a new world order based upon international reform and the enforcement of peace. Principle and practicality alike motivated him. Though never a pacifist, Wilson had begun to despair at the evidently endless, fruitless, man-devouring carnage of the Western Front. Sometime during 1916, most likely in November, Wilson had written in a private memorandum, "Where is any longer the glory commensurate with the sacrifice of millions of men required in modern warfare to carry and defend Verdun?" Practical considerations also moved Wilson to act. Ever since his endorsement of the league idea, its ardent advocates in both America and Britain – where mediation and peacekeeping programs had attracted significant left-wing and trade union support – had appealed to the president to try to end the war, negotiate a just, nonimperialistic peace settlement, and inaugurate a new world order based on international enforcement. There were also multiplying signals of renewed threats of being dragged into the war. Private reports were coming from Germany that pressures were mounting to reopen and expand submarine warfare.[17]

In response Wilson mounted a multifaceted, high-stakes diplomatic offensive to mediate the war. He injected the league idea into the maneuver in a public diplomatic note to the belligerents asking them to state their terms for ending the war. He asserted that all of those nations

16. Republican platform, quoted in Bartlett, *LEP,* 58; Hughes speech of July 31, 1916, in Charles Evans Hughes Papers, Library of Congress, Box 182. On Lodge's role in dropping the endorsement, see Bartlett, *LEP,* 57–58, and William C. Widenor, *Henry Cabot Lodge and the Search for an American Foreign Policy* (Berkeley, Calif., 1980), 240–241.

17. Wilson, "prolegomenon" to peace note, [ca. Nov. 1916], in Link, ed., *Papers of Wilson,* XL, 71.

had declared themselves "ready to consider the formation of a league of nations to ensure peace and justice throughout the world." Therefore, Wilson offered American membership in such a league as an inducement to the belligerents to make peace. Americans, the president avowed, "stand ready, and even eager, to cooperate in the accomplishment of these ends when the war is over with every influence and resource at their command."[18]

Wilson's move stirred up hornets' nests of recrimination on both sides of the Atlantic. The sharpest attacks at home emanated from Roosevelt and other Republicans who strongly favored the Allied side, but the most significant debate revolved around Wilson's offer to commit the United States to a league of nations. In early January 1917, Senator William E. Borah, Republican of Idaho, denounced the proposal with an isolationist argument that was strikingly similar to Bryan's earlier blasts at the LEP. Borah charged that Wilson was proposing to allow "other nations to make war upon the United States if we refuse to submit some vital issue of ours to the decision of some European or Asiatic nations. This approaches, to my mind, moral treason." Such an "alliance" would thrust America "to the very storm center of European politics. We have abandoned the policy of nearly a century and a half and entered directly and at once upon that policy which was condemned by the Father of our Country in the very beginning of the Government."[19]

Those remarks heralded the emergence of a major contender in the upcoming League fight. Recently reelected to a third term in the Senate, the fifty-three-year-old Borah had not previously interested himself much in foreign policy. Instead, this square-jawed orator whose thick mane of hair earned him the nickname of the "Lion of Idaho" had distinguished himself as a formidable though theatrical advocate of domestic reform against Taft and party conservatives. The events of 1915 and 1916 – especially the combination of the threat of entering the world war, increased military preparedness, and the spread of the league idea – had impelled Borah to think more deeply about world politics. Now, at the beginning of 1917, he was coming out as an isolationist. Between his oratorical gifts and his dogged, studious, moralistic approach to political issues, Borah brought formidable talents to the nascent debate.[20]

18. Diplomatic note to belligerent nations, Dec. 18, 1916, ibid., 274. "Ensure" was Wilson's own word, which he substituted for "enforce" in an earlier draft. Ibid., 276 n. 2.
19. *Congressional Record*, 64th Cong., 2nd Sess. (Jan. 5, 1917), 892–895.
20. On Borah's espousal of isolationism, see Cooper, *Vanity of Power*, 136–142.

Borah's entry into the debate also indicated shifts in alignments for and against the league idea. Both Bryan and Roosevelt wrote to commend him for attacking Wilson's proposal. The ex-president waxed especially wrathful against the linkage of international enforcement to an attempt to end the world war. Wilson's use of the league idea to boost possible mediation likewise prompted Senator Lodge to make a public about-face on international enforcement. Privately, Lodge had condemned the LEP as early as the previous April for trying "to bind us to all kinds of things which the country would not hold to." When Wilson had opened the peace initiative in December, Lodge told Roosevelt, "I regret that I ever got mixed up with it [the LEP]." Publicly, Lodge accused Wilson of partiality toward Germany and of attempting to effect "a departure from the hitherto unbroken policy of this country."[21]

Dissent at home and the wary-to-harsh responses from the belligerent nations failed to deter the president from pressing forward. On January 22, 1917, in a surprise speech to the Senate, Wilson delivered the most sweeping and significant foreign policy pronouncement yet of his career. Declaring that America "must lay afresh and upon a new plan the foundations of peace among the nations," he called for a "covenant of cooperative peace" undergirded with "a force . . . so much greater than the force of any nation." The key to those foundations must be to end the present war in "a peace without victory," not a "victor's terms imposed upon the vanquished. . . . Only a peace between equals can last. Only a peace the very principle of which is equality and a common participation in a common benefit." Other parts of those foundations would be equality of rights among nations and the ability of peoples to choose their own governments. He pointed to the nonexistence of "a united, independent, autonomous Poland" as a universally conceded example of a wrong to be righted, and he called for free access to and use of the ocean lanes and limitation of armaments on land and sea. In laying down these principles, Wilson claimed to speak not just for the government and people of the United States, but "for the silent mass of mankind everywhere who have as yet had no place or opportunity to speak their real hearts out."

Bold as Wilson was, he also showed signs of his having heard his domestic critics. The reference to overwhelming force was his only implicit allusion to the league idea, and he closed the speech with the assertion:

21. Lodge to Sturgis Bigelow, Apr. 5, 1916, Henry Cabot Lodge Papers, Massachusetts Historical Society; Lodge to Roosevelt, Dec. 21, 1916, Theodore Roosevelt Papers, Library of Congress, Box 316; *Congressional Record,* 64th Cong., 2nd Sess. (Jan. 3, 1917), 792–797.

> I am proposing, as it were, that the nations should with one accord adopt the doctrine of President Monroe as the doctrine of the world: . . . that all nations henceforth avoid entangling alliances which would draw them into competitions of power, catch them in a net of intrigue and selfish rivalry, and disturb their own affairs with influences intruded from without. There is no entangling alliance in a concert of power. . . . These are American principles, American policies. We could stand for no others.

Clearly, Wilson was trying to disarm his critics by appealing to both Democratic pacific and Republican activist foreign policy approaches.[22]

This escalation of the president's peace offensive met with a mixed response. Except for the newspapers published by William Randolph Hearst, nearly every Democratic politician and journal praised Wilson in glowing terms. Even Bryan lauded the president's "brave and timely appeal to the war-mad rulers of Europe." On the league question Bryan said that he hoped further development of Wilson's ideas would show "that there is no reason for difference." That endorsement foreshadowed another about-face on international enforcement, which would lead Bryan to become a steady, though never terribly enthusiastic, supporter of Wilson in the League fight. Likewise, among Republican progressives, Senator La Follette conspicuously praised the "peace without victory" speech, while Senator Norris called a peace-enforcing league "something worthy of a trial and fair consideration of honest men everywhere in the civilized world."[23]

A few other Republicans also endorsed the president's peace initiative and his use of the league idea. Taft, despite privately snarling at the linkage to mediation, declared that the LEP's members "rejoice sincerely" at Wilson's utterance. One Republican senator, Porter J. McCumber of North Dakota, applauded "the idea of world-enforced peace" and declared that an international organization to promote that principle was "no more an entangling alliance than the compact of our States for a general government." Later, during the League fight, McCumber would emerge as by far Wilson's staunchest Republican supporter in the Senate.[24]

Other prominent Republicans, such as Elihu Root, the party's elder statesman in foreign policy, and Charles Evans Hughes, the recently

22. Wilson address, Jan. 22, 1917, in Link, ed., *Papers of Wilson,* XL, 533–539.
23. Bryan to Wilson, Jan. 26, 1917, ibid., XLI, 29; Bryan speech, Feb. 2, 1917, in *The Commoner,* XVII (Mar. 1917), 8; *Congressional Record,* 64th Cong., 2nd Sess. (Jan. 24, 1917), 1883.
24. Taft in *New York Times,* Jan. 23, 1917; McCumber in *Congressional Record,* 64th Cong., 2nd Sess. (Feb. 1, 1917), 2231–2235.

defeated presidential candidate, remained publicly noncommittal. But the main reaction among both Republicans and former Progressives was unmistakably hostile to the league idea. Most Republican senators greeted the "peace without victory" address with derision and dissent. Lawrence Sherman of Illinois thought the president's proposal "will make Don Quixote wish he had not died so soon." Borah declared, "What this passion-torn world needs and will need are not more leagues and alliances, but a great untrammeled, courageous neutral power, representing not bias, not prejudice, not hate, not conflict, but order and law and justice."[25]

The most formidable opposition came from Lodge. In a lengthy, carefully prepared speech, he argued that genuine peace "rests upon justice and righteousness," which could just as easily be gained by conquest as by mutual concessions. To Wilson's invocation of the Monroe Doctrine, Lodge answered, ". . . if we have the Monroe Doctrine everywhere we may be perfectly certain that it will not exist anywhere." The league idea struck him as tempting but perilous. "There is no halfway house to stop at," Lodge maintained. "The system must be either voluntary or there must be force behind the agreement." Admitting his own earlier attraction to the league idea, he observed that "the more I have thought about it the more serious the difficulties in the way of its accomplishment seem to be."

Lodge also condemned Wilson's proposal because it required the abandonment of America's traditional diplomatic isolation. He insisted that he had "no superstition in regard to Washington's policy," but he also believed "that we should not depart from it without the most powerful reasons and without knowing exactly where that departure would lead." For Lodge, Wilson's vision justified no such departure. He saw "in this tortured and distracted world nothing but peril in abandoning our long and well-established policies." The nation's traditional avoidance of alliances contained "no lurking place" for the president's conception of a league and a new world order. Rather, America's isolationist principles were "as clear as the unclouded sun at noonday, and are not collections of double-meaning words under which men can hide and say they mean anything or nothing."[26]

These debates and alignments at the beginning of 1917 offered a

25. Sherman in *New York Times*, Jan. 23, 1917; Borah in *Congressional Record*, 64th Cong., 2nd Sess. (Feb. 7, 1917), 2749.
26. Ibid. (Feb. 1, 1917), 2364–2370. For an excellent analysis of this speech and the thinking behind it, see Widenor, *Lodge and American Foreign Policy*, 256–260.

foretaste of things to come. Some elements in this dress rehearsal for the League fight – especially the roles played by such leading actors as Wilson, Taft, Lodge, and Borah and the centrality of partisan conflict in the events of 1917 and 1920 – accurately foreshadowed the main event. The biggest difference between 1917 and 1919 would involve the peace-inclined and left-leaning elements that Wilson had attracted to his foreign policies. The president would lose much of their support because he took the country into the war and then allowed a hate-filled, repressive climate to flourish during the fighting. Except as a dress rehearsal for the League fight, however, this debate over "peace without victory" was beside the point. On January 31, 1917, the Germans announced that they were immediately resuming submarine warfare against all shipping to the Allied nations. The threat of involvement in the world war at once shoved aside all other issues, and two months later, after much agonizing by President Wilson and debate in Congress and the press, the United States did take up arms.

American intervention transformed the league idea into a war aim. Wilson used his vision of "peace without victory" as a justification for belligerency. On April 2, in his address to Congress asking for a declaration of war, he affirmed, "I have exactly the same things in mind now that I had in mind when I addressed the Senate on the twenty-second of January last." But now, he insisted, "a steadfast concert for peace can never be maintained except by a partnership of democratic nations. . . . It must be a league of honour, a partnership of opinion." Wilson pledged that

> we shall fight for the things which we have always carried nearest our hearts – for democracy, for the right of those who submit to authority to have a voice in their own governments, for the rights and liberties of small nations, for a universal dominion of right by such a concert of free peoples as shall bring peace and safety to all nations and make the world itself at last free.[27]

In his appeal to righteousness and honor, Wilson seemed to echo the original Rooseveltian expressions of the league idea as a directorate of like-minded "righteous" great powers. Actually, the resemblance owed

27. Wilson speech, Apr. 2, 1917, in Link, ed., *Papers of Wilson*, XLI, 523–524, 526. In his second inaugural address, on March 5, 1917, as he struggled to find the proper response to the crisis, Wilson restated his ideas for a new world order as seven principles that "we shall stand for, whether in war or peace." Those included the proposition "that peace cannot securely or justly rest upon an armed balance of power." Ibid., 334.

more to the need to rally an uncertain, reluctant people and congress than to any shift in Wilson's views. The president had undertaken his most delicate foreign policy task. He was attempting to implement his vision of a new world order through American belligerency and coalition warfare alongside, but at a distance from, the Allies.

Fortuitously, Wilson found a golden opportunity to pursue those aims when the Bolsheviks seized power in Russia at the end of 1917 and denounced both sides in the war as imperialistic. At this critical juncture, the American president restated his views in such a compelling way as to bend the Allies at least temporarily and ostensibly toward his vision of a new world order. In an address to a joint session of Congress on January 8, 1918, Wilson laid down a "programme of the world's peace, . . . the only possible programme" under a set of Roman numerals that became known as the Fourteen Points.

Timing and specificity, not novelty, made this speech so significant. War weariness and dissent among liberal and left-wing elements in the Allied countries required a persuasive response to Bolshevik charges that both camps of belligerents were sacrificing their peoples, especially their working classes, on the altar of capitalist greed and imperialistic power politics. Wilson responded by proposing such concrete steps as the evacuation and indemnification of Belgium; restoration of Alsace and Lorraine to France; and territorial adjustments in Central and Eastern Europe, the Balkans, and Asia Minor on the basis of nationality and fair adjustment of colonial claims. On broader issues, Wilson broke new ground with Point I: "Open covenants of peace, openly arrived at," but otherwise he merely restated the principles that he had been presenting for almost two years, such as insistence upon "freedom of navigation upon the seas," removal of trade barriers, and reduction of armaments. Perhaps most important, he conflated international enforcement and equal treatment of nations into the single statement of Point XIV: "A general association of nations must be formed under specific covenants for the purpose of affording mutual guarantees of political independence and territorial integrity to great and small states alike."[28]

Wilson's declaration fired the imaginations of liberals and progres-

28. Wilson speech of Jan. 8, 1918, ibid., XLV, 536–538. It should be noted that the words "self-determination" do not appear in the Fourteen Points address, and Wilson did not lay down any such general principle in this speech. The phrase originated, in fact, three days earlier in a speech by the British Prime Minister David Lloyd George, in which he asserted "the right of self-determination." See Lloyd George, *War Memoirs* (Boston, 1937), V, 63–73.

sives at home and abroad because of who he was and the nation he led. His earlier enunciations of international principles and peace without victory had given the president unmatched credibility as the champion of a new, more just, more peaceful world order. From the Fourteen Points speech on, Wilson dominated the formulation of war aims and the negotiations of the end of the war, often despite Allied leaders' covert disagreement and intentions to subvert his policies. Wilson likewise continued to enjoy much domestic support for his synthesis of pacific aims and power politics activism. In fact, he encountered little open opposition for over a year after the United States entered the war.

By the middle of 1918, however, the situation had started to change. Abroad, Allied leaders were girding for upcoming diplomatic struggles over what they regarded as their legitimate fruits of victory. At home, isolationist and nationalist critics of Wilson's foreign policies were getting ready to renew their attacks. Unfortunately, in this situation Wilson chose to slight the domestic side of the task that he had set for himself. During the war he failed to build a sufficiently strong base of popular support for the position that he subsequently took in the League fight. This failure had two dimensions. One was neglect of the task that he himself had always regarded as indispensable to democratic leadership – education of public opinion. Wilson knew that he was neglecting this aspect of his leadership. Partly at the urging of his politically canny secretary, Joe Tumulty, he planned a cross-country speaking tour to the West Coast in conjunction with the Liberty Loan campaign but then canceled the trip. In a statement to the press September 9, 1918, Wilson explained, "I have keenly felt again and again the privation of being confined to the Capital and prevented from having the sort of direct contact with the people I am serving which would be of so much benefit and stimulation to me."[29]

Wilson did want contact with the people. He enjoyed campaigns and speaking tours, and he believed that he renewed himself through them. Perhaps if delicate and urgent diplomatic issues had not intervened as they did in September 1918, he might have made a full-scale speaking tour to explain his larger aims for the postwar world. But those demands did not provide the underlying reason for his comparative silence on the subject. Factors deep within the president's character dictated this choice. In his basic approach to all large political questions,

---

29. Wilson statement, Sept. 9, 1918, in Link, ed., *Papers of Wilson*, XLIX, 490. See also Tumulty to Wilson, Sept. 4, 1918, ibid., 439. On Wilson's neglect of educating public opinion during the war, see Cooper, *Warrior and Priest*, 342–343, and Knock, *To End All Wars*, 148–154, 157–166.

Wilson first established his general principles and approaches and then moved carefully into the specifics of debate and implementation. Wilson followed this approach in his foreign policy in 1917 and 1918. He refused to commit himself publicly further than stating his support for the principles of international enforcement, equality of national rights, and freedom from aggression, and he repeatedly declined to endorse plans advanced by the LEP or others. Also, with one significant exception, he did not approve any ideas about a structure for a league of nations until the negotiations in Paris at the beginning of 1919. In one way, Wilson acted wisely to avoid specifics. Not until he began dealing with the Allied leaders could he know how far he could push his vision of a liberal peace settlement.

Wilson was also failing to mend political fences. He could have held himself aloof from trying to educate public opinion with less harm if he had let others do some of the job for him. Congress could have supplied eager recruits for a domestic campaign on behalf of his foreign policies. With few exceptions, Democrats on Capitol Hill enthusiastically backed him. So did some Republicans, although such earlier advocates of the league idea and a compromise peace as senators Norris and La Follette had vehemently opposed intervention, and now they were deeply alienated from the militant, often repressive home front atmosphere. In any event, Wilson seldom reached out to sympathizers in Congress or elsewhere. The principal overtures toward such liberal journalistic supporters as the editors of *The New Republic* came from Wilson's confidant Colonel Edward M. House, not on the president's initiative.[30]

Wilson delivered his worst political slight to the LEP. In the three and a half years between its founding and the end of World War I, the LEP had grown into a formidable organization. Its state chapters blanketed the country and enlisted officeholders, including thirty-four state governors, as well as prominent businessmen, journalists, educators, and clergymen. Its lobbying efforts secured adoption by the legislatures of sixteen states of resolutions favoring judicial settlement of international disputes and enforcement by a league of nations. The LEP had a monthly budget of just under $12,000 in the latter part of 1918. Its national headquarters were on the twenty-third floor of a new office building on Fifth Avenue in New York, and it had a large professional staff headed by William H. Short, a veteran of philanthropic endeavors and earlier peace efforts. Taft continued to lend his prestige as the organization's president, and after

30. On the overtures toward the *New Republic* editors, see ibid., 119–120, 157, and Ronald Steel, *Walter Lippmann and the American Century* (Boston, 1980), 63, 107–110.

him the most active and prominent officer was Lawrence Lowell, the president of Harvard. Its national coverage, prestigious members, big budget, energy, and resourcefulness made the LEP arguably the most influential foreign policy lobbying group in American history.[31]

Intervention in the war had spared Taft, Lowell, and other prominent Republican members of the LEP further embarrassment at Wilson's linkage of the league idea to a compromise peace. After April 1917, the organization joyously climbed aboard the war bandwagon. The LEP supplied speakers, leaflets, and advertising to official and unofficial campaigns to whip up enthusiasm for the war effort. LEP stationery emblazoned across its letterhead the slogan, *"Clinch the Victory – Keep the World Safe by a League of Nations."* Taft and most LEP speakers sold international enforcement as the indispensable way to keep the Allies on top and Germany downtrodden once the war was won. As a result, public acceptance of the league idea as a war aim owed more to the LEP than to Wilson.[32]

The LEP's strength and effectiveness did not endear the organization to the president. Partisan rancor left over from the 1916 election kept personal relations cool between Wilson and Taft. Wilson also harbored a dislike for Lowell that evidently went back to their days as fellow university presidents. But Wilson's main reason for shunning the LEP sprang from his resolve to avoid specific plans for international enforcement. In March 1918 a tense exchange took place between the president and the LEP leadership. Wilson feared, as he told Colonel House, that "the League to Enforce Peace butters-in" and "wool-gatherers" would embarrass him with "discussion now of the *constitution* of the league of nations." He met with Taft and Lowell at the White House on March 28 and asked them to get the LEP to back off from adopting plans for a league.[33]

Keeping his distance from the LEP and the Allies dovetailed for Wilson during the summer of 1918. Under pressure from the mounting

---

31. On the LEP's budget, see William H. Short to Hamilton Holt, Aug. 16, 1918, Hamilton Holt Papers, Rollins College Library, Box 2; on its size and effectiveness, see John Milton Cooper, Jr., "The Not So Vital Center: The League to Enforce Peace and the League of Nations, 1919–1920," in Michael Wala, ed., *Gesellschaft und Diplomatie im transatlantischen Kontext* (Stuttgart, 1999), 119–132.

32. On the LEP's wartime role, see Bartlett, *LEP*, 83–112.

33. Wilson to House, Mar. 20, 1918, in Link, ed., *Papers of Wilson*, XLVII, 85; Taft memorandum, [Mar. 29, 1918], ibid., 200–202. For Taft's description of the meeting, see also Edwin M. Borchard to John Bassett Moore, Apr. 4 [*sic* – Apr. 11], 1918, John Bassett Moore Papers, Library of Congress, Box 57.

enthusiasm in liberal and labor circles for Wilson's approach to peace and international order, the British government had earlier appointed a commission headed by a distinguished jurist, Sir Walter Phillimore. That commission produced a report that called for an "alliance" in which member states would pledge to refrain from war with each other, use sanctions against violators, consider coming to the aid of victims of aggression, and adopt arbitration and mediation procedures. Prime Minister David Lloyd George gave the Phillimore Report a cool reception, but he did authorize its confidential transmission to the United States. One of the report's recipients was Colonel House. This small, sly, ingratiating Texan enjoyed a reputation as the president's confidant, and he was overseeing the work of the Inquiry, the group of scholars and other experts who had been gathered to advise on war aims and plans for the peace conference. Unlike Wilson, House wanted close relations with the Allies, and he saw an opportunity to use the LEP to serve that end. In his typically devious and manipulative way, House told the LEP leaders about the existence of the Phillimore Report, He also persuaded Lowell to urge Wilson to appoint a similar commission and coordinate work on plans for a league with the British.[34]

At first, House's ploy seemed to backfire. Wilson curtly told Lowell and the LEP to mind their own business. In August he also told Sir William Wiseman, the British Secret Service agent who was his government's main channel of communication with House and Wilson, that publication of the Phillimore Report and any involvement with the LEP would cause "endless trouble and controversy if immature conclusions are made public." According to Wiseman, Wilson specifically feared that, "[o]ne section of the Senate, led by Lodge, would say that he had gone to[o] far in committing the United States to a Utopian scheme, and, on the other hand, the League enthusiasts would criticize him for not going far enough."[35]

The matter did not end there. Wilson also responded to the Phillimore Report by asking House and his legal expert on the Inquiry,

34. On the Phillimore Commission, see George W. Egerton, *Great Britain and the Creation of the League of Nations: Strategy, Politics, and International Organization, 1915–1919* (Chapel Hill, N.C., 1978), and Link, ed., *Papers of Wilson*, XLVIII, 502 n. 1. On House's enlistment of Lowell, see Lowell to House, July 5, 1918, ibid., 561–562; Lowell to Wilson, July 10, 1918, ibid., 586. In forwarding Lowell's letter to him, House disavowed any support of the LEP effort. House to Wilson, July 8, 1918, ibid., 561.

35. Wilson to Lowell, July 11, 1918, ibid., 591; Wiseman to Lord Reading, Aug. 16, 1918, ibid., XLIX, 273–274. On Wiseman, see W. B. Fowler, *British-American Relations, 1917–1918: The Role of Sir William Wiseman* (Princeton, N.J., 1969).

David Hunter Miller, to come up with an alternative plan for a league. Miller drafted a "Suggestion for a Covenant of a League of Nations." This "covenant" consisted of a preamble and twenty-three articles. It incorporated features from the Phillimore Report, particularly those specifing sanctions, and it reiterated views earlier stated by Wilson about territorial integrity of nations. The document also included statements about disarmament and an international court.[36]

This draft did not satisfy Wilson. He now made the single exception to his refusal to discuss plans specific for a league. Wilson revised the House–Miller draft in line with his own thinking. Obviously liking the title word, he called his own draft a "COVENANT." Wilson retained, revised, and consolidated thirteen articles from the earlier draft and wrote his own preamble and three new articles. Wilson made significant changes in four areas. First, he guaranteed equality of representation to small nations. Second, he dropped any mention of a world court. Third, he strengthened the call for disarmament and requirements for arbitration. Finally, he strengthened the commitment to international order when he stated, "The Contracting Powers unite in guaranteeing to each other political independence and territorial integrity," but with the proviso that "territorial adjustments" could be made, "pursuant to the principle of self-determination," with the approval of three-quarters of the league's members. Wilson also declared, "The Contracting Powers accept without reservation the principle that the peace of the world is superior in importance to every question of political jurisdiction and boundary."[37]

Wilson went over this "covenant" with House in August during a visit to the colonel's summer home in Magnolia, on Massachusetts' North Shore. For that reason, this document later became known as the "Magnolia Draft." It was, as Thomas Knock has written, "a fine document distinguished by the salient principles of progressive internationalism" and would be "the most important document that he would take with him to the Paris Peace Conference." Both what Wilson wrote in the Magnolia Draft and what he did with it revealed his ideas about how to design and bring to fruition a league of nations. He differed from the LEP in not favoring a world court and judicial settlement of international disputes – one of the hallmarks of that organization's approach to peacekeeping. Also unlike them, he also wanted compul-

36. "A Suggestion For A COVENANT OF A LEAGUE OF NATIONS," encl. with House to Wilson, July 16, 1918, in Link, ed., *Papers of Wilson*, XLVIII, 630–637; House to Wilson, July 14, 1918, ibid., 608.
37. "COVENANT," encl. with Wilson to House, Sept. 7, 1918, ibid., XLIX, 467–471.

sory arbitration and efforts toward disarmament and assurance of equality among nations. Specifically, he disagreed with LEP leaders such as Taft and with the British in rejecting a league that was primarily a great power directorate. As this draft implied, such a league would be political organization backed by military force if necessary.[38]

Despite House's entreaties, Wilson kept the Magnolia Draft strictly secret. He allowed only two copies to be made – one for House and one for himself. Likewise, he continued to reject any idea of communicating with the British about plans for a league. This treatment of the document again reflected the pattern of behavior that he had established in foreign policy since 1915. His refusal to let anyone else in on his thinking – except, in a limited and occasional way, House – sprang from his determination to retain as much freedom of action as he could. In coming days, Wilson would repeatedly act this way at various stages in the League fight, particularly when he appointed the American delegation to the peace conference.

As the summer of 1918 wore on, the truce over the league idea and more generally over war aims collapsed. The ever brighter prospect for victory removed the need for pretenses of domestic unity. Roosevelt began firing heavy salvos at Wilson's war aims, denouncing them as "silly" and "mischievous" and calling on Americans "emphatically to repudiate the 'fourteen points' offered by President Wilson as a satisfactory basis for peace." Interestingly, however, Roosevelt began to see merit again in the league idea. He now suggested that by joining with the Allies and other right-minded nations "we may be able to make a real and much needed advance in international organization." Taft made much the same argument in the fall of 1918. "The point now is to secure a workable League of Nations required in the maintenance of the purposes of this war," he asserted. Later international conferences could create "a larger League of Nations based on this, the product of the necessity of the present situation."[39]

The American electoral calendar conspired with the approach of victory to reheat the political pot. Campaigns for state and congressional elections in November 1918 arrayed the respective parties into hostile camps. Republicans of nearly all stripes found reasons to pitch in

38. Knock, *To End All Wars*, 153–154.
39. Roosevelt newspaper columns, Oct. 17, Nov. 17, 1918, in Ralph Stout, ed., *Roosevelt in the Kansas City Star: Wartime Editorials by Theodore Roosevelt* (Boston, 1921), 378, 400; Taft newspaper column, Oct. 25, 1918, William Howard Taft Papers, Library of Congress, microfilm edition, reel 557.

together in their common loathing for Wilson and his works. Even those two foes, Roosevelt and Taft, patched up their long broken friendship, and Roosevelt's kind words for the league idea owed something to their newfound reconciliation. Taft's energetic partisanship, his reunion with Roosevelt, and his increasingly pointed attacks on Wilson in the fall campaign – these moves caused some in the LEP to fear alienating Wilson and the Democrats. Conversely, the continued unwillingness of such leading Republicans as Root, Hughes, and the party's national chairman, Will Hays, to join the LEP – together with reports of renewed nationalist and isolationist criticism – raised concerns about the opposite danger.[40]

Wilson also apparently worsened the situation with a partisan ploy of his own. On October 25, the president issued an appeal to voters to elect Democrats. "If you have approved of my leadership," he declared, "and wish me to continue to be your unembarrassed spokesman in affairs at home and abroad, I earnestly beg that you will express yourselves unmistakably to that effect by returning a Democratic majority to both the Senate and the House of Representatives." The gamble failed. On November 5, the Republicans won a 44-seat majority in the House and a one-vote margin the Senate. The Senate result insured that Lodge would become both majority leader and chairman of the Foreign Relations Committee. Those would be positions of enormous influence in the consideration of any post-war treaties. Roosevelt, Taft, Lodge, and other Republicans gleefully greeted the electoral outcome as precisely a repudiation of the president's leadership.[41]

The worst effect of this partisan sparring sprang from an unfortunate coincidence. Less than a week after the election, on November 11, 1918, the war ended with the Armistice. From the standpoint of debate about the shape of future peace and questions of international enforce-

---

40. On the distress within the LEP, see LEP Exectuive Committee minutes, Nov. 23, 1918, Holt Papers, Box 73.

41. Wilson statement, [Oct. 19, 1918], released Oct. 25, 1918, in Link, ed., *Papers of Wilson*, LIII, 381. This presidential appeal has been almost universally judged to be possibly the greatest political blunder of Wilson's career, and it has been condemned for getting him off on the wrong foot in the League fight. Those judgments are overdrawn. His appeal did not appreciably worsen the already nasty partisan atmosphere. Conversely, the appeal may have helped save Democrats from worse defeat, and Wilson may have strengthened his ties with his fellow partisans by showing that he was willing to go out on a limb for them. For an analysis of the election results, see Seward W. Livermore, *Politics Is Adjourned: Woodrow Wilson and the War Congress, 1916–1918* (Middletown, Conn., 1966), 224–227.

ment, this was bad timing. In the United States, political sourness, barely resumed discussions about peace plans, and murky prospects abroad greeted the silence of the guns. Wilson himself caught the odd mood when he unveiled the Armistice terms to a joint session of Congress. "It is not now possible to assume the consequences of this great consummation," he observed. Though hopeful, the president also feared such aftereffects of four years of bloody carnage as fear, hunger, misery, disorder, and vengeance: "There is here matter for no small anxiety and misgiving. When peace is made, upon whose promises and engagements besides our own is it to rest?"[42]

II

Preliminaries for the League fight began as soon as the guns of November 1918 fell silent. President Wilson's question – who would shape the peace and how? – now took center stage. Two competing approaches to peacemaking emerged at once. The first approach came from Wilson, who carried forward the attitudes and behavior that he had previously displayed toward the league question and war aims. As before, he strove to keep the initiative and freedom of maneuver in his own hands. The second approach to peacemaking emanated from certain Republicans, particularly Roosevelt, Lodge, Root, and Senator Philander C. Knox, who was also a former secretary of state. They and others sought to supplant Wilson and his vision of the peace settlement.

The first bone of contention in this struggle for primacy in shaping the peace settlement involved who would speak and act for the United States in the negotiations. No one disputed the president's sole authority to appoint the American plenipotentiaries, but plenty of people, friends and foes alike, did question whom he should appoint. Wilson's first and later most controversial appointment was himself. When he aired the idea to his cabinet the day after the Armistice, Secretary of State Robert Lansing strongly disagreed and afterward told the president so in a private meeting. Wilson, Lansing recorded in his diary, "did not like what I said. His face assumed that harsh, obstinate expression which indicates resentment at unacceptable advice. He said nothing but looked volumes." Wilson also consulted with two Democratic senators, who canvassed their colleagues and found opinion divided about the wisdom of his going. The dissents did not deter Wilson, and a week after the

42. Wilson address, Nov. 11, 1918, in Link, ed., *Papers of Wilson*, LIII, 4–42.

Armistice the president announced that he would head the delegation to the peace conference.[43]

Lansing and other skeptics voiced the main criticism of the president's personal involvement – namely, that by not going he could remain, as some Democratic senators put it, "a superman residing afar off in the citadel of power beyond that of all nations." Others believed, however, that only Wilson himself could effectively implement his ideas for a liberal, nonpunitive peace and international enforcement. One friendly senator split the difference and suggested that the president might make only a brief trip to the conference, at a time "when your presence would enable you to speak with the most telling effect." These private discussions highlighted the main points that have been raised about Wilson's presence among the peacemakers at Paris in 1919. The notion of his maintaining a distant moral high ground may have had an appealing ring, but the argument that no one else could have adequately represented Wilson and his thinking was much more persuasive. That argument at once recognized his abilities and leveled a devastating criticism. Ever since Bryan's resignation as secretary of state in 1915, Wilson had kept the conduct of major policies toward the world war almost entirely to himself. He had treated Bryan's successor, Lansing, strictly as a functionary and Colonel House as a negotiator and facilitator rather than an advisor. This practice had prevented him from grooming strong, trustworthy lieutenants who could carry on his work in foreign affairs.[44]

There was little public reaction to Wilson's decision to go to the peace conference himself. Instead, attention focused on the question of who else would be appointed to the delegation. When the names of other members appeared in the press on November 29, cries of outrage erupted. That outrage fell equally on whom Wilson did and whom he did not appoint. Two of the four other members of the delegation, Lansing and General Tasker H. Bliss, aroused no strong feelings because they simply brought technical expertise in diplomatic and military matters. By contrast, House found himself derided as a crony and syco-

43. Robert Lansing Diary, Nov. 12, 1918, in Link, ed., *Papers of Wilson*, LIII, 65–66. See also Josephus Daniels' Diary, Nov. 12, 1918, ibid., 65, and Key Pittman to Wilson, Nov. 15, 1918, ibid., 93–95.
44. Pittman to Wilson, Nov. 15, 1918, ibid., 94; Peter G. Gerry to Wilson, Nov. 16, 1918, ibid., 103. The best discussion of the pros and cons of Wilson's going to Paris is still Thomas A. Bailey, *Woodrow Wilson and the Lost Peace* (New York, 1944), 73–86.

phant. The one outsider, Henry White, a former ambassador, struck most observers as just another technical expert. People at home and abroad could not help asking whether Wilson chose the best team that the United States could field for what promised to be the diplomatic game of the century. Criticism of who was included dovetailed with criticism of who was excluded. Wilson's choices came in for heavy censure because were no senators, no figures of national stature, and no prominent Republicans.[45]

The Senate's role in treaty making – particularly the requirement of consent by a two-thirds majority in order to complete the process of ratification – spoke to the wisdom of naming some members of that body to the delegation. The last time the United States had made peace, in 1898 at the end of the Spanish-American War, William McKinley had sent three senators, two of his majority Republicans and one from the Democratic minority, to help negotiate the settlement – a move that was generally believed to have helped garner the necessary margin for consent. Compelling as the case and precedent for senatorial inclusion appeared, however, there was a seemingly insurmountable obstacle – Henry Cabot Lodge. The president could not offer a place on the delegation to any senator without including Lodge. The Massachusetts senator was about to become the chairman of the Foreign Relations Committee and majority leader, and he was his party's senior member in length of service and the body's preeminent spokesman in foreign affairs. Not to offer a place to Lodge would insult both the Senate and the Republican party.[46]

In view of these two men's cordial hatred for each other, it seems

---

45. For example, Senator Lodge asserted, "Our delegation with the exception of Mr. White are merely mouthpieces of the President, and if Mr. White should differ he will be overridden." Lodge to Lord Bryce, Dec. 14, 1918, Lodge Papers.

46. On peacemaking at the end of the Spanish-American War, see W. Stull Holt, *Treaties Defeated by the Senate: A Study of the Struggle between President and Senate over the Conduct of Foreign Relations* (Baltimore, 1922), 165–177; H. Wayne Morgan, *William McKinley and His America* (Syracuse, N.Y., 1963), 400–401; and Lewis L. Gould, *The Presidency of William McKinley* (Lawrence, Kans., 1980), 130–131, 143–149. Interestingly none of these authors attributes much of McKinley's success in getting Senate approval of the treaty to his having included senators among the peace negotiators. Holt emphatically argues that the quixotic gesture by Bryan in asking Democratic senators to vote for the treaty in order to make the Philippines an issue in the next presidential election was the most important element in its narrowly securing the necessary margin.

hard to fault Wilson for not wanting to have Lodge at his side during what promised to be difficult weeks or months of negotiation. Yet he may have missed a bet. During the Civil War, Abraham Lincoln had preferred to have his main rivals and critics in his cabinet where he could keep an eye on them. Wilson might have done well to follow that example and keep the greatest potential spoiler of his plans where he could watch and perhaps control him. Moreover, there was a strong chance that Lodge would decline the offer in order to preserve his freedom to criticize and oppose the peace treaty. In that event, Wilson could have named any senators he pleased.[47]

The other criticisms of Wilson's exclusions from the peace delegation – lack of national figures and lack of prominent Republicans – amounted to the same thing. Except for Bryan, the only people of political and international stature whom Wilson could have appointed were Republicans. Speculation and advice about suitable appointees revolved around three names: Taft, Root, and Charles Evans Hughes. As Wilson's predecessor in the White House and head of the LEP, Taft seemed a logical choice. In Republican eyes, Root's long service as secretary of war under McKinley and Roosevelt and secretary of state under Roosevelt gave the austere but witty seventy-three-year-old New Yorker unmatched stature as an authority on foreign policy. The bearded, dynamic Hughes was a former governor of New York, former justice of the Supreme Court, and the party's last presidential candidate, and he was expected to be a future contender for the nomination.[48]

In refusing to pick a member of this Republican triumvirate, Wilson seems to have acted for situational, ideological, and personal reasons. Situationally, there was that unfortunate coincidence between the 1918 elections and the war's end. Republican attacks during the congressional campaign, especially by Roosevelt and these three Republicans, had left sore feelings among the denizens of the White House just when the matter of appointing the peace delegation arose. At a cabinet meeting, when Hughes was suggested as a possible delegate, Wilson snapped, "No – there is no room big enough for Hughes & me to stay in." Unquestionably, any of these men would have supplied domestic

47. If Lodge had declined, the next-ranking Republican member of the Foreign Relations Committee was McCumber, who had already shown himself to be one of the most pro-league senators of either party. The ranking Democrat on the committee was Gilbert Hitchcock of Nebraska, an administration loyalist.
48. Wilson to Henry L. Myers, Nov. 20, 1918, in Link, ed., *Papers of Wilson*, LIII, 141.

political standing and savvy, together with renowned legal skills and, in the cases of Taft and Root, diplomatic knowledge and experience. Lodge thought that Wilson's refusal to take such men with him reflected a "love of inferiority" and "the fear of able men as assistants [which] is one of the marks of a small man." Nasty as that assessment was, it contained a kernel of truth. During the previous four years, Wilson had seldom sought or taken counsel on foreign policy with anyone of real stature. More charitably viewed, the president's refusal to surround himself with strong, independent-minded associates allowed him greater freedom of maneuver in the negotiations.[49]

Wilson also rejected these Republicans because he recognized that deep differences over the terms of the peace settlement and international enforcement separated him from them. Privately he disdained what he regarded as the legalistic ideas of Taft and the LEP, and he resented the way that Taft had linked the LEP program during the fall campaign to Roosevelt's and Lodge's demands for a harsh, punitive peace. Likewise, he told House that Root, with his "lawyer's mind," had "the wrong idea" about a peace league. Wilson disclosed how different his own thinking was in a confidential talk with a Swiss visitor on November 22. "*I'm going to Europe because the Allied governments don't want me to,*" he joked. He saw international enforcement as a basically political enterprise – namely, "to extend the Monroe Doctrine so as to make it a principle of mutual protection. '*Not a big-brother affair, but a real partnership.*'"[50]

Still, the question needs to be asked whether the potential reward of including one or more of these men might not have been worth the price. The biggest possible reward lay in tying leaders of the Republican party to the peace settlement. Their inclusion in the delegation could have insured that the treaty and any commitment to international enforcement would be the product of a bipartisan foreign policy. In short, the president was failing to practice bipartisanship.

To be fair to Wilson, it has to be noted that bipartisanship offered no panacea at the end of 1918. The term itself would not come into use until the late 1940s. Despite McKinley's gesture in 1898, bipartisanship belongs to a later era in American history, when Franklin Roosevelt and Harry Truman embraced Republicans during and after World War II in a

49. Entry, Nov. 19, 1918, Daniels Diary, ibid., 135. Lodge to George Harvey, Dec. 25, 1918, Lodge Papers.
50. House Diary, Aug. 15, 18, 1918, in Link, ed., *Papers of Wilson*, XLIX, 267, 286; William Emmanuel Rappard memorandum, [Nov. 20, 1918], ibid., LXIII, 626–627.

conscious effort to avoid what they viewed as Wilson's mistakes. Before the end of World War I, all discussions of the politics of foreign policy had revolved around partisanship versus nonpartisanship. The previous May, Wilson had declared, "Politics is adjourned," and far more than any wartime president before him, he had kept that promise. He had not tried to gain partisan advantage from the war, except in his October 1918 appeal for a Democratic congress. He had perhaps savored some morsels of personal and partisan revenge when he spurned his bitter political foe Roosevelt – who had wanted to raise a division to fight on the Western front – and his harsh policy critic General Leonard Wood – who had coveted command of the American Expeditionary Force in France. In fact, the civilian and military heads of the War Department had heartily agreed with Wilson's decisions. Furthermore, he had departed from the previous practices of all wartime presidents. Wilson had declined to give the most highly visible wartime military, diplomatic, and civilian leadership posts to Democrats. He had also tapped such Republicans as Taft and Root for special assignments.[51]

But those circumstances did not fully excuse Wilson's failure to practice bipartisanship. Of all American politicians in 1918, he was best able to understand the need to involve the opposition party in such a momentous enterprise as this peace settlement. As a close student of parliamentary systems, Wilson was familiar with the workings of coalition governments, under which both of the principal Allies, Britain and France, were then operating. In fact, Wilson did make a stab at bipartisanship when he named Henry White to the delegation. White enjoyed the friendship and admiration of Roosevelt, Lodge, and Root, all of whom he consulted before accepting the appointment. Both the president and White's Republican friends expected him to act as a liaison between the two camps – a role that he would play assiduously, if not happily, throughout the peace negotiations and the League fight.[52]

Finally, it must be asked whether Wilson's health may have affected his decision making. Several observers later noted that some time in 1918, the president began to show uncharacteristic signs of rigidity, suspicion, and irascibility. Moreover, in the last months of the war, Wilson's

51. Wilson address to Congress, May 27, 1918, in Link, ed., *Papers of Wilson,* XLVIII, 164. The one exception to the practice of not promoting Democrats was William Gibbs McAdoo, who became administrator of the government-run railroads, but partisan calculation played no role in that appointment.

52. For White's consultations and expectations, see Lodge to George Harvey, Dec. 9, 1918, Lodge Papers.

established routines for avoiding overwork had broken down, and the burden of his office began to weigh on him much more heavily. His worst ordeal of sheer volume of work, crushing responsibility, and emotional stress lay ahead at Paris. It would be a tribute to Wilson's stamina and will that he performed as well as he did for so long a time in 1919. The fact remains, however, that this man who would turn sixty-two in another month and who suffered from neurological and circulatory problems was no longer at the height of his powers. He had lost much of his earlier freshness and resourcefulness. Whether a younger, healthier Wilson would have handled the appointment of the peace conference delegation differently can only remain a matter of conjecture.[53]

As it was, the president moved fast in preparing to implement his ideas. Wilson persisted in refusing to disclose what shape his efforts would take. On December 2, 1918, he gave his sixth and, as it turned out, last state-of-the-union address to Congress. Wilson dwelled mainly on domestic affairs and made only brief mention of the world situation. He reiterated "the sincere desire of our Government to contribute without selfish purpose of any kind to the settlements that will be of common benefit to all the nations concerned." He also confessed, "I realize the magnitude of the duty I am undertaking; I am poignantly aware of its grave responsibility." The next day the president and the delegation to the peace conference sailed for Europe without further elucidation of his plans or program. One high-ranking member of the shipboard party privately complained that he "did not know a God-dam thing about what the President was thinking."[54]

This presidential silence and freedom of maneuver infuriated leading Republicans. Roosevelt and Lodge were working to undercut Wilson. Publicly, they repeatedly broadcast their claim that the president no longer spoke for the American people. Privately, they communicated their views directly to the Allied leaders. To the British foreign secretary, Arthur Balfour, Roosevelt declared that the Republican "party stands

53. For observations on Wilson's condition during and after the summer of 1918, see Edwin A. Weinstein, *Woodrow Wilson: A Medical and Psychological Biography* (Princeton, N.J., 1981), 320–323.

54. Wilson address to Congress, Dec. 2, 1918, in Link, ed., *Papers of Wilson*, LIII, 285–286; Clive Day to Elizabeth D. Day, Dec. 10, 1918, ibid., 349. Day, a younger member of the delegation staff, was quoting George Creel, chairman of the Committee on Public Information. According to one Republican senator, Reed Smoot of Utah, he and his fellow partisans from both houses of Congress gave Wilson a cold reception when he spoke. See entry, Dec. 2, 1918, in Harvard Heath, ed., *In the World: The Diaries of Reed Smoot* (Salt Lake City, 1997), 405.

for the unconditional surrender of Germany and for absolute loyalty to France and England in the peace negotiations. . . . America should act, not as an umpire between our allies and our enemies, but as one of the allies bound to come to an agreement with them." Roosevelt also maintained that "while we gladly welcome any feasible scheme for a League of Nations, we prefer that it should begin with our present allies, and be accepted only as an addition to and in no sense as a substitute for the preparedness of our own strength and for our own defense." He sent similar letters to the premiers of the principal Allied nations, Britain's Lloyd George and France's Georges Clemenceau.[55]

To this vision of international power politics-as-usual Lodge added a further twist. Also to Balfour, the senator declared that effective international enforcement still seemed to him "almost hopelessly impracticable in many respects. Any agreement for a League, if such a thing can be made, should be in a separate instrument. It should not be made an integral part of the peace terms." Strong opposition existed in the United States to any kind of supranational authority over such matters as tariffs, immigration, the armed forces, or the Monroe Doctrine. For that reason, he warned, ". . . it would be most unfortunate to have an agreement for a League attached to the peace treaty, for it might lead to great and most undesirable delays and probable amendments to the treaty of peace, which would be greatly to be deplored." Between them, Roosevelt and Lodge were setting out the three main tenets of a Republican alternative approach to the peace settlement: first, a united front with the major Allies, coupled with hints about a postwar alliance; second, harsh terms to be imposed on the defeated Germans; and third, separation of any possible arrangements for a league from the treaty that ended the war.[56]

Even before the war had ended, another major Republican foreign policy spokesman had also enunciated such a three-pronged approach to peacemaking. This was Philander Knox. The cherubic-looking, deceptively low-keyed Knox presently a held Senate seat from the GOP bastion of Pennsylvania, where he enjoyed close ties to the party's staunchest big business backers. Previously he had served as attorney general under McKinley and Roosevelt and secretary of state under Taft. That background gave Knox special claims to speak to and for mainstream Republican thinking. On October 28 he had lambasted Wilson's diplomatic leadership for both executive usurpation and soft

55. Roosevelt to Balfour, Dec. 15, 1918, in Elting E. Morison, ed., *The Letters of Theodore Roosevelt* (Cambridge, Mass., 1954), VIII, 1415.

56. Lodge to Balfour, Nov. 25, 1918, Lodge Papers.

much more attention to thus standing by them than to . . . the League of Nations." Roosevelt favored "a working agreement between the British Empire and the United States; indeed, I am now content to call it an alliance." But to a friendly journalist he confided in December that any pledge involving continental European nations "is a pretty big guarantee and I don't know whether it would be made good. Indeed, I don't know whether it ought to be made good." Schemes for international enforcement elicited even greater skepticism. Roosevelt warned another journalist who visited him that month in the hospital, "Any treaty adopted under the influence of war would be like the good resolutions adopted at a mass meeting . . . [where] we adopt resolutions abolishing vice. But vice isn't abolished that way." Publicly, Roosevelt sang the same song, although he sometimes stressed different notes. "It is our business to act with our allies," he wrote in his newspaper column at the end of November, "and to show an undivided front with them against any move of our late enemies."61

Yet Roosevelt did not believe that solidarity with the Allies and harsh treatment of Germany were necessarily incompatible with a league of nations. At the beginning of January 1919, in the last newspaper column that he wrote, Roosevelt chided Wilson for failing to disclose his plans for a league of nations. "We all of us earnestly desire such a league," he declared, and the best possible one was "the league which we already have in existence, the league of the Allies who have fought through this great war." Let America avoid "the position of international Meddlesome Matty." Let the European Allies watch over their own sphere. Let the United States continue to manage the Western Hemisphere. Let all civilized nations "introduce some kind of police system in the weak and disorderly countries at their thresholds." If America and the Allies did those things, Roosevelt concluded, "I believe that such an effort made moderately and sanely, but sincerely and with utter scorn for words that are not made good by deeds, will be productive of real and lasting international good."62

In all, the Republicans' prospects for gaining the upper hand in

61. Roosevelt to Rudyard Kipling, Nov. 23, 1918, *Letters of Theodore Roosevelt*, VIII, 1404; Roosevelt to Andrew J. Haskell, Dec. 18, 1918, ibid., 1417; Roosevelt quoted in Stout, ed., *Roosevelt in the Kansas City Star*, xlvi; Roosevelt, *Kansas City Star*, Nov. 26, 1918, in Hagedorn, ed., *Works of Roosevelt*, XIX, 399.
62. Roosevelt, *Kansas City Star*, Jan. 13, 1919, ibid., 406–408. Roosevelt dictated that last column on January 3, 1919, two days before his death. Ibid., 406 n. 1.

peacemaking looked good as the year 1919 opened. By stressing solidarity with the Allies, harshness toward Germany, and postponement of the league, their principal spokesmen were putting forward a traditional great power approach. This promised to appeal strongly both abroad to America's diplomatic partners and at home to a large segment of public opinion. This situation allowed Roosevelt to gather nearly all shades of Republican opinion into his big tent of unrepentant nationalism supplemented by consideration of limited international commitments and possible collective security arrangements. Meanwhile, Lodge journeyed to Roosevelt's hospital room in New York in December 1918 to plot strategy for the Senate's handling of any peace treaty and league arrangement that Wilson might bring back from Paris.[63]

Unfortunately, these seemingly bright prospects had a literally fatal flaw. This Republican foreign policy also relied on the fragile health of a man in his sixties. The visits to the hospital in December 1918 offered the latest evidence that all was not well with Theodore Roosevelt. The lingering ravages of tropical diseases contracted on his expedition to the Brazilian jungles in 1914, coupled with untreated hypertension, inflammatory rheumatism, and, possibly, the emotional impact of his son Quentin's death in combat the previous July all had weakened this national symbol of vigor and shortened his remaining days on earth. Still, Roosevelt's death in his sleep from a coronary embolism on January 6, 1919, struck like a bolt of lightning from a seemingly cloudless sky. Suddenly and without warning, one of the two most powerful and best-known figures in American politics was gone. The Republicans had lost their all but certain next presidential nominee and their best hope for regaining the White House in 1920.[64]

None of the consequences of Roosevelt's death was more imponderable and possibly drastic than its effect on the shape and outcome of the upcoming League fight. President Wilson received the news of his great rival's passing while he was traveling in Italy on his preconference tour

63. What Roosevelt and Lodge agreed upon in those last meetings is a matter of some controversy. The only fragmentary first-hand accounts, set down after the fact, are Lodge to Brooks Adams, Dec. 23, 1918, Lodge Papers; Lodge to Henry White, Apr. 8, 1919, ibid.; and Corinne Roosevelt Robinson, *My Brother Theodore Roosevelt* (New York, 1922), 362–363.

64. How central Roosevelt was to Republican hopes was indicated by his last written words, a memorandum scribbled just before he went to bed that last night. "Hays [Will H. Hays, the Republican national chairman] see him; he must go to Washington for 10 days; see Senate & House; prevent split on domestic policies." Roosevelt memorandum, [Jan. 5, 1919], in Morison, ed., *Roosevelt Letters*, VIII, 1422.

of the principal Allied countries. He immediately sent a telegram of sympathy and wrote a generous eulogy. Gloating or sighing with relief would have been unseemly, but Wilson and his fellow Democrats and other League advocates may well have thought that fortune had just dealt them a strong card. In some ways, they were right to think that their task had grown easier abroad and at home. Without such a well-known and sympathetic opposition leader standing in the wings as a possible president-in-waiting, the Allied leaders came to believe that they had no choice but to reach an accommodation with Wilson on peace terms and a league of nations. The president would not be home free in the negotiations at Paris, but his chances of shaping a more liberal and less punitive settlement, and erecting a new structure of international security and enforcement seemed to have grown much brighter.[65]

In the larger scheme of things, however, Roosevelt's death may have dealt a heavy blow to the chances for a lasting peace. His long advocacy of American great power activism and his erstwhile espousal of collective security – together with his now uniquely unifying role among Republicans – had made him the single person most likely to get the bulk of his party brethren to accept postwar international commitments. With a living, leading Roosevelt, the grounds of Republican opposition to Wilson might have been much more favorable to overseas commitments and much less susceptible to isolationist influences. A second Roosevelt presidency in the 1920s might well have featured either a face-saving American entry into the League of Nations or some other overtures toward global security and peacemaking.

Roosevelt's death had a deep impact on Lodge. His passing removed the one influence that might have swayed the senator toward greater willingness to give international enforcement a fair trial and to work constructively toward other measures of collective security. That influence went deeper than the bonds of one of the strongest personal friendships in American political life. As William Widenor has pointed out, for Lodge his fallen friend had embodied the "Rooseveltian solution" – which meant leadership that combined transcendent nationalism, wisdom about power politics, and charisma in enlisting popular support. In Lodge's thinking, that kind of leadership offered the only way to overcome the obstacles to pursuit of a great power role that he saw as inherent in a democratically governed, commercially infused, geographically unthreatened nation like the United States. In the coming months, not

---

65. For the Allied leaders' acquiescence in the Wilsonian approach despite their own attraction to the Republican position, see Egerton, *Great Britain and the League of Nations*.

the now lost "Rooseveltian solution," but the far feebler tactical exigencies of partisan and senatorial leadership, would restrain Lodge's oppositional impulses.[66]

As before, Wilson was deliberately maintaining silence in an effort to preserve his freedom of action. In private, he was pursuing his own approach to the proper American role in world affairs. He disclosed the main tenets of his thinking twice on the voyage to Europe in December 1918. On December 8, his physician and newfound confidant, Cary Grayson, wrote in his diary that the president "declared emphatically that it [the league] must constitute part and parcel of the peace treaty itself and not be left to later consideration" and that the United States and the major Allies would form the "nucleus of the league." Two days later, Wilson held a meeting with the Inquiry – that small group of young, male, mostly academic advisors whom House had gathered to supply information and interpretations about war aims and a peace settlement. To them he vowed his unswerving determination to forge a peace settlement on the basis of the Fourteen Points, even in the face of likely opposition from the Allied leaders. Two of his hearers recorded the president as declaring, "Tell me what's right and I'll fight for it; give me a guaranteed position."[67]

On the subject of the league, noted one of the members of the Inquiry, Wilson continued to doubt "that any hard and fast constitution of the 'League to Enforce Peace' variety can be established at the present time." But he did believe that "the idea of covenants . . . could be worked out in general form and agreed to and set in motion, and he particularly emphasised the importance of succeeding experience to guide subsequent action." A nascent league formed by these covenants would guarantee members' "political independence and territorial integrity" and would set up a council "to report to the Governments composing the League, if it considered that war was likely to break out in any quarter of the globe and [it would then be] the business of the

66. See Widenor, *Lodge and American Foreign Policy*, esp. 130–131, 149–150, 154–155, 161–162.
67. Cary T. Grayson Diary, Dec. 8, 1918, in Link, ed., *Papers of Wilson*, LIII, 337; William C. Bullittt Diary, Dec. 9 [*sic* – Dec. 10], 1918, ibid., 350–352; Isaiah Bowman memorandum, Dec. 10, 1918, ibid., 353–356. The version of Wilson's famous declaration quoted here is Bowman's. Bullitt's version reads: "'Tell me what is right and I'll fight for it.' 'I want a guaranteed position.'" Ibid., 352. For a third, briefer account of this meeting, see Charles Seymour to family, Dec. 10, 1918, ibid., 356–357. The next day Wilson painted a similar picture of his task at Paris, though without discussing the league, to another advisor and trusted friend, Raymond Fosdick. See Fosdick Diary, Dec. 11, 1918, ibid., 365–366.

Governments to step in and stop it." Under this arrangement, the president explained, "any war must be considered as affecting the whole world. If any nation refused to listen to the powers composing the league it is my idea that they should be boycotted by the other powers, . . . cut off absolutely."[68]

Those remarks on the way to Paris showed that Wilson was bent on following a course that was largely, though not totally, opposed to the Republican approach. He agreed with his partisan adversaries that an Allied–American coalition should form the core of the league. But he intended to include the league in the peace treaty, and he was determined to resist the Allies' expected push for harsh terms and territorial, financial, and colonial spoils. Also, Wilson's vision of a peacekeeping league was different from, though not necessarily incompatible with, the thinking of the LEP and other league advocates. He wanted an essentially political organization that would enforce peace settlement of disputes through such economic means as the boycott and such political means as diplomatic ostracism. Interestingly, Wilson never referred to military force in these conversations. According to one of the Inquiry members, he stated that

> just as the Monroe Doctrine had developed in time to meet changing conditions, so would the League of Nations. In fact, he could not see how a treaty of peace could be drawn up or how both *elasticity* and *security* could be obtained save under a League of nations; the opposite of such a course was to maintain the idea of the Great Powers and of balance of power, and such an idea had always produced only aggression and selfishness and war.[69]

68. Bowman memorandum, Dec. 10, 1918, ibid., 354–355.
69. Ibid., 354. In distancing himself from the LEP, Wilson may have overstated his differences and inadvertently misled Lodge. On December 18, while still aboard ship, he issued a statement to the press declaring that "the particular plan of the League to Enforce Peace I have never, directly or indirectly, endorsed." Wilson statement, Dec. 18, 1918, ibid., 420. That same day he had a talk with Henry White, who was "much relieved to find that the President's idea as to the League is rather a general one. . . ." White memorandum, Dec. [18], 1918, quoted in Allen Nevins, *Henry White: Thirty Years of American Diplomacy* (New York, 1930), 359. Soon afterward, White reported to Lodge, ". . . you may be perfectly certain that he [Wilson] does not contemplate any organization of that League, whereby our army and navy would be placed under the orders of a combination of Powers or any orders but our own." White assured Lodge that Wilson wanted the peace conference to establish only a "very slender organization . . . as a first start for that proposed League." White to Lodge, Dec. 24, 1918, Lodge Papers.

Even before the conference opened, Wilson moved to make his ideas real. He used his preconference tour of Britain, France, and Italy to expound his approach to a sound and just peace. In his first speech in Europe, on December 21, he urged that a league of nations should "operate as the organized moral force of men throughout the world," turning the "searching light of conscience" on all potential aggressors. A week later, he lauded the Allied and American soldiers for having "fought to do away with an old order and establish a new one," to overthrow "that unstable thing which we used to call the 'balance of power.'" Two days afterward, he conceded that the peace conference probably would produce, in his view, "unsatisfactory settlements," but it was far more important to "see to it that they are rendered more and more satisfactory by the subsequent adjustments which are made possible." For those adjustments the world needed "a machinery of good will and friendship. Friendship must have a machinery."[70]

Fervent crowds turned out to cheer the American president on this tour. Groups and individuals lined the railroad tracks to watch his train pass. In London and Paris, vast throngs turned out to shout themselves hoarse cheering him. In Rome, children threw flowers at his feet, and men and women throughout Allied and neutral countries lighted candles in front of his portrait, like a religious icon. It was a heady, moving time that one writer has called "America's moment." The power and ideals of the United States embodied in this man really did seem capable of transforming the world for the better. Even without Roosevelt's death, this triumphal march through Europe and the flood of newspaper accounts, photographs, and newsreels back home gave Wilson a powerful boost in his pursuit of world peace.[71]

Also before the peace conference opened, he began to take steps toward establishment of a league of nations. Wilson took heart when he learned that since the Phillimore Report officials in the British government had drafted other plans for an international organization. Two drafts of these British plans struck him as especially promising. The drafts came from Lord Robert Cecil, a junior British cabinet minister who combined an almost mystical religious faith with hard-hitting politics, and Jan Christiaan Smuts, a deeply learned South African general who had fought against Britain in the Boer War but was now a member of the British and Imperial War Cabinets. Wilson studied Smuts's draft

70. Wilson speech at Paris, Dec. 21, 1918, ibid., 462; speech at London, Dec. 28, 1918, ibid., 532; speech at Manchester, Dec. 30, 1918, ibid., 550–551; speech at Rome, Jan. 3, 1919, ibid., 603.
71. See Arthur Walworth, *America's Moment: 1918: American Diplomacy at the End of World War I* (New York, 1977).

during his Italian tour, and he incorporated the South African's ideas into the new draft that he wrote of what he again called the "Covenant" of the league of nations.[72]

Later known as the "First 'Paris Draft,'" this document contained thirteen articles and six supplementary provisions. The first two articles dealt sketchily with the league's structure. They stated that there should be a "Body of Delegates" to include all members and an "Executive Council" to be made up of the "Great Powers," together with other nations on a rotating basis. Article III went to the heart of Wilson's thinking: "The Contracting Powers unite in guaranteeing to each other political independence and territorial integrity;" boundary changes could be made "pursuant to the principle of self-determination," by a three-fourths vote of the members, but all "Contracting Powers accept without reservation the principle that the peace of the world is superior in importance to every question of Political jurisdiction or boundary." Articles IV and V called for arms reduction and set out procedures for peaceful settlement of disputes by the Executive Council. Article VI affirmed that any member not submitting to those procedures "shall *ipso facto* become at war with all the members of the League, which shall immediately subject it to a complete economic and financial boycott," while the council would also "recommend what effective military or naval force the members of the League of Nations shall severally contribute." The remaining seven articles provided for blockade of offending powers; asserted concern by the whole league whenever and wherever war threatened; stated a procedure for admission of new members; and abrogated all treaties inconsistent with the covenant. Six supplementary provisions addressed the fate of former German colonies and Austro-Hungarian and Turkish territories, with "mandatory" authority to be conferred by the league over some of those places, and assured humane conditions for labor and fair treatment of minorities in former enemy territories.[73]

Several minds and hands lent themselves to this draft of a covenant for a league of nations. Some of the provisions came from the Magnolia Draft; other ideas and language derived from Smuts's plan. But Wilson himself furnished the words – typed on eleven letter-sized pages on his own machine and corrected and amended in his handwriting. Also, his alone was the central tenet – that the members of the league would mutually guarantee each other's independence and borders and pledge

72. Entry, Jan. 6, 1919, Grayson Diary, in Link, ed., *Papers of Wilson*, LIII, 621–622; House Diary, Jan. 8, 1919, ibid., 694.
73. Wilson Draft Covenant, [ca. Jan. 8, 1919], ibid., 678–686.

to boycott and perhaps use military force against any offender. This document showed unmistakably that Wilson had taken his stand on the principle that international enforcement must be carried out by a political body. That body would consist of a great power directorate and a widely inclusive membership of other nations; together, they would undertake to maintain peace throughout the world. Boldness had always been the strongest trait of Wilson's political character. The world would soon note how much in character he remained.[74]

Having established his basic position, Wilson was now willing to share his thoughts. He showed this draft to House on January 8 and discussed it with the American delegation two days later. Lansing, who shared the skepticism of Lodge and others about international enforcement, found the president "so vain of his ability" that he adopted "a curt, almost insulting manner of refuting valid objections to the document which he has drawn. House says that he must have been unwell." That may have been the case, because shortly afterward Wilson welcomed General Bliss's detailed written comments. He adopted Bliss's suggested addition to Article III – the guarantee of independence and territorial integrity – which added the words "as against external aggression." This change, together with others suggested by Bliss, formed the basis for the revised covenant that Wilson wrote around the middle of January.[75]

This new document, which came to be known as the "Second 'Paris Draft,'" now included a sharper definition of the mandate system as a reform of colonialism, a stronger statement on behalf of the rights of laboring people, a clearer commitment to disarmament, a more prominent inclusiveness toward all nations great and small, and a stronger commitment to peaceful change along lines of self-determination. Thomas Knock has called this Second Paris Draft "Wilson's most important formulation of the League." It built the platform on which the president would hammer out and unveil to the world as the fundamental charter of the League of Nations – the Draft Covenant.[76]

---

74. A photographic copy of this typed draft is in ibid., 655–677.
75. House Diary, Jan. 8, 1919, ibid., 694; Bliss to Newton D. Baker, Jan. 11, 1919, ibid., 720; Lansing memorandum, "The President's Draft of a Covenant for a League of Nations," Jan. 11, 1919, ibid., LIV, 3–4; Bliss to Wilson, Jan. 15, 1919, ibid., 84; Bliss memorandum, "Suggestions in Regard to the Draft of the Covenant," Jan. 14, 1919, ibid., 85–88; Wilson to Bliss, Jan. 17, 1919, ibid., 123; Wilson Draft Covenant [ca. Jan. 18, 1919], ibid., 138–148. See also entry Jan. 18, 21, 1919, Edith Benham Diary, ibid., 149, 196.
76. Knock, *To End All Wars*, 207. On this draft see also ibid., 204–206.

In the four weeks from mid-January to mid-February 1919, Wilson displayed both gifts as negotiator and his major weakness in pursuit of peacemaking. The peace conference formally opened on January 18, and the president moved at once on the league question. During the first week of the conference he pulled off a coup. He persuaded the conference's governing body, the Council of Ten, to set up a League of Nations Commission that included only representatives from the more important powers. Next, he capitalized on that move by getting the Council of Ten to stack the membership of the League Commission further in his favor by appointing himself, House, Cecil, and Smuts, along with two representatives each from France, Italy, and Japan, and one member each from nine other countries. On January 25, when the full conference met for its second plenary session, Wilson reported on the project. Declaring that the League of Nations was essential to both achieving and maintaining the peace settlement, he urged that its framers "make this League of Nations a vital thing – not merely a formal thing, an occasional thing, . . . but always functioning in watchful attendance upon the interests of the nations, . . . it should be an eye of the nations to keep watch upon the common interest, an eye that does not slumber."[77]

The League Commission met ten times between February 3 and 14. Wilson, House, Smuts, Cecil, and their technical advisors gathered frequently between those sessions to hash out disputed points and go over several further drafts. In addition, the president had informal talks with less senior members of the American delegation, including Herbert Hoover, who was in Paris to advise on food aid to Europe and other technical aspects of the peace settlement. It was grueling work for Wilson, particularly because he was the only head of government on the commission. He had to attend its sessions and conduct the behind-the-scenes discussions on top of taking part in the almost daily conclaves of the Council of Ten and the Supreme War Council. Those encounters with his fellow plenipotentiaries, especially France's aged, obdurate premier, Clemenceau; Britain's wily, mercurial prime minister, Lloyd George; and Italy's smooth but shallow premier, Vittorio Orlando, merely reinforced his suspicions about their selfish war aims. Physically, the succession of fifteen-hour days took a toll, as his family, physician,

---

77. House to Wilson, Jan. 19, 1919, ibid., 150; Sir William Wiseman Diary, Jan. 19, 1919, ibid., 151; Cecil Diary, ibid., Jan. 1919, 152; Sir Maurice Hankey minutes of Council of Ten, Jan. 22, 23, 1919, ibid., 206–210, 218; Wilson speech, Jan. 25, 1919, ibid., 266–267.

and newspaper reporters noticed. Wilson was paying a price for his lonehandedness in making major foreign policy decisions.[78]

Three other matters added to his effort and anguish. One was the language of the proposed covenant. According to Hoover, who argued the merits of a gradualist approach, Wilson stated, "We must have a great state instrument which will be like the Declaration of Independence and the Constitution of the United States, and make a great step forward in international relations." Because of that desire – along with Wilson's renowned concern for language – the compromises with other representatives and the requirements of diplomatic and international legal usage pained him. One British draft had, Wilson told House, "no warmth or color in it," while the Draft Covenant struck him as inferior to his earlier version which, House agreed, "was more human and a little less legal." One person who would agree with Wilson about the literary merits of the Draft Covenant was Lodge. The senator later reportedly sneered at the president's presumed authorship of the document: "As an English production it does not rank high. It might get by at Princeton but certainly not at Harvard."[79]

Also draining the president's energies and emotions were two challenges to the guarantee of independence and territorial integrity. From one side, Cecil proposed to drop the words "and preserve as against external aggression" from the guarantee. Wilson held the other members of the League Commission firmly against Cecil, although they did soften the language somewhat by adding, "In case of any such aggression, the Executive Council shall advise the plan and the means by which this obligation shall be fulfilled." This challenge stemmed from personal friction between Cecil and Wilson, neither of whom liked the other much, and from British attitudes that resembled Republican thinking back home in wanting only limited security commitments. "I am afraid there will be trouble with the Dominions," Cecil recorded in his diary, "who do not appreciate the idea of having to fight for the integrity of Bohemia, or some such place." Cecil's observation eerily anticipated Neville Chamberlain's words about Czechoslovakia during

78. For the strain on Wilson, see Grayson Diary, Feb. 4, 5, 9, 1919, ibid., 473, 489, LV, 36; Edith Benham Diary, Feb. 4, 6, 10, 1919, ibid., LIV, 489, 521, LV, 66; *New York Herald,* Feb. 15, 1919, ibid., 162.
79. Hoover account in Henry L. Stimson Diary, Mar. 18, 1920, Yale University Library; House Diary, Feb. 2, 13, 1919, in Link, ed., *Papers of Wilson,* LIV, 459; LVI, 155–156. For Lodge's remark, see Stephen Bonsal, *Unfinished Business* (New York, 1944), 275.

the Munich crisis of 1938 – "a faraway country of which we know little" – and it offered a foretaste of the arguments that Wilson would face
in the Senate from Lodge, Knox, and other Republicans.[80]

The president was only too keenly aware of the limitations imposed
by his country's Constitution and political leanings. When the French
pushed for creation of an international military force under unified
command, Wilson told the League Commission, "We must make a distinction between what is possible and what is not. No nation will consent to control." The American Constitution forbade any such action,
and the main argument of American league opponents "is that the army
of the United States would be at the disposal of an international council, that American troops would thus be liable to fight at any moment
for the most remote of causes." Speaking directly to the French members, Wilson asserted that the only path to international security "lies in
our having confidence in the good faith of the nations who belong to
the League. . . . When danger comes, we too will come, and we will
help you, but you must trust us. We must all depend on our mutual
good faith." Wilson's words were not too different from what Roosevelt, Lodge, and Knox had said and from what those senators and
others would say again and again during the League fight.[81]

III

On February 14, 1919, Wilson proved how great a feat he had wrought
through the League of Nations Commission. Without advance notice,
he presented the finished Draft Covenant to the plenary session of the
peace conference. The day was damp and rainy, and the president quietly read the document article by article before speaking only briefly.
"Slowly as he read," wrote the American journalist William Allen
White, "the hearers realized that they were getting some new declaration of independence, of the world's national independence." Still,
White thought that Wilson's "spoken words were as gray and drab and
soggy as his reading." His performance probably certainly owed a lot to
fatigue. Riding back from the meeting, Mrs. Wilson noticed that he
leaned his head back on the seat of the car. "Are you so weary?" she

80. League Commission minutes, Feb. 6, 1919, Link, vol. LIV, 510, 512. See
    also Cecil Diary, Feb. 6, [1919], ibid., 514. On the two men's mutual dis-
    like, see Cecil Diary, Jan. 19, Feb. 3, 1919, ibid., 152, 460–461; Benham
    Diary, Feb. 6, 1919, ibid., 522.
81. League Commission minutes, Feb. 11, 1919, ibid., LV, 79–80.

recalled asking him. "Yes, I suppose I am," he reportedly answered, "but how little one man means when such vital things are at stake."[82]

Wilson was also deliberately downplaying the drama of the event in an attempt to control reactions at home. Just before the plenary session, he held a press conference with American reporters, which one of them described as "cordial and frank." At this conference, the reporter noted, the president "described intimately, but not for publication how the League of Nations Commission worked and spoke confidently about the society's prospects." Also before the session, Wilson cabled the members of the Senate Foreign Relations Committee and House Foreign Affairs Committee asking them to meet with him for dinner at the White House on February 26. In the meantime, he asked "that I be permitted to go over with you, Article by Article the Constitution reported before this part of the work of the Conference is made the subject of debate in Congress." The following day, February 15, the president left Paris to make a quick trip back to the United States.[83]

Still, Wilson could not disguise what a giant step he had taken. Though longer, more detailed, and less eloquent than his previous drafts, the Draft Covenant retained the essential features of his program. His all-important guarantee of independence and territorial integrity, in almost exactly the same words, was now Article X. Article XI asserted the League's concern about "war or threat of war" anywhere in the world. Articles XII through XV laid down requirements for mediation and arbitration and called for establishment of a "Permanent Court of International Justice." Article XVI established the League's authority to institute an economic boycott and recommend the use of force. Also remaining from Wilson's earlier drafts were arms reduction, mandates over former enemy colonies, humane labor conditions, and the bicameral structure with a Body of Delegates composed of all members and an Executive Council comprising the United States, Britain, France, Italy, and Japan as permanent members. In sum, Wilson had achieved his aim of creating an essentially political international organization – not the primarily judicial one favored by the LEP and others – with potentially broad, muscular enforcement powers.[84]

Despite himself, Wilson let a sense of momentousness and notes of

82. White in New York *World*, Feb. 16, 1919; Edith Wilson, *My Memoir*, 239.
83. *New York Herald*, Feb. 15, 1919, in Link, ed., *Papers of Wilson*, LV, 161–162; Wilson to Joseph P. Tumulty, Feb. 14, 1919, ibid., 184.
84. The Draft Covenant, as Wilson read it to the plenary session, is in ibid., 164–173.

hope creep into his speech presenting the Draft Covenant to the conference. "Armed force is in the background of this program," Wilson
acknowledged, "but it *is* in the background, . . . the last resort, because
this is intended as a constitution of peace, not as a league of war."
These structures and procedures were "not a straitjacket, but a vehicle
of life, . . . in which power may be varied at the discretion of those who
exercise it and in accordance with the changing circumstances of the
time." Firm but elastic, this document offered "a definite guarantee of
peace. It is a guarantee by word against aggression." Wilson characterized the Draft Covenant as "at one and the same time a practical document and a humane document. There is a pulse of sympathy in it. There
is a compulsion of conscience about it."[85]

The Draft Covenant also expressed Wilson's lonehanded, radically
executive approach to foreign policy. Except for airing the First Paris
Draft to the American delegation in January, he had shared his inner-
most thoughts with no one other than Colonel House – whom he continued to use as a minion rather than a real advisor. Wilson ignored
pleas from sympathetic Democrats to take them and others into his confidence. He likewise brushed aside suggestions to publicize his views in
the right quarters from Ray Stannard Baker, the delegation's press officer, and from Herbert Bayard Swope, the chief correspondent of the
nation's leading Democratic newspaper, the New York *World*. This tactic reflected Wilson's long-standing practice of keeping reporters at a
distance, and it presaged future trouble in press relations at the conference. "The battle for some things is a bit lonely," the president admitted
to Swope. But he maintained that "it is very important just now that I
should not say anything. I am surrounded by intrigue here, and the only
way I can succeed is by working silently, saying nothing in public unless
it becomes necessary to bring about an open contest."[86]

Now the arena was about to change. An "open contest" was about
to start at home. How well Woodrow Wilson would fare in this new
theater of operations would become the paramount question of the
League fight. He and everyone else would begin to answer that question
when he returned to America at the end of February 1919.

85. Wilson remarks, Feb. 14, 1919, ibid., 175–178.
86. Wilson to Swope, Feb. 1, 7, 1919, ibid., LIV, 427, 550–551. For Demo-
    crats' suggestions, see House Diary, Jan. 2, 1919, ibid., LIII, 587–588, and
    for Baker's urging, see Baker to Wilson, Jan. 21, 1919, ibid., LIV, 189–191.

2

Round Robin and Revision

On March 3 and 4, 1919, the U.S. Senate was meeting around the clock. Under the congressional calendar that existed before the adoption of the Twentieth Amendment to the Constitution in 1933, all-night sessions were common at such times as this. The previous calendar required that the life of a congress end at noon on March 4 of an odd-numbered year. The deadline usually occasioned a frantic rush to pass legislation and, hence, all-night sessions like this one in 1919. To the Senate, with its privilege of unlimited debate, the deadline also offered a standing temptation to filibuster. Two years before, in March 1917, as the country had teetered on the brink of intervention in World War I, a dozen senators led by Robert La Follette and George Norris had staged a filibuster to block passage of the bill to arm American merchant ships. President Wilson had denounced them as a "little group of willful men, representing no opinion but their own," and their action had prompted the Senate in its next session to adopt its first cloture rule to limit debate.[1]

Now, in 1919, another filibuster was under way. This time, however, the instigators were not a small band of despised dissidents, but rather, the Republican leadership. Since late February, Henry Cabot Lodge and his cohorts had been consuming the Senate's legislative days in order to prevent passage of necessary appropriation bills. Their undisguised aim was to grab a share of power. By blocking indispensable legislation, they were forcing the president to call the next congress – in which they, the Republicans, held majorities in both houses – into session long before the constitutionally mandated date of the following December. In addition, Lodge and other leading Republicans such as Knox had a more sharply focused aim. On February 25, within hours of his arrival in Washington on his return from France, the Democratic leaders in the Senate informed Wilson that the Republicans were trying to seize control of the debate over the peace treaty and the League of Nations. This filibuster was a tactic in the now-raging League fight.[2]

---

1. Wilson statement [Mar. 4, 1917], in Arthur S. Link, ed., *The Papers of Woodrow Wilson* (Princeton, N.J., 1990), XLI, 320. On the armed ships bill filibuster, see Arthur S. Link, *Wilson: Campaigns for Progression and Peace* (Princeton, N.J., 1965), V, 359–361.
2. On the meeting with the Democratic leaders, see Link, ed., *Papers of Wilson*, LV.

That situation formed the background to the move that Senator Lodge made just before midnight on March 3, 1919. He entered the Senate chamber carrying a rolled-up document. At his desk, he unrolled the document, read it over, and waited for Representative Medill McCormick of Illinois, who was a Republican senator-elect, to come and sign it. Then, having gotten permission to interrupt the senator who was speaking, Lodge read the document, which was a resolution that he wished to put before the Senate. The resolution opened with three "whereas" clauses; these observed that the Senate must give its advice and consent to treaties, that the peace conference was meeting in Paris, and that a committee of the conference had drafted a constitution of a League of Nations. The resolution's two operative clauses stated that, first, ". . . the constitution of the league of nations in the form now proposed by the peace conference should not be accepted by the United States," and, second, ". . . it is the sense of the Senate that the negotiations on the part of the United States should immediately be directed to the utmost expedition of the urgent business of negotiating peace terms with Germany" satisfactory to the Allies before consideration of any proposal for a league.[3]

A Democratic senator, Claude Swanson of Virginia, immediately objected to the introduction of the resolution. Lodge bowed to the objection and commented, "I merely wish to add by way of explanation the following:" whereupon he read the names of thirty-seven Republican senators and senators-elect who had signed the resolution. He added that three or four other senators, whom he had not been able to contact, would probably add their names to the list. Lodge later recalled that he had expected objection to be raised and that, by reading the resolution and the names of the signers, "our purpose, however, had been served."[4]

Lodge read the situation right. The press immediately resorted to a 150-year-old term to describe such a method of introduction and dubbed his resolution the "Round Robin." Nobody missed the significance of the Round Robin. With all ninety-six members of the Senate voting, thirty-three was the number needed to deny consent to a treaty. The Round Robin's signatories numbered thirty-seven, and within hours two absent Republican senators telegraphed their support. In addition, at least one Democrat, James Reed of Missouri, had denounced the league

3. *Congressional Record*, 65th Cong., 3rd Sess. (Mar. 4, 1919), 4974.
4. Ibid.; Henry Cabot Lodge, *The Senate and the League of Nations* (New York, 1925), 118.

idea and the Draft Covenant. The Round Robin likewise served to remind the Allied negotiators in Paris that powerful Americans favored an approach to peacemaking that differed from Wilson's and was more like theirs. With the Round Robin, Lodge and his Republican colleagues fired a warning shot across the bow of Wilson's fast-moving project to establish a League of Nations with the United States as a charter, leading member. It struck a hard blow in the League fight.[5]

I

The Republicans were correct in believing that they needed to stop Wilson's momentum. Before the unveiling of the Draft Covenant, his tactics had succeeded in keeping the Republicans off base. Still reeling under the impact of Roosevelt's death, they had seethed at Wilson's silence. "The difficulty in dealing with the [league] question," Lodge confessed privately at the end of January, "is that everything is in the air." Several Republican senators did attack the league idea during January and early February 1919, and the isolationists also chimed in. At the end of January Borah raised the level of hyperbole when he told reporters, "If the Saviour of mankind should revisit the earth and declare for a League of Nations, I would be opposed to it." When the news of the Draft Covenant reached the United States during the afternoon of February 14, the main reactions, however, were less apocalyptic. Public opinion, judging by the best measures available, responded warmly and positively. *Literary Digest* and *Current Opinion*, two magazines that surveyed newspaper responses, initially found coolness and doubt among some Republican journals, but widespread expressions of enthusiasm and even adulation from Democratic, independent, and other Republican organs.[6]

---

5. The other two Republican senators were Albert Fall of New Mexico and Stephen Elkins of West Virginia. See *New York Times*, Mar. 4, 5, 1919; New York *World*, Mar. 4, 5, 1919. The term "round robin" originally referred to a practice, evidently begun in the eighteenth century by British sailors, of signing a petition in a circular fashion in order to conceal the names of the originators. In America, it had come to refer simply to the practice of presenting a petition and reading the names of its signers into the record of an official meeting.

6. Lodge to Albert J. Beveridge, Jan. 30, 1919, Lodge Papers; *Congressional Record*, 65th Cong., 3rd Sess. (Jan. 14, 1919), 1385–1387; New York *World*, Feb. 1, 1919; *Current Opinion*, LXVI (Mar. 1919), 139; *Literary Digest*, LX (Mar. 1, 1919), 13.

Literary Digest conducted the broadest newspaper poll in mid-March, after a month of discussion of the Draft Covenant and the Republican counterattack with the Round Robin. This poll canvassed 1,377 editors. It recorded 718 (52 percent) of them in favor of accepting the Draft Covenant as it stood, 478 (35 percent) wanting some changes, and 181 (12 percent) opposed. Republican papers registered 22 percent for unconditional acceptance, 56 percent wanting changes, and 22 percent against. Democratic papers registered 85 percent for unconditional acceptance, four percent for changes, and 11 percent – mostly Hearst's papers – against. Independent papers registered 78 percent for unconditional acceptance, 19 percent for changes, and three percent against. Sectional variations largely followed party lines. The Republican stronghold regions, the Northeast and Midwest, stood lowest for unconditional acceptance, whereas the Democratic bastion of the South stood highest. The one true two-party region, the West, stood in between but closer to the Republican regions. Opinion may also have diverged between urban and rural areas and between larger and smaller cities. A yes-or-no questionnaire printed during February and March in sixteen large-circulation metropolitan newspapers yielded a response in which 107,700 readers (76 percent) answered yes to unqualified acceptance of the Draft Covenant, versus 33,427 (24 percent) who answered no.[7]

This strongly favorable reception owed less to Wilson than to assiduous organizing and publicizing by the LEP. Taft and other LEP leaders were mounting a series of ten regional congresses throughout the country that started in early February. The ex-president and other prominent pro-league spokesmen traveled over 8,000 miles and addressed 175 meetings, which were attended by about 300,000 people. These regional congresses adopted resolutions calling for "the formation of a League of Nations with adequate economic and military sanctions to guarantee the peace." When Taft read the Draft Covenant, he bubbled with delight. "It is a real League with *cinch* and *clinch* in it," he wrote his wife. "It does not quite come up to the League to Enforce Peace program but it is very near it." Taft and the other LEP leaders instantly converted the remainder of their tour and the regional congresses into rallies in support of the new document. Taft also used his speeches and his newspaper column to fend off Republican criticisms in the Senate and elsewhere, and he tried to enlist Root's backing. That elder states-

---

7. Ibid., LXI (Apr. 5, 1919), 13–16, 120–129; newspaper questionnaire, cited in Warren F. Kuehl, *Seeking World Order: The United States and International Organization to 1920* (Nashville, Tenn., 1969), 299.

man, Taft told another LEP leader, "would influence Republicans in the Senate more than any man you could secure."[8]

Taft was right to worry about the attitudes of Republican senators and other members of his party. Lodge, for one, greeted the Draft Covenant with scorn and fear. As Republican leader in the Senate and soon to be chairman of the Foreign Relations Committee, he felt bound to honor Wilson's request to withhold comment until after the meeting at the White House on February 26. Privately, however, Lodge minced no words. "It is in the highest degree dangerous," he wrote to Albert Beveridge. ". . . One single clause [Article X] requires us to guarantee the territorial integrity and political independence of every nation on earth." Such a guarantee "can only be sustained by arms," and he did not think that the American public would buy into that kind of commitment. To another friend Lodge confided, "I cannot accept this draft as it stands. I should be false to every conviction which I have were I to do so. I cannot be carried away by a gust of emotion or passion on a matter so important as this." But he was worried about opposing the Draft Covenant. "We must be careful, however, in handling it [the League]," Lodge told still another confidant, and to a plea for outright opposition, he replied, "I shall not oppose a blank negative to any League. I shall discuss the one that is before us."[9]

Lodge's revulsion toward the Draft Covenant, rather than Taft's endorsement, came closer to typifying the reaction of leading Republicans. His general unease and his pouncing on Article X found faithful reflection in the responses of Root and Hughes. Those men also refrained from public comment at first, but in private they likewise sounded harsh notes. Behind his pose of sphinxlike silence, Root expressed doubts about the Draft Covenant. According to his friend

---

8. Taft to Helen H. Taft, Feb. 15, 1919, Taft Papers, reel 27; Taft to Herbert S. Houston, Feb. 27, 1919, ibid., reel 555; LEP regional congress resolution quoted in Ruhl J. Bartlett, *The League to Enforce Peace* (Chapel Hill, N.C., 1944), 115. For Taft's unassuaged doubts about Wilson, see, e.g., Taft to Oscar S. Straus, Jan. 19, 1919, Oscar S. Straus Papers, Library of Congress, Box 15; Taft to Gus J. Karger, Feb. 14, 1919, Taft Papers, reel 555. For the LEP's activities, see Bartlett, *League to Enforce Peace*, 114–115; and for some of Taft's speeches and columns, see Theodore Marburg and Horace Flack, eds., *The Taft Papers on the League of Nations* (New York, 1920), 228–257.
9. Lodge to Beveridge, Feb. 18, 27, 1919, Lodge Papers; Lodge to Robert M. Washburn, Feb. 22, 1919, ibid.; Lodge to Louis A. Coolidge, Feb. 17, 1919, ibid.

and protégé Henry Stimson, Root said on February 15, "Article X, for
example, completely abrogated the Monroe Doctrine." He also objected
"that the instrument rested upon the strength of covenants rather than
upon the establishment of international law." After a night's reflection,
however, Root added to Stimson "that he thought the instrument, with
proper amendments, might constitute a beginning." When Taft asked
Root to speak in support of the Draft Covenant, however, Root
declined. "Thanks, I think I will not speak," was his laconic reply.[10]

Hughes reacted almost identically to the Draft Covenant As he later
told his biographer, he first read the document in his morning newspaper
over breakfast on February 15. "When he came to Article X," wrote the
biographer, "he knit his brow in disapproval. . . . Reading it to his wife,
who sat across the table, he snapped, 'The American people will never
stand for that.'" In autobiographical notes, Hughes later recalled, "I
thought this proposal was a grave mistake." After the Round Robin,
Hughes broke his public silence to tell reporters, "I do not favor the constitution of the League as it stands." Implicitly attacking Article X, he
warned that "we must not involve ourselves in a League of Nations that
may make us the pawn of selfish people in other lands and in the end
destroy the peace and happiness of our own people." Later in March,
Hughes gave a speech that contained a lengthy critique of the Draft
Covenant and leveled the strongest attacks at Article X.[11]

Wilson's plea to avoid premature discussion of the Draft Covenant
did not silence the isolationists. Several of them pounced on the Draft
Covenant, including three members of the president's own party. The
agrarian radical and racist demagogue, James K. Vardaman of Mississippi, scoffed at Wilson's "little gold rattle" and excoriated the pro-

---

10. Entry, Feb. 15, 1919, Henry L. Stimson Diary, Yale University Library; note
at Dec. 29, 1918 entry, ibid.; Root to Taft, Feb. 28, 1919, quoted in
Richard L. Leopold, *Elihu Root and the Conservative Tradition* (Boston,
1954), 135. Leopold calls Root's reply "worthy of Calvin Coolidge." Ibid.
For Stimson's own views, which generally mirrored Root's, see Stimson to
Will Hays, Feb. 18, 1919, copy in Elihu Root Papers, Library of Congress,
Box 137; Stimson to Taft, Feb. 20, 1919, Taft Papers, reel 205.

11. Merlo J. Pusey interview with Hughes, Nov. 26, 1946, cited and quoted in
Pusey, *Charles Evans Hughes* (New York, 1951), I, 395; David J. Danelski
and Joseph S. Tulchin, eds., *The Autobiographical Notes of Charles Evans
Hughes* (Cambridge, Mass., 1973), 210; *New York Times*, Mar. 7, 1919.
For Hughes' critique, see speech of Mar. 26, 1919, in Charles Evans
Hughes Papers, Library of Congress, reel 138; the parts of this speech
attacking Article X are in Danelski and Tulchin, eds., *Autobiographical
Notes of Hughes*, 210–212.

posed League as a "superstate" and a "Trojan horse" of mainly British pedigree. His fellow agrarian radical, Thomas Hardwick of Georgia, asked, "Are you willing to enter into a covenant of death secretly arrived at? . . . to become the policeman of the world? . . . to plunge our people forever into the maelstrom of European and Asiatic slaughter?" Because Vardaman and Hardwick had fallen victim to a party purge by Wilson the year before, they would not be in the Senate to bedevil him after March 4. But another isolationist Democrat would be. This was Reed, who had attacked the League idea since 1917. Reed now denounced the Draft Covenant for proposing to set up a League controlled by the British Empire.[12]

Familiar Republican isolationist voices likewise rained damnation down on the Draft Covenant. Borah told reporters on February 15 that the document meant the destruction of the Monroe Doctrine. Although he was a member of the Foreign Relations Committee, he decided not to attend the meeting at the White House so that he could deliver a scathing indictment on the Senate floor. On February 21, Borah denounced the Draft Covenant as "the most radical departure from our policies hitherto obtaining that has ever been proposed at any time since our Government was established." Citing Article X as a triumph of British diplomacy, he claimed that it would destroy the Monroe Doctrine by allowing Europeans to intervene in the Americas and by requiring the United States to intervene outside its own hemisphere. Instead, America must help the world by renewing "the national spirit; not isolation but freedom to do as our own people think wise and just."[13]

12. New York *World*, Feb. 16, 1919; *Congressional Record*, 65th Cong., 3rd Sess. (Feb. 18, 1919), 3657–3658; ibid. (Mar. 1, 1919), 4704; ibid. (Feb. 22, 1919), 4026–4033. Reed would go on to express greater personal animus against Wilson than almost any other senator. Why he did was not clear. Reed, who was close to the political machine run by Tom Pendergast in his hometown of Kansas City, had previously clashed with Wilson over policy and patronage, but he had also grasped the president's coattails in running for reelection in 1916.

13. Ibid., 3911–3915. In this speech, as in some of his earlier pronouncements, Borah also sounded anti-imperialist notes that would later make him a hero among anticolonial rebels in Asia and Latin America. On Borah's later idolization in Latin America, see Robert David Johnson, *The Peace Progressives and American Foreign Relations* (Cambridge, Mass., 1995), 115–116, 137–139. Other Republicans who raised isolationist arguments against the Draft Covenant were Miles Poindexter of Washington and Albert Cummins of Iowa. See *Congressional Record*, 65th Cong., 3rd Sess. (Feb. 19, 1919), 3746–3756, (Feb. 26, 1919), 4310–4313.

Several signs boded ill for the president's meeting with the congressional committees on February 26, 1919. Wilson evidently felt some foreboding about the trip back, because in a shipboard dinner conversation he coined the phrase that he would later use often in the League fight: "The failure of the United States to back it [the League] would break the heart of the world." Wilson's luck started to run out as soon as he set foot back in the United States. A longshoremen's strike in New York required the presidential liner to dock in Boston. That circumstance stirred up criticism about offending Senator Lodge by appearing in his hometown. To make matters worse, local officials in Boston staged elaborate ceremonies to greet the president, including a parade and a speech to a crowd of 8,000. Wilson avoided making any direct references to the Draft Covenant, and he stuck to generalities in the speech. Lodge's friends assured the senator that the public reception was "cool, apathetic, and without enthusiasm." But newspaper reports and other accounts painted a different picture, and Lodge's need for reassurance showed how bothered he and the Senate Republicans were.[14]

With those events as a prelude, it was small wonder that the meeting at the White House on February 26 was not a smashing success. No stenographic record was kept, and, like any such meeting, this one was rife with self-serving interpretations. After the thirty-four senators and representatives arrived, President and Mrs. Wilson took them in to dinner in the State Dining Room. Then the all-male official conclave moved to the East Room, where the attendees sat in a U-shaped arrangement, with the president at the middle of one side of the "U." The discussion lasted over two hours, until nearly midnight, and by most accounts everyone remained polite and pleasant. Dr. Grayson, who was not present but presumably heard an account from the president right afterward, wrote in his diary, "The meeting was more or less of a free and easy character, as the President invited questions, and his invitation was taken advantage of by many of those present."[15]

14. Grayson Diary, Feb. 22, 1919, in Link, ed., *Papers of Wilson*, LV, 224; Lodge to Calvin Coolidge, Feb. 26, 1919, Lodge Papers. For other accounts of Wilson's reception in Boston, see Louis A. Coolidge to Lodge, Feb. 25, 1919, ibid.; William S. Felton to Lodge, Feb. 25, 1919, ibid.; New York *World*, Feb. 25, 1919; *New York Times*, Feb. 25, 1919; Grayson Diary, Feb. 24, 1919, in Link, ed., *Papers of Wilson*, LV, 235–237.

15. Grayson Diary, Feb. 26, 1919, ibid., 267; *New York Times*, Feb. 27, 1919. For the seating arrangement, see Tom Connally and Alfred Steinberg, *My Name is Tom Connally* (New York, 1954), 96. Two senators, Borah and Albert Fall of New Mexico, and one representative, Dorsey Shackleford of Missouri, did not attend the meeting.

Dispute about the spirit and usefulness of the meeting arose at once. As Grayson also noted in his diary, "the various Senators who were interviewed by the newspaper correspondents failed to agree in their stories of what actually happened." The *New York Times* and New York *World,* both pro-League papers, carried stories stressing the "good humor" of the president and his guests and quoted several senators, including even the normally irascible Republican Frank Brandegee of Connecticut, as appreciating Wilson's openness. "For myself," Brandegee added, "I can say that nothing the President said changed my mind about the League of Nations. I am against it, as I was before." Anonymous skeptics also expressed "great astonishment" at Wilson's "lack of information" about such matters as the status of the Monroe Doctrine under the Draft Covenant and members' rights to withdraw from the League or to refuse to accept mandates. Actually, according to the account in the *New York Times,* Wilson discoursed knowledgeably on such topics as disarmament, arbitration, and collective security. In answer to a question about whether the United States would relinquish sovereignty under the League, he conceded that there might be some sacrifice of sovereignty – a point that would weigh heavily and negatively with many Republicans in the League fight. Some other anonymous sources alleged that Wilson had brushed aside self-rule for Ireland as a purely British concern that could not come before the peace conference. The White House issued a quick statement that the remark about Ireland "has no foundation in fact, and is a deliberate falsehood."[16]

In private, both the president and his senatorial critics had harsher things to say. The day after the meeting Lodge told a friend that it had been "uneventful" and that Wilson had not known "so much as some of the men who questioned him" about the Draft Covenant. "We learned practically nothing," Lodge later wrote to Henry White. Predictably, Frank Brandegee was more scathing. This lonely, brooding bachelor was the Senate's leading curmudgeon and a well-known alcoholic. To the Republican lawyer and foreign policy advisor Chandler P. Anderson, Brandegee confided that the dinner was "a miserable affair." No alcohol was served; each guest got only "one rather small cigar of indifferent quality," and Mrs. Wilson displayed dirty fingernails. Brandegee also criticized Wilson for not having brought a copy of the Draft Covenant to the discussion and for having shown "dense ignorance as

16. Grayson Diary, Feb. 26, 1919, in Link, ed., *Papers of Wilson,* LV, 267; *New York Times,* Feb. 27, Mar. 1, 1919; New York *World,* Feb. 27, 1919; New York *Sun,* Feb. 27, 1919; *Congressional Record,* 65th Cong., 3rd Sess. (Feb. 28, 1919), 4528–4530, (Mar. 1, 1919), 4881.

to its meaning and effect." For his part, the president revised his initially positive recollection of the meeting in light of the Round Robin. Back in Paris, Wilson later told Colonel House, who had suggested this format rather than a speech to Congress, "Your dinner to the Senate Foreign Relations Committee *[sic]* was a failure as far as getting together was concerned."[17]

Even before the Round Robin, Lodge lent credence to the president's sour second thoughts. On February 28, the senator delivered one of his long, erudite addresses. He admitted he had written the speech before the White House meeting and had not altered it afterward. Lodge assailed the Draft Covenant as a product of haste, full of "crudeness and looseness of expression," and requiring abandonment of traditional American foreign policies. Article by article, he dissected what he saw as the Draft Covenant's shortcomings, particularly the sweeping pledge of Article X and threats to the Monroe Doctrine and control of immigration. "Unless some better constitution of a league than this can be drawn," Lodge concluded, "it seems to me . . . that the world's peace would be much better, much more surely promoted by allowing the United States to go on under the Monroe doctrine, . . . and if a league is desired it might be made up by the European nations whose interests are chiefly concerned, and with which the United States could cooperate fully and at any time, whenever cooperation was needed." After all, he

17. Lodge to Louis A. Coolidge, Feb. 27, 1919, Lodge Papers; Lodge to Henry White, Apr. 8, 1919, ibid.; entry Mar. 13, 1919, Chandler P. Anderson Diary, Library of Congress, reel 2; House Diary, Mar. 14, 1919, in Link, ed., *Papers of Wilson*, LV, 499. Wilson also recalled, incorrectly, "Knox and Lodge remained perfectly silent, refusing to ask any questions or to act in the spirit in which the dinner was given." Ibid. House evidently repeated this story to others. There is an account of this conversation in Stephen Bonsal memorandum, Mar. 24, [1919], Bonsal Papers, Box 18. Henry White related the part about Lodge's silence to the Senator, who replied, "He [Wilson] is mistaken in saying that neither Knox nor I asked him any questions. I asked at least three and Knox asked at least two; but we were not the principal questioners, although I think the questions we did ask covered some rather essential points." Lodge to White, Apr. 8, 1919, Lodge Papers. For another first-hand account of the meeting, from an anti-League Republican congressman, which supports Brandegee's points about Wilson's lack of a text and detailed knowledge of the Draft Covenant but lauds his "apparent candor" and patience under Brandegee's "pressing him rather closely," see John Jacob Rogers to White, Mar. 3, 1919, quoted in Allen Nevins, *Henry White: Thirty Years of American Diplomacy* (New York, 1930), 392–393, and Rogers memorandum, [ca. Mar. 5, 1919], Henry White Papers, Columbia University Library, Box 1.

noted, wars like the one just finished "are, fortunately, rare; so rare that one has never before occurred, and when the time came we took our part." The real guarantee against the recurrence of such a war lay in letting the peace conference get on with its real job, which was to shackle Germany with severe reparations and concessions. "We must not lose by an improvident attempt to reach eternal peace," Lodge concluded, "all that we have won by war and sacrifice."[18]

The next day, Knox took his swing at the Draft Covenant. In an equally long and carefully prepared speech, he argued that the proposed League of Nations was "merely an offensive and defensive alliance . . . formed with an avowed and published purpose to impose upon stranger powers the will of the coalition." This proposal amounted to "tyranny, nothing more, nothing less," and, worse, "instead of abolishing war, actually sanctions, breeds, and commands it. Moreover, it absolutely requires that every future war will be a potential world war, and that we shall be an active participant in every such war." Such a departure was totally unnecessary because war "is further away to-day than it has been for a century," and America could be "trusted again to come to the rescue" in the event of great international peril. As surer paths to peace, Knox urged three measures. The first was expanded, multilateral arbitration. The second was "an alliance [by the United States] with the strongest other power or two powers of the world for mutual protection." The third was a "true league of nations . . . to stop war" by strengthening international law and establishing a world court under which major powers would enforce its decrees within their respective spheres. Knox likewise called for shelving the League until after the peace treaty was completed, and in closing he declared, ". . . if the Hun flood again threatened to engulf the world, we should again be found fighting for the right, with the same accord and cooperation as in the past, all for the defense of civilization."[19]

Between them, Lodge and Knox were presenting the Republican alternative to both the Draft Covenant and Wilson's approach to peacemaking. They insisted that they did not want the United States to shrink from an involved role in the world. Of the two men's arguments, Knox's endorsement of an alliance seemed more in line with previous Republican great power activism, but basically he and Lodge stressed the same two themes in opposition to Wilson's vision of a new world order. One was a preference for regionalism over globalism within a framework of great power suzerainty over smaller nations and colonial areas. The

18. *Congressional Record,* 65th Cong., 3rd Sess. (Feb. 28, 1919), 4520–4528; New York *World,* Mar. 1, 1919.
19. *Congressional Record,* 65th Cong., 3rd Sess. (Mar. 1, 1919), 4687–4694.

other was their belief that, despite the world war's destruction and upheaval, the international political system had not changed and that established diplomatic approaches still sufficed. These two themes delineated the core of the Senate Republicans' position toward the Draft Covenant.[20]

Lodge's and Knox's attacks came as no great surprise, and they did not appear to sow much consternation among Senate Democrats or at the White House. After Lodge and Knox spoke, two other Republicans abetted their party's filibuster with further denunciations of the Draft Covenant. Lawrence Sherman of Illinois called it "a Pandora's box of evil to empty upon the American people the aggregated calamities of the world." Joseph France of Maryland spurned this "league to preserve the present condition of the world." It would erect an armed camp, at a time when America ought to providing the example "of our own exalted purposes . . . [to] lead all the nations toward that better, more perfect civilization."[21]

Meanwhile, Wilson was trying to show a conciliatory face toward critics. At the meeting with the congressional committees, he insisted that he would welcome proposals for changes in the Draft Covenant. He also responded favorably to a suggestion by Senator Thomas J. Walsh, Democrat of Montana, that the president might meet with him and a few like-minded pro-administration senators to consider revisions. On February 28, Wilson delivered a rambling speech to the Democratic National Committee in which he did stray from sweetness

20. There was an irony in Lodge's and Knox's implicit denials of revolutionary change. In the wake of the Bolshevik Revolution, the word and concept of "revolution" occupied a large place in the press and political discussion in Europe and the United States, where antiradical sentiment was already building up toward the "Red Scare" that blossomed at the end of 1919. In criticizing the Draft Covenant, both Poindexter and Lodge had played on the word "internationalism" to allege a guilt-by-association between Bolshevism and advocacy of the League. See *Congressional Record*, 65th Cong., 3rd Sess. (Feb. 19, 1919), 3755; (Feb. 28, 1919), 4528. Conversely, League advocates also played the anti-Bolshevik card, arguing that the League was needed as part of a strong international defense against revolutionary radicalism. Senator McCumber made such an argument in a pro-League speech on March 3 (ibid., 4883), and Taft had done the same in a speech in St. Louis on February 25 (Marburg and Flack, eds., *Taft Papers*, 258).

21. *Congressional Record*, 65th Cong., 3rd Sess. (Mar. 3, 1919), 4844–4850, 4865–4867, 4872–4888.

by alluding to his critics and "the fatuity of these gentlemen with their poor little minds." His main message, however, was to warn that the prospect of not supporting the League "reaches the depth of tragedy." He argued that the Draft Covenant made "a workable beginning of a thing that the world insists on" and that its plan "comes as near to being a guarantee of peace as you can get." Such rambling was not in character for Wilson, and it underscored what reporters had noticed the day before when the president had spent two hours at the Capitol conferring with representatives and senators – that he seemed tired. Wilson publicly insisted otherwise, but privately he admitted as much when the historian William E. Dodd called at the White House on March 1. The first thing Wilson said was, Dodd recalled, "I am tired, so tired."[22]

The Round Robin came into the picture at this point as a move to upset the presidential applecart of persuasion and conciliation. Lodge was its mover, and he and Knox were its principal authors, but the idea had originated with Brandegee. The Connecticut senator had gotten his inspiration from a letter of an anti-League constituent who urged the Senate to pass a resolution or make a public declaration against the Draft Covenant. Brandegee had taken the suggestion to Lodge at his home on Sunday, March 2. They had telephoned Knox to come over, and the three men worked into the evening on the text. The next day Brandegee showed the document to Albert Cummins of Iowa, who approved and signed it, and then began to circulate it. The three authors and Cummins agreed to keep the Round Robin secret unless they could get signatures from more than thirty-three of their colleagues – the number needed to block a treaty. After encountering some initial difficulty, Brandegee garnered twenty-one signatures within an hour. Another twelve senators clambered on board when they learned how strong the support was. The original foursome of Brandegee, Lodge, Knox, and Cummins also decided, according to Lodge, to keep the

22. Wilson speech of Feb. 28, 1919, in Link, ed., *Papers of Wilson*, LV, 309–324; Dodd to _____ Childers, Apr. 3, 1920, William E. Dodd Papers, Library of Congress, Box 150. For Wilson's openness to proposed changes, see John Jacob Rogers memorandum, [Mar. 5, 1919], Henry White Papers, Columbia, Box 1; Thomas J. Walsh to Wilson, Feb. 25, 1919, in Link, ed., *Papers of Wilson*, LV, 262–263; Wilson to Walsh, Feb. 26, 1919, ibid., 280. For reports of the meeting at the Capitol, see *New York Times*, Feb. 28, 1919, and entry, Feb. 27, 1919, Raymond Clapper Diary, Clapper Papers, Library of Congress, Box 6.

In contrast to his predecessor's lengthy, detailed, low-keyed presentation, Wilson's shorter speech flashed with his wonted eloquence and fire. Decrying his critics' "comprehensive ignorance of the state of the world," the president declared that the "great tides of the world . . . rise in their majesty and overwhelming might, and those who stand in the way are overwhelmed. Now the heart of the world is awake, and the heart of the world must be satisfied." Reminding the audience of "those splendid boys in khaki," he pledged, "I do not mean to come back until it's over over there." Wilson vowed that

> when the treaty comes back gentlemen on this side will find the Covenant not only in it, but so many threads of the treaty tied to the Covenant that you cannot dissect the Covenant from the treaty without destroying the whole vital structure. The structure of peace will not be vital without the League of Nations, and no man is going to bring back a cadaver with him.

Wilson closed with a peroration that echoed the closing lines of his war address two years before: "God give us the strength and the vision to do it wisely! God give us the privilege of knowing that we did it without counting the cost, and because we were true Americans, lovers of liberty and of the right!"[28]

In response to these words, the audience applauded wildly and then stood silently in their places until the president left the stage. But his eloquence exacted a price. As several pro-League Republicans noted, Wilson's sharply worded defiance stood in stark contrast to Taft's mildness and conciliation. Privately, Taft and others in the LEP had latched onto the phrase in the Round Robin that rejected the Draft Covenant "in the form now presented," and they were already suggesting changes to mollify the senators. From the Democratic side, Gilbert Hitchcock of Nebraska, the outgoing chairman of the Foreign Relations Committee, hastened to assure Wilson that many of the signers of the Round Robin could be won over, particularly if certain revisions were made to the Draft Covenant. Those might include specific exclusion of domestic jurisdiction over tariffs and immigration, exemption of the Monroe Doctrine, clarification of the right of withdrawal, and disclaimer of any obligation for the United States to accept a mandate under the League to govern a former German colony. Such considerations, together with Wilson's admitted fatigue, again raise questions about whether his health was affecting his performance. In the past, Wilson had rarely risen to the bait of provocation, and he had often used his eloquence to dwell on the sweet reasonableness of compromise. As matters stood,

28. Wilson speech, Mar. 4, 1919, in Link, ed., *Papers of Wilson*, LV, 413–421.

this defiant declaration matched the Round Robin almost too perfectly. Together, they ended this first major engagement in the League fight on a sour, adversarial note.[29]

II

As soon as he returned to Paris in the middle of March 1919, the president tried to accommodate his critics at home. Wilson's mood of defiance evidently lasted for a while after his departure from New York. On the voyage back, the peace conference delegation's press secretary, Ray Stannard Baker, commented in his diary, "He is a good hater – & how he does hate those obstructive Senators. He is inclined now to stand by the Covenant word for word as drawn, accepting no amendments." When Wilson arrived in Paris, Colonel House noted in his diary, "The President comes back very militant and determined to put the League of Nations into the Peace Treaty." Those impressions spoke more to the state of Wilson's physical and emotional health. House, who had not seen the president for a month, found him "worn and tired." One of the colonel's aides, Stephen Bonsal, commented privately that a "change for the worse" in Wilson's health "is increasingly noticeable and is being generally commented upon." According to Bonsal, his left cheek twitched with an "almost chronic" tic, and he seemed "in a highly nervous condition" and showed "a certain peevishness of manner."[30]

In spite of his initial defiance, Wilson immediately started to consider changes in the Draft Covenant. On March 18, he met with House, Lord Robert Cecil, and David Hunter Miller, the legal advisor to the American delegation. They discussed four provisions that had drawn fire from

29. New York *World*, Mar. 5, 1919; *New York Times*, Mar. 5, 1919. For observations on the contrast between Taft and Wilson, see Nicholas Murray Butler to Alfred Holman, Mar. 4, 1919, Nicholas Murray Butler Papers, Columbia University Library; George W. Wickersham to Henry White, Mar. 9, 1919, White Papers, LC, Box 40. For the early feelers toward compromise, see Taft to Gus J. Karger, Mar. 5, 11, 1919, Taft Papers, reel 555; Taft to Stimson, Mar. 9, 1919, ibid.; Taft to Casper S. Yost, Mar. 9, 1919, ibid.; Taft newspaper column, Mar. 5, 1919, ibid., reel 588; Hitchcock to Wilson, Mar. 4, 1919, in Link, ed., *Papers of Wilson*, LV, 439.
30. Ray Stannard Baker Diary, [Mar. 8, 1919], in Link, ed., *Papers of Wilson*, LV, 465; House Diary, Mar. 14, 22, 1919, ibid., 499, ibid. LVI, 179; Bonsal memorandum, Mar. 24, [1919], Stephen Bonsal Papers, LC, Box 18. Baker, by contrast, believed that Wilson "looked gray & worn when he came aboard: . . . but he soon recuperated, under Dr. Grayson's care, so that now he looks as well as ever." Baker Diary, Mar. 13, [1919], in Link, ed., *Papers of Wilson*, LV, 490.

American critics: Article X, the right of withdrawal, the Monroe Doctrine, and domestic questions. Cecil found Wilson "in a very different and more malleable frame of mind," and House thought him "more reasonable than he was the other day as to meeting the wishes of the Senate." House conceded that they "found it nearly impossible to write what the Senate desires into the Covenant," mainly because other nations would not agree to such changes and those changes might "cause more difficulties than they cure." For example, according to Miller, Wilson argued that Article X "was the one on which the French relied and he did not see how it could be weakened." Everyone agreed, both Miller and House recorded in their diaries, that a specific exemption of the Monroe Doctrine would prompt Japan to claim comparable suzerainty in Asia. Both Wilson and House worried that an exclusion of domestic questions might inflame pro-Irish senators by appearing to bow to British pressure. The right of withdrawal struck the discussants as already implicit, and evidently no one raised the question of separating the League from the peace treaty.[31]

Wilson was genuinely seeking to accommodate critics of the League plan. He welcomed the suggestions offered by Taft, who sent a brief telegram on March 18 in which he urged "more specific reservation of the Monroe Doctrine," together with a statement that the League Council must vote unanimously to recommend any action and an express exclusion of such domestic matters as immigration and tariffs. During the next ten days, Taft cabled twice more to elaborate on these suggestions and to argue that the Monroe Doctrine exemption would sway enough Republican senators to approve the treaty: "A strong and successful stand will carry the League." At the same time, acting through intermediaries, Wilson tried to sound out Root about changes that would make the Draft Covenant acceptable to him and other Republicans. Root responded with his usual wariness. Although he declined to render "matured" judgment on the Draft Covenant, he did say that he regretted the absence of an international court and specific exemption of the Monroe Doctrine, and he worried that Article X "committed the various nations including the U. S. of America to intervention in many boundary disputes in which they were not concerned."[32]

31. Cecil Diary, Mar. 18, [1919], ibid., LVI, 82; House Diary, Mar. 18, 1919, ibid., 82–83; David Hunter Miller Diary, Mar. 18, 1919, ibid., 78–80.
32. Taft to Wilson, Mar. 18, 21, 28, 1919, ibid., 83, 157–159, 398–399; enclosure with Thomas W. Lamont to Wilson, Mar. 19, 1919, ibid., 99–100. The men who talked with Root were Lamont's business partners on Wall Street: J. P. Morgan, Jr., and Dwight W. Morrow. On the effort to contact Root, see also Henry White to Root, Mar. 19, 1919, Root Papers, LC, Box 137.

Root was also involved in another effort at communication between the president and his Republican critics. Henry White had remained true to his agreed-upon role as liaison between the peace conference delegation and his party's foreign policy leadership, and he now tried to ascertain what changes to the Draft Covenant Lodge wanted. Acting on his own initiative on March 9, while the president was still at sea, White cabled Lodge asking him to "cable, in cipher, through the State Department, to me the exact phraseology of amendments modifying the League of Nations covenant which the Senate considers important." Unfortunately, the New York *Sun*, a Republican paper, got wind of the story in Paris and contacted Lodge even before he received White's cable. In the light of this publicity, the senator sought protective cover. As soon as he received the cable on March 12, he telephoned Knox, who was away from Washington, for advice, and he met with Brandegee, who told him, "In my opinion the gentleman who sent the cable is being used as a catspaw."[33]

Most likely at Lodge's behest, Brandegee then consulted a Republican lawyer and foreign policy advisor, Chandler Anderson, who, he insisted, must come to see him in person. The senator wanted a face-to-face meeting because, Anderson recorded in his diary, he "explained that his telephone line had been tapped for some time, and it was unsafe for him to use it." Brandegee showed Anderson White's cable, called it a "trap," and confided that "he was afraid Lodge would fall into it unless Lodge was stiffened up." Brandegee asked Anderson to go see Root "and if possible get him to write to Lodge, suggesting the danger of the situation, and also the form of a reply." Anderson took an overnight train to New York, where he met Root the next morning. After listening to his visitor, Root paced around the room, "thinking aloud," while Anderson took notes. Together, they outlined a reply for Lodge to send to White. Root then called in his secretary and dictated a letter to Lodge that explained their thinking and gave him the text of the proposed reply. In the letter Root maintained that it would be highly improper for Lodge to discuss any aspect of the treaty with anyone except the president himself or in any way other than through official channels. Root also noted that "it is a fair presumption that he [Wilson] knew of this approach. I think White would hardly have sent it without communicating with the President."[34]

33. White to Lodge, Mar. 7, 9, 1919, Lodge Papers; New York *Sun* to Lodge, Mar. 10, 1919, ibid.; Brandegee memorandum, Mar. 12, 1919, ibid.; Lodge, *Senate and League*, 124.

34. Anderson Diary, Mar. 13, 1919, Anderson Papers, LC; Root to Lodge, Mar. 13, 1919, Lodge Papers. This letter is reprinted in Lodge, *Senate and League*, 124–127. For an interpretation that views Root's role in the best possible light, see Philip C. Jessup, *Elihu Root* (New York, 1937), II, 388.

Lodge adopted Root's language verbatim in his reply to White:

> Have considered your cable March 9th. The President expressed no
> willingness to receive any communication from the Senate while
> that body was in session. If he now wishes to have amendments
> drafted which the Senate will consent to, the natural and necessary
> course is to convene the Senate in the customary way. Manifestly I
> cannot now speak for the Senate or consult its members nor can
> they consult with each other nor can the President consult them
> while they are at their homes in forty-eight states.

To Root, Lodge added, "I cannot tell you how grateful I am. . . . I saw
the net spread and was determined not to get into it; but I could not satisfy myself with the form of the reply until your analysis cleared my
mind and gave me just the words I was seeking for." This stiff-necked
insistence upon senatorial prerogative brushed aside the olive branch
that White had tried to extend. Neither Lodge's stand nor Root's
behind-the-scenes part augured well for further attempts to build
bridges between Wilson and the Republicans. Worse was to come
before the month of March was over.[35]

On March 19, four days after Lodge rebuffed White's request, the
senator engaged in a debate in Boston with Lawrence Lowell, the president of Harvard and an LEP stalwart. In the void in the League fight
left by Wilson's departure and the adjournment of Congress, their
debate drew a big local crowd and attracted nationwide press coverage
and commentary.

The heightened attention also sprang from the standing and reputations of the two men involved. This was a battle of the Boston brah-
mins. It is hard to imagine two more striking specimens of that particular branch of the American upper crust. Both the sixty-eight-year-old
Lodge and the sixty-two-year-old Lowell traced their ancestry back to
the earliest Puritan settlers of Massachusetts, and they had both inherited great wealth from their families' long involvement as merchants in
the days of sailing ships and as leaders and investors in textiles, railroads, and other spearheads of the industrial revolution during the preceding century. Also, like Wilson, both of these Harvard men had pur-
sued careers that bridged the worlds of learning and public affairs.
Lodge, who had long basked in being called the "scholar in politics,"
had also earned a Ph.D. and taught history briefly at Harvard before
entering politics in the early 1880s. Lowell had also earned a law degree

---

35. Lodge to White, Mar. 15, 1919, Lodge Papers; Lodge to Root, Mar. 14,
    1919, ibid. For Lodge's explanation of his reply, see Lodge to White, Apr.
    8, 1919, ibid.

at Harvard and practiced law in Boston before he returned to teach government at Harvard in 1897 and became its president in 1909. The only contrast between the two men lay in their physical appearance and speaking style. Lodge was slender, had a perfectly trimmed pointed beard, and was widely reputed for speaking vigorously and sharply. Lowell was beefier, wore a walrus mustache, and was known for speaking ponderously.[36]

The Lodge–Lowell debate followed a time-honored format for such encounters in American politics. It was the format that had been used in the celebrated debates in 1858 between Abraham Lincoln and Stephen Douglas. As the opening speaker, Lodge spoke for an hour. As the respondent, Lowell followed with an hour-and-a-half speech. Then Lodge closed with a half-hour response. The senator delivered his opening statement in a quiet, often almost apologetic manner, mainly covering points that he had made earlier in his Senate speeches. "I am anxious to have the nations, the free nations of the world united in a league," he protested, but the main question before the country was "of a practical nature" – namely, whether this proposed League of Nations would secure peace and would not endanger American sovereignty. He insisted that the Monroe Doctrine must be specifically exempted from the "very loosely and obscurely drawn" provisions of the Draft Covenant, as must immigration and tariffs. He noted that Article X, "the most important article in the whole treaty," made "a tremendous promise . . . to guarantee the political independence and territorial integrity of every nation on earth." Were Americans, he asked, really ready "to send the hope of their families, the hope of the nation, the best of our youth, forth into the world on that errand"?[37]

Friends and supporters on both sides later claimed that their man won the debate, but LEP colleagues had complained earlier that Lowell

36. The best biography of Lodge is John A. Garraty, *Henry Cabot Lodge* (New York, 1953). On Lowell, see Henry A. Yeomans, *Abbott Lawrence Lowell, 1856–1943* (Cambridge, Mass., 1948). Both men had crossed paths with Wilson earlier in their careers. In 1879, as editor of the *International Review*, Lodge had published Wilson's first article in a journal. A few years later, Lowell had debated Wilson in the pages of the *Atlantic Monthly*. Although Wilson had reminded Lodge of their earlier encounter when he first became president, their relationship quickly degenerated into political enmity. With Lowell, by contrast, their debate led to an amiable acquaintanceship. On these encounters, see Garraty, *Lodge*, 295–296, and Henry W. Bragdon, *Woodrow Wilson: The Academic Years* (Cambridge, Mass., 1967), 56–57, 136–138, and Link, ed., *Papers of Wilson*, III, 170 n. 2.

37. *New York Times*, Mar. 20, 1919. On the Lincoln–Douglas debate format, see David Herbert Donald, *Lincoln* (New York, 1995), 214.

was a lackluster, pedantic speaker. One of the few detached observers present that night in Boston regretted the Harvard president's "rather rambling and Lowellish style." Nor did the substance of his remarks make up for deficiencies in delivery. Striking a consistently defensive tone, Lowell admitted that the League plan was "very defective in its drafting. In places it is so obscure that the meaning is often inaccurately expressed and easily misunderstood." He undertook to correct such misunderstandings by explaining how limited were the powers of the League Council and the obligations of the United States under Article X. Again conceding that the Draft Covenant was "imperfect and poorly drawn," Lowell nevertheless called it a great step toward preventing a repetition of the horrors of the world war. Rising to his one moment of true eloquence, he closed by asking "whether our country shall take its place, like a great and generous nation, side by side with others as guardians of law and order, or whether it shall turn its face away from a world in agony."[38]

Lowell's lukewarm advocacy gave Lodge the perfect opening to soar in his closing remarks. "I repeat again," the senator declared, "I want a League of Nations that will advance the cause of peace on earth, that will make war as nearly impossible as it can be made." But, he questioned, did the present plan fill that bill? Yoking the League to the peace settlement struck him as doubly dangerous. Negotiating the Draft Covenant had already wasted precious time at the peace conference, and intertwining it with the settlement would imperil the experiment in international enforcement. Most of all, Lodge wanted to keep America unsullied "as a great moral asset to Christian civilization. . . . I want to keep America as she has been – not isolated, not prevent her from joining other nations for these great purposes – but I wish her to be master of her fate." Shouting that he was "an American" who had "never had but one flag, never loved but one flag," Lodge closed with the demand that the nation must remain true to its character and values: "Let her go on in her beneficent career, and I want to see her stand as she has always stood, strong and alive, triumphant, free."[39]

38. William Phillips to Robert Lansing, Mar. 22, 1919, Lansing Papers, LC; *New York Times*, Mar. 20, 1919. For comments on Lowell's shortcomings as a speaker, see Horace Dutton Taft to William Howard Taft, Jan. 21,1919, Taft Papers, reel 203; W. H. Taft to H. D. Taft, Jan. 30, 1919, ibid.

39. *New York Times*, Mar. 20, 1919. For descriptions of the debate and Lodge's delivery, see Phillips to Lansing, Mar. 22, 1919, Lansing Papers; New York *World*, Mar. 20, 1919; Richard W. Hale to Jules Valery, Mar. 20, 1919, Lodge Papers; Beveridge to Lodge, Mar. 20, 1919; Garraty, *Lodge*, 360.

For all the publicity surrounding it, the Lodge–Lowell debate broke no new intellectual ground and swayed no committed partisans on either side. What it did do was to help shift the balance of middle-of-the-road opinion, especially among Republicans. Such people now began to lean away from urgent embrace of the League plan and toward sympathy with Lodge's ostensibly cautious, reasonable stance. As Warren Kuehl has pointed out, the readiness of Lowell and others from the LEP to acknowledge flaws in the Draft Covenant made that document look worse than it really was. With friends like those, Wilson's plan did not need enemies or critics to wrest the ideological initiative away from their side. Conversely, Lodge's avowals of sympathy for the league idea and love of world peace struck responsive chords in many circles, coupled as they were with his fervent invocation of such symbols of national loyalty as home, hearth, and flag. His stance also made some headway toward broadening and shoring up the Republican party front on the League issue. That front stretched from great power traditionalists such as Root, who told Lodge "you availed yourself with skill and wisdom of an opportunity for a real public service," to outright opponents such as Albert Beveridge, who told Lodge "your leadership has been so wise and astute that disagreements on methods & approach do not amount to much with me."[40]

Still, many leading Republicans recognized that they needed to do more in the way of presenting a constructive alternative to the president's plan. Most notable among those who worried about political damage from appearing negative or obstructionist was the party's energetic, adept national chairman, Will Hays. With his small-town Indiana ways and teetotaling habits, the skinny, energetic Hays stood out among that era's big-city, hard-drinking denizens of smoke-filled rooms. Such deviations from type did not prevent this Hoosier from becoming the best party manager of the time, a worthy successor to his fellow Republican Mark Hanna. Recognized for his talents only late in the 1916 campaign, Hays had shaped up the Republican presidential effort almost enough to allow Hughes to beat Wilson. True to his calling, he wanted only one thing – party unity that would ensure victory in the next election.[41]

Just as Taft had done earlier, Hays saw Root as the key to a Republican response to Wilson on the League. He had better luck in eliciting a public commitment from the party's foreign policy guru. Root's protégé,

40. Kuehl, *Seeking World Order;* Root to Lodge, Apr. 4, 1919, Lodge Papers; Beveridge to Lodge, Mar. 20, 1919, ibid. See also Root to Lodge, Apr. 4, 1919, ibid.
41. On Hays, see Will H. Hays, *Memoirs* (Garden City, N.Y., 1955).

former Secretary of War Henry Stimson, acted as a go-between. Stimson broached the idea of a public statement to Root, and then he took Hays to see him on March 19, the same day as the Lodge–Lowell debate. Stimson recorded in his diary that Hays began the conversation by asserting, "Mr. Root, fifty or sixty million Republicans are in a fluid condition on this subject. . . . I think the time has come for you to speak." Root replied, "If I thought I can be of help I will do it." Explaining that he wanted to strengthen the Allies in "preserving the victory," he argued, "If I could I would make an alliance with England and France for that purpose." But he objected strongly to confusing such a "political alliance to preserve peace" with "a legal union for the arbitration of disputes," as the Draft Covenant had done. After discussing revisions such as exemption of the Monroe Doctrine and immigration and further criticizing Wilson's plan, Root agreed to make a statement. Afterward Hays told Stimson, ". . . what he is going to say will coincide exactly with the need of the political situation in the Middle West, and what people want to find out, what they are groping for." After further conversations, Hays wrote to Root on March 24 formally requesting that he furnish "further light on the question of the so-called League of Nations."[42]

Root replied five days later with a long, carefully drafted letter. He professed to find "great value" in the Draft Covenant, but he also detected "serious flaws" that could prevent the United States from joining the League. After noting that both Taft and Lodge favored revisions and demanding that the Senate be called into immediate session, Root posed the question of whether this plan would prevent wars. He welcomed the provision that "makes international conferences on political questions compulsory in times of danger," but he deplored the total disregard of international law. He recommended, therefore, six changes in the Draft Covenant. He called, first, for provisions for judicial settlement of disputes and, second, for review and expansion of international law. Third – concerned about not making too large a breach in "the long-established policy of the United States to keep the Old and New World from becoming entangled in each other's affairs and embroiled in each other's quarrels" – Root suggested exemption of the Monroe Doctrine and immigration from the League's jurisdiction.

In his fourth suggested change Root leveled his strongest fire at Arti-

42. Stimson Diary, Mar. 19, 1919, Stimson Papers; Hays to Root, Mar. 24, 1919, Root Papers, Box 137. This letter is also printed in James Brown Scott, ed., *Men and Policies: Addresses by Elihu Root* (Cambridge, Mass., 1925), 250.

cle X. "Looking at this article as part of a perpetual league for the preservation of peace," he confessed, "my first impression was that the whole article should be stricken out. If perpetual, it would be an attempt to preserve for all time unchanged the distribution of power and territory made in accordance with the views and exigencies of the Allies in this present juncture of affairs. It would necessarily be futile." Still, Root admitted, in the present chaotic condition of Europe, "the United States cannot quit. It must go on to the performance of its duty, and the immediate aspect of Article X is to do that. I think, therefore, that Article X should be amended so that it shall hold a limited time, and thereafter any member may withdraw from it." As his fifth revision, Root proposed international inspection to enforce arms-reduction agreements, and, finally, he called for provisions to make future revisions in the Covenant. "The whole arrangement is at present necessarily tentative," Root concluded, and the League must presently move away from "an alliance of one half of the active world against or for control of the other half" and toward "a league of peace." Such a transformation would require rethinking arrangements and obligations "in a calmer atmosphere, and when the world is less subject to exciting and disturbing causes."[43]

This letter, which Hays immediately released to the press, was a masterly performance. It displayed the skills that had made Root the nation's leading corporate lawyer and one of its ablest diplomats. He had artfully woven together virtually every Republican foreign policy position. Like Taft and his brethren in the LEP, Root said some nice things about the Draft Covenant, and he revived their earlier emphasis on international law. In a bow to Lodge and Knox and their senatorial colleagues, he offered functional substitutes for separating the League from the peace treaty and for concluding a security pact with the Allies. Root even echoed the isolationists when he genuflected toward traditional American policies and the Monroe Doctrine and when he detected in Article X the potential for reviving something like the Holy Alliance. Yet Root called for no radical changes in the Draft Covenant. The one real revision he suggested was to limit the duration of Article X. Otherwise, Root wanted to make only widely desired additions to the Draft Covenant, including the arms inspection provision that would actually strengthen the League. Most important, Root outdid Lodge in breathing a spirit of sweet reasonableness and constructive concern.

---

43. Root to Hays, Mar. 29, 1919, Root Papers, Box 137. This letter is also printed in Scott, ed., *Men and Policies*, 251–268.

The letter fulfilled Hays's hopes for a nearly united party front. Except for isolationists, Republicans of all stripes praised the letter. On one side, Lowell gushed, "Mr. Root's letter seems to have settled the position of the great mass of the Republican party, and of all but a few of the Republican senators, and if Mr. Wilson makes the amendments, . . . the ratification of the Covenant would seem to be assured." On the other side, George Harvey, a bitter foe of the Draft Covenant and of Wilson personally, was, according to Stimson's diary, "very enthusiastic about it [Root's letter]." On March 29, at a meeting with Root, Hays, and Stimson, Harvey told them, "This will unite everybody in both wings. It brings me as a radical and Borah and the other radicals, and it will also bring in the conservatives, Taft and the others." That was an exaggeration. Neither Borah nor any other isolationist rushed to join him, while Beveridge professed himself "disgusted" at changes that did not "amount to a hill of beans." Likewise, contrary to Lowell's prediction, neither Lodge nor any other senator committed himself to approving the League if Root's suggested changes were made.[44]

The final and worst news in March 1919 for League advocates came from their diehard opponents, who were organizing and, evidently, making fresh converts. For almost four years, the LEP had enjoyed a free field in the effort to influence public opinion on the questions of international enforcement and a postwar American role in the maintenance of world order. The opposition, by contrast, had mounted only sporadic, individual efforts, mostly speeches by such isolationist senators as Borah and Reed. Things began to change early in 1919, even before the publication of the Draft Covenant. In January and February, Beveridge, a former senator from Indiana and Roosevelt's one-time cohort in the imperialist and Progressive causes, made a stab at raising money and organizing publicity for campaigns against any league of nations. Beveridge met several times with such anti-League publicists as Harvey and Frank Munsey. At the same time, Borah conferred with William Randolph Hearst to shore up the press baron's continued opposition to League membership. Another activist against Wilson's proposals was the Chicago lawyer Salmon Levinson, who sought to reform international relations through what he called the "outlawry of war." Levinson vowed to work against the League as "not [a] solution of war

44. Lowell to F. F. Ayer, Apr. 2, 1919, Lowell Papers; Stimson Diary, Mar. 29, 1919; *New York Times,* Apr. 3, 1919; Beveridge to John T. McCutcheon, Apr. 13, 1919, Beveridge Papers, Box 216.

problem but mere compromise which keeps war legal and supersovereign of the world."[45]

The initial efforts at organizing the anti-League forces proved disappointing. One meeting in Boston struck Beveridge as attracting "a poor looking lot . . . no crowd for live wires," while Munsey worried about Hays's unwillingness to tie the Republican party to opposition to the League. The main impetus toward formation of a national organization came from George Wharton Pepper, a lively amateur politician who was leading lawyer and member of a socially prominent family in Philadelphia. Acting on his own, Pepper drew up an outline for an organization, which he showed to Lodge early in March. The senator declined to associate himself publicly with Pepper's plan, but he arranged for the Philadelphian to receive a check for $10,000 from a donor who wanted to fight "against the Wilson–Taft form of peace." On March 13, Pepper went to Washington for "a most unsatisfactory" meeting with anti-League senators, each of whom "had a different idea" and was unwilling "to yield to anybody else." Only a brand-new freshman Republican, George H. Moses of New Hampshire, was any real help, Pepper later recalled, and the two of them took the lead a few days afterward in chartering the League for the Preservation of American Independence.[46]

This organization would usually be referred to as the "Independence League." It maintained a nonpartisan facade by choosing as its figurehead president an anti-Wilson Democrat, the aged Louisville newspaper publisher Henry Watterson. Its board of directors included such Repub-

---

45. Beveridge to Harvey, Jan. 26, 1919, Beveridge Papers, Box 215; Beveridge to John C. Shaffer, Feb. 12, 1919, ibid., Box 281; Beveridge to Munsey, Feb. 18, 1919, ibid., Box 216; Beveridge to Borah, Feb. 25, 1919; ibid., Box 214; Borah to Hearst, Feb. 20, 1919, Borah Papers, Box 769; Hearst to Borah, Feb. 22, 1919, ibid.; Levinson to John H. Clarke, Jan. 4, 1919, Salmon O. Levinson Papers, University of Chicago Library, Box 54; Levinson to John Haynes Holmes, Jan. 20, 1919, ibid., Box 4; Levinson to William E. Dodd, [Feb. 14, 1919], ibid., Box 16. On the isolationist senators' speaking activities, see Ralph A. Stone, *The Irreconcilables: The Fight against the League of Nations* (Lexington, Ky., 1970), 82–83. On Levinson and the outlawry of war, see John E. Stoner, *S. O. Levinson and the Fact of Paris: A Study in the Techniques of Influence* (Chicago, 1942).

46. Beveridge to Shaffer, Feb. 12, 1919, Beveridge Papers, Box 281; Munsey to Beveridge, Mar. 7, 1919, ibid., Box 216: Pepper to Lodge, Mar. 9, 10, 1919, Lodge Papers; Lodge to Pepper, Apr. 7, 11, 1919, ibid.; Thomas Harris Powers to Lodge, Mar. 7, 1919, ibid.; George Wharton Pepper, *Philadelphia Lawyer* (Philadelphia, 1944), 125–126.

lican senators as Miles Poindexter of Washington, Moses, Joseph France of Maryland, and Harry New of Indiana, as well as Democratic ex-Senator Thomas Hardwick of Georgia. The Independence League imitated LEP by maintaining a headquarters in New York and a Washington office for lobbying, along with eight district units and chapters in most states and larger cities. Also like the LEP, the Independence League organized speaking tours by its oratorical stars, most notably Borah, Beveridge, and a new recruit to the isolationist ranks, Hiram W. Johnson. Though only a first-term Republican senator, the moon-faced, bespectacled Johnson brought formidable skills and reputation to the anti-League cause. Before he entered the Senate in 1917, Johnson had served six years as California's ever-pugnacious, crusading reform governor. He had also run at Roosevelt's side in 1912 as the Progressive party's vice-presidential nominee. Most observers of the League fight subsequently rated Johnson as the most effective stump speaker on the anti-League side, even better than Borah.[47]

Although its most prominent spokesmen were isolationists, the Independence League did not advocate total rejection of League membership. Its charter called only for opposition to "unconditional ratification" of any treaty that contained the Draft Covenant. In April the organization's first official statement, a "Declaration of Principles," demanded immediate conclusion of a peace treaty, with separate consideration of the League Covenant by the Senate "with due care and reasonable opportunity for amendment." The declaration opposed membership in the League "in its present form" and gave as reasons such standard objections as violation of the Monroe Doctrine, lack of provision for withdrawal, interference in domestic matters, and obligation to fight in distant quarrels. The document did deplore abandonment of Washington's and Jefferson's warnings against alliances and also repeated charges that Wilson's plan legalized war. Conversely, the state-

47. On the organization and structure of the Independence League, the best account is Stone, *Irreconcilables*, 78–82, which pieces together a coherent picture from extremely fragmentary sources. The organization evidently left no records, and there is nothing relating to its formation and organization in the George Wharton Pepper Papers, University of Pennsylvania Archives. On Johnson, see Richard Coke Lower, *A Bloc of One: The Political Career of Hiram W. Johnson* (Stanford, Calif., 1993). Beveridge played a less active part on the speaking circuit than the other two because he suffered several illnesses during the summer of 1919 and because he was reluctant to take too much time away from his biography of John Marshall.

ment lambasted the Draft Covenant's alleged "ambiguity, vagueness, and uncertainty" but suggested that those defects might possibly be remedied through "its thorough reconstruction." Also, some leaders of the Independence League, most notably George Harvey and Pepper, strongly favored an alliance with Britain and France.[48]

Yet the Independence League never matched the LEP in reach, scope, and impact. Some of its shortcomings stemmed from its late start; other problems boiled down to money. The organization's financial situation brightened at the beginning of May when Knox suggested that he and Harvey solicit funds from two of their multimillionaire friends, the steel tycoon Henry Clay Frick and the financier Andrew Mellon. When Harvey approached Frick, he readily agreed, asking, "How much do you want?" Mellon soon kicked in an equal sum, probably $10,000, and Medill McCormick, another anti-League Republican senator, promised to raise the same amount in Chicago. Welcome as those contributions were, however, they did not put the Independence League on an equal footing with the LEP. League advocates supplied ten speeches and pieces of printed matter to everyone from the opposition, Salmon Levinson estimated in June. This disparity also sprang from the Independence League's lack of staff, which forced Pepper to write most of its pamphlets himself. Nor did the problem posed by senatorial egos diminish. Early on, Reed had a spat with Pepper, which left relations between that senator and the organization "purely formal." Pepper also recalled that "in all my contacts with them [the anti-League senators], I was made conscious that I was dealing with Olympians whose condescension to a mere mortal was not to be lightly esteemed."[49]

48. "Declaration of Principles," enclosed with James E. Clarke to Watterson, Apr. 23, 1919, Henry Watterson Papers, Library of Congress, Box 8. Several prominent members of the organization, such as Beck and Pepper, were conspicuous Anglophiles who had favored American intervention in the world war on the Allied side before 1917. Someone from the organization privately approached the British ambassador in April 1919 to apologize for anything they said that might appear to be "tail-twisting" or in any way "unfriendly at the bottom to the British people." See Frank L. Polk to Lansing, [n.d., ca. Apr. 29, 1919]), in Link, ed., *Papers of Wilson*, LIX, 452–453.

49. George Harvey, *Henry Clay Frick: The Man* (New York, 1928), 324–330; Levinson to W. Bourke Cochran, June 13, 1919, Levinson Papers, Box 54; Pepper, *Philadelphia Lawyer*, 127–128. On Harvey's role in the opposition to the League, see also Lodge to Ellerton James, Apr. 17, 1921, Lodge Papers.

Actually, those handicaps did not hamper the work of the Independence League all that much. Difficulties with the senators mirrored the tribulations that the LEP suffered from Wilson's cold shoulder. Organizational shortcomings made less difference than they might have done otherwise thanks to Pepper, whose energy and oratorical gifts later enabled him to join the senatorial Olympians who condescended to him in 1919. Most important, the Independence League had an easier case to make with public opinion than did the LEP. Unlike its rival, it was not trying to sell people on a major departure in American foreign policy, nor did it have to persuade them to support a positive program. Instead, by opposing the Draft Covenant "in its present form," the Independence League could embrace a broad spectrum of critics and opponents. Those ranged from isolationists who demanded rejection in any form to people who professed various degrees of willingness to acquiesce in League membership, provided sufficient limits and safeguards were attached. The Independence League showed how comfortably isolationists could consort with advocates of traditional Republican great power foreign policy and how strong a strategic advantage their side enjoyed in the League fight.[50]

That advantage was not readily apparent in the readings of popular sentiment during March and April 1919. In those days before carefully devised methods for sampling public opinion, observers resorted to culling editorial opinion and canvassing local journalists and politicians. Surveys of newspaper opinion continued to show widespread support for League membership and an American role in upholding a peace settlement. Those sentiments were frequently coupled with concerns about protecting national sovereignty and the Monroe Doctrine and avoiding unnecessary overseas involvement. Also, as earlier, these surveys found that how warmly people embraced Wilson's program and how deeply they doubted it varied primarily along partisan lines and secondarily somewhat along sectional lines. The South remained well-nigh solid for the Democrats and their president on this question. To Lodge's chagrin, his state of Massachusetts and New England in general registered strong support for League membership. To the comparable chagrin of Beveridge and Illinois' two anti-League Republican senators, McCormick and Sherman, the Midwest also reported a lot of pro-League sentiment. Even Borah's Idaho reportedly leaned toward

---

50. For a witty, incisive portrait of Pepper, see John Lukacs, *Philadelphia: Patricians and Philistines* (New York, 1981), 219–239.

membership. The main reports of popular anti-League sentiment came from Kansas and Montana and from Irish-American organizations throughout the country.[51]

League supporters would have done well not to take too much heart from those surveys. Clear signs of growing opposition to their program were emanating from one of the president's erstwhile constituencies – domestic reformers who were international idealists. Salmon Levinson supplied one focal point for such opposition, as he simultaneously joined up with the Independence League and pushed his "outlawry of war" as an alternative scheme for international reform. Others on the left – especially those who had either opposed intervention or warily supported the war – now denounced the Draft Covenant and Article X. For example, the iconoclastic economist Thorstein Veblen claimed that that article underwrote imperialism and would "block the path to a new order." The editor of the *Nation*, Oswald Garrison Villard, accused Wilson of "insincerity" and of fashioning a peace based on "intrigue, selfish aggression, and naked imperialism." More ominously, reformers who had previously ridden the war bandwagon with gusto were beginning to defect. On March 29, the *New Republic,* formerly Wilson's most influential supporter among progressive journals, ran an editorial titled "Defeat Article X." The magazine's editors declared that since "[f]inal justice cannot be done at Paris . . . America must not be pledged to uphold injustices." The *New Republic* withheld final judgment on the League until the terms of the peace settlement were concluded, but the journal made it

---

51. For surveys of editorial opinion, see New York *World,* Mar. 9, 17, 1919; *Literary Digest,* LX (Mar. 8, 1919), 11–13; ibid. (Mar. 29, 1919), 32. On New England sentiment, see Francis B. Loomis to Lodge, Mar. 6, 1919, Lodge Papers. On Midwestern opinion, see Frank B. Kellogg to Lodge, Mar. 13, 1919, ibid.; S. S. Gregory to Levinson, Mar. 14, 1919, Levinson Papers, Box 49; William C. Bobbs to Beveridge, Apr. 12, 1919, Beveridge Papers, Box 214; Munsey to Beveridge, Apr. 14, 1919, ibid., Box 216. On Idaho, see William Gibbs McAdoo to Antoinette Funk, Apr. 21, 1919, William Gibbs McAdoo Papers, Library of Congress, Box 219. On Kansas, see Chester J. Long to Taft, Apr. 28, 1919, Taft Papers, reel 208. On Montana, see various letters reporting opinion to Senator Walsh, Mar.–Apr. 1919, Thomas J. Walsh Papers, Library of Congress, Box 284. For more general assessments of opinion, see also Ellery Sedgwick to Tumulty, Mar. 21, 1919, in Link, ed., *Papers of Wilson,* LVI, 162–163; Newton D. Baker to Wilson, Mar. 27, 1919, ibid., 331; and Antoinette Funk to McAdoo, Apr. 3. 1919, McAdoo Papers, Box 219.

clear that its support hinged on those terms' living up to a high standard of fairness, unselfishness, and nonpunitiveness.[52]

III

Wilson found some revisions to the Draft Covenant easy to effect. A clause stating the right of withdrawal, with two years' notice, sailed through the League Commission. House and Cecil maneuvered behind the scenes to push through other changes, including a statement that unanimity was required for the League Council to take any action – which guaranteed a veto to its members, especially the great powers – and exclusion from the League's purview of matters "solely within the domestic jurisdiction" of a nation – effectively, such questions as tariffs and immigration. But revisions on the two matters that had drawn the strongest fire at home – Article X and the Monroe Doctrine – spawned a nasty clash among the English-speaking powers. On his return to Paris, Wilson found awaiting him a critique written by the Canadian prime minister, Sir Robert Borden. Sounding like Article X's American doubters, Borden argued that it "should be struck out or materially amended" because of "national aspirations to which the provisions of the treaty would not do justice" and the danger of involvement in distant conflicts. Conversely, the French tried again to convert the League into an alliance against Germany. In the face of these contradictory assaults, Wilson thought it best to leave Article X unchanged.[53]

Not only did Lloyd George refuse to sanction exemption of the Monroe Doctrine, but he also made threatening noises about wanting to sep-

52. Veblen, "Peace," *The Dial,* LXVI (May 17, 1919), 485–487; Villard, "The Truth about the Peace Conference," *Nation,* CVIII (Apr. 26, 1919), 646–647; *New Republic,* XVIII (Mar. 29, 1919), 263–265. On Levinson's activities, see Levinson to W. Bourke Cockran, June 13, 1919, Levinson Papers, Box 33; Levinson to Knox, June 19, 1919, ibid., Box 26. On left-wing defections from Wilson during this period, see also Thomas J. Knock, *To End All Wars: Woodrow Wilson and the Quest for a New World Order* (New York, 1992), 252–254.

53. Draft of League Covenant, [Apr. 28, 1919], in Link, ed., *Papers of Wilson,* LVIII, 189, 190, 193; Borden memorandum, n.d., quoted in ibid., LV, 502 n. 1. See also Borden to Wilson, Mar. 14, 1919, ibid., LV, 501–502. For an excellent account of the workings of the Anglo-American front and the Cecil–House partnership, see Lloyd Ambrosius, *Wilson and the American Diplomatic Tradition: The Treaty Fight in Perspective* (New York, 1987), 113–118.

arate the League Covenant from the peace treaty. The wily Welshman was using these issues to try to gain leverage in other areas, particularly to spike America's ambitious naval building program, which was aimed at having a navy larger than Britain's. This scrap occurred just when Wilson fell ill with back and stomach pains and a high fever that kept him confined to bed for four days. As soon as he recovered, he faced the British down and secured agreement to a clause that stated: "Nothing in this Covenant shall be deemed to affect any international engagement or understanding for securing the peace of the world such as treaties of arbitration or the Monroe Doctrine." The League Commission adopted this language, changed to read "regional understandings like the Monroe Doctrine," as Article XXI of the final Covenant. Inasmuch as no European power had ever before recognized the Monroe Doctrine, this revision represented a great diplomatic victory for the United States.[54]

Revising the Draft Covenant was only part of Wilson's mission at Paris. His major task lay in hammering out the peace settlement, and there the heaviest cross that he had to bear was French determination to crush Germany and erect a multilateral military system. At meetings of the inner circle of leaders that now ran the conference – the "Big Four" – the president clashed almost daily with the aged, sharp-tongued "Tiger of France," Clemenceau. Matters reached such a pass in early April that Wilson threatened to leave the conference. From his sickbed he issued orders for his ship to be readied for a return voyage. The French relented and caused less friction afterward. But Wilson also made major concessions to the French. He agreed to larger financial reparations to be imposed on Germany, and he approved a collateral security pact with Britain and France that gave, in Wilson's words, "[a] pledge by the United States, subject to the approval of the Executive Council of the League of Nations, to come to the assistance of France

---

54. Memorandum [ca. Apr. 10, 191], in Link, ed., *Papers of Wilson*, LVII, 218. On the flap with the British, see esp. entry, Mar. 27, 1919, House Diary, ibid., LVI, 335; and on Wilson's illness, see entry, Apr. 3, 1919, Grayson Diary, ibid., 556–557. The exact nature of this illness has remained a matter of some speculation and controversy. Grayson later reported that the president had succumbed to influenza, but Lloyd George said some years later that he thought Wilson had suffered a slight stroke. Several scholars, including physicians, have examined both hypotheses, as well as the additional suggestion that Wilson might have suffered from a form of encephalitis. Because of the brevity of the illness and its symptoms, it seems more likely to several physicians who have recently examined the records of the illness that Wilson had a viral infection. For an extended discussion of the illness, see ibid., 557 n. 2.

so soon as any unprovoked movement of aggression is made against her by Germany." This treaty embodied the idea that Lodge and Knox had put forward, and it later gained their verbal support for a while.[55]

Those concessions and others prompted observers then and later to question whether Wilson was giving up too much for the sake of the League. Actually, in these cases, such linkage seems to have played only a small, indirect part. On reparations, Wilson gave in evidently because he felt sympathy for the French position and because had never concerned himself much with economics as a subject or policy area. He assented to the security pact in part because Clemenceau's appeals to French history, especially to his nation's terrible losses in the world war, moved him and in part because French intransigence made him anxious to grasp at some way to get the question behind him. Likewise, on two territorial matters involving Italy that later earned Wilson great but contradictory opprobrium – cession of the South Tyrol and resistance to designs on Fiume and the Dalmatian coast – his decisions had nothing to do with the League. About the South Tyrol, Wilson admitted to Ray Stannard Baker, "I am sorry for that decision. I was ignorant of the situation when the decision was made." The dispute over Fiume and Dalmatia, which would drag on for the next three years, showed Wilson's stubbornness and perhaps his insensitivity to Italian sentiments, but it was hard to deny that he was standing up for self-determination.[56]

The one place where concern over the League may have swayed him to make a concession was in Asia. When the Japanese members of the League Commission had earlier sought to include a statement affirming racial equality, Wilson had bowed to his own country's and British white supremacist sentiments and vetoed the proposal. Sensitivity over that incident and concern that Japan might refuse to join the League made him more amenable to the short-term cession of Shantung, Germany's former protectorate in China, which Japan had conquered and was occupying. More than any other single provision of the peace settlement, the Shantung cession would stir up furious opposition in the United States. Wilson later defended his decision by arguing that the League would compel Japan to honor its promise to withdraw from Shantung within five years, which eventually did happen. At bottom, like American presidents before and after him, Wilson was bowing to

55. Wilson draft, Mar. 28, 1919, in Link, ed., *Papers of Wilson,* LVI, 371; House Diary, Mar. 27, 1919, ibid., 336. On the reparations decision, see John Foster Dulles memorandum, Apr. 1, 1919, ibid., 498–499; Vance McCormick Diary, Apr. 1, [1919], ibid., 501–502; Thomas W. Lamont Diary, [Apr. 1, 1919], ibid., 502.
56. Entry, May 28, [1919], Baker Diary, ibid., LIX, 574.

power realities in Asia. "It is the best that could be accomplished out of a 'dirty past,'" he told Grayson soon after the decision.[57]

The influences that affected Wilson's negotiating most may have been such personal factors as emotion, fatigue, impatience, and insufficient attention. At Paris in the spring of 1919, he fit the profile of an aging, infirm, overburdened leader at what later generations would call a "summit meeting." Wilson's physician, Grayson, commented nearly every day in his diary and letters on the unremitting strain and fatigue. "He is working beyond his endurance," Grayson confided to William Gibbs McAdoo in April. But, Grayson added, when he implored the president to ease up, ". . . he answers me by saying that in the midst of this imminent crisis he feels that he should participate in the things for which he is responsible. . . . He feels that a mess would be made of things in his absence." That last remark referred to both Wilson's lone-handed approach and his growing alienation from House. Although he blamed the colonel unfairly for making certain concessions, he had reason to doubt House's loyalty. Behind his pose of fawning confidant, the colonel had always fancied himself a superb manipulator and a vastly superior diplomatist and negotiator, and, as Ray Stannard Baker noted in his diary, House "sides with the group which desires a swift peace on any terms: the President struggles almost alone to secure some constructive & idealistic result out of the ruin."[58]

Justified as the estrangement with House may have been, it also supplied disturbing evidence about Wilson's physical and mental condition. Besides fatigue, he was also displaying uncharacteristic traits of forgetfulness, inarticulateness, irritability, and suspicion bordering on paranoia. Some scholars – particularly the editors of *The Papers of Woodrow Wilson* and a group of neurologists whom they consulted – have speculated that Wilson suffered a small stroke at the end of April

57. Grayson Diary, Apr. 30, 1919, ibid., LVIII, 245.
58. Grayson to McAdoo, Apr. 12, 1919, in Link, ed., *Papers of Wilson*, LVII, 304–305; Baker Diary, Apr. 4, 1919, ibid., 589. Those comments did not misrepresent House. For example, on April 1, he had written in his diary, "The President is becoming stubborn, and he never was a good negotiator. So there you are. The President is becoming unreasonable, which does not make for solutions." House Diary, Apr. 1, 1919, ibid., LVI, 518. Three days later he wrote in his dairy that at a meeting of the Big Four which he had attended in Wilson's absence, "I told them that in my opinion it was more important to bring about peace quickly than it was to haggle over details. That I would rather see an immediate peace that brought world order than I would see a better peace and delay." House Diary, Apr. 4, 1919, ibid., LVII, 587. For Mrs. Wilson's recollection of the break, see Baker Diary, May 25, [1921], ibid., LXVII, 289–291.

and that he also had severe hypertension. The major, debilitating stroke that felled Wilson five months later, together with his family health history, makes those speculations seem well grounded. It is not clear what effect the president's physical condition may have had on his performance at Paris, but there was no question that he was in poor shape for facing the tasks that loomed ahead of him back in the United States.[59]

Also auguring ill for Wilson's prospects in the League fight at home was his reluctance to reveal much about the workings of the conference or to speak out to explain his program. Those attitudes frustrated Ray Stannard Baker, the delegation's press secretary, who unavailingly urged the president to hold press conferences and meet with reporters. Wilson's one stab at a dramatic gesture – the order to ready his ship to sail during the fight with Clemenceau – fell flat. Many newspapers looked upon the move, his secretary Joe Tumulty reported, "as an act of impatience and putulance [sic] and not accepted here in good grace by either friends or foes." When Wilson allowed the text of the Monroe Doctrine exemption in the revised Covenant to be published, he got some favorable press reactions, but when word began to leak out about the Shantung award, public anger flared. "Am afraid of the impression it will make," Tumulty cabled, but he worried that "an attempt to explain the compromise, why it was made, would weaken our position instead of strengthening it."[60]

When Wilson made the revised Covenant public on April 26, 1919, the response at home was predictable and ultimately disappointing. Taft

---

59. See "Wilson's Neurological Illness at Paris," ibid., LVIII, 607–611, which includes facsimiles of his handwriting; Bert E. Park, "The Impact of Wilson's Neurological Disease during the Paris Peace Conference," ibid., 611–630; Edwin A. Weinstein, "Woodrow Wilson's Neuropsychological Impairment at the Paris Peace Conference," ibid., 630–635; James F. Toole, "Some Observations on Wilson's Neurologic Illness," ibid., 635–638; "Editors' Commentary," ibid., 638–640. Some hints of Wilson's health problems were filtering back to the United States. Shortly afterward, Beveridge passed on to Senator McCormick a report "from a man who has been there [Paris], and is close to Wilson, that Wilson is badly off physically and his health seriously impaired." Beveridge to Medill McCormick, June 19, 1919, Beveridge Papers, Box 216.

60. Tumulty to Grayson, Apr. 9, 1919, ibid., LVII, 177; Tumlty to Grayson, Apr. 30, [1919], ibid., LVIII, 273; Tumulty to Wilson, [May 1, 1919], ibid., 329. An insightful explanation for Wilson's reluctance to open up to the press came from Baker, who wrote in his diary, "One reason the President so dislikes publicity when events are in the making is due to a certain artistic repuganance to expose half-done work to the light of day. He wants to present a workmanlike result (in his messages & speech not alone, but in his decisions in conference)." Baker Diary, [May 17, 1919], ibid., LIX, 245.

and the LEP praised this Covenant for meeting all previous criticisms, especially concern about the Monroe Doctrine. The LEP's efforts at public persuasion peaked during the following two months. Taft, Lowell, and other leaders mounted renewed speaking tours, and the LEP staged a series of "ratifying conventions" from late May to early July. Striving to compare the Covenant with the Constitution, the LEP sponsored a collection of thirteen papers by Taft and others, written in open imitation of the *Federalist*. Called "The Covenanter," these papers appeared in full in 80 newspapers and in summary in 30 others; they were also distributed to 1,000 journals and printed as a pamphlet. In all, the LEP enrolled around 300,000 members, sponsored over 36,000 speakers, and distributed some of its publications in runs of 500,000 copies. No wonder that the Independence League leaders felt outgunned in the propaganda wars of 1919 or that most observers reported continued widespread support for League membership in some form.[61]

Initial straws in the wind indicated that some Republican senators might have been won over by the revisions in the Covenant. Charles McNary, a freshman from Oregon, declared, "In my opinion the covenant has been amended to meet all legitimate objections raised against it." Others, including some signers of the Round Robin, expressed guarded approval. Predictably, such isolationists as Borah and Hiram Johnson denounced the revisions. They scoffed at the Monroe Doctrine exemption and harped on the lack of change in Article X. More ominous signs were similar objections to Article X by voiced other Republicans, especially Lodge. Publicly, in his capacity as incoming majority leader, he and the assistant leader, Charles Curtis of Kansas, telegraphed to urge their party brethren "to reserve final expression of opinion respecting the amended League Covenant until the latest draft has been carefully studied and there has been opportunity for conference."[62]

61. On the LEP activities and finances, see Bartlett, *League to Enforce Peace*, 128–129; Herbert S. Houston to McAdoo, June 19, 1919, McAdoo Papers, Box 221; Hitchcock speech, *Congressional Record*, 66th Cong., 1st Sess. (June 30, 1919), 2065; W. H. Short to Borah, June 30, 1919, *New York Times*, July 1, 1919. For estimates of public support for League membership, see *Current Opinion*, LXVI (June 1919), 346–348; McAdoo to Bernard Baruch, May 29, 1919, McAdoo Papers, Box 230; Taft to Gus J. Karger, May 31, 1919, Taft Papers, reel 556.

62. McNary in *New York Times*, Apr. 30, 1919; Borah in ibid., Apr. 28, 1919; Lodge and Curtis telegram, Apr. 29, 1919, *New York World*, Apr. 30, 1919. For other senators' reactions, see *New York World*, Apr. 29, 1919; *New York Times*, Apr. 30, 1919; and Herbert F. Margulies, *The Mild Reservationists and the League of Nations Controversy in the Senate* (Columbia, Mo., 1989), 30.

Lodge's less openly broadcast but by no means private stance was even more ominous. When the senator returned to Washington on April 28, he told reporters that he planned to confer during the next week with colleagues of all stripes of opinion about the Covenant. Lodge explained to Beveridge that he was striving "to get together, assure the Republican organization of the Senate, then take up amendments [to the Covenant]." To Albert Cummins he added, "The League, in my opinion, needs further amendment. Nothing has been done to Article 10, which I think and I believe you thought was the most dangerous proposition in the whole scheme." The exclusion of immigration and other domestic questions struck him as "in a worse position than it was in the original League," while the Monroe Doctrine exemption seemed to him "entirely worthless" because the League, not the United States alone, could say where and when it applied.[63]

Lodge used foreign policy to help ensure Republican control of the Senate. Ever since the Republicans had won their one-vote majority the preceding November, he had been cultivating fellow partisans regardless of his differences on domestic views or previous clashes with them. With conservatives he stressed personal and domestic arguments, as he did when he avowed "that the Republican party is the only organized force we have to rely upon to defeat the Wilsonian movement toward socialism." Conversely, with progressives he stressed foreign policy. Such erstwhile insurgents and bolters as Borah, Johnson, Medill McCormick, and Miles Poindexter had already taken stands against the League, and that opposition gave Lodge leverage in getting them to bury the hatchet for the sake of stronger resistance against Wilson.[64]

Reports about domestic reactions bothered Wilson's advisors, who tried without success to get him to speak out and explain his actions. Tumulty gingerly warned the president of trouble at home when he

---

63. New York *World,* Apr. 30, 1919; Lodge to Beveridge, Apr. 30, 1919, Lodge Papers; Lodge to Cummins, Apr. 30, 1919, ibid. Lodge later wrote a longer account of his conversation with Borah in *The Senate and the League of Nations,* which embellishes but essentially agrees with what he told Beveridge right after the event. See Lodge, *Senate and League,* 146–148.

64. Lodge to Harvey, Apr. 18, 1919, Lodge Papers. Cf. Lodge to Cummins, Apr. 30, 1919, ibid. For Lodge's cultivation of La Follette, see Lodge to Beveridge, Feb. 7, 1919, ibid.; La Follette to family, Nov. 16, 1918, Robert M. La Follette Papers, Library of Congress, Box A 24; La Follette to Robert M. La Follette, Jr., May 8, 1919, ibid., Box A 27. For an insightful interpretation of how Lodge played party solidarity and foreign policy off against each other, see William C. Widenor, *Lodge and the Search for an American Foreign Policy* (Berkeley, Calif., 1980), 310, 310 n. 42, 321.

cabled, "Hope you will consider making tour of country on League of Nations. It would be a great stimulant and mean utter rout of your political enemies." Wilson replied coldly that a speaking tour was "impossible to predict with certainty." There was, however, one domestic task the president could not avoid. On May 7, he issued the call for the Sixty-sixth Congress to convene on May 19. As he prepared an address to send the new Congress, Wilson passed up another opportunity to make his case to the country. "This message must necessarily be very short," he told Grayson, "because I am leaving my real message until my return home, when I can deliver it in person." The message consisted almost entirely of a list of domestic measures that he urged Congress to adopt, including passage of the constitutional amendment to guarantee woman suffrage. About the terms of the peace treaty, he said only, "It would be premature to discuss them or to express a judgment about them before they are brought to their complete formulation by the agreements which are now being sought at the table of the conference."[65]

The call to convene Congress prompted Lodge to intensify his effort to firm up the Republican majority in the Senate. His chief problem lay in the legacy of more than a decade of Republican divisiveness over domestic issues. The party's steady rightward drift since 1914 – together with Roosevelt's scuttling of the Progressives and return to the fold in 1916 – had dampened the earlier causes of conflict. Still, in 1919 enough reverberations from those Old Guard versus insurgent and conservative versus Progressive battles lingered to endanger Republican hopes for effective control of the Senate. The touchiest problem involved committee chairmanships. A group of erstwhile insurgents, including Borah and Johnson, threatened to fight against the selection of pro-business conservatives to head the Appropriations and Finance committees, but their own disunity doomed the gesture. Still, the insur-

---

65. Wilson address to conference, Apr. 28, 1919, in Link, ed., *Papers of Wilson*, LVIII, 199–201; editors' note, ibid., 202 n. 1; Tumulty to Wilson, [Apr. 29, 1919], ibid., 214; Wilson to Tumulty, May 2, 1919, ibid., 364; Grayson Diary, May 13, 1919, ibid., LIX, 79; Wilson message to Congress, May 20, 1919, ibid., 290. The full message is in ibid., 289–297. These performances were what prompted Baker to make the comment on May 17 cited earlier in note 60. On the day of the message to Congress, Baker further mused, "I am never quite able to make up my mind whether his unwillingness to meet people – and it is growing upon him – his extreme reticence in talking except in public speeches – . . . is due to a secretiveness of nature, or to a kind of shyness which shrinks from contact with people who are either likely to be hostile or may crudely misunderstand." Baker Diary, [May 20, 1919], ibid., 317.

gents gave Lodge a few anxious hours, and Borah worried him most of all. Here the League issue gave him a strong card to play. Lodge urged an editor who was an outspoken opponent of the League and a friend of Borah's to point out to him, "If we do not control the Senate – I am now including the committees – . . . all prospect of resisting or amending the League will vanish." Lodge also evidently promised Borah that Johnson would join them on the Foreign Relations Committee.[66]

Observers noted that all the new seats on that committee went to critics and opponents of the League. Enlarging the majority–minority ratio to ten to seven – up from nine to eight in the previous Democratically controlled Congress – Lodge gave the other two new places to Moses of New Hampshire, a League opponent and a collaborator with the Independence League, and Harry New of Indiana, an ultra-dependable party regular. In choosing them and Johnson, Lodge offended other senators who were more friendly to the League. One of them, Frank Kellogg of Minnesota, who fancied himself an expert in foreign affairs, wanted very much to be on the committee. In what Lodge recalled as "a frank talk," Kellogg admitted to him that "you did not care to take any committee with anything resembling a pledge or an explanation of views, that you wished to be entirely independent, a feeling which I understood and respected." It was also a feeling that made Lodge turn Kellogg down. Conversely, he required no oaths of fealty from senators who did not lean toward the League.[67]

66. Lodge to James T. Williams, Jr., May 13, 1919, Lodge Papers. Williams evidently did as Lodge asked, probably either by telephone or by going to see Borah, because he wrote soon afterward, "Thank you again, my dear Senator, and again my congratulations on the courage and vision you are showing." Williams to Borah, May 23, 1919, Borah Papers, Box 769. On the Senate situation, the political reporting in the New York *World* for May 1919 is excellent, and the reporting in the *New York Times* is also good. Another insightful assessment is Frank Polk to Lansing and House, May 17, 1919, in Link, ed., *Papers of Wilson*, LIX, 202. For a fine treatment of the Republican maneuvers, see Stone, *Irreconcilables*, 95–99.

67. Lodge to Kellogg, May 28, 1919, Lodge Papers. As a likely candidate for the Republican presidential nomination in 1920, Johnson was pleased with his appointment, as he wrote to his son: "The net result, however, of the whole situation has been that I am on the most important committee in the Senate, the Foreign Relations Committee, and the one I am most anxious to be on during this period." Johnson to Hiram Johnson, Jr., May 27, 1919, in Robert E. Burke, ed., *The Diary Letters of Hiram Johnson* (New York, 1983), III. On his appointment, see also Gus J. Karger to Taft, May 27, 1919, Taft Papers, reel 209; and on Kellogg's exclusion, see Taft to Karger, May 31, 1919, ibid., reel 556.

As matters stood, McCumber was the only pro-League Republican on the committee. The remaining majority party members included, besides Lodge, such announced opponents of the League as Borah, Brandegee, and Albert Fall of New Mexico, together with Philander Knox and Warren G. Harding of Ohio, another party loyalist and a presidential aspirant. "I think when you hear of the membership of the committee on foreign relations," Knox told Salmon Levinson, "you will be satisfied that the league of nations is going to have the time of its life when it is officially submitted." For Knox and Lodge, it seems, packing the Foreign Relations Committee in order to bring Borah and Johnson and others along on domestic matters was a matter of eating their cake and having it too.[68]

These Republican moves in the Senate occurred just as the final terms of the peace settlement were becoming known. The terms imposed on Germany struck many liberals as punitive and unjust. When he read a draft of the treaty early in May, Ray Stannard Baker found it "a terrible document: a document of retribution to the verge of revenge." The president himself conceded, Baker recorded in his diary, "If I were a German I think I should never sign it." Wilson soon quelled those qualms, and he later told a meeting of the American delegation, "I think that it is a good thing for the world and for Germany that the terms should be hard, so that Germany may know what an unjust war means." Wilson also believed, according to Baker, "that the treaty is in the main based securely on the 14 points – his interpretation of them."[69]

Wilson's fellow commissioners, Lansing, Bliss, and White, all found the terms too harsh and suggested revisions to soften their impact; only House refrained from raising questions. Herbert Hoover also made a plea to modify the treaty. "I feel that even if Germany signed the present terms," Hoover argued, "we would not secure stability, and that if she

---

68. Knox to Levinson, May 23, 1919, Levinson Papers, Box 26. Adopting reasoning just the opposite of Johnson's, La Follette rejected the offer because he did not want to give up his seat on either the Finance or the Interstate Commerce committee. As he explained to his sons, "While Foreign Relations is a big committee at any time and the center of interest just now – in ordinary times either of the other committees out-ranks it in public interest." La Follette to Philip and Robert M. La Follette, Jr., May 23, 1919, La Follette Papers, Box A 27. On the offer to New, see New to Beveridge, June 7, 1919, Beveridge Papers, Box 217. Cf. the interpretation of Lodge's actions in Widenor, *Lodge and American Foreign Policy*, 323, 323 n. 101.

69. Baker Diary, May 3, 26, 1919, in Link, ed., *Papers of Wilson*, LVIII, 419, LIX, 480; Grayson Diary, May 7, 1919, ibid., LVIII, 500; Charles Seymour to family, June 3, 1919, ibid., LX, 78.

refuse we will have extinguished all possibility of democracy in favor of either Communism or reaction, and that we will have wrecked the very foundations of the League of Nations." Dissent from the peace terms penetrated down into the ranks of the delegation. Several of the young experts, including such later renowned figures as the liberal lawyer A. A. Berle and the historian Samuel Eliot Morison, wrote private letters of protest. Another of these young men went further. On May 17, William C. Bullitt publicly resigned and wrote an open letter to Wilson accusing him of having "consented now to deliver the suffering peoples of the world to new oppressions, subjections and dismemberments – a new century of war. . . . I am sorry that you did not fight our fight to the finish and that you had so little faith in the millions of men, like myself, in every nation who had faith in you." Later, Bullitt and, less spectacularly, Berle would lend their intelligence and energy to the cause of blocking American consent to the peace treaty and membership in the League.[70]

As Bullitt implied in his parting shot, others besides Americans felt betrayed by the peace terms. In the British delegation no one felt greater dismay at the peace terms than the brilliant young economist John Maynard Keynes. "I've been as miserable for the past two or three weeks as a fellow could be," Keynes wrote a friend on May 14. "The Peace is outrageous and impossible and can bring nothing but misfortune." Unlike Bullitt, Keynes did not publicly resign, since he was about to return to his fellowship at King's College, Cambridge. He left Paris quietly early in June, because, as he told Lloyd George, "I can do no more good here. . . . The battle is lost." Keynes now began a personal battle against what he regarded as the twin infamies of the treaty and the League. As soon as he got back to England, he started writing *The Economic Consequences of the Peace*. In that book, which Keynes produced at lightning speed, his superb literary gifts, inside knowledge of the conference, and economic expertise would come together to furnish Wilson's opponents on both sides of the Atlantic with potent ammunition later in the League fight.[71]

70. Hoover to Wilson, June 4, 1919, ibid., 137; Bullitt to Wilson, May 17, ibid., LIX, 232–233. The private letters of protest, including Berle's and Morison's, are in Lansing Papers, Vol. 43. Not all the younger staff members shared this disillusionment with Wilson. For an account of a much more favorable but not uncritical discussion of his work at the conference, see Seymour to family, May 14, 1919, in Link, ed., *Papers of Wilson*, LIX, 158–159.

71. Keynes to Duncan Grant, May 14, 1919, quoted in Robert Skidelsky, *John Maynard Keynes: Hopes Betrayed, 1883–1920* (New York, Penguin ed., 1994), 371; Keynes to Lloyd George, June 5, 1919, quoted in ibid., 375.

Dissent in the ranks of his delegation did not seem to affect Wilson's health. In May and June 1919, several observers remarked on how much stronger and more vigorous he seemed. Ray Stannard Baker noted, for example, that Wilson was "looking and fit and alert as ever. He is a wonder!" The president also began to defend his approach to peace outside the confines of the peace conference. In early May, in a speech in Paris to the Institute of International Law, he warned against "the unqualified hope that men have entertained everywhere of immediate emancipation from the things that have hampered them and oppressed them. You cannot in human experience rush into the light." Three weeks later, in a Memorial Day address at the American military cemetery at Suresnes, Wilson appealed to the spirit of those who had given their lives "to defeat forever the things for which the Central Powers stood . . . [and] to see to it that there should never be a war like this again. . . . The League of Nations is the covenant of governments that these men shall not have died in vain." Onlookers saw tears streaming down the cheeks of battle-hardened veterans. Baker, who recognized that both the occasion and Wilson's phrasing recalled the Gettysburg Address, called this "the greatest speech . . . of any I ever heard."[72]

Wilson's newly revived eloquence availed him little with disillusioned liberals and idealists at home. During April and May, as details of the settlement leaked out, those on the left who had already crossed over into opposition – most notably Oswald Garrison Villard and his magazine, the *Nation* – repeatedly excoriated Wilson for failure to live up to his promises. In the middle of May, from the Women's International Conference for Permanent Peace, which was meeting in Zurich, several leading feminist peace advocates, including Jane Addams, Florence Kelley, and Lillian Wald, who had formerly given Wilson strong backing, issued a statement demanding radical softening of the treaty's terms. The heaviest blow of all from the left fell on May 24, when the *New Republic* abandoned its wait-and-see attitude to blast the settlement in an issue emblazoned with the headline, "THIS IS NOT PEACE." As for their erstwhile champion, the *New Republic* added two weeks later, "Wilson, for lack of courage and knowledge and administrative capacity, has yielded to a settlement which means a Europe of wars and revolution and agony." Offering mock congratula-

72. Entry, May [May 30, 1919], [June 20, 1919], Baker Diary, in Link, ed., *Papers of Wilson*, LIX, 621–622, LXI, 34; Wilson speech, May 9, 1919, ibid., LVIII, 598–600; speech, May 30, 1919, ibid., LIX, 607. See also Edith Benham Diary, May 30, 1919, ibid., 621.

tions to cynics and reactionaries, the editors conceded, "They were right about Mr. Wilson. We were wrong. We hoped and lost. They did not hope and did not lose."[73]

Sarcasm could not disguise the anguish that the *New Republic* editors and other liberals felt over their choice. Should they support the treaty and League membership, despite their imperfections? Or should they take the morally more satisfying but still troubling stance of opposition? The *New Republic*'s chief editor, Herbert Croly, secluded himself and paced the floor for three days, his wife remembered, before he made up his mind. Walter Lippmann, who was Croly's junior colleague on the magazine and until recently one of House's bright young men on the Inquiry, later claimed that the magazine's "decision to oppose ratification was Croly's. I followed him, though I was not then, and am not now, convinced that it was the wisest thing to do. . . . If I had it to do all over again, I would take the other side; we supplied the Battalion of Death [Senators Borah, Johnson, and company] with too much ammunition." Lippmann's memory played tricks on him. At the time, he confided to Secretary of War Newton D. Baker, ". . . I suppose that you keep your faith in the future by hoping that the League of Nations can modify the terms and work out a genuine settlement. I can't share that belief."[74]

Other progressives did share that belief. Croly's and Lippmann's intimate friend Learned Hand tried to make a case for supporting the treaty to them, but to so little avail, he told his wife, "that I am out of temper with the whole outfit; . . . for their arrogance and assumption really have made me sick." One important figure on the left also stuck with the League despite a history of bitter disappointment from Wilson and dislike of much that transpired at the peace conference. This was W.E.B. DuBois, the nation's leading African-American thinker and spokesperson. DuBois had witnessed the doings in Paris first-hand as a delegate to the Pan-African Congress there in February 1919, and he deplored the scramble for colonial spoils and the shortcomings of the

73. *Nation,* CVIII (May 24, 1919), 845–851; Addams, Kelley, and Wald statement, *New York Times,* May 15, 1919; *New Republic,* XIX (May 24, 1919), 100–106, (June 7, 1919), 170. For a sensitive treatment of liberal disillusionment with the treaty, see Knock, *To End All Wars,* 252–256.

74. Lippmann, "Notes for a Biography," *New Republic,* LXIII (July 16, 1930), 252; Lippmann to Baker, June 9, 1919, N. D. Baker Papers, Box 10. On Croly's position, see David Levy, *Herbert Croly of the New Republic* (Princeton, N.J., 1985), 263–266; on Lippmann's, see Ronald Steel, *Walter Lippmann and the American Century* (Boston, 1980), 157–166.

mandate system. Nevertheless, in the May issue of *The Crisis*, the magazine of the National Association for the Advancement of Colored People, which DuBois edited, he issued a ringing declaration in favor of League membership. "A league of nations is absolutely necessary to the salvation of the Negro race," declared DuBois. Not only would such a world body "from the beginning recognize the Negro nations," but it would give them a forum in which to speak and act against "the selfish nations of white civilization" which threatened to plunge the world into a "Great War of Races" even more terrible than the conflict just ended. "The refusal to adopt the Japanese race equality amendment is deplorable," DuBois conceded, "but it is an argument for and not against a nation of nations. It is the Beginning of a mighty End."[75]

Disaffected idealists aided the opposition to the treaty and the League less through their numbers than through their resourcefulness and articulateness. Lippmann did not exaggerate when he remembered having supplied "ammunition" to the isolationists. Thanks to his former position on the Inquiry, he was able to leak embarrassing information about the peace conference to Johnson and Borah and helped to arrange damaging testimony when the Foreign Relations Committee held hearings on the treaty. Between Villard's obsessively righteous prosecution of Wilson in the *Nation* and Croly's and Lippmann's more thoughtful dissection of the peace settlement in the *New Republic*, the president's senatorial opponents and the Independence League acquired a rich arsenal of well-targeted, highly destructive rhetorical missiles to launch in coming engagements in the League fight. During the next two decades, those arguments would lend intellectual luster to the anti-Wilsonian, anti-League isolationist persuasion that grew to dominate the American left, especially during the 1930s.[76]

In the short run, however, few others objected to the harsh terms imposed on Germany. Most newspapers, magazines, and public figures applauded that aspect of the treaty. "This country wanted hard measure

75. Learned Hand to Frances Hand, June 15, 1919, quoted in Gerald Gunther, *Learned Hand: The Man and the Judge* (New York, 1994), 265; DuBois, "The League of Nations," *The Crisis*, XVIII (May 1919), 10–11. On DuBois's thinking about the world war and the League, see Manning Marable, *W.E.B. DuBois, Black Radical Democrat* (Boston, 1986), 91–103, and David Levering Lewis, *W.E.B. DuBois: Biography of a Race* (New York, 1993), 535–580.
76. On Lippmann's cooperation with the senators, see Lippmann to Hiram Johnson, Aug. 17, Sept. 9, 1919, Walter Lippmann Papers, Yale University Library; Johnson to Lippmann, Aug. 18, 23, 28, 1919, ibid.

meted out to Germany and is pleased that the terms are as drastic as they are," commented Lodge in rare kind words about the peace conference. For Wilson, the erosion of support from the idealistic side meant that he would have to try to appease his Republican critics. Those critics' reactions to the revised Covenant showed how wide a gulf still separated them from the president, and their approval of the terms with Germany did not appear to soften their resistance to full-fledged participation in the League. Lodge broke his stance of withholding public comment on the treaty just once at this time to remark in the Senate about the Covenant, "Then he [Wilson] took it back and they amended it. They made it much worse than it was before." Clearly, the president would have his bridge-building work cut out for him when he returned from the peace conference.[77]

How hard that work would be became apparent with the first reactions to the Covenant and the treaty in the newly convened, Republican-controlled Senate. Lawrence Sherman of Illinois unleashed a rambling, scathing attack on the League Covenant as the "miserable delusion" of one man, whom he again likened to Don Quixote. The dissident Democrat James Reed indulged in one of the League fight's rare appeals to unvarnished prejudice. He called the League "a colored league of nations; that is to say, the majority of the nations composing the league do not belong to the white race of men." He cited population statistics and quoted from DuBois's editorial in the *Crisis* to show that the League was an opening wedge for racial equality. To his fellow Democrats, Reed thundered, "Chew on that quid in your reflective moments, you men of the South!" Hiram Johnson delivered a long denunciation of "the sordid, cunning, secret, and crafty designs of European and Asiatic governments," which, under Article X of the League Covenant, required Americans to shed their blood to uphold unjust boundaries around the world and colonial oppression in such places as Ireland, Korea, and China. Johnson broached a now-familiar argument among insurgents and former Progressives that linked his hatred of big business to his opposition to the League to excoriate it as "a gigantic war trust . . . a great world economic trust, wherein a few men sitting in secret may control the economic destinies of peoples."[78]

Republican senators also stirred up what Tumulty called "a tempest

77. *Congressional Record*, 66th Cong., 1st Sess. (May 23, 1919), 161.
78. Ibid. (May 23, 1919), 157–171; (May 26, 1919), 235–246; (June 2, 1919), 501–509. For descriptions and analyses of the Senate situation, see New York *World*, June 5, 7, 9, 1919; Frank Polk to American Mission, June 6, 1919, in Link, ed., *Papers of Wilson*, LX, 245; Gus J. Karger to Taft, June 5, 1919, Taft Papers, reel 209; Hitchcock to Taft, June 6, 1919, ibid., reel 210.

in a teapot" over publication of the text of the treaty. Borah announced
to the Senate on June 9 that he had obtained a copy of the treaty and
asked unanimous consent to read it into the *Congressional Record.*
Democrats objected and brought out, in the words of one newspaper
reporter, "all the artillery that is part of the regular strategy of a filibuster." The fiery John Sharp Williams of Mississippi "did the heavy
fighting," calling League opponents "Prussian junkers" who wanted
"unlimited American sovereignty and unlimited preparation for universal war." Brandegee and Williams got into a nasty spat, as Brandegee
mocked Williams' deafness and Williams shot back with a thinly veiled
slur on Brandegee's alcoholism. Borah eventually read the treaty to a
largely empty chamber for about half an hour, until there was motion for
unanimous consent to have the rest of the text printed for the *Record.*[79]

In the second week in June, Knox introduced a new version of his
resolution to separate the League from the peace treaty. This version
also restated his earlier "Knox doctrine," with the fifth clause stating:

> That, finally, it shall be the declared policy of our Government, in
> order to meet fully and fairly our obligations to ourselves and to
> the world, that the freedom and peace of Europe being again
> threatened by any power or combination of powers the United
> States will regard such a situation with grave concern as a menace
> to its own peace and freedom, will consult with other powers
> affected with a view to devising means for the removal of such
> menace, and will, the necessity arising in the future, carry out the
> same complete accord and cooperation with our chief cobelligerents
> for the defense of civilization.[80]

79. Tumulty to Wilson [June 13, 1919], in Link, ed., *Papers of Wilson,* LX, 536;
Congressional Record, 66th Cong., 1st Sess. (June 9, 1919), 781–802; New
York *World,* June 10, 1919. The reporter was Charles Michelson. For other
descriptions of the scene, see *New York Times,* June 10, 1919, and La Follette
to Robert M. Jr. and Philip La Follette, June 9, 1919, La Follette Papers, Box A
27. It was estimated that reading the entire text would have taken more than
twenty hours. It appears in *Congressional Record,* 66th Cong., 1st Sess. (June
9, 1919), 802–857. The Foreign Relations Committee also investigated leaks of
the text of the treaty. Borah demanded that four international bankers,
Thomas W. Lamont, Henry P. Davison, Frank C. Vanderlip, and J. P. Morgan,
be subpoenaed to appear before the committee. The four financiers explained
that they had known of no prohibiton on showing around copies of the treaty
that they had brought back from Paris. Despite expectations of fireworks, there
was, as one newspaper noted, "no inquisition . . . it was all pleasant." New
York *World,* June 10, 12, 1919; *New York Times,* June 10, 12, 1919.
80. *Congressional Record,* 66th Cong., 1st Sess. (June 10, 1919), 894.

Lodge claimed that Knox had not consulted him, but this resolution was clearly intended to reassert the established Republican approach to foreign policy. The resolution was also intended, Republican senators admitted, to put Wilson on the defensive. Knox told reporters that he believed the Foreign Relations Committee would approve his resolution and, even if the Senate failed to pass it, there would be a convincing demonstration of Republican strength. The committee took up the Knox resolution on June 12, in a heated three-hour session. The main item of contention was the fifth clause, which Johnson found "as obnoxious as the League of Nations itself." After some jockeying, Knox consented to have that clause removed. He later told reporters that the previous statement had sufficed as assurance to the Allies. The committee concurred in its excision and approved the resolution, with all the Republicans in favor except McCumber, who joined the Democrats in opposition. This alignment demonstrated again the willingness of mainstream Republicans like Knox and Lodge to make common cause with the isolationists against Wilson. The committee's approval meant that this alternative to the president's foreign policy could hover in the wings to be called forward if the situation warranted.[81]

But that time had not yet come. Few Republicans outside the Senate sprang to support the Knox resolution. Hays, the party chairman, refrained from making any comment and took care to mend his fences with Taft. Other Republicans joined the search for a middle way between the Knox resolution and unconditional acceptance of the League. Nicholas Murray Butler, the president of Columbia University and a leader in prewar international law movements, journeyed to Washington to meet with senators Frank Kellogg of Minnesota (whom Lodge had just blackballed from the Foreign Relations Committee), Frederick Hale of Maine, and several others. Butler agreed to draft reservations to Senate consent to League membership that would specify further the exemptions of domestic questions and the Monroe Doctrine and limit obligations under Article X. "As was said last night by so many of those who participated in our conversation," Butler told Hale the next day, "the Republican party cannot afford to leave on the country the impres-

---

81. New York *World,* June 11, 12, 1919; *New York Times,* June 11, 12, 1919; Johnson to Hiram Jr. and Arch M. Johnson, June 12, 1919, in Burke, ed., *Johnson Letters,* III. See also Tumulty to Wilson, [June 13, 1919], in Link, ed., *Papers of Wilson,* LX, 535; Karger to Taft, June 12, 1919, Taft Papers, reel 210; La Follette to Robert M. Jr. and Philip La Follette, June 12, 1919, La Follette Papers, Box A 27.

sion of mere negation in this matter of a League of Nations." Those meetings marked the first gathering of the little band of Republican senators who would later be known as the "mild reservationists."[82]

Opponents and harsh critics of League membership reacted furiously to their fellow Republicans' moderation. Brandegee tried to bully Root into coming out for the Knox resolution. Though himself a thorough-going conservative, Brandegee scrawled an angry note on June 9 in which he told Root, "We are 'Americans' and no international Banking Syndicate can terrify or bulldoze us!" In a second, rambling note the same day Brandegee grew livid at the prospect that "you fellows over in N.Y., with what you represent & control – in newspapers, banks, trust cos. et al. et al. et al. are going to bend in the middle or truckle to Wilson & Taft. God help you!" He claimed that he and his fellow opponents were "tak[ing] the bayonet thrusts, the poisonous gas, and the cold blue steel, while they [Wall Street moguls] count their profit. I am getting a trifle weary of being the Goat! Do you get me?" The near incoherence of these letters made it seem likely that Brandegee had been drinking when he wrote them. He soon calmed down enough to call a meeting of sixteen Republican senators at his house, where they discussed the Knox resolution and their party's attitude toward the League. "Confidentially, I don't like the look of things," Johnson reported to his son. The senators at the meeting concluded that the Knox resolution would get no more than thirty-six votes because, Johnson said, "we have too many weak-kneed brethren." The identity of everyone who attended that meeting is not known, but, given the presence of Brandegee and Johnson, it most likely marked the first gathering of the diehard opponents of League membership who would soon be known as the "Irreconcilables."[83]

---

82. Butler to Hale, June 12, 1919, Nicholas Murray Butler Papers, Columbia University Library. For Butler's reservations, see Butler memorandum, [June 12, 1919], ibid. On his meetings with Republican senators, see also Butler memorandum, June 4, 1938, ibid.; Chandler P. Anderson Diary, June 11, 1919, Anderson Papers; and Margulies, *Mild Reservationists*, 35–37. On Hays' position, see Hays to Taft, June 18, 1919, Taft Papers, reel 210.

83. Brandegee to Root, June 9, 1919 [two letters], Root Papers, Box 137; Johnson to Archibald M. Johnson, June 16, 1919, in Burke, ed., *Johnson Letters*, III. On the meeting at Brandegee's house, see also Gus J. Karger to Taft, June 16, 1919, Taft Papers, reel 210, and New York *World*, June 17, 1919. For Root's private reactions to the revised Covenant, see entry May 15, 1919, Stimson Diary.

Knox himself took a more sober stance in the furor over his resolution. After he announced that he would speak on June 17, a large audience packed the galleries, and most of his colleagues took their seats. Knox defended his resolution at length as a simple expedient to separate the League Covenant from the rest of the treaty so that "the Senate may advise and consent to that part of it which shall bring us peace." Knox criticized this Covenant as no improvement over its predecessor. He leveled his strongest fire at "the pernicious provisions in article 10." That article proposed to fix current boundaries, regardless of the wishes of peoples affected, along lines dictated "by imperial governments and kings with dynastic and other interests to serve alien to us." Knox read from the Farewell Address to warn against too quickly abandoning Washington's warning against permanent alliances in order "to guarantee their [the Allies'] perpetual possession of these spoils, as is proposed in article 10 of the covenant. . . . Beware of the possible consequences of haste. God forbid that 'the war that was to end all wars' shall conclude with a peace that may end all peace."[84]

Although Republican senators spoke most often, the Democrats did not sit by silently. Thomas Walsh of Montana delivered a thoughtful defense of the League, in which he called Article X "the soul and spirit of the covenant. Cut it out and the heart is cut out of the only plan the statesmanship of the world has been able to devise or has ever been able to offer for the preservation of the peace of the world." Other Democrats furiously assailed both the Knox resolution and the motives of the Republicans on the Foreign Relations Committee, whom one called an "infernal gang" bent on defeating the League by devious means. League opponents likewise did their part to lower the level of debate. Sherman staged another exhibition of demagoguery when he charged that Catholic nations subservient to the Pope would dominate the league. "The sway of those people," he asserted, "and their implicit faith in the infallibility of the head of this great organization is [sic] supreme." Sherman's performance infuriated one Democrat, Henry Ashurst of Arizona, so much that he launched an impromptu attack on the Illinois senator for having demonstrated "the remarkable phenomena of a man being foggy and windy at the same time." Ashurst admonished his fellow senators to recast their debate as "a Home-

---

84. *Congressional Record*, 66th Cong., 1st Sess. (June 17, 1919), 1216–1222. It is not clear whether Knox, like Lodge earlier, meant to taunt Wilson with one of his own phrases when he referred to "the war to end all wars." If he did, he was attributing something to Wilson that he never said. Like "self-determination," this phrase came from Lloyd George.

ric contest, let patriotism speak, let logic and the powers of thought speak, and not prejudice of any kind, either political or religious prejudice."[85]

Meanwhile, at Lodge's urging, Root had come to the capital and spent much time in Knox's office conferring with him and other Republicans. Some newspapers reported that the Knox resolution was "in extremis" and that Root had been summoned to advise its supporters on how to extricate themselves from an awkward situation, perhaps to prepare some new proposition. The reports were accurate. Lodge was privately complaining about "the difficulties of the fight to make here in the Senate. We are at the awful disadvantage of being 50 men fighting 1 and each one of the 50 wants to fight him in his own way." In an attempt to remedy the situation, Lodge asked Root to write a letter both criticizing the Covenant and stating a number of suggestions for limiting and safeguarding American membership in the League. While Root was in Washington, he, Knox, and Lodge, later joined by Brandegee, went over a draft of what Lodge called "a masterly letter," which he believed "will do us a lot of good."[86]

This new letter of Root's, like its predecessor, lived up to Lodge's expectations. The eleven-page document was dated June 19, but it was

85. *Congressional Record*, 66th Cong., 1st. Sess. (June 18, 1919), 1261–1276; (June 19, 1919), 1372–1379; (June 20, 1919), 1430–1450. Sherman admitted in this speech that friends had tried to dissuade him from making these charges. On this point, see Borah to Elmer Peterson, June 24, 1919, cited in Stone, *Irreconcilables*, 104 n. 16. The response to Sherman's speech was mixed. Although many newspapers deplored his utterance, the senator received, according to Ralph Stone's estimate, twice as many favorable as unfavorable letters. Many of the letters praising him came from Protestant ministers in the South. Sherman also had 27,000 copies of the speech mailed out, including a large number to Missouri, at the request of his fellow irreconcilable and indulger in demagoguery, Reed. See ibid., 105. For his part, Ashurst was less of an uncritical administration loyalist than other Democratic senators, and he frequently criticized Wilson privately for neglecting to mend his fences at home.

86. New York *World*, June 21, 22, 1919; *New York Times*, June 21, 22, 1919; Lodge to W. Sturgis Bigelow, June 21, 26, 1919, Lodge Papers. On the origin of Root's letter and the meeting at Lodge's house, see also entry Feb. 28, 1920, Stimson Diary; Knox to Beveridge, June 21, 1919, Beveridge Papers, Box 215; Brandegee to Beveridge, Nov. 28, 1919, ibid., Box 214. Why Lodge referred to "50 men" on his side is not known. Perhaps he was adding Reed to the forty-nine Republicans, but several of them, such as McNary, were openly favorable to the League, and one, McCumber, was as ardently pro-League as any Democrat.

revised over the next two days and released to the press on June 21. It opened with a blistering four-page critique of the League Covenant for having failed to incorporate Root's earlier suggestions. The revisions that had been made were, he judged, "very inadequate and unsatisfactory." The peace negotiators had still done nothing "towards providing for the revision and development of international law" and nothing "to limit the vast and incalculable obligation which Article X of the Covenant undertakes to impose." Neither the statement of the right of withdrawal nor the exclusions of domestic questions and the Monroe Doctrine did much to protect American sovereignty and interests. "On the other hand," added Root, in a bow to League advocates, "it still remains that there is in the covenant a great deal of very high value that the world ought not to lose." As before, he likened the provisions for meeting threats of war with automatic international conferences, for compulsory delay in going to war, and for some forms of joint response to aggression. He also conceded that current conditions in Europe and elsewhere required "prompt action" to restore peace and order.

"Under these circumstances," Root then asked, "what ought to be done?" If the Covenant remained part of the peace treaty, then the Senate must adopt "in its resolution of consent to the ratification of the treaty an expression of such reservations and understandings as will cure so far as possible the defects which I have pointed out." Equally important, he insisted, those reservations must "be made part of the instrument of ratification." Root briefly sketched three areas to be covered by such reservations. First, with respect to Article X, it must be made clear that the Senate "refuses its consent." Second, the ability to withdraw from the League on two years' notice must be made absolute, subject to no other power's review or approval. Third, joining the League must not "imply a relinquishment by the United States of America of its traditional attitude toward purely American questions [i.e., the Monroe Doctrine], or to require the submission of its policy regarding questions which it deems to be purely American, to the decision or recommendation of others." Root implicitly answered pro-League critics who charged that amendments to the treaty, such as Lodge and other Republicans were suggesting, would require reopening negotiations. He stated that reservations covering these areas would not require renegotiation but would be accepted simply by other signatories' not objecting to them.

Both Root's opening swipe at obligations under Article X and his suggestion of a reservation of nonconsent to it showed again that he basically agreed with Lodge and Knox rather than with Wilson and Taft. He underscored this position by devoting the longest section of the letter to a much harsher attack on Article X than he had made earlier.

Root dismissed this article as "not an essential or even an appropriate part of the provisions for a League of Nations to preserve peace." On the contrary, that provision constituted "an independent alliance for the preservation of the *status quo*," which sought to commit Americans to enter into wars in faraway places where they would almost certainly not want to fight. "If it is necessary for the security of western Europe that we should go to the support of say France if attacked," Root observed, "let us agree to do that particular thing plainly. . . . I am in favor of that." But not Article X, which raised in his view precisely the dangers that Washington had warned against in his Farewell Address. "Just so far as it is necessary to modify this historic American policy," he added, "in order to put into effect a practical plan for a League of Nations to preserve peace we ought to go, and we ought not to go one step farther. The step proposed in Article X is not necessary for such a plan, and we ought not to take it." Root closed the letter by stating that he did not regard "the League covenant in its present form as the final word upon an organization for the preservation of the peace of the world," and he urged future efforts to strengthen international law and arbitration, to reduce armaments, and to revise and improve the League.[87]

Once more the Republicans' foreign policy mandarin had worked his magic. Although Root had unmistakably distanced himself from Taft and the LEP, he still smiled upon the League and harked back again to their own earlier stress on international law. Although he plainly differed with Borah and other isolationists, his invocation of the Farewell Address, his insistence upon unilateral maintenance of the Monroe Doctrine, and his revulsion toward Article X did not leave them out in the cold. He endorsed neither Knox's demand to separate the Covenant from the peace treaty nor Lodge's pledge to seek amendments, but he again offered an alternative to those expedients. As a substitute for amendments, which would require going back to the negotiating table, Root proposed that the Senate attach strictly worded, tightly binding reservations to the instrument of ratification. Likewise, although the Covenant might remain in the treaty, a reservation refusing to consent to Article X offered a way to nullify what many Republicans regarded as Wilson's most obnoxious and dangerous handiwork. Best of all, with his suggestion of a pledge to France and his statement of willingness to depart from the Farewell Address, Root undid the concession that Lodge and Knox had made to the isolationists on the Foreign Relations Committee when they dropped the

87. Root to Lodge, June 19, 1919, Lodge Papers. This letter is also reprinted in Scott, ed., *Men and Events*, 269–277. Manuscript notes for parts of the letter are in Root Papers, Box 161.

fifth clause of the Knox resolution – the pledge to defend "the freedom and peace of Europe." Thereby, Root reaffirmed their party's established great power foreign policy. Withal, Root's letter resurveyed broad grounds upon which Republicans of many stripes could unite, and it put a positive face on their stance during this final stage of the peace negotiations.[88]

Root's letter rallied Republicans both inside and outside the Senate. Hays and Hughes quickly endorsed his position, and one Republican newspaper published an editorial titled, "Root to the Rescue." According to some estimates, as many as forty-nine senators would vote for reservations along the lines that he proposed. The strongest testimony to the effectiveness of Root's letter came from Lodge. "In my opinion it is more disastrous to the League than any statement that has been made by anyone," he told Henry White. "It has consolidated feeling in the Senate. It is obvious that it is producing an immense effect upon public opinion throughout the country." To a friend in Massachusetts he added that framing reservations along Root's lines "is precisely what we are trying to do. . . . [Root's letter] proposes exactly what many of us hope to succeed in securing." In his heart of hearts, Lodge may not have abandoned his desire to separate the Covenant from the treaty, but, as William Widenor has pointed out, Root had shown another way to reach the same end. He had set the course that Lodge and the mainstream of the Republican party would follow during the next nine months. They were now ready to do battle when Wilson returned from Paris for the main campaign of the League fight.[89]

88. The distinction between an amendment and a reservation can be elusive and would generate much debate during the coming months. According to Henry Stimson, as he recorded in his diary, Root explained the distinction to him this way on June 2: "While an amendment to the League must go before the other nations, if our Senate should, instead of amending, ratify the treaty, expressing its construction of a given provision, and no other nation expressly objects to that construction, it will stand. Similarly we could ratify the covenant, reserving our ratification as to a specific point, and the remainder would hold." Entry June 3, 1919, Stimson Diary. Not every Republican senator was won over to Root's position. Johnson commented privately, "Every little scrub in the Senate jumps at the idea of ratifying 'with reservations' beli[e]ving that he can hereafter justify himself as being upon both sides of the matter. If we ratify in this manner, nobody will every [*sic*] again hear of the reservations, and we'll be in the League, bound hand and foot." Johnson to Hiram Jr. and Archibald M. Johnson, June 22, 1919, in Burke, ed., *Johnson Letters*, III.
89. Lodge to White, June 23, 1919, Lodge Papers; Lodge to Charles C. Jackson, June 28, 1919, ibid.; Widenor, *Lodge and American Foreign Policy*, 328–329. On Root's role at this stage in the League fight, see also Bartlett, *League to Enforce Peace*, 139, and Leopold, *Root*, 139.

3

Long, Hot Summer

The signing of the treaty of peace with Germany on June 28, 1919, was a French show. The event displayed two renowned traits of that nation – grandeur and revenge. Nothing could have conveyed grandeur better than the ceremony's setting. It was at that symbol of the power and the glory of France under the "Sun King," Louis XIV – the Hall of Mirrors in the Palace of Versailles. Revenge also dictated the setting. Not quite fifty years before, the victorious Prussians had insisted on crowning their king as the first emperor of a united Germany in the Hall of Mirrors. An added touch of revenge came with an old, plain table in the center of the great hall. This was Louis XIV's writing table. In 1870, the victorious Germans had forced the vanquished French to sign the treaty ending the Franco–Prussian War on this table. Now, the German delegates had to sign the Treaty of Versailles on the same table, under the baleful stare of Premier Clemenceau and other Allied leaders.[1]

Given the setting, this ceremony could not help being impressive. But there were odd notes. Negotiations among the victors had lasted so long and proved so fractious that Wilson and the Allied leaders had scrapped their original plan for a preliminary conference, to be followed by bargaining with the Germans. Instead, they imposed the terms that they had so arduously hammered out. The Germans thereupon threatened to refuse to sign the treaty. Their threat impelled Lloyd George to break ranks and argue for softening some of the terms. This time, Wilson sided with Clemenceau to stymie this last-minute stab at revision of the treaty. The only speech at the ceremony on June 28 was a short statement by Clemenceau in which he noted that no change had been made in the terms previously communicated to Germany. Afterward, the Big Four held a brief final meeting and then left at once for their respective countries.[2]

1. For descriptions of the scene, see *New York Times,* June 29, 1919; Lansing memorandum, "THE SIGNING OF THE TREATY OF PEACE WITH GERMANY AT VERSAILLES ON JUNE 28TH, 1919," in Arthur S. Link, ed., *The Papers of Woodrow Wilson* (Princeton, N.J., 1990), LXI, 321–328; William Linn Westerman, "The Signing of the Treaty of Versailles," ibid., 328–332; entry, June 28, 1919, House Diary, 332–333.
2. On the conflict with Lloyd George, see esp., transcript of Peace Commission meeting, [June 3,1919], ibid., LX, 71.

This muted end to the peace conference suited the mixed message that Wilson wanted to send back home. The day before the ceremony at Versailles, the president telegraphed a 500-word statement to be released in the United States at the time of the signing. He called this treaty "the charter for a new order of affairs in the world." He acknowledged that it was "a severe treaty" but only because "great wrongs done by Germany are to be righted. . . . And it is much more than a treaty of peace with Germany." It liberated peoples; it abolished the right of conquest; it put force behind international law; it set colonial subjects on the path to self-rule; it laid a basis for freer world trade; it provided for humanitarian services; and it guaranteed fairer treatment of labor. Because the treaty did all these things, Wilson called it "a great charter for a new order of affairs. There is ground here for deep satisfaction, universal reassurance, and confident hope." Immediately after the ceremony at Versailles, the president boarded a train that took him to Brest, where his ship sailed for home that night.[3]

Wilson was already trying to sell the treaty and the League to the Senate and the American people. In fact, he had started his lobbying before the treaty was signed. On June 11, he sought to mollify Irish-Americans, who still felt aggrieved at Britain's actions in their homeland, by meeting with two of their leaders and explaining the difficulty and delicacy of peacemaking. Grayson, who was at that meeting, believed that the president's eloquence and sincerity moved his visitors. On June 19, Wilson told the Belgian parliament, "The League of Nations is . . . a league of right," and its opponents were those who wished "to turn back to those bad days of selfish contest" that had caused the war. On June 27, he met with fifty American reporters for an hour of no-holds-barred questions. Ray Stannard Baker believed that Wilson, as he noted in his diary, "never appeared to a better advantage than on this occasion." He used humor, drew homely analogies, and told affecting stories. "I didn't say it [the treaty] adheres to the Fourteen Points," Wilson said in response to one question. "But really, I think it adheres more closely to them than I had a right to expect." On Shantung, he stated, "That seemed the best that could be got out of a complicated situation in which two of the other powers [Britain and France] were bound."[4]

3. Wilson telegram, June 27, 1919, ibid., LXI, 292–293.
4. Wilson speech to Belgian parliament, June 19, 1919, ibid., 18–19; entry, June 27, [1919], Baker Diary, ibid., 252–254; Walter E. Weyl notes, June 27, 1919, ibid., 240–245. See also entry, June 27, 1919, ibid., 235–237, and Charles T. Thompson notes, June 27, 1919, ibid., 246–252. On the meeting with the Irish-American leaders, see entry, June 11, 1919, Grayson Diary, ibid., LX, 383–387.

Wilson gave conflicting signals as to how he might behave when he got back to the United States. On the way to the station after the signing ceremony, Colonel House talked with him in what turned out to be the last meeting of their lives. House recorded in his diary that he urged Wilson "to meet with the Senate in a conciliatory spirit." Wilson replied, "House, I have found one can never get anything in this life that is worth while without fighting for it." The day before, Wilson had breathed a different spirit to the reporters, but he had agreed to meet with them only on condition that what he said could not be quoted or even attributed to him. As Ray Stannard Baker observed, this was the only press conference that the president held during his six months in Paris. "I wish he would do it oftener," Baker wrote in his diary; "but he dreads it, & is keenly sensitive to those who are hostile in their questioning & is likely to assume a defensive tone." These reactions did not bode well for Wilson's performance in the coming months.[5]

I

By the time he boarded his ship to come back to America, Wilson was receiving conflicting advice about how to deal with the task of selling the treaty and the League in the United States. His closest advisors were pushing divergent strategies. On one side stood Tumulty and William Gibbs McAdoo, who had been secretary of the treasury and wartime director of the railroads and was Wilson's son-in-law. They urged the president to take his case for the treaty and the League directly to the people by making a speaking tour soon after his return. On the other side stood Democratic senators and Postmaster General Albert Burleson. They urged him to let a decent interval of time elapse before he made any appeal to the public. Those strategies were not mutually exclusive, and Tumulty assured Burleson, "The President never had any intention of making his tour immediately upon returning to this country." Instead, he would first seek to sway the senators.[6]

That was not going to be an easy job. Nearly every knowledgeable observer agreed that the senators had aligned themselves into three well-defined factions. First, there were League supporters. Next came those who

5. Entry, June 27, [1919], Baker Diary, ibid., 252.
6. Tumulty to Burleson, June 25, 1919, Albert S. Burleson Papers, Library of Congress, Vol. 24. On plans for a speaking tour, see Tilson to Tumulty, June 16, 1919, in Link, ed., *Papers of Wilson*, LXI, 610; Wilson to Thomas Lamont, June 17, 1919, ibid., 641; Tumulty to Wilson, June 28, 1919, ibid., LXI, 350; I. T. Jones memorandum, [ca. June 20, 1919], Jospeh P. Tumulty Papers, Library of Congess, Box 50; Tumulty to Wilson, June 20, 1919, ibid.

were willing to accept membership, but only with reservations. Finally, diehard opponents stood apart and unto themselves. Shortly before the signing of the treaty, the *Chicago Tribune* counted forty senators as pro-Leaguers, forty-three as reservationists, eight as opponents, and five as undecided. According to this count, the pro-Leaguers were all Democrats except McCumber. The reservationists were all Republicans except Charles S. Thomas of Colorado and Thomas P. Gore of Oklahoma. The opponents included such outspoken foes of the League as Borah, Johnson, Reed, Brandegee, Albert Fall, and Miles Poindexter. Also counted as opponents were Robert La Follette and his fellow insurgent Republican Asle J. Gronna of North Dakota. Both of them had opposed intervention in the war and had repeatedly criticized Wilson, but neither one had publicly taken a stand against the treaty and the League. The undecideds were all Democrats, four of them from the South. This estimate turned out to forecast most senators' stands with remarkable accuracy.[7]

Either way – dealing with the Senate or going to the people – Wilson faced a tough situation. In the Senate nowhere near a majority, much less two-thirds, favored the League as it stood. Also, the long summer of 1919 had begun, and the spirit of that season would infect the League fight. Temperatures in the capital soared above even their normally miserable levels. Meanwhile, the nation's cities, including Washington, exploded in a series of race riots that left several hundred people dead – most of them African-Americans – thousands more injured, hundreds of stores and homes looted and destroyed, and emotions rubbed raw. Simultaneously, strikes embroiled or threatened to shut down such major industries as coal mining, iron and steel making, and railroads. In various places, particularly in the West but not only there, the antiradical hysteria that would come to be called the "Red Scare" was already rife. By itself, the League fight generated plenty of passion and rancor, but this background of heat and turmoil in the summer of 1919 made matters worse.[8]

7. *Chicago Tribune,* June 24, 1919. For other estimates, see Taft to Helen H. Taft, May 26, 1919, Taft Papers, reel 27; entry, May 29, 1919, Ashurst Diary, in George F. Sparks, ed., *A Many-Colored Toga: The Diary of Henry Fountain Ashurst* (Tucson, Ariz., 1962), 96; W. R. Boyd to W. H. Short, [ca. June 25, 1919], A. Lawrence Lowell Papers, Harvard University Archives; and Stone, *Irreconcilables,* 89. On the lack of reaction to the treaty signing, see Karger to Taft, June 28, 1919, Taft Papers, reel 210.
8. On the domestic troubles of the summer of 1919, see William L. Tuttle, Jr., *Race Riot: Chicago in the Red Summer of 1919* (New York, 1970); Burl Noggle, *Into the Twenties: The United States from the Armistice to Normalcy* (Urbana, Ill., 1974); and Francis Russell, *A City in Terror: The 1919 Boston Police Strike* (New York, 1975).

Everyone expected that Wilson's presentation of the treaty to the Senate would be a major event. People on all sides in the conflict prepared for it as the president's ship sailed across the Atlantic at the end of June and beginning of July. League opponents redoubled their efforts to sway public opinion. Early in July, staff members of the Independence League met with several senators to plan speaking tours. Ironically, two of their cause's oratorical powerhouses, Borah and Reed, faced a dilemma similar to Wilson's: Should they remain in Washington, or should they get out on the hustings? Johnson did not share their qualms. On July 2 he spoke at Carnegie Hall in New York, where his first mention of Wilson's name brought cries of "Traitor! Traitor!" Johnson got similar responses at rallies in New England. The Independence League also arranged for Albert Beveridge to go to the Midwest later in July, but race riots prevented him from speaking in Chicago and poor arrangements elsewhere made the rest of the trip a bust.[9]

Beveridge and others in the Independence League were also consulting with the Republican national chairman. Hays continued to straddle the League question himself. "It is impossible to take a party position," he told Beveridge, "when the party is 'split this way and that.'" Complaining that senators on both sides were demanding that he commit the party to their stand, Hays hoped "that the senators will reach some common ground so that the party organization can get right behind that position and back it up with all power." Pinning his hopes on Root's reservations, Hays issued a statement to the press on July 15. "The situation respecting the covenant is simply this," he declared. "There must be effective reservations. These reservations must safeguard the sovereignty of the United States in every particular"; and they must include an absolute right of withdrawal, total exemption of the Monroe Doctrine, elimination or drastic limitation of obligations under Article X, and unabridged control of tariffs, immigration, and "all other purely domestic questions."[10]

Hays never would have issued that statement without Lodge's approval. It seems certain that Root had passed the senator's views

9. Johnson to Hiram Jr. and Arch Johnson, July 2, 1919, in Robert E. Burke, ed., *The Diary Letters of Hiram Johnson* (New York, 1983), III. On these arrangements and tours, see also Johnson to Hiram Jr. and Arch Johnson, July 16, 1919, ibid.; Borah to Reed, July 16, 1919, Borah Papers, Box 767; Thomas R. Shipp to Beveridge, July 5, 15, 1919, Beveridge Papers, Box 218; Beveridge to Knox, July 31, 1919, ibid., Box 215; Louis A. Coolidge to Lodge, July 11, 1919, Lodge Papers.
10. Hays to Beveridge, July 8, 1919, Beveridge Papers, Box 215; New York *World,* July 16, 1919.

along to him. On July 7, Lodge wrote to Root that forty-eight, possibly all forty-nine, of the Senate's Republicans would approve Root's reservations on the Monroe Doctrine and domestic matters, and forty-seven would also accept his Article X reservation. "The more I have thought of it," Lodge told Root, "the more satisfied I am that this is the right course to take. I am not interested in rescuing Europe from Article X. All I want to do is save the United States. If we can take the United States out by reservations my purposes are fulfilled." Therefore, Lodge believed, ". . . when we are so thoroughly united on the substance of your reservations Hays ought to come out and back us up, not with vague generalities but with something properly definite. I wish you could say a word to him in regard to it." Evidently Root did speak to Hays, because the party chairman only waited to gauge reactions to the president's presentation to the Senate before he issued his statement.[11]

Hays would also not have issued his statement if he had feared serious opposition from Taft or other pro-League Republicans. In fact, by the time he spoke out, the party chairman knew that he could count on the ex-president's support. Root's reservations, especially the one aimed at limiting obligations under Article X, had angered most of the top LEP activists, including Taft. Publicly, the LEP insisted upon full, unqualified membership in the League. Privately, however, Taft had begun to assure fellow Republicans that he could agree to reservations so long as they were not amendments that would require reopening negotiations with other nations. "It may be that Root's letter may suggest a compromise," Taft confided to his wife. He proved how amenable he was to pursuing the search for mutually agreeable reservations when Hays telephoned him at his summer home at Murray Bay, Quebec, on July 9. Taft agreed "to get together on some reservations in the treaty," provided they were "sufficiently innocuous as not to take the heart out of the League, and reservations to which Wilson can agree."[12]

How formidable a task Taft faced was already becoming apparent to

---

11. Lodge to Root, July 7, 1919, Root Papers, Box 161. Actually, Lodge's estimate of Senate opinion agreed with those of several different observers, including Hays himself. See Hays to Root, July 1, 1919, ibid., Box 137; LEP memorandum, July 7, 1919, Herbert Parsons Papers, Columbia University Library, Series III, LEP File; *New York Times*, July 8, 1919.
12. Herbert S. Houston to McAdoo, June 19, 1919, McAdoo Papers, Box 221; Taft to Gus J. Karger, June 9, 1919, Taft Papers, reel 556; Taft to Helen H. Taft, June 23, 1919, ibid., reel 77; Taft to Henry C. Wallace, July 9, 1919, ibid., reel 557. See also Taft to Arthur H. Vandenberg, June 4, 1919, ibid., reel 556.

two of his closest associates. Taft's brother Henry, a prominent Wall Street attorney, and his law partner George W. Wickersham, who had been attorney general in Taft's administration, described to him their efforts to draft reservations for Senator Kellogg. "I cannot find any satisfactory provision," Henry Taft reported to his brother, "between a mere reference to the provisions of our Constitution [about Congress's war power] and a condition precedent which would result in modification of the treaty [i.e., an amendment]." Henry Taft had put his finger on the conundrum that would dog every effort at compromise on Article X – how to stake out common ground on international enforcement between Wilson's idea of a commitment and more restricted Republican conceptions. Henry Taft recoiled in disbelief when he learned that his brother was seeking an accommodation on the basis of the Root reservations. He telegraphed at once to urge caution, and in a letter he warned, "Murray Bay is pretty far removed from this atmosphere, and we are just a bit concerned here that you should not answer too quickly suggestions coming from those who have been recently engaged in unmeasured denunciation of the League and scarcely less violent denunciations of you."[13]

The brotherly warning fell on deaf ears. Taft had already drafted six ponderously worded reservations. The first two dealt with Article X. They limited America's obligation to five years, unless the president chose to extend it with the consent of two-thirds of the senators. One of these reservations also stated:

> That the obligations of the United States are to be fulfilled only by action of the Congress of the United States, in which is vested the final power of determining the good faith of the United States, the extent of such obligations, the happening of the conditions on which they become immediate, and the means and method of their fulfillment.

The other four reservations dealt with "solely domestic questions," the Monroe Doctrine, withdrawal, and British Empire voting in the League Council. Taft refrained from sending the reservations to Hays until he received his brother Henry's letter. When the letter arrived, he brushed aside its cautious counsel. Taft sent the reservations to Hays and then followed them up with subsequent letters in which he tinkered with the wording. He also forwarded a copy of the reservations to several Republican senators. These reservations would do great damage when they were subsequently leaked to the press. In the meantime and in private, they sufficed to assure Hays that he had the ex-

13. Henry W. Taft to Taft, July 9, 1919, letter and telegram, ibid., reel 210.

president in his pocket when he issued his statement to the press on July 15.[14]

Wilson sailed into this political situation only partially aware of how firmly the Republican front was hardening against him. While he was still in Paris, reports of growing Republican coalescence behind Root's reservations had prompted him to shoot back: "My clear conviction is that the adoption of the Treaty by the Senate with reservations would put the United States as clearly out of the concert of nations as a rejection. We ought either to go in or to stay out." Only pleas from Democratic senators had prevented the president from issuing that defiant declaration as a statement to the press. As earlier, Wilson's mood of defiance waned. The relaxed conditions on shipboard revived his spirits and made him look the picture and health of vitality when he landed in New York on July 8.[15]

Those appearances were deceiving. On the return voyage, Wilson uncharacteristically struggled for several days to produce a draft of the speech that he would give when he took the treaty to Capitol Hill. Ray Stannard Baker noted in his diary on July 1 that Wilson "found probably for the first time in his entire life that his work of the day before had not satisfied him, so he was forced to begin all over. . . . He said he found it a difficult message to write." Wilson claimed the trouble was that "he had so very little respect for the audience to which he would deliver the address." But he also told Baker and Grayson that he wanted to produce a speech that would "fill the bill" as worthy of the momentous occasion. Because Wilson had heretofore composed speeches so easily, those difficulties and worries did not offer promising signs.[16]

The president's struggle also gave unsettling hints about his political judgment. On July 5, he read the address to five of his advisors. They were the financiers Thomas W. Lamont, Bernard Baruch, and Norman

14. Taft reservations, July 10, 1919, ibid., reel 557; Taft to Henry Taft, July 10, 12, 1919, ibid.; Taft to Hays, July 12, 13, 16, 1919, ibid., reel 210; Taft to Le Baron Colt, July 15, 1919, ibid.; Taft to Selden P. Spencer, July 16, 1919, ibid.; Taft to McCumber, Colt, and Charles McNary, July 17, 1919, ibid. Although he delayed sending the reservations to Hays, Taft did send them to his agent and confidant in Washington, Gus Karger, with the suggestion that he show them to Senator Hitchcock, who, he hinted, might pass them on to the president. Taft to Karger, July 10, 1919, ibid., reel 557.

15. Wilson to Tumulty, June 23, 1919, in Link, ed., *Papers of Wilson,* LXI, 115. For Democrats' advice not to issue the statement, see Tumulty to Wilson, June 25, [1919], ibid., 184. On Wilson's appearance, see Irwin H. Hoover memoir, ibid., LXIII, 632; and entry, July 8, 1919, Breckinridge Long Diary, Breckinridge Long Papers, Library of Congress, Box 2.

16. Entry, July 1, [1919], Baker Diary, in Link, ed., *Papers of Wilson,* LXI, 363; entry, July 1, 1919, Grayson Diary, ibid., 360–361.

Davis; the Democratic progressive activist Vance McCormick; and the academic economist Frank Taussig. "We had few changes to suggest," McCormick recorded in his diary, "as it was an excellent general statement of the situation at Paris and the problems that confronted him." Wilson had rarely sought advance reactions to a speech before, especially with such great pronouncements as "peace without victory," the war address, and the Fourteen Points. His reaching out now betrayed uncharacteristically shaky self-confidence and questionable judgment in his choice of a test audience. Able as they were, these selected wise men were not, except possibly for McCormick, people versed in domestic politics and public opinion. One person on board the ship was so versed and might have given him tougher advice. This was Baker, but there is no record of Wilson's having discussed the content of the speech with him. The only advice that he sought from Tumulty and leading Democrats in Washington was about whether to present the treaty to a joint session of Congress or just to the Senate. They advised that the Senate was so jealous of its prerogative in treaty making that the president should address that body alone, and Wilson bowed to their judgment.[17]

Large crowds lined the sidewalks of New York when Wilson disembarked on July 8. He spoke briefly at Carnegie Hall, alluding to the vision of a better world that he had brought back from Paris. "I am afraid that some people, some persons do not understand that vision," he commented, but he knew that after studying the treaty most of his fellow citizens "will see that it is a just peace." When the presidential train arrived in Washington around midnight, a throng estimated at 100,000 people had gathered in and around Union Station. The president did not speak to his welcomers, but in the car on the way to the White House, he told Mrs. Wilson and Grayson, "The reception here tonight is one of the greatest surprises of my life. It is very touching." Not everyone welcomed him. Theodore Roosevelt's high-spirited daughter, Alice, who was married to Republican Congressman Nicholas Longworth of Ohio, later recalled that she had gotten out of her car to watch Wilson pass. Standing on the curb, she had crossed her fingers, made the sign of the evil eye, and uttered an Irish curse: "A murrain on him, a murrain on him."[18]

17. Entry, July 5, 1919, Vance McCormick Diary, ibid., 385. On this meeting, see also entry, July 5, 1919, Lamont Diary, ibid., 386–387; entry, July 5, 1919, Grayson Diary, ibid., 383. On the question of whether to address a joint session or the Senate alone, see Tumulty to Wilson, July 5, 1919, ibid., 388; Wilson to Tumulty, July 6, 1919, ibid., 397.
18. Wilson speech, July 8, 1919, ibid., 403–404; entry, Grayson Diary, July 8, 1910, July 8, 1919, ibid., 401; Alice Roosevelt Longworth, *Crowded Hours* (New York, 1933), 285.

After a day's respite, Wilson plunged into his new task of selling his program at home. First, he held a press conference at which over a hundred reporters gathered in the East Room of the White House. For a change, his statements were on the record. He answered a range of questions, most of them about Article X and reservations. Wilson defended Article X by asserting "that if you leave that out, it [the League] is only a debating society, and I would not be interested in a debating society. I have belonged to them and have found them far from vital." He argued that in the event of an invocation of Article X by the League Council, the president would have to seek legislative authority in order to furnish "the necessary means of action," and he scoffed at the notion that Congress's constitutional power to declare war might be impaired in this process. Reservations he called "a complicated problem." He maintained, incorrectly, that a two-thirds majority was required in order to attach reservations to the instrument of ratification. To allegations that a reservation could be "innocuous," he responded, "But who is to say that it is innocuous?" Wilson closed by asserting, "The Senate is going to ratify the treaty."[19]

That press conference showed him again at his best – crisp, informative, firm but not combative. He tackled the issues of obligations under Article X and reservations in a way that held his ground but did not rule out the possibility of accommodation. It is interesting to speculate about what might have happened if Wilson had followed this performance with a similar speech to the Senate and also with other, less formal addresses in various settings and with additional meetings with reporters. If Wilson had done those things, he might have seized command of the debate and staked out an area of interpretation of Article X that might have gained assent from major Republican figures, such as Henry Stimson and, possibly, Root or Hughes. As it was, Wilson did nothing like that until much later. By then political circumstances and his own health would make his regaining a commanding role unlikely if not impossible.

For League advocates, the situation soured within the space of an hour on the afternoon of July 10. This was when Wilson went to Capitol Hill for formal delivery of the treaty. It was the first time a president had presented a treaty in person to an open session of the Senate. Crowds had been milling around the Capitol for hours despite heavy rains, even though only people with special tickets could enter the building. When Wilson arrived, a five-man delegation consisting of Lodge, Borah, McCumber, Hitchcock, and John Sharp Williams met

19. Wilson press conference, July 10, 1919, in Link, ed., *Papers of Wilson*, LXI, 417–424.

him and escorted him into the chamber. Lodge commented on the bulky copy of the document under Wilson's arm, asking, "Mr. President, can I carry the Treaty for you?" Wilson got a laugh by replying, "Not on your life." Inside the chamber, loud applause, mixed with rebel yells, erupted from the galleries and from Democratic senators. Reporters noticed, however, that just two or three Republican senators applauded at the beginning and that McCumber was the only one to clap at the end. Otherwise, everyone in the chamber listened closely but silently during the thirty-seven-minute speech.[20]

Wilson opened with the assertion that the treaty "constitutes nothing less than a world settlement" but was too complicated to explicate at this time. Besides, he observed, the senators already knew most of its contents. Their country's part in the treaty flowed from both America's role in the war and worldwide expectations that Americans "would do everything that was within our power to make the triumph of freedom and right a lasting triumph." In spite of "old entanglements of every kind" that had stood in the way, America had succeeded in founding new nations in eastern Europe, safeguarding minorities, regulating waterways, and, most important, establishing the League of Nations. The League pointed the way out of the old international system based on "force" and into a new order that was "the hope of the world" and must not be disappointed. "Shall we or any other free people hesitate to accept this great duty?" Wilson asked. Then he uttered the speech's only memorable line, "Dare we reject it and break the heart of the world?"

Answering that question took up the rest of the speech. Wilson argued that American "isolation was ended twenty years ago" and that the United States could not cease "to be a world power. . . . The only question is whether we shall accept or reject the confidence of the world." He closed with an attempt at one of his typically soaring invocations:

> The stage is set, the destiny disclosed. It has come about by no plan of our conceiving, but by the hand of God who led us into this way. We cannot turn back. We can only go forward, with lifted eyes and freshened spirit, to follow the vision. It was of this that we dreamed at our birth. America shall show the way. The light streams upon the path ahead, and nowhere else.[21]

The speech was a dud. In view of the occasion's partisan cast, Democrats dutifully praised the address, and Republican opponents were predictably scathing. "Soap bubbles of oratory and souffle of rhetorical

20. Entry, July 10, 1919, Grayson Diary, ibid., 417; *New York Times*, July 11, 1919.
21. Wilson speech, July 10, 1919, in Link, ed., *Papers of Wilson*, LXI, 426–436.

phrases" was Brandegee's characterization, and George Moses dismissed the League as "an international come-on game." Other Republicans were more polite, but even future mild reservationists expressed disappointment. Privately, Democratic senators groaned. The best assessment came from Henry Ashurst of Arizona, who noted in his diary, "Everyone in the Senate was on the tiptoe of expectation. The President's opponents as well as supporters expected a masterpiece. . . . Here were League supporters hungry for arguments in support of the League, whilst supporter and opponent alike expected explanation of obscure portions," such as the Shantung cession, safeguarding the Monroe Doctrine, the meaning of Article X, the lack of mention of Ireland, and withdrawal from the League. "These and many other vital questions were ignored." Ashurst found himself "petrified with surprise," whereas League opponents "were in a state of felicity; they winked, thrust tongue against cheek, and whispered that Wilson had failed to 'make good.'" Ashurst likened Wilson to the president of a company who, when asked to explain major obligations to his board of directors, "tonefully read Longfellow's Psalm of Life. Wilson was called upon to render an accounting of the most momentous cause ever entrusted to an individual. His audience wanted raw meat, he fed them cold turnips."[22]

Why did this happen? Why did Wilson make such a botch of what he intended to be a great occasion? Part of the problem unquestionably stemmed from his physical condition as he spoke. The *New York Times* reporter commented, "He was not at his best in the delivery of the speech. . . . Several times during the first half he dropped a word in reading the typewritten copy, . . . and then reread these sentences." Such fumbling and faltering were totally unlike Wilson. He prided himself on his ability to speak flawlessly, usually from sketchy notes or none at all. Senator Ashurst also observed, "There was a contraction of the back of his neck and a transparency of his ears; infallible indicia of a man whose vitality is gone." Those signs, note the editors of the *Papers of Wilson,* indicated that he was experiencing tension, probably suffering from a headache, and not getting enough blood to his head. These may have been symptoms of the cardiovascular condition that would culminate in a stroke three months later.[23]

Wilson's failure with this speech went deeper than poor delivery. The main flaw lay in its content. Ashurst and other observers thought that he had given the wrong speech in the wrong place at the wrong time. Only

22. New York *World,* July 11, 1919; entry, July 11, 1919, Ashurst Diary, in Link, ed., *Papers of Wilson,* LXI, 445–446.
23. *New York Times,* June 11, 1919; entry, July 11, 1919, Ashurst Diary, in Link, ed., *Papers of Wilson,* LXI, 446; editors' note, ibid.

impaired political judgment could explain this misstep. Wilson's troubles in writing and delivering this speech showed that he could no longer draw upon the full range of political talents that had previously served him and his causes so well. This loss dealt a blow to the pro-League forces. They were counting on the president's persuasive powers to be one of the biggest guns in their arsenal. "He is a pretty formidable speaker," Taft had recently confided to his wife, "and he may frighten the Republicans into a reasonable frame of mind." This speech to the Senate made it clear that no such turnaround was immediately in the offing.[24]

Wilson's next action helped somewhat in recovering from this bad start. A week after he presented the treaty, he started to confer with senators individually. For two weeks, from July 18 to August 1, Wilson met in the East Room of the White House one-on-one with twenty-six senators, all but four of them Republicans. Two other Republicans were invited but did not come. Each senator spent about an hour with the president. After each such encounter the senator told waiting reporters that the conversation had been cordial but that he had not changed his mind about the need for reservations. Private evaluations of these meetings varied considerably. Taft's principal informant in Washington reported to him that the president's "attitude has been courteous and even gracious . . . and I believe he has done some good." In later meetings, however, Wilson may not have made such a good impression. Those meetings seem to have gone less well partly because Wilson was dealing with Republicans whose attitudes were closer to Lodge's thinking. In the view of one historian, the tactic may have backfired because the publicity surrounding these conferences forced each Republican senator to reaffirm his support for reservations.[25]

24. Taft to Helen H. Taft, June 23, 1919, Taft Papers, reel 77. For other reactions to the speech, which are consonant with Ashurst's and come from pro- and anti-League observers, see New York *World,* July 11, 1919; Casper S. Yost to Taft, July 11, 1919, Taft Papers, reel 210; Belle Case La Follette to "children," July 10, 1919, La Follette Papers, Box A 24; Lodge to Louis A. Coolidge, July 15, 1919, Lodge Papers. Even McAdoo hinted at disappointment with the speech in a letter urging Wilson to get out on the hustings. See McAdoo to Wilson, July 11, 1919, in Link, ed., *Papers of Wilson,* LXI, 459.

25. Gus J. Karger to Taft, July 19, 1919, Taft Papers, reel 211; the judgment of overall failure comes from Herbert F. Margulies, *The Mild Reservationists and the League of Nations in the Senate* (Columbia, Mo., 1989), 50. Senators' statements to the press after their meetings can be found in the *Washington Post* and *New York Times.* For some private assessments of the meetings, see Truman H. Newberry to Charles Townsend, July 30, 1919, in Link, ed., *Papers of Wilson,* LXI, 602 n. 2; entry, July 30, 1919, Chandler Anderson Diary, and James W. Watson, *As I Knew Them* (Indianapolis, 1936), 201–203.

Well-wishers continued to urge the president to speak out. Thomas Lamont warned that "the public itself, taking its cue from headlines of opposing newspapers, seems to a certain extent, to have the feeling that information is being with-held from them." Rather than mount a speaking tour, Lamont suggested that Wilson explain his positions in a series of memoranda to the Foreign Relations Committee or, preferably, in speeches to the full Senate, which could then be distributed "to every hamlet in the United States." Lamont conceded that his suggestion "will sound to you very crude. But some such direct challenge as this would draw instant and enthusiastic response from the public, I believe."[26]

Far from crude, those would have been good moves. It is something of a mystery why Wilson did not seek some middle way between confidential talks with senators and a full-fledged tour around the country. Pressure from domestic affairs may have accounted for some of this neglect. Both rampant inflation, popularly dubbed "HCL" for "high cost of living," and the threat of a nationwide railroad strike demanded presidential attention, especially because the Republicans were trying to turn those matters to partisan advantage. Still, distraction by other concerns did not fully explain Wilson's actions during these weeks. McAdoo told Grayson that postponing a speaking tour was wise "because of his health." The head usher of the White House later recalled that the president "was making an effort to conserve his health," by playing golf, taking automobile rides, retiring for frequent rests during the day, staying away from the Oval Office, and "shutting himself off from the world." At the beginning of August, Wilson himself uncharacteristically complained about how he was enduring "strenuous times" and carrying the "weight of this weary, unintelligible world."[27]

More than fatigue was weighing him down. On July 19, after his first round of senatorial conferences, Wilson started to feel sick during his meeting at the Capitol with Senator Gilbert Hitchcock of Nebraska, the

26. Tumulty to McAdoo, July 16, 1919, McAdoo Papers, Box 222; Lamont to Wilson, July 25, 1919, in Link, ed., *Papers of Wilson*, LXI, 641–643. For similar advice, see Charles H. Grasty to Wilson, July 24, 1919, ibid., 616.

27. McAdoo to Grayson, July 30, 1919, McAdoo Papers, Box 223; Irwin H. Hoover manuscript memoir, in Link, ed., *Papers of Wilson*, LXIII, 632–633; *Washington Post*, July 21, 22, 1919; Edith Wilson to Henry White, Aug. 9, 1919, in Link, ed., *Papers of Wilson*, LXII, 156; Wilson to E. P. Davis, Aug. 1, 1919, ibid., 102; Wilson to Thomas Dixon, Aug. 2, 1919, ibid., 115. On the weekend illness, see also Grayson to McAdoo, July 26, 1919, McAdoo Papers, Box 223. For a similar description of Wilson as tired and worn from a meeting with him on July 31, see Edward N. Hurley, *The Bridge to France* (Philadelphia, 1927), 327–328.

ranking Democrat on the Foreign Relations Committee. He remained indisposed for the next two days, and Grayson told reporters that the president was suffering from a touch of dysentery. Mrs. Wilson privately maintained that the illness was not serious, just a sign of strain. Some interpreters have given a more ominous reading to this incident. They have speculated that Wilson may have suffered another small stroke, which often prefigures the kind of major stroke that he would soon suffer. Whether or not that was the case, evidence was accumulating to show that Wilson was not playing the political game at anywhere near his usually exalted level of performance.[28]

II

Others rushed in to occupy the space that the president was leaving unfilled in public discussion. The LEP kept up its public relations offensive across the country, but the organization's leaders necessarily began to concentrate more of their attention to lobbying in the capital. In August, the LEP opened a Washington office. Meanwhile, Taft maintained a personal lobbying and intelligence-gathering operation through Gus Karger, who was the veteran Washington correspondent of the *Cincinnati Times-Star,* which was owned by Taft's half-brother, Charles. Both the LEP office and Karger devoted most of their efforts to working with "mild reservationist" Republican senators. The Independence League laid plans to "trail" Wilson with a group of senators if and when he made his long-bruited speaking tour. In the capital, a journalist named Lee Meriwether coordinated the organization's activities.[29]

Senators likewise did not hurry to speak out about the Treaty of Versailles. Most of the action in the Capitol took place off the floor, as dif-

---

28. For an assessment of Wilson's condition and the illness over the weekend of July 19–21, see Bert E. Park, "Wilson's Neurological Illness during the Summer of 1919," in Link, ed., *Papers of Wilson,* LXII, 628–638. Park, who is a trained neurologist, is more willing than I am to conclude that Wilson suffered a small stroke over that weekend, but he makes a strong case for the larger, progressive effects of Wilson's condition and its effects on his personality and political performance.
29. On the LEP's activities, see esp., McAdoo to Vance McCormick, Aug. 1, 1919, McAdoo Papers, Box 223; McAdoo to Wilson, Aug. 4, 1919, ibid., Box 526; Herbert S. Houston to Lowell, Aug. 2, 1919, Lowell Papers. And on those of the Independence League, see Lee Meriwether, *Jim Reed: "Senatorial Immortal"* (Webster Groves, Mo., 1948), 68–69, 72, 77–78; Ralph A. Stone, *The Irreconcilables: The Fight against the League of Nations* (Lexington, Ky., 1970), 131–133.

ferent groups of senators met to exchange views and map out possible strategies. The day after Wilson's speech, six of the Republicans on the Foreign Relations Committee, including Lodge and Knox, gathered to talk about trying to compel the president to testify before them and to furnish papers from the peace conference. That group soon expanded its membership to include twenty or so of their party brethren who were disposed to some degree against the League. Most of those Republican senators reportedly regarded reservations as a consolation prize if they could not pass amendments and, as one of them put it, "take an axe and go through the treaty."

The first speech on the Senate floor came on July 14, when a Democrat and Wilson loyalist, Claude Swanson of Virginia, defended the president and scoffed at charges that American sovereignty would be impaired under Article X. That opening performance established the pattern of floor debate that lasted through the summer and fall of 1919. At the opening of the session on a given day, several senators would insert material into the *Congressional Record,* usually speeches, magazine articles, and newspaper editorials. Then, after the conclusion of procedural matters, one or more senators would deliver a prepared address. Comments, questions, or challenges from allies or adversaries would sometimes interrupt or follow the speech. During the next five months, three-quarters of the members of the Senate, seventy-two senators in all, would make at least one speech on the treaty and the League. Among the opponents, Borah, Reed, and Sherman would speak often and at length. Among the president's Democratic supporters, John Sharp Williams, Gilbert Hitchcock, and Key Pittman would also speak frequently. In the annals of senatorial eloquence, these debates did not match the Olympian heights attained in the previous century by such immortals as Daniel Webster, John C. Calhoun, and Charles Sumner, and they did fall short of Ashurst's "homeric" ideal. For all that, these debates set a standard that would not be matched again in the twentieth century except at a few times during the civil rights debates of the 1950s and '60s.[30]

30. New York *World,* July 12, 1919. See also *New York Times,* July 14, 1919; *Congressional Record,* 66th Cong., 1st Sess. (July 14, 1991), 2532–2543. Of the twenty-four senators who did not speak, three were ailing during all or most of the debate. Martin (D-Va.), the minority leader, missed the entire session and died in November before the Senate voted on consent to the peace treaty; Bankhead (D-Ala.) and Culberson (D-Tex.) were able to leave their sickbeds only to vote about half the time during the session, and Bankhead died in March 1920. Like them, the remaining twenty-one were all reliable party men, whose records on votes surrounding the treaty cleaved closely to their respective party stands.

During the second half of July there was only one truly notable speech. It came when the insurgent Republican George Norris of Nebraska delivered what one historian has called "a wild, three-day address, arguably the most intemperate speech delivered in his Senate career." Norris announced at the outset that he could not vote for the treaty "in its present form." He recounted his long-standing beliefs in disarmament and international enforcement to prevent war, even if that meant substantial sacrifices of sovereignty or abandonment of the Monroe Doctrine. But, in Norris's view, this League of Nations, tied as it was to this peace treaty, was infected with "the germs of wickedness and injustice." The Shantung cession and Japanese mistreatment of Korea struck Norris as the most egregious examples of "the greed and avarice shown by the nations that . . . are to control the league." Could there be any possible gains, any assurances of peace, he asked, "so dear that we can afford to perpetuate them by giving our official approval to an act brought about by a procedure that would be a disgrace to the civilization of the wild man and the barbarian?"[31]

An unusually large number of senators came to the chamber to listen to Norris, and his speech touched a nerve among them. Though constrained by his leadership position from jumping into the debate, Lodge could not resist seconding Norris's denunciation of the Shantung cession as "a gift to Japan; it was a price paid, and all the world knows it." Lodge scorned the action as "the robbing of China," the betrayal of "a friendly people who were our allies in the war," for the sake of Japanese aggrandizement. Several Democrats defended both Japan's conduct and the necessity of ceding Shantung while several Republicans disputed how much Japan had really contributed to the Allied victory. "No nation has ever played its diplomatic game with greater ingenuity and greater ability and greater foresight," declared Borah, "than did Japan at Versailles [sic]."[32]

As before, the main action in the Senate was taking place off the floor. It occurred in two arenas. One was the Foreign Relations Com-

---

31. Johnson, *The Peace Progressives and American Foreign Relations* (Cambridge, Mass., 1995), 100; *Congressional Record*, 66th Cong., 1st Sess. (July 15, 1919), 2592–2600. Norris received many letters of thanks and support from Americans who were sympathetic to Korea and from Koreans, including a future president of South Korea. See Syngman Rhee to Norris, July 17, 1919, George W. Norris Papers, Library of Congress, Box 46.

32. *Congressional Record*, 66th Cong., 1st Sess. (July 15, 1919), 2605–2616; New York *World,* July 16, 1919. Borah, like many people at the time and since, was confusing the peace conference, which took place in Paris, with the signing of the treaty at Versailles.

mittee. As expected, this committee chaired by Senator Lodge did not greet the Treaty of Versailles with open arms. At their first meeting, on July 15, the members reportedly engaged in an acrimonious wrangle over procedures, particularly over whether and how to get the president to meet with them. At one point, Lodge issued a statement to the press to clear up "a great deal of misunderstanding" about presidential testimony. "No committee of Congress has any right or ought to have any right to summon the President of the United States before them," insisted Lodge, "and no suggestion has been made that they should do so." The chairman and his cohorts soon belied that mild posture toward the president. When Wilson requested interim authority to name American delegates to the Reparations Commission, a separate body created by the treaty, Republican committee members reportedly sniffed that they "could recognize a trap when they saw one" and voted to deny the president's request. Next, the committee's Republican majority passed a resolution that attacked Wilson for not having submitted the French security pact along with the peace treaty. The committee did not hold its first public hearing until July 31, when Bernard Baruch was called to testify about the treaty's financial provisions.[33]

The other arena for off-the-floor action was in Capitol cloakrooms and senators' offices and homes. Two distinct groups of fewer than ten Republicans began to meet regularly to exchange views and plot strategy. The longer established of these groups comprised the opponents of the League and the treaty. This group was soon to be dubbed the "Irreconcilables" and, after a heroic wartime unit, the "Battalion of Death." Its original members were Borah, Johnson, Sherman, Brandegee, Moses, Poindexter, Fall, and McCormick. Reed, the Democratic anti-Leaguer, cooperated with them but did not join in their gatherings. Another openly negative Democrat, Thomas of Colorado, had not yet declared his unalterable opposition to League membership, and even after he did, he went strictly his own way. Likewise, the three men still in the Senate who had opposed intervention in the war in 1917 – Republican insurgents Norris, La Follette, and Gronna – were not part of this group. Thus far, Norris had staked out his opposition to the Shantung cession and other treaty provisions, but he had not yet declared himself one way or the other on the League. La Follette and Gronna were maintaining a sullen silence. Other Republicans who were critical of the League

33. New York *World*, July 16, 18, 22, 23, 25, Aug. 1, 1919; *New York Times*, July 23, 1919. The official publication of the hearings is U.S. Senate, 66th Cong., 1st Sess., Committee on Foreign Relations, Document No. 106, *Treaty of Peace with Germany: Hearings* (Washington, 1919). Baruch's testimony and the senators' questioning appear in ibid., 5–14, 29–30.

and the treaty, such as Knox and Joseph France of Maryland, had been hinting that stringent reservations might win them over. On July 20 Knox dashed those hopes when he announced, "I cannot vote for the treaty unless the league covenant is separated from it and unless material modifications are made to the body of the treaty."[34]

These Irreconcilables – both the original members and the others who eventually joined them – comprised a diverse lot. They were, as Ralph Stone has observed, "more a cross section of the nation than an ideologically homogeneous minority." This group later included one devotee of traditional great power politics, Knox, and two theoretical internationalists, Norris and La Follette. Therefore, not all of the Irreconcilables can fairly be labeled "isolationists." That controversial categorical shoe does fit the group's original core, but their political identities defied most of the theories that journalists, historians, and political scientists would subsequently spin to explain twentieth-century American isolationism. Contrary to interpretations that would link isolationism to alleged Midwestern insularity, these isolationists came from every section of the country except the South. Even that bastion of Democratic and Wilsonian loyalty had spawned such other isolationists of 1919 as former senators Thomas Hardwick of Georgia and James K. Vardaman of Mississippi, as well as the agrarian radical Tom Watson. Likewise, interpretations that would link isolationism to sentiments of German Americans and Irish Americans applied only to the latter-day Irreconcilables, Gronna, La Follette, and Norris, who did represent states with sizable constituencies of either of those ethnic groups. Also, attempts then and later to tar isolationism with the brush of ignorance and provinciality fall flat. One of the original Irreconcilables was Medill McCormick, a wealthy graduate of Yale who had gone to school in England, lived in France, and learned to speak French fluently while his father had held diplomatic posts. Another was George Moses, a Dartmouth graduate who was also fluent in French and who had served during the Taft administration as American minister to Greece. Most tellingly, a later recruit to the ranks of the Irreconcilables would be a former secretary of state, Knox.[35]

Other interpretations have sought to link isolationism with domestic

34. *Washington Post,* July 20, 1919. On the group at this time, see Stone, *Irreconcilables,* 115.
35. Ibid., 178. On McCormick's background, see Christie Miller, *Ruth Hanna McCormick: A Life in Politics, 1880–1944* (Albuquerque, N.M., 1992), and Richard Norton Smith, *The Colonel: The Life and Legend of Robert R. McCormick* (Boston, 1997), esp. 59, 82–84, 210–211. On Moses's background, see Taft to Charles P. Taft, Nov. 6, 1918, Taft Papers, reel 200.

political views. Some of these explanations fit the Irreconcilables better. Among the original group, Borah, Johnson, McCormick, and Poindexter and, among the later adherents, Gronna, Norris, and La Follette all sprang from the insurgent and reformist wing of the Republican party. The presence of all three former Progressives in the Senate – Johnson, McCormick, and Poindexter – established a tie to Roosevelt, as did the adherence to their views of such other erstwhile third-party activists as Beveridge. Likewise, his daughter, Alice Roosevelt Longworth, threw herself into lobbying on the Irreconcilables' behalf during the summer and fall of 1919. These ex-Progressives repeatedly claimed that they were faithfully upholding Roosevelt's views. They and other reformer-insurgents also tirelessly charged that "our masters of Wall Street," as Johnson called them, were scheming to get the country into the League in order to defend their financial stakes in Allied war debts and British and European imperialism.[36]

Still, despite similar expressions of sentiment by such veteran radicals as Oswald Garrison Villard of the *Nation,* domestic reformism was by no means perfectly congruent with isolationism. Such other former Rooseveltian Progressive stalwarts as Chase Osborn and William Allen White were active members of the LEP. Conversely, such doughty conservatives as Brandegee, Moses, and Sherman were charter members of the Irreconcilables group. They, too, saw international bankers lurking behind every pro-League bush, as sometimes did Lodge and other impeccably nonreformist Republicans.

The best explanation for why members of this group of senators embraced isolationism in 1919 lies in the interplay of partisan and personal circumstances. Only a few years before, isolationist views had found their main home among Bryanite Democrats. Now, however, despite the persistence of unreconstructed isolationism in Reed, Thomas, Hardwick, Vardaman, and Tom Watson, such views were rare on their side of the partisan fence. In his own party at least, Wilson had succeeded in selling his foreign policy views. By contrast, former Progressives and insurgents among the Republicans, who held domestic views that were similar to those of many Democrats, could more easily remain faithful to an antimilitarist, anti-imperialist brand of isolationism. But the pull of such views only partly explained such Republicans'

---

36. For Alice Roosevelt Longworth's activities, see her *Crowded Hours,* 284–289. The most extended recent effort to link these domestic views and foreign policy views comes in Johnson, *Peace Progressives,* which either eschews the term "isolationism" or tries, unsuccessfully in my view, to deny its applicability to these reformers during this period and the succeeding decade.

attraction to those views. Poindexter and Beveridge, for example, still subscribed to a Rooosevelt-style nationalism that smacked of unreconstructed imperialism. Nearly all the Irreconcilables blended affirmations of self-interest and national glory with appeals to idealism. Moreover, sheer partisan distaste for Democrats and loathing of Wilson moved such irascible conservatives as Brandegee, Moses, and Sherman to damn the man, the party, and their works in totality.[37]

Similar partisan and personal circumstances evidently occasioned the off-the-floor activity of the second group of Republican senators. This was the band of pro-Leaguers who had earlier sought counsel from Nicholas Murray Butler. Soon to be dubbed "mild reservationists," they included Porter McCumber of North Dakota, Le Baron Colt of Rhode Island, Charles McNary of Oregon, Knute Nelson and Frank Kellogg of Minnesota, Irvine Lenroot of Wisconsin, Albert Cummins of Iowa, Selden Spencer of Missouri, and Frederick Hale of Maine. This group of nine met off and on throughout July in an effort to forge a position that might bridge the gap between Wilson's insistence on unabridged assent to the treaty and their own and others' misgivings about possible sacrifices of American sovereignty. Like the Irreconcilables, they hailed from across the country, although the majority of them were Midwesterners. They likewise held a variety of domestic views, ranging from the conservatism of McCumber, Colt, and Spencer to the erstwhile insurgency of Cummins and Lenroot. Moreover, just as the Irreconcilables worked closely with the Independence League, these senators communicated constantly with Taft, Lowell, and others within the LEP.[38]

37. For a similar characterization of the blending of idealism and self-interest which tries to draw a sharper distinction among these senators, see Stone, *Irreconcilables*, 178–180. Their anti-imperialism would make one of these isolationsists, Borah, a hero among anticolonial rebels in Asia and Latin America. When the journalist Vincent Sheean traveled to Asia in 1925, he recalled that one letter of introduction proved to be "a document almost as valuable to me as my passport. It was an open letter ('To Whom It May Concern') written by the senior Senator from Idaho. Mr. Borah's fame throughout the world was at its height during the reactionary era of Harding and Coolidge, and his reputation for liberalism and anti-imperialism was nowhere greater than in China; his letter was to constitute my best introduction to the leaders of the national revolution." Sheean, *Personal History* (Garden City, N.Y., 1937), 189.
38. On these senators' activity, see McCumber to Taft, July 24, 31, 1919, Taft Papers, reel 211; McNary to Taft, July 24, 1919, ibid.; Kellogg to Taft, July 28, 1919, ibid.; Karger to Taft, July 31, 1919, ibid.; Kellogg to Nicholas Murray Butler, July 28, 1919, Butler Papers; New York *World*, Aug. 1, 1919; *New York Times*, Aug. 1, 1919.

Why these mild reservationists assumed a more moderate, pro-League stance than the rest of their party brethren is not completely clear. McCumber was like Wilson in believing passionately that only international enforcement and new ways to maintain order could save the world from future wars; he also believed that a strong League of Nations would form a bulwark against the spread of Bolshevism. McNary and Colt held similar views, though less ardently. Kellogg and Lenroot were ambitious freshmen senators anxious to get ahead in the party; Kellogg also wanted to make a name for himself in foreign affairs. Despite the closeness of some of these senators to the LEP, none of them was personally intimate with Taft – which said something about his standing in his party. Most of these senators also shared a distaste for overheated intra-party and partisan conflict. Unlike the Irreconcilables and Lodge and some of the Democrats, the mild reservationists were not fierce fighters, and they displayed no taste for zealotry.[39]

The mild reservationists had an immediately critical role to play at this juncture in the League fight. Later in July, McCumber, McNary, and Kellogg started to draft a set of reservations that McCumber told Taft "might be made without injury to the treaty" and might "secure the number necessary for ratification." These three, together with Cummins, Lenroot, Spencer, and Colt, held a series of meetings at which they tentatively agreed on four reservations covering the main points of controversy. Those points were exclusion of the Monroe Doctrine and domestic affairs, withdrawal from the League, and obligations under Article X. Most of those reservations were, noted Chandler Anderson, who consulted with Kellogg, "in the form proposed by Mr. Root." These senators decided not as to offer their reservations yet for criticism or approval to Lodge or Hitchcock, who was now, because of the illness of Senator Thomas Martin of Virginia, serving as acting Democratic

---

39. For some interpretations of their views and distinctions among their positions, see Margulies, *Mild Reservationists,* esp. xii, xiv, 60–61. One of these mild reservationists, Lenroot, had gotten badly burned several times in the highly charged ideological politics of his home state of Wisconsin during the preceding decade. Another Republican senator, Arthur Capper of Kansas, had earlier, as governor, joined the LEP and shepherded a resolution approving its program through his state's legislature, but he kept his distance from the mild reservationists and followed Lodge's lead. Spencer had some ties to Taft as a fellow Yale man, and his chief journalistic support in Missouri came from the strongly pro-League St. Louis *Globe-Democrat.* Nevertheless, he proved to be the least reliable member of this group. After initially meeting with the mild reservationists, he grew frightened at reports of anti-League sentiment in Missouri and seemed to talk out of both sides of his mouth about the League and reservations. Ibid., 61.

leader. Instead, they sought support from additional Republicans, preferably twenty or so, in an effort to command enough swing votes to make up two-thirds in combination with the Democrats.[40]

At the same time, outside the Senate, Hays's campaign to enlist the broadest possible swath of Republicans behind the banner of reservations got a big boost when a pair of the party's most prominent figures unveiled their versions of reservations. The first unveiling came from the party's most recent nominee for president, Hughes. Responding to urging by Root, Hughes produced a long public letter in which he affirmed, "There is a plain need for a league of nations," particularly one that would foster the development of international law, establish and maintain a world court, and generally promote international cooperation. "I perceive no reason why," he added, "these objects cannot be attained without sacrificing the essential interests of the United States. There is a middle ground between aloofness and injurious commitments." This particular League of Nations struck him, however, ". . . as a mere beginning, and while it is important that we should have a beginning, it is equally important that we should not make a false start." He still regarded Article X as "a trouble-breeder and not a peace-maker." Hughes offered four reservations, covering the usual subjects of withdrawal from the League, domestic questions, the Monroe Doctrine, and Article X. Unlike Root's suggestion, Hughes's reservation did not call for nonadherence to Article X but stated that the United States

> assumes no obligation under said Article to undertake any military expedition, or to employ its armed forces on land or sea, unless such action is authorized by the Congress of the United States of America, which has exclusive authority to declare war or to determine for the United States whether there is any obligation on its part under said Article and the means or action by which any such obligation shall be fulfilled.[41]

Considering who Hughes was, his reservations should have made a bigger splash than they did. An unfortunate coincidence robbed them of attention and significance. The day before Hughes's letter was made

40. Entry, July 30, 1919, Anderson Diary. See also McCumber to Taft, July 31, 1919, Taft Papers, reel 211.
41. Hughes to Frederick Hale, July 24, 1919, ibid. See also Lodge to Root, July 7, 1919, Root Papers, Box 161. Interestingly, in the autobiographical notes that he wrote in 1943, Hughes quoted only the first portion of the letter, not the more critical remarks and the texts of the reservation. See David J. Danelski and Joseph S. Tulchin, eds., *The Autobiographical Notes of Charles Evans Hughes* (Cambridge, Mass., 1973), 212.

public, someone leaked Taft's reservations to the press. These reservations bore out his closest associates' worst fears. When he first saw the reservations before they were leaked, his brother recoiled at "quite so radical a suggestion" as the five-year time limit on adherence to Article X. "I am just a trifle concerned," Henry Taft added, "that you have put yourself a little too unreservedly in the hands of Hays. He seems to be extremely anxious to pull off a 'Hays coup.'" Senator McCumber likewise told Taft that his Article X reservation went "farther . . . than is necessary. . . . I regard Article 10 as the real heart of the compact and I don't want to cut it out." Taft himself had second thoughts, and he bombarded Hays with long letters, further explaining his position, enjoining Hays to maintain confidentiality, and asking Hays not to show the reservations to Lodge or Root.[42]

A savvier politician would have known that such injunctions were futile. Hays had already sent copies of Taft's reservations to Lodge and Root. Lodge had instantly recognized that their publication "would strengthen the cause of reservations . . . and would greatly weaken the opponents as coming from Mr. Taft." As is usual in such cases, no one would admit to being the leaker. The strongest suspicions fell on two senators – Knox, who may have gotten a copy of the reservations from Lodge, and McNary, who may have thought that he was helping the cause of getting the treaty approved. There was a flurry of excitement on the Senate floor when Borah interrupted another senator's speech to read the text of Taft's reservations. According to some reporters, some senators dismissed their importance while several of the Irreconcilables felt gleeful. At the White House, Tumulty used some impolite epithets to describe Taft, but the president sympathized with his predecessor's private correspondence being leaked to the press.[43]

The best assessment of the political impact of Taft's reservations came from Lodge. He dismissed the reservations as "not very effective, but the main thing is that he is accepting reservations, which is all the country will care to know. It is a sign of weakness." The leadership of the LEP agreed. At a hastily called meeting on the eve of the press leaks, members of the executive committee, including Henry Taft, Wickersham, Lowell, and McAdoo, conceded, as was reported to Taft, "that

---

42. Henry Taft to Taft, July 16, 1919, Taft Papers, reel 210; Henry Taft to Taft, July 18, 1919, ibid., reel 211; McCumber to Taft, July 18, 1919, ibid.; Taft to Hays, July 20, 1919, ibid. See also Taft to Hays, July 13, 1919, ibid., reel 210; Taft to Hays, July 19, 20 [second letter], 23, 1919, ibid., reel 211.
43. Lodge to Hays, July 17, 1919, Lodge Papers. On the source of the leak and White House reactions, see Karger to Taft, July 23, 24, 28, 31, 1919, Taft Papers, reel 211. On Senate reactions, see New York *World*, July 24, 1919.

any suggestions from the League and its leading members at this time, suggesting reservations, would be used to convince the country that we were weakening and were ready to compromise, in which case opposition would finally force us to compromise at a point much further within their territory than we had any idea of going." For his part, Taft was full of chagrin at having been "impulsive, earnest, and anxious to do things quickly." He asked Lowell to tender his resignation as president of the LEP at the next meeting of the executive committee. When the committee met, the subject of his resignation never came up. Instead, the committee unanimously adopted a resolution affirming that the LEP favored "unconditional ratification of the Covenant of the League of Nations," was "opposed to any amendments or reservations thereto," and was "in accord with the position of its President, the Honorable William Howard Taft."[44]

The LEP's face-saving resolution fooled nobody. As Lodge and the executive committee both recognized, Taft's reservations gravely weakened the bargaining position of those who opposed limits on participation in the League. Although compromise of some sort might eventually prove necessary, by giving away so much at the outset, especially on Article X, Taft was ensuring that any such compromise would be closer to what critics and opponents wanted. This incident also supplied unmistakable evidence of disunity within the top ranks of the LEP. Relations between Taft and the rest of the leadership would never be the same again. His impulsive blundering and political naiveté inescapably brought back bad memories of his floundering conduct in the White House. Taft quickly got over his remorse, and he began to disparage the LEP both for apparent ineffectiveness in its Washington lobbying and for what he saw as excessive influence by and leaning toward the Democrats. From this time on, the LEP would never again speak with one voice. The sun was setting swiftly on the heyday of this once-formidable organization.

At this time, the end of July and beginning of August, Wilson was having to divert his attention increasingly to domestic problems. Rampant inflation and a threatened railroad strike were the sole subjects taken up at a cabinet meeting on July 31. A few days later, the White

---

44. Lodge to James T. Williams, July 24, 1919, Lodge Papers; Short to Taft, July 22, 31, 1919, Taft Papers, reel 211; Taft to Charles D. Hilles, July 25, 1919, ibid.; Taft to Lowell, July 27, 1919, ibid. On Lodge's reactions to the Taft reservations, see also entry, July 30, 1919, Anderson Diary. On the July 31 LEP meeting, see also McAdoo to Wilson, July 31, 1919, in Link, ed., *Papers of Wilson*, LXII, 70–71; and Herbert S. Houston to Lowell, Aug. 2, 1919, Lowell Papers.

House announced that the president was suspending his meetings with senators about the treaty in order to address a joint session of Congress on the high cost of living. In that speech, on August 8, Wilson did attempt to connect troubles at home with delay in ratifying the peace treaty. He made such vague injunctions as, "In the presence of a world confused, distracted, she [America] must show herself self-possessed, self-contained, capable of sober and effective action." Like Wilson's address to the Senate a month before, this one showed signs of difficulty in composition and delivery. Wilson was also pondering the question of releasing persons imprisoned under wartime laws, most notably Eugene Debs, and how to respond to anti-Bolshevik and antiradical sentiments. Curiously, the one problem at home that he never seems to have discussed publicly or privately was the racial violence that had recently raged just blocks from the White House and still rocked Northern cities and small towns and the countryside in the South.[45]

During August, twelve more senators gave speeches on the floor about the League and the treaty. The most important of these speeches were those delivered by the pair of Republicans with the greatest influence in foreign affairs. On August 12, Lodge delivered his first prepared address as majority leader and chairman of the Foreign Relations Committee. He opened with several learned references, including quotations from the preamble to the Holy Alliance of 1815. That preamble – which Lodge called, "Brave words, indeed!" – took him straight to his main point: that the League of Nations was the same sort of enterprise, namely an alliance charged to intervene anywhere in order to maintain the existing distribution of power in the world. "If Europe desires such an alliance or league with a power of this kind, so be it," Lodge conceded. But he objected "in the strongest possible way" to having the United States controlled by such a league. Not only Article X of the Covenant but also articles XI and XV – which asserted the League's concern about threats to peace everywhere and set up procedures for the Council to settle disputes among members – raised grave dangers of

45. Wilson speech, Aug. 8, 1919, in Link, ed., *Papers of Wilson*, LXII, 209–219. This speech was, in the judgment of the editors of *Papers of Wilson*, so "rambling, loquacious, repetitive, and chatty" that they speculate that he was suffering from "dementia" brought on by his deteriorating physical condition. See editors' note, ibid., 209 n. 1. See also *New York Times*, Aug. 2, 6, 1919; *Washington Post*, Aug. 5, 6, 1919. On the release of prisoners and antiradical sentiment, see Wilson to A. Mitchell Palmer, Aug. 4, 1919, in Link, ed., *Papers of Wilson*, LXII, 126; entry, Aug. 7, [1919], Lansing Desk Diary, ibid., 202; Lansing to Wilson, Aug. 7, 1919, ibid., 203.

interference in the internal affairs of other nations and America. He likewise rejected any designation of the Monroe Doctrine except as "a purely American policy," with the United States always "to be the sole judge of what it means." In sum, he believed, "[t]his league to enforce peace does a great deal for enforcement and very little for peace."

The United States could join this League, Lodge argued, only with ironclad safeguards that made "perfectly clear that no American soldiers, not even a corporal's guard, that no American sailors, not even the crew of a submarine, can ever be ordered anywhere except by the constitutional authorities of the United States." He rejected "all this empty talk about isolation" and maintained that America would continue "to help in all ways to preserve the world's peace. But we can do it best by not crippling ourselves." Lodge warned that it would become impossible to "Americanize" immigrants "if we are continually thrusting them back into the quarrels and difficulties" of their former countries. He sneered at Wilson's claim "that we shall 'break the heart of the world'" by not joining the League, "this deformed experiment upon a noble purpose, tainted, as it was," with the intrigues and spoils of the peace settlement. Nor did the League's friends enjoy "a monopoly of idealism." He and others like him

> have our ideals. . . . Our first ideal is our country. . . . We would not have our country's vigor exhausted or her moral force abated, by everlasting meddling and muddling in every quarrel, great and small which affects the world. Our ideal is to make her ever stronger and better and finer, because in that way alone, as we believe, can she be of the greatest service to the world's peace and the welfare of mankind.[46]

This was a typical Lodge performance. He privately admitted that he had aimed for oratorical excellence. The finished product was elegantly constructed, but it was not as tightly organized nor as trenchant a piece of analysis as might have been expected. Likewise, despite the learned references – which also included quotations from Charles Lamb and a line from Horace recited in Latin – Lodge did not get much more concrete or engage in any sharper critical thinking than Wilson had done before the Senate a month earlier. The only novel element in the speech was the reference to immigrants and avoidance of agitating them by American involvement in their old countries' affairs. Overall, Lodge's argument seemed to be that the United States had previously done fine under Republican presidents, especially Roosevelt, and that it could once more play its greatest role in the world by getting back to their tried and true policies rather than by being led astray by this crackpot

---

46. *Congressional Record*, 66th Cong., 1st Sess. (Aug. 12, 1919), 3778–3784.

scheme of Wilson's. Still, Lodge stated that argument vaguely, and he offered no clear indication of where he was heading. In tone, style, and much of its substance, the speech could have come from one of the Irreconcilables, yet Lodge did not call for rejection of the treaty or the League. Conversely, he did not say what revisions to the treaty might satisfy him. At bottom, the speech was a political document. He meant to keep options open for himself and other Republican senators, so that they could still jump either way on the question of consent to the treaty.[47]

Whatever Lodge's speech may have lacked in specificity or intellectual rigor, it more than made up in the political fireworks that it set off. Thanks to publicity and arrangements by the Independence League lobbyists, a sympathetic crowd packed the Senate galleries, including some Marines in uniform, who cheered Lodge and booed and hissed the Democrats who rose to answer him. Rise they did. First, John Sharp Williams delivered a rambling, impassioned extemporaneous reply. Charging that Lodge "always attempted to make a show of himself," Williams excoriated the "cold, New England, Brahmin cynicism" that allowed him to scoff at "breaking the heart of the world," and he denounced Lodge's scare tactics regarding immigration, especially the specter of feelings inflamed among the foreign-born. The intemperate tone of Williams's performance raised speculations about whether he had been drinking again. Hitchcock took a gentler line of criticism by quoting from the 1915 speech in which Lodge had endorsed the league idea. By contrast, Borah commended Lodge for having changed his mind about the league idea, and Johnson seconded Lodge's condemnation of Article X by quoting from John Quincy Adams's 1820 reply to the Holy Alliance, adding ". . . what he said there is true to-day."[48]

The other major speech came on August 29, from Knox. He called

47. *"Post equitem sedet atra cura"* was the line from Horace that Lodge recited. It was recognizable to most of his listeners as the source of one of Roosevelt's best remembered sayings: "Black care seldom sits behind a rider whose pace is fast enough." On his aiming for oratorical effect, see Lodge to John T. Morse, Aug. 18, 1919, Lodge Papers.

48. *Congressional Record*, 66th Cong., 1st Sess. (Aug. 12, 1919), 3784–3791. On the scene in the Senate, see entry, Aug. 12, 1919, Ashurst Diary, in Sparks, ed., *Many-Colored Toga*, 101; Lodge to Ellerton James, Aug. 15, 1919, Lodge Papers; Lodge to John T. Morse, Aug. 19, 1919, ibid.; Williams to E. J. Doering, Aug. 18, 1919, Williams Papers, Box 47; Williams to William H. Fleming, Aug. 22, 1919, ibid.; New York *World*, Aug. 13, 1919.

the document before the Senate "not the treaty but the truce of Versailles," and he found that, "stripped of its meaningless and beatific provisions, [it] provides merely and simply for an alliance between the five great powers against the balance of the world." Such an alliance could not work, Knox believed, for two reasons. One was that, historically, victors' coalitions like this one quickly broke down in dissension and conflict. The other reason stemmed from the terms to be imposed upon the vanquished. Knox protested that he felt "no maudlin sympathy for Germany." He faulted the negotiators at Paris for a softness toward the foes that "left them beaten but proud and arrogant, . . . and with a will fired by hate to mete out revenge." Nevertheless, he criticized its commercial, colonial, and financial terms as violations of international law and injurious to the international economy in ways that would "kill the goose that we expect to lay the golden eggs." He also lambasted the treaty's labor provisions as unenforceable sops toward "class antagonism between capital and labor."

This review of the treaty – entirely apart from the League Covenant – led Knox to conclude "that the only safe way for us to deal with it is to decline to be a party to it at all." The United States must forgo any gains or compensation under the treaty and refuse to participate in any of the bodies set up to enforce its terms. America's "general policy" should be, Knox declared, "to regard with concern any threat of disturbance to world peace, but at the same time we should reserve complete liberty of action either independently or in conjunction with other powers in taking such steps as we determine wise for preserving the peace." Further, the president should convene an international conference to codify international law, reduce armaments, "and go as far as possible in the direction of securing peace through justice, through a league to which all the world are parties in its formation. This would be a fitting, generous, and dignified exit from a situation in which primarily we had no direct concern." Beyond that, Knox warned, the United States must not go. America must steer clear of the "hard and cruel peace that this treaty stipulates," because involvement with this settlement risked "wrecking our beloved country, earn[ing] the odium of its treasonable betrayal."[49]

Knox was making a number of departures. He was publicly taking his stand with the Irreconcilables. He sweepingly condemned the treaty and cited no amendments or reservations that might make it palatable to him. Knox left no room for anything but total opposition to consent on any basis. He did talk about responding to future threats to world peace, but there was reference to the "Knox doctrine." Nor did Knox

49. *Congressional Record,* 66th Cong., 1st Sess. (Aug. 29, 1919), 4493–4501.

reiterate his willingness to accept an alliance with Britain and France but called instead for reserving "complete liberty of action."[50]

Most startling of all was Knox's condemnation of the peace terms imposed on Germany. Until now, no senator had publicly criticized that aspect of the treaty. Knox was placing himself in the unaccustomed company of the editors of the *Nation* and the *New Republic* and other radicals. His indictment of the peace terms anticipated John Maynard Keynes's as-yet-unpublished attack. His faulting of the peacemakers for having antagonized but not crushed Germany foreshadowed the main line of criticism of the Treaty of Versailles for the rest of the twentieth century. Most tellingly, Knox called for a new, American-sponsored international conference to refine international law, promote disarmament, and establish a separate international organization that would include all nations but, presumably, have no enforcement powers. This suggestion anticipated the Republicans' 1920 campaign cries that condemned "Wilson's League" and called for an "association of nations." It also laid down the main lines of foreign policy that Republican presidents and secretaries of state would pursue during the next decade. In all, Knox had dealt the heaviest blow that any senator had yet rained down on the cause of membership in the League and participation in the peace settlement.

This speech also set off a few fireworks on the Senate floor. A mild reservationist Republican, Knute Nelson, told reporters that Knox's policy would have America "take on the ignominy of deserting the stricken world in this hour of its crisis." A Democrat, Robert Owen of Oklahoma, accused Lodge of "seeing ghosts which do not exist" in Article X.

As before, however, most of the senators' activity took place off the floor. During August, the Foreign Relations Committee held thirteen days of hearings, at which thirty-three witnesses appeared to testify and present documents and resolutions. In addition, on August 19, the committee went to the White House, at the president's invitation, for a three-hour exchange of views and information. These hearings featured both friends and foes of the treaty. The first four witnesses came from the American delegation to the peace conference, including Secretary of State Lansing. Thereafter, these gatherings in the Senate Office Building featured solely representatives of nations or groups that had quarrels to pick with parts of the peace settlement, especially China and Shantung. Also, a delegation of African Americans headed by the renowned militant William Monroe Trotter appealed to the Senate to amend the treaty to affirm racial equality for the sake of nonwhite peoples at home as much as abroad. The month's hearings concluded with a six-and-a-half-

50. Ibid., 4501.

hour session devoted almost entirely to Ireland. Prominent Irish-American Democrats denounced Britain's recent treatment of Ireland and the peacemakers' failure to consider Irish independence. They also told stories about their own frustrated attempts to gain Wilson's ear and support. Their testimony led one Democratic senator to lament, "These Irishmen, alas, are *lost* to the Democratic party at the next election."[51]

These hearings before the Foreign Relations Committee served the purposes of its chairman and all but one of his party colleagues. Occasionally, Lodge disingenuously claimed that he and his fellow Republicans were just discharging their legislative duties, but no one believed him. The welcome mat extended to blatantly hostile spokesmen and the badgering tone toward the administration witnesses, especially by Brandegee, created a bad impression in the press. Even a dedicated foe of the League and the treaty found fault with the hearings. As an experienced trial lawyer and one-time special prosecutor, Hiram Johnson tried to use his skills in examining witnesses, but he felt frustrated at not getting more credit for his efforts. "Our real difficulty," he wrote to his sons, "is that we are utterly without leadership, and that there is no real solidarity of action. The Republicans are generally suspicious of each other." He attributed the suspicion and disunity to there being "so many candidates for President among them." That remark smacked of hypocrisy since Johnson himself was one of those candidates.[52]

Only two of the committee's sessions made much of an impact on the League fight. One was when Lansing underwent five hours of often hostile questioning. He responded as laconically as possible, while the Republicans on the committee behaved, in one reporter's description, "as if the Secretary of State was suspected of having connived at international horse stealing and a commission of country lawyers were bent on making him admit the accusation." In his typically badgering manner, Brandegee probed for information about how the League Covenant had been drafted. Lansing did hint at disagreements within the American delegation about Shantung and seemed to tell the committee members that only the president could really answer their questions. Irked at

51. *New York Times,* Aug. 31, 1919; *Congressional Record,* 66th Cong., 1st Sess. (Aug. 30, 1919), 4547–4551; entry, Aug. 30, 1919, Ashurst Diary, in Sparks, ed., *Many-Colored Toga,* 164. The August testimony is in U.S. Senate, 66th Cong., 1st Sess., Doc. 106, *Peace Treaty Hearings,* 75–945.

52. Johnson to Hiram Jr. and Arch M. Johnson, Aug. 23, 1919, in Burke, ed., *Johnson Letters,* III. See also Johnson to Hiram Jr. and Arch M. Johnson, Aug. 7, 15, 1919, ibid. For other estimates of the hearings, see Stone, *Irreconcilables,* 123; and Lloyd Ambrosius, *Wilson and American Diplomatic Tradition,* 168–170.

the ineffectiveness of the questioning and the dilatoriness of the answers, Johnson jumped in to ask about how well the peace treaty had fulfilled the promises of the Fourteen Points. Smiling as he responded, Lansing said that he believed that the treaty conformed to the Fourteen Points "so far as it was possible to do so with twenty-three nations around the table." In answer to Lodge's question whether the Shantung cession violated the principle of self-determination, he answered, "Yes." When questioned about Article X, Lansing offered the opinion that it imposed no "legal obligation."[53]

The secretary's appearance made no public stir. Many newspapers did not cover it but devoted their front pages, instead, to such domestic matters as the railroad situation and the high cost of living. Lansing's testimony was more significant than it appeared. His failure to sound a ringing endorsement of the treaty and the League and his deadpan manner – which struck Johnson as "the picture of indifference, vacillation, hesitation and downright ignorance" – betokened deeper troubles. Ever since his return from Paris, Lansing had been smarting under what he saw as the president's indifferent, contemptuous treatment, and he confided to his diary that he meant to resign at the first opportune moment. He also commented in his diary that he found the hearing "a disagreeable experience," less because of the Republicans' evident hostility and more because "I felt I could not disclose the truth as to the negotiations." Still, by implication, his performance before the committee exposed the division at the top of the administration's foreign policy team. Lodge privately called Lansing's appearance "rather a pathetic exhibition," and he told his daughter that one of the Democrats on the committee had said to him during the hearing, "What do you suppose Lansing did while he was in Paris?"[54]

The other session that made an impact on the League fight came when President Wilson met with the committee. This was, as everyone recognized, a historic occasion. The only comparable encounter that

53. New York *World,* Aug. 7, 1919. Lansing's testimony is in U.S. Senate, 66th Cong., 1st Sess., Doc. 106, *Peace Treaty Hearings,* 139–214. On August 11, Lansing testified for another two hours, see ibid., 215–252. For Johnson's reaction, see Johnson to Hiram Jr. and Arch M. Johnson, Aug. 7, 23, 1919, in Burke, ed., *Johnson Letters,* III.
54. Johnson to Hiram Jr. and Arch M. Johnson, Aug. 7, 1919, ibid.; entry, Aug. 7, 1919, Lansing Diary; Lodge to Louis A. Coolidge, Aug. 7, 1919, Lodge Papers; Lodge to Constance Lodge Gardner, Aug. 9, 1919, ibid. For similar reactions to Lansing's testimony, see Karger to Taft, Aug. 8, 1919, Taft Papers, reel 211. On Lansing's desire to resign, see entry, Aug. 1, 1919, Lansing Diary, and Edward N. Smith to Lansing, Aug. 25, 1919, Lansing Papers, Vol. 46.

had ever occurred before had been Wilson's invitation the previous March to members of the Senate and House committees to discuss the Draft Covenant. That earlier meeting had been different because it was an informal gathering with no stenographer present, and it had not involved a matter of business then before either house of Congress. Also, as Lodge had noted in July, the constitutional separation of powers forbade congressional committees from summoning a president to testify. For his part, Wilson maintained a proper sensitivity about not breaching executive privilege in his dealings with Congress. For several weeks he had been sparring with the Foreign Relations Committee over requests for submission of the French security pact and various papers from the American delegation, particularly ones that reportedly disclosed Lansing's and General Bliss's protests against the Shantung cession. On August 8, in public letters to the Senate and to Lodge, Wilson conceded that Lansing and Bliss had disagreed with the Shantung cession, but he also stated that he could not release their papers or other documents because of pledges of confidentiality to other governments.[55]

At the same time, the president responded to Thomas Lamont's earlier suggestion and, to more recent urgings by McAdoo and others that he speak out. Wilson tried to draft a statement about reservations. Uncharacteristically, he fretted for more than a week about what to say in that statement, and, also uncharacteristically, he finally let Tumulty draft most of the language that he used. Wilson also bowed to Tumulty's advice that the best way to keep "the initiative with you" would be either to release the statement to the press or to read it as opening remarks to a meeting with the Foreign Relations Committee. On August 14, the White House sent word through Senator Hitchcock that the president was willing to meet with the committee, which immediately voted to instruct Lodge to make the necessary arrangements.[56]

Five days later, at ten o'clock in the morning on August 19, the members of the committee gathered with the president around a table in the East Room of the White House. Wilson sat at one corner, between Lodge and Williams, directly opposite Borah and Brandegee. No one else except two stenographers and the head usher of the White House

55. Wilson to Senate, Aug. 8, 1919, in Link, ed., *Papers of Wilson*, LXII, 208–209; Wilson to Lodge, Aug. 8, 1919, ibid., 219.
56. Tumulty to Wilson, Aug. 15, 1919, ibid., 309. On the drafting of the statement, see entries, Aug. 4, 13 [1919], in Desk Diary, Lansing Papers; Tumulty to Wilson, Aug. 14, 1919 [two letters], in Link, ed., *Papers of Wilson*, LXII, 272–275; Wilson to Lodge [draft], [Aug. 14, 1919], ibid., 276–280; editorial notes, ibid., 275 n. 1, 309 n. 1. On the meeting, see Lodge to Wilson, Aug. 14, 1919, ibid.

was present during the meeting, which lasted for three-and-a-half hours and was followed by lunch.[57]

Wilson opened the meeting by reading his prepared statement. He stressed the hardships caused by delay in ratification of the treaty, and he asserted that the only barrier to ratification lay in "certain doubts with regard to the meaning and implication of certain articles of the covenant of the league of nations." Professing himself "unable to understand why such doubts should be entertained," Wilson reviewed such points at issue as exemption of the Monroe Doctrine and domestic questions and found no ambiguity about those matters. With regard to Article X, he maintained that two conditions – the requirement for unanimity in the League Council and the strictly advisory character of its decisions – would protect the United States against any actions that it did not wish to undertake. Moreover, Wilson asserted, not only was Congress' war-making power unimpaired, but Article X imposed "a moral, not a legal, obligation, and leaves our Congress absolutely free to put its own interpretation upon it." Those limitations notwithstanding, he still deemed Article X "to constitute the very backbone of the whole covenant. Without it the league would be hardly more than an influential debating society."

Turning to reservations, the president declared that he had no objection "provided that they do not form a part of the formal ratification itself." But if the United States did attach reservations to its instrument of ratification, he knew that other nations would do likewise. That process would cause "long delays" and ensure "that the meaning and operative force of the treaty would presumably be clouded from one end of its clauses to the other."[58]

Lodge opened for the committee. He commented that he and his fellow senators "have no thought of entering upon an argument as to interpretations"; they merely wanted information about points in the treaty that were not clear. The chairman then asked specific questions about the peace treaties with other former Central Powers and about earlier drafts of the League Covenant. The president answered these questions crisply and informatively. Lodge's disclaimer notwithstanding, the main points at issue in the debate over reservations soon surfaced. Borah asked about who else, in the event of America's withdrawal from the League, would pass judgment on whether it had fulfilled its obliga-

57. For descriptions of the scene, see New York *World,* Aug. 20, 1919; *New York Times,* Aug. 20, 1919.
58. Wilson statement, Aug. 19, 1919, in Link, ed., *Papers of Wilson,* LXII, 340–344. The statement is also in U.S. Senate, 66th Cong. 1st Sess., Doc. 106, *Peace Treaty Hearings,* 499–503.

tions. "Nobody," Wilson answered, adding that the League Council had no say in the matter. McCumber then asked about adopting a reservation that would restate this proposition. Wilson responded by reiterating both his distinction between a moral and a legal obligation – "Only we can interpret a moral obligation" – and his opposition to attaching a reservation to the instrument of ratification – "because then it would be necessary for other governments to act upon it." Lodge interjected a distinction between amendments and reservations. He argued that reservations applied only to the enacting power. Wilson responded by observing that authorities differed on that point. Borah thereupon asked whether Article X imposed only a moral obligation. The president answered yes, and Borah countered that any action under the article would create a legal obligation.

Obligations under Article X occupied much of the rest of the meeting. McCumber asked about including a reservation that stated congressional authority to authorize any forcible action under that article. Wilson responded by stating once more that it would be a mistake to include such a reservation in the instrument of ratification. Knox then asserted that other powers could assent to reservations simply by replying to them. Next came the only exchange that reportedly tried Wilson's patience. Another Republican, Warren Harding of Ohio, engaged him in a lengthy colloquy about whether articles X and XI really meant anything if they imposed only moral obligations. Wilson asserted, "Now a moral obligation is of course superior to a legal obligation, and, if I may say so, has a greater binding force." In his view, a legal obligation was binding only "to do a particular thing under certain sanctions," whereas with a moral obligation "there is an element of judgment," which made a moral obligation "[n]ot less binding, but operative in a different way." Borah interjected a question about whether the French security pact imposed a legal obligation. Wilson answered – mistakenly – "No, sir," and he compounded the error by asserting, "In international law, 'legal' does not mean the same thing as in national law, and the word hardly applies."

At this point, the president committed the worst gaffe of the meeting. Borah asked him when he had first learned about the wartime secret treaties among the Allies. Wilson replied that he and Lansing had not known about them until six months earlier. Critics later accused Wilson of lying when he gave that answer. Yet even such an unfriendly eyewitness as Johnson – who had learned from Walter Lippmann that the president had known about those treaties at the end of 1917 – commented only that "his memory played him false." Immediately after giving that answer to Borah, Wilson also contradicted himself in responding to questions about Shantung by Johnson and Brandegee. First he denied and then he admitted that he had agreed to the cession because of Japanese threats not to sign the treaty.[59]

The president recovered his aplomb when Harding and Brandegee next badgered him further about Article X. He emphatically disagreed with Harding's contentions about "surrendering the moral obligation of this Republic to the prejudices and necessities of the Old World." Harding again asked, if there were only moral obligations under Article X imposed, then what value was there in it? Wilson argued that by serving notice of its moral obligation, the United States "steadies the whole world in advance by its promise beforehand that it will stand with other nations of similar judgment to maintain the right of the world."

By all accounts, Wilson next responded good-naturedly to a volley of questions from Brandegee about the origins of Article X and what part Americans had played in the creation of the League. Their colloquy ended when the sharp-tongued Brandegee asked rhetorically why the United States could not make peace by congressional resolution or by ratifying the treaty without joining the League. Either of those expedients would permit Americans, Brandegee maintained, "not to have any entanglements or connections with European powers, but to pursue our course as before the war." Wilson answered that those actions would create an "unworkable peace, because the league is necessary to the working of it." But, Brandegee persisted, the United States could opt out of the League and other obligations under the treaty. "We could, sir," Wilson replied, "but I hope the people of the United States would never consent to do it." Brandegee snapped back, "There is no way by which the people can vote on it."

By this time, the meeting had gone on for more than three hours, and Lodge ended the exchange between Brandegee and the president by asking about resumption of trade with Germany. Two other Republicans, Harry New and George Moses, then inquired about aspects of the peace settlement in eastern Europe and about mandates over former German colonies. In answering those inquiries, Wilson committed several more errors by denying that the United States was involved in those matters in any way. New asked how the League Covenant would have affected America during the War of 1812 and the Spanish-American War, and

59. Johnson to Hiram Jr. and Arch M. Johnson, Aug. 23, 1919, in Burke, ed., *Johnson Letters*, III. The editors of *Papers of Wilson* note that it is unclear whether Wilson had read the copies of those treaties that the British had given to him shortly after the United States entered the war in April 1917, but other evidence shows that long before the war's end he knew about what the British and French had promised to the Italians and the Japanese in the way of territorial gains. Link, ed., *Papers of Wilson*, LXII, 365 n. 27.

Wilson responded that although he "tried to be a historical student," he could only "figure that out if you give me half a day." At this point Lodge interjected, "Mr. President, I do not wish to interfere in any way, but the conference has now lasted about three hours and a half, and it is half an hour after the lunch hour." The president replied, "Will not you gentlemen take luncheon with me? It will be very delightful." By all accounts, the lunch was pleasant, if not delightful, but Wilson may have remembered the verse from Psalm 23, "Thou preparest a table before me in the presence of mine enemies."[60]

This meeting marked the only time before or since in American history that a president came close to allowing himself to be questioned by a congressional committee. In the view of some of the participants, the senators did not subject the president to much of an examination. Once more, Johnson privately deplored the "desultory" questioning, especially by Lodge, and the absence of "legitimate cross-examination." With his usual mixture of insight into the conduct of others and blindness about his own, Johnson again blamed the public spotlight for bringing out the worst in "sixteen vain men, sitting around a table, each of whom was certain that the world hung upon his words, and each of whom knew his own ability to outshine his fellows." Johnson grudgingly acknowledged that Wilson "bore himself, I think, with equanimity and courtesy, and generally excellently." Albert Fall, another anti-League member of the committee, agreed, declaring the next day in the Senate, "The President of the United States was, I think, frank and open and manly in his treatment of the Senators; he was patient, and endeavored to give them what information he thought he could give them."[61]

60. Ibid., 344–411. The complete transcript of the meeting is also in U.S. Senate, 66th Cong., 1st Sess., Doc. 106, *Peace Treaty Hearings,* 503–553.
61. Johnson to Hiram Jr. and Arch M. Johnson, Aug. 23, 1919, in Burke, ed, *Johnson Letters,* III; *Congressional Record,* 66th Cong., 1st. Sess. (Aug. 20, 1919), 4027. In December 1862, Lincoln had met twice in the White House with a "committee" appointed to represent the Republican caucus in the Senate to hear and deal with complaints about his cabinet. These were strictly private meetings and did not involve either a standing committee of Congress or any pending legislation or, as in this case, a treaty. On Lincoln's meetings with the senators, see James G. Randall, *Lincoln the President: Springfield to Gettysburg* (New York, 1945), II, 243–247; Philip Shaw Paludan, *The Presidency of Abraham Lincoln* (Lawrence, Kans., 1994), 173–177; and David Herbert Donald, *Lincoln* (New York, 1995), 403–405. At other times, presidents have met informally with members of various committees, and from the 1950s to the 60's, Truman, Eisenhower, Kennedy, and Johnson often conferred with members of the Foreign Relations Committee and sometimes the committee as a whole, particularly at times of national crisis.

Those assessments were noteworthy because other observers at the time and most interpreters since then have judged Wilson's conduct before the committee a failure. Lodge privately scoffed that "the performance of yesterday . . . amounted to nothing" and showed Wilson's "ignorance and disingenuousness." Others have seen the president's mistaken notions about legal obligations and his lapse about the secret treaties as evidence of physical and mental deterioration. That judgment seems overdrawn. Obviously, as the White House head usher later recalled, "the President was not at his best at that meeting." Yet even in his younger, healthier days, Wilson had never excelled in encounters like this one, which required quick responses to shifting questions and arguments. Moreover, given his difficulties during the past month in composing and delivering speeches, it was remarkable that he came off as well as he did at this meeting with the Foreign Relations Committee.[62]

Those judgments of Wilson's performance were really beside the point. All that he had really accomplished in the meeting was not to lose ground. To win in any meaningful way he needed to do much more. The most significant outcome of this meeting lay in what did not

62. Lodge to James T. Williams, Jr., Aug. 20, 1919, Lodge Papers; Lodge to W. Sturgis Bigelow, Aug. 25, 1919, ibid.; Hoover memoir, in Link, ed., *Papers of Wilson*, LXIII, 632. For interpretations that stress Wilson's poor performance as a function of his deteriorating health, see Edwin A. Weinstein, *Woodrow Wilson: A Medical and Psychological Biography* (Princeton, N.J., 1981), 350–352, and Park, "Wilson's Neurological Illness during the Summer of 1919, " in Link, ed., *Papers of Wilson*, LXII, 631. Drawing upon his long courtroom experience, Johnson caught some of the quality of Wilson's personality and judged him with much malice when he wrote to his sons,

> I observed him very carefully during all of the time. I think he was interested in me too. He is alert and fairly quick thinking, but with a mind which does not and can not grasp detail. He is an uncanny thing to look at. When he turned, as he did as I began my few questions, he was quite tense, and his whole expression, although not so intended, was quite wicked. His face in repose is hard, and cold, and cruel. When he smiles, he smiles like certain animals curling his upper lip and wrinkling his nose. His is not the infectious laugh of the red-blooded individual. His ponderous lower jaw gives a very strange appearance of a vicious horse, has in connection with the lower part of his face a singular sort of fascination. As one watches his profile, it is not of the intellectual man you might think, but of some mysterious ill-defined monster.

Johnson to Hiram Jr. and Arch M. Johnson, Aug. 23, 1919, in Burke, ed., *Johnson Letters*, III.

happen. This meeting had presented Wilson with a golden opportunity to pull off a coup. Preferably in his opening statement or perhaps in response to a prearranged inquiry by McCumber, he could have taken much of the wind out of his critics' and opponents' sails. He could have announced a new position on reservations that might have gathered in the Republican mild reservationists. Better yet, he could have dropped a bombshell by announcing that he had already worked out a bipartisan agreement with those senators. This was probably the greatest single missed opportunity of the League fight. The question that needs to be asked is, why? Why did the major actors involved fail to seize this moment?

The moment did indeed seem promising. The month of August marked the high point in the mild reservationists' activity and potential influence in the League fight. They were concentrating their efforts on two subjects – amendments and reservations. On amendments, these Republican senators, who numbered between seven and ten according to various reporters' counts, succeeded in forming a cohesive bloc. On future votes, they would join with virtually all the Democrats to oppose any amendments to the text of the treaty that might require reopening negotiations. They made their stand clear when the Republicans on the Foreign Relations Committee adopted their first amendment. On August 23, those Republicans moved to strike out all references to Japan and substitute "China" in the clauses of the treaty that referred to Shantung. This "Shantung amendment," as it was christened, struck many commentators as an insult to Japan and a ploy to wreck the treaty. The mild reservationists immediately denounced this amendment and helped to firm up a majority to defeat all such measures when they reached the Senate floor.[63]

Their second subject – reservations – was a different story. Internal cohesion among the mild reservationists and cooperation across party lines proved difficult This was not for want of effort. McCumber, McNary, and Kellogg in particular conferred almost constantly among themselves and with other Republican senators. They also corresponded with Taft and Root and met with Lowell and other LEP leaders. Article X remained a stumbling block. Three of these senators – McCumber, McNary, and Nelson – wanted to preserve as much of an obligation as possible. Another three – Cummins, Lenroot, and Spencer – insisted on a limiting reservation. Kellogg and Colt fell somewhere in between. Spencer vexed his fellow mild reservationists when reports of anti-

---

63. On the coalition to defeat amendments, see New York *World*, Aug. 27, 28, Sept. 1, 1919; *New York Times*, Sept. 1, 2, 1919; Karger to Taft, Aug. 21, 28, 1919, Taft Papers, reels 211, 212.

League sentiment in Missouri scared him into, in McNary's words, "flop[ping] like a herring on dry land." Nevertheless, by the middle of the month these eight senators appeared to agree that four reservations, along the lines of those proposed by Hughes, should be attached to the instrument of ratification. They also claimed that another dozen or so of their party colleagues would support such reservations, thereby delivering a total of twenty Republican votes. Together with forty-five likely Democratic votes, these Republicans could supply the two-thirds needed for consent to the treaty.[64]

Prospects for such a bipartisan coalition looked bright at the middle of August. Several of the mild reservationists were already reaching out across party lines. Gus Karger, Taft's agent in Washington, reported back to his patron that McNary had talked with Claude Swanson about Taft's suggested reservations and that Swanson had "told McNary that if he could get twenty Republicans to come in on them the Democrats would join them in putting them over." Charles Michelson of the New York *World* likewise reported "a get-together movement" between Democrats and mild reservationists that was "still in the conference stage." One Democratic senator, Key Pittman of Nevada, later recalled, "The situation was such at one time that we all felt confident that an agreement had been reached substantially as between those who were negotiating."[65]

Actually, the prospects for bipartisan cooperation were not all that bright. The mild reservationists could not go too far in accommodating the Democrats without appearing to be unfaithful to their own party. Moreover, their logic in opposing amendments required them to support reservations that might not be mild. Also at the middle of August, Lodge enlisted Root's help in trying to bring Kellogg and Colt back in line behind "a real and effective reservation on Article 10" – one that would be attached to the instrument of ratification and would require assent from the Allies. Those two senators and most of the other mild reservationists soon did come back into the party fold, although it is questionable how much Lodge or Root influenced them. They got back together with their party brethren because the other cloud over these

---

64. McNary quoted in Karger to Taft, Aug. 4, 1919, Taft Papers, reel 211. On these efforts by the mild reservationists, see ibid.; entry, August 6, 1919, Straus Diary, Straus Papers, Box 24; New York *World*, Aug. 16, 1919; *New York Times*, Aug. 15, 1919. On the internal divisions among these senators, see Margulies, *Mild Reservationists*, 90–91.
65. Karger to Taft, Aug. 11, 1919, Taft Papers, reel 211; New York *World*, Aug. 11, 1919; Pittman to William Hard, July 7, 1926, Pittman Papers, Box 13.

bipartisan prospects – from the White House – unloaded a downpour of disappointment on these hopes for accommodation.[66]

Wilson's attitude always hung a sword of Damocles over any possibility of bipartisan cooperation. At first, the president seemed willing to meet the mild reservationists halfway. According to McAdoo's recollection, Wilson told him around this time, "Mac, I am willing to compromise anything but the Ten Commandments." A delegation of LEP leaders also met with the president on August 7 and discussed the four areas covered by Taft's and Hughes's proposed reservations. One of those LEP leaders, Oscar Straus, found Wilson "very frank, confidential and outspoken" in expressing his interest in an exchange of public letters with the mild reservationists in order to clarify their respective positions. Four days later, however, when Lansing recommended that he reach an agreement with the mild reservationists, he recorded in his diary that Wilson "would have none of it, and his face took on that stubborn and pugnacious expression which comes whenever anyone tells him a fact which interferes with his plans." Similarly, on August 15, Wilson authorized Senator Hitchcock to tell reporters, "In the opinion of the President, no compromise issue is now before the friends of the treaty and the League. This is not the time to think of a compromise, much less to discuss it or negotiate it. . . . There may have to be a compromise in the end, but at present that bridge is not being crossed."[67]

Why did Wilson take such an intransigent attitude? In their meetings with him in July, Republican senators had repeatedly warned that they would not vote for the treaty without reservations. Likewise, Root and

---

66. Lodge to Root, Aug. 15, 1919, Root Papers, Box 161.
67. William Gibbs McAdoo, *Crowded Years* (Boston, 1931), 514; entry, Aug. 7, 1919, Straus Diary, Straus Papers, Box 24; entry, Aug. 11, 1919, Lansing Diary, in Link, ed., *Papers of Wilson*, LXII, 258–259; *New York Times*, Aug. 16, 1919. On Wilson's meeting with the LEP leaders, see also Lowell to Taft, Aug. 7, 1919, Lowell Papers. McAdoo also recalled that Wilson

> said he would not be averse to the ratification of the treaty with the so-called 'mild' reservations, but that the opponents of the treaty had not advanced them in good faith and the moment there was any indication on his part of a willingness to accept them, partisan opponents would immediately propose other and more objectionable reservations which it would be impossible to consider. They were, he said determined to prevent ratification of the treaty at whatever cost; therefore, it was impossible for him to discuss compromise.

McAdoo, *Crowded Years*, 514.

Hughes had both insisted that reservations must be attached to the instrument of ratification. There was no room for doubt about what kind of reservations would be required. It looked as if Wilson was not fully connecting with the political reality of the situation around him. It is also worth noting that this time, the first week in August, was when the president had to divert his attention from the treaty and the League to deal with domestic problems. His intransigence and unwillingness became much more pronounced when he returned to those previous concerns during the second week in August. For many years Wilson had self-deprecatingly complained about his "one-track mind." Now, however, this lack of flexibility and sensitivity raised doubts about how well he could function even on a single track.[68]

Oddly, no storm of protest arose in the face of Wilson's announced attitude. Senator Pittman had written to him, "The desire upon the part of a number of Democratic Senators to pass the treaty with reservations is steadily, if not rapidly growing." Any declaration by Wilson, warned Pittman, "that may be construed into a determination not to ratify with any reservations" would cause "an immediate and definite alignment in the Senate," including many Democratic defections. Yet neither intra-party dissension nor outcries from the mild reservationists greeted Wilson's statement through Hitchcock. The lack of reaction seems to have stemmed from fixation on the upcoming encounter between the president and the Foreign Relations Committee. Even then, neither Wilson's opening remarks to the Foreign Relations Committee nor his answers to the members' questions – in which he consistently held out against attaching reservations to the instrument of ratification – dashed expectations of accommodation.[69]

The storm that doused those unwarranted hopes broke the day after that historic meeting. A good intention gone awry triggered the downpour. Pittman, who was one of the Democrats on the committee, introduced a resolution that stated four propositions as an "understanding as to the present and future construction and interpretation of the treaty." His propositions covered withdrawal from the League, exclusion of domestic questions, and exemption of the Monroe Doctrine. On Article X, Pittman's wording held that "suggestions" by the League

68. There is some speculation that this behavior pattern may have stemmed from an undetected small stroke that Wilson could have suffered around this time, although there is no record of any illness to suggest that he did. See Park, "Wilson's Neurological Illness," in Link, ed., *Papers of Wilson,* LXII, esp. 633–638.
69. Pittman to Wilson, Aug. 15, 1919, ibid., 310–312. Pittman evidently wrote this letter before reading Hitchcock's statement to reporters.

Council that might involve military force or economic measures "can only be carried out through the voluntary separate actions" of each government. Failure to follow such "suggestions . . . shall not constitute a moral or legal violation of the treaty." Pittman called Article X "the heart of the covenant," but he argued that it "does not provide any machinery for the enforcement of the obligation . . . we will determine for ourselves what method we shall utilize; and when we do that there is no ground of complaint throughout the world." Borah and Fall repeatedly pushed Pittman on the distinction between a legal and a moral obligation and on what actions the United States would really be compelled to take under Article X. "I am just as much at sea now," Fall asserted, "as I was before the explanation." As for trying to represent the president's position, Fall added, "I wonder if sometimes . . . he may not say, 'God deliver me from my friends; I can take care of my enemies myself.'"[70]

As an overture toward a bipartisan compromise, Pittman's resolution backfired. All of the mild reservationists immediately repudiated the plan. With the exception of McCumber, they insisted that any reservations must be part of the instrument of ratification, and they vowed to reporters that they would never budge from this stand. Outside the Senate, pro-League Republicans reacted the same way. "I feel as if the president weakened his case by his lack of clarity and his insistence on no reservations," Taft told Kellogg. "Pittman, too, was asinine in his resolutions." The White House wasted no time in pulling the rug out from under Pittman. The day after he introduced his resolution, Hitchcock was authorized to tell reporters, "The President had no knowledge of the resolution or of its introduction."[71]

The collapse of Pittman's move ended for the time being any further efforts at cooperation between the Democrats and the mild reservationists. Wilson's defiance flared up again after the meeting with the Foreign Relations Committee. The following day, Lansing recorded in his diary

70. *Congressional Record,* 66th Cong., 1st Sess. (Aug. 20, 1919), 4035–4039, 4048–4054, 4059.
71. New York *World,* Aug. 21, 22, 1919; *Washington Post,* Aug. 22, 1919; Taft to Kellogg, Aug. 23, 1919, Taft Papers, reel 211; *Philadelphia Public Ledger,* Aug. 24, 1919. The editors of *Papers of Wilson* speculate, based upon circumstantial evidence, that Pittman may have consulted with Wilson before he introduced his resolution. See editorial note in Link, ed., *Papers of Wilson,* LXII, 432 n. 2. Pittman, however, later stated, "I purposely refrained from consulting with the president with regard to such resolution, as I realized it was not proper or advisable for him to approve or [sic] any reservations at that time." Pittman to William Hard, July 7, 1926, Pittman Papers, Box 13.

that Wilson told him that the current conduct of the European nations, "the great and utter selfishness of it all," made him "almost inclined to refuse to permit this country to be a member of the League of Nations when it is composed of such intriguers and robbers. I am disposed to throw up the whole business and get out." Lansing also noted, "This is the *third* time that the President has said that the conduct of the nations makes him consider withdrawing from the League, though he never before said it so emphatically." That remark did not make Wilson a closet isolationist. Rather, this all-or-nothing attitude betrayed the increasing difficulty that he was having with his intellectual and emotional balance.[72]

An equally vivid illustration of his difficulty in keeping on an even keel came with Wilson's response to the Shantung amendment. On Capitol Hill, the Irreconcilables had also been busy. The ones on the Foreign Relations Committee went into a huddle as soon as they returned to the Capitol from lunch at the White House, and they met again the next day. The second of those meetings took place in Knox's office. Reporters correctly viewed this meeting as a sign that Knox had cast his lot with the Irreconcilables, which he revealed in his speech on August 29. These Irreconcilables kept up the pressure on Lodge and other Republicans on the committee to amend the text of the peace treaty. That pressure bore its first fruit on August 23, when the Foreign Relations Committee passed the Shantung amendment. Swanson protested that the committee should first take up the treaty itself, and not this measure, which he said the Allies would never accept. By contrast, Knox exulted, "The committee decided it would take independent action."[73]

Wilson's reaction came two days later. On August 25, Lansing recorded in his diary, "Prest very angry at Senators for proposed amendment as to Shantung." Lansing further recorded that Wilson "[t]old me confidentially that he planned to got to the people at once and that if they wanted war he would 'give them a belly full.'" Two days later the White House announced the decision, and within a week, on September 3, the president left on a trip that was scheduled to take him across the country and back in the space of four weeks packed with speeches and public appearances. A speaking tour had remained a live

72. Entry, Aug. 20, 1919, Lansing Diary, in Link, ed., *Papers of Wilson*, LXII, 428–429. For another expression of that attitude, see entry, Aug. 11, [1919], Lansing Desk Diary, ibid., 253.

73. New York *World*, Aug. 20, 22, 24, 1919; *New York Times*, Aug. 22, 24, 1919.

option from the time that Wilson had gotten back to the United States. Tumulty had been laying the groundwork for one all along. Many observers noted that people were growing less interested in foreign policy and more worried about domestic problems. With a speaking tour, Wilson hoped to reignite popular support for his position on the League and thereby improve his bargaining position with the Senate.[74]

The decision to go to the people did not rule out further efforts to reach out to the men on Capitol Hill. Senator Swanson saw Wilson twice between the meeting with the Foreign Relations Committee and his departure on the speaking tour. On August 25, the president spent forty-five minutes in the senator's office while Mrs. Wilson waited outside in the presidential limousine. Swanson later claimed that he had urged Wilson to accept reservations in the instrument of ratification. "What difference does it make whether the baby is tied with blue ribbons or pink ones," Swanson remembered saying, "– as long as we get the baby." In response, he also recalled, Wilson "listened attentively and declined to commit himself but promised to think the matter over." Evidently he did. After Swanson came to the White House for an hour's talk on September 2, the senator told reporters that the president had "frowned upon" amendments or drastic reservations and was "unalterably opposed" to any changes that would require resubmission of the treaty to the peace conference. But, Swanson also told the reporters, "If interpretative reservations were deemed imperative, the President said he would not oppose them. . . ."[75]

That statement represented more than just an offhand remark or an overly hopeful reading on Swanson's part. The next evening, just before he boarded his train for the speaking tour, Wilson met with Hitchcock at the White House and gave the senator a document that he had typed on his own typewriter and revised in his own hand. Titled "Sugges-

---

74. Entry, Aug. 25, [1919], ibid., 507. The editors of *Papers of Wilson* observe that Wilson made the decision "without much thought, in anger, and on the spur of the moment," and they conclude that it was "irrational." Editorial note, ibid., n. 2. This judgment strikes me as overdrawn. On the decision to undertake the tour, see John Milton Cooper, Jr., "Fool's Errand or Finest Hour? Woodrow Wilson's Speaking Tour in September 1919," in Cooper and Charles E. Neu, eds., *The Wilson Era: Essays in Honor of Arthur S. Link* (Arlington Heights, Ill., 1991), 199–205.

75. New York *World*, Aug. 26, 1919; *New York Times*, Sept. 3, 1919; Swanson quoted in Henry C. Ferrell, Jr., *Claude Swanson of Virginia: A Political Biography* (Lexington, Ky., 1985), 126, and in George Wharton Pepper, *Philadelphia Lawyer* (Philadelphia, 1944), 129.

tion," it consisted of five one-sentence paragraphs – a preamble and four points. In the preamble, Wilson addressed the question of where reservations would be attached. He stated that the Senate should advise and consent "with the following understanding" and the president would "communicate these interpretations to the several States signatory to said treaty at the same time that he deposits the formal instrument of ratification." The four points covered the same matters as previous reservations and suggestions. On withdrawal, Wilson asserted that there was "no limitation . . . except such as may lie in the conscience of the Power proposing to withdraw," and he did not mention any advance notice. On domestic matters, Wilson held that "no question" could be raised in the League that might give that organization "the right to report on or to make any recommendation upon the policy of any Member State with regard to such matters as immigration, naturalization, or tariffs." On the Monroe Doctrine, he affirmed that "nothing contained in the Covenant shall be interpreted in any way impairing or interfering with the application of the Monroe Doctrine in the Western Hemisphere."

None of those three points differed much from Taft's and Hughes' proposed reservations or from drafts that were being circulated around the Senate by the mild reservationists. Only on Article X did Wilson depart from earlier approaches. His point read:

> It [the United States] understands that the advice of the Council of the League of Nations with regard to the employment of armed force contemplated in Article Ten of the Covenant of the League is to be regarded only as advice and leaves each Member State free to exercise its own judgment as to whether it is wise or practicable to act upon that advice or not.

By not mentioning Congress' constitutional powers, Wilson was attempting to retain some presidential flexibility, and he implicitly left open his idea of a moral obligation. Whether this approach would satisfy Republican senators was questionable, but it did mark a significant unbending on the central issue of international enforcement.[76]

How promising this gesture was should not be exaggerated. It was not likely that the mild reservationists would have welcomed these proposals with open arms. As Herbert Margulies has pointed out, Wilson persistently failed to appreciate how deeply committed all of those sena-

---

76. Wilson, "Suggestion," [Sept. 3, 1919], in Link, ed., *Papers of Wilson*, LXII, 621. The original document is enclosed with Hitchcock to Edith Wilson, Jan. 5, 1920, Woodrow Wilson Papers, Library of Congress, reel 106.

tors, except McCumber, were to limitating obligation under Article X. A fresh illustration of the gulf between the two sides came on September 2, when Lenroot also spent an hour at the White House with the president. As Lenroot later recalled, "I pointed out to him that the only real obstacle to the ratification of the Treaty was Article X and that if he would agree to a reservation relieving the United States from the obligation of that article, ratification would be certain and his speaking trip would be unnecessary." Wilson replied, Lenroot remembered, "that he would not agree to such a reservation, for, in his opinion, Article X was the heart of the Covenant and without it the League would be of no value in maintaining the peace of the world." It would have taken a remarkably gifted dialectician and a commandingly persuasive legislative leader to bridge this gulf. None of the mild reservationists possessed the skills or the stature to pull off such a feat. Probably the only person who could have brought it off on Capitol Hill was Root, if he had been in the Senate and joined the mild reservationists, or Knox, if he had cast his lot with them instead of the Irreconcilables.[77]

Further afield among Republican senators, the situation looked even less promising. Wilson did not err in viewing the Foreign Relations Committee's Shantung amendment as a slap in the face. Far from reluctantly appeasing the Irreconcilables with the amendment, Lodge gladly supported it, as he told Chandler Anderson. Moreover, Anderson recorded in his diary on August 22 that Lodge favored a reservation on Article X that "was much more drastic than anything heretofore drafted" and declared "that no compromise was possible." Three days later, Anderson further recorded that Lodge "wanted to nullify the treaty with respect" to Article X. That same day Lodge also told a friend, "It is a great pity that the treaty with France, cutting out the League of course, should not be ratified. . . . But the curse of the League is on it, and it is that which has delayed peace, it is that which endangers the treaty with France." Clearly, prospects of attracting enough Republicans to command the necessary two-thirds for consent to the treaty were not bright.[78]

Those obstacles on Capitol Hill left the burden of working out any compromise squarely on Wilson's shoulders. He vitiated the usefulness of his proposed reservations by forbidding Hitchcock to tell anyone that he had written them. This embargo on disclosing his authorship, Hitch-

77. Lenroot in *Washington Post*, Mar. 4, 1945. For Margulies' observations, see *Mild Reservationists*, 72, 88–89.
78. Entries, Aug. 22, 25, 1919, Anderson Diary; Lodge to Charles A. Prince, Aug. 25, 1919, Lodge Papers.

cock later recalled, stemmed from Wilson's fear that "his enemies would make use of his yielding to demand more and more because they wanted not only to defeat the league but to discredit and overthrow him." In view of that embargo, it was questionable what use, if any, Hitchcock could make of the reservations. Moreover, even if Hitchcock could have disclosed that they came from the president, no one besides Wilson could have put them on the table for bargaining, and he was absenting himself from the scene for the next four weeks.[79]

Actually, the linkage between these reservations and the speaking tour reflected sound political judgment. Wilson did not say so explicitly, but it seems likely that he was drawing upon his experience in 1916, when he had made a speaking tour and conducted negotiations with congressional leaders over his military preparedness program. At that time, Wilson had first given a series of speeches and then made a critical concession on the most controversial issue, thereby winning approval of his overall program. If, as seems probable, Wilson was thinking along such lines, the reservations that he left with Hitchcock might plant the seed for a similar concession when he returned from this speaking tour.[80]

This analogy contained flaws, the most serious of which arose from Wilson himself. For him to prevail as he had done earlier he would have to return from his speaking tour willing and able to do the kind of tough, intricate bargaining that might assemble a bipartisan coalition large enough to gain consent to the treaty. Although his physician, Grayson, could not grasp the true nature or full extent of the president's illness, he did know that Wilson was not a well man. Grayson correctly worried that a campaign-style speaking tour would badly strain Wilson's fragile health, and he was trying to persuade the president to stay in Washington. According to his later recollection, Grayson went so far as to advise Wilson at the end of August against making the tour. "I do not wish to do anything foolhardy," he recalled the president's saying in response,

> but the League of Nations is now in its crisis, and if it fails, I hate to think what will happen to the world. You must remember that I, as Commander in Chief, was responsible for sending our soldiers to

79. Hitchcock, "Events Leading to the World War," [Jan. 13, 1925], Gilbert M. Hitchcock Papers, Library of Congress.

80. On that earlier tour, see Arthur S. Link, *Wilson: Confusions and Crises* (Princeton, N.J., 1964), 15–54, and John Milton Cooper, Jr., *The Vanity of Power: American Isolationism and the First World War, 1914–1917* (Westport, Conn., 1969), 90–98.

Europe. In that crucial test in the trenches they did not turn back – and I cannot turn back now. I cannot put my safety, my health in the balance against my duty – I must go.[81]

Wilson may have said something like that, but his casting himself in the role of heroic martyr sounded more like Theodore Roosevelt. According to another recollection, by Secretary of the Navy Josephus Daniels, the president brushed aside warnings that the tour would injure his health. "You are mistaken," Daniels recalled Wilson as saying. "It will be no strain on me – on the contrary, it will be a relief to me to meet the people. No, the speeches will not tax me. The truth is, I am saturated with the subject and spoiling to tell the people about the Treaty. I will enjoy it." That sounded more like Wilson. He had always enjoyed campaigning, and he believed that democratic leaders renewed their political strength through contact with the people. Unfortunately, perhaps even tragically, this optimism was misplaced. Wilson would return from the tour incapable of ever again playing a constructive role in the League fight. No one knew it at the time, but the best chance for a happy ending to the League fight had passed.[82]

81. Cary T. Grayson, *Woodrow Wilson: An Intimate Memoir* (New York, 1960), 95. Other flaws in the analogy with the 1916 situation involved political circumstances. Earlier, Wilson's principal opponents had been fellow Democrats, followers of Bryan, and even the most obdurate among them had felt great qualms about balking their own party's president. In 1919 few Republicans, even mild reservationists, felt that way. Likewise, earlier Wilson had only needed to win over simple majorities in a Congress controlled by his own party and in which Republicans generally supported him on the issue. Now he faced the far more difficult task of securing a two-thirds margin in a Senate controlled by an opposition party in which few of them supported him on this issue.
82. Josephus Daniels, *The Life of Woodrow Wilson* (Philadelphia, 1924), 326–327. Also, as Edwin Weinstein has shown, Wilson was long habituated in the ways of psychological denial toward physical problems or limitations, as were most American males of his generation. On Wilson's practice of psychological denial, see Weinstein, *Wilson*, 147–148.

4

Ill-Fated Journey

O n the night of September 3, 1919, Woodrow Wilson left Washington on his speaking tour to advocate ratification of the Treaty of Versailles and membership in the League of Nations. The presidential train traveled overnight to Columbus, Ohio, where Wilson made his first major speech on September 4. Sparse crowds lined the streets as the motorcade moved through downtown Columbus because a streetcar strike kept people away. Still, an audience of 4,000 filled the auditorium where the president spoke at noon. Another 2,000 people clamored outside to get in. In the speech Wilson declared, "The terms of the treaty are severe, but they are not unjust." He jumped around a bit in touching on various points about the settlement, but he devoted most of his hour-long address to the League. Wilson expressed astonishment at the ignorance and "radical misunderstanding" of what the League was intended to do. It was intended "not . . . merely to end this war. It was intended to prevent any similar war. . . . The League of Nations is the only thing that can prevent the recurrence of this dreadful catastrophe and redeem our promises." As for the rest of the treaty, the "heart" did not lie in punishing Germany – "That is a temporary thing." Rather, the treaty was aimed at righting "the age-old wrongs which characterized the history of Europe" and which had caused the world war. Near the end of the speech, Wilson called attention to "that line of youngsters in khaki." He saluted them proudly "because I have done the job in the way I promised them I would do it. And when this treaty is accepted, men in khaki will not have to cross the seas again."[1]

The president then left for Indianapolis. There, after making whistle stop appearances along the way, he gave his second major speech that evening. The big crowd – estimated between 16,000 and 20,000 – and poor acoustics in the huge auditorium hampered Wilson's efforts to make himself heard. He spoke in an unusually husky voice, and again he rambled a bit as he discussed different aspects of the treaty. Wilson claimed that Article X "goes to the heart of this whole bad business" of deterring the kind of aggression that had caused the world war. Diplomatic and eco-

1. Wilson speech at Columbus, Sept. 4, 1919, in Arthur S. Link, ed., *The Papers of Woodrow Wilson* (Princeton, N.J., 1990), LXIII, 7–18. On the scene, see entry, Sept. 4, 1919, Grayson Diary, ibid., 3; and New York *World*, Sept. 5, 1919.

nomic boycotts, in his view, would be the chief means of enforcement under Article X: "The most terrible thing is outlawry. The most formidable thing is to be absolutely isolated." Military action was "on the outskirts. War is a secondary threat." Wilson also insisted that he was not speaking in any partisan way, and he praised Article XI for making any potential threat to peace "everybody's business." He defended the Shantung cession as necessary and proper, and he challenged his critics to "'put up or shut up.' Opposition is not going to save the world." Despite the acoustics, the speech seemed to go over well. The audience applauded often and enthusiastically, and people called out, referring to Indiana's two Republican senators, "Better tell that to Harry New and Jim Watson."[2]

Much of the remainder of Wilson's tour followed the pattern set on that first day. He revealed the main strengths and weaknesses in his appeal to the people. "Intensive" would be too weak a word to describe Wilson's efforts in September 1919. This foray onto the hustings would feature forty speeches in the space of twenty-one days. Wilson had never before spoken so often or made so many public appearances in so short a time, not even during his presidential campaigns in 1912 and 1916. The very intensity of the tour attested to his basic problem. Wilson was trying to make up for lost time and missed opportunities in educating the public about his program. This circumstance compelled him to try to do so many things so quickly at a belated hour in the debate. Rather than an example of too little too late, this speaking tour would be a case of too much too late. The sheer volume of speaking and extent of the travels would put a strain on both Wilson's persuasive powers and his deteriorating health. Likewise, having to explain a big, complicated program and at the same time appeal to people's thoughts and emotions would sometimes make his speeches poorly focused and confused. In all, the wonder of this speaking tour would be not that Wilson displayed shortcomings but that he performed as well as he did.[3]

2. Wilson speech at Indianapolis, Sept. 4, 1919, in Link, ed., *Papers of Wilson,* LXIII, 19–29; entry, Sept. 4, 1919, Grayson Diary, ibid., 4.
3. For a comparable estimate of Wilson's having tried to do too much, based upon a conversation with him a year later, see Homer S. Cummings memorandum, Oct. 5, 1920, in Link, ed., *Papers of Wilson,* LXVI, 195, and the estimate of Wilson's speeches by the *Papers of Wilson* editors, ibid., LXIII, vi–xi. For accounts of the tour, see Thomas A. Bailey, *Woodrow Wilson and the Great Betrayal* (New York, 1945), 105–130; Dexter Perkins, "Woodrow Wilson's Tour," in Daniel Aaron, ed., *America in Crisis* (New York, 1952), 245–265; and John Milton Cooper, Jr., "Fool's Errand or Finest Hour? Woodrow Wilson's Speaking Tour in September 1919," in John Milton Cooper and Charles E. Neu, eds., *The Wilson Era: Essays in Honor of Arthur S. Link* (Arlington Heights, Ill., 1991), 198–220.

I

During the first week of the tour, the presidential train made overnight trips between cities, and the president usually gave two speeches each day. The second day, September 5, found Wilson in St. Louis. A parade greeted his arrival, and he spoke first at a chamber of commerce luncheon and at night to an audience of 12,000. The next day featured parades and speeches in Kansas City and Des Moines. A day off on Sunday, September 7, gave the president some rest. It also bowed to his and others' strict sabbatarian views. Then came another round of twice-daily parades and speeches in Omaha, Sioux Falls, Minneapolis, and St. Paul. Only when the itinerary took the presidential party across the sparsely settled Great Plains did the pace slacken temporarily. The slower pace came as a relief to Wilson's physician. From the outset of the trip, Dr. Grayson had worried about the strain that the packed schedule would put on his patient. Several times he dissuaded Wilson from speaking at whistle stop appearances. Late-summer heat in the Midwest added to the wear and tear. At Kansas City, the president quipped to reporters after his speech, "I believe I lost at least two pounds." Grayson also noted that Wilson had begun the trip with "a severe headache" that apparently persisted for several days.[4]

Wilson's speeches showed general though not completely consistent improvement in delivery as he got into the swing of the tour. In part, the upswing stemmed from experience. As in his previous campaigns, Wilson took a little time to hit his stride. Starting with the speeches in St. Louis, he tended to stick more closely to a few basic points, mainly explanations of how the League and Article X would work. Wilson also began to speak more often from typed outlines, as he did in most of his better performances on the tour. This need for notes also betrayed, however, a weakening in his previously formidable gifts as an extemporaneous speaker. The improvement in his performance correlated as well with his opportunity to rest. The speech at Omaha, which was one of the most effective ones in this segment of the tour, came right after the Sunday break.[5]

Improved content matched improved delivery in these speeches. As a reasoned explicator of ideas and programs, Woodrow Wilson knew no equal in his time and few equals in all of American history. He put these

4. *Kansas City Star,* Sept. 6, 1919; entry, Sept. 4, 1919, Grayson Diary, in Link, ed., *Papers of Wilson,* LXIII, 3. For other observations on Wilson's health, see entries, Sept. 5, 6, 1919, ibid., 12, 64; and *New York Times,* Sept. 9, 1919.

5. On Wilson's use of typed outlines, see editors' note, in Link, ed., *Papers of Wilson,* LXIII, 42 n. 2.

talents on display once more in his disquisitions on the League and Article X. To the business leaders in St. Louis, he expounded on their stake in the restoration of world trade and the economic rehabilitation of Europe. At Omaha, he compared the international system without Article X to a community with "unsettled land titles." In such a community, he told the Nebraskans, "[a]ll the farmers would be sitting on fences with shotguns." Wilson also told them that the League gave "no absolute guarantee" against war. But, he argued, some guarantee was better than none: "I can predict with absolute certainty that, within another generation, there will be another world war if the nations of the world – if the League of Nations – does not prevent it by concerted action." At Minneapolis, Wilson held up a copy of the treaty, "a great thick volume," and explained "some of the things that it provides for" with short statements that began "It provides" or "It abolishes." The president delivered those statements, eleven in all, in a staccato style that was reminiscent of the Fourteen Points.[6]

Wilson also wanted to move his listeners emotionally. With his salute to the "boys in khaki" at Columbus, the president had shown that he could aim for the heart as well as the head. At Sioux Falls, Wilson called attention to the mothers who had lost their sons on the battlefield and whose sacrifices "we are going to redeem." In St. Louis, he warned that the alternative to the League and Article X would be America's going it alone in the world, armed to the teeth, and ruled over "by the only sort of government that could handle an armed nation" – a "Prussian" military despotism. Also in St. Louis, he closed a speech with lines that echoed Rudyard Kipling's well-known poem, "Recessional," and in St. Paul he ended an address with sentences that recalled Bryan's "Cross of Gold" speech. In Kansas City, he declared that he was fighting for a cause "as great as the cause of mankind" and meant "to fight that battle as long as I live. My ancestors were troublesome Scotchmen, and among them were some of that famous group that were known as Covenanters. Very well, here is the Covenant of the League of Nations. I am a Covenanter!"[7]

6. Wilson speech in Omaha, Sept. 8, 1919, ibid., 99–102; speech in Minneapolis, Sept. 9, 1919, ibid., 131–132. See also speech in St. Louis, Sept. 5, 1919, ibid., 36–37.
7. Wilson speech at Sioux Falls, Sept. 8, 1919, ibid., 117; speech at St. Louis, Sept. 5, 1919, ibid., 48; speech at Kansas City, Sept. 6, 1919, ibid., 75. One recent commentator, who has found that prediction at St. Louis extremely prescient is Senator Daniel Patrick Moynihan. See Moynihan, *On the Law of Nations* (Cambridge, Mass., 1990), 105–108. Although the comparison is anachronistic, Wilson's declaration at Kansas City is strikingly reminiscent of John F. Kennedy's "Ich bin ein Berliner."

That defiant declaration revived fears among Wilson's advisors and supporters that he would antagonize Republican senators. These emotional appeals also pointed to the danger inherent in impassioned public persuasion. Wilson faced sore temptations to tap base and unattractive sentiments. One such sentiment was a hatred of Germany spawned by the war. League advocates such as Taft and Senator McCumber frequently touted the organization as a means to keep Germany downtrodden. Wilson would occasionally play the anti-German card, but what seems remarkable and creditable to him is how sparingly he resorted to anti-German appeals.

Similarly, rising antiradical and anti-Bolshevik sentiments – which were about to explode into the "Red Scare" – offered another tempting way to sell the League to the public. At Kansas City, Wilson denounced the Bolsheviks' "monopoly of power at Petrograd." He also protested that "I am not comparing any of my respected colleagues to Bolsheviki," but he observed that "the Bolshevik spirit lacks every element of constructive opposition," as did some anti-League elements. That was the closest that Wilson ever came to outright demagoguery. This slur on his opponents may have owed something to the circumstance that he was speaking in the hometown of one of his bitterest and most demagogic opponents, Senator Reed, whom most Democrats regarded as a party traitor. Wilson never again said anything like this about his opponents. He would later make a few additional anti-Bolshevik remarks, but here, too, what is noteworthy is how little he resorted to such appeals.[8]

Other omissions in his speeches were less salutary. Wilson still seemed unwilling to engage the main issues that his critics and opponents had raised. At St. Louis he talked about Shantung again, and at Omaha he admitted that personally he did not like the cession to Japan. But, he argued, "[w]e can't sign the treaty with the Shantung provision out of it, and, if we could, what sort of service would that be doing China?" Also at Omaha, he called a reservation "an assent with a 'but,'" and he dismissed the ones regarding the Monroe Doctrine and domestic questions as unnecessary. He also maintained that the other reservations would require renegotiating the treaty with other powers, including Germany. Wilson likewise failed to reach out to senators or suggest possible areas for compromise. The only time on the entire tour that he mentioned any senators by name occurred in Omaha. There, he declared "how proud I have been to stand alongside of Senator Hitchcock in this fight. I would be just as glad to stand by Senator Norris if

8. Wilson speech at Kansas City, Sept. 6, 1919, in Link ed., *Papers of Wilson*, 73.

he would let me." Otherwise, with one clear and two possible exceptions, Wilson let senatorial friends, foes, and fence sitters alike go unmentioned when he spoke in their states. He made the one clear exception in St. Paul. Without naming them, he exempted Minnesota's two Republican mild reservationists, Kellogg and Nelson, from a blanket charge of ignorance about the League. His only move toward reaching out to Republicans was repeated eschewal of partisanship. "Forget that I am a Democrat," he said in St. Louis. "Forget that some of you are Republicans. Forget all about that. That has nothing to do with it."[9]

Whether those gestures cut much ice on Capitol Hill is doubtful. Estimates of the tour's impact varied widely. His critics and opponents scoffed at Wilson's efforts. A week into the tour, Lodge told a friend, ". . . the President's trip is evidently a failure. People go to hear him because he is the President, but he is making no effect on anyone." Conversely, supporters put the best face on the tour. The LEP's Washington lobbyist reported to headquarters: "So far Senators are receiving more despatches than they expected to on the President's speeches and many less on Irish protest," which he thought might well stir up "a back fire on the Senate Chamber." Taft gave probably the most balanced assessment when he noted privately that the tour was "rousing partisan opposition, but it is focusing the attention of the public on the treaty, and I think it is going to create a sense of impatience at the delay." Ironically, the best testimony to how well Wilson was attracting public attention came from Lodge. He wrote to an anti-League activist about a move in the Foreign Relations Committee: "Our reservations made a hit and shared the front page with Wilson."[10]

The tour's success in generating publicity was no accident. The presidential train carried twenty-one newspapermen, including such ace political reporters as Charles Grasty and Walton Bean of the *New York Times,* Louis Seibold of the *World,* and David Lawrence of the *Evening Post.* There were also five wire service correspondents and one each from such papers as the *Chicago Tribune,* Philadelphia *Public Ledger,* and Louisville *Courier-Journal.* Whenever the train reached a city, local reporters and photographers joined in covering the visit. Between stops, Tumulty circulated regularly among the correspondents, most of whom

9. Wilson speech at Omaha, Sept. 8, 1919, ibid., 101–102, 107; speech at St. Paul, Sept. 9, 1919, ibid., 50; speech at St. Louis, Sept. 5, 1919, ibid., 50.
10. Lodge to Walter V. R. Berry, Sept. 11, 1919; Lodge to James T. Williams, Jr., Sept. 6, 1919, ibid.; Talcott Williams to Short, Sept. 7, 1919, Lowell Papers; Taft to Short, Sept. 10, 1919, LEP Papers. Cf. Taft to Karger, Sept. 10, 1919, Taft Papers, reel 212.

he knew well. Wilson also sometimes came forward to the club car to talk with the press contingent. On September 10, as the train crossed North Dakota, he enunciated to reporters "fundamental principles" of the peace settlement. He expressed those principles in "ten points," such as "the substitution of public discussion and arbitration for war, using the boycott rather than arms," "disarmament," and "the liberation of oppressed peoples." Likewise, Wilson lightened the burden that he put on reporters by not speaking from prepared texts. As soon as he finished a speech, his stenographer, Charles Swem, produced an official transcript, which was immediately mimeographed and distributed.[11]

Comparably elaborate arrangements ensured that the president's utterances reached as broad an audience as possible. Tumulty and the LEP provided texts of the speeches, printed in readily usable formats, to be furnished to 1,400 small daily newspapers throughout the country. This distribution system cost an estimated $1,000 a day and totaled $41,000 for the whole tour. Most of the money to finance the effort came from the multimillionaire automobile magnate Henry Ford – who was a peace advocate, League supporter, and recent Democratic senatorial candidate. Tumulty also kept the telegraph wires from the train humming with requests for information to use in Wilson's speeches and for reports on conditions back in Washington. He even arranged a special code for messages to him from Gus Karger, Taft's man in the capital. Tumulty similarly tried to compensate for Wilson's not mentioning senators in the speeches by telegraphing occasional personal messages from the president to selected senators when the president was in their states.[12]

Opponents of the League strove to offset the presidential edge in publicity by using a variety of public forums. On the Senate floor, critical and opposing speeches outnumbered those supporting Wilson two-to-one. Borah charged that the major powers were "building up the greatest armament that the world has ever known" in order to pursue their imperialistic projects throughout the world. Norris spun an acidic fable titled "The Troubled Community" about a bunch of farmers:

11. *Billings* (Montana) *Gazette*, Sept. 11, 1919, in Link, ed., *Papers of Wilson*, LXIII, 163. On the arrangements about the train, see also entry, Sept. 3, 1919, ibid., LXII, 626–627; *New York Times*, Sept. 9, 1919.
12. On the finances, see Short to Louis Liebold, [Sept. 1919], LEP Papers; Short to Taft, Sept. 22, 1919, ibid.; H. N. Rickey memorandum for Tumulty, [Sept. 1919], ibid.; Herbert S. Houston to Taft, Sept. 6, 1919, Taft Papers, reel 212. On the code arrangement, see Karger to Taft, Sept. 13, 1919, ibid. For a telegram to a senator, see Wilson to Henry L. Myers, [ca. Sept. 11, 1919], in Link, ed., *Papers of Wilson*, LXIII, 197.

"Mr. Jap" stole land from his peaceful neighbors, "Miss Korea" and "John Chinaman," while the other big farmers, "John Bull," "Mr. French," and "Miss Columbia," excused the thievery. Poindexter also dismissed the need for the League. The world war had been, he maintained, "a special occasion. . . . Such a European emergency, threatening civilization and menacing the independence of the United States, is not likely to arise again for 50 years." Wilson's supporters got in a few licks, too. Hitchcock contrasted Knox's newfound solicitude for Germany with his wartime demands for crushing defeat and unconditional surrender. McCumber pleaded once more for sensible reservations, especially one that would not eviscerate Article X. Williams scorned Lodge's "cool, diabolical insolence" and indulgence in "opera bouffe Americanism."[13]

One speech by a Republican senator during the president's speaking tour outshone all others in importance and attention. It came from Lodge, and it was more than just a speech. Such remarks as Lodge's earlier crowing about sharing the front page and Williams's slurs on "insolence" and "opera bouffe Americanism" sprang from the measures that the majority on the Foreign Relations Committee were adopting. On September 10, Lodge presented forty-five amendments and four reservations in the form of a Senate Report. Reading the report to the Senate, he scoffed at the "unthinking outcry" for the League. He warned against the influence of "certain great banking firms which had a pecuniary interest" in the terms of the treaty, and he praised these amendments. Nothing, Lodge insisted, "is more groundless than the sedulously cultivated and constantly expressed fear that textual amendments would require a summoning of the conference, and thereby cause great delay." One amendment, he explained, was intended to equalize American voting rights in the League assembly with those of the British Empire. The five amendments that related to Shantung expressed the committee's unwillingness to be associated with "what they consider a great wrong." Most of the other amendments would relieve the United States from participation in international commissions that involved no American interests.[14]

Because the prospects for passing amendments were doubtful, greatest interest centered on the four reservations that the committee also adopted. The Republicans, minus McCumber, had adopted those reser-

---

13. *Congressional Record,* 66 Cong., 1st Sess. (Sept. 3, 1919), 4726–4731, 4896–4902; (Sept. 5, 1919), 4960–4963; (Sept. 8, 1919) 5024–5031; (Sept. 11, 1919), 5232–5236. The exact distibution of speeches was seventeen against, eight in favor.
14. Ibid. (Sept. 10, 1919), 5113.

demonstration had been seen there since Roosevelt[']s time. We made the news."[18]

The senators did make news. Johnson found reporters traveling with him for the rest of his tour. At Kansas City, he attracted a crowd estimated at 18,000; Borah drew big, enthusiastic audiences in Nebraska and Iowa, and Reed did the same in Oklahoma and Arizona. The lion's share of the trailing of Wilson fell to Johnson. He followed the president to the West Coast and remained away from the capital until well into October. Johnson's absence fed well-founded suspicions that he was using the tour as his warm-up for a bid for the Republican presidential nomination. The Independence League and such organizations as the Friends of Irish Freedom advanced big sums of money to pay for tours by these senators and others, including Albert Beveridge and George Wharton Pepper. On another front, Salmon Levinson enlisted the recently imprisoned wartime conscientious objector and civil liberties activist Roger Baldwin to give a series of speeches against the League. How successful these efforts were in counteracting the impact of Wilson's tour is open to question. One historian has argued that they prevented a publicity stampede in favor of Wilson and the League. Lodge agreed. In late September, he retracted his previous doubts and called the Independence League "a first-rate thing."[19]

By that time, the senator could take pride in having inflicted an even heavier blow to Wilson's cause. The blow fell on September 12, at the final hearing held by the Foreign Relations Committee. This was when

18. Johnson to Hiram Jr. and Arch Johnson, Sept. 22, 1919, in Robert E. Burke, ed., *The Diary Letters of Hiram Johnson* (New York, 1983), III. On the inception of the tour, see Johnson to Hiram Jr. and Arch Johnson, Aug. 31, Sept. 3, 1919, ibid.; Borah to James T. Williams, Jr., Sept. 9, 1919, Borah Papers, Box 769; Lee Meriwether, *Jim Reed: "Senatorial Immortal"* (Webster Groves, Mo., 1948), 77–78. On the Chicago meeting, see also *Chicago Tribune*, Sept. 11, 1919, and Max [last name unknown] to Taft, Sept. 14, 1919, Taft Papers, reel 212.

19. Lodge to Sturgis Bigelow, Sept. 25, 1919, Lodge Papers. The estimate of the impact of these efforts is in Ralph A. Stone, *The Irreconcilables: The Fight against the League of Nations* (Lexington, Ky., 1970), 133. On the various efforts, see ibid., 131–133; Louis A. Coolidge to Lodge, Sept. 5, 1919, Lodge Papers; Reed to Beveridge, Sept. 24, 1919, Beveridge Papers, Box 217; John E. Milholland to Levinson, Sept. 24, 1919, Levinson Papers, Box 33, Folder 9; Levinson to Meriwether, Oct. 4, 7, 9, 10, 1919, ibid., Box 54, Folder 5.

William C. Bullitt testified. The handsome, socially prominent twenty-eight-year-old Bullitt had been among the younger men who had resigned from the American delegation to the peace conference in May. They had protested what they regarded as President Wilson's betrayal of the Fourteen Points and acquiescence in an unjust, imperialistic settlement. Unlike the others, Bullitt had made his protest public, and Walter Lippmann of the *New Republic* had subsequently informed senators Borah and Johnson that Bullitt might give damaging testimony about the doings at Paris. A summons had gone out to Bullitt on August 23, but because he had been fishing for trout in the Maine woods he had received the summons just a few days before the hearing. Although only six senators – all Republicans – were on hand to question Bullitt, a full complement of reporters was present. They had been alerted, probably by Lodge or Brandegee, that something sensational might happen.[20]

The reporters and spectators who anticipated fireworks must have felt let down at first. For more than two of the three hours of Bullitt's testimony, Knox conducted the examination. He led the witness through a leisurely review of how the Draft Covenant had emerged from the work of Wilson, House, Smuts, and Cecil and a recollection of Bullitt's own aborted mission to make contact with the Bolsheviks. In the course of his testimony, Bullitt produced thirty documents that were entered into the record and printed as exhibits. Thus far, little of what he said or supplied to the committee was noteworthy. The only ammunition that he gave to the president's foes consisted of confirming that others besides Americans had played a big part in shaping the League. He also maintained that Article X was Wilson's main contribution, and he tried to show how far Wilson had been willing to go at one time in an effort to reach an accommodation with the Bolsheviks.[21]

The bombshell burst near the end of Bullitt's testimony. Lodge asked

---

20. On Lippmann's role, see Lippmann to Johnson, Aug. 17, 25, 1919, in John M. Blum, ed., *Public Philosopher: Selected Letters of Walter Lippmann* (New York, 1985), 128–131, and Ronald Steel, *Walter Lippmann and the American Century* (Boston, 1980), 163. On the anticipation of something sensational by Lodge and Brandegee, see entry, Sept. 21, 1919, Anderson Diary.
21. Bullitt's testimony and exhibits are in U.S. Senate, 66th Cong., 1st Sess., Committee on Foreign Relations, Document No. 106, *Treaty of Peace with Germany: Hearings* (Washington, 1919), 1161–1297.

him about his resignation and about disagreements within the delegation. To Lodge's delighted surprise, Bullitt read from a memorandum
that he had written on May 19, immediately after a conversation with
Secretary of State Lansing. Lansing had told Bullitt

> that he, too, considered many parts of the treaty thoroughly bad,
> particularly those dealing with Shantung and the league of nations.
> He said: "I consider that the league of nations at present is entirely
> useless. The great powers have simply gone ahead and arranged the
> world to suit themselves. England and France in particular have
> gotten out of the treaty everything that they wanted, and the league
> of nations can do nothing to alter any of the unjust clauses of the
> treaty except by unanimous consent of the members of the league,
> and the great powers will never give their consent to changes in the
> interests of weaker peoples."

In forecasting the treaty's prospects in the Senate, Bullitt had noted,
"Mr. Lansing said: 'I believe that if the Senate could only understand
what this treaty means, and if the American people could really understand, it would unquestionably be defeated, but I wonder if they will
ever understand what it lets them in for.'"[22]

The publicity impact of Bullitt's revelation exceeded all the hopes of
Wilson's opponents. This recitation of Lansing's anti-League views
appeared on the front page of every major newspaper, beneath big
headlines. Then Lansing's response made matters worse. He was on
vacation at his family home in Watertown, New York, where he issued
a one-sentence statement to the press, "I have no comment to make,"
and immediately left for a fishing trip on Lake Ontario. Meanwhile,
the State Department buzzed with talk and conferences, and William
Phillips, who was acting secretary in Lansing's absence, met with Senator Hitchcock to discuss ways to respond to Bullitt's testimony. For
his part, Lansing continued to stonewall reporters. He now offered the
excuse that he would not comment until he had read the full, official
transcript of the testimony. This ploy backfired. As one administration
loyalist observed, "He [Lansing] lost the value of an instantaneous
statement and left in the public mind the impression that Bullitt's
statements were true – and incidentally did the President and the cause
a great injury." Lansing's problem was, he confided to Undersecretary
of State Frank Polk, that Bullitt's "garbled" account "was founded on
a measure of truth, enough truth so that I would have to explain my

22. Ibid., 1276–1277.

statements as quoted by the little traitor. I could not flatly deny the testimony."[23]

Bullitt's disclosures and Lansing's lack of response also strained the already bad relations between the president and the secretary of state. Wilson got the news about Bullitt's testimony while his train was traveling westward across the state of Washington. Lansing did not contact the president personally for five days. He finally telegraphed his own brief account of the May 19 meeting with Bullitt, whose conduct he called "most despicable and outrageous." This tardy communication evidently infuriated Wilson. Tumulty later recalled that the president summoned him into his private compartment and showed him the telegram. "Read that," Wilson said, "and tell me what you think of a man who was my associate on the other side and who expressed himself to an outsider in such a fashion?" He said that Bullitt's testimony confirmed "suspicions that I have had with reference to this individual. I found the same attitude of mind on the part of Lansing on the other side." What bothered Wilson most, recalled Tumulty, was that these statements "came from a man whom I raised from the level of a subordinate to the great office of Secretary of State of the United States." If he were back in the capital, Wilson also declared, he would fire Lansing at once.[24]

On his side, the secretary was equally bent on getting out. He planned to resign as soon as he got back from his fishing trip, Lansing recorded in his diary, "because the more I have thought of it the more keen has been my mortification as to my treatment at Paris." Nor did he mean to go quietly. Toward the end of September Lansing drafted a letter of resignation that he had privately printed and showed to some cabinet colleagues. In this letter he expressed "the bitter disappointment that I have suffered in the outcome of the negotiations at Paris, at the failure of the Fourteen Points." Wilson's "grave breach of faith" was, he

---

23. New York Times, Sept. 13, 1919; entry, Sept. 21, 1919, Breckinridge Long Diary; Lansing to Polk, Oct. 1, 1919, in Link, ed., *Papers of Wilson*, LXIII, 540. On the discussions at the State Department and with Hitchcock, see William Phillips to Lansing, Sept. 13, 15, 1919, Lansing Papers, Vol. 46; Lansing to Phillips, Sept. 15, 17, 1919, ibid.; Phillips to Lansing, Sept. 18, 1919, ibid., Vol. 47.

24. Joseph P. Tumulty, *Woodrow Wilson As I Know Him* (Garden City, N.Y., 1921), 442. For another description of Wilson's reaction when he received Lansing's telegram, see Breckinridge Long memo., 1924, cited and quoted in Link, ed., *Papers of Wilson*, LXIII, 339 n. 4.

asserted, "very far from the idealism voiced by you that made it possible to put the country into the war. A glorious chance to rearrange the world has been lost." Only Wilson's illness kept Lansing from loosing this blast.[25]

II

The furor over Bullitt's testimony and Lansing's lack of response hit Wilson at a particularly vulnerable moment. At the beginning of the second week of the speaking tour, the presidential party crossed the Great Plains. Because this area was sparsely populated, the train made fewer stops and Wilson was able to get more rest. But Grayson worried about the accumulated effects of fatigue and the recurring headaches. Moreover, the journey across the Plains brought still hotter temperatures, drier air, and higher altitudes. All of these conditions affected Wilson badly. By the time the train reached Montana, he began to suffer from what Grayson called "asthmatic attacks," which clogged his throat and prevented him from sleeping lying down. Wilson had to try to sleep sitting up and could not doze off for more than two hours at a time. Nasal sprays administered every few hours eased the pain in his throat, but the "asthma" and coughing persisted. In fact, Wilson's difficulty in breathing almost certainly stemmed from congestive heart failure caused by his arteriosclerosis. The virtually unrelieved headaches and his difficulty in breathing offered signs of further deterioration in his physical condition.[26]

Wilson's speeches during the second week of the tour sometimes showed the effects of his health problems. When he spoke at Bismarck, he rambled, as he did again the next day at Billings. That evening at Helena he gave his longest and most disjointed speech on the tour, as he meandered on about Article X, reservations, Shantung, and the Monroe Doctrine. Toward the end Wilson shifted abruptly to domestic affairs to make his only public reference to that summer's race riots, expressing "my shame as an American citizen." These lapses may have been what prompted Tumulty to write two memoranda in which he suggested that Wilson lend specificity to his speeches by giving the

25. Entry, Oct. 16, 1919, Lansing Diary; draft letter, [ca. Sept. 27, 1919], Lansing Papers, Vol. 47.

26. See entries, Sept. 10, 25, 27, 1919, Grayson Diary, in Link, ed., *Papers of Wilson*, LXIII, 152, 489, 527; and entry, Nov. 5, 1919, R. S. Baker Diary, ibid., 620. On the likelihood of congestive heart failure, see Bert E. Park, "Woodrow Wilson's Stroke of October 2, 1919," ibid., 640.

numbers of people killed in the war. He also advised mentioning Republicans who had espoused the league idea, particularly Roosevelt, and appealing to the sacrifices that American soldiers had made. In fact, Wilson had closed the speech at Helena by recalling the American cemetery at Suresnes, with "those voiceless graves, those weeping women." He vowed, "My fellow citizens, the pledge that speaks from those graves is demanded of us."[27]

Wilson's performance improved later during this second week. When he spoke at Coeur d'Alene, his only stop in Idaho, and at Spokane, he concentrated mainly on the need to prevent future wars. The League of Nations promised, he declared, "the one chance that has ever been offered to insure the peace of the world" – in his view, "a 98 per cent insurance against war." He also praised Republicans for supporting the League, and he gave specific answers to criticisms, especially of Article X and votes for the British commonwealths. When the presidential party reached the more populous coastal areas of the Pacific Northwest, the pace of the tour reverted to the earlier whirl of parades, receptions, and more frequent speeches. Wilson spoke twice in Tacoma, once in Seattle, and twice in Portland. He also gave interviews to local reporters and went on board ship to review the fleet. As usual, Wilson took Sunday off on September 14, and he enjoyed the longest break of the entire trip as the train traveled all day and night through the sparsely settled regions between Portland and San Francisco.[28]

In one of the speeches at Tacoma, Wilson followed Tumulty's advice. He used figures that the secretary had supplied about deaths in the world war, and he singled out for special praise such Republican leaders of the LEP as Taft. At Seattle, he called Article X "the heart of the pledge that we have made to other nations of the world. Only by Article X can we be said to have underwritten civilization." On reservations, he unbent a bit by conceding, "If all you desire is to say what you mean, no harm can be done by saying it." But he rejected "reservations which give the United States a position of special privilege or special exemption from responsibility among members of the League." At Portland, Wilson rushed through his dire depiction of a militarized America and his defiant self-identification as a Covenanter, and he practically slobbered over age-old dreams of "America as the savior of the world." That evening, in his second appearance, he redeemed himself somewhat.

---

27. Wilson speech at Helena, Sept. 11, 1919, ibid., 180–197. See also Tumulty to Wilson, Sept. 12, 1919, ibid., 221–223.
28. Wilson speech at Spokane, Sept. 12, 1919, ibid., 224–225. On the breaks and respites, see entries, Sept. 14, 16, 1919, Grayson Diary, ibid., 273, 300.

He cooled down, praised the LEP, quoted Lodge's 1915 endorsement of the league idea, and insisted that he did not object to interpretative reservations.[29]

Wilson still declined to mention senators by name. The oversight was particularly glaring in North Dakota. This was the home state of McCumber, who was by far the mildest of the mild reservationists and the strongest Republican advocate of League membership. The slight was almost as conspicuous in Montana, the home state of Thomas Walsh, one of the ablest and staunchest administration loyalists. The president did take implicit jabs at two of his senatorial opponents. He insisted on making a stop in Idaho, in order to show the flag in Borah's state. "I have been amazed," he observed in Coeur d'Alene, "that there are some men in responsible positions who are opposed to the ratification of the treaty of peace with Germany altogether." A few hours later in Spokane, the hometown of the irascible Irreconcilable Poindexter, Wilson quipped, "I have forgotten who it was that said it, but I wouldn't mention his name if I remembered it, that this Covenant was an arrangement for the dominance of the British Empire."[30]

Wilson appealed again to antiradical and anti-German sentiment in some of these speeches, but now with mitigating twists. In Montana, Wilson felt obliged to say something about radicalism, because of the western states' experiences with the IWW. "There is only one way to meet radicalism," he argued at Billings, "and that is to deprive it of food, and wherever there is wrong, there is an abundance of food for radicalism. The only way to keep men from agitating against grievances is to remove the grievances, and as long as things are wrong I do not intend to ask men to stop agitating." Wilson likewise charged again that staying out of the League was to play Germany's game. He warned that the Germans "expect the isolation of the United States to bring about an alienation of the United States and the other free nations of the world, which will make it impossible for the world ever to combine again against such enterprises as she was defeated in attempting." Now, however, Wilson frequently praised those "other free nations." In Seattle, he lauded Belgium and Italy for having fought and bled to "underwrite civilization." He also commended such features of the treaty as

29. Wilson speech at Seattle, Sept. 13, 1919, ibid., 262; speech at Portland, Sept. 15, 1919, ibid., 277–283.
30. Wilson speech at Coeur d'Alene, Sept. 12, 1919, ibid., 212; speech at Spokane, Sept. 12, 1919, ibid., 231. For descriptions of these appearances, see entry, Sept. 12, 1919, Grayson Diary, ibid., 210–211; and G. W. Davis to Borah, Sept. 23, 1919, Borah Papers, Box 768.

the restoration of Poland. Yet he admonished, ". . . without the League of Nations the whole thing is a house of cards. Just a breath of power will blow it down, whereas with the League of Nations it is as strong as Gibraltar."[31]

Wilson also began to sharpen his emotional appeal for the League as the means to prevent another world war. In whistle stop remarks at Mandan, North Dakota, Wilson saluted "the boys . . . who carried their guns with them over the sea. We may think that they finished the job, but they will tell you that they did not; that unless we see to it that peace is made secure, they will have the job to do over again, and, we, in the meantime, will rest under a constant apprehension that we may have to sacrifice the flower of our youth again." In brief remarks during an automobile ride through Tacoma, he noted that children were present. "Our work now," he declared, "is to care for the future, so that the world may be a better place for our children, and to this factor we have given much thought in our plans for peace." At Portland after the Sunday break, Wilson started to merge and build upon these observations. "As I have come along through the country and stopped at station after station," he began his main speech, "the first to crowd around the train have always been little children – bright-eyed little boys, excited little girls. . . . And I thought, as I looked upon them from the car platform, that, after all, it was they to whom I had come to report." He feared that they would face another horrendous ordeal because "the task – that great and gallant task which our soldiers performed – is only half finished."[32]

Wilson also continued to eschew partisanship. He referred to past and present Republican advocacy of the League, and he renewed his disavowals of any personal political stake in the outcome of the League fight. Twice, he made pointed, possibly portentous references to the next presidential election. "I leave the verdict with you," Wilson declared at Spokane, "and I beg my fellow citizens, that you will not allow yourselves for one moment, as I do not allow myself for one moment, as God knows my conscience, to think of 1920 when thinking about the redemption of the world." The following day at Tacoma Wilson further avowed, "I hope there is not a real thoughtful, conscientious

31. Wilson speech at Billings, Sept. 11, 1919, in Link, ed., *Papers of Wilson*, LXIII, 177; speech at Portland, Sept. 15, 1919, ibid., 292; speech at Seattle, Sept. 13, 1919, ibid., 256; speech at Tacoma, Sept. 13, 1919, ibid., 250.
32. Wilson speech at Mandan, Sept. 10, 1919, ibid., 162; speech at Tacoma, Sept. 13, 1919, ibid., 240–241; speech at Portland, Sept. 15, 1919, ibid., 283–284.

person in the United States who will determine his or her opinion about this matter with any thought that there is an election in the year 1920. And, just because I want you to realize how absolutely nonpartisan this thing is, I want you to forget, if you please, that I had anything to do with it."[33]

It is tempting to read those statements as lead-ins to a pledge not to run again in 1920. There is no evidence to suggest that Wilson contemplated such a move. Plenty of sound political considerations militated against any disavowal of third-term intentions – at least not yet. The possibility that he might run again in 1920 was the biggest saber that Wilson could rattle in the ears of friend and foe alike. With Roosevelt gone, no one commanded anything approaching Wilson's stature in the public eye. One of the primary purposes of this speaking tour was to use that stature to awe his opponents and bolster his supporters. Maintaining a solid phalanx among Senate Democrats presented a special challenge because there were persistent reports of possible defections in their ranks. If Wilson had declared himself out of the running in 1920, Democratic senators might have stampeded toward reservations.[34]

Yet why did Wilson come as close as he did to broaching the subject? Was this another instance where a younger, healthier Wilson might have risked a bold gamble? Renunciation of a third term would have rung out like a cannon blast and would have made the Bullitt–Lansing business sound like a popgun. Such a gesture might have had a meliorating, air-cleaning effect on the debate. It could conceivably have put Wilson

---

33. Wilson speech at Spokane, Sept. 12, 1919, ibid., 234; speech at Tacoma, Sept. 13, 1919, ibid., 247.
34. For reports of possible defections among Senate Democrats, see *New York Times,* Sept. 9, 10, 1919; Ashurst statement, *Congressional Record,* 66th Cong., 1st Sess. (Sept. 9, 1919), 5070; Burleson to Wilson, Sept. 13, 1919, in Link, ed., *Papers of Wilson,* LXIII, 266; N. D. Baker to Wilson, Sept. 15, 1919, ibid., 296. Speculation and advice about a third term had inevitably arisen in Wilson's inner circle. At Paris in May, Henry Morgenthau and Mrs. Wilson's secretary, Edith Benham, had both speculated that he might run again in 1920. See entry, May 12, 1919, Edith Benham Diary, ibid., LIX, 74–75. Colonel House, on the other hand, was strongly of the opinion that Wilson would not and should not run again. See entry, May 27, 1919, Oscar Straus Diary, Straus Papers, Box 24. More recently, Wilson's old acquaintance and friendly rival from days as college presidents, Charles William Eliot, had advised Tumulty that the president should tell senators in confidence that he would not run again and then announce it publicly later. See Eliot to Tumulty, July 21, 1919, in Link, ed., *Papers of Wilson,* LXI, 577–578.

in an unassailable bargaining position as the totally disinterested seeker of world peace. Perhaps – perhaps not. Such speculations can never be more than teasing might-have-beens. If Wilson entertained any thoughts along those lines, he shared them with no one. After Tacoma, he made no further references to 1920, and he dropped no more hints about his own intentions until the last day of the tour. In what turned out to be his next to last speech, Wilson again would seem to crack open the door again to this possible approach to resolution of the League fight.

With excitement erupting elsewhere during the second week of the president's tour, it was not surprising that not much happened on the Senate floor. Sherman delivered a predictably bilious excoriation of Wilson once more as "our Executive Don Quixote," who had been bamboozled by Europe's "wily diplomats, grizzled in the ways of this naughty earth." By contrast, McCumber spoke as the lone Republican on the Foreign Relations Committee who had voted against both the amendments and the reservation on Article X. He condemned the committee's report because it contained "[n]ot one word, . . . not a single allusion" about the purposes of the League but substituted "[i]rony and sarcasm . . . for argument." McCumber found the proposed reservation to Article X offensively worded and intended "to take the United States as a power for the peace of the world out of the League entirely." McCumber proposed six substitute reservations, including one on Article X that termed "suggestions" for implementation by the League Council "only advisory" and stated that anything requiring military, naval, or economic measures "can under the Constitution be carried out only by the action of Congress."[35]

As earlier, the most important activity in the Senate was taking place off the floor. Since the beginning of September, the mild reservationists had been talking among themselves and negotiating with Lodge in an effort to find a position that might satisfy all Republican senators. Party leaders outside the Senate weighed in on both sides. Taft plumped for milder reservations, whereas Root and Hays called for ones closer to the committee's version. Lodge enlisted Root to work on several mild reservationists, all of them reportedly beginning to lean toward Lodge's way of thinking. The busiest would-be bargainer and framer of proposed language among the mild reservationists was Kellogg, who met constantly with Lodge and corresponded regularly with Root. Lodge felt pleased with how things were going. "The real trouble is not Kellogg, however," he confided to an anti-League friend; "it is McCumber.

35. *Congressional Record,* 66th Cong., 1st Sess. (Sept. 15, 1919), 5356–5359, (Sept. 16, 1919), 5491–5501.

He is the one who is kicking up all the trouble and although he has accepted three of the reservations he wants a mushy one in place of No. 2 [on Article X]."[36]

In the middle of September, Capitol Hill correspondents reported that all of the mild reservationists, including McNary and McCumber, had reached an agreement with Lodge on that key reservation. Those reports proved premature. McCumber told Taft's agent, Gus Karger, not to "fear precipitate action. There is no agreement." Unfortunately, Taft and the LEP were not giving McCumber as much help as they might have provided. That was because they continued to speak with a divided voice. Privately, Taft was pressing the mild reservationists to compromise, and he continued to criticize the LEP's Washington lobbyists and executive committee, whom he found too pro-Wilson. McCumber, by contrast, urged the LEP not to endorse any reservations, in order to strengthen his hand in resisting the committee's proposals.[37]

McCumber and like-minded Republicans faced an even greater problem in the president's absence from Washington and the nonparticipation of Democratic senators in these negotiations. Another premature report of an agreement between Lodge and the mild reservationists reached Wilson on September 18. A presidential confidant immediately telegraphed the text of a reservation on Article X that was a slightly softened version of the committee's proposal. As soon as Wilson read this, he fired back instructions to tell Hitchcock "that I should regard any such reservation as a practical rejection of the Covenant." In fact, McCumber and several other mild reservationists were still dickering over how far to go in trying to reach an accommodation with Lodge. According to a report by an LEP lobbyist, another of them, Lenroot, "expressed himself as being disappointed and discouraged over the situation. He feels every day the President is out adds to the injury being done the treaty cause. 'It is the greatest mistake he ever made,' he said,

---

36. Lodge to James T. Williams, Jr., Sept. 6, 1919, Lodge Papers. On the negotiations, see Lodge to Root, Sept. 3, 1919, Lodge Papers; Root to Lodge, Sept. 10, 1919, ibid.; Kellogg to Root, Sept. 11, 1919, Root Papers, Box 137; entry, Sept. 21, 1919, Anderson Diary.

37. Karger to Taft, Sept. 17, 1919, Taft Papers, reel 212. For reports of an agreement on reservations, see *New York Times,* Sept. 15, 1919; New York *World,* Sept. 15, 1919. On Taft's estrangement from the LEP, see Taft to Caspar Yost, Sept. 16, 1919, Taft Papers, reel 212; Taft to Short, Sept. 18, 1919, LEP Papers. On McCumber's advice to hold out against reservations, see LEP executive committee minutes, Sept. 20, 1919, Taft Papers, reel 212; McCumber to Edward Cummings, Sept. 25, 1919, Lowell Papers.

[']this tour of his is.'" Democratic loyalists such as Swanson shared that opinion, the lobbyist added.[38]

Meanwhile, on the other side of the continent, Wilson was beginning the third week of his tour. He spent six days in California, including the usual Sunday break. The longest working stop on the trip occurred in and around San Francisco. During the course of two days, Wilson delivered five speeches, attended parades and rallies, and met with local journalists, politicians, and LEP leaders. Grayson did his best to curtail the president's activities because he was increasingly worried about the accumulating effects of strain. Nearly every day the doctor noted "constantly recurring headaches" in his diary, and he also commented on the heat. On the other hand, Grayson had not mentioned "asthma" since the train reached the West Coast. Those omissions may have indicated that lower altitudes were placing less strain on the president's heart. Surprisingly to Grayson, Wilson's health problems did not seem to affect his speeches. In San Francisco, he recorded in his diary, "I had done everything possible to relieve his [headache] pain. He drank a cup of coffee, and then made a splendid address."[39]

Grayson judged Wilson's performances correctly. The speeches that he gave in California were the best of the tour. They ranked among some of the finest of his life. At some appearances he again used notes. He also continued to incorporate information and advice that were supplied by Tumulty and reinforced by the local League supporters with whom he conferred. In San Francisco, Wilson devoted one speech to a careful explanation of the obligation under Article X. He charged that its opponents "want to make it a matter of opinion merely, and not a matter of action." Wilson also explained the Shantung cession as an unfortunate necessity ("I think it ought to be different"), and he praised the Open Door in China as originally a Republican foreign policy. He also chided his opponents for "the alternative that they offer" – which was "that we shall arm as Germany was armed, that we shall submit our young men to the kind of constant military service that the young men of Germany were subjected to." Wilson made his most stirring emotional appeal in a speech at Oakland. Remarking again on "those

38. Wilson to Rudolph Forster, [Sept. 19, 1919], in Link, ed., *Papers of Wilson*, LXIII, 296; Charles D. Warner memorandum to H. N. Rickey, [Sept. 19, 1919], Taft Papers, reel 212. For the telegram to Wilson with the text, see Vance McCormick to Wilson, Sept. 18, 1919, in Link, ed., *Papers of Wilson*, LXIII, 363.

39. Entry, Sept. 17, 1919, Grayson Diary, ibid., 309. See also entries, Sept. 18, 20, 21, 23, Grayson Diary, ibid., 345, 397, 425, 446.

ranks of little children [who] seemed to be my real client," he warned
that "unless we concert measures and prevent it, there will be another
and final war, just about the time these children come to maturity."[40]

Circumstances now conspired to make a speech that Wilson gave at
San Diego on September 19 the finest of the whole tour. The enthusiastic reception that he got in San Francisco elated him, Grayson observed,
especially because the city was Senator Johnson's "stamping ground."
According to the doctor, the tonic effect of this outpouring of support
even offset the president's persistent headache. Wilson also profited
from the rest that he got on the long train ride to San Diego, which
included only three short, nonspeaking stops. In San Diego, the president spoke at an outdoor stadium, before a crowd of 30,000. The
arrangements required him to stand inside a glass enclosure on a raised
platform and speak through a "voice phone" with electric wires running to "megaphones" aimed at the stands. This was an early use of a
microphone and electric amplification. "The President did not relish
this experience," Grayson recorded in his diary. "He said afterwards
that it was the most difficult speech he had ever tried to deliver in his
life. He could not be free and natural because it was necessary that he
remain at one spot talking so that his voice carried directly to the megaphones in front of him."[41]

This handicap did not prevent Wilson from excelling. He sought to
inform his listeners and the American people "as to the real character
and scope of the great treaty of peace," which was to put war out of
business and to overturn autocracy. Wilson affirmed "that the great
heart of humanity beats in this document," and he harked back to the
Republican origins of the league idea, quoting from Roosevelt's and
Lodge's earlier endorsements. He answered various criticisms and
dwelled particularly on the British Empire's six votes in the League
Assembly. This was the subject of one of the Foreign Relations Committee's proposed amendments. It was popularly known, thanks to its

40. Wilson speeches at San Francisco, Sept. 17, 18, 1919, ibid., 311–322,
    323–336, 341–350; speech at Berkeley, Sept. 18, 1919, ibid., 350–352;
    speech at Oakland, Sept. 18, 1919, ibid., 352–361.
41. Entries, Sept. 18, 19, 1919, Grayson Diary, ibid., 340, 369–370. Wilson
    was not alone among orators of his generation in finding this new technol-
    ogy distasteful. The next year, at the Democratic convention in San Fran-
    cisco, Bryan indignantly waved aside the microphone on the speakers' dais.
    As one of his biographers points out, this innovation robbed Bryan of the
    advantage that he had heretofore enjoyed because of his greatest physical
    gift, his powerful voice. See Paolo E. Coletta, *William Jennings Bryan* (Lin-
    coln, Neb., 1969), III, 128, 131.

authorship, as the "Johnson Amendment." If such American protectorates as Cuba and Panama each had a vote in the League Assembly, Wilson asked, "could it reasonably be denied to the great Dominion of Canada?" Or to South Africa, or to New Zealand, or to Australia, "that great independent republic in the Pacific, which has led the world in so many liberal reforms?" Wilson praised Article XI, which allowed members to bring any threat to peace before the League, "for it draws all men together in a single friendly court, where they may discuss their own affairs and determine the issue of justice." He scorned anew reservations that sought "an unjust position of privilege" in the League. "Neither will I be a little American. America, in her makeup, in her purposes, in her principles, is the biggest thing in the world, and she must measure up to the measure of the world."

Wilson closed with another reference to seeing the children who thronged up to his train. "Why, my fellow citizens," he declared, "nothing brings a lump into my throat quicker . . . than to see the thronging children that are everywhere the first, just out of their curiosity and no doubt of glee, to crowd up to the train when it stops. Because I know, if, by any chance, we should not win this great fight for the League of Nations, it would be their death warrant." These children would have to fight "that final war" in which "[t]he very existence of civilization would be in the balance." That would betray the sacrifice of the mothers whose fallen sons

> helped to save the world. And there was that light in the eyes of the boys who went over there, that light of men who have caught the gleam of inspiration of a great cause. The armies of the United States seemed to those people on the other side of the sea like bodies of crusaders come out of a free nation to give freedom to their fellows, ready to sacrifice their lives for an idea, for an ideal, for the only thing that is worth living for – the spiritual purpose of redemption that rests in the hearts of humanity.[42]

This was the rhetorical and emotional apogee of the speaking tour. Wilson stayed close to this exalted point for a while. In a brief after-dinner talk that night in San Diego, he called the League "a parliament of nations at last, where everyone is under covenant himself to do right, to respect and preserve the territorial integrity and existing political independence of the others." The next day in Los Angeles, Wilson revived one of his old arguments when he called Article X "the Monroe Doc-

42. Wilson speech at San Diego, Sept. 19, 1919, in Link, ed., *Papers of Wilson*, LXIII, 371–382. In quoting from Lodge and Roosevelt, Wilson was evidently following a suggestion made by Tumulty on the train earlier in the day. See Tumulty to Wilson, Sept. 19, 1919, ibid., 371.

trine applied to the world." Continuing in that vein, he argued that "entangling alliances" were exactly what the League's opponents "want to lead us back to . . . a day of alliances . . . a day of balances of power." By contrast, the "process of the League of Nations is a process of disentanglement." Wilson also explained the Shantung cession again and defended giving votes in the League to "the great energetic republic of South Africa" and "that stout little commonwealth of Australia." He argued once more that it was "impossible for the United States to be isolated, . . . to play a lone hand." The only choice was "to be either provincials – little Americans – or big Americans – statesmen. You either have to be ostriches with your heads in the sand or eagles."[43]

Wilson lingered a little longer on this height of persuasive power. Another Sunday off the hustings gave him a bit of peace and quiet. The schedule remained light as the train traveled all day Monday, September 22, with just a brief stop at Sacramento. His one extended speech that day came when the train made a two-hour stop at Reno. Evoking the spirit of the frontier, Wilson called the League similarly "forward-looking" and evoked the spirit that had lighted a fire in 1776 that "has consumed every autocratic government in the world, every civilized autocratic government. And now at last the flame has leaped to Berlin, and there is the funeral pyre of the German Empire."[44]

From there the speaking deteriorated for Wilson. The higher altitudes and drier climate of the Rockies brought a recurrence of his breathing troubles. In Nevada and Utah Grayson noted in his diary that "the irritation in his throat brought coughing spells that interfered greatly with his rest, [and] caused me great concern." Nor was that all that concerned the physician. Wilson's headaches continued without remission,

43. Wilson speech at San Diego, Sept. 19, 1919, ibid., 382–388; speeches at Los Angeles, Sept. 20, 1919, ibid., 400–418. In the Los Angeles speeches, Wilson again appears to have been following Tumulty's advice about subjects to include. See Tumulty to Wilson, Sept. 20, 1919, ibid., 397–398. In the second speech in San Diego, he also may have brushed on the subject of running again when he said, "And, after all, personal remarks are neither here nor there. What does any one of us matter in so great a thing as this?" Ibid., 388.

44. Wilson speech at Reno, Sept. 22, 1919, ibid., 428–441. That Sunday in Los Angeles featured a parade of visitors. Among them was Mary Allen Peck, who had been Wilson's confidant and perhaps lover some years before, in a relationship that had once threatened to create a scandal when Wilson first ran for president in 1912. Also among the president's visitors that day was a Los Angeles businessman and active Democrat named George S. Patton, father of the famous and controversial general in World War II. See ibid., 419 n. 1, 424 n. 3.

while the accumulated fatigue of more than two weeks of constant train travel and the campaign-style schedule struck Grayson as "calculated to exhaust every possible bit of vitality that the President had." The doctor also later claimed to have noticed a yet more ominous sign of physical deterioration in Los Angeles. "Little drops of saliva appeared at the corners of Mr. Wilson's mouth," a friend of Grayson's recorded him saying in 1924. "His lips trembled slightly. The saliva continued. His pallor increased." Those were premonitory symptoms of a stroke. Because Grayson did not write this observation in his diary, the description may have been apocryphal. Still, indications were growing that all was not well with Wilson. A reporter for a Wyoming newspaper who saw the president on September 24 remarked that "the utter weariness showed plainly in deep lines around his eyes."[45]

As earlier in the Rockies, Wilson's speeches soon showed the effects of his deteriorating health. The region's sparse settlement gave him another chance to rest on September 23, since the train did not make a stop until it reached Ogden in the afternoon. There, a telegram arrived to inform the president, this time correctly, of an agreement between McCumber and Lodge on a reservation to Article X. Initially, Wilson took the news calmly. He had Tumulty wire back to the White House instructing a senior staff member to "ask Hitchcock what present status of League situation is and what his advice to the President on the League should be." Wilson also wanted to know, "Who are the Democrats who joined McCumber in the deal?" Immediately afterward, however, in brief remarks during a motorcade in Ogden, he accused his opponents of pro-Germanism. "All the elements that tended toward disloyalty are against the League," Wilson avowed, "and for a very good reason" – staying out of the League would in effect put the United States in cahoots with Germany.[46]

Things got worse as the day wore on. Wilson spoke that evening in Salt Lake City at the Mormon Tabernacle. With 15,000 people packing the unventilated space, Mrs. Wilson recalled the "fetid air . . . unlike anything I have ever experienced." She said that she had nearly fainted and that the president's clothes were drenched with perspiration at the end of the meeting. The speech that Wilson delivered was unquestionably the worst of the whole tour. He began by charging – erroneously –

45. Entry, Sept. 23, 1919, Grayson Diary, ibid., 446; Breckinridge Long memorandum of Grayson conversation, 1924, ibid., 339 n. 4; *Wyoming State Tribune*, Sept. 25, 1919, ibid., 487.
46. Tumulty to Forster, Sept. 23, 1919, ibid., 447; Wilson speech at Ogden, Sept. 23, 1919, ibid., 448. On this telegram and the next two speeches, see the comment of the editors of *Papers of Wilson*, ibid., n. 1.

"Reservations are to all intents and purposes equivalent to amendments." He compounded this error by maintaining that all the signatories to the treaty must agree to reservations, including Germany. Next he read the text of McCumber's and Lodge's proposed reservation to Article X. When the audience applauded, he lashed back, "Wait until you understand the meaning of it, and if you have a knife in your hand with which you intend to cut out the heart of the Covenant, applaud." Wilson recovered sufficient aplomb as he explained that the requirement for unanimity in the League Council and Congress' sole power to declare war would protect the United States from military entanglements. Besides, he argued, common sense ruled out far flung escapades: "If you want to put out a fire in Utah, you don't send to Oklahoma for the fire engine." Still, he maintained, reservations like this one would destroy any moral obligation under Article X and serve to play Germany's game. Wilson closed with vague references to Americans' being "friends of each other as well as friends of mankind," who would bring "the same sort of comradeship and intimacy of spirit and purity of purpose to the counsel and achievements of mankind."[47]

Wilson did such a poor job that even the faithful Tumulty told him, "Frankly your 'punch' did not land last night in Salt Lake City." Tumulty admonished the president to make his points more forcefully. He especially wanted Wilson to stick to the argument that refusal to enter the League wholeheartedly would betray the sacrifices of American boys in the war. Tumulty also drafted a speech for him that likened Article X to Roosevelt's last public statement on international security and appealed to the legacy of that "wise and brave American, who today, had God spared him, would be leading the Republican party." Wilson took some of that advice, and his performance did perk up a bit. He spent the next day mostly resting until the train reached Cheyenne, where a motorcade and a cavalry parade preceded a late-afternoon speech. Wilson charged again that "forces that showed the hyphen during the war" now opposed the League, but he talked more about votes for British commonwealths and the children who "will be sacrificed on the altar" of another world war. Also, following an earlier suggestion of Tumulty's, he warned that "new instruments of destruction" would be used in that war. Most of all, Wilson dwelled on Article X – "That cuts at the taproot of war." He urged reservationist senators, "men whom I

47. Edith Bolling Wilson, *My Memoir* (Indianapolis, 1939), 282; Wilson speech at Salt Lake City, Sept. 23, 1919, in Link, ed., *Papers of Wilson*, LXIII, 449–463. Curiously, Grayson did not comment in his diary on the conditions in the Mormon Tabernacle. See entry, Sept. 23, 1919, Grayson Diary, ibid., 446.

greatly respect," to reconsider what they were proposing: "That we should make no general promise, but leave the nations associated with us to guess in each instance what we were going to consider ourselves bound to do, and what we were not going to consider ourselves bound to do."[48]

Still, Wilson's failing health was becoming apparent to outsiders as well as to his inner circle. As the train moved on, Grayson noted that the president "had a very trying night but his nerve worked overtime." Sheer determination evidently carried him through the two speeches that he gave in Colorado on September 25. He spoke in the morning at Denver and in the afternoon at Pueblo. At the first appearance, Wilson seemed to zigzag on the subject of reservations. He again scorned measures that sought "to give the United States exceptional advantages in the League of Nations, to exempt it from the obligations that the other members assume." There was, he maintained, a "straight-cut line – adoption or rejection. Qualifying adoption is not adoption." Then, in the next breath, he added, "It is perfectly legitimate, I will admit, to say in what sense we understand certain articles. They are perfectly obvious, so far as I can see, but if you want to make the obvious more obvious, I see no objection." Whether Wilson meant to extend an olive branch toward the reservationists was not clear, however, because he immediately reiterated that America could not ask for "special privileges. . . . We must either go in or stay out."[49]

Rambling on among several subjects, Wilson managed to make one of his most powerful emotional appeals on the tour when he once more recalled the mothers and wives and children who flocked to see him. "And I thought," he said, "these are the little people I am arguing for. These are my clients." Think, the president implored his audience, what another world war would be like. The last war, he stated, "is not to be compared with the one we would have to face next time. There were instruments possessing methods of destruction inconceivable, which were just ready for use when the war ended – great projectiles which guided themselves, capable of one hundred miles or more, and bursting tons of explosives on helpless cities." The weapons of the last war were "toys as compared with what would be used in the next war." Wilson asked if any soldier from the war "wants to go through any hell like that again. That is what the next war would be. And that is what would

48. Tumulty to Wilson, Sept. 24, 1919 [two letters], Tumulty Papers, Box 50; Wilson speech at Cheyenne, Sept. 24, 1919, in Link, ed., *Papers of Wilson*, LXIII, 467–482.
49. Entry, Sept. 25, 1919, Grayson Diary, ibid., 487; Wilson speech at Denver, Sept. 25, 1919, ibid., 493–494.

be the destruction of mankind. And I am for any kind of insurance against it and the barbarous reversal of civilization."[50]

Wilson concluded with two important but ambiguous arguments. One was a reminder that the final decision on a treaty rested, not with the Senate – which gave advice and consent – but with the president – who actually ratified the document. "When the Senate has acted," Wilson warned, "it will be up to me to determine whether its action constitutes an adoption or rejection." He softened the threat by also insisting, "I do not wish to do injustice to the processes of any honest mind." Then he further mixed his message by closing with remarks about "election time" and how it would be "easy for applause to go to the head, it is easy for applause to seem more than it is." For his own part, however, Wilson protested, "I thank God, on this occasion, the whole issue has nothing do with me." Rather, the issue was "so big that it transcends all party and personal interests. . . . We ought, above all else, to forget that we ever divide ourselves into parties when we vote. We are all democrats because we believe in a people's government, and what I plead for is nothing less than a people's peace." This was the first reference that Wilson had made to 1920 and his own possible prospects since he had spoken at Tacoma twelve days earlier. Once more, whether he meant to convey anything more than standard disdain for petty partisanship is not clear.[51]

The last speech of the tour came that afternoon at Pueblo. All day, Wilson had a splitting headache. It was so bad, Grayson recorded, "that he could hardly see." Mrs. Wilson recalled that he told her as he mounted the speakers' platform at Pueblo, "This will have to be a short speech." Instead, he gave a long address that was one of his best performances of this part of the tour. Wilson again declared that "any man who carries a hyphen carries a dagger that he is ready to plunge into the vitals of this republic," but he urged everyone to "sweep aside all this language of jealousy. Let us be big enough to know the facts and welcome the facts." Adopting Tumulty's suggestion, he quoted Roosevelt on the need for organized peace, and he equated Roosevelt's argument with his own stand on Article X. On its obligations and on the League

50. Ibid., 494–495.
51. Ibid., 499–500. The complete text of the speech is in ibid., 490–500. The phrase "we are all democrats" was a paraphrase of Jefferson's declaration in his first inaugural, "We are all federalists, we are all republicans." The auditorium where Wilson spoke was the place where the Democratic national convention had met in 1908 and nominated Bryan for the last time. Wilson never mentioned Bryan or any other Democrat except Senator Hitchcock by name on the tour.

Covenant generally, he continued to insist that "we have got to adopt or reject it. There is no middle course. You cannot go in on a special-privilege basis of your own." As the alternative to the League, he once more painted a picture of a militarized America, and he recalled the scene at the cemetery at Suresnes on Memorial Day. He wished that his opponents could "visit such a spot as that. I wish that the feeling which came to me could penetrate their hearts." For emotional impact, Wilson should have stopped there. Instead, he went into a discussion of the League's machinery for delay of disputes, and he ended with an evocation of the American people's having seen "the truth of justice and of liberty and of peace. We have accepted that truth, and we are going to be led by it, and it is going to lead us, and, through us, the world out into the pastures of quietness and peace such as the world has never dreamed of before."[52]

Those words at Pueblo later acquired special significance. They were not only the last words that Wilson spoke on this journey, but they were also the last extended public utterance of his life. They became the closing lines of one of the greatest speaking careers in American history. To say that Wilson had inklings of finality when he spoke that day seems fanciful, but he did seem to make a special effort that day in Colorado. The tour's itinerary projected five more stops with major addresses in Wichita, Oklahoma City, Little Rock, Memphis, and Louisville, but the appearances in those cities never came off. At Pueblo Grayson noted that Wilson "was very tired and suffering as he entered the [train] car." About twenty miles out of town, Grayson ordered the train to make a stop so that the president could take an hour's walk. On the walk Wilson shook hands with a farmer and climbed over a fence to talk with a young soldier. The respite seemed to do him good, and Grayson noted that at dinner that evening he ate better than he had done for several days. Wilson insisted upon staying up until 10 o'clock for a stop at Rocky Ford, but Grayson prevailed upon him not to go out on the platform.[53]

At two in the morning, Mrs. Wilson called for Grayson. The doctor recorded in his diary that he found the president "unable to sleep and in a highly nervous condition, the muscles of his face twitching, and he

52. Entry, Sept. 25, 1919, Grayson Diary, ibid., 489; Edith Wilson, *My Memoir*, 283; Wilson speech at Pueblo, Sept. 25, 1919, in Link, ed., *Papers of Wilson*, LXIII, 500–513.

53. Entry, Sept. 25, 1919, Grayson Diary, ibid., 487–490. Daniel Patrick Moynihan judges the speech at Pueblo "as moving as anything in the language of the American presidency" and calls it "[a] speech from the cross." Moynihan, *On the Law of Nations*, 52, 53.

was extremely nauseated." Wilson was also having "a very bad asthmatic attack – the worst that he had on the trip. For a few minutes it looked as if he could hardly get his breath." Grayson did what he could to relieve the president's pain and get him to sleep, and he felt obliged to tell him that he should call off the trip. Wilson protested, insisting that he would be better in the morning, and finally he went to sleep. "That night was the longest and most heart-breaking of my life," Mrs. Wilson later wrote.[54]

Grayson wanted to cancel the rest of the tour because Wilson was plainly exhausted and suffering from great pain. Whether the doctor yet suspected that the president was in danger of suffering a stroke is not clear. At some point, probably that night or soon afterward, he noticed something related to what he subsequently recalled having seen in Los Angeles. The doctor did not record this observation at the time, either, but a few weeks later Ray Stannard Baker wrote in his own diary after a visit to the White House, "Coming east one day the doctor saw a curious drag or looseness at the left side of his mouth – a sign of danger that could no longer be obscured." That may have been a sign of what neurologists call a "transient ischemic attack," a blockage in the arteries in or to the brain that prefigures a major stroke. Grayson was not a neurologist, and he did not use the word "stroke" then or ever in his diary. But he did send out an urgent summons to Dr. Francis X. Dercum, who was one of the country's leading neurologists and the specialist who had treated Wilson in 1906 when he had suffered a circulatory blockage that had left him partially blind in one eye. Dercum was scheduled to examine the president at the White House on October 3.[55]

That night on the train, according to Grayson's diary, he waited until the president was asleep. Then he woke Tumulty to tell him that the rest of the trip had to be canceled. After Wilson awoke, the doctor went back to his compartment, where he found the president shaving and expecting to go through with the appearance at Wichita. A long argument ensued. Grayson kept insisting that for the president to continue "might prove fatal." Eventually, Wilson conceded, "If you feel that way about it, I will surrender." Grayson thereupon summoned Tumulty to make arrangements to call off the remainder of tour. At this point, Wilson broke down and said to Tumulty, "I don't seem to realize it, but I

54. Entry, Sept. 26, 1919, Grayson Diary, in Link, ed., *Papers of Wilson*, LXIII, 518; Edith Wilson, *My Memoir*, 284.
55. Entry, Nov. 5, 1919, Baker Diary, in Link, ed., *Papers of Wilson*, LXIII, 620. On the question of whether Wilson was suffering a transient ischemic attack or severe, uncontrolled hypertension, see Park, "Wilson's Stroke," ibid., 641–642.

have gone to pieces. The Doctor is right. I am not in condition to go on. I have never been in a condition like this, and I just feel as if I am going to pieces." Then, Grayson recorded, the president looked out the window, choked up, and began to cry.[56]

When the train pulled into Wichita, Tumulty told reporters and the reception committee that the president was suffering from "a nervous reaction in his digestive system" and the rest of the tour was being suspended on doctor's orders. The party waited while the railroad put on a new engine and arranged for the tracks to be cleared. Then the train made a straight run of 1,700 miles back to Washington. During this last part of the trip, Wilson stayed in his compartment. He continued to suffer badly from nausea, coughing, and sleeplessness. Because the train was moving so fast, the president's private car at the end swayed and rocked severely, adding to his discomfort. Twice, Grayson had to order railroad officials to slow the train down, and on the last leg of the trip the doctor demanded that the speed could not go over twenty-five miles an hour. Finally, on Sunday, September 28, Wilson's journey ended. A photograph taken on his arrival at Union Station told the story of what had happened when it showed the left side of his face drawn and his mouth fixed in a haggard grimace. There is no record that Alice Roosevelt Longworth was there to see this spectacle. If she had been, she would certainly have thought that her evil eye and "murrain" had worked on Wilson. The presidential limousine whisked him away to the White House, where Grayson prescribed complete rest and seclusion until the neurologist could come to examine him.[57]

Even without foreknowledge of the impending stroke, it was painfully clear that the speaking tour had taken a terrible toll on Wilson. The price that he was paying revived the question of whether he had been wise or foolish to make this journey. At the time, assessments of the public response to Wilson on his journey differed widely. Critics and opponents tended to downgrade both the president's performance and how people reacted to it. Pro-Leaguers gave him high marks and stressed how warm his reception was. Perhaps the most balanced assess-

56. Entry, Sept. 26, 1919, Grayson Diary, ibid., 518–519. There are also accounts of the events of this night in Edith Wilson, *My Memoir*, 283–286, and Tumulty, *Wilson as I Know Him*, 446–448. Mrs. Wilson's account generally agrees with Grayson's Diary, but the accuracy of Tumulty's account is doubtful especially because he claims that Wilson was paralyzed on his left side that night. The paralysis did not occur until Wilson suffered his stroke on October 2.

57. Tumulty statement, Sept. 26, 1919, in Link, ed., *Papers of Wilson*, LXIII, 520; entries, Sept. 27, 28, 1919, Grayson Diary, ibid., 527, 532–533.

ment came from Secretary of War Newton Baker, who noted privately at the end of the tour:

> He seems to have been received with very great enthusiasm and to have had every evidence given him of the popularity of the treaty and the covenant, but I do not believe, so far as I can discover from the talk here, that his work among the people has had any effect one way or the other upon the Senate. As one of the Senators said to me the other day, "Nearly every Senator has from four to six years yet to serve, and they are perfectly willing to let future events cover up any present disapproval of their course of action."[58]

In the eight decades since Wilson made the tour, most interpreters have seconded that assessment. Many have carried it further still, to argue that he went on a fool's errand and brought back little or nothing to show for it. Plenty of fault can be found. Failure to target senators for praise or criticism and the often scattered and weakened arguments in the speeches undeniably diminished the tour's effectiveness. Wilson's declining health likewise clearly affected his performance. This was his first foray onto the hustings in three years, and the contrast between then and now was sometimes startling. Yet when those faults and shortcomings are accounted for, Wilson still acquitted himself well. Taken together, these speeches presented the most compelling case for his side made during the whole League fight. Wilson answered the main criticisms that had been advanced against the treaty – particularly Article X, the Shantung cession, and British Empire votes. Moreover, he had repeatedly delivered deeply moving appeals to save the next generation, today's children, from the horrors of another, more terrible world war. He had occasionally stooped to base appeals, such as when he raised the specter of Bolshevism, cast aspersions on his opponents' motives, and tapped veins of leftover enmity toward Germany. Yet what was

58. Baker to Hugh C. Wallace, Sept. 27, 1919, N. D. Baker Papers, Box 11. Earlier, Senator Ashurst had agreed: "A President who essays a speaking trip is assured of an audience, but W. W. has made no converts to the Treaty." Entry, Sept. 12, 1919, Ashurst Diary, in George F. Sparks, ed., *A Many-Colored Toga: The Diary of Henry Fountain Ashurst* (Tucson, Ariz., 1962), 105. For some of the varying assessments, see David T. Hoag to Taft, Sept. 8, 1919, Taft Papers, reel 212; Caspar S. Yost to Taft, Sept. 10, 1919, ibid.; Robert M. La Follette, Jr., to Philip and Belle La Follette, Sept. 8, 1919, La Follette Papers, Box A 26; Thomas W. Lamont to Wilson, Sept. 10, [1919], in Link, ed., *Papers of Wilson*, LXIII, 165; Dorothy Black to Senator and Mrs. Lenroot, Sept. 20, 1919, Irvine L. Lenroot Papers, Libary of Congress, Box 26; Lawrence Y. Sherman to Elmer Youngman, Sept. 25, 1919, Lawrence Y. Sherman Papers, Illinois State Library, Box 62.

noteworthy was not how often but how seldom Wilson strayed onto those low roads. If this was not his finest hour, it was one of the noblest moments of his life.[59]

This tour in September 1919 represented the most extensive effort at public persuasion that any president has ever made on behalf of a foreign policy. True to his fundamental conception of democratic leadership, Wilson was attempting to educate people. He sought to inform them and draw forth thoughtful support from them. The main flaws in this effort stemmed from health, timing, technology, and follow-through. It is interesting to speculate about how he might have done if he had been younger and stronger, or how this tour would have gone over if he had made several smaller ones at earlier stages in the League fight. Also, as the encounter with the microphone in San Diego showed, a technological breakthrough was just around the corner. Thomas A. Bailey and others have wondered whether Wilson could not have rallied greater public support at far less cost to himself if radio had been available to him. Something like the "fireside chats" that Franklin Roosevelt developed only a decade later might have proven a singularly effective means for making a case for the League.[60]

In the final reckoning, any assessment of what Wilson accomplished on his tour comes back to what happened next. One of the newspaper correspondents on the trip, Grasty of the *New York Times,* told a friend soon afterward "that the President would have produced an enormous effect if he had continued." Grasty was probably referring both to the rest of this tour and to another one planned for the Northeast in October. Even without another tour, a ringing return from this tour would have given Wilson a great psychological lift. There was always the danger that the echoes of the cheering on the tour would renew his intransigence in dealing with the Senate. But there was also the chance that those demonstrations of public support would give him the leeway to work out a face-saving compromise on Article X – which now stood out unmistakably as the key to any accommodation. Even in his irascible and weakened state in the last speeches, he had not completely rejected reservations, and Tumulty privately told Gus Karger "that at no time has the President been opposed to 'clarifying reservations.'" Likewise, the renewed hint about his own prospects in 1920 may have pointed toward a possible trade-off. But any such possibilities depended

59. This assessment differs somewhat from my earlier one in "Fool's Errand or Finest Hour?" in Cooper and Neu, eds., *The Wilson Era,* 198–220. See also "Introduction," in Link, ed., *Papers of Wilson,* LXIII, vi–xi; and Park, "Wilson's Stroke," ibid., 640, 646.

60. See Bailey, *Wilson and the Great Betrayal,* 104.

upon there being a Wilson who could play an active part in the rest of this round of the League fight. This was not to be.[61]

III

Back in Washington, events had not stood still during the latter part of the president's tour. Appearances by anti-League senators tapered off. This was in part because Lodge, acting in his capacity as majority leader, sent out a message on September 18 urging all Republicans to be present for impending votes on the Foreign Relations Committee's amendments to the treaty. All the main Republican speakers honored the summons, as did Reed. When the votes were delayed, however, Johnson took off again, much to the annoyance of his fellow senators. The Independence League continued to send out other speakers, but those efforts did not come close to matching the president's tour in their impact. For his critics and opponents, the locus of action shifted back to Capitol Hill, both on and off the Senate floor.[62]

The pace of speechmaking picked up bit. Of the ten senators who spoke about the League and the peace settlement, eight were critics or opponents. Borah attacked the LEP and other internationalists, whom he blamed for such domestic troubles as the bombings of the homes of public officials the previous May and the wave of lynching of African Americans in the South. He charged that "underlying this condition of discontent and restlessness is . . . an utter absence of true Americanism." Why Borah stooped to such uncharacteristic demagoguery is not clear. He may have felt rattled at the prospect of a compromise that would put America in the League. Likewise, Reed showed once more that no one in the Senate, with the possible exception of Sherman, could hurl harsher vituperation at Wilson. "He hears the echo of his own voice," Reed sneered, "and the next day proclaims them the voice of God." Reed warned again that a majority of the members of the League "belong to the dark-skinned races" and would be able to "vote for race equality." As for Wilson's prediction of another world war, Reed scoffed, "I am not scared about this thing." This speech caused quite a

61. Gilbert Parker to Theodore Marburg, Dec. 18, 1919, in Latane, ed., *Development of the League Idea*, II, 61; Karger to Taft, Sept. 30, 1919, Taft Papers, reel 212.

62. Lodge's message is in Lodge and Charles Curtis to "Senator," Sept. 18, 1919, Lodge Papers. On the senators' ill feelings toward Johnson, see Karger to Taft, Sept. 30, 1919, Taft Papers, reel 212; and on the concern of pro-League leaders, see McAdoo to Tumulty, Sept. 30, 1919, McAdoo Papers, Box 526.

stir, in part because the anti-League organizations had again packed the galleries with cheering, foot-stamping, handkerchief-waving spectators. Several members of the House also came over to hear Reed, including the grizzled Republican former speaker, "Uncle Joe" Cannon, who reportedly claimed that he had just heard "the greatest forensic effort that has resounded since the days of Webster and Calhoun." Apart from the speech's length – over four hours – it was hard to see what prompted Cannon's claim.[63]

Some Democrats denounced Republican tactics in considering the treaty, and Lodge heatedly denied allegations that he was abetting a filibuster of the treaty. His denial smacked of disingenuousness. Both Lodge and his Democratic opponents resorted to delaying tactics during the last days of Wilson's tour. This was because the wheeling and dealing off the Senate floor had grown tense and complicated. Lodge was still striving to draw all of his Republicans and possibly a few Democrats together behind a common front of reservations and perhaps some amendments. The task required him to talk out of both sides of his mouth, or at least to give the appearance of doing that. There were conflicting reports about whether he really wanted to see amendments adopted. Henry Stimson recorded in his diary that Lodge had told Root "that the amendments were reported mainly to please their respective proponents, and that Lodge expected that they would be defeated in the Senate, and that the only things that would pass were the four reservations." Yet Lodge urged his former Senate colleague from Massachusetts, John W. Weeks, to lobby several of their fellow Republicans in favor of the Johnson amendment. "How anyone can vote against it passes my comprehension," Lodge asserted. ". . . There is literally no argument that can be made in favor of giving Great Britain six votes to our one."[64]

The Johnson amendment and the reservation to Article X dominated the behind-the-scenes discussions. "I personally went over this reservation to Article 10 again and again with groups of Senators and with individual members," Lodge recalled later. On September 21, he achieved a breakthrough when he invited McCumber to lunch at his house. "After much discussion he and I agree upon the reservation in the form in which it was presented to the Senate and finally adopted." It was this version that informants immediately communicated to the

63. *Congressional Record*, 66th Cong., 1st Sess. (Sept. 22, 1919), 5700–5716; (Sept. 29, 1919), 6076–6080; Meriwether, *Jim Reed*, 89–90. See also *New York Times*, Sept. 23, 1919; New York *World*, Sept. 23, 1919.
64. Entry, Sept. 26, 1919, Stimson Diary; Lodge to Weeks, Sept. 22, 1919, Lodge Papers.

president. These informants also reported that McCumber, McNary, Nelson, Lenroot, Colt, and Kellogg – virtually the entire mild reservationist cadre – had agreed to it. The text read:

> The United States assumes no obligation under the provisions of Article X to preserve the territorial integrity or political independence of any other country or to interfere in controversies between other nations whether members of the League or not or to employ the military and naval forces of the United States under any article of the treaty for any purpose unless in any particular case the Congress, which has the sole power to declare war or authorize the employment of military and naval forces of the United States, shall by act or joint resolution so declare.[65]

Wilson's impolitic denunciation of this reservation at Salt Lake City infuriated some of the mild reservationists. "Kellogg is so mad that he feels like voting against the entire treaty and for the Johnson amendment," Karger reported to Taft. Kellogg also believed that Wilson was engendering among Republican senators "the thought on the part of some of them that it might be just as well to die for a sheep as for a lamb." One such senator was Reed Smoot of Utah. Smoot felt torn between being a stout party regular and a high-ranking official of his church, the Mormons, which fervently supported League membership. "I had intended to vote against all amendments," Smoot told Karger after Wilson's speech in Salt Lake City. "I shall vote for them now." Speaking on the Senate floor, Lenroot declared that "unless a reservation substantially such as that read by the President is incorporated as part of the ratification resolution, this peace treaty is not, in my judgment, going to be ratified by the Senate." As for himself, Lenroot vowed that in the absence of such a reservation ". . . I shall unhesitatingly vote for the rejection of the treaty."[66]

Wilson did not err in thinking that this reservation posed a grave threat to any obligation under Article X. The reservation sought to reconcile

---

65. Henry Cabot Lodge, *The Senate and the League of Nations* (New York, 1925), 183; William Phillips to Wilson, Sept. 22, 1919, in Link, ed., *Papers of Wilson*, LXIII, 444. See also Breckinridge Long to Wilson, Sept. 22, 1919, ibid., 444–445; Guy Mason to Tumulty, Sept. 22, 1919, ibid., 445; Forster to Tumulty, [Sept. 22, 1919], ibid., 445. The only difference between this text and the final version of the reservation was the last word which, instead of "declare," read "provide."

66. Karger to Taft, Sept. 24, 1919, Taft Papers, reel 212; *Congressional Record*, 66th Cong., 1st Sess. (Sept. 25, 1919), 5912. On Smoot, see Milton R. Merrill, *Reed Smoot: Apostle in Politics* (Logan, Utah, 1989), esp. 251, 265.

opposing viewpoints – Lodge's determination to nullify anything legally or morally binding in American adherence to the article and McCumber's wish to preserve something morally binding – and this version of the reservation tilted heavily, perhaps decisively, in Lodge's direction. McCumber soon had second thoughts. He admitted to Lowell that "the thread that binds us to that side of the question [enforcement under Article X] is somewhat slander [*sic*], and I shall vote for it only as a last resort necessary to secure sixty-four votes for this treaty." Such second thoughts worried Lodge enough that he again enlisted Root in an effort to keep the mild reservationists in line. The reservations were, he insisted to Root, "moderate," and all the Republicans were "very nearly agreed" on Article X. But Lodge claimed to "fear that if we do not make the reservations strong and effective – those of the committee, with perhaps a slight modification in language – the whole treaty will be killed on the floor of the Senate. You do not realize how strong the feeling has grown against it."[67]

Lodge did not exaggerate by much. The immediate danger did not lie in outright defeat of the treaty. Rather, the danger lay in amendments that would require renegotiation of the treaty and in a Democratic rush toward strong reservations. Rumors of possible defections in the ranks of the president's party continued to circulate around Capitol Hill, mentioning Shields of Tennessee, Ashurst of Arizona, Thomas P. Gore of Oklahoma, David I. Walsh of Massachusetts, and Hoke Smith of Georgia. In Smith's case, the stories were true. "Hoke Smith has prepared some [reservations] of his own," Lodge quipped to Root, "but we shall find them 'Hoaxmith (Ha-ha) this will give you pain.'" Wilson's political operatives took these reports seriously. Postmaster General Burleson consulted with Hitchcock and other loyalists in the Senate. Afterward he begged Wilson to say something nice about Shields, when the president was to speak in Tennessee near the projected end of the tour. The situation regarding amendments seemed to change daily. Supporters and opponents alternately claimed that they held the votes to win. At one

---

67. McCumber to Lowell, Sept. 26, 1919, Lowell Papers; Lodge to Root, Sept. 29, 1919, Lodge Papers. The historian who has studied the mild reservationists most closely, Herbert Margulies, has concluded that they were sacrificing any vestige of predicability and universality in what was already a weak collective security system. Margulies has also questioned whether these senators realized how much they were giving away. See Herbert F. Margulies, *Mild Reservationists and the League of Nations in the Senate* (Columbia, Mo., 1989), 106–107, and also Lloyd Ambrosius, *Woodrow Wilson and te American Diplomatic Tradition: The Treaty Fight in Perspective* (New York, 1987), 184–185. On mild reservationists' second thoughts, see also McNary to Taft, Sept. 26, 1919, Taft Papers, reel 212, and entry, Sept. 24, 1919, Breckinridge Long Diary, Box 2.

point, the Democrats evidently considered trying to force a vote on the Johnson amendment, but they backed off and seemed content to drag out the debate until the president returned.[68]

Lodge's summons to Republican senators to come back for a vote on amendments sowed dissension in the Republican ranks. Karger reported to Taft that "the old-line Republicans" had started to realize "that they are permitting Johnson to run away with the Republican party, and said realization is giving them pause." Other Republicans resented Johnson's taking credit for both the amendment and opposition to the treaty, and some were hinting that a reservation on British Empire voting would satisfy them. For his part, Johnson stormed around Capitol Hill in a fury when he found out that a vote on his amendment was being delayed. "I have won this fight in California, to surrender it in the Capitol," he was reported as saying at one point. Johnson blanketed even fellow Irreconcilables with his ire, also reportedly remarking, "You can rest assured of one thing, and that is if Borah and I were crossing the Sahara desert, I'd carry the water flask."[69]

Just before Wilson's tour ended, the Senate took its first vote on a treaty-related matter, and it showed a few straws in the wind. On September 23, Lodge offered a motion to postpone consideration of some other amendments offered by Fall. According to newspaper reports, the Republican leadership did not feel confident about passing either these measures or Johnson's amendment. Lodge's motion carried, 43 to 40, on nearly solid party lines. Of the Democrats, only Reed voted for the motion; all the others, including most of the rumored potential defectors, opposed it. Conversely, among the Republicans, only McCumber joined the Democrats in opposition; all of the other Republicans, including the rest of the mild reservationists, voted for the delay. For Lodge, this was a pyrrhic victory. Given the near certainty of mild reservationist defections, the three-vote margin did not bode well for passage of any of the proposed amendments.[70]

68. Lodge to Root, Sept. 29, 1919, Lodge Papers. See also Burleson to Wilson, Sept. 22, 1919, in Link, ed., *Papers of Wilson*, LXIII, 443; Talcott Williams memorandum, Sept. 23, 1919, Lowell Papers.

69. Karger to Taft, Sept. 28, 1919, Taft Papers, reel 212; T. Williams to Taft, Sept. 28, 1919, ibid. Over two decades' service together in the Senate and common devotion to the isolationist cause never endeared these two great oratorical egotists to each other. Later, when they were fellow members of the insurgent Republican bloc in the 1920s, Johnson coined a memorable putdown of Borah when he called him "our spearless leader."

70. *Congressional Record*, 66th Cong., 1st Sess. (Sept. 23, 1919), 5780. See also *New York Times*, Sept. 24, 1919.

That vote marked the end of the threat of amendments to the treaty. Administration and LEP lobbyists began to issue optimistic private reports on the situation, and newspaper correspondents picked up similar estimates. But this likely victory came at a price. The price was the reservation to Article X that the mild reservationists were joining Lodge in approving. Any further Republican resistance was crumbling. Publicly, Taft continued to urge compromise, but privately he groused about the LEP even more than earlier. Lowell likewise began to find fault with Article X, and he was telling others in the LEP that it differed fundamentally from their own program. Only the president's own party continued to hold out against reservations. The vote on September 23 buried any further talk about substantial numbers of Democratic senators voting for amendments or reservations. What brought them around is not entirely clear. It may have been Wilson's tour itself, which demonstrated his drawing power with the public. Or it may have been his collapse, which gave vivid proof of the sacrifices he was willing to make for what was supposed to be their party's cause.[71]

By the end of September, Senator Swanson was confidently predicting that no Democrats would defect on either amendments or reservations. Democratic senators were also reported to be plotting a strategy for confronting the Republicans. It went this way: With their forty or so votes, they would defeat a resolution of ratification that contained the proposed reservations. Then they would move consent either without reservations or with merely interpretive ones. Finally, if as seemed certain, their resolution was also defeated, the treaty would go back to the president, who would then be in a position to broker a compromise. This was an intriguing scheme, and it was significant that Democratic senators were talking about it at this point in the consideration of the treaty. What they were contemplating was also a recipe for stalemate. Real danger existed that the different sides would become so locked into their respective positions that compromise would prove impossible. Was such stalemate to be the outcome of the League fight? The answer to that question would hinge mainly on the actions of the sick man who had just come back to the White House.[72]

71. For Taft's public advocacy of reservations and compromise, see Philadelphia *Public Ledger,* Sept. 28, 1919; for Lowell's argument, see Lowell to Short, Sept. 27, 1919, Lowell Papers.
72. Swanson's prediction and the Democrats' strategy is reported in *New York Times,* Sept. 30, 1919.

5

Stroke and Stalemate

During the early hours of the morning of October 2, 1919, the dread blow fell. Woodrow Wilson may not have known that anything was wrong with him when he got up from bed. But when he tried to walk to the bathroom, his left leg gave way, and he sank down on the floor in the middle of the bedroom.

As soon as Mrs. Wilson learned what had happened, she summoned Grayson. The doctor found numbness and weakness on the president's left side – a condition that grew worse but finally stabilized as the day wore on. Grayson did not use the word at the time, but he knew that the president had suffered a massive stroke.[1]

After conferring with two other physicians who consulted at the White House, Grayson telephoned Dr. Dercum, the neurologist who was scheduled to examine the president the next day. Grayson asked Dercum to come right away. When Dercum's train arrived from Philadelphia, Grayson met him at the station and briefed him in the car on the way to the White House. Dercum began his examination at 4:20 in the afternoon. As he wrote two and a half weeks later, the neurologist found Wilson's left arm and leg "in a condition of complete flaccid paralysis, [and] the lower half of the left side of the face was drooping." He also detected a loss of feeling on Wilson's entire left side and some loss of vision. Throughout the examination, Dercum noted, Wilson "was conscious though he was somewhat somnolent." He answered

1. See Francis X. Dercum memorandum, [Oct. 20, 1919], in Arthur S. Link, ed., *The Papers of Woodrow Wilson* (Princeton, N.J., 1990), LXIV, 500–50l; Grayson memorandum, ca. Jan. 1920, ibid., 508; entry, Oct. 2, 1919, Irwin H. Hoover Diary, Library of Congress, microfilm reel 3. These accounts of the onset of Wilson's stroke are closest to the event and were written by physicians. In later accounts both Mrs. Wilson and Ike Hoover, the head usher of the White House, claimed that Wilson fell in the bathroom, gashed his face, and lost consciousness. See Edith Bolling Wilson, *My Memoir* (Indianapolis, 1939), 287; and Irwin H. Hoover, "The Facts about President Wilson's Illness," in Link, ed., *Papers of Wilson*, LXIII, 634–635. If Wilson did in fact suffer such a traumatic fall, it seems odd that neither physician mentioned it in his memorandum.

questions "a trifle slowly, but without evident impairment of articulation and the answers were always entirely responsive."[2]

Dr. Dercum's diagnosis on October 2 – which he confirmed nine days later – "was that of a severe organic hemiplegia, probably due to a thrombosis of the middle cerebral artery of the right hemisphere." He ruled out an "ingravescent hemorrhage," because of "the extremely gradual onset, the final arrest of the progress of symptoms, [and] the absence of marked disturbance of respiration and of consciousness." Those words conveyed the neurologist's technical description of a particular kind of massive stroke. When Dercum ruled out an "ingravescent hemorrhage," he was saying that Wilson had not suffered what is commonly called an apoplectic stroke. That type of stroke occurs suddenly, renders the person unconscious, frequently affects speech and reasoning, and is often life-threatening. Instead, according to Dercum's diagnosis, the president had suffered a more common form of stroke. This type of stroke occurs gradually over several hours, leaves the person conscious, and is not in itself life-threatening. Also – as Wilson's alertness in answering questions and unimpaired speech indicated – this kind of stroke does not normally affect a person's intellectual capacity.[3]

Despite those encouraging signs, there was no question that the president was gravely ill. He was paralyzed on his left side, and he suffered from diminished eyesight and double vision. He was unable to leave his bed and unable to pay attention to anything for more than a few minutes. Moreover, these were only the immediately apparent effects of the

---

2. Dercum memorandum [Oct. 20, 1919], in ibid., LXIV, 500–501.
3. Ibid., 503. In his own memorandum, which was probably written three months later, Grayson states, "THE DIAGNOSIS made October 2nd and confirmed at the subsequent examinations was that of a *thrombosis* ["vascular lesion" crossed out] involving the internal capsule of the right cerebral hemisphere." Ibid., 510. The cause of this stroke is a matter of some question among three neurologists who later examined various records. Edwin Weinstein, who did not have these two memoranda available to him but who also interpreted Wilson's earlier medical history, believes that narrowing and blockage of internal carotid arteries caused this stroke and earlier incidents. See Edwin A. Weinstein, *Woodrow Wilson: A Medical and Psychological Biography* (Princeton, N.J., 1981), 141, 163, 357. James Toole and Bert Park, who have examined these memoranda, also lean toward carotid artery occlusion as the likely cause of the stroke, although Park does not rule out a hemmorhage deep within the brain. See Toole to Link, June 12, 1990, in Link, ed., *Papers of Wilson*, LXIV, 505–506; Park to Link, [June 1990], ibid., 506–507.

stroke. Time would tell how extensive and lasting the physical impairment and the emotional and psychological consequences would be.
Unfortunately, too, this stroke occurred at a time when the agenda of
public affairs was groaning under the weight of pressing concerns.
Besides the peace treaty debate, strikes were racking the coal and steel
industries, popular hysteria against radicals was exploding, unemployment was ballooning, and inflation remained rampant. The year 1919
was shaping up as one of the worst in American history, and from this
time on the president would know little or nothing about what was
happening. For the rest of Wilson's term of office, the country would
stumble along virtually without a president. The government's functioning at all would owe much to established routines and to Wilson's collegial style of administration, which had given cabinet officers a largely
free hand in running their departments in domestic affairs.

Foreign affairs would be a different story. Bad blood continued to
fester between Wilson and Secretary of State Lansing in the wake of
Bullitt's testimony before the Foreign Relations Committee. If the stroke
had not intervened, it would have been a toss-up to see who would have
moved faster, Lansing to resign or Wilson to fire him. Instead, for the
next four months the White House would ignore almost daily pleas
from the state department for advice about negotiations and diplomatic
appointments. Worse still, Wilson suffered his stroke at a singularly
inopportune moment in the League fight. Debate and maneuvering had
reached a critical stage on Capitol Hill. Now, however, the major players would have to act in the face of sphinxlike silence from the White
House. This situation would totally alter the complexion of the League
fight – with dire consequences.

I

Wilson's stroke immediately posed two questions: Could he remain in
office? Who would make that decision? The answer to the first question
depended, to an extent, on advice from physicians. The answer to the
second question depended entirely on two circumstances. The first was
who knew the nature and severity of his illness; the second was who
seized the initiative to supply the answer. Neither the Constitution nor
previous experience offered any help. Article II, Section 1, of the Constitution states: "In case of the removal of the President from office, or of
his death, resignation, or inability to discharge the powers and duties of
the said office, the same shall devolve on the Vice President." Before
1919, that provision had sufficed to cover the five times when presidents
had died and vice-presidents had succeeded to the office. In four of those

previous instances the president had died within days or hours after being taken ill or being felled by an assassin's bullet. Only one previous instance seemed to bear any resemblance to Wilson's present incapacity: in 1881, when James A. Garfield had lain bedridden but fully conscious for two-and-a-half months between the time he was shot and when he died. At that time little pressing public business had excited the country, and no question had arisen about whether, how, how long, or by whom Garfield might have been removed from office. Clearly, Wilson's case was going to be different from anything that had happened before.[4]

The one person who does not seem to have had a say about whether he should be removed from office was Wilson himself. No contemporary record or later recollection mentions anyone's broaching to him the subject of his resigning or temporarily stepping aside. On his own accord, Wilson mentioned the possibility of resigning only once. That would happen four months later, when, ironically, he had recovered somewhat. It was no surprise that Wilson did not offer to resign immediately after the stroke. For more than a month, he seemed to be so incapacitated that he could give almost no attention to any public business. The stroke itself was not life-threatening, but two weeks later a probably unrelated prostate blockage developed. This caused an infection and high fever that did appear to imperil his life. Grayson sent out an urgent summons to a leading urologist, Dr. Hugh Young of the Johns Hopkins University School of Medicine, to examine the president and advise about an operation to relieve the blockage. Surgery would have been risky for an exhausted sixty-two-year-old man who had just suffered a massive stroke. Instead, Young recommended continued application of hot compresses. Fortunately, this treatment cleared the obstruction after four days. Wilson's life would not be in danger again, but this added illness left him weaker and less capable of attending to public business.[5]

In any event, Wilson almost certainly would not have contemplated resigning. He was a strong-willed, determined man. Furthermore, like most males of his time and background, he believed in stoic pursuit of duty in the face of setbacks, and he practiced psychological denial of ill-

4. Wilson's case is discussed in the context of both previous and subsequent instances of presidential incapacity in John Milton Cooper, Jr., "Disability in the White House: The Case of Woodrow Wilson," in Frank Freidel and William Pencak, eds., *The White House: The First Two Hundred Years* (Boston, 1994), 75–99.

5. On Wilson's later contemplation of resignation, see Chapter 6. On the prostate blockage, see *New York Times,* Oct. 18, 1919; and editor's note in Link, ed., *Papers of Wilson,* LXIII, 579 n. 1.

ness and infirmity. In the past, Wilson had dealt with illnesses by mini-
mizing them, ignoring them, or wishing them away. He would deal with
this massive stroke the same way. Amazing as it seems, there is no evidence that he ever admitted even to himself that he had suffered a
stroke. Moreover, despite his one-time flirtation with the idea of resigning, Wilson would later entertain fantasies about being able to run for a
third term. As it was, the person who first answered the question of
whether he should step down was Mrs. Wilson. She almost certainly
acted in exactly the same way that he would have done if someone had
put the question to him. Edith Wilson knew her husband's mind and
character better than anyone else. She mirrored his thinking faithfully
when she rejected the idea of his resigning as president.[6]

As Mrs. Wilson recalled nearly twenty years later, Dr. Dercum gave
her his diagnosis probably just after the middle of October. He prescribed complete rest for the president. She said that she asked at once,
"Then had he better not resign, let Mr. Marshall [the vice-president]
succeed to the Presidency and let himself get that complete rest that is
so vital to his life?" According to Mrs. Wilson, the doctor had replied,

> No. . . . For Mr. Wilson to resign would have a bad effect on the
> country, and a serious effect on our patient. He has staked his life
> and made his promise to the world to do all in his power to get the
> Treaty ratified and make the League of Nations complete. If he
> resigns, the greatest incentive to recovery is gone; and, as his mind
> is clear as crystal he can still do more with even a maimed body
> than anyone else.[7]

It is extremely doubtful that Dercum or any responsible physician
would have said those things. Mrs. Wilson's recollection filtered the
doctor's words through two decades of emotion-charged memory. At
the time, it was far more likely that she grasped at straws that the
physicians held out. Those included Wilson's undiminished intellectual
capacity, uncertainty about the extent and permanency of the stroke's
effects, and the likelihood of some improvement. All of those conditions are typical with strokes of this type. Some interpreters have
faulted Mrs. Wilson for putting wifely devotion to her husband's
health ahead of the public good. The notion that his remaining in
office offered "the greatest incentive to recovery" probably did sway

6. Dr. Edwin Weinstein uses the term "anosognosic" to describe what he calls
   Wilson's "denial personality." See Weinstein, *Wilson,* esp. 147–148,
   358–359.
7. Edith Wilson, *My Memoir,* 289.

her. But that was not her main motive in ruling out resignation. Edith Wilson believed that she was doing what her husband would want her to do for the good of the country and his most cherished policies. She read his mind right.[8]

Mrs. Wilson's rejection of resignation led her to make two fateful decisions. From the start, she embargoed any public disclosure of the nature of her husband's illness. She acted against the advice of Grayson and the other physicians who were attending Wilson. They, in turn, felt obligated by their professional canons to abide by the wishes of their patient, as expressed by his next of kin. Grayson repeatedly told the press that the president was suffering from "nervous exhaustion." He also said that Wilson was responding well to treatment and would make a "complete recovery." The other attending physicians went along with Grayson's charade for nearly five months. Then, in February 1920, Dr. Young, the urologist, inadvertently disclosed the truth when he told a reporter that Wilson was making excellent progress for a man who had suffered "a cerebral thrombosis."[9]

Mrs. Wilson's second fateful decision was to restrict access of both people and information to the president. She forbade anyone besides herself, Wilson's daughters, physicians, and nurses, and selected White House servants from seeing him for nearly a month. His secretary, Tumulty, would not see him until mid-November. Instead, regarding information about public business, as she recalled, she heeded Dr. Dercum's admonition "that every time you take him a new anxiety or problem to excite him, you are turning a knife in an open wound." Acting on that advice, Mrs. Wilson recalled:

> I studied every paper . . . and tried to digest and present in tabloid form the things that, despite my vigilance, had to go the President.

8. Neither Dercum's nor Grayson's memorandum mentions giving any advice about how resignation might affect Wilson's prognosis for recovery. The unlikelihood that Dercum said what Mrs. Wilson remembered him saying is also raised by Weinstein who was himself a distinguished and experienced neurologist. See Weinstein, *Wilson*, 360.
9. Young in *New York Times*, Feb. 11, 1920. Grayson's statements to the press are in Link, ed., *Papers of Wilson*, LXIII and LXIV. For the disagreement over disclosure of the natue of Wilson's illness, see Grayson memorandum, [ca. Jan. 1920], ibid., 510. The doctors were evidently less tight-lipped among themselves, because a prominent Chicago physician stated in February, "It soon became fairly widely known, in spite of every effort at secrecy, that the President had suffered a stroke, with resulting paralysis of one arm and leg." Dr. Arthur Dean Bevan in *Philadelphia Press*, Feb. 16, 1920, ibid., 431.

> I, myself, never made a single decision regarding the disposition of public affairs. The only decision that was mine was what was important and what was not, and the *very* important decision of when to present matters to my husband.[10]

This decision by Mrs. Wilson had both private and public consequences. Privately, she may unwittingly have worsened the impact of the stroke and hindered her husband's recovery. She was isolating him from outside contacts and stimulation. A later generation of neurologists would discover that such isolation provides the worst convalescent environment for a stroke victim. Mrs. Wilson's categorical recollection of Dr. Dercum's opinion makes it seem likely that she was following his and the other physicians' advice. Besides, the prostate blockage and infection left Wilson so weak that he could do little besides lie in bed for much of October. The ill effects of this isolation would become apparent when he regained enough energy and attention to deal with public business. Then, the psychological effects of the stroke, worsened by isolation, would have a devastating impact on his decisions in the League fight.[11]

The public consequences of Mrs. Wilson's decision to restrict access to the president became apparent much sooner. At the time and later, critics would accuse her of usurpation. Contemporary attacks quickly charged that – horror of horrors! – the country was being run by a woman. Such obviously biased allegations missed the mark. If anyone was going to act in Wilson's stead, his wife was the best-qualified person for the job. After all, she had been his closest advisor for more than four years. The far more important point was that no one should have played such a role of surrogate president. Mrs. Wilson's disclaimer

10. Edith Wilson, *My Memoir,* 289. In this case there is less question about whether Mrs. Wilson remembered Dr. Dercum's words correctly. Two weeks after the stroke, she wrote to Col. House's wife, ". . . we keep every thing from him which it is not important to have his advise *[sic]* about & which would annoy or distress him. . . ." Edith Wilson to Loulie Hunter House, Oct. 17, 1919, in Link, ed., *Papers of Wilson,* LXIII, 580.
11. I am grateful to Dr. Thomas Sutula, chair of the Department of Neurology of the University of Wisconsin Medical School, for pointing out the changes in treatment since Wilson's time and the likelihood that his subsequent behavior reflected the effects of isolation. In fairness to Dr. Dercum, it must be reiterated that no other record of what he said exists apart from Mrs. Wilson's account. It does seem odd that he would have suggested that staying in office would have given Wilson an incentive for recovery and then counseled against exposure to the business of his office.

about making decisions for her husband smacked of disingenuousness. Anyone could see that the person who controlled access to the president assumed much of the power of the office.

For the first month and a half after the stroke, Wilson attended to no public business at all. Then and afterward, it was not only Lansing's pleas to fill diplomatic posts that went unanswered. Other posts likewise went unfilled, and when appointments were made the choices were often poor. Of the three cabinet changes that occurred after Wilson's stroke, only one resulted in a first-rate replacement. Moreover, no clear line could separate administration from policy, and Wilson's policies suffered at home and abroad. An example occurred just three weeks after the stroke when Congress passed the Volstead Act, which would enforce nationwide prohibition under the recently ratified Eighteenth Amendment. Almost certainly with Mrs. Wilson's consent, Tumulty wrote a veto message, which Secretary of Agriculture David F. Houston revised. Because Wilson had consistently opposed prohibition, there was no question about acting contrary to his policy, but he almost certainly knew nothing about this veto. In coming weeks Wilson would be able to pay some attention to public business, but this incident set the pattern for the rest of his presidency. Tumulty would write nearly all of his messages and public statements, albeit later with the president's approval. Beforehand, however, Tumulty would usually have to try to guess at Wilson's position.[12]

Mrs. Wilson's answer to the question of whether the president should step down did not prevent others from trying to give a different answer. There was a move within the administration to consider the president's removal from office. It originated, unfortunately, with Secretary of State Lansing. On the evening of October 2, Lansing learned from Grayson that the "President's condition [was] bad." The next day, he went to the White House, where he asked Tumulty what was wrong with the president. "He did not answer me in words," Lansing wrote a few months later, "but significantly he put his right hand to his left shoulder and drew it down along the left side. Of course the implication was that the President had had a shock [i.e., stroke] and was paralyzed." Tumulty then

12. It is also the judgment of the editors of *Papers of Wilson* that he knew nothing about the veto. See Link, ed., *Papers of Wilson*, LXIII, 602 n. 3. Congress had passed the Volstead Act by large majorities and promptly overrode the veto. In view of those circumstances, Secretary of the Navy Daniels and, he claimed, three other cabinet members considered the veto "a big mistake & indefensible." See entry, Oct. 27, 1919, Daniels Diary, ibid.

asked Grayson to join them, and the three men conferred for nearly two hours in the Cabinet room. "Grayson was extremely reticent as to the President's malady," Lansing recalled, "giving no indication of any trouble other than a nervous breakdown." Then, one of them, most likely Lansing, introduced "the possible necessity of Vice President Marshall taking over the executive authority temporarily and the absence of precedents as to what constituted disability under the Constitution." After further discussion, they agreed that Lansing should call a Cabinet meeting to consider the situation for the following Monday, October 6. Lansing later talked with Secretary of War Baker and Secretary of the Interior Franklin K. Lane, both of whom supported the move to have the Cabinet consider what to do if the president could not perform his duties.[13]

On October 6, the Cabinet did briefly consider the question of whether Wilson should remain in office. Daniels recorded in his diary that Lansing opened the meeting by suggesting that they "ought to consider what steps to take" in light of the president's possible incapacity. "Should the V. P. be called upon [?]," Daniels recorded him asking. "He [Lansing] thought so. Referred to the Constitutional provision 'in case of the inability of the President.' What constitutes 'inability' & who is to decide it [?]" Grayson then joined them and, according to Daniels, "said the President was better but no business should come before him now. His condition encouraging but we are not out of the woods. President wanted to know why meeting of Cabinet was held – did *not* like it." Grayson himself wrote a memorandum immediately afterward in which he noted that Lansing

> asked me the direct questions as to what was the matter with the President, what was the exact nature of the President's trouble, how long would he be sick and was his mind clear or not. My

13. Lansing Desk Diary, Oct. 2, 1919, ibid., 543; Lansing memorandum, "Cabinet Meetings during the Illness of the President," Feb. 23, 1920. ibid., LXIV, 455–456. Tumulty left a conflicting, more lurid account of these discussions, in which he depicted Lansing as actively seeking Wilson's removal and himself and Grayson heatedly spurning all such notions. See Tumulty, *Woodrow Wilson as I Know Him* (Garden City, N.Y., 1921), 443–444. In fact, Lansing's recollection seems accurate. It agrees with brief entries that he made in his Desk Diary, Oct. 3, 4, 1919, in Link, ed., *Papers of Wilson*, LXIII, 547, 552, and a fuller account in Lansing to Polk, Oct. 4, 1919, ibid., 541, and with Baker's recollection in Baker to Julius W. Pratt, July 5, 1928, N. D. Baker Papers, Box 191. Lansing recounts how he wrote the memorandum in Lansing to Daniels, Feb. 21, 1924, Lansing Papers, Vol. 61.

reply was that the President's mind was not only clear but very active, and that he clearly showed that he was very much annoyed when he found that Cabinet had been called and that he wanted to know by whose authority the meeting had been called and for what purpose. Secretary Lansing was somewhat astounded when I spoke thus.

Secretary Baker smoothed things over by asking Grayson to tell the president that they had "only met as a mark of affection" to him and were attending to business as usual. "Please convey our sympathy to the President," Baker added, "and give him our assurance that everything is going to be all right."[14]

That discussion in the Cabinet constituted the only reliably recorded attempt within official circles to deal with the possibility of Wilson's removal from the presidency. It was a botched effort. Blame for the failure fell on both Lansing and Grayson. The blow-up over Bullitt's testimony and Lansing's determination to resign – which he had shared with other Cabinet members – made any suggestion from him about replacing the president suspect in the eyes of those closest to Wilson. In his memorandum about the meeting on October 6, Grayson also noted, "From what the French ambassador had said previously to Mr. Forster [of the White House staff] it appeared as if Secretary Lansing was particularly anxious to have Vice-President Marshall act in the President's place." That was just gossip, but it seems to have been well-founded. On October 4, Lansing wrote to Frank Polk, the second-ranking official in the State Department, "The distressing thing about the present time is the illness of the President and his inability to take part in public affairs." Lansing speculated that Wilson's "monomania concerning the League" had brought him to the verge of "a complete nervous collapse." A short while later, Colonel House recorded in his diary that Polk told him "when he [Lansing]

---

14. Entry, Oct. 6, 1919, Daniels Diary, in Link, ed., *Papers of Wilson*, LXIII, 555; Grayson memorandum, Oct. 6, 1919, ibid., LXIV, 496. Lansing recorded, "Grayson gave us report on Prest's condition which is encouraging." Entry, Oct. 6, 1919, Lansing Desk Diary, ibid., LXIII, 554. In his later memorandum, Lansing amplified only slightly: ". . . Grayson gave a very encouraging report on the President's condition, which, he said, showed decided improvement and seemed to indicate a speedy recovery. Because of Grayson's optimistic report the possibility of the Vice President was not discussed and only incidentally mentioned before Grayson made his statement." Lansing memorandum, Feb. 23, 1920, ibid., LXIV, 457.

first called the Cabinet together he had it in mind to thresh out the disability of the President. Polk confirmed that Lansing had in mind more than the interchange of ideas on departmental matters." Lansing may have felt so keen about raising this matter simply out of conscientious concern for the public good. It was more likely, however, that his determination to press the issue sprang from his deep personal alienation from Wilson.[15]

Grayson deserved equal or greater blame for aborting the discussion. He gave misleading reports about the president's condition first to Lansing and Tumulty on October 3 and then to the Cabinet on October 6. Strictly speaking, Grayson did not lie on either occasion. As of those dates, Dr. Dercum had offered only a preliminary diagnosis, which he did not confirm definitively until October 11. Grayson correctly characterized Wilson's intellectual capacities and state of consciousness. Moreover, the president's awareness of and annoyance at the Cabinet meeting on October 6 indicated that he was somewhat more in touch with events than he would be after he suffered the prostate blockage and infection. Still, Grayson's statements left mistaken impressions about both the severity of Wilson's illness and his ability to function as president. The doctor knew what he was doing. He persisted in issuing vague, optimistic reports to the press about "nervous exhaustion." Worse, on October 12, after Dercum had confirmed his diagnosis, Grayson misled reporters. Responding to allega-

---

15. Lansing to Polk, Oct. 4, 1919, ibid., 540; Grayson memorandum, Oct. 6, 1919, ibid., 496; entry, Mar. 28, 1920, House Diary, ibid., LXV, 139. In a private conversation with me (May 1996), Arthur Link suggested another possible motive on Lansing's part, namely, that he may have wanted to become president himself. Under the law of succession then in effect, the secretary of state stood next in line after the vice-president, and if Marshall had resigned after replacing Wilson, Lansing would have become president. Wilson himself had concocted such an arrangement in 1916, in the event he had lost the election, whereby he would have appointed Hughes secretary of state, secured Marshall's resignation, and then resigned himself. See Arthur S. Link, *Wilson: Campaigns for Progressivism and Peace* (Princeton, N.J., 1965), V, 154–156. It must be added that there is no evidence to support this speculation, that Lansing and Marshall were not close to each other, and that, as a matter of fact, the two men were at this moment engaged in a spat over an apparent slight to Marshall in connection with the official visit of King Albert of the Belgians. See Marshall to Lansing, Oct. 6, 9, 1919, Lansing Papers, Vol. 47; Lansing to Marshall, Oct. 7, 1919, ibid.

tions by Senator George Moses that the president had suffered a stroke and was paralyzed, he quipped "Senator Moses must have information that I do not possess." That was a lie, and Grayson compounded it by continuing to obfuscate the few bits of information that he did give out.[16]

Yet the truth about the president's illness would not stay secret, and others in Washington, particularly some of the men on Capitol Hill, were also raising questions about Wilson's being replaced. Those discussions produced an unlikely hero, Vice-President Thomas Riley Marshall. To all appearances, Marshall remained invisible during these events. He initiated no contacts with the White House, and he refused to talk to reporters. In fact, Marshall was much better informed about the president's condition than he let on. According to later recollections, soon after the stroke someone at the White House, most likely Tumulty acting at Mrs. Wilson's behest, briefed a friendly reporter, J. Fred Essary of the Baltimore *Sun,* about the president's condition and asked him to visit the vice-president in secret. Essary recalled that when he went to Marshall's office in the Capitol and related the information, the vice-president sat dumbfounded, stared down at his hands clasped on his desk, and did not say a word. "It

16. *New York Times,* Oct. 13, 1919. For a more sympathetic treatment of Grayson's conduct, see Link, "Dr. Grayson's Predicament," *Proceedings of the American Philosophical Society,* CXCVIII (1994), 487–494. Moses's comment, in fact, described Wilson's condition accurately. On October 10 or 11, in a letter to a constitutent that the recipient gave to the press, Moses characterized the illness as "some kind of cerebral lesion," and added, "His condition is such that while this lesion is healing, he is absolutely unable to undergo any experience which requires concentration of mind. . . . Physicians here describe the cerebral lesion, when followed by paralysis, as a shock or rupture of the cerebral arteries. It might take the form of apoplexy and is sometimes called cerebral hemmorhage." *New York Times,* Oct. 12, 1919. In response to Grayson's denial, Moses commented, "I do not pretend to have any straight line on the White House. In these letters I have merely given my constutents a statement of the facts as I understand them in light of the best evidence that I have been able to obtain here." Ibid., Oct. 13, 1919. Moses was not the only Republican senator who had an accurate idea of Wilson's condition. Sherman also privately told a correspondent, "He has had a lesion of a blood vessel in the brain. . . . It is believed that he had a slight stroke about the time he started for home." Sherman to Walter A. Rosenfield, Oct. 17, 1919, Sherman Papers, Box 61.

was the first great shock of my life," Essary remembered Marshall saying to him afterward.[17]

Marshall's unsung finest hour occurred sometime during the next month or two. The president's total removal from public view and the trickle of information from the White House proved so frustrating on Capitol Hill that talk persisted about a congressional inquiry into Wilson's condition and efforts to remove him from office. According to later recollections, on two separate occasions different groups of senators tried to persuade Marshall to take over the presidency. The first overture came from two prominent but unnamed Democrats; the second came from four leading Republicans. Marshall spurned both offers and told almost nobody about the incidents. "I could throw this country into civil war, but I won't," his wife remembered him telling her. The vice-president's secretary later recalled that he had pressed Marshall to reconsider his course. What would the vice-president do, he had asked, if Congress passed a resolution declaring that the president was unable to remain in office? The only way that he would agree to assume the presidency, Marshall had maintained, would be if Congress passed a resolution and Mrs. Wilson and Grayson approved it in writing. But the vice-president adamantly refused to make any moves in that direction. "I am not going to seize the place," he declared, "and then have Wilson – recovered – come and say 'get off, you usurper.'"[18]

It is interesting to speculate what might have happened if different people had held those offices. Wilson, and his wife acting on his behalf, suffered from the defect of his greatest virtues – drive, vision, and strength. A president less bent on masterful leadership and on achieving great aims might well have stepped aside or been induced to step aside. Marshall later said as much in the only implicit criticism that he uttered about Wilson in his memoirs: "I have sometimes thought that great men are the bane of civilization; that they are the real causes of

17. Essary quoted in Charles M. Thomas, *Thomas Riley Marshall: Hoosier Statesman* (Oxford, Ohio, 1939), 207. The account of this incident is in ibid., 206–207, and it is based upon Thomas's correspondence with Essary and with Marshall's secretary, Mark Thistlethwaite, in July 1937. See ibid., 266.

18. Marshall, quoted in ibid., 211, 227. Thomas evidently also based this account on correspondence with Marshall's secretary, together with other correspondence in July 1937 with senators Watson and Moses and with Mrs. Marshall in August 1937. Ibid., 266.

all the bitterness and contention that amounted to anything in the world."[19]

It is also interesting to speculate about what might have happened if a different person had been vice-president in 1919 – someone who enjoyed Wilson's admiration and trust – or what might have happened if a different conception of the office had existed. In fact, such a person and such a conception almost were in place then. In 1916, some high-ranking Democrats, including Colonel House, had tried to dump Marshall and replace him with Newton Baker, but Wilson had rejected the scheme. "He felt Baker was too good a man to be sacrificed," House recorded in his diary. The colonel disagreed and argued that

> if the right man took it [the vice-presidency], a man who had his confidence as Baker has, a new office could be created out of it. He might become Vice President in fact as well as in name, and be a co-worker and co-helper of the President. He [Wilson] was interested in this argument but was unconvinced that Baker should, as he termed it, be sacrificed. He was afraid that he could not educate the people in four years up to the responsibilities of the office.[20]

It was unfortunate, perhaps even tragic, that Wilson did not let his interest in House's idea of a form of co-presidency sway him further. If he had endorsed this idea and chosen Baker or someone like him as his running mate in 1916, much might have been different in 1919. After his stroke, Wilson might well have chosen or been persuaded to let the vice-president act in his stead. Better still, the chance to share the burdens of wartime leadership and peacemaking might have eased the strain on his health. If any leader could legitimately be faulted for not gazing better into the future in this instance, it was Wilson. He had previously shown great boldness and vision in shaking up established

19. Thomas Riley Marshall, *Recollections of Thomas R. Marshall* (Indianapolis, 1925), 363. Leaving little doubt that he would have compromised on the treaty and League membership, Marshall followed those sentences with the observation, "Pride of opinion and pride of authorship, and jealousy of the opinion and authorship of others wreck many a fair hope." Ibid.
20. Entry, May 24, 1916, House Diary, in Link, ed., *Papers of Wilson*, XXXVII, 105. House also recorded Wilson as saying, erroneously, "that no Vice President had ever succeeded a President by election." Ibid. On the attempt to dump Marshall, see John Milton Cooper, Jr., "A Shadowed Office: The Vice Presidency and Its Occupants, 1900–1920," in Timothy Walch, ed., *At the President's Side: The Vice Presidency in the Twentieth Century* (Columbia, Mo., 1997), 17–18.

notions of political conduct. This was one of the worst possible times for his political imagination to fail him. As things transpired, responsibility for dealing with the worst crisis of presidential disability in America history fell on such people as Mrs. Wilson, Grayson, Tumulty, Lansing, and Marshall. For once, fate had not dealt at all kindly with the United States.

II

The League fight did not stop because of the president's incapacity. The Independence League continued to send out speakers and hold rallies. According to the organization's publicity director, the staff mailed out over two million documents, mostly copies of speeches by senators Borah, Johnson, and Reed. But of those senatorial stars, only Johnson and, to a lesser extent, Reed now spent much time on the speaking circuit. The Independence League also continued to suffer from internal dissension. Some within the organization complained that Pepper was diverting funds to Will Hays and the Republican National Committee. Much of the propaganda effort on both sides turned toward reaching targeted subgroups and gaining endorsements from influential organizations. Women offered one field for such activity. Pro-League advocates gained endorsement of membership without reservations from the American Federation of Women's Clubs. Anti-League forces formed the Special Campaign Committee of American Women Opposed to the League of Nations. This organization featured as its honorary chair the renowned suffragist Harriet Stanton Blatch and as one of its vice-chairs former Representative Jeanette Rankin of Montana, the first woman to serve in Congress.[21]

The LEP concentrated its efforts mostly on lobbying in Washington and in other arenas around the country. In September, pro-League forces scored a coup when the American Bar Association endorsed unqualified ratification of the peace treaty. Foes of the League complained that friends of Taft prevented debate on the floor of the ABA convention. "It was a characteristically scurvy trick," an anti-League activist complained to Lodge. A month later, Lodge himself suffered special embarrassment when the Massachusetts Republican convention

---

21. On the Independence League, see John E. Milholland to Salmon Levinson, Oct. 6, 1919, Levinson Papers, Box 33, Folder 9; Lee Meriwether to Henry A. Wise Wood, Dec. 8, 1919, ibid., Folder 6; Meriwether to Levinson, Dec. 18, 1919, ibid. On the anti-League women's organization, see Olive Stott Gabriel to John Sharp Williams, Oct. 24, 1919, Williams Papers, Box 48.

declared for ratification of the treaty "without amendment." Ironically, the Massachusetts Democratic convention endorsed strong reservations on League membership and condemned the peace treaty for failing to secure independence for Ireland. That juxtaposition epitomized the continuing state of public opinion toward the League and the treaty as well as it could be judged. Surveys by magazines and private soundings indicated continuing support for both League membership and reservations. At the same time, many observers also detected a distinct waning of public interest in the issue. An Indianapolis publisher noted that people in his state "were so tired of the League that they yawned when it was mentioned." Instead, Hoosiers wanted "to get it disposed of and have the Senate and President settle down to give attention to the serious economic questions of the hour."[22]

No such shift of attention occurred in Washington. The treaty and the League shoved other concerns off the political stage even more thoroughly than earlier. With the president in seclusion, the Senate dominated the scene completely. Talk and action on the floor faithfully reflected this newfound focus. Between the beginning of October and the final votes on November 19, the Senate met thirty-four times. These sessions featured 128 speeches and 89 votes related to the peace treaty and League membership. The tempo of speaking increased sharply. Half the sessions featured at least four speeches, as well as briefer exchanges in debate. The largest number of speeches occurred, predictably, on November 19, just before the votes. Then the Senate was operating under a cloture rule that limited the time of each speaker.[23]

Now, the senators were also voting. The subjects of these votes included procedural motions and quixotic gestures by individual senators, amendments and reservations, and, finally, consideration of the

22. Louis A. Coolidge to Lodge, Sept. 5, 1919, Lodge Papers; William C. Bobbs to Beveridge, Sept. 8, 1919, Beveridge Papers, Box 215. On the Massachusetts Republicans' action, see Lodge to Charles Sumner Bird, Oct. 8, 1919, Lodge Papers; Lodge to Courtenay Crocker, Oct. 18, 1919, ibid.; Beveridge to Knox, Oct. 6, 1919, Beveridge Papers, Box 215. For other estimates of public opinion, see Beck to Lodge, Sept. 12, 1919, Lodge Papers; Max [name unknown] to Taft, Sept. 14, 1919, Taft Papers, reel 212; Arthur Vandenberg to Taft, Sept. 18, 1919, ibid.; Charles D. Hilles to Taft, Sept. 25, 1919, ibid.

23. Most of the speeches during these weeks came from senators who had spoken before and spoke again several times. Borah was by far the most frequent speaker, and at least 80 percent of the speeches came from critics and opponents.

treaty itself. The voting fell into three distinct groups. The first twelve votes involved amendments to the treaty, all of which lost. The second and largest group of votes – sixty-two in all – involved reservations. With two exceptions, only reservations presented by Lodge and the Foreign Relations Committee passed. All efforts by Democrats and McCumber to soften these reservations failed. So did every attempt by Irreconcilables to strengthen them or add other reservations. The last set of votes – 15 in all – occurred on November 19 and involved consideration of the treaty itself, including three votes on consent to the Treaty of Versailles.[24]

How to assess these votes poses a fundamental interpretative question at the outset: how to judge their relative significance. By one criterion, the only votes that really mattered were the three on consent to the treaty. Two of those votes included, as part of the instrument of ratification, fourteen reservations popularly known as the "Lodge reservations." There was also a vote on consent without reservations. These three votes determined the fate of the treaty. The acid test of any senator's convictions was how he stood up and was counted on these votes. By another criterion, however, the complete spectrum of these votes needs to be considered. Nearly all of these votes sharply and consistently differentiated supporters and opponents of the stand favored by the Wilson administration. These votes revealed groupings and gradations in support and opposition. They also showed what, if any, common ground might have existed for compromise.

Off the Senate floor, discussion and dealing among senators and lobbying from outside likewise intensified. The most active lobbying continued to come from the LEP. The organization operated through its Washington office and through Gus Karger, while Taft, Lowell, and other leaders made frequent trips to the capital. As earlier, the LEP concentrated its attention mostly on the mild reservationists, especially McCumber, McNary, Colt, and Kellogg, and occasionally on some Democrats. By coincidence, Taft arrived in Washington on Friday, October 3, just after Wilson suffered his stroke, and he spent the weekend conferring with senators and LEP lobbyists. Although McAdoo told Taft that Wilson was "in a state of collapse," the subject of the president's condition evidently did not come up during his meetings on Capitol Hill. Instead, Taft strove to persuade several Republicans to vote against all amendments to the treaty, and he went over the wording of proposed reservations. Taft found the situation among Republicans discouraging. As he related to Lowell, ". . . the truth is nobody's judgment

---

24. Adding the earlier move on September 23, delay consideration of Fall's amendments, brings the total number of votes to ninety.

is very good, because I think there are quite a number of people that don't know how they are going to vote themselves."[25]

The Democrats seemed to Taft to offer more hopeful prospects. At a meeting with Oscar Underwood, the Alabama senator struck Taft as being "as level-headed a man as I saw." Underwood explained that forty Democrats would vote for the treaty without changes. They could not yet agree to any proposed Republican reservations because that would open the door to other possible reservations. Of the remaining seven Democrats, Underwood dismissed Reed and Gore as "of course hopeless." He claimed that David Walsh of Massachusetts felt obliged to vote for the Johnson amendment on British Empire voting, but otherwise "he is acting very well and will help where he can." Other reportedly shaky Democrats had promised to vote against the Johnson amendment. Therefore, forty-four Democratic votes – combined with four Republicans who Taft said were solid, McCumber, McNary, Colt, and Nelson – would be enough to produce a 48-to-48 tie. That tie would be broken against the amendment by the vice-president's vote. "Underwood said that his plan was this," Taft further recounted:

> That after the amendments were defeated, they would see whether they could come to an agreement with enough Republicans to carry the treaty. If the Republicans agreed on reservations that they could not concur in, they [the Democrats] would vote against the resolution [of ratification], which would prevent a two-thirds vote but would not defeat the treaty under the rules of the Senate.

Instead, Underwood stated that there would be a postponement and "an opportunity for a compromise on reservations. He thus gave me a new phase of the situation."[26]

Why Taft took heart from Underwood's scenario was puzzling. Underwood was restating the position that Swanson had outlined earlier. This entailed the risky strategy of deliberate stalemate. "Underwood was anxious, too," Taft added, "that his plan should not be revealed. He thinks that the pressure for ratification of the treaty is going to be so strong that his plan may work out, though I was so hoping that they can reach an agreement before they get to a final vote on the resolution of ratification." Taft's misgiving pointed again to the main danger – that both sides might become so rigidly committed to their respective stands that agreement would prove impossible. Further-

---

25. Taft to Lowell, Oct. 5, 1919, Lowell Papers. Cf. Taft to Le Baron Colt, Oct. 5, 1919, Taft Papers, reel 213. For a comparable assessment of the situation, see Lansing to Polk, Oct. 1, 1919, in Link, ed., *Papers of Wilson*, LXIII, 540.

26. Taft to Lowell, Oct. 5, 1919, Lowell Papers.

more, there was an unstated assumption behind this strategy of confrontation and compromise – that Wilson would be able to play some part in the eventual meeting of the minds. No evidence indicates that Underwood or any other Democrats contemplated either defying or trying to work around the president. Given the optimistic reports that periodically emanated from the White House, these men were behaving reasonably when they assumed that Wilson would either approve or not block a later effort at compromise. It would soon become apparent how wrong they were.[27]

Three votes on October 2, the day that Wilson suffered his stroke, offered the first tangible evidence of where senators stood on amending the treaty. Deletions proposed by Albert Fall went down to defeat by wide margins: thirty for, fifty-eight against; twenty-eight for, forty-six against; and thirty-one for, forty-eight against. Only one Democrat, Gore, voted for any of these amendments. By contrast, seventeen Republicans voted against them. To the press, both sides claimed victory. Speaking for the pro-League forces, the acting Democratic leader, Hitchcock, affirmed, "No textual changes, I am convinced, will be made in the treaty." Lodge, by contrast, professed to be "delighted beyond measure at the showing" because there were the "weakest of all amendments" and because, combined with those announced in favor, his forces had mustered "considerably more than the thirty-three votes necessary" to defeat consent to the treaty without major changes. Both men were right. Of the remaining amendments, five – the Shantung provision, Johnson's and two others related to British Empire voting, and one on the labor clauses – would gain a few more adherents, but the alignment on these votes supported Hitchcock's contention that no amendments would pass. Still, the support for these measures showed that Lodge was not talking through his hat when he claimed to be able to block any expansive construction of American obligations under the treaty and the Covenant. Genuine compromise was going to be a hard sell.[28]

Speeches on the Senate floor swung back and forth between amendments and broader discussions of the League and the treaty. On Wilson's side, McCumber ridiculed notions of British domination because Australia, Canada, India, New Zealand, and South Africa were to have

27. Ibid.
28. Ibid., 6269, 6271, 6280; *New York Times*, Oct. 3, 1919. Cf. the analysis of these votes in Herbert F. Margulies, *Mild Reservationists and the League of Nations in the Senate* (Columbia, Mo., 1989), 114, and Lloyd Ambrosius, *Woodrow Wilson and the American Diplomatic Tradition: The Treaty Fight in Perspective* (New York, 1987), 198.

additional votes. He observed that the United States controlled votes in the League from what McCumber dubbed "our begotten child Panama, our foster-child Cuba, our wards Nicaragua, Haiti, Guatemala, Honduras, Uruguay, Ecuador, Bolivia, Peru, and even Brazil." One of the Irreconcilables, Joseph France of Maryland, expounded his highly idealistic brand of isolationism. He scorned "this monstrous scheme" of the League as the handiwork of "European statesmen – men dominated by bigotry, hatred, intolerance." America's "peculiar national destiny," declared France, was "that of demonstrating to the world the transcendent excellency and universal applicability of free republican government and of persuading all other peoples to the adoption of those institutions and ideals." Many of the speeches sent a strong signal that amendments would fail. A succession of Republicans, joined by Democrats known to be critical of the treaty, announced their opposition. To a man, however, these senators predicated their rejection of amendments on a call for strong reservations.[29]

The vote on the amendment to strike the Shantung clause from the treaty revealed almost exactly the same alignment as the earlier votes on Fall's amendments. The thirty-five supporters included three Democrats: Reed, Gore, and Walsh of Massachusetts. The fifty-five senators voting against the amendment included fourteen Republicans. Two more of their party brethren were announced against, along with three Democrats – bringing the total number of opponents to sixty. As before, pro-League forces could feel gratified that a comfortable bipartisan majority was holding out against amendments. But also as earlier, an amendment to the text of the treaty had drawn support from more than a third of the senators, including such leading foreign policy spokesmen as Lodge and Knox. That support – together with the stated grounds upon which Republicans opposed the amendment – again showed how hard it would be to gain a two-thirds vote for consent on any basis short of emasculation of nearly all obligations under the League Covenant.[30]

Except for Shantung and Article X, no part of the peace settlement aroused more argument than the League membership of the dominions of the British Empire. Even at the time, the issue looked to many observers like the proverbial tempest in a teapot. It was true that, combined with the mother country, dominion votes would give the empire six votes in the League Assembly, but that was not the action arm of the League. There was also a chance of multiple votes for the empire in the

---

29. *Congressional Record*, 66th Cong., 1st Sess. (Oct. 3, 1919), 6337; (Oct. 9, 1919), 6600–6614.
30. Ibid. (Oct. 16, 1919), 7012–7013. See also New York *World*, Oct. 18, 1919. Cf. the analysis in Margulies, *Mild Reservationists*, 124.

League Council when one or more of the dominions rotated onto the Council and supplemented Britain's permanent vote. Given the sensitivities of not only the United States but also France, that did not seem likely to happen often. Nevertheless, more than twenty senators spoke to support or oppose amendments that would have either deprived the dominions of full voting strength or given the United States an equal number of votes. Lodge avowed that America must never "occupy a place of inferiority in power and representation." Hitchcock praised "these great self-governing dominions" that were "part of the great Anglo-Saxon race like ourselves." Seven Republicans, mostly mild reservationists, again made rejection of amendments conditional on adoption of reservations to accomplish the same result.[31]

On October 27 and 29, the Senate voted on the amendments to alter British Empire voting in the League. All three of these amendments failed. As predicted, Johnson's measure garnered the most support of any amendment proposed during the entire League fight. It had thirty-nine votes in favor and forty against. That paper-thin margin was deceptive. Of the eighteen senators not voting, only four more were announced in favor, whereas nine were announced as opposed. That brought the count to forty-three for and forty-nine against. The other two amendments fell short by wider margins. Three Democrats – Gore, Shields, and Walsh of Massachusetts – voted for all three of these amendments. This time, the pro-League forces felt no jubilation. There was no gainsaying how narrow their victory was and how many senators favored a drastic change in the treaty.[32]

31. *Congressional Record*, 66th Cong., 1st Sess. (Oct. 25, 1919), 7491; (Oct. 27, 1919), 7551. McCumber also favored a reservation on the subject, but he did not make his opposition to the amendments conditional on such a reservation.

32. Ibid. (Oct. 27, 1919), 7548; (Oct. 29, 1919), 7679, 7680. The *Record* states the number of votes in favor of the Johnson amendment incorrectly as thirty-eight. Of the three senators besides Davis Elkins of West Viriginia who did not announce their stands, Reed almost certainly would have favored the Johnson amendment, and Martin and Pittman, as administration loyalists, would have opposed it. Adding those speculative assignments to the actual votes and announcements would bring the alignment to forty-four for and fifty-one against. On these votes, another Republican once counted among the moderates, Arthur Capper of Kansas, ignored a "personal & confidential" handwritten plea from Taft "not to vote for an amendment changing the text of the treaty and sending it back for a reconference, or definitely taking us out of the League and sending us to seek a separate peace with Germany." Taft to Arthur Capper, Oct. 12, 1919, Arthur Capper Papers, Kansas State Historical Society, Box 31.

The Senate voted down four more proposed amendments during the last days of October and first week of November, all by wide margins. Of these proposed amendments, the one that stimulated the greatest debate and attracted the largest number of votes was a move to strike out the clauses of the treaty that dealt with labor. The author of this amendment was Robert La Follette. The fiery, unrepentant Wisconsin progressive was now beginning to shed the shroud of pariahdom imposed by his opposition to the war. Unlike other critics of this part of the treaty, La Follette ardently supported labor unions. He denounced the treaty's labor clauses as "the deadly joker which may at any time . . . subject American labor to a direct attack upon its existing protective statutes." La Follette had not yet announced where he stood on the treaty and League membership, but he left little doubt about his eventual position when he avowed his conviction "that America's best gift to the world . . . would be the example and perfection of our democracy unhampered and unrestrained by outside influences."[33]

The rest of the debate on La Follette's amendment consisted of attacks on the labor clauses by senators who excoriated what they saw as rampant radicalism among unionists at home and abroad. Several western Democrats gave vent to the bitterness spawned by three decades of often violent conflict in their region between labor and capital. Thomas of Colorado declared that any labor arm of the League "may advocate the extremes of revolution . . . [and] disseminate the doctrines of I.W.W.ism over the world." William King of Utah agreed that these clauses "will destroy nationalism . . . and will not conduce to the world's peace." Henry Myers of Montana alluded to the incipient Red Scare at home when he denounced the treaty's labor clauses for spreading "to the entire world the industrial disturbance, dissatisfac-

---

33. *Ibid.* (Oct. 29, 1919), 7670–7677. La Follette had gone through a terrible personal and political ordeal during World War I. His adversaries in Wisconsin had used his opposition to the war as a weapon against him in a drive to break his power and the power of his movement in the state. Vilification and denunciation had included resolutions of censure by the state legislature and by the faculty of his alma mater, the University of Wisconsin, and his being burned in effigy on the university campus. La Follette's bitterness over these attacks can be seen in the letters that he wrote in 1919 to his wife and sons, in the La Follette Papers (Library of Congress). See also Belle Case La Follette and Fola La Follette, *Robert M. La Follette* (New York, 1952), II, 761–908, and Bernard A. Weisberger, *The La Follettes of Wisconsin* (Madison, Wis., 1994), 179–224. As already noted, La Follette's partial rehabilitation and reconciliation with Senate Republicans had begun after the 1918 elections, when his vote was needed to give them their one-vote majority.

tion, and unrest which now unhappily exists *[sic]* in this country." La
Follette's amendment garnered thirty-four votes in favor, including five
from Democrats – Gore, Myers, Reed, Thomas, and Walsh of Massachusetts; four others, all Republicans, were announced in favor.[34]

As November began, the senators shifted their attention to reservations. There were repeated roll-call votes either on reservations or on
motions to amend those reservations and substitute others for them.
These votes made up the largest group of roll calls in the entire League
fight – sixty in all. The doings on the Senate floor were finally catching
up with where the main focus of attention had been for several weeks.
Even before Wilson returned from his speaking tour, many of the main
actors in the League fight had been discussing, drafting, and dealing
with each other over reservations that would almost certainly be
attached to the instrument of ratification. The overweening subject of
their attention and the crux of their differences always lay in Article X.

Others besides Americans were also trying their hand at influencing
people on both of the main sides in the debate. Ever since the signing of
the treaty in June and Wilson's departure for home, the European Allies
had viewed the struggle over American ratification with growing apprehension. Lloyd George and Clemenceau had never put much stock in
the League of Nations, but they desperately desired an American commitment to uphold other parts of the settlement and, in the case of the
French, the tripartite security pact. Both diplomatic etiquette and fear of
Wilson's reaction restrained the ambassadors of Britain and France
from making anything but the quietest, most tentative contacts on Capitol Hill.

The British did, however, make one stab at reaching out to the opposition. Viscount Grey of Fallodon, who had earlier served as Britain's
foreign secretary, spent the last four months of 1919 in the United
States, to get medical treatment for his failing eyesight at Johns Hopkins. Grey also conducted an informal mission sanctioned by Lloyd
George to sound out the situation. During this time, Grey made several
trips to Washington and New York to meet with Lansing, Root, and
Lodge – but not Wilson. The president refused to receive him. Lodge,
who had known Grey for years, saw him two or three times. The senator evidently did most of the talking at their meetings, because he told a
mutual friend that he felt satisfied Grey "will have the best possible
effect in the work which he will have to do & in the position which he

---

34. *Congressional Record*, 66th Cong., 1st Sess. (Oct. 31, 1919), 7797–7805;
    (Nov. 4, 1919), 7939; (Nov. 5, 1919), 7957, 7969. Despite his denuncia-
    tion of the labor clauses, King voted against the amendment, as did nearly
    all of the other western Democrats.

will be sure to take." In other words, Lodge believed that the former foreign secretary would try to convince the British government and public to accept the Republican stand on the treaty and the League. Lodge judged his man right. Grey would later do what the senator wanted at a critical moment in the League fight.[35]

The main efforts at exerting influence on reservations sprang, however, from sources closer to home. The most important of these came from leaders of the LEP and from senators themselves. Several LEP leaders made repeated visits to augment the activity of their organization's lobbyists. On October 10, Lowell and Oscar Straus held meetings with McCumber and Lodge, to try to work out acceptable language for a reservation to Article X. It was a measure of how far the LEP had retreated that they now concentrated on trying to restrict any limitations in reservations solely to Article X. Lowell admitted, as he told the LEP's chief lobbyist, "I am not sure whether this reservation leaves any moral obligation whatever upon the United States to act under Article X, . . . but it certainly leaves the economic obligations under Article XVI untouched, and that is not a little to preserve." For once Taft disagreed, at least temporarily. When he read the language that the mild reservationists had approved, he told a Democratic senator that it was "a stunning blow to me, from which I have not recovered." The reservation meant "destruction of the universal boycott, about which all the provisions of the League center, [and] that takes the heart out of me."[36]

Taft soon calmed down. McCumber explained to him, "Considering the intense feeling of senators on this subject of Article X, I think we have got it [the reservation] in the best shape that we could get it." So many Republicans, McCumber added, together with some Democrats, wanted to restrict all obligations. The "best we could do," therefore, was to settle for this reservation, "which avoids any reference to coercive measures under any other articles of the treaty." This situation left the LEP in a quandary. When the executive committee met on October 28, the members were sharply divided. Some favored acquiescence in

35. Lodge to Bryce, Oct. 8, 1919, Lodge Papers. See also Lodge to Lord Charnwood, Jan. 24, 1920, ibid.; Lodge to Louis Coolige, Feb. 2, 1920, ibid. On the British position toward the conflict in the United States and Grey's mission, see George W. Egerton, *Great Britain and the Creation of the League of Nations* (Chapel Hill, N.C., 1978), 179–194.

36. Lowell to Talcott Williams, Oct. 22, 1919, Lowell Papers; Taft to John Sharp Williams, Oct. 24, 1919, Williams Papers, Box 48. On the October 10 meeting, see also Short to Vance McCormick, Oct. 11, 1919, LEP Papers. On Taft's dismay at the reservation, see also Taft to Colt, Oct. 23, 1919, Taft Papers, reel 213; Taft to McCumber, Oct. 23, 1919, ibid.; Taft to Henry W. Franam, Oct. 24, 1919, ibid.

the Foreign Relations Committee's reservations; others wanted to back the Senate Democrats' plan to block consent in hope of future compromise. In the end, the committee adopted a resolution that simply disapproved "reservations that would involve delay by negotiation." Afterward, Lowell made another trip to Washington and came away convinced that, as he told the LEP's secretary, "we must not oppose the different reservations except 14 [a stinging exclusion of American 'honor' and 'vital interests']; but hold our peace upon them, except for minor changes." Such diminished influence showed that the LEP was continuing to pay the price of speaking with a divided voice.[37]

The most potent effort at exerting influence over reservations came from senators themselves. They engaged in protracted, often testy pulling and hauling over two matters. One was Article X; the other was the "preamble" to the package of reservations that laid down requirements for other nations to accept them. On the Article X reservation, McCumber had stated the main question: Could pro-League senators salvage any vestige of an obligation to join in international enforcement measures? The issue with the preamble involved whether to require explicit agreement to the reservations from the major Allies – Britain, France, Italy, and Japan. Lodge and the majority on the Foreign Relations Committee demanded that three of those four powers must formally accept these reservations to American ratification of the treaty. League advocates countered that, under established international usage, such formal acceptance was not necessary. They also charged that the preamble was a thinly veiled ploy to goad more than one of those four Allies into rejecting the reservations. Britain would plainly dislike any measure that refused to allow more than one vote to Britain and the dominions in disputes involving the United States. Japan would obviously bristle at the reservation that stated American nonacceptance of the Shantung clauses. Italy also posed a problem, in view of the unresolved dispute raised by Wilson's opposition to that nation's expansionist designs on Fiume and the Adriatic coast.[38]

Given the gravity of the issues at stake in the Article X reservation and the preamble, surprisingly few senators involved themselves in the

37. McCumber to Taft, Oct. 24, 1919, ibid.; LEP executive committee minutes, Oct. 28, 1919, McAdoo Papers, Box 225; Kellogg to Lowell, Oct. 31, 1919, Lowell Papers; Lowell to Short, Nov. 1, 1919, ibid. For a similar interpretation of the LEP's loss of influence due to its divided counsels, see Ruhl J. Bartlett, *The League to Enforce Peace* (Chapel Hill, N.C., 1944), 158–195.
38. For the reservations and the preamble, see *Congressional Record,* 66th Cong., 1st Sess. (Oct. 24, 1919), 7417–7418.

efforts to hammer out an agreement on them. No more than seven or eight men took part in these dealings. On one side, Lodge appears to have acted largely alone in representing the twenty-five to thirty Republicans who insisted upon strong reservations along the lines of those adopted earlier by the Foreign Relations Committee. On the other side, a handful of mild reservationists strove to soften those reservations. McCumber, Kellogg, and Lenroot took the most active parts.

Lodge won. His victory owed something to his skill and patience as a negotiator, but much more to the high cards that he held in his hand. His ace of trumps was numbers. Not only the Irreconcilables but also a few Democrats and less-committed mild reservationists were almost certain to join Lodge and his followers in supporting the committee's reservations. Thereby, they were sure to garner enough votes for those reservations to be adopted. The mild reservationists also continued to suffer from internal divisions and lack of stomach for a protracted fight. Kellogg admitted as much when he told Taft at the end of October, "I am getting very tired of this long drawn out contest and the additional work of the Senate."[39]

Besides those advantages, two other factors favored Lodge and his side. One was what Republican after Republican had stated during the debate over amendments. For them, the price of voting for consent was reservations that negated American acceptance of certain clauses and circumscribed obligations under the League Covenant. McCumber, who remained as always the mildest of all reservationists, made this reality plain when he told a League advocate that

> in order to secure the 64 votes required to ratify the treaty, it is necessary to include certain reservations in the resolution of ratification. . . . If we make the reservations as mild as I would wish to have them, the treaty would be defeated. I wish, therefore, to concede as little as possible and still be certain of ratification. To accomplish this, I must agree to a compromise, even though that compromise is far from my convictions of what should be done.[40]

The outcome of these senatorial dealings was what McCumber ruefully implied. It was not a compromise; it was a capitulation. This happened mainly because of the other factor that favored Lodge's side. Nobody except the mild reservationists was trying to soften the terms

39. Kellogg to Taft, Oct. 27, 1919, Taft Papers, reel 213. On the internal divisions, see also entry, Oct. 31, 1919, Anderson Diary. For a more detailed account of the mild reservationist side of the dealings, see Margulies, *Mild Reservationists*, 110–145.

40. McCumber to Courtenay Crocker, Oct. 29, 1919, Lowell Papers. See also *New York Times*, Oct. 20, 1919.

under which the Senate might consent to the treaty. The Irreconcilables took no part in these dealings. They played the role of sullen bystanders, especially as their proposed amendments were defeated. Borah summed up their attitude when he told a friend in Idaho, "What I expect to see, although hoping and praying for another result, is that the reservations will be adopted and then the whole treaty ratified." In Borah's eyes, the only glimmer of hope lay in the Democrats' threats "to defeat the whole treaty" if these reservations were adopted. But, he sighed, "that is too good to be true."[41]

The Irreconcilables' hopes were not so faint as they feared. What hobbled the mild reservationists' efforts to get anything worthwhile out of these dealings was the Democrats' absence. The Democratic senators stood in an uncomfortable position. According to knowledgeable journalists, most of them wanted a compromise. Taft, LEP lobbyists, and mild reservationists met repeatedly with Hitchcock, Underwood, and other Democrats and tried to draw them into negotiations over reservations. But the Democrats refused to participate. The stumbling block was Wilson. "If it were not for the feeling among [Democratic] Senators that to act with the mild reservationists would be a betrayal of the President," a New York *World* correspondent noted early in October, "the peace treaty and the League of Nations would be near ratification." If Wilson would meet with some of those senators, the reporter added, "there would be a dozen advocates of the compromise, of his own party, endeavoring to persuade him that this is the best possible solution to the problem." There was the rub. No one could get in to see Wilson. As the LEP's chief lobbyist reported in mid-October, "The President cannot be considered as a factor in the treaty situation. There is no possibility that he will be able to take any part whatever in the fight."[42]

Actually, Wilson's removal made him a negative influence. The paucity of news about the president's condition – abetted by Grayson's misleading assurances and combined with the failure to delegate anyone to act in his stead – created a vacuum on the side of the pro-League forces. Democratic senators might want to broker a compromise and get the treaty behind them, but they dared not strike out on their own. Their debts to Wilson and the requirements of party loyalty, especially

41. Borah to Alfred J. Dunn, Oct. 9, 1919, Borah Papers, Box 768. For a similarly pessimistic assessment from an Irreconcilable, see Johnson to Hiram Jr. and Arch Johnson, Nov. 1, 1919, in Robert E. Burke, ed., *The Diary Letters of Hiram Johnson* (New York, 1983), III.
42. New York *World*, Oct. 6, 1919; H. N. Rickey to Short, Oct. 14, 1919, LEP Papers. See also *New York Times*, Oct. 7, 1919.

with national elections just a year away, restrained them from making any moves that the president might disavow. On October 24, Vice-President Marshall met with most of his party's senators. They formally decided not to take any action on reservations unless and until the president advised them. Also, according to the *World*, eighteen of those Democrats pledged that, if Wilson wished, they would vote against the treaty with reservations. Together with the Irreconcilables, they could supply more than the one-third needed to block consent.[43]

The Democratic senators' nonparticipation meant that no one represented their side in the dealings in October. Some observers at the time and later judged this absence a major blow to the cause of the treaty and the League. One of the mild reservationists, McNary, told reporters, "The proponents of the treaty among the Democrats missed a great opportunity. The mild reservationists were forced to deal with the radical element on their own side. The result is the committee report on reservations, which to my mind must be adopted if the treaty is to be ratified." That judgment is hard to gainsay. Active involvement by the Democrats might have strengthened the mild reservationists' hand in dealing with Lodge. Conversely, the Democrats' noninvolvement undoubtedly weakened the mild reservationists' bargaining position. Yet the likelihood that a majority or near-majority favored the Lodge reservations threw doubt on how much room for maneuver really existed. Moreover, the alignment that was about to emerge in the voting on reservations would underline how little latitude remained for genuine compromise. Still, any participation by the Democrats would have been better than nothing, and nothing was what the Democrats gave the mild reservationists in these dealings. For that, Wilson's stroke and the way that the people around him were handling it were solely to blame.[44]

Lodge's success in securing a united Republican front became evident when he unveiled his fourteen reservations on the Senate floor on October 24. During the preceding three days, he had gathered all the Republicans on the Foreign Relations Committee, including McCumber, behind the preamble and twelve of the reservations. The Article X reservation, though altered a little, was no less restrictive and scarcely less

---

43. New York *World*, Oct. 25, 1919. See also *New York Times*, Oct. 25, 1919.
44. St. Louis *Post-Dispatch*, Oct. 24, 1919, quoted in Margulies, *Mild Reservationists,* 145. Cf. Margulies' interpretation, ibid. 147. Also cf. the judgment of the LEP's chief lobbyist: "The Republican majority and its Democratic recruits offer a compromise. The Democratic minority offers nothing thus far." Talcott Williams to Lowell, Nov. 4, 1919, Lowell Papers.

offensively worded than the previous version – the one that Wilson had so hotly denounced at Salt Lake City. It now read:

> The United States assumes no obligation to preserve the territorial integrity or political independence of any other country or to intervene in controversies between nations – whether members of the league or not – under provisions of article 10, or to employ the military or naval forces of the United States under any article of the treaty for any purpose, unless, in any particular case, the Congress, which, under the Constitution, has the sole power to declare war or authorize the employment of the military or naval forces of the United States, shall by act or joint resolution so provide.

Small wonder McCumber and other mild reservationists felt as if they had swallowed a bitter, possibly poisonous, pill.[45]

The remaining Republican-sponsored reservations covered other parts of the treaty and the Covenant. One withheld assent to the Shantung clauses. Several required congressional approval for appointments to League commissions and other treaty-enforcing bodies. One permitted the United States to maintain relations with Covenant-breaking nations. One allowed the United States to exceed limitations on armaments that might be agreed upon by the League. One reserved all American legal rights. Previously rejected amendments had covered some of those matters. The committee did not present a reservation on British Empire voting because the Senate had not yet acted on the amendments that dealt with that subject. The complete set of reservations attained the ironic number of fourteen because two additional ones came from a Democrat. John Shields of Tennessee, who had voted for the Republicans' reservations in the committee, got them to reciprocate by agreeing to two of his reservations. One was a disclaimer of any American mandates over former German colonies. The other was the stinging assertion of exclusive American rights to exclude matters of national honor and vital interests.[46]

III

The thirteen days that the Senate met between the beginning of November and the final votes on the 19th witnessed an all-time high in the

---

45. *Congressional Record*, 66th Cong., 1st Sess. (Oct. 24, 1919), 7417.
46. The reservations are in ibid., 7417–7418. The idea for the exclusion of honor and vital interests had originated with a non–committee Democrat, Reed. On the deliberations and actions within the Foreign Relations Committee, see Ambrosius, *Wilson and Diplomatic Tradition*, 199–201.

number of speeches delivered during the League fight – sixty-six. As before, critics and opponents dominated the speechmaking. Despite the preponderance of negative speaking, more real debate and interchange among senators took place now than at any time yet in the League fight. More and more of the debate concentrated on Article X. One of the Democratic dissidents, Gore, rejected the obligation "to take part in every war that ever happens on this planet" and found "a league to enforce peace, a contradiction in terms." Another dissident Democrat, Hoke Smith of Georgia, declared himself "utterly opposed to any kind of a league of nations that has a constitution with the power of physical force." Borah argued that Article X must fail because it was either too weak or too strong. "If the council has no authority, no power, no reserve force until it consults with Congress," he asked, "what reason have we to believe that its authority will preserve peace any more than the actions of Congress itself, without any contract binding us?" Still, Borah feared that the article would suck America into "the rapacious power of the imperial system of Europe. . . . I know that instead of Americanizing Europe, Europe will Europeanize America."[47]

The two most noteworthy speeches during this run-up to the final votes came from Irreconcilables. Speaking for the first time in two months, Knox introduced a reservation of his own "to make the United States a consulting member of the league of nations, . . . in the league, in principle, without making us an integral part of the league in all its complicated and questionable details." Thereby, he argued, America would "do a great service to the world. By becoming more, America would stultify herself for the service of right in the world, and would at the same time put in jeopardy her precious heritage." "Fighting Bob" La Follette finally took his stand among the Irreconcilables when he delivered a two-day diatribe against Wilson and the treaty. Denouncing the president's "departure from the letter and the spirit of the Constitution," La Follette reviewed Wilson's previous writings to expose "the peculiar sinuous workings of that mind." He also dismissed Wilson as "a gentleman who had failed as a lawyer and had become a college professor." In view of the president's transgressions and "the injustice involved in the treaty," La Follette demanded that his colleagues must ensure that "this treaty will be either materially amended, or . . . rejected so decisively that no President in the future will ever attempt to make a treaty involving matters of supreme importance in our international relations, to say nothing of an attempt to reconstruct our Gov-

47. *Congressional Record*, 66th Cong., 1st Sess. (Nov. 4, 1919), 7948; (Nov. 5, 1919), 7953–7957; (Nov. 7, 1919), 8058–8062.

ernment, without at least advising the Senate in his monumental undertaking."[48]

The first measures in the package of reservations to come to a vote
were the preamble and the reservation stating a unilateral right of withdrawal from the League. These reservations passed and proposed
amendments failed, nearly all by similar margins. Virtually every
Republican – joined by Gore, Reed, Walsh of Massachusetts, and,
sometimes, Shields and Smith of Georgia – supplied between forty-eight
and fifty votes for the winning side. Opposing them were between
thirty-seven and forty votes, all from Democrats, together with
McCumber and, once, Knute Nelson of Minnesota. These votes established a pattern that would prevail on all but two of the reservations
reported out from the Foreign Relations Committee.[49]

The next reservation to come before the Senate was the one dealing
with Article X. This measure prompted the most tightly focused debate
of the entire League fight. On November 10, the two Democrats named
Walsh clashed over the article and the treaty. Thomas Walsh of Montana charged that this reservation virtually nullified Article X, whose
"purpose is to stop the war and compel the aggressor to submits its
controversy . . . to the arbitratment of the council." Walsh did concede
that the "removal of the chance to aid deserving revolutionaries is an
evil" inherent in this plan and that those "who regard this chance as
sacred" should oppose "any league of nations." David Walsh of Massachusetts responded that "my objection to article 10 is that it perpetuates
the status quo condition." He professed to be "a believer in a league of
nations" who expected to vote for a covenant, provided there was sufficient protection against such objectionable features as Article X, Shantung, and British Empire votes.[50]

More speechmaking and attempts to change this reservation took
place before it finally came to a vote on November 13. A Democrat,
Robert Owen of Oklahoma, defended the treaty as a fulfillment of the
Fourteen Points and Article X as the means necessary to enforce a just
peace. Norris retorted that Article X was just the opposite – an insidious device "to stifle the cry of freedom" of the peoples of Ireland,
Egypt, Korea, and Shantung and thus "uphold the cruel aristocratic
reign of greedy kings and pagan monarchs the world over." Thomas
Walsh acknowledged that Wilson had failed to embody all of the Four-

48. Ibid. (Nov. 6, 1919), 8000, 8001–8010.
49. Ibid. (Nov. 6, 1919), 8020; (Nov. 7, 1919), 8065; (Nov. 8, 1919), 8136.
50. Ibid. (Nov. 10, 1919), 8192–8200, 8207.

teen Points in the peace settlement, but he blamed those shortcomings on "constant derision upon the Republican side of this Chamber." Lodge restated his insistence on bulwarks against Germany, but he also maintained, "I never for a moment contemplated that we were to be handed a document which bound us for all time, without any possible limit anywhere." Reed launched into a two-day denunciation of Wilson and the League. Reviewing what he regarded as the real reasons that America had gone to war, Reed asked, "Do you find anything there about making the world safe for democracy? Do you find anything . . . that can be construed into the voice of God calling the American people to regenerate the earth, to change the Governments that have existed?"[51]

Interspersed among these speeches were votes on six efforts to mitigate the terms of the reservation. All of them fell short of adoption. Between thirty-one and thirty-four senators voted in favor – all Democrats. Between forty-four and forty-six voted against – all Republicans, joined by the same five Democrats: Gore, Reed, Shields, Smith of Georgia, and Walsh of Massachusetts. With those straws in the wind, approval of the reservation itself was a foregone conclusion. It passed, forty-six for and thirty-three against. The votes in favor came from Republicans – including such mild reservationists as Colt and McCumber – joined by a predictable Democratic foursome – Gore, Reed, Smith, and Walsh; Shields did not vote but announced in favor. Three other nonvoters, all Republicans, also announced in favor. All of the opposing votes came from Democrats, with four more announced against. Effectively, slightly more than an absolute majority – fifty senators – favored this stringent limitation on obligations under Article X. Of the eight other nonvoting senators, who did not announce their stands, two were Irreconcilables (Knox and McCormick) and two were mild reservationists (Kellogg and Nelson) – all of whom were either sure or highly likely to have favored this reservation. Conversely, counting the four Democrats announced against and adding the four other unannounced Democrats, the largest possible number in opposition only came to forty-one. In all, between fifty and fifty-four senators favored and between thirty-seven and forty-one opposed stringent

51. Ibid. (Nov. 11, 1919), 8271–8275, 8286–8292, 8296; (Nov. 12, 1919), 8365–8373. Reed had to curtail his speech because word arrived that Senator Martin of Virginia had just died, and the Senate followed its established custom of adjourning for the rest of the day out of respect for a deceased member.

restrictions on adherence to Article X. Those numbers did not augur well prospects for any agreement that might satisfy Wilson and his Democratic loyalists. Except for the final votes on consent to the treaty itself, this was the most significant vote that the Senate took during the entire League fight.[52]

After that vote, the incidence of speechmaking on reservations and the treaty fell off until November 18 and 19, the last two days of consideration. This abatement in oratory stemmed from two circumstances. One was the introduction of a related measure to limit debate or to impose – in the Senate's parlance – "cloture." No such possibility had existed until two years before. The Senate had first adopted cloture procedures on March 8, 1917, in the angry aftermath of the filibuster of the armed ships bill by La Follette, Norris, and other anti-interventionists, whom Wilson had dubbed "a little group of willful men." This new procedure required that upon presentation of a petition signed by at least sixteen members, a vote on limiting debate must be held within two legislative days. If two-thirds of the Senate voted for cloture, then each member would be limited to one hour of speaking time on the measure before the body and no amendments could be offered without unanimous consent.[53]

On November 13, before the vote on the Article X reservation, Gilbert Hitchcock attempted to present a cloture petition signed by twenty-three Democrats, but the president pro tempore ruled the petition out of order and was sustained on a roll-call vote. After the vote on the reservation, however, Lodge presented his own cloture petition, signed by thirty Republicans. The next legislative day fell on Monday, November 15, and after some sparring over procedures, the Senate imposed cloture on its members for the first time, by a vote of seventy-eight to sixteen. Eleven of the opposing votes came from announced Irreconcilables, and three more came from harsh critics of the League. Cloture would have a big impact on the length of speeches but not on the number of senators who spoke. The other circumstance that really curtailed speechmaking was a one-day adjournment on November 16. The adjournment was to allow a number of senators, including Lodge and most of the senior Democrats, to go to Charlottesville, Virginia, for

52. Ibid. (Nov. 13, 1919), 8437. The nonvoting, unannounced Democrats were Bankhead, Chamberlain, Culberson, Smith (Arizona), and Swanson.

53. On the adoption of cloture, see ibid., 65th Cong., Special Session of Senate (Mar. 8, 1917), 45; *New York Times,* Mar. 9, 1917. On the armed ships filibuster, see Link, *Wilson,* V, 359–367.

the funeral of Senator Thomas Martin, the long-ailing Democratic leader, who had died on November 12.[54]

Cloture evidently delivered a salutary shock. Within minutes after the vote on cloture, the senators started voting on reservations. On November 15, the senators voted seventeen times, the second highest number of votes on any day that they considered the treaty. Most of the votes followed the now-established pattern. Usually favoring the position of Lodge and the Foreign Relations Committee were between fifty and fifty-four senators – all Republicans except for the familiar Democratic quintet of Gore, Reed, Shields, Smith of Georgia, and Walsh of Massachusetts. Opposing them were usually between forty and forty-three senators – all Democrats. There were occasional variations. The reservation requiring congressional approval to accept a League mandate passed on a voice vote, without a roll call. Two other reservations – one exempting such domestic matters as tariffs and immigration and one excluding the Monroe Doctrine – attracted fifty-five and fifty-nine votes in favor. At the end of the day, Lodge noted with satisfaction that "we have now been in session for more than six hours and have disposed of 10 reservations."[55]

Only the last two of the Foreign Relations Committee's reservations remained to be voted on. These reservations – one declining to assume mandates over former German colonies in Africa and the Pacific and the other excluding all matters of national honor and vital interests – reportedly enjoyed less support than the others. Debate and voting on November 17 bore out those earlier predictions. The reservation against mandates produced some curious arguments. Two Republicans, Harry New of Indiana and Charles Townsend of Michigan, and a Democrat, James D. Phelan of California, invoked anti-Japanese sentiments as reasons for supporting or opposing this reservation. Africa loomed largest

54. *Congressional Record,* 66th Cong., 1st Sess. (Nov. 13, 1919), 8413–8417, 8437; (Nov. 15, 1919), 8547, 8549, 8555–8556. The other two votes against cloture came from two Democrats normally counted among Wilson's supporters, King and Pomerene. The only senator not to vote was Fall. On the background to cloture, see also *New York Times,* Nov. 13, 1919; New York *World,* Nov. 13, 1919; and H. N. Rickey to Short, Nov. 14, 1919, LEP Papers.

55. *Congressional Record,* 66th Cong., 1st Sess. (Nov. 15, 1919), 8571. The votes are in ibid., 8556–8571. For a comparable assessment of the day's business, see entry, Nov. 15, 1919, Ashurst Diary, in George F. Sparks, ed., *A Many-Colored Toga: The Diary of Henry Fountain Ashurst* (Tucson, Ariz., 1962), 114.

in the minds of two others on opposite sides. Shields of Tennessee supported the reservation because "no possible benefit" could derive from
American involvement "in a barbarous country far away" in Africa.
Joseph France of Maryland reiterated his total rejection of the League
but opposed this reservation because he saw in a possible American
mandate a chance to promote "the advancement of the peoples of
Africa." This reservation became the first of the committee's proposals
to be defeated. Its sixty-four opponents included twenty-two Republicans. Most of the mild reservationists voted against it, as did some
harsh critics of the League and two Irreconcilables, France and Norris.[56]

The final reservation – the sweeping exclusion of national honor and
vital interests – provoked a debate that was both pointed and predictable. Knox supported the reservation, denying that as secretary of
state in 1911 he had proposed to submit such matters to arbitration.
Similarly, Lodge quoted Falstaff on the meaning of honor from Shakespeare's *Henry IV* and demanded that America "keep its vital interests
and its honor clear from the dictation of any other power on the face of
the earth." This reservation also failed to be approved, though by a narrower margin. Opposing it were fifty-six senators – of whom sixteen
were Republicans, including all of the mild reservationists. Of the
thirty-seven supporters, three were Democrats – Gore, Reed, and
Shields. It was significant that more than a third of the Senate favored a
measure that everyone acknowledged would nullify any obligation
under the League and the rest of the treaty.[57]

Disposing of the committee's proposals opened the way for senators
to present reservations of their own. McCumber immediately introduced one to withhold assent from the labor clauses, which he found
"the only feature of the treaty that is obnoxious and abhorrent." By
unanimous consent this reservation was put aside for a day. Owen then
offered a reservation withholding assent from articles in the treaty that
recognized British domination in Egypt, which he called "a matter
affecting the honor and dignity of liberty throughout the world."
Affirming a common bond of anticolonial sentiment that existed
between some League advocates and Irreconcilables, Norris praised
Owen for having "outlined one of the sinful things contained in this
treaty," and he compared Britain's treatment of Egypt with Japan's
aggression in Korea and Shantung. This reservation also fell short of
adoption, with thirty-seven for and forty-five against. Owen next

56. Ibid., 8619, 8629–8630, 8634.
57. Ibid. (Nov. 17, 1919), 8618, 8634–8635, 8637, 8640.

offered a reservation affirming the Fourteen Points. It was rejected on a voice vote.[58]

By the end of the day on November 17, the senators had approved twelve reservations, all of which had come from the Foreign Relations Committee. Besides the preamble – which would require the assent of three of the four major Allies – these measures included assertions on such matters as the right of unilateral withdrawal from the League and maintenance of relations with treaty-breaking powers, exclusion of domestic questions and the Monroe Doctrine from the League's jurisdiction, the ability to exceed possible limits on armaments, and disavowal of the Shantung cession. Most important, the reservation to Article X severely circumscribed any obligation under that article and required approval by both houses of Congress for any enforcement actions. In all, these reservations embodied a limited, suspicious, grudging conception of approval of the peace treaty and membership in the League of Nations that stood poles apart from President Wilson's expansive vision. At the conclusion of the voting, Lodge moved that the Senate should meet for two hours earlier the next day and "remain in session until we dispose of the amendments [sic] and reach the ratifying resolution." The senators passed the motion on a voice vote and went home to get ready for the last two days of debate and voting.[59]

58. Ibid., 8641, 8642, 8643–8644.
59. Ibid., 8644.

6

Showdown

November 18 and 19, 1919, proved to be the busiest and most intense time in the whole League fight. These two days ranked with the great clashes before the Civil War and during Reconstruction afterward as among the most momentous encounters in the then-130-year history of the U.S. Senate. The first of these days' meetings began two hours earlier than usual, at 10 o'clock in the morning, and lasted until 10:15 at night. The second and last day's meeting began at the normal hour of noon and lasted until 11:15 at night. At that point, the first session of the Sixty-sixth Congress officially adjourned. Only during filibusters and those round-the-clock marathons that customarily preceded the expiration of a congress did the Senate hold such long meetings. Cloture made these two days more unusual still, because of the limit on the length of speeches. Instead of delivering their usual lengthy disquisitions, the senators filled these long days with sharper, more-pointed remarks and roll-call votes. In all, it was a tense, exciting moment.

I

Cloture ruled the day from the outset. Of the nine senators who spoke on November 18, all but three briefly addressed additional reservations that were being proposed. One of the exceptions was La Follette. Other senators yielded time to him so that he could excoriate the League as "an instrument for the preservation of the status quo. Like the Holy Alliance of 1815, it is couched in the language of idealism and peace. But, like the Holy Alliance, it will be used for the suppression of nationalities and for the prosecution of aggressive warfare." At last daring to allude to his opposition to the war, La Follette denounced "the imperialists who dominate the British Foreign Office" for having seduced the United States into the war and now for seeking "the crushing of the German Republic and the German people, who, according to the President's own terms, were not responsible for the war." Another exception was Knox, who once more urged separating the League from the treaty and demanded that the United States assume "no obligations whatsoever to go forward in reference to matters which we regard as improper or unjust."[1]

Voting, not speaking, occupied most of the Senate's time on November 18. This twelve-hour session witnessed the largest number of votes of any day in the consideration of the treaty – twenty-one. All of the votes dealt with reservations, which fell into three categories. One category consisted of efforts by individual senators and groups of senators to attach even stricter reservations than those presented by the Foreign Relations Committee. For example, Hiram Johnson offered a substitute for one of his defeated amendments. His reservation would have equalized American and British dominion voting in all League bodies. It failed, forty-three for and forty-six against. Most of the reservations in this category fell short by margins of around thirty in favor and fifty against. The second category of proposed reservations consisted of more or less quixotic gestures toward weakening or strengthening American participation in the League. In this category, the two most significant reservations were an effort by Knox to keep the United States out of the League and a move by Walsh of Massachusetts to restrict Article XI – the clause that authorized the League to take cognizance of threats to international order – from applying to efforts to gain national independence. Knox's reservation attracted thirty votes, with sixty-one against. The Walsh reservation, which he admitted was aimed at Ireland, gained thirty-six votes, with forty-two against.[2]

The final group of reservations numbered just three. These were the only ones to be adopted. One was a proposal by McCumber not to accept the labor clauses unless Congress approved them by joint resolution. This measure passed, fifty-four for and thirty-five against. Joining Republicans in voting for this reservation were nine Democrats, including the usual deviant foursome, Gore, Reed, Shields, and Walsh of Massachusetts. The second successful reservation was Lenroot's move to exempt the United States from obligations to comply with any League action in which members of the British Empire cast more than one vote. The fifty-five in favor included six Democrats, while McCum-

1. *Congressional Record*, 66th Cong., 1st Sess. (Nov. 18, 1919), 8720–8729, 8742–8743. For accounts of the day's debate and action see entry, Nov. 18, 1919, Ashurst Diary, in George F. Sparks, ed., *Many-Colored Toga: The Diary of Henry Fountain Ashurst* (Tucson, Ariz., 1962), 114; *New York Times,* Nov. 18, 1919; New York *World,* Nov. 18, 1919.

2. These and the other votes are in *Congressional Record,* 66th Cong., 1st Sess. (Nov. 18, 1919), 8729–8759.

ber joined thirty-seven Democrats in voting against. The last reservation to be adopted was the Foreign Relations Committee's proposal to require congressional approval to accept a League mandate, which had been approved earlier on a voice vote. Now, on a roll call, fifty-two senators favored the reservation, including seven Democrats; thirty-one Democrats and no Republicans opposed it. These votes – together with unsuccessful attempts to water down the preamble and to revive previously rejected proposals – completed the roll calls. The number of reservations, exclusive of the preamble, still stood at the ironic total of fourteen. All that remained, besides jockeying for position among the different sides, was to vote on the treaty itself.

By this point, the senators had voted seventy-five times on matters relating to the treaty and the League. The final day's meeting on November 19 would produce another fifteen votes, three of which would be on consent to the treaty. The alignment of senators on those final roll calls, as well as on the other, mostly procedural votes that last day, would come as no surprise to anyone who had been following the earlier roll calls. Those last fifteen votes would bear out the patterns established during the preceding seven weeks. It is worth examining what those patterns were.

The best way to see how senators stood on these votes is to rate them for their support of and, conversely, opposition to the Wilson administration's position. Table 6.1 lists senators according to a descending level of support on the votes taken between late September and November 19, 1919.

This tabulation gives numerical confirmation to the impressions that anyone could have gathered from senators' speeches during the preceding five months. As in those speeches, two qualities loomed above all others in the voting – polarization and partisanship. On the Democratic side, all but one of the two Irreconcilables, Reed, and the three non-Irreconcilable dissidents – Gore, Shields, and Walsh of Massachusetts – supported Wilson on seventy-five percent or more of the votes that they cast. Oddly and anomalously, the other Democratic Irreconcilable, Thomas, supported the administration's position 84 percent of the time that he voted. All but seven Democrats backed their president on 90 percent or more of their votes, and more than half of the party's forty-six senators – twenty-six in all – supported the administration's position on at least 98 percent of their roll calls. Overall, the mean percentage of support among non-Irreconcilable Democrats was 92.5. Excluding the dissident trio raises that percentage to 97.2.

On the Republican side, only one senator, McCumber, supported Wilson more than half of the times that he voted. Only nine other Republicans joined him in casting 40 percent or more of their votes that

Table 6.1 *Senatorial Support for Wilson Administration Position on Treaty of Versailles, 66th Congress, 1st Session**

Percent support	Senators (Democrat, *Republican,* <u>Irreconcilable</u>)
100	Ashurst, Gerry, Harris, Harrison, Jones (N.M.), Nugent, Sheppard, Smith (S.C.), Smith (Md.), Smith (Ariz.), Wolcott
99	Fletcher, Gay, Henderson, Hitchcock, Kendrick, Robinson, Simmons, Stanley, Swanson, Williams
98	Bankhead, Culberson, McKellar, Ransdell, Johnson (S. Dak.)
97	Overman, Pittman, Pomerene, Walsh (Mont.)
96	Dial
95	Chamberlain, Kirby, Owen, Underwood
94	King, Phelan
92	Trammell
90	Myers
86	Beckham
84	<u>Thomas</u>
75	Smith (Ga.)
66	*McCumber*
49	*Nelson*
47	*Lenroot*
46	*Sterling*
45	*Hale*
44	*Kellogg,* Walsh (Mass.)
43	*Edge, McNary*
41	*Colt, Keyes*
38	*Spencer*
37	*Townsend*
32	*Smoot*
27	*Warren*
25	*Kenyon*
23	*Dillingham*
21	*Wadsworth*
20	*Cummins, Newberry,* Jones (Wash.), *Phipps,* <u>*Poindexter*</u>
19	Shields
18	*Harding*
17	*Frelinghuysen,* Gore
16	*Capper, Sutherland*
15	*Curtis*
14	*New*
13	*McLean*
12	*Ball,* <u>*Brandegee,*</u> *Page,* <u>Reed</u>
11	*Elkins,* Lodge, <u>*McCormick*</u>
10	<u>Borah,</u> *Calder,* <u>*Fall, Fernald, Sherman*</u>
9	<u>*Knox, Moses, Norris*</u>
8	<u>*Gronna,*</u> Penrose, Watson
7	<u>*La Follette*</u>
6	<u>*France, Johnson*</u> (Calif.)

*The total number of votes is ninety. The total number of senators is ninety-five, because Martin is not included. Percentage scores are based upon the number of times each senator voted, not the total number of roll calls.

way. Of the forty-nine Republican senators, thirty-seven supported the administration position on fewer than one-third of their votes, whereas over half of their total membership – twenty-seven – favored that position on less than 20 percent of their votes. Overall, the mean percentage of support among non-Irreconcilable Republicans was 27.4. Excluding McCumber lowers the percentage to 26.2. By way of comparison, the mean percentage of support among Irreconcilables was 14.6. Excluding their deviant, Thomas, lowers the percentage to 12.4.

One factor alone helps to explain these divisions – partisanship. No other factor serves to differentiate the senators' voting. For example, the three main groups show striking similarities in age, length of service, and sectional representation, as illustrated in Table 6.2.

The only other apparent difference among these groups was sectional. That difference was really a function of partisanship, as shown in Table 6.3.

Plainly, sectional factors divorced from partisanship explained nothing about those divisions. How high the senators from any section scored on the average depended entirely upon how many of them were Democrats. Both the high average score of southern senators and the absence of southerners from the Republican and Irreconcilable ranks stemmed from the same source – the Democrats' total domination of that section. The partisan underpinning of these sectional differences was likewise clear elsewhere. Four senators apiece from the Northeast and Midwest made up the Democrats' total senatorial strength in those

Table 6.2 *Characteristics of Senators by Voting Groups on Treaty of Versailles, 66th Congress, 1st Session*

Group	Number	Mean Age	Mean Years of Service	NE	S	MW	W
				Section*			
Democrats	44	55	6.2	4	25	3	12
Republicans	35	58	7.4	15		15	5
Irreconcilables (14 *Rep.*, 2 *Dem.*)	16	57	6.4	5		6	5
Senate as Whole	95	56	6.6	24	25	24	22

*Sections are defined as follows: "NE" = Northeast, includes New England and Middle Atlantic states, plus Maryland, Delaware, and West Virginia; "S" = South, includes former Confederate states, plus Kentucky and Oklahoma; "MW" = Midwest, includes Great Lakes, North Central, and Plains states, plus Missouri; "W" = West, includes states in the Rocky Mountains and on the West Coast.

Table 6.3 *Sectional Distribution of Senators' Votes on Matters Related to the Treaty of Versailles, 66th Congress, 1st Session*

Region	Northeast	South	Midwest	West
Mean percentage support of Wilson admin.	27.4	90.4	31.0	65.3
No. of Democrats	4 (15%)	25 (100%)	4(15%)	13(50%)
No. of Republicans	22 (85%)		22(85%)	13(50%)

regions; two of the four northeasterners were from the border states of Maryland and Delaware. Nothing quite matched the Democrats' racially reinforced stranglehold on the South, but the Republicans had enjoyed comfortable dominance in the Northeast and Midwest since the mid-1890s. The only serious challenges to their dominance there had come from insurgencies within their own ranks. Roosevelt's bolt in 1912 had shaken this sectional hegemony, but, it appeared, only temporarily. Despite Wilson's reelection in 1916, the Republicans had recaptured most of the Northeast and Midwest. In 1918, despite upsets in New York and Massachusetts, they had apparently completed their restoration in those regions. As before, the West remained the only genuinely competitive two-party region of the country.[3]

3. In fact, the display of southern solidarity behind Wilson on the League and the treaty was a bit deceptive. Two of the three non-Irreconcilable Democratic dissidents, Gore and Shields, were southerners. In the previous congress, two other southern Democrats, Hardwick of Georgia and Vardaman of Mississippi, had stated that they would have taken their stands with the Irreconcilables if they had remained in the Senate. Hardwick, who had since become a leader in the Independence League, would make a political comeback in 1920, when he won the governorship of Georgia. In the same Democratic primary that Hardwick won, the veteran racist demagogue Tom Watson would defeat both the reservationist Hoke Smith and a more ardently pro-Wilson candidate on a platform of total rejection of the League and "Wilsonism." On Hardwick's and Watson's victories, see C. Vann Woodward, *Tom Watson: Agrarian Rebel* (New York, 1938), 470–474, and Dewey W. Grantham, Jr., *Hoke Smith and the Politics of the New South* (Baton Rouge, La., 1958), 351–357.
   On the broader question of sectional influences, none of the measures later used by interpreters of isolationism and internationalism really helps to explain these divisions in senatorial voting. Isolationism would be associated with the Midwest because of such factors as insularity – meaning distance

(continued)

Table 6.4   *Characteristics of Mild Reservationist Republican Senators, 66th Congress, 1st Session*

Number	Mean Age	Mean Years of Service	Section NE	MW	W
10	52.6	6.4	4	5	1

The one set of differences over the treaty and the League that partisanship does not explain is deviance within the parties. It is hard to say what does explain that deviance. For example, as the numbers in Table 6.2 show, the Irreconcilables were strikingly congruent with the other two groups in mean age and length of service. Their sectional distribution mainly reflected their comprising fourteen Republicans and only two Democrats. Similarly, the three non-Irreconcilable Democratic dissidents, Gore, Shields, and Walsh of Massachusetts, had a mean age of 52 and length of service of 6.3 and a sectional distribution of two southerners and a northeasterner – all of which mirrored the overall shape of their party's representation in the Senate. The Republicans who supported Wilson's position more than 40 percent of the time, the mild reservationists, showed little difference from their party as a whole, as shown in Table 6.4.

"Cosmopolitanism" – the notion that later interpreters would usually invoke to explain receptivity to overseas involvement – likewise explained almost nothing about how senators voted in the fall of 1919.

from oceans and ingrained notions of self-sufficiency – and ethnicity – meaning large concentrations of German and Scandinavian Americans. Conversely, the most internationalist region should have been and was usually presumed to be the Northeast, thanks to its greater proximity to Europe, greater involvement in international finance and trade, and concentrations of elite colleges and universities and cosmopolitian cultural institutions. The evidently anomalous circumstance of high southern support for overseas involvement and intervention was explained by invoking such factors as the region's economic attachment to low tariffs and fondness for things military and "British-American" ethnicity among the dominant white caste. Oddly, Democratic partisanship seldom figured much in interpretations of southern "internationalism." For discussions of these interpretations, see John Milton Cooper, Jr., *Vanity of Power: American Isolationism and the First World War* (Westport, Conn., 1969), 250–257.

One frequently cited measure of cosmopolitanism would be an elite education. But among these senators, the twelve who were graduates of Harvard and Yale, six apiece, ranged across virtually the entire spectrum of support. The lone Democrat among the Harvard men, Peter Gerry of Rhode Island, scored 100 percent; among the five Republicans the highest scorer was Frederick Hale of Maine, at 45 percent. None of the Harvard men joined the Irreconcilables at this time, but two of them, Lodge and Boies Penrose of Pennsylvania, scored among the lowest in support for the treaty and the League, at 11 and 8 percent, respectively. Of the Yale men, all of whom were Republicans, two, Brandegee and McCormick, were Irreconcilables; their highest scorer among them was Colt, at 41 percent.[4]

Other measures of cosmopolitanism, such as study and residence abroad, fluency in foreign languages, and diplomatic service, actually tended to correlate negatively with support for the treaty and the League. The Senate's one former envoy to a foreign country was George Moses of New Hampshire, a Dartmouth graduate who had served earlier as minister to Greece and who spoke French and Greek. He was an Irreconcilable. So was the former secretary of state, Knox. Of the three senators who had studied at foreign universities, all of them in Germany, the two Democrats, Hitchcock and Williams, supported the administration position on 99 percent of their votes. The other one was Joseph France. He was both an Irreconcilable and one of the pair of senators who scored at the bottom of the scale of support – 6 percent. By background, the most cosmopolitan member of the Senate was McCormick. As a child, he had lived and gone to school in England and Europe while his father served in diplomatic posts. He boasted that he had learned to

4. The Harvard men were *Elkins,* Gerry, *Hale, Keyes, Lodge,* and *Penrose.* The Yale men were *Brandegee, Colt, McCormick, Newberry, Spencer,* and *Wadsworth.* Among the senators were also two Princeton alumni, both Democrats, Pomerene and Gay, who had studied there when Wilson was a professor and president. Among the southern Democrats, three were graduates of Vanderbilt and four had studied law at the University of Virginia. Three senators were Civil War veterans: Bankhead, who had fought for the Confederacy, and *Nelson* and *Warren,* who had fought for the Union. At age 77, Bankhead was the oldest member of the Senate. The youngest, at 38, was his fellow Democrat, Harrison of Mississippi, who had defeated Vardaman in 1918. *Nelson,* a native of Norway, was the only foreign-born senator. Six senators were veterans of the Spanish-American War – all Republicans – *Edge, Ekins, Fall, Frelinghuysen, Newberry,* and *Wadsworth.* Only *Newberry* had also served in the world war.

speak French before he spoke English, and he had attended the most anglophilic of New England boarding schools, Groton, before going to Yale. Besides being an Irreconcilable, McCormick favored the treaty and the League on only 11 percent of the votes that he cast.[5]

Insofar as differences among senators can be explained other than along party lines, two other considerations have to be included. One consideration involves such elusive matters as temperament and personal experience. Both the high level of support for Wilson's position among Democrats and the comparatively low level among Republicans derived almost entirely from party loyalty. Most of the senators who seldom or never spoke in the debates and took little part in the behind-the-scenes maneuvers clustered in their voting around the positions of their respective leaders, Wilson and Lodge. Not every senator cared passionately about the treaty and the League, and the ones who did not made up many of those in the clusters at either end of the spectrum. This was especially true among the Democrats. Among them, Williams, Owen, and Walsh of Montana seemed to be the only ones who felt a deep personal stake in supporting Wilson's position. The Republicans who ranged between 10 and 30 percent in their support affected to care greatly about the defense of American sovereignty, but much of their speaking and voting likewise seemed perfunctory.

It was the men of more intense temperament and stronger feelings who tended to become the party deviants. Of the five Democrats who went their own way – the two Irreconcilables, Reed and Thomas, and the three strong reservationists, Gore, Shields, and Walsh of Massachusetts – at least three of them had shown maverick tendencies before. Reed was an ally of the subsequently fabled Pendergast machine in his hometown of Kansas City, but he was something of a political loner and a fiery orator. Also, despite his protestations of good will toward the president, Reed seemed to feel a need to demean and defy him. Thomas was an eccentric, even by the permissive standards of the Senate of that day. He was also a political loner, an unreconstructed advocate of silver money, and a fierce opponent of labor radicalism. His anomalous voting record bore witness to his wrenching personal conflict. Thomas liked Wilson and admired his idealism, but he recoiled from the treaty's labor clauses and harbored a deep pessimism about any possible melio-

5. On McCormick's speaking French before English, see McCormick to Cyrus H. K. Curtis, Nov. 2, 1923, Hanna-McCormick Papers, Library of Congress, Box 10.

ration of international affairs. Gore was a one-time Populist who had been blind since boyhood. He had already broken party ranks to vote against going to war in 1917. Some observers were surprised that he did not join the Irreconcilables.[6]

Less easy to explain were the motives of the other Democratic deviants. Shields was another of the southern Democrats whom Wilson had tried to purge in 1918. In his speeches, Shields sounded more like a Republican nationalist and a "realist" than any other Democrat except Reed. Most observers attributed the Massachusetts Walsh's deviancy to his Irish-American background and constituency, who resented Ireland's treatment at the peace conference. It is also noteworthy that Walsh represented a younger generation and new breed of Democrats who owed nothing politically to Wilson. These were the mobilizers of a rising urban, ethnic constituency in the Northeast. Fittingly, Walsh's election to the Senate from Massachusetts in 1918 coincided with Al Smith's capturing the governorship of New York. Also fittingly, the one other outspoken Democratic reservationist and the only other one to fall below 80 percent in his support of the Wilson position was Hoke Smith of Georgia. Smith was a successful lawyer and businessman, an ex-governor and erstwhile political powerhouse

6. On Reed and Thomas, see Ralph A. Stone, *The Irreconcilables: The Fight against the League of Nations* (Lexington, Ky., 1970), 187–188. On Gore, see Monroe Billington, *Thomas P. Gore: Oklahoma's Blind Senator* (Norman, Okla., 1967). Little in the James A. Reed Papers, University of Missouri–Kansas City, sheds much light on the reasons for his apparent hostility to Wilson. In several speeches at the time and later, he insisted that he felt no personal animosity toward the president. Speaking in Kansas City in April 1921, however, he also declared, "Let me say to you the most dangerous man who has ever lived on this earth is the phrase-monger, is the man who can say something in a catchy way, who disregards the plain and practical facts of life. The man who talks about democratizing Europe and puts that phrase into the brains of the American people; that we are going out to democratize the world. I do not speak now of any individual; he is a type." Reed speech, Apr. 5, 1921, ibid., Box 41. Cf. speeches, July 23, 1920, and n.d. [ca. 1936], ibid. Thomas straightforwardly states both his personal regard for Wilson and reasons for opposition to his peace plan in his manuscript autobiography, which was written in 1923 and 1924, Charles S. Thomas Papers, Colorado Historical Society, Box 9; and in Thomas to Paul A. Hill, Jan. 13, 1920, ibid., Box 10. Portions of the autobiography are reproduced in Sewell S. Thomas, *Silhouettes of Charles S. Thomas: Colorado Governor and United States Senator* (Caldwell, Ida., 1959).

in his state. Besides Knox, he was the only former Cabinet member in the Senate. In his youth Smith had practiced law alongside Wilson in Atlanta and done much better at the bar. For all those reasons, he never felt so grateful or awestruck toward the president as did some other Democratic senators.[7]

Among the Republicans, the Irreconcilables claimed such renowned paragons of independence and devotion to principle as Borah, Johnson, La Follette, and Norris. Also, in addition to Johnson, the Senate's other two former Roosevelt third-party Progressives, McCormick and Poindexter, became Irreconcilables. All three of them avowed fealty to Rooseveltian nationalism, but the common bond among them may have more in their taste for defiant, emotionally charged posturing. Likewise, Asle Gronna of North Dakota, La Follette, and Norris had opposed the war and had suffered the slings and arrows of outrageous calumny for their stand. La Follette and Norris claimed that they remained internationalists in theory, but their bitterness toward Wilson made it virtually impossible for them to support any peace settlement or collective security scheme that he might propose. Joseph France had not voted against the declaration of war, but he was perhaps the most ardent international idealist and anti-imperialist in the Senate. With him, too, it is difficult to see how any international organization with enforcement powers could have lived up to his expectations. Not all of the Irreconcilables were former insurgents or even outspoken on the League and the treaty. Bert Fernald of Maine was as obscure and unengaged as any of his low-profile colleagues. Albert Fall seems to have been an amiable wheeler-dealer throughout his checkered political career. But such other Irreconcilables as Brandegee, Sherman, and, to a lesser extent, Moses were also men of passionate intensity who excoriated both Wilson and internationalist idealism

7. On Shields, see the biographical sketch and comments of his Senate colleague, McKellar, in Kenneth D. McKellar, *Tennessee Senators As Seen by One of Their Successors* (Kingsport, Tenn., 1942); on Walsh, see Joseph P. Huthmacher, *Massachusetts People and Politics, 1919–1933* (Cambridge, Mass., 1959); and on Smith, see Grantham, Jr., *Hoke Smith*. Smith had served as secretary of the interior during Grover Cleveland's second administration. Wilson reciprocated this lack of respect. At this time, he said to Hitchcock about Smith, "Don't bother about him. That is his usual attitude. He is always wrong in debate but he votes right. You need not pay any attention to him." Grayson memorandum, Nov. 17, 1919, in Arthur S. Link, ed., *The Papers of Woodrow Wilson* (Princeton, N.J., 1990), LXIV, 45.

with a harshness and a venom that seemed excessive on even such an earthshaking issue as this.[8]

Of all the senators who deviated from their party's norms, the oddest ones were the mild reservationist Republicans. They were not intense or defiant men. All but one of them desired harmony and reconciliation. In their devotion to the League and international reform they resembled Taft more than Wilson, and they similarly gave way on the critical issue of obligations under Article X. As Herbert Margulies has pointed out, these men were not temperamentally suited to the trials and tribulations of mediating between Wilson and Lodge. Even if they had gotten help from Wilson and the Democrats, Lodge's strategic advantages and their own distaste for protracted conflict made it doubtful that they could have achieved much more than they did. The single exception among these mild reservationists was McCumber. He believed as passionately as Wilson did in the League of Nations. His speeches and his voting record had already shown that he would go much further than any other Republican to support the president's position. McCumber would demonstrate that support a final time on November 19, when he became the only member of his party to vote for consent to the treaty without reservations.[9]

8. On these Irreconcilables, see Stone, *Irreconcilables,* 183–186. McCormick proudly noted that he was also differing with his brother and his family's newspaper, the *Chicago Tribune,* which supported League membership with strong reservations. See McCormick to Bryan, Nov. 22, 1919, William Jennings Bryan Papers, Library of Congress, Box 32. Although it may be only coincidental, both Brandegee and McCormick were alcoholics and both later committed suicide. McCormick also suffered from a manic-depressive condition and had been treated by the Swiss psychoanalyst Carl Gustav Jung. See Christie Miller, *Ruth Hanna McCormick: A Life in Politics, 1880–1944* (Albuquerque, N.M., 1992), esp. 44–57, 113–119, 146–147. Fall later became the first Cabinet officer in American history to be convicted of a crime committed in office and to serve a term in prison. He was found guilty of perjury because he lied under oath when he testified before a Senate committee investigating his part in the Teapot Dome affair as Harding's secretary of the interior. The interrogator to whom he gave his perjured answers was Walsh of Montana. On this encounter, see Francis Russell, *The Shadow of Blooming Grove: Warren G. Harding and His Times* (New York, 1968), 609–616.

9. On the mild reservationists, see Herbert F. Margulies, *Mild Reservationists and the League of Nations Controversy in the Senate* (Columbia, Mo., 1989); on McCumber, see ibid., 14–15.

Another consideration is the question of what these differences really amounted to. Down-the-line League advocates and most of the Irreconcilables diverged fundamentally. They formed the opposite poles of opinion in the Senate. Among the rest of the senators, the differences were less stark and less substantial. This was especially the case between the camps of reservationists, mild and strong, and between strong reservationists and Irreconcilables. With the single exception of McCumber, no senator who supported the Wilson position at a level below 86 percent voted for consent without reservations. Even such relatively mild reservationists as Smith of Georgia, with a level of support of 75 percent, Lenroot at 47 percent, and Hale at 45 percent repeatedly warned that they would not vote for consent unless obligations under Article X were severely curtailed or eliminated. Since this remained the crux of the conflict between League advocates and reservationists, questions persist about whether any possible meeting ground for compromise really existed.

Two facts about the strong reservationists and Irreconcilables are noteworthy. First, six Republicans, including Lodge, supported the Wilson position at as low a level as nearly all of the Irreconcilables, yet they still voted for consent with the Lodge reservations. Second, Knox became an Irreconcilable. His presence among them was especially significant. Unlike most of his newfound comrades, he in no way fit the profile of an impassioned loner or insurgent. Furthermore, he and Lodge thought, spoke, and voted almost identically. These facts raise the question of what, if anything, League membership with these restrictions would have meant. Clearly, Lodge and the five other non-Irreconcilable Republicans who scored so low believed that his reservations nullified any obligation under Article X and thereby rendered membership in the League of Nations harmless. Other Republicans, particularly those who voted in the 12 to 37 percent range of support, also shared those beliefs. These circumstances also raise the question of where any real ground for compromise lay.

In order to reach the constitutionally required two-thirds (sixty-four out of ninety-five members), it would have been necessary to delve as low as the 18 percent level of support. If consent had become a live option, some of the senators at or near that level might well have gone over to the Irreconcilables. One of those senators, Shields, later did go over four months later when the treaty came up for another vote with virtually the same reservations. If, on the other hand, Republicans in this range of support had still voted for consent, the other question then became paramount: With such people willing to acquiesce in League membership, could it have amounted to anything meaningful in the way of international enforcement and reform? The ground for genuine compromise seemed to be as elusive as ever.[10]

II

All the while that the speechmaking and voting were going on in November, efforts had continued off the Senate floor to achieve a meeting of the minds between the two main camps. As before, the LEP's lobbyists and leaders strove to promote reconciliation and compromise, but they continued to suffer from their unresolved dilemma over whether or not to swallow the Lodge reservations. The organization's chief lobbyist, Talcott Williams, described the two horns of the dilemma. The preamble and the reservations would, he conceded in a letter to Lowell, make American participation "less effective than it should be, but able to create a League in being which can develop." Besides, he added, the Republican senators "offer a compromise. The Democratic minority offers nothing thus far." But Williams also argued in a memorandum to LEP headquarters that the present set of reservations "is not a compromise and it cannot be accepted as a compromise." Moreover, he warned, "Any declaration [by the LEP] in favor of accepting the existing Reservations cannot hasten action and it will strengthen opposition." Which was it to be for the LEP: The devil or the deep blue sea?[11]

If the devil of that dilemma was the Lodge reservations, then the men who carried the most weight in the LEP were willing to make a pact with that side. Lowell had now convinced himself, as he told the LEP's executive secretary, "So far as these reservations affect the Covenant, which they do not by any means all do, I am inclined to

10. On that second vote, Penrose also went over to the Irreconcilables. Johnson wrote to his sons two days after the last votes that he thought Harding switched at the last minute to support consent with the Lodge reservations. See Johnson to Hiram Jr. and Arch Johnson, Nov. 21, 1919, in Robert E. Burke, ed., *The Diary Letters of Hiram Johnson* (New York, 1983), III. Also, according to Borah's biographer, Harding told him early in 1919, "Bill, I'd like to get into the fight against this League of Nations, but the people of my state are all for it I'm afraid." Harding quoted in Claudius O. Johnson, *Borah of Idaho* (New York, 1936), 233. Harding's most recent biographers have tended to discount these stories of his being a closet Irreconcilable.

11. Williams to Lowell, Nov. 4, 1919, Lowell Papers; Williams memorandum, [Nov. 4, 1919], ibid. See also Williams to Taft, Nov. 4, 1919, Taft Papers, reel 214.

think that the Covenant is about as good with them, as without them." Taft made a comparable capitulation, in stages and mostly in public. In his newspaper column, the ex-president conceded that the Article X reservation left only "an imperfect obligation," but he maintained that there would still be "teeth in the treaty" through the economic boycott and through other nations' adherence to Article X. "The real friends of the treaty should be willing to sacrifice something of their hopes and ambitions," Taft concluded, in order to save what was left. Taft soon likewise convinced himself, as he told a sympathetic newspaper editor, that the Article X reservation "does not modify the original article nearly so much as a good many people have supposed it did, and with the boycott unimpaired the League is one with a great deal of force in it."[12]

With its two most influential leaders leaning so strongly and openly toward acquiescence in the reservations, the LEP could not long avoid officially following suit. The showdown on what stand to take came at a stormy four-hour meeting of the executive committee on November 13. After the LEP's lobbyists reported on the situation in the Senate, there ensued, as the minutes dryly recorded, "extended discussion, which developed the attitude of the Committee on different phases of the question." In fact, the committee members took two conflicting stands as they debated a resolution that opposed the Lodge reservations. This resolution lost, five in favor and ten against. Although the minutes did not name those who supported the resolution, all but one can be identified. They were William Gibbs McAdoo and Vance McCormick, the LEP's two most prominent Democrats; Hamilton Holt, a magazine editor who had introduced the resolution; and Theodore Marburg, a lawyer and one of the original proponents of the league idea. In announcing the result of the vote, Lowell, who was serving as chairman of the meeting, stated, "The opinion of this committee is that we had better accept this treaty with such reservations as the majority pass rather than have it rejected by the present session of the Senate." Taft thereupon moved that Lowell's statement of the LEP's position be publicized and communicated at once to the

12. Lowell to Short, Nov. 4, 1919, Lowell Papers; Philadelphia *Public Ledger,* Nov. 8, 1919; Taft to Casper S. Yost, Nov. 13, 1919, Taft Papers, reel 214. McCumber, for one, upbraided Taft for coming out so flatfootedly in favor of this reservation and worried that his statement would tempt some reservationists to excise the economic boycott as well. See McCumber to Taft, Nov. 8, 1919, ibid.

White House and to Hitchcock, the acting Democratic leader in the Senate.[13]

This bare recording in the minutes conveyed neither the heat of the argument at the meeting nor the decisive role played by Taft. The executive secretary, William Short, hinted at how fractious things got and how persuasive Taft was when he told McAdoo "how deeply I regretted last night having to disagree with you on one of the fundamental questions before the Executive Committee. . . . I shrink as much as any one does from being considered a quitter or a turncoat." But, Short explained, he had "become fully persuaded that Senator Hitchcock's program for a defeat of ratification on the first vote, followed by compromise on more favorable terms, could not succeed. I don't think that Senator Hitchcock himself believes it can be." Another staff member, H. N. Rickey, underscored Taft's role when he told Short, "I was quite sure last night that Mr. Taft's presentation was unanswerable, and I am equally sure of it today." Given Taft's overwhelming influence, it was unthinkable that the LEP could have acted differently. By his own lights, the ex-president had convinced the organization to back a compromise that he found increasingly reasonable and attractive. By his critics' lights, the organization had surrendered to the enemies of their program. At all events, this meeting marked the LEP's swan song. It would play a diminished part in the remainder of the League fight.[14]

As the reference to Hitchcock indicated, the other main source of efforts at compromise continued to be among the senators themselves. The growing prospect of a deadlock worried a number of Democrats inside and outside the Senate. The LEP's lobbyists were predicting at that at least twenty of the party's senators, whom they listed in a memo-

13. Minutes, LEP Executive Committee meeting, Nov. 13, 1919, McAdoo Papers, Box 225. For the identification of those who favored the resolution, see Short to McAdoo, Nov. 14, 1919, ibid.; and Marburg to John Walker Holcombe, Mar. 22, 1920, in John H. Latane, ed., *Development of the League of Nations Idea: Documents and Correspondence of Theodore Marburg* (New York, 1933), II, 673. Bartlett identifies the same four and also speculates that the fifth man was probably Herbert Hoover. Ruhl J. Bartlett, *The League to Enforce Peace* (Chapel Hill, N.C., 1944), 151–152. Hoover's voting for the resolution seems unlikely, because the minutes identify him, along with Lincoln Colcord and Raymond Fosdick, as guests at the meeting.
14. Short to McAdoo, Nov. 14, 1919, McAdoo Papers, Box 225; Rickey to Short, Nov. 14, 1919, LEP Papers.

randum, might vote for consent with the Lodge reservations. In fact, those men did not vote that way November 19, but many of them would prove willing to accept these reservations when the treaty came up for a vote again four months later. The LEP lobbyists had identified a major fault line within the Democrats' Senate contingent. Some recognized national party spokesmen were also swinging around to acquiescence in the reservations. The editor of the country's leading Democratic newspaper, Frank Cobb of the New York *World,* told Taft, "I think you are right in your suggestion, that it would be a great mistake to kill the Treaty because of the reservations."15

As ranking Democrat on the Foreign Relations Committee and acting minority leader, Gilbert Hitchcock was the person who tried hardest to fill the breach in this situation. Late in October, he had started to float the idea of a second round of reservations and votes. "It is Senator Hitchcock's plan," his colleague Ashurst recorded in his diary, "immediately upon the defeat of the Lodge Resolution of Ratification, to introduce another Resolution of Ratification with reservations of such character as will, so he hopes, secure the votes of the 'mild reservationists.'" Hitchcock's plan represented a refinement of the Democratic tactic outlined earlier by Swanson and Underwood. This was to block consent with the Lodge reservations as the opening move in a continuing game. The reservations that Hitchcock wanted to present were the ones that Wilson had given to him in September on the eve of the speaking tour. "We are willing to support and shall propose reservations which will cover all legitimate points," Hitchcock told Taft on November 12, "but that cannot be done until men now bound by promises to support the Lodge resolution are released by its defeat and until they see that support of such reservations means defeat of the treaty."16

The LEP's stand on November 13 did not help Hitchcock's cause, but

15. Cobb to Taft, Nov. 12, 1919, Taft Papers, reel 214. Earlier, both Baruch and McAdoo had stated privately that a compromise on reservations was necessary. See entry, Oct. 17, 1919, Anderson Diary; and McAdoo to Grayson, Oct. 17, 1919, McAdoo Papers, Box 225. For the breakdown of senators, see Rickey to Short, Nov. 14, 1919, LEP Papers; memorandum, "Possible Line-Up of the Senate on the Final Vote to Ratify the Treaty on the Basis of the Reservations Adopted in the Committee of the Whole," [Nov. 14, 1919], ibid. The worst inaccuracies in this prediction involved Republicans, of whom the lobbyists predicted only five – Fall, Gronna, Johnson, Knox, and La Follette – would vote against consent with the Lodge reservations.

16. Entry, Nov. 1, 1919, Ashurst Diary, in Sparks, ed., *Many-Colored Toga,* 111–112; Hitchcock to Taft, Nov. 12, 1919, Taft Papers, reel 214.

he persisted in this strategy. "In my opinion," he told Lowell, "it is better to defeat the Lodge resolution as the first step to a compromise which would eliminate the obnoxious preamble and possibly [permit] a moderate change in the reservation on Article X being secured." This strategy held both promise and danger. As the senators debated under the cloture rule and voted on the Foreign Relations Committee's reservations, talk abounded about both deadlock and compromise. On the afternoon of November 17, Charles Michelson of the *World* observed that senators were holding "almost innumerable conferences." He and the *New York Times'* correspondent also picked up rumors about compromise and defections among the mild reservationists. Still, any real breakthrough was going to require the cooperation of one or both of the most important players in the currently stalemated contest, Lodge and Wilson. Hitchcock met with both of them on November 17. What transpired at those meetings would determine the outcome of this phase of the League fight and perhaps of the whole conflict.[17]

The significance of Hitchcock's meeting with Lodge lay less in what the two senators said than in what one of them, Lodge, probably did not say. Four weeks later, he and Hitchcock clashed on the Senate floor about what the majority leader had agreed to do. Hitchcock maintained that Lodge had promised at this meeting to consult with his party colleagues about recessing the Senate for a day or two after the initial votes on consent, in order to work out a compromise. "After that time," Hitchcock asserted, "I heard no word from the Senator from Massachusetts." Lodge rejoined that he had told Hitchcock "that we were ready to receive proposals, but they must be made before we went to a vote." Hitchcock then charged that Lodge had really wanted to defeat the treaty and had conspired with the Irreconcilables to that end. Lodge closed the exchange by replying, "My only object was to get the treaty ratified with the reservations that had been put on by a majority of the Senate. I did not go and consult with the Senator from Nebraska and the others to whom he refers, because their votes were not their own." That last remark was a slam at the Democrats for following Wilson's lead. On Lodge's part, the question was not whether he openly or implicitly agreed to a recess and further efforts at compromise but, rather, what he really wanted. Was he trying, as Hitchcock charged, to defeat the treaty through deadlock? Or

17. Hitchcock to Lowell, Nov. 15, 1919, Lowell Papers; New York *World*, Nov. 18, 1919; *New York Times*, Nov. 18, 1919. On Hitchcock's strategy, see also Lansing to Polk, Nov. 14, 1919, Lansing Papers; Grey of Fallodon to Lansing, Nov. 19, 1919, ibid.

was he striving, as he maintained, for ratification under the terms of his committee's reservations?[18]

Lodge dropped hints that pointed both ways. On Sunday, November 16, he conferred at his home with Borah, Brandegee, and Knox, and the next day he told reporters that he opposed dropping the preamble, which the Democrats and some mild reservationists regarded as superfluous. Lodge also talked with Lenroot at his house that Sunday. Lenroot had become the most active of the mild reservationists in seeking grounds for compromise, and he indicated that some of them might be willing to drop the preamble. But the most intriguing hint that Lodge gave about willingness to compromise came in his talks with Stephen Bonsal, a journalist and former member of the staff of the peace conference delegation, who was acting as an emissary for Colonel House. This was the most mysterious incident in the whole League fight.[19]

The business with Bonsal began sometime after the middle of October 1919. There was dickering over whether Colonel House, who had just returned from Paris, would be called to testify before the Foreign Relations Committee. House, who understandably wanted to avoid repeating the experiences of Lansing and Bullitt, pleaded ill health. Because he had recently suffered a recurrence of gallstones, House explained to Hitchcock, "I shall not be physically able to make the trip for sometime." He also asked Bonsal, who had been a boarding school friend of Lodge's recently deceased son-in-law, "Gussie" Gardner, to go and see the chairman and plead his case. Bonsal met with Lodge twice, first on October 28 in the senator's private office in the Capitol, and again on the evening of October 30 in the library of his home on Massachusetts Avenue. The matter of House's not testifying raised no difficulty. In a memorandum to House the next day, Bonsal quoted Lodge as saying, "The question of reopening the hearings is so uncertain that I think Colonel House should have no other thought but as to what is best for his health."[20]

18. *Congressional Record,* 66th Cong., 2nd Sess. (Dec. 13, 1919), 533–535. Lodge recounted the meeting along the same lines nine months later in Lodge to Frederick Gillett, July 26, 1920, Lodge Papers. Hitchcock describes his dealings with Lodge, although not the meeting specifically, at second-hand in entry, Nov. 18, 1919, Bonsal Diary, in Stephen Bonsal, *Unfinished Business* (New York, 1944), 276–277.

19. On these meetings, see *New York Tribune,* Nov. 17, 1919; *New York Times,* Nov. 18, 1919.

20. House to Hitchcock, Oct. 25, 1919, Hitchcock Papers, Vol. I; Bonsal memorandum, Nov. 1, 1919, Edward M. House Papers, Yale University Library, Box 17. On this aspect of the meetings, see also Bonsal memorandum, [Nov. 1919], Bonsal Papers, Box 12; entry, Oct. 30, 1919, Bonsal Diary, in Bonsal, *Unfinished Business,* 271–272.

What made these two meetings noteworthy was something that evidently arose during Bonsal's first encounter with Lodge. Bonsal recorded in his diary that Lodge gave "the impression that he was not as confident as some of his adherents claimed to be, that he could defeat the treaty and so alter the Covenant as to 'hamstring' it. . . . Indeed, I came to the conclusion that the chairman of the Foreign Relations Committee was in the mood to compromise, but with whom?" As soon as he could get to a telephone, Bonsal called House in New York. The colonel instructed Bonsal to stick with Lodge and ascertain his terms for compromise. The two men met again on October 30. As Bonsal recorded in a diary entry made on November 16, he brought along a printed copy of the Covenant, on which

> the Senator made the changes and inserted the interlineations which if accepted, he thought, would smooth the way to ratification. The changes ran to forty words, the "inserts" to about fifty. It seemed to me that they were more concerned with verbiage than with the object and intent of the instrument. In my judgment, they were complementary to, rather than limiting, any substantial purpose of the Covenant.[21]

Because no copy of this document has survived, it is impossible to say for sure what Lodge proposed. In another diary entry made on November 12, Bonsal noted that the senator "made additions to Article X and Article XVI which, in his opinion, restored to the Senate and also to the House, as the 'money power,' the constitutional authority which, as he claimed, was their constitutional right and which he asserted the president had ignored." In the diary entry of November 16, Bonsal added that Lodge "stated that his interest or, as he put it several times, his anxiety, centered around Article X, . . . and his suggestion, indeed

21. Entries, Oct. 30, Nov. 16, 1919, Bonsal Diary, ibid., 272–273, 274–276. The main difficulty in judging the accuracy of these accounts is that they appear only in this published version. The Bonsal Papers contain no handwritten or typed manuscript version of this diary against which to check this version. There are, however, enough other contemporary and nearly contemporary items about this incident to rule out the notion that Bonsal made up his accounts out of whole cloth. In addition to the two memoranda cited in the previous note, see also Bonsal pencil note [ca. Nov. 1919], Bonsal Papers, Box 12; note, "add to Lodge business," n.d., ibid., Box 20; note, "Lodge-League-House Oct. 1919 and also Nov.," [ca. 1923], ibid., Box 19; Bonsal to Fanny B. Denton, Apr. 8, 1928, ibid., Box 3; Bonsal to Charles Seymour, June 11, 1928, Apr. 12, 1944, Charles Seymour Papers, Yale University Library; Seymour to Bonsal, June 26, 1928, ibid.; Seymour to House, June 15, 1928, House Papers, Box 100.

his demand, was to the effect that none of the obligations or commitments should be undertaken without the approval of the Senate and the concurrence of the House." When Bonsal replied that "it goes without saying" that such limitations were already implicit in Article X, Lodge retorted, "If it goes without saying, there is no harm in saying it – and much advantage." Bonsal also recorded that the senator "chaffed" him good-naturedly about the Covenant's literary failings: "It might get by at Princeton, but certainly not at Harvard."[22]

Bonsal later recalled that he had rebutted Lodge's allegation, but in his November 16 diary entry he noted that they amiably changed the subject and discussed the writings of an author whom they both knew. Bonsal evidently had to quell his excitement as they chatted for a while longer before he took his leave. As soon as he got out of the senator's house, Bonsal hurried to the post office at Union Station, where he sent the annotated copy of the Covenant to House by registered mail. "And when this was out of the way," Bonsal also recorded, "I by telephone called up the Colonel, who was in bed, and told him in veiled language of the important document that would be in his hands in the morning. I was rewarded with a whoop of joy." Earlier, in a diary entry presumably jotted down right after this telephone call, Bonsal noted that House commented, "The situation is brighter, much brighter." Bonsal commented to himself, "I trust he is right – he generally is – but after all the President is still silent and darkness enshrouds the White House."[23]

Those forebodings were well taken. No reply ever came from the White House. When Bonsal saw House soon after the first votes on the treaty, Bonsal speculated that Wilson had snubbed Lodge. That would have wounded the senator "in his vanity, which is enormous," and caused him to harden in his attitudes. Or perhaps, thanks to Mrs. Wilson and Grayson, ". . . the olive branch may never have reached him – an unfortunate mess." There was, however, another, more likely explanation. In that conversation with Bonsal, House blamed the Irreconcilables, not the president or those who ran what Bonsal later called the "sickroom regime," for hardening Lodge's attitude. Then, nearly a decade later, Bonsal recorded another conversation with House in his diary. This time, the colonel went to great lengths to defend himself on two counts. First, he justified his not having intervened further after having, he said, "sent your letter and memorandum on to the President,

22. Entries, Nov. 12, 16, 1919, Jan. 10, 1926, Bonsal Diary, in Bonsal, *Unfinished Business,* 273–276.
23. Entries, Oct. 30, Nov. 16, 1919, ibid., 273, 276.

giving it my warmest support." House agreed with Bonsal that Wilson may never have seen those documents, but he said that he had not wanted to add to the burdens of the invalided president by trying to reach him to urge compromise. Moreover, House maintained, he had suspected Lodge's motives. "This I can best describe," Bonsal recorded the colonel as saying, "in the words of one of my Texas friends, who said: 'To have followed Lodge in that Treaty battle would have broken the back of the most supple rattlesnake.'"24

House's explanation smacked of protesting too much. That seems especially to be the case in light of the other count on which the colonel was defending himself. He was talking to Bonsal shortly after the publication of the last volume of *The Intimate Papers of Colonel House.* This was the highly selective rendition of his diary and papers edited by the Yale historian and another former member of the peace conference staff, Charles Seymour. Except for Bonsal's memorandum of November 1, 1919, which referred solely to the question of House's testifying before the Foreign Relations Committee, the colonel had insisted on omitting any reference to the meetings with Lodge or the annotated

24. Entries, Nov. 27, 1919, Jan. 10, 1926, Jan. 1929, ibid., 280, 276 n. 4, 285–289. One of Lodge's biographers, John Garraty, gives this interpretation a special twist, arguing, "Had Wilson seized upon the offer, it would have been very difficult for Lodge to have backed down. Perhaps Lodge, who considered himself a master judge of the President, was counting on Wilson's stubbornness and the strong dislike he entertained for Lodge himself." John A. Garraty, *Henry Cabot Lodge* (New York, 1953), 375 n. 8. One objection to this interpretation is that if Lodge meant to embarrass Wilson in this business, he would have publicized his willingness to compromise.

This was not the only time that House defended himself and claimed to have tried to get a compromise proposal to Wilson. In October 1920, he told Lansing that he had gotten Thomas W. Gregory, the former attorney general, to give a letter urging compromise to Mrs. Wilson for the president to read. "Whether Mr. Wilson ever saw this letter is doubtful," Lansing commented in his diary. "He was then very ill and unable to do business." Entry, Oct. 11, 1920, Lansing Diary, Lansing Papers. No copy of this letter, if it ever existed, has survived. Again, in fairness to House, it must be noted that his suspicions about his loss of influence were fully justified. Early in November 1919, Ray Stannard Baker noted in his diary after a visit at the White House with Mrs. Wilson, "The Colonel's stock has fallen to zero. He is no longer a factor. He tried at Paris to conciliate away everything that the President stood for." Entry, Nov. 5, 1919, Baker Diary, in Link, ed., *Papers of Wilson,* LXIII, 621.

copy of the Covenant. No mention of anything about a possible com-
promise on the League would see the light of print until 1944, after
House's death, when Bonsal published his own diary as a book titled
Unfinished Business.[25]

25. Entry, Jan. 1929, Bonsal Diary, in Bonsal, *Unfinished Business,* 285–289.
Also, possibly in the vein of protesting too much, House noted around this
time, "I am not keeping my diary regularly for present events seem unimportant compared with the work I have been doing in Europe." Entry, Dec.
15, 1919, Edward M. House Diary, Yale University Library. In addition, he
noted, "I am not keeping a daily record and it is doubtful I shall do so in
the future." Entry, Dec. 20, 1919, ibid.

In assessing the colonel's behavior, it may be useful to note what Arthur
Walworth, a historian sympathetic to House and personally close to Seymour, wrote about Bonsal's account to one of the last surviving members of
the Wilson circle, Robert Woolley: "But no scholar has been able to find
any documentary evidence of the story except the letters printed in *The
Intimate Papers of Colonel House,* vol. iv, pp. 504–506. These letters prove
that Bonsal had *one* talk with Lodge in October, but do not confirm Bonsal's story of a compromise offer on the Senator's part." Walworth to Woolley, Dec. 22, 1953, Robert Woolley Papers, Library of Congress, Box 22.

After noting Garraty's comment in his then newly published biography
of Lodge, Walworth added, "Mr. Seymour and I have been able to find no
confirmation in the House Collection – not even in the Diary; in fact, when
Mr. Seymour raised the question with Miss Denton [House's secretary] several years ago, she could remember nothing definite. Furthermore, there is
no trace, in the Wilson Papers in the L[ibrary of] C[ongress], of the letters
that House is said to have forwarded to the White House with Lodge's suggestions for compromise. (Of course, Mrs. Wilson may be holding these, or
they may have been destroyed; perhaps the President never saw them.)

"While we think Mr. Bonsal a thoroughly reliable authority, we cannot
understand the absence of documentary evidence or the void in the memory
of Miss Denton and we hesitate to accept the story as historical without
evidence." Ibid.

Evidently, Walworth and Seymour had not examined the Bonsal Papers,
which contain enough bits of evidence to corroborate his story in general
outline, if not in every detail. Seymour's role in this business also seems
equivocal. Despite Bonsal's having told him about Lodge's offer in 1928,
Seymour either forgot or affected to forget about it when Bonsal published
Unfinished Business in 1944, and he did contact House's secretary, Frances
Denton, in an effort to learn more about it. See Seymour to Bonsal, Apr. 6,
1944, Seymour Papers; Seymour to Denton, Apr. 6, 1944, ibid.; Denton to
Seymour, Apr. 12, 1944, ibid. See also Woolley to Walworth, Jan. 4, 1953,
ibid.; Walworth to Seymour, Dec. 22, 1953, ibid.

There is a more likely explanation for the silence that greeted this overture from Lodge – namely, that House never sent the papers to the White House and was lying when he claimed to have done so. By the time this volume of the *Intimate Papers* was published, both Wilson and Lodge had been dead for four years. But Mrs. Wilson and Grayson were still living and could have unmasked the colonel's duplicity. The Texan's remark about the rattlesnake may have applied better to House than to Lodge.

It is questionable whether this overture through Bonsal amounted to a great deal and whether its failure disappointed Lodge. No other evidence indicates that Lodge felt anything but cool and collected as the stalemate loomed in the Senate between the Democrats and his Republican reservationists. Furthermore, in view of Lodge's unwavering and amply documented insistence upon virtual nullification of any obligation under Article X, it is doubtful that any annotations that he may have written on that copy of the Covenant were as inconsequential as Bonsal, who only had a chance to glance at them, believed them to be. Besides, insistence upon involving both houses of Congress in assenting to any actions under Article X was nothing new. Such language had been in every version of this reservation adopted by the Foreign Relations Committee and previously agreed to by the mild reservationists. More than fear of involvement may have deterred House from forwarding this proposal to the White House. Either by himself or with the advice of his international lawyer son-in-law, Gordon Auchincloss, the colonel could easily have grasped that Lodge was giving away little or nothing from his rejection of commitments to international enforcement. Yet, despite all those likely limitations, Lodge had been willing to involve himself in such a scheme. No hint of that involvement seems to have leaked out to his fellow senators, unless the otherwise hard to fathom talk about compromise on November 17 and 18 somehow reflected a glimmer of possible flexibility on his part.

Wilson left no doubt about how he might have greeted this compromise effort when Hitchcock met with him on November 17. This was the senator's second face-to-face meeting with the president since his stroke. Hitchcock had previously seen Wilson on November 7. At that time, he was only the third person outside the immediate circle of family, physicians, and selected White House personnel who had seen the president since the stroke. The other outsiders were the king and queen of the Belgians, who had made a brief, carefully staged, strictly ceremonial visit on October 30. Hitchcock was also the first outsider who was permitted to discuss business with Wilson. Even the president's secretary, Tumulty, did not get to see him until the middle of the month.[26]

At that first meeting on November 7, Hitchcock conferred for half an hour with Wilson. "I was shocked to see that he had become an old man," the senator recalled several years later. "As he lay in bed slightly propped up by pillows with the useless arm concealed beneath the covers I beheld an emaciated old man with a thin white beard which had been permitted to grow. But his eye was clear and his resolve strong." Judging from what Hitchcock told reporters immediately after this meeting, the senator must have done most of the talking, as he apprised the president of the situation at the Capitol and his own strategy of deadlock in hopes of compromise. "The President gave his very ardent approval to what had been done," Hitchcock told the reporters. But the senator later recalled that Wilson had grown anxious when he learned that there were not enough votes to gain consent without reservations. "He asked how many votes we could get for ratification without reservations," Hitchcock related. "I told him not over forty-five out of ninety-six. He fairly groaned: 'It is possible, it is possible.'" When the reporters asked whether Wilson would prefer defeat of the treaty to approval with strong reservations, Hitchcock answered, "He did not say outright whether he would favor rejection rather than acceptance of the majority reservations. He said he would accept any compromise the friends of the treaty thought necessary to save the treaty, so long as it did not destroy the terms of the pact itself. He made it plain that the Lodge reservations would kill the treaty."[27]

Between that time and Hitchcock's second meeting with Wilson ten days later, the president's physical condition took a turn for the better. Such improvement, which comes in stages, is common following this type of stroke. On November 11, Wilson left his bed for the first time and sat in a wheelchair for about an hour. The next day, he asked to be shaved, to get rid of the white beard that had startled Hitchcock. Before being shaved, according to Grayson, he asked to see himself in a mirror

---

26. The editors of *Papers of Wilson* speculate that Hitchcock had met with Wilson around October 20, but they appear to have confused a visit by him at that time to the White House, where he talked with Grayson, with the meeting on November 7. See Link, ed., *Papers of Wilson*, LXIV, 45 n. 1. On the October 20 visit to the White House, see Hitchcock to Grayson, Oct. 20, 1919, ibid., LXVI, 547; Grayson to Hitchcock, Oct. 23, 1919, ibid., LXIII, 593.

27. Hitchcock memoir, "Wilson's Place in History," Hitchcock Papers; *New York Times*, Nov. 8, 1919.

and recited a favorite limerick of his about his looks, which began, "For beauty I am not a star." Three days later, on November 14, the president received another royal visitor, the Prince of Wales. During the visit, Wilson observed that during a stay at the White House in 1860, the prince's grandfather had slept in the same bed in which he was now sitting. The two men chatted about a number of matters, Dr. Grayson told reporters, and the prince's visit lifted the president's spirits. That same day, Wilson sat for a while outside on the south portico of the White House. Then, on November 17, the day of his second meeting with Hitchcock, he spent an hour in his wheelchair on the lawn. These small gains prompted Dr. Dercum, the neurologist, to tell the Wilson family after an examination on November 15 that the president was making steady recovery. "He jumped with joy literally when he examined Father last Sat[urday]," Wilson's daughter Margaret wrote to her sister Eleanor.[28]

Wilson was also beginning to take a more active interest in public business, particularly the peace treaty. At Mrs. Wilson's request, the senator sent her two reports on the situation in the Senate, which she read to the president. On November 13, in his first report, Hitchcock called the Article X reservation, which had just passed, "not quite as obnoxious as it was when the President denounced it in Salt Lake. . . . Still it is bad." Hitchcock reaffirmed his plan for the Democrats to block consent with the Lodge reservations and then to offer five reservations of their own as substitutes. Enclosing a copy of those reservations, Hitchcock noted, "The first four are substantially in accordance with the suggestions made to me by the President and the last one is, I think, in accordance with his views on the true meaning of the league covenant." Two days later, Hitchcock reiterated his previously stated strategy of defeating consent with the Lodge reservations and requested another meeting with Wilson. "In order to make the democratic vote as nearly solid as

28. Grayson memorandum, n.d., in Link, ed., *Papers of Wilson*, LXIV, 489; *New York Times*, Nov. 12, 16, 19, 1919; *Washington Post*, Nov. 14, 1919; Margaret Wilson to Eleanor Wilson McAdoo, [Nov. 19, 1919], McAdoo Papers, Box 59. By contrast, Grayson had painted a much gloomier picture to Baker when he visited the White House on November 5. "The President will be much longer in getting up & about than anyone knows – & he may never get up," Baker recorded in his diary. ". . . The President is undeniably better, but the doctor is guarding him closely, keeping everyone away – & preventing, as much as possible, any business coming to his attention. This is hard to do because the President's mind is exceedingly acute, as good as it ever was, & he chafes at the inactivity." Entry, Nov. 5, 1919, Baker Diary, in Link, ed. *Papers of Wilson*, LXIII, 620.

possible, however," he explained, "I would like to have definite word
from the president if possible that in his judgment this is the proper
course to take." In Wilson's judgment, that was the proper course. After
receiving this report and reading it to her husband, Mrs. Wilson wrote
on the envelope in which it came, "Program he [Hitchcock] out lines
has his [Wilson's] approval. He could not accept the Lodge Reservations
in any case."[29]

When Hitchcock entered the president's bedroom on the morning of
November 17, he found a changed man. Wilson opened the discussion
defiantly, as Grayson, who was present, recorded immediately afterward in a memorandum. He scorned the resolution of ratification with
the Lodge reservations: "I consider it a nullification of the Treaty and
utterly impossible." Wilson intended the word "nullification" to carry
its most pejorative sting, because he explicitly compared those reservations to South Carolina's attempts to nullify federal laws before the
Civil War. When Hitchcock asked him about the Article X reservation,
Wilson replied, "That cuts the very heart out of the Treaty; I could not
stand for those changes because it would humiliate the United States
before all of the allied countries." Ratification with the Lodge reservations would earn the United States "the contempt of the world. We will
be playing in to Germany's hands." Evidently mistaking the preamble as
requiring German approval, he added, "Think of the humiliation we
would suffer in having to ask Germany whether she would accept such
and such a reservation!"

For Wilson, the most important consideration was pinning blame
where it belonged. "If the Republicans are bent on defeating this
treaty," he went on to Hitchcock,

> I want the vote of each, Republican and Democrat, recorded,
> because they will have to answer to the country in the future for
> their acts. They must answer to the people. I am a sick man, lying
> in this bed, but I am going to debate this issue with these gentlemen
> in their respective states whenever they come up for re-election if I
> have breath enough in my body to carry on the fight. I shall do this
> even if I have to give my life to it. And I will get their political
> scalps when the truth is known to the people. They have got to
> account to their constituents for their actions in this matter. I have
> no doubts as to what the verdict of the people will be when they
> know the facts. Mind you, Senator, I have no hostility towards
> these gentlemen but an utter contempt.

29. Hitchcock to Edith Wilson, Nov. 13, 15, 1919, ibid., LXIV, 28–29, 37–38;
    Edith Wilson note, [ca. Nov. 15, 1919], ibid., 38.

When Hitchcock tried to suggest compromise, the president retorted, "With the exception of interpretations, which would not alter substance, I am not willing to make any compromise other than that we agreed upon at our meeting on [November 7]." He would accept nothing that required submission to the approval of other nations. After that, the rest of the meeting consisted of Hitchcock's reporting on various matters. He related to Wilson that both Lord Grey and Jules Jusserand, the French ambassador, had told him that their countries would reject the Lodge reservations. At Wilson's insistence, Hitchcock described the recent debates and votes in the Senate in detail. The president pressed him about why he had followed certain strategies and made cracks about individual senators. This colloquy took some time, and the interview lasted for more than an hour. When he rose to leave, Hitchcock apologized for tiring the president by going on so long. "No, Senator," Wilson replied, "you have strengthened me as against the opponents."[30]

After he left the president's bedroom, Hitchcock commented to Grayson about how much better Wilson seemed since their previous meeting. "He is very combative today as he sits up there in that bed," the senator observed. "On certain compromises he is as immovable as the Rock of Gibraltar." Hitchcock also told Grayson, "I would give anything if the Democrats, in fact, all the Senate, could see the attitude that man took this morning. Think how effective it would be if they could see the picture as you and I saw it this morning." When he talked with the reporters gathered outside the White House, Hitchcock gave a softened rendition of Wilson's stand. Although he used the word "nullification" to characterize the president's opinion of the Lodge reservations, he omitted any reference to pre–Civil War South Carolina. Likewise, on the subject of holding Republicans accountable for their votes, Hitchcock quoted Wilson as saying, "I would like to have some of the Senators go home to their constituents while the treaty is still pending." Hitchcock also sent a message that was both contradictory and misleading when he explained what Wilson would do if the Senate voted for consent with the Lodge reservations. Referring to the president's constitutional power as the final ratifying agent, he told the reporters, "President Wilson will pocket the treaty if the Lodge program of reservations is carried out." But, he added, Wilson had not said "that all the Lodge reservations were unacceptable."[31]

30. Grayson memorandum, Nov. 17, 1919, ibid., 43–45. One of the senators about whom Wilson made a crack was Hoke Smith. See n. 7 of this chapter.
31. Ibid., 44–45; *New York Times,* Nov. 18, 1919.

The threat of refusal to ratify was one of the two most important statements that Hitchcock made to the reporters. The other one was his answer to their questions about which of the Lodge reservations Wilson might accept: "I know the President's ideas on the subject but I do not feel free to quote him." Hitchcock did not want to offer a quotation because he was going to let Wilson appear to speak for himself. Later in the day, Hitchcock sent to the White House a draft of a letter that Mrs. Wilson read to the president. She edited the draft at his dictation, and then returned to the senator as a letter from the president dated November 18. The letter read:

> You were good enough to bring me word that the democratic senators supporting the treaty expected to hold a conference before the final vote on the Lodge resolution of ratification and that they would be glad to receive a word of counsel from me. I should hesitate to offer it in any detail but I assume that the senators desire my judgment only upon the all-important question of the final vote on the resolution containing the many reservations by Senator Lodge. On that I can not hesitate, for in my opinion the resolution in that form does not provide for ratification, but rather for the nullification of the treaty. I sincerely hope that the friends and supporters of the treaty will vote against the Lodge resolution of ratification. I understand that the door will probably then be open for a genuine resolution of ratification. I hope therefore that all true friends of the treaty will refuse to support the Lodge resolution.[32]

That letter exploded like the bombshell that Hitchcock evidently meant it to be. It sealed the fate of any further attempts to bridge the gap between the Democrats and Republican reservationists. The only remaining hope for eventual American ratification of the Treaty of Versailles would now lie in the uncertain enterprise of starting all over again on reservations and interpretations. Many observers at the time and most later interpreters would regard this move by Wilson as one of the two greatest blunders of his life – the other one being his similarly defiant refusal to accept the Lodge reservations a second time four

32. *New York Times*, Nov. 18, 1919; Wilson to Hitchcock, Nov. 18, 1919, in Link, ed., *Papers of Wilson*, LXIV, 58. On the drafting of the letter, see Hitchcock to Edith Wilson, Nov. 17, 1919, ibid., 50; letter draft with Mrs. Wilson's additions and emendations, ibid., 51. The idea of Wilson's making a statement had been circulating for several days, as indicated in Hitchcock's letter of November 15. Four days earlier, Tumulty had drafted a similar, though longer and somewhat more softly worded, letter. See Tumulty to Wilson, Nov. 11, 1919, ibid., 15.

months later. These presumed blunders would fix for future generations Wilson's reputation as a self-righteous, impractical idealist who committed infanticide on his own cherished creation rather than bend in the face of an unavoidable reality. Virtually the only argument about Wilson's behavior would revolve around which of his flaws was chiefly to blame. Was it his warped personality, which had given rise to a messiah complex? Or was it his damaged health, which had kept him out of touch with events and uninformed about the true state of affairs?[33]

Wilson's behavior at this stage in the League fight could be defended on the ground that the Lodge reservations raised serious doubts about whether the United States could really do much toward building a new world order. Moreover, a stalemate at this stage did not necessarily mean that all was lost for League advocates. During the next four months, they would get a second chance to make their dreams come true. Still, despite such defenses, Wilson's behavior did stem from his shortcomings, not his strengths. In a way, those who blamed his personality and those who blamed his health were both correct.[34]

Wilson's stroke had affected him both physically and psychologically. The limitations on his mobility and personal contacts prevented him from getting as much information and opinion as he needed to make well-informed judgments in this political situation. Unfortunately, however, those were not the stroke's only or most damaging effects. If they had been, then the gradual improvement in his physical condition might have permitted him to play a more constructive role in the League fight. Instead, Wilson's behavior would grow worse. The performance that Grayson and Hitchcock witnessed on November 17 offered a foretaste of the way that the president would act during the rest of the League fight and all of his remaining days in office.

Wilson's stroke had its cruelest and most politically damaging impact

---

33. The most recent incarnation of this argument occurred in the conflict between Weinstein and Link on one side and Alexander and Juliette George on the other, with each side supported by sympathetic medical experts. For critical assessments of this controversy, see Dorothy Ross, "Woodrow Wilson and the Case for Psychohistory," *Journal of American History*, LXIX (Dec. 1982), 659–668, and Lloyd E. Ambrosius, "Woodrow Wilson's Health and the Treaty Fight," *International History Review*, IX (Feb. 1987), 73–84.

34. For a recent expression of the argument that Wilson might have had sound reasons for rejecting the Lodge reservations, see Thomas J. Knock, *To End All Wars: Woodrow Wilson and the Quest for a New World Order* (New York, 1992), 264–268.

on his psychological balance. Along with his limited physical recovery, he was displaying typical symptoms of this kind of stroke, which impairs the victims' emotional balance and control. The isolation imposed upon Wilson by his wife's well-meaning sickroom regime had worsened those effects. As a result, like many stroke victims, Wilson became barely able or unable to adapt to changing circumstances. For him, this impairment proved especially harmful. Perhaps the single quality, in addition to his formidable intellect, that had made him such an effective political leader had been precisely his emotional balance. On one side, Wilson had previously possessed such traits as driving will, overweening self-confidence, denial of weaknesses, and passionate commitment. But, on the other side, he had also usually shown detachment, self-criticism, humor, and patience. The death of his first wife, Ellen, in 1914 had robbed him of his strongest outside influence toward calm and restraint; his second wife, Edith, rarely played a similar role in his life. Aging and the possible earlier effects of his cardiovascular condition had also left him less flexible and adaptable. All of these influences devastated his psychological balance and, thereby, his political judgment. Thereby, Woodrow Wilson became the greatest single obstacle to a more amicable, less damaging outcome to the League fight than would finally occur.[35]

III

When the Senate met on November 19, 1919, for the last day of debate and voting on the peace treaty, it quickly became apparent how big a spoiler the president had become. The Democrats gathered for a caucus before the Senate convened, and Hitchcock read them the letter that had come from the president. Either he or the White House also released the text to the press. Newspapers that printed the letter were circulating in the Senate chamber within minutes after the opening of the session at noon. Only a little business transpired before those newspapers arrived. A quorum call was held. Lodge and Hitchcock had clashed over what measures the senators would vote on, and two sena-

---

35. On the possible psychological effects of the stroke, see Bert E. Park, "Woodrow Wilson's Stroke of October 2, 1919," in Link, ed., *Papers of Wilson*, LXIII, 639–646. This aspect of Wilson's illness is also examined in John Milton Cooper, Jr., "Disability in the White House: The Case of Woodrow Wilson," in Frank Freidel and William Pencak, eds., *The White House: The First Two Hundred Years* (Boston, 1994), 75–99.

tors spoke briefly. At this point in the proceedings, Lodge broke in to read Wilson's letter aloud to the Senate. At the end, he added, "I think comment is superfluous, and I shall make none." One of the Democratic senators, Ashurst, noted in his diary that his party brethren were flabbergasted that the letter had been made public, while "it enraged the 'Mild Reservationists' and two or three of them let off oaths in an undertone."[36]

After that bombshell exploded, the senators engaged in ten hours of debate and voting. To his sons Hiram Johnson described what transpired as "exciting but not particularly interesting." Ten more senators spoke before the first votes were taken. With one exception, none of them said much that was new or noteworthy. The exception came from the senator who had spoken the most often and usually the most eloquently. Delivering a last plea against joining the League and involving America in international power politics, Borah made explicit something that he had left ambiguous in his earlier utterances. This was that, for him, unfettered American sovereignty was not an end in itself. Rather, such sovereignty was a means, albeit an essential means, to an end. That end was democracy, which was, Borah argued, "vastly more than a mere form of government. . . . It is a moral entity, a spiritual force as well." Try to yoke democracy with "the discordant and destructive forces of the Old World," and democracy would lose its soul. "We may become one of the four dictators of the world, but we shall no longer be master of our own spirit." Even if the League could assure peace, he added, "I would not pay the price. But your treaty does not mean peace – far, very far from it. If we are to judge the future by the past it means war." Borah concluded by pleading that "America disenthralled and free in spite of all these things will continue her mission in the cause of peace, of freedom, and of civilization."[37]

Borah's speech offered a fitting close to the debate over the peace treaty. Well-connected personages filled the galleries in the Senate chamber, while less fortunate folk jammed the corridors outside. "It was the greatest crowd I have ever seen there," recalled one of the privileged spectators, Alice Roosevelt Longworth. She and her friend Ruth Hanna McCormick, the wife of the Illinois senator, were there to cheer Borah

36. *Congressional Record,* 66th Cong., 1st Sess. (Nov. 19, 1919), 8768; entry, Nov. 19, 1919, Ashurst Diary, in Sparks, ed., *Many-Colored Toga,* 115.
37. Johnson to Hiram Jr. and Arch Johnson, Nov. 21, 1919, in Burke, ed., *Johnson Letters,* III; *Congressional Record,* 66th Cong., 1st Sess. (Nov. 19, 1919), 8781–8784.

as he delivered his presentation. Even his jealous rival Johnson admitted
to his sons that Borah "excelled himself, and made the one great speech
of the whole fight. It was not so much the matter, but the manner of the
delivery and his carefully prepared sentences were very effective. I
should like to have attempted to do the same, but I would not have succeeded." Evidently Borah had risen to the "homeric" standard that
Ashurst had challenged his colleagues to attain. He had spoken with the
kind of eloquence that Wilson had tried and failed to marshal on his
side when he had presented the treaty to the Senate on that hot day in
July four months before.[38]

The greatest excitement of this chilly day in November came when
the senators at last began to vote. As the last senator to speak sat down,
cries arose around the chamber, "Vote," "Vote." The first vote came at
5:30 in the afternoon, on Lodge's resolution of ratification. It went
down to defeat, thirty-nine in favor and fifty-five against. The only senator absent was Fall, who was announced against. Voting in favor of
consent with the Lodge reservations were thirty-five Republicans; joining them were the expected quartet of Democrats, Gore, Shields, Smith
of Georgia, and Walsh of Massachusetts. Against the resolution stood
forty Democrats, who were supporting the president's position, and fifteen Irreconcilables – with another of them, Fall, announced against. A
possibly hopeful development occurred next. Reed, of all people, moved
to reconsider this vote. This was the parliamentary device for keeping
the question before the Senate. The motion passed, sixty-three in favor
and thirty opposed. This vote gave perhaps the best indication of which
senators really wanted consent under some conditions. In favor of
reconsideration were forty-five Democrats – including the four reservationists and, oddly, Reed. Joining them were eighteen Republicans –
mainly mild reservationists but also several who had favored some
amendments and stronger reservations. In opposition stood fourteen
Irreconcilables and sixteen other Republicans, including Lodge. If this
were to be read as a straw vote on a limited form of League membership, then Reed must be counted among the opponents, along with Fall.
The other nonvoter, John Kendrick of Wyoming, a Democrat who was

38. Alice Roosevelt Longworth, *Crowded Hours* (New York, 1933), 292; John-
son to Hiram Jr. and Arch Johnson, Nov. 21, 1919, in Burke, ed., *Johnson
Letters*, III. See also *New York Times*, Nov. 20, 1919. Around this time,
"Princess Alice" conducted a well-known and lengthy love affair with
Borah. See Anthony Lukas, *Big Trouble: A Murder in a Small Western
Town Sets Off a Struggle for the Soul of America* (New York, 1997), 291 n.

paired with Fall, should be added to the supporters. That left the alignment at sixty-three for, thirty-two against – one vote short of the necessary two-thirds.[39]

With Lodge's resolution of ratification now still before the Senate, the Democrats resorted to several expedients in an effort to buy time for possible compromise. Seven votes were taken before consent with the Lodge reservations came up for the second time. None of these measures attracted more than forty-three votes – all from Democrats joined by McCumber. Against them were arrayed between forty-eight and fifty-one votes – from Republicans, with Gore, Reed, and Shields joining them. Only two of these measures involved some substance. One was a proposal by a Democrat, Atlee Pomerene of Ohio, to appoint a bipartisan committee of conciliation to present a new set of reservations. The other was an attempt by Hitchcock to gain reconsideration of the five reservations that he had presented earlier. Even now, Hitchcock did not disclose that Wilson had written four of those reservations before he had left on his speaking tour. Then came the second vote on the same resolution of ratification as before. It failed again by nearly but not exactly the same margin – forty-one for, fifty against. This time two more Democrats, Myers and Owen, switched to support the resolution.[40]

These votes took place in a tense atmosphere on and off the Senate floor. According to both Taft's informant, Gus Karger, and Hiram Johnson, Democrats and mild reservationists scurried around trying to break the deadlock. Karger faulted Hitchcock for stymying these efforts. "He

39. *Congressional Record*, 66th Cong., 1st Sess. (Nov. 19, 1919), 8786–8787; *New York Times*, Nov. 20, 1919. Of the Republicans who opposed reconsideration, the highest scorer in support of the Wilson position on all the votes was Warren at 27 percent. Of the Republicans who scored at less than that level, five – Capper, Curtis, Dillingham, Kenyon, and McLean – favored and fifteen opposed reconsideration. Johnson related to his sons just after these votes, "There was a time when twenty-eight men on the Republican side agreed to vote against the Treaty." Johnson to Hiram Jr. and Arch Johnson, Nov. 21, 1919, in Burke, ed., *Johnson Letters*, III. Although Johnson was probably not talking about exactly the same Republicans who voted against reconsideration, it is noteworthy that his number and this vote, which included one Democrat, were nearly identical.

40. *Congressional Record*, 66th Cong., 1st Sess. (Nov. 19, 1919), 8787–8802. Of the three nonvoters, one, Nelson, was announced for, while the other two, Culberson of Texas, a Democrat, and Fall, an Irreconcilable, were announced against.

seemed obsessed with the thought that ratification without reservations could yet be forced through," Karger reported to Taft. Johnson thought that both sides acted, as he told his sons, "like little children who were at variance, and with whom a very slight and trivial matter leads to serious disagreement, and finally blows." On the floor, blame became the name of the game. At one point, Swanson walked over to Lodge and pleaded, "For God's sake, can't something be done to save the treaty?" Lodge replied, "Senator, the door is closed. You have done it yourselves." Warren Harding took the same line when he interrupted the voting to deliver the last speech of the day. He charged that blame for the defeat of the treaty fell solely on Wilson's "towering ambition. . . . It is a very grave misfortune, and I am sorry about it; but I tell you, Senators, the independence of action and the preserved inheritance of this Republic are infinitely more important than the wounded feelings of him who negotiated it without admitting the existence of the Senate."[41]

Only one item of business remained. Lodge honored an earlier promise to Hitchcock and permitted a vote on consent without reservations. Underwood now introduced a resolution of unconditional ratification. This resolution lost – thirty-eight in favor, fifty-three against. Only McCumber joined the thirty-seven Democrats who voted it. Knute Nelson might also have voted for it, but he had left the chamber without announcing his position. Opposing this resolution were fifteen Irreconcilables, thirty-one other Republicans, and five Democrats – the expected four and, unexpectedly and without explanation, Park Trammell of Florida. An attempt to reconsider this vote failed, by almost the

41. Karger to Taft, Nov. 20, 1919, Taft Papers, reel 214; Johnson to Hiram Jr. and Arch Johnson, Nov. 21, 1919, in Burke, ed., *Johnson Letters,* III; *New York Times,* Nov. 20, 1919; *Congressional Record,* 66th Cong., 1st Sess. (Nov. 19, 1919), 8791–8792. For another account of the scene, see entry, Nov. 19, 1919, Ashurst Diary, in Sparks, ed., *Many-Colored Toga,* 116. See also Margulies, *Mild Reservationists,* 174–175. Technically speaking, Harding was not the last senator to deliver a speech. Shields entered a speech into the *Appendix* to the *Congressional Record,* in which he called the League a "superstate" and "supergovernment," lauded the Lodge reservations as attempts to preserve American sovereignty, denounced British dominance in the League, and predicted that if America became "a party to such supergovernment and entangling alliance we have reached the beginning of the end of the world's greatest Republic." *Congressional Record,* 66th Cong., 1st Sess., *Appendix* (Nov. 19, 1919), 9222–9227. Inasmuch as he held those views, it should have come as no surprise that Shields later joined the Irreconcilables. The only surprise was that he did not join them now.

same margin. Lodge's substitute motion to table, and thus kill, reconsideration passed – forty-eight in favor, forty-two against. After that vote, a Democrat raised a question about whether the president should be informed. The gargantuan, curmudgeonly old guard Republican Boies Penrose retorted, "Oh, he'll know about it well enough." The senators then disposed of some routine business and voted to adjourn. The first session of the Sixty-sixth Congress ended at 11:10 in the evening of November 19.[42]

There was no question that this was the end of an important round in the League fight. The only question was whether this was the end of the whole League fight. Some people close to the scene expected speedy resumption of debate and renewed action when the next session of Congress opened in December. "End only for the present, of course," Karger reported to Taft. ". . . If their pride of opinion and their personal rancors can be mollified, there may yet be hope. Your own work, it seems to me, is not yet done. There's no rest for the righteous." Hiram Johnson regretfully agreed. "The victory, however, I think is temporary," he told his sons. "The treaty will probably be handed to us again in December, and I look for an agreement between the two pussyfooting factions." Not everyone among the Irreconcilables shared Johnson's pessimism. Brandegee chortled soon afterward to Lodge about "the broken heart of the world which according to last accounts was feebly and intermittently palpitating." Alice Roosevelt Longworth threw a party at her house that night after the votes. "We were jubilant," she recalled later. ". . . And by we, I mean the Irreconcilables, who were against joining any League no matter how 'safeguarded' with reservations."[43]

What happened next would depend upon what happened in two quarters. One was the White House. It was not clear what steps the president might take. Wilson made no public comment on the Senate's actions. He did try to dictate a statement to Mrs. Wilson, but he could

---

42. Ibid. (Nov. 19, 1919), 8803. Why Trammell voted against consent without reservations remains a mystery. His papers (University of Florida) contain no statements or correspondence about this vote, and the Florida newspapers made no comment on his vote. See Stephen Kerber, "Park Trammell of Florida: A Political Biography" (Ph.D. diss., University of Florida, 1979), 215–217.

43. Karger to Taft, Nov. 20, 1919, Taft Papers, reel 214; Johnson to Hiram Jr. and Arch Johnson, Nov. 21, 1919, in Burke, ed., *Johnson Letters*, III; Brandegee to Lodge, Nov. 27, 1919, Lodge Papers; Longworth, *Crowded Hours*, 292. For another example of jubilation among the Irreconcilables, see Borah to James T. Williams, Jr. Nov. 22, 1919, Borah Papers, Box 769.

only manage to utter some disconnected remarks about the sacrifices of the war, reservations being "in effect redifinitions *[sic]* of responsibilities & duties undertaken by us under the Treaty," and "This is the field & function of nego[ti]ation not of ratification." Wilson's physical incapacity and his sentiments offered little hope that he might work to break the current deadlock.[44]

Nor were the signs promising from the other main quarter where initiatives would have to originate for any future compromise. Alice Roosevelt Longworth recalled that "the reservationists," including Lodge, also came to her party and that "they seemed quite as happy as we were." Writing to George Harvey the next day, Lodge remarked, "Of course I am sorry to have my reservations beaten." But he also commented, "Brandegee and I thought of you last night after the thing was over and wished we could have an opportunity to exchange with you a few loving words." Evidently they wanted to share with their Wilson-hating friend their delight at his pain. Writing about the scene several years later, Lodge noted that Brandegee had said to him, "We can always depend on Mr. Wilson. He never has failed us. He has used all his powers to defeat the Treaty, because we would not ratify it in just the form in which he desired." Lodge recalled that he had replied, "This is quite true. Without his efforts the Treaty would have been accepted by the Senate to-day." Neither Lodge's coziness with the Irreconcilables nor his joy over Wilson's predicament boded well for his working to break the deadlock. Whether others influential with these men could change their attitudes would determine what happened next in the League fight.[45]

44. Wilson draft, [Nov. 19, 1919], in Link, ed., *Papers of Wilson,* LXIV, 65.
45. Longworth, *Crowded Hours,* 292; Lodge to Harvey, Nov. 20, 1919, Lodge Papers; Henry Cabot Lodge, *The Senate and the League of Nations* (New York, 1925), 214.

Woodrow Wilson at the peace conference, Paris, 1919.
A painting by Sir William Orpen.
Wilson sat for this portrait in June 1919, near the end of the conference
and shortly before the signing of the peace treaty.
Source: Courtesy of the White House Historical Association.

The Council of Ten of the peace conference in the Hall of the Clock,
French Foreign Ministry, Quai d'Orsay, 1919.
A painting by Sir William Orpen.
Seated, left to right, are Secretary of State Robert Lansing, President Wilson, Prime
Minister David Lloyd George of Great Britain, British Lord Privy Seal Andrew
Bonar Law, and British Foreign Secretary Arthur James Balfour. Standing behind
Wilson is Colonel Edward M. House, the president's confidant. Bending over between
Clemenceau and Lloyd George is Professor Paul Mantoux, interpreter and one
of the two principal minute-takers of the conference.
This was the room in which Wilson presented the Draft Covenant of the
League of Nations to the peace conference on February 14, 1919.
Source: Courtesy of the Imperial War Museum, London.

**The signing of the peace treaty in the Hall of Mirrors,
Palace of Versailles, June 28, 1919.
A painting by Sir William Orpen.**

The American delegation to the conference is seated in the front row, left to right: General Tasker H. Bliss, House, Ambassador Henry White, Lansing, and Wilson. To Wilson's left, bending over between Clemenceau and Lloyd George, is Colonel Sir Maurice Hankey, secretary to the British cabinet and the other principal minute-taker of the conference.

Source: Courtesy of the Imperial War Museum, London.

**Former President
William Howard Taft**
As president of the League
to Enforce Peace, Taft was
the leading Republican
advocate of the
League of Nations.
Source: Courtesy of the
Princeton University Libraries.

Elihu Root
Formerly secretary of war and state
under Republican presidents,
Root exercised greater influence
than anyone else in his party
over foreign policy.
Source: Courtesy of the
Princeton University Libraries.

**Senator Henry Cabot Lodge
of Massachusetts**

Holding the posts of majority leader and
chairman of the Foreign Relations
Committee, Lodge exercised the greatest
influence among the Republicans in the
Senate over disposition of the treaty and
membership in the League of Nations.

Source: Courtesy of the
Princeton University Libraries.

**Senator Gilbert M. Hitchcock
of Nebraska**

As acting minority leader and ranking
Democrat on the Foreign Relations
Committee, Hitchcock served as Wilson's
principal spokesperson in the Senate.

Source: Courtesy of the
Princeton University Libraries.

Woodrow Wilson arriving in St. Paul, Minnesota, September 9, 1919.
Six days into his whirlwind speaking tour on behalf of the treaty and the League, Wilson
showed no outward sign of the strain of the trip and his deteriorating health. Standing
in front of Wilson is his physician, Admiral Cary T. Grayson.
Source: Courtesy of the Princeton University Libraries.

This appearance at Tacoma, Washington, on September 13, 1919, was typical of events on Wilson's tour. He spoke most often at outdoor stadiums to large crowds with his unaided voice. Only once on the tour did he use the then brand-new technology of the microphone and amplifier.

Source: Courtesy of the Princeton University Libraries.

Each stop in a city on Wilson's tour featured a parade and motorcade. This flag festooned journey through San Francisco on September 17, 1919, followed the standard set from the beginning of the trip.

Source: Courtesy of the Princeton University Libraries.

**Woodrow Wilson at Union Station, Washington, D.C.,
September 28, 1919.**
The strain of the speaking tour showed unmistakably on Wilson's return, after his
physician had canceled the remainder of the speeches two days earlier. Four days
after this photograph was taken, Wilson suffered a massive stroke.
Source: Courtesy of the Princeton University Libraries.

This photograph, taken at the beginning of Wilson's administration, shows the president's secretary, Joseph P. Tumulty, in a pose of observing and advising him. After Wilson's stroke, Tumulty collaborated with Mrs. Wilson and Dr. Grayson in covering up his incapacity and wrote public messages for Wilson such as the call for a "great and solemn referendum" on the League in the 1920 election.

Source: Courtesy of the Princeton University Libraries.

This retouched photograph with Mrs. Wilson was taken after the president's stroke. Intended to convey an image of health and competence, the picture instead emphasizes how dependent he had grown on his wife in maintaining a semblance of continuing to occupy his office.

Source: Courtesy of the Princeton University Libraries.

In 1919, the most gifted American editorial cartoonist was Rollin Kirby of the New York *World*. Both Kirby and his newspaper ardently supported Wilson in the League fight. "Give the Lady a Seat" depicts Senators Borah, Johnson, and Lodge as obstructionists opposed to peace.

Source: Courtesy of the Library of Congress.

7

Last Chance

The next and final round of the League fight lasted exactly four months. It opened immediately after the Senate debate and votes on November 19, 1919, and ended on March 19, 1920, when the Senate voted a final time on consent to the Treaty of Versailles. The outcome in March was the same as in November. The treaty again failed to gain the two-thirds necessary for consent, and the ratification process once more ground to a halt. This may have been history repeating itself, but there were some variations. For one thing, this time the Senate took only one vote on the treaty itself. This was a take-it-or-leave-it roll call on a resolution of ratification that included a slightly changed version of the Lodge reservations. By the time of that second vote, a number of senators had struggled repeatedly to find common ground for compromise. Nearly every League advocate now called for swallowing membership with these reservations as better than nothing. On March 19, consent with those reservations received the votes of a majority of senators that included twenty-three Democrats and fell only seven votes short of the necessary two-thirds. This effort failed solely because Wilson adamantly rejected all reservations proposed in the Senate and openly threatened to refuse to ratify. Perhaps this round of the League fight did bear out Karl Marx's dictum that history repeats itself the first time as tragedy and the second time as farce. But this was a grim farce. It was the last chance for the United States to ratify the Treaty of Versailles and join the League of Nations.

I

If the views of the two principal actors, Senator Lodge and President Wilson, had prevailed, no effort at reconsideration of the treaty would have gotten off the ground. At the end of November and beginning of December 1919, the two men vied in venting their bitterness and obduracy and in demanding surrender from the other side. To friend and foe of the League alike, Lodge snorted about Wilson, "The time has come for him to concede," and "It is for him to move – not for us." Lodge even grew querulous and peremptory toward Elihu Root. The Republicans' foreign policy demigod now suggested a set of cosmetic changes in the previously adopted reservations that might serve as a basis for reopening consideration of the treaty. Lodge responded by calling Wilson "a marplot from the beginning." He also complained, "I am getting a little weary of Taft and those who are continually asking us to make further concessions. Why do they not put pressure on Wilson and make him yield?" Besides, Lodge maintained, it would be "extremely difficult to get our men to accept any further modifications. A considerable number of Republicans who voted with me really desired to vote against the treaty in any form but I was able to hold them for ratification with reservations."[1]

The invalid in the White House was equally stiff-necked. He refused to discuss the treaty with anyone until a special, threatening incident forced him to speak out. Immediately after the votes on November 19, Hitchcock and Underwood, who would soon be running against each other for the post of Democratic leader in the Senate, wrote to urge the president to resubmit the treaty and seek a basis for compromise. Likewise, Colonel House diffidently asked Mrs. Wilson to forward two letters to her husband in which he pleaded for compromise. The gist and language of these letters did reach the president. Around the beginning of December he dictated a statement to Mrs. Wilson that was evidently intended for release to the press. Wilson noted that the Germans were refusing to complete their ratification of the peace treaty. He argued that they were "treating it as only one more 'scrap of paper'" and would "respect no treaty which has not the united force of the free nations behind it." Unfortunately, the president concluded, "The action of the Senate has convinced her [Germany] that no force or influence of America will be put behind the execution of the treaty[.]"[2]

That fragmentary statement, which was not made public, was the closest that Wilson came to saying anything about the treaty for more

1. Lodge to J. A. Lowell Blake, Dec. 3, 1919, Henry Cabot Lodge Papers, Massachusetts Historical Society; Lodge to John H. Sherburne, Dec. 4, 1919; Lodge to Root, Dec. 3, 1919, Elihu Root Papers, Library of Congress, Box 161. For Root's suggested reservations, see Root to Lodge, Dec. 1, 1919, Lodge Papers.
2. Edith Bolling Wilson draft, [ca. Dec. 2, 1919], in Arthur S. Link, ed., *The Papers of Woodrow Wilson* (Princeton, N.J., 1990), LXIV, 118. See also Underwood to Wilson, Nov. 21, 1919, ibid., 69–70; Hitchcock to Wilson, Nov. 22, 24, 1919, ibid., 70, 93–94; House to Edith Wilson, Nov. 24, 27, 1919, ibid., 88–89, 95–97; House to Wilson, Nov. 24, 27, 1919, ibid., 89–90, 96. Norman Davis, a respected Democratic banker and former member of the peace conference delegation, also wrote to Tumulty to urge that the president negotiate with senators about reservations. See Davis to Tumulty, Dec. 1, 1919, ibid., 104–105.

than two weeks after the Senate votes. He did not answer or even acknowledge the attempts to communicate with him. Likewise, at his direction, Mrs. Wilson deleted all references to the treaty from the draft that Tumulty prepared of the state-of-the-union message to the session of Congress that opened on December 2. Moreover, when Senator Hitchcock called at the White House on November 29, the president refused to see him. Hitchcock took offense at this treatment and said so to reporters, who pressed Tumulty for an explanation. "The President has made wonderful improvement," Tumulty insisted, but just now Mrs. Wilson thought "it unwise for him to hold a conference with Mr. Hitchcock or anyone else." This act of barring the door to the presidential sickroom was the straw that broke the camel's back of frustration on Capitol Hill. Four days later the *New York Times* reported that Wilson's refusal to see Hitchcock was feeding "unease . . . over the President's prolonged lack of participation in public activities." It was bolstering beliefs "that the President is in much worse condition than his physicians have indicated," and it was escalating demands that "Congress and the country should know the facts."[3]

Congressional leaders seized upon current Mexican affairs as a pretext for probing Wilson's condition. Chronic turmoil spawned by the revolution in Mexico and recurrent friction between the United States and the government of Venustiano Carranza – which in October had seized and detained an American citizen, William O. Jenkins – had fomented calls for military intervention. Those calls found their loudest and most persistent champion in Senator Albert Fall, the Republican Irreconcilable from New Mexico, who owned property in Mexico and was close to Mexican conservatives. Also on November 29, Tumulty or someone else at the White House divulged to reporters that the president had taken no part in consideration of either the current coal strike at home or the Mexican situation. Then, on December 4, under questioning before the Foreign Relations Committee, Secretary of State Lansing admitted that neither he nor anyone else in his department had talked with Wilson about Mexico since August. In response to Lansing's admission, the committee went into closed session and voted six to five,

3. *Washington Post*, Nov. 30, 1919; *New York Times*, Dec. 4, 1919. For the deleted portion of the state-of-the-union message, see Tumulty draft, [Nov. 24, 1919], in Link, ed., *Papers of Wilson*, LXIV. On the refusal to see Hitchcock, see also Tumulty to Edith Wilson, Dec. 1, 1919, ibid., 103; Hitchcock to Bryan, Nov. 30, 1919, Bryan Papers, Box 32; and Charles D. Warner memorandum, Nov. 29, 1919, Lansing Papers, Vol. 49. For a review of the Mexican situation and Fall's efforts to promote intervention, see Link, ed., *Papers of Wilson*, LXIV, 121–122 n. 1.

strictly along party lines, to appoint a subcommittee, consisting of Fall and Hitchcock, to go to the White House and discuss the Mexican situation with the president. Everybody knew and many privately admitted that the real motive behind this move was to check up on Wilson's physical and mental condition. Washington wags dubbed the Fall–Hitchcock duo the "smelling committee."[4]

The president's physician had anticipated something like this happening. "I had a plan of my own to meet this situation when the time arose," Grayson noted in a memorandum at the time. At his instigation, Wilson put on an artful performance that concealed the true extent of his incapacity. As soon as Grayson learned about the smelling committee, he announced publicly that the president would be glad to receive the senators. The next day, December 5, when Fall and Hitchcock telephoned to arrange a time for their visit, the answer was "2:30 this afternoon." When the senators arrived at the White House, Fall asked the doctor how long they would be permitted to stay. Grayson replied that Fall could judge that for himself. "This was a staggering blow," Grayson chortled in his memorandum, "because there is no doubt that the Republican majority in the Senate was hopeful that I would, even if I permitted the committee to see the President, limit the time and make it very brief." As it was, Fall and Hitchcock spent about three-quarters of an hour with Wilson.[5]

Ushered into the bedroom, the senators found the president propped up in bed. According to Grayson, Wilson had ordered all the lights in the room turned on so that the visitors could get a good look at him. He did lie with his partially paralyzed left side bundled in the bedcovers and with papers placed on a bedside table where he could reach them easily with his right hand. The senators both shook hands with the president. According to Mrs. Wilson's notes from the meeting, Fall opened the conversation by stating, "I hope you will consider me sincere. I have been praying for you, Sir." Years later, Mrs. Wilson recalled that her husband shot back, "Which way, Senator?" It is a shame to spoil a good story, but neither Mrs. Wilson's notes nor Grayson's memorandum at the time mentions that witty comeback. Grayson also recorded

4. *New York Times*, Dec. 5, 1919. See also entry Dec. 4, 1919, Lansing diary, in Link, ed., *Papers of Wilson*, LXIV, 125; and Grayson memorandum, Dec. 5, 1919, ibid., 135–136. The party-line vote in the Foreign Relations Committee was six to five, because McCumber was absent then and during most of this round of the League fight.
5. Ibid., 137. Grayson states that the meeting lasted "for more than forty-five minutes," whereas news reports said that it lasted forty minutes. See *New York Times*, Dec. 6, 1919.

that the president responded by saying that he was getting along well and hoped to be up on his feet soon so that he could come down to the Capitol and deal with public business.[6]

"Senator Fall did most of the talking," Hitchcock told reporters afterward, "and presented a very good summary of conditions to which the President gave the deepest attention." Wilson also reached out and took some papers from the senators, Grayson noted. A little later, the doctor came back into the room to announce, as he related to reporters, "Pardon me, gentlemen, but Secretary Lansing had asked me to tell you immediately that Jenkins has been released." Grayson admitted to reporters that he felt like an actor making a sensational entrance.[7]

Wilson's attentiveness and the dramatic ploy of announcing Jenkins' release satisfied the pretext for the senators' visit. When reporters asked Fall immediately afterward about Mexico, he answered, "In my opinion, Mr. Wilson is perfectly capable of handling the situation." Wilson's performance likewise achieved the larger purpose of quashing doubts about his ability to fill his office. "He seemed to me in excellent trim for a man who has been in bed for ten weeks," Fall added to the reporters. "Of course, I am not an expert, but that's how it appeared to me." Wilson reinforced the impression of his fitness by telling jokes about Mexico, including a quip by one of Finley Peter Dunne's humorous characters that "Mexico is so contagious to us that I'm thinkin' we'll have to take it." Wilson also referred to

6. Edith Wilson notes, [Dec. 5, 1919], in Link, ed., *Papers of Wilson*, LXIV, 134–135; Grayson memorandum, Dec. 5, 1919, ibid., 137–138; Edith Bolling Wilson, *My Memoir* (Indianapolis, 1939), 299. As might be expected, accounts of this incident differed on certain points. One was whether the senators could get a good look at Wilson. As noted, Grayson claimed that all the lights were turned on, to offset the gloom of that December afternoon, whereas Fall told reporters, "His bed was in a shaded portion of the room." Ibid. The one other eyewitness account of the meeting, written some years later by "Ike" Hoover, the head usher of the White House, claims that the room was deliberately darkened and only one light was left on. I. H. Hoover memoir, in Link, ed., *Papers of Wilson*, LXIII, 637. As for "Which way, Senator?" that was probably what Wilson wished he had said to Fall, and he later may have come to believe that he had said it. In February 1921, when Wilson recounted the incident to Secretary of the Treasury David Houston, he said that after Fall made his remark, "If I could have got out of bed, I would have hit the man. Why did he want to put me in bad with the Almighty?" David F. Houston, *Eight Years with Wilson's Cabinet* (Garden City, N.Y., 1926), II, 141.
7. *New York Times*, Dec. 6, 1919.

Senator Moses' earlier allegations about his having suffered a stroke. According to Fall, "The President said that as a result of the conference the Senator [Moses] would be reassured, although he might be disappointed."[8]

The smelling committee's visit also elicited Wilson's first public statement since the Senate votes on the peace treaty. Hitchcock spoke up at the end of the meeting to ask Wilson what he intended to do with the treaty. "The President said," Hitchcock recounted to reporters, "that he regarded responsibility as having been shifted from his shoulders to others, and that he was disposed to let it rest there awhile." Hitchcock added that he took that statement to mean that Wilson would do nothing for the present but leave it to the Senate to seek a compromise. A few days afterward, when Hitchcock finally got to see Wilson by himself, he found the president even more obdurate. "Let Lodge compromise," Hitchcock later recalled Wilson replying to suggestions about initiatives toward compromise. "Let Lodge hold out the olive branch."[9]

Heated though it was, Wilson's defiance did not spring primarily from hatred of Lodge. His attitude now and during the rest of the League fight mainly reflected the psychological effects of his stroke. With a stroke of this kind, its psychological impact can grow more pronounced as the patient's physical condition improves. Wilson demonstrated the link between his physical health and his political stance most clearly when he took two actions on December 14. First, as Grayson announced to reporters, the president overruled his doctors and insisted on taking his first steps since his stroke, and he walked around the bedroom without ill effect. At the same time, Dr. Dercum, the neurologist, who was making his weekly visit to examine Wilson, publicly pronounced him "markedly better." This news heartened Democratic party leaders, who told reporters that they hoped the president would soon take part in politics and might attend the party's annual Jackson Day dinner on January 8. Wilson's other action on December 14 was to issue a public statement about the peace treaty. He dictated a press release "from the highest authority in the executive department" that brushed aside talk about his making any move as

8. Ibid.

9. Ibid.; Hitchcock, "Brief View of the Late War and the Struggle for Peace Aims," speech to Nebraska State Historical Society, Jan. 13, 1925 (pamphlet, Nebraska State Historical Society), 21. Hitchcock seems to have seen Wilson on December 8 or 9. See *New York Times*, Dec. 10, 1919; entry, Dec. 11, 1919, House Diary, in Link, ed., *Papers of Wilson*, LXIV, 182–183.

"entirely without foundation." Rather, speaking in the third person, the president declared, "He has no compromise or concession of any kind in mind, but intends, so far as he is concerned, that the Republican leaders of the Senate shall continue to bear the undivided responsibility for the fate of the treaty and the present condition of the world in consequence of that fate."[10]

This statement foreshadowed similar actions by Wilson during this round of the League fight. His defiance would flare up most often at times when his recovery from the stroke took a turn for the better. At those times, the president would feel what the editors of the *Papers of Wilson* have called "euphoria," and this mood would lead him to entertain fantasies about his ability to function as president. In reality, his recovery was only partial and was strictly relative to his previous debility. Despite the adroit handling of the smelling committee, he was not paying any attention to Mexico or other pressing domestic and foreign policy concerns. The most glaring proof of his continued incapacity came on December 2, when for the first time he failed to deliver a state-of-the-union address. One of Woodrow Wilson's proudest innovations had been to revive the practice of the president's appearing in person before Congress. He had done so twice during the last session. Furthermore, Wilson had always taken great pride in writing his own speeches. Now, he had to rely on Tumulty to draft nearly all of his messages.[11]

In these moments of euphoria, Wilson's ingrained habits of denial of obstacles and weakness blossomed into full-blown illusions. He believed that he comprehended political conditions better than anyone else and that he could best his adversaries. These euphoric moments would become the most dangerous times for presidential intervention in this round of the League fight. Around the middle of December, Wilson privately revealed how far his fantasies were taking him. He had Tumulty draft a statement, which he revised by dictating changes to Mrs. Wilson. The statement asserted again that Germany was plotting to keep the United States from ratifying the peace treaty and joining the League and then declared, "There is but one way to settle such questions, and that is by direct reference to the voters of the country." Because the Constitution did not provide for a referendum, Wilson proposed an alternative

10. *Washington Post*, Dec. 14, 1919; *New York Times*, Dec. 15, 1919. On Wilson's having dictated this statement, see Link, ed., *Papers of Wilson*, LXIV, 187 n. 1.
11. For the characterization of Wilson's "euphoria," see ibid., viii.

method: "I challenge the following named gentlemen, members of the Senate of the United States, to resign their seats on the issue of their several records with regard to ratification of the Treaty." He listed the names and states of fifty-six senators and promised that "if all or a majority of them are re-elected, I will resign the presidency." In addition, Wilson pledged that the vice-president would also resign, so that "one of the acknowledged leaders of the Republican party," having been previously appointed secretary of state and thus next in the line of succession, would become president.[12]

If Wilson had made this scheme public at the middle of December 1919, the attempts to reopen the League fight might have ground to a screeching halt. Wilson did not pursue the idea at this time, although he did have Mrs. Wilson write to the attorney general to find out how senators' seats were filled when they resigned. This referendum scheme would soon rear its head again. That would not happen, however, until after a number of initiatives at compromise had acquired sufficient momentum to overcome both Lodge's and Wilson's resistance. Some outside pressures abetted these moves. To the disgust of Republican Irreconcilables, their party chairman, Will Hays, lobbied for disposal of the treaty before the upcoming election. Among Democrats, William Jennings Bryan exerted himself in the same direction. These party warhorses wanted to get the treaty debate behind them. They did not

---

12. Draft statement, [ca. Dec. 17, 1919], ibid., 199–202. The list of senators was carelessly prepared, as the editors of the *Papers of Wilson* note, because it included such reliable Democrats as Bankhead, Kirby, and Kendrick. See ibid., 202 n. 1. In addition, among the Republicans, the list omitted one of the Irreconcilables, Norris, and included all of the mild reservationists except McCumber and Nelson. Wilson had given a hint of something like this scheme during his second meeting with Hitchcock before the Senate votes in November. He was drawing upon some long-standing ideas of his about making the American political system work more like a parliamentary one. Besides his belief in appealing over the heads of legislators, which he had acted upon most recently with the speaking tour in September, he was drawing upon the plan that he had secretly concocted to resign from the presidency after the 1916 election if he had lost, meanwhile getting the vice-president to resign and naming Hughes secretary of state so that he could become president immediately. That plan would not become publicly known for many years. Lansing alludes to it somewhat cryptically in his *War Memoirs* (Indianapolis, 1935), 165–166. For a full account, see Arthur S. Link, *Wilson: Confusions and Crises* (Princeton, N.J., 1964), V, 153–155.

fear outraged public opinion one way or the other, but they did want to fight the next election on tried-and-true domestic issues. As far as can be determined, no great outcry arose from either the press or the public following the deadlock in November. All surveys continued to find widespread support for League membership but also concern for safe-guarding American sovereignty, with newspapers still largely divided according to their party affiliations.[13]

Unlike earlier, this round of the League fight would feature little in the way of speeches or rallies around the country. That was because nearly all knowledgeable observers detected a growing lack of interest in these issues on the part of the public. "It will be hard to get up any meetings," Beveridge commented to Borah, "because the people are fed up – literally gorged – . . . [so] that the ordinary citizen is sick of them and starts to a movie show every time a meeting is mentioned." One of the LEP's lobbyists agreed. He found in all his conversations "a very marked difference of opinion, where there was any opinion at all. . . . Mostly, whatever discussions I had about the treaty I had to initiate." Both the LEP and the Independence League virtually closed up shop. They slashed their budgets because of lack of funds and reduced their staffs to a corporal's guard. With one major exception, neither organization tried to organize mass meetings or mount large-scale petition drives. Individual LEP leaders did continue to lobby, and they later sent a delegation to Washington that represented a number of large organizations, most notably the American Federation of Labor. In the main,

13. Privately, Wilson remained as obdurate as ever against compromise. Writing through his wife, he told Hitchcock "that it would be a serious mistake for him (or for our side), to *propose* anything." Edith Wilson to Hitchcock, Dec. 19, 1919, in Link, ed., *Papers of Wilson*, LXIV, 206. When Bernard Baruch saw Wilson around this time and suggested compromise, Baruch, as he told Chandler Anderson, "had almost been kicked out of the room for doing so." Entry, Jan. 11, 1920, Anderson Diary, Chandler P. Anderson Papers, Library of Congress. For the inquiry to the attorney general, see Edith Wilson to A. Mitchell Palmer, Dec. 18, 1919, in Link, ed., *Papers of Wilson*, LXIV, 202–203; and Palmer to Wilson, Dec. 22, 1919, ibid., 214–215. For Hays' activities, see *New York Times*, Nov. 24, Dec. 9, 1919; for the Irreconcilables' disgust with him, see Brandegee to Beveridge, Dec. 9, 1919, Albert J. Beveridge Papers, Library of Congress, Box 214. For Bryan's activities, see Bryan to Hitchcock, Nov. 24, 1919, William Jennings Bryan Papers, Library of Congress, Box 32. One survey of newspaper opinion is in the New York *World*, Nov. 21, 1919.

however, the time for trying to arouse popular opinion and interested organizations had passed.[14]

The real initiative to reopen the League fight came from within the Senate. Two groups of senators took the lead in seeking to bring the peace treaty up again for consideration and build a basis for compromise. As was to be expected, the Republican mild reservationists pushed hard for renewed debate and action. Kellogg, Lenroot, and, to a lesser extent, McNary started working around the middle of December to explore modifications in the Lodge reservations. In part, these Republicans were reacting to a move by Lodge and Knox to revive their earlier scheme to bypass ratification of the peace treaty by passing a congressional resolution to declare an end to the state of war with Germany. On December 20, the Republicans on the Foreign Relations Committee approved a new version of the Knox resolution. The mild reservationists responded by going to Lodge's house the next day and informing him of their strong opposition. They also insisted that Lodge open discussions with the Democrats, and they suggested specific concessions on reservations.[15]

Certain Democrats were likewise pushing for renewed debate and compromise. Their newfound initiative marked a big change from the previous session, when few of them had shown any stomach for departing from the president's presumed lead. Their activism sprang in part from a division in their ranks. Hitchcock and Underwood were vying for the post of party leader left vacant by Martin's death a month earlier. Of the two, Underwood initially took a bolder stand in favor of compromise. Speaking on the Senate floor on December 13, he revived

14. Beveridge to Borah, Dec. 3, 1919, William E. Borah Papers, Library of Congress Box 769; H. N. Rickey to Short, Dec. 9, 1919, A. Lawrence Lowell Papers, Harvard University Archives. On the curtailed activities of the Independence League, see Lee Meriwether to Levinson, Dec. 2, 9, 1919, Levinson Papers, Box 33; Meriwether to J. S. Baches, Dec. 17, 1919, ibid. On the LEP's curtailment, see Short memorandum [Dec. 20, 1919], Lowell Papers; H. S. Houston to Taft, Dec. 23, 1919, Taft Papers, Library of Congress, reel 216.

15. Herbert F. Margulies, *Mild Reservationists and the League of Nations Controversy in the Senate* (Columbia, Mo., 1989), 193. On their activities and meetings, see also *New York Times,* Dec. 17, 21, 1919; New York *World,* Dec. 18, 22, 1919; McNary to Taft, Dec. 22, 1919, Taft Papers, reel 215; and Alice Roosevelt Longworth, *Crowded Hours* (New York, 1933), 294–295. On the new version of the Knox resolution, see entries, Dec. 18, 19, 20, 1919, Anderson Diary; and Lodge to James, T. Williams, Jr., Dec. 20, 1919, Lodge Papers.

the previous session's last-ditch proposal to appoint a committee of conciliation between the two parties as "a common-sense treatment of the situation." Underwood conceded that "a compromise has to be made. I think that if the members on this side of the chamber were not willing to meet Senators on the other side of the chamber halfway and agree upon a reasonable compromise to bring peace to the land, they would be subject to criticism, and just criticism."[16]

Underwood's proposal sparked the first floor debate about the peace treaty since the convening of this session of Congress. Lodge and Hitchcock sparred over what each of them had agreed upon before the votes on November 19 and about who was to blame for the ensuing defeat and deadlock. Lodge insisted that Wilson must make the first move toward any reconsideration of the treaty, and he scoffed at Underwood's and Hitchcock's remarks as evidence "of competition between the two distinguished aspirants for the Democratic leadership." Underwood responded by making a significant though perhaps unwise concession. If all other efforts to resolve differences failed, he declared, "I would be willing by reservation . . . to strike out of the treaty of peace all clauses relating to the league of nations, so far as we are concerned." Under questioning from Knox and Lenroot, Underwood reiterated, "I would be willing to purchase peace by reserving the question as to whether we should become parties to the league of nations until the people of the United States could act on it."[17]

Underwood's initiative directly and indirectly heated the pot of senatorial consideration of the treaty. His evident willingness to shelve League membership may have played a role in prompting the Republicans on the Foreign Relations Committee to approve Knox's resolution, which in turn stirred up the mild reservationists. Knox's resolution, together with Underwood's statements, also prompted some further debate. But that brief flurry of discussion marked the last floor debate, except for one more speech by a Democrat urging compromise, for the next month and a half. This would be another contrast with what had

16. *Congressional Record,* 66th Cong., 2nd Sess. (Dec. 13, 1919), 533.

17. Ibid. (Dec. 13, 1919), 533–534, 536, 540–541. Also participating in this debate were Lenroot, who also urged compromise but placed the onus for opening discussions on the Democrats; Brandegee, who sneered that the treaty was dead, just a "defunct piece of paper with some printing on it"; and Underwood's Alabama colleague, Bankhead, who seconded the proposal for a conciliation committee. Ibid., 539–540, 542, 543–544. See also Underwood to S. C. Jenkins, Dec. 17, 1919, Oscar W. Underwood Papers, Alabama State Archives, Box 38.

home on December 31, Pomerene told reporters, "We are going to act together."[22]

Such optimism was premature, but not too much so. In public Lodge was giving more guarded readings of his meetings with Pomerene and the mild reservationists. Privately, he continued to reassure League opponents that nothing was afoot. "Do not be disturbed about talk of compromise in the newspapers," Lodge told Beveridge. He insisted that he was just going through the motions of letting the Democrats try to come up with compromises. The senator was protesting a bit too much to his anti-League friends. At the beginning of January 1920, Lodge met with a bipartisan foursome that consisted of Swanson, McNary, Lenroot, and Arthur Capper of Kansas.[23]

Meanwhile, Hoke Smith of Georgia was attempting to assemble a cohort of reservationist Democrats. According to some reports, Smith enlisted twelve of his party brethren behind him, while another seven, including Pomerene, were said to be leaning his way. By the end of the first week in January, McKellar and Kendrick were proposing the appointment of an informal committee of conciliation and outlining specific changes in the Lodge reservations. Underwood also talked with Lodge, and he announced on the Senate floor that he was so pleased with his colleagues' efforts that he was temporarily stepping aside, "as I do not desire to throw any monkey wrenches into any machinery that would look to the ratification of the treaty of peace." As before, however, Wilson's attitude remained a question mark. By common consent, as newspapers reported, the senators who were engaged in these compromise negotiations agreed to suspend their work until they heard what the president had to say at the Jackson Day dinner on January 8.[24]

---

22. *New York Times,* Jan. 1, 1920. On McKellar's contacts with Colt and Kenyon, see McKellar memorandum, [June 1926], Kenneth D. McKellar Papers, Shelby County Public Library, Memphis, Box 7. A copy of this memorandum is also in the Hitchcock Papers, along with a letter explaining its composition. McKellar to Hitchcock, June 26, 1926, ibid. The only contemporary reference made to these contacts is in Bryan to McKellar, [ca. Dec. 21, 1919], McKellar Papers, Box 56, and McKellar to Bryan, Dec. 22, 1919, ibid.

23. Lodge to Beveridge, Jan. 3, 1920, Lodge Papers; *New York Times,* Jan. 4, 1920.

24. *Congressional Record,* 66th Cong., 2nd Sess. (Jan. 7, 1920), 1158. On Smith's effort and on McKellar's and Kendrick's proposal, see New York *World,* Jan. 3, 7,1920; *New York Times,* Jan. 4, 8, 1920. For reports on the situation in the Senate, see also Karger to Taft, Dec. 31, 1919, Jan. 3, 1920, Taft Papers, reel 215.

II

"Throw a monkey wrench" aptly described what Wilson tried to do with his letter to that Democratic party gathering. His action sprang from both his delusions of strength and the reality of his weakness. He was determined to seize control of consideration of the peace treaty, and he still wanted to stage some kind of referendum on League membership. But Wilson was not able to appear in person to deliver a speech at the Jackson Day dinner or even write his own message to the assembled Democrats. Instead, on January 6, two days before the dinner, he ordered Tumulty to draft a letter for him. This draft dripped with bitter remarks about how the Senate's refusal to act was threatening to undo the victory over Germany, which would mean a "resumption of the old offensive and defensive alliances" and failure to restore Alsace and Lorraine to France. The only way out of this predicament, the letter charged,

> is by a direct referendum; . . . it is our duty as a party to give the next election the form of a great and solemn referendum to the voters of the country in this great matter, a referendum as to the part the United States is to play in completing the settlements of the war and in the prevention in the future of such outrages as Germany attempted to perpetrate, and these are matters of such supreme importance that they can be settled only by the sovereign voice of the voters of the Republic.[25]

It was a tribute to Tumulty's familiarity with Wilson's mind that he could coin the phrase "great and solemn referendum." Those words captured his chief's lofty cadence and removal from political reality. It was a tribute to Tumulty's own sense of political reality that he enlisted some administration insiders to revise and soften this message. He asked Secretary of Agriculture David Houston to meet with him, Attorney General A. Mitchell Palmer, and Undersecretary of State Frank Polk in Houston's office to go over the draft. "It was unsatisfactory," Houston later recalled himself thinking. ". . . I could not understand how he [Wilson] could have made such statements." These three advisors urged Tumulty to drop the references to Alsace-Lorraine's not being restored to France and the treaty provisions' not being implemented. Those references were glaringly false and would stir up bad feelings in Europe. Furthermore, although it is not clear whether he said so at the meeting, Houston thought the referendum idea "unwise. It was a flat declara-

25. Tumulty draft, [Jan. 6, 1920], in Link, ed., *Papers of Wilson,* LXIV, 247–249.

tion, in effect, against further attempts to agree on reservations and would, if assented to, make the Treaty a partisan issue in an election, while the people were in a bad humour and might be interested in other things besides the Treaty."[26]

Houston also recalled that he had recognized the futility of trying to talk Wilson out of the referendum scheme. He offered instead to revise the draft. He wanted to eliminate errors and, as he stated in a memorandum the next day, "to make clear again what has already been said that *Interpretative reservations* are not objectionable." To that end, Houston added five sentences, to precede the "great and solemn referendum." These sentences barred amendments to the treaty but stated that Wilson had "no reasonable objection to interpretations accompanying the act of ratification, provided they do not form a part of the formal ratification itself." Wilson accepted Houston's changes, but he also dictated to Mrs. Wilson another sentence to follow the call for "a great and solemn referendum." This sentence read, "We have no moral right to refuse now to take part in the execution & administration of these settlements than we had to refuse to take part in the fighting of the last few weeks of the war which brought victory & made it possible to dictate to Germany what the settlements should be[.]" These additions – Houston's modification and Wilson's further challenge – bracketed the call for a referendum in the letter that was read at the Jackson Day dinner on January 8.[27]

The president's attempt to derail compromise failed. Houston's additions took some of the sting out of the letter, and senatorial negotiations had acquired too much momentum. "The Democratic Senators do not seem to feel that all hope of getting together is over," one of the mild reservationists noted privately the next day. William Short of the LEP, who was at the banquet, agreed. He did report, however, that Republican senators thought that the letter was "likely to make the

26. Houston, *Eight Years with Wilson's Cabinet*, II, 47–48. There is some question about who originated the idea of revising this draft. Polk told Colonel House soon afterward that Lansing had asked to see a draft and Tumulty refused but consulted with Polk. Entry, Jan. 11, 1919, House Diary, in Link, ed., *Papers of Wilson*, LXIV, 270. In his own diary, however, Lansing simply said that the draft "was shown to Polk, Palmer and Houston by Tumulty." Entry, Jan. 10, 1920, Lansing Diary, ibid., 269. In his memoir, Houston also states that Tumulty asked for the meeting.

27. Houston memorandum, [Jan. 7, 1920], ibid., 250–252; Edith Wilson handwritten addition to Tumulty redraft, [Jan. 7, 1920], ibid., 254. The final text is in ibid., 257–259.

Democratic Senators more timid about yielding the points necessary to agreement."28

Much of the muffled impact of this would-be bombshell also derived from the fractious, uncertain state of intraparty Democratic politics. Bryan was the featured speaker at the banquet. He used much of his speech, which followed the reading of Wilson's letter, to urge compromise on whatever basis possible. Bryan also maintained that the importance of Article X was "very much magnified." Sensible as many Democrats found this message, some of them distrusted the messenger. "What does W. J. B. mean to do?" wrote Senator Ashurst, who was also present, in his diary. "Is he seeking a fourth nomination? He was the guest who was suspected – feared and hated." Bryan compounded that distrust by proposing two days later in a speech in Chicago that, if no compromise could be reached, the Democratic senators should simply stand aside and let the Republicans alone vote through consent with the Lodge reservations. This suggestion roused howls of derision even among Democrats who ardently wished to get the League and the treaty behind them.29

The other intraparty circumstance that evidently dampened reaction to Wilson's letter in the Senate was the race for the Democratic leadership there. Both Hitchcock and Underwood moved cautiously. Out of a wish to avoid offending potential supporters, the two men neither agreed nor disagreed with the president. Two days before the Democrats met to vote on January 15, Hitchcock wrote to Mrs. Wilson asking for her husband to intercede on his behalf. His plea was to no avail. She replied that the president "feels he is bound in conscience to take no part in the choice to which you refer." When the Democratic senators voted on January 15, the result was a tie. Underwood could have prevailed if the man whom the governor of Virginia had just appointed to fill Martin's seat, Secretary of the Treasury Carter Glass, had voted. The

28. Frederick Hale to Nicholas Murray Butler, Jan. 9, 1920, Butler Papers; Short memorandum, [Jan. 10, 1920], Lowell Papers.

29. Entry, Jan. 11, 1920, Ashurst Diary, in George F. Sparks, ed., *A Many-Colored Toga: The Diary of Henry Fountain Ashurst* (Tucson, Ariz., 1962), 121–122. For other accounts of the dinner, see Karger to Taft, Jan. 10, 1920, Taft Papers, reel 217; Louis F. Post to William E. Dodd, Feb. 16, 1920, William E. Dodd Papers, Library of Congress, Box 16. Press reaction to the letter also seems to have been muted, with many calling for getting on with compromise over the treaty. See *Literary Digest*, LXIV (Jan. 17, 1920), 11–13. On Bryan's role, see also Paolo E. Coletta, *William Jennings Bryan* (Lincoln, Neb., 1969), III, 96–99.

senators voted to allow Glass, who had not yet resigned from the cabinet, to cast a ballot, but Underwood demurred, saying that he did not
wish to cause discord. As a stopgap, the senators agreed to postpone
another vote until sometime after Glass had taken his seat. In the meantime, Hitchcock would continue to serve as acting leader.[30]

From the standpoint of drawing the Senate Democrats together and
promoting compromise on the treaty, this tie vote and postponement
may have been the worst possible outcome. Not being full-fledged party
leader, neither Underwood nor Hitchcock could try to unite his party
brethren. Instead, they had to keep them divided in order to win the
leadership. Worse, in view of Wilson's downplayed but really undisguised intransigence, any Democratic leader who sought to forge a compromise on the treaty and League membership would almost certainly
have to stand up to the president, even defy him. Of these two senators,
Underwood was far better suited to that role than Hitchcock. A month
earlier, Secretary of State Lansing had summed up the difference
between the two senators when he wrote in his diary, "Hitchcock will
obey orders. Underwood prefers to give them. One is a lieutenant, the
other a commander." The trouble was, neither Underwood nor his rival

30. For the breakdown and maneuvering of the Democratic senators, see *New
York Times,* Jan. 16, 1920. By custom, the candidates themselves did not
vote. Each one received nineteen votes, with each having two others
announced for him. Johnson of South Dakota neither voted nor announced
for either, and Smith of Georgia refused to endorse either man. Sectional
differences in their support were striking. Of Underwod's twenty-one supporters, sixteen were from the South or border states, and three others were
natives of the South who had moved west. Of Hitchcock's supporters, fifteen represented states west of the Mississippi. Domestic differences played
a part, too, inasmuch as Underwood's supporters leaned toward the more
conservative southern or "Bourbon" side, whereas Hitchcock's backers
leaned toward the progressive side. Foreign policy seems to have played
some role, too, since the Irreconcilable Reed and three of the four reservationists – Gore, Shields, and Walsh of Massachusetts – backed Underwood.
Underwood himself read the division as entirely sectional. See letters in
Underwood Papers, Box 38. Conversely, one of the progressive Democrats
who eventually supported Hitchcock did so most reluctantly. A month earlier, Owen had written to Bryan, "I very much regret that the leadership of
the Senate is in such bad condition. Unfortunately, a number of the more
progressive Senators were induced to think that it would be a reflection on
Hitchcock if he were denied the chairmanship when he had stood as vice-
chairman under Martin. I do not feel willing to support either of these gentlemen, and I agree with you that it would handicap our Party in the next
campaign." Owen to Bryan, Dec. 9, 1919, Bryan Papers, Box 32.

was yet commander of the Senate Democrats. Both of them had to continue to carry water on both shoulders by maintaining good relations with both Wilson's critics and his defenders.[31]

Wilson's opponents were the ones who read his Jackson Day letter at face value. "Mr. Wilson has taken the right means of settling the question," Borah told reporters. "His position is consistent." Lodge likewise declared, "The President has made his position very plain. He rejects absolutely the reservations accepted by a decisive majority of the Senate." Yet, though their responses sounded similar, Borah and Lodge were not coming from the same place. The Irreconcilables relished the prospect of fighting the next election on the issue of League membership because they felt sure Wilson would lose. Lodge, on the other hand, was only seeking to mollify the anti-League forces. "The situation is very good, so far," he wrote to Beveridge on January 18, "but not quite so ideal as you think." Lodge warned that a number of their party colleagues were refusing to join him in trying to pass the Knox resolution:

> There are Republicans who are not willing to vote for it until it is apparent that no agreement of any sort can be come to for ratifying the treaty with reservations. I doubt if any such arrangement is possible, in view of Wilson's attitude. . . . The President seems to be perfectly reckless about the whole thing, and I do not myself believe that he means to yield anything at all.[32]

None of these attempts to throw cold water had much effect. Among the Republicans, Short of the LEP reported after a visit to the capital that not only were established mild reservationists pushing for an agreement, but joining them now were a "new group of mild reservationists." These Republicans were evidently the ones who drew the line against any attempt as yet to pass the Knox resolution. They also got into specifics with some Democrats about which of the Lodge reservations might be changed. As McNary reported to Taft, they found few problems with dropping the earlier preamble and modifying the reservations to the labor clauses and British Empire voting. By contrast, McNary added, "We reported that we would hold fast to Reservation X, which qualifies Article 10," as well as some other ones. "Our chief

---

31. Entry, Dec. 16, 1919, Lansing Diary, in Link, ed., *Papers of Wilson*, LXIV, 194. For an analysis of Underwood's and Hitchcock's predicament in trying to promote a compromise on the treaty, see Karger to Taft, Jan. 10, 1920, Taft Papers, reel 217.
32. *New York Times*, Jan. 9, 1920; Lodge to Beveridge, Jan. 13, 1920, Beveridge Papers. See also Knox to Beveridge, Jan. 13, 1920, ibid.; and Lodge to Harvey, Jan. 16, 1920, Lodge Papers.

controversy now hinges over Article 10." Wilson's and Lodge's attitudes bothered him, but he felt "satisfied yet that compromise can be reached."[33]

Democratic senators now exerted themselves even more strongly for compromise. In the days following Wilson's Jackson Day utterance, there was talk about revolt against him, but one Democrat dismissed this as "cloakroom courage." Out in the open, Owen gathered twenty of his party colleagues at his apartment on the evening of January 11. Those attending the meeting included Underwood, Pomerene, Kendrick, McKellar, and Smith of Georgia. According to the New York *World,* they discussed the modifications to the Lodge reservations outlined earlier by Kendrick and McKellar. Those modifications included elimination of the preamble, softening of some of the others, and a position on Article X that retained some obligation. According to one estimate, thirty Democrats were promising to support such a compromise, although it remained unclear exactly what they might agree to. One unnamed senator echoed Wilson when he told the *New York Times,* "You can say that the Democratic side is willing to compromise reservations that will be only interpretative but will not accept reservations that nullify." By contrast, a powerful party insider, Furnifold Simmons of North Carolina, told the New York *World,* "I believe that it is too late to ratify the treaty with nothing stronger than interpretations. . . . Something between interpretations and nullification must be agreed upon."[34]

Outside pressure was also promoting compromise. This was the only time in this round of the League fight when public opinion played an overt role in the course of events. At the beginning of January, over Taft's objections and without his participation, the LEP's executive committee, led by Oscar Straus and Theodore Marburg, decided to mount one last public lobbying drive and join forces with organized labor in making this effort. Twice during the previous year, Samuel Gompers had gotten the AFL to endorse League membership without reservations. Besides cementing his labor federation's political alliance with the Democrats, Gompers wanted to resist what he saw as the anti-union thrust of the reservation to the treaty's labor clauses. On January 13, a large convocation chaired by Straus met in Washington. Present were representatives from twenty-six organizations with an estimated membership of 20 million people; these included the AFL, the Federal Coun-

33. Short memorandum, [Jan. 10, 1920], Taft Papers, reel 217; McNary to Taft, Jan. 13, 1920, ibid.
34. Philadelphia *Public Ledger,* Jan. 11, 1920; *New York Times,* Jan. 12, 1920; New York *World,* Jan. 12, 1920.

cil of Churches, the National Education Association, Rotary, the American Federation of Women's Clubs, and individual unions and farm groups. This meeting drafted a resolution urging speedy ratification of the peace treaty on the best terms possible, and a delegation went to Capitol Hill to meet with senators Lodge and Hitchcock. Probably not coincidentally, the next day the Associated Press released a poll of students and faculty at 475 colleges and universities, which found 46,259 for ratification of the treaty without reservations, 33,304 for compromise, 23,577 for the Lodge reservations, and 11,690 for rejection.[35]

The main difficulty in responding to the various pressures for compromise lay in channeling them constructively. During the second week of January, at least six different proposals popped up among the Senate Democrats. One, floated by Hoke Smith and Pat Harrison of Mississippi, called for a new round robin, this time in support of a compromise plan that was to be signed by sixty-four senators. However, as the New York *World* observed, "somehow it foundered." Next, the idea of an informal conciliation group emerged. At the same time William King of Utah offered a list of reservations and Owen suggested a nonpartisan caucus to discuss reservations. Kendrick and McKellar also urged a general meeting to consider their proposals for modifications to the Lodge reservations, but they got no response.[36]

The plan that finally bore fruit grew out of the meeting at Owen's apartment on January 11. Sometime during the next three days, the Oklahoma Democrat went to see Lodge to discuss changes in Article X that had been suggested at that meeting. He found the Republican leader willing to conduct a bipartisan meeting only with others present. Owen took up the challenge and arranged a gathering on January 15 in one of the Foreign Relations Committee's rooms. Representing the Democrats, in addition to Owen, were Hitchcock, McKellar, Simmons, and Walsh of Montana. Representing the Republicans were Lodge, Kellogg, Lenroot, and Harry New of Indiana. The nine senators talked for two hours, beginning what became known as the "bipartisan conference." This conference lasted, on-again, off-again, through the rest of January 1920. It would mark the most promising moment for compro-

35. On this convocation, see minutes, Jan. 13, 1920, William Gibbs McAdoo Papers, Library of Congress, Box 228. On the LEP's involvement and Taft's objections, see LEP executive committee minutes, Jan. 4, 1920, ibid., Box 227; Taft to Wickersham, Jan. 5, 1920, Taft Papers, reel 558; Taft to Karger, Jan. 5, 1920, ibid., reel 216. For the Associated Press poll, see *Congressional Record*, 66th Cong., 2nd Sess. (Jan. 16, 1920), 1603–1604.

36. New York *World*, Jan. 17, 1920. See also ibid., Jan. 15, 1920; *New York Times*, Jan. 15, 16, 1920.

mise and consent to the peace treaty, at least as far as the Senate was concerned.[37]

Both the problems and the promise of the bipartisan conference showed up strikingly at its first meeting on January 15. For a change, the participants remained tight-lipped about their discussions not only with the press but also with their fellow senators. They were so uncommunicative that Borah later complained, half-jokingly, on the Senate floor, ". . . that committee put it all over the Versailles conference on secrecy" – to which Walsh rejoined, "We did the best we could." Newspapers carried only a brief account of the meeting, including Lodge's comment, "We just talked. The conference was a beginning. There is nothing that can be given out at this time."[38]

Actually, a lot could have been given out. Secretly, Hitchcock reported what happened to Tumulty at the White House. The composition of the respective sides struck Hitchcock as disparate. Lodge, in his view, had chosen two Republicans, Lenroot and New, "who are almost as irreconcilable as Lodge himself." Only Kellogg was "more reasonable." Hitchcock depicted himself as "accompanied by Senators who desire a compromise." They stood in contrast to Lodge's "rather uncompromising lot except Kellogg." Discounting its obvious bias, Hitchcock's characterization was accurate up to a point. Lodge himself later privately conceded that "Lenroot was never mild" as a reservationist. New subsequently admitted on the Senate floor that he had participated in the bipartisan conference "with great reluctance" and that he opposed any weakening of the Lodge reservations. Hitchcock was in no position to throw stones. Only one of his fellow Democrats, McKellar, favored for his rival in the party leadership, and only one of them, Owen, had broken ranks in November to vote for consent with the Lodge reservations.[39]

Hitchcock also complained that the Republicans "made no sugges-

37. *New York Times*, Jan. 15, 16, 1920.
38. *Congressional Record*, 66th Cong., 2nd Sess. (Feb. 21, 1920), 3232; *New York Times*, Jan. 16, 1920.
39. Hitchcock to Tumulty, Jan. 16, 1920, in Link, ed., *Papers of Wilson*, LXIV, 283; Lodge to Frederick Gillett, July 26, 1920, Lodge Papers; *Congressional Record*, 66th Cong., 2nd Sess. (Mar. 6, 1920), 3955. As he stated publicly and privately, Lodge chose the Republicans, but it is not clear how the Democrats were chosen. McKellar later claimed that Kendrick was asked to serve but declined and that Pomerene attended some of the meetings. See McKellar memorandum, [June 1926], McKellar Papers, Box 7.

tions at all." Despite that apparent coolness, the two-hour meeting covered a lot of ground. The senators took up the Lodge reservations one by one. At the outset, when one of the Democrats urged that an objectionable part of the preamble be stricken, Hitchcock recounted, "Lodge indicated that this could probably be arranged." Next, on the withdrawal reservation, when the Democrats suggested that notice of withdrawal from the League might come through a joint congressional resolution rather than a concurrent one, "Lodge and his friends did not seem to think there would be much difficulty with that." Likewise, on several of the other reservations no one objected to some minor alterations. The participants did not get to the last reservation, which covered British Empire voting.[40]

The sticking point, as expected, came on the reservation to Article X. Simmons offered a substitute stating that there would be "no obligation to employ the military and naval forces" except as provided by a joint congressional resolution. "Lodge and New both indicated," Hitchcock noted, "that they thought it would be very difficult to procure support for this substitute." McKellar then proposed a revision of the Lodge reservation that twice added "<u>by its military or naval forces</u>" to the eschewal of the obligation and substituted "<u>until</u>" Congress acted for "unless in any particular case." Hitchcock told Tumulty that both of these proposals went further than he felt willing to go, "but Lodge indicated that they could not be assented to by his side." Those differences apparently did not stir up an argument, and the senators agreed to meet again on January 17.[41]

Their second meeting lasted more than twice as long, and it produced some meeting of minds across party lines. Once more, the participants divulged little to reporters. Lodge commented that the conferees had discussed "minor matters." Hitchcock agreed that they had started out with "less difficult matters." In fact, as Hitchcock reported to Tumulty, "No

40. Hitchcock to Tumulty, Jan. 16, 1920, in Link, ed., *Papers of Wilson*, LXIV, 283–284. Lodge later gave a similar account of these and later discussions. "I never liked the language of the preamble, which was suggested by Root. I wanted to draw it differently and I have done so, and in our conversation the Democrats said they would accept it. . . . The other changes on which we tentatively agreed were mere changes of phraseology with no effect whatever upon the reservations." Lodge to James T. Williams, Jr., Feb. 2, 1920, Lodge Papers.

41. Hitchcock to Tumulty, Jan. 16, 1920, in Link, ed., *Papers of Wilson*, LXIV, 283–284.

final agreement was reached on anything though agreements were reached on a number of things." He enclosed a printed copy of the Lodge reservations annotated in his own handwriting. This document showed that the senators discussed the first nine reservations. On six of those numbered reservations, they agreed to changes on such matters as withdrawal, exclusion of domestic questions, mandates, and representation on League bodies. Most of these changes involved matters of no great weight. On the Shantung reservation, however, the deletion of the reference to China and Japan by name represented a face-saving gesture. Hitchcock's proposal to soften the reservation regarding the reparations commission got marked "not favorably considered," and the Monroe Doctrine reservation had "no change" written beside it. Also, curiously, the preamble bore the annotation, "Passed over for the present." Most important of all, the Article X reservation had "Passed over for the day" written in the margin. Nevertheless, the bipartisan conferees had made good progress, and they agreed to meet again on January 19.[42]

At that third meeting and at two subsequent meetings over the next two days, the discussions seemed to bog down. The only one of these meetings that received any mention in the press was the one on January 19. Hitchcock told reporters afterward that the conferees were stuck "on a sandbar" over the British Empire voting reservation. Lodge sounded more positive. "If this group of Senators cannot agree," he told reporters, "no group can." Hitchcock must have read the mood of the meetings more accurately because he sent no further reports to the White House until the sixth meeting, on January 22. Meanwhile, Karger reported to Taft, "The efforts at compromise lack responsibility . . . and although there is plenty of compromise talk in the air, it remains in the air." This apparent stall in the discussions provoked some of the mild reservationists to threaten to revolt and join the Democrats in calling up the treaty for consideration on the Senate floor. "We are going to give these 'impossibles' who are meeting in Senator Lodge's office a day longer," an unidentified mild reservationist, most likely McNary, told reporters. "They won't be able to agree in a thousand years." That threat may have thrown a scare into Lodge. Also, the friendly influences of Henry White and possibly Root, both of whom

42. *New York Times,* Jan. 18, 1920; Hitchcock to Tumulty, Jan. 17, 1920, in Link, ed., *Papers of Wilson,* LXIV, 288; photostatic copy of annotated reservations, ibid., 289–295. On the change in the Shantung reservation, see also remarks by Lodge and Kellogg, *Congressional Record,* 66th Cong., 2nd Sess. (Mar. 4, 1920), 3839, 3841.

were in Washington at this time, may have induced him to unbend. At any rate, the conference abruptly took a more hopeful turn when the senators met on January 22.[43]

The apparent breakthrough came on the least promising ground of all, the Article X reservation. The Republican conferees told reporters that a "sudden change in the situation" had occurred during the discussion of that reservation. They "indicated that tomorrow would probably bring an agreement on Article X." Lodge declined to supply details, but he allowed himself to be quoted as believing that "the thing is going to work out." New was more expansive, declaring, "At no time in the discussions has the possibility of agreement appeared so bright as it is tonight." Privately, Hitchcock confirmed how well founded these hopes were. He reported to the White House, this time directly to the president, "On Article X the effort to reach a compromise has now reached a state where both sides are seriously considering a proposition as indicated by the enclosed clipping." The enclosure was a printed copy of the Lodge reservation to Article X with deletions and insertions in Hitchcock's handwriting. That intelligence from Hitchcock may prompted what was almost certainly a leak to the press by Tumulty. As the *New York Times* stated, "While the conferees were meeting today a report reached the Capitol that president Wilson had conveyed indirectly to leading Democrats that if they are able to reach a reasonable settlement with the Lodge group, he will not stand in the way of its ratification by the Senate. Confirmation of this report was lacking however."[44]

Just how close the two sides were to an agreement on this crucial

43. *New York Times,* Jan. 20, 21, 1920; Karger to Taft, Jan. 19, 1920, Taft Papers, reel 217. On the likelihood that McNary was the mild reservationist quoted, see *New York Times,* Jan. 23, 1920. White was openly trying to promote compromise and frequently meeting with Lodge. See Allen Nevins, *Henry White: Thirty Years of American Diplomacy* (New York, 1930), 480–482. Whether Root was also working in that direction is debatable. His biographers disagree over whether he involved himself in these talks. See Philip C. Jessup, *Elihu Root* (New York, 1937), II, 408, and Richard L. Leopold, *Elihu Root and the Conservative Tradition* (Boston, 1954), 142. He did meet with Kellogg and Watson and went over the text of several reservations with them. See Kellogg to Root, Mar. 12, 1920, Root Papers, Box 139. For a private expression of Lodge's more sanguine view of the conference at this stage, see Lodge to J.D.H. Luce, Jan. 21, 1920, Lodge Papers.

44. *New York Times,* Jan. 23, 1920; Hitchcock to Wilson, Jan. 22, 1920, in Link, ed., *Papers of Wilson,* LXIV, 312; enclosure, ibid., 313.

matter would soon become the subject of heated disagreement. Lodge subsequently maintained that he had never wavered in his stand on Article X. "The point was a simple one," he explained six months later to his Massachusetts colleague, Speaker of the House Frederick Gillett. "They [the Democrats] insisted on some form of reservation which would leave an obligation in existence. We were determined that there should be no obligation of any kind left under Article 10. They went pretty far in offering exceptions to the obligation but they kept the obligation alive." That was a fair description of the version of the reservation that the conference discussed on January 22. Hitchcock's most important change, at the end of Lodge reservation, read, *"Nothing herein shall be deemed to impair the obligation of Art 16 concerning the economic boycott[.]"* Furthermore, within a week to the press and later again on the Senate floor, Kellogg and Lenroot claimed that neither they nor Lodge and New had agreed to another of Hitchcock's additions, which inserted *"to employ its military or naval forces or the economic boycott"* between the words "obligation" and "preserve the territorial integrity or political independence of any other country." That much in the way of the participants' recollections supports the claim that no deal on the Article X reservation was in the offing on January 22.[45]

But if the two sides stood so far apart, why did Lodge and New publicly and Hitchcock privately voice such high hopes? Later, on the Senate floor, three of the five Democrats from the bipartisan conference maintained that the Republicans had tentatively agreed to the changes in the reservation. In his own statements on the Senate floor, Lodge did not say one way or the other whether he had agreed to this compromise. Interestingly, the *New York Times* reported that after the meeting on January 22 Lodge and New showed McNary a copy of what they had done. Seventeen years later McNary told the historian Thomas A. Bailey that he still retained a copy of that revised Article X reservation with annotations in Lodge's handwriting. McNary's papers contain a printed copy of the Lodge reservations with typewritten additions and with other

---

45. Lodge to Gillett, July 26, 1920; enclosure, [Jan. 22, 1920], in Link, ed., *Papers of Wilson*, LXIV, 313. For Kellogg's and Lenroot's claims, see *New York Times*, Jan. 28, 1920; and *Congressional Record*, 66th Cong., 2nd Sess. (Feb. 20, 1920), 3179, (Mar. 15, 1920), 4323. Two historians' interpretations that agree with these claims are Lloyd E. Ambrosius, *Woodrow Wilson and the American Diplomatic Tradition: The Treaty Fight in Perspective* (New York, 1987), 232, and Margulies, *Mild Reservationists*, 206.

changes and marginal notes in handwriting that resembles Lodge's. The revisions to the Article X reservation are virtually identical to the ones on the copy that Hitchcock forwarded to the White House. Lodge and the other Republicans at the bipartisan conference do seem to have committed themselves to a compromise on the Article X reservation.[46]

This deal involving the Article X reservation immediately came unstuck. The mere hint of softening on that reservation was enough to send other Republicans to the barricades to defend the original version. Two strong reservationists spoke out just before and after the bipartisan conference meeting on January 22. Joseph Frelinghuysen of New Jersey told reporters that he and a number of other Republicans demanded that there be "no compromise upon Article 10." Howard Sutherland of West Virginia made a similar statement to the press and to Lodge personally. Moreover, according to Kellogg, Frederick Hale of Maine, who was usually counted among the mild reservationists, also berated Lodge for contemplating any change in the Article X reservation.[47]

The Irreconcilables reacted even more hotly. Mrs. La Follette informed her husband, who was ailing and away from Washington, that Borah had telephoned their house on January 22 to say that "the treaty situation was very serious and [he] wanted you informed of the fact immediately." The next day, Borah told anti-League newspaper publisher Frank Munsey that the Republican leaders were "engaged in the cowardly and pusillanimous enterprise of . . . compromise upon those things which were declared to be the least we could accept and protect American interests." Likewise, Johnson, who had spent most of the last two months out campaigning for the Republican presidential nomination, came back to Washington on January 22 to discover, as he told his

46. *New York Times*, Jan. 23, 1920. For the Democratic senators' claims, see *Congressional Record*, 66th Cong., 2nd Sess. (Feb. 20, 1920), 3179, (Feb. 21, 1920), 3232, (Mar. 15, 1920), 4323, (Mar. 18, 1920), 4534, (Mar. 19, 1920), 4583. For Lodge's statement, see ibid. (Feb. 21, 1920), 3238. For McNary's recollection, see Thomas A. Bailey, *Woodrow Wilson and the Great Betrayal* (New York, 1945), 231. The copy of the reservation is in McNary Papers, Box 65. It is filed together with another revised printed copy of the Lodge reservations with the notation in McNary's handwriting, "Senator Simmons proposal March 18–20." There is also a piece of Senate stationery with the handwritten comment, "Note to Executor: Senator considered these very important." Ibid.

47. Frelinghuysen, quoted in Margulies, *Mild Reservationists*, 207. See also *New York Times*, Jan. 24, 1920; and Taft to Karger, Feb. 2, 1920, Taft Papers, reel 217.

sons, "that Lodge had broken under the pressure, and that he was engaged in compromising on his reservations."[48]

Borah and Johnson both later claimed credit for what happened next. On January 23, one or the other of them called a meeting of the Republican Irreconcilables. In addition to themselves, Knox, Brandegee, Sherman, McCormick, France, Moses, and Poindexter attended. These nine senators then sent word to Lodge, who was in his office with the bipartisan conference. They demanded that he come immediately and meet with them. Lodge, accompanied by New, complied. There followed possibly the most dramatic confrontation of the whole League fight. As Borah repeatedly told the tale during the next two decades, a scared-looking Lodge protested, "Can't I discuss this matter with my friends?" Borah answered, "No, Cabot, not without telling your other friends." After leaning silently against a wall, Lodge finally rejoined, "Well, I suppose I'll have to resign as majority leader." Borah shot back, "No, by God! You won't have a chance to resign. On Monday, I'll move for the election of a new majority leader and give the reason for my action." Most historians, including Thomas Bailey, to whom Borah recounted the story in 1937, believe that he embellished, especially about Lodge's offer to resign and his own threat to try to depose Lodge.[49]

Even without those particular fireworks, the encounter featured plenty of sound and fury. "We had three corking hours," Johnson wrote to his sons. "There was bitterness and indignation on our side and apologies on his." Inklings of those emotions did leak out into the press. The *New York Times* reported that the discussion grew heated and that Sherman made a "vigorous speech" in which he charged that "Wall Street financial interests had obtained control of certain Republican Party leaders, preventing them from taking a stand against the League of Nations." To the *Chicago Tribune* Sherman avowed that "if

48. Belle C. La Follette to La Follette, Jan. 22, 1920, Robert M. La Follette Papers, Library of Congress, Box A 28; Borah to Frank Munsey, Jan. 23, 1920, Borah Papers, Box 770; Johnson to Hiram Jr. and Arch Johnson, Jan. 23, 1920, in Robert E. Burke, ed., *The Diary Letters of Hiram Johnson* (New York, 1983), III.

49. Bailey, *Wilson and Great Betrayal*, 230–231. A similar version of the story is in Claudius O. Johnson, *Borah of Idaho* (New York, 1936), 246–247. For other expressions of doubts about Borah's story, see Ralph A. Stone, *The Irreconcilables: The Fight against the League of Nations* (Lexington, Ky., 1970), 157 n. 37, and John A. Garraty, *Henry Cabot Lodge* (New York, 1953), 386.

there is the slightest yielding I am through with the party. . . . In plain language, I'll bolt."[50]

Borah made the same threat privately and even more ominously. The next day, he sent Lodge a fourteen-page letter in which he quoted extensively from Lodge's own statements about the necessity to nullify all obligation under Article X. Therefore, Borah charged, "Either this conference is trifling with a great and grave subject and doing a foolish and useless thing for insincere purpose or it is proposing to surrender the vital interests of the American people." If Lodge did mean to change the reservations, Borah warned "that I can no longer respect or cooperate with the party organization. I must refuse even by implication to seem to go along with an organization which according to its own announcement is now engaged in compromising American honor and security. I propose to appeal from the organization to the voters." Perhaps Borah's memory did not embellish so much after all.[51]

The Irreconcilables' ploy worked. To the press, Lodge downplayed his reaction to their attacks. The *Washington Post* reported that he "seemed to enjoy the ordeal." But judging by Lodge's subsequent behavior toward the bipartisan conference, Johnson and Borah seem to have been closer to the mark when they described him as fearful and contrite. What must have struck fear into him was seeing the prospect of his handiwork of holding the Senate Republicans together crumble before his eyes. When some of these senators talked about bolting, they were not uttering idle threats. Three of them, Johnson, McCormick, and Poindexter, had earlier followed Roosevelt over to the Progressives. Borah had never formally renounced the Republican label, but he, together with three other Irreconcilables who were not at this meeting – La Follette, Norris, and Gronna – had long histories of insurgency and disdain for party loyalty.[52]

50. Johnson to Hiram Jr. and Arch Johnson, Jan. 24, 1920; *New York Times,* Jan. 24, 1920; *Chicago Tribune,* Jan. 24, 1920.
51. Borah to Lodge, Jan. 24, 1920, Lodge Papers.
52. *Washington Post,* Jan. 24, 1920. The only other contemporary accounts by participants at the meeting came from New and Moses, both of whom wrote to Beveridge. New minimized the seriousness of the exchanges, whereas Moses stressed the Irreconcilables' efficacy in getting Lodge to see the light. New to Beveridge, Jan. 24, 1920, Beveridge Papers, Box 223; Moses to Beveridge, Jan. 27, 1920, ibid., Box 222. The only oddity about the threats to bolt was that the only publicly uttered one came from Sherman. He was a strong Republican partisan who had earlier scorned Progressives and insurgents for seeking to injure the party.

What evidently filled Lodge with contrition was having his own previous stand against Article X thrown in his face the way Borah did in
that letter. None of the public or private accounts at the time indicated
which senators said what at the meeting, except for Sherman's accusation of nefarious Wall Street influence. It was unlikely, however, that
Borah or others would have neglected to rub Lodge's nose in his apparent apostasy on Article X. Whether Knox talked much is not known,
but his mere presence was a reproof to Lodge. Both Knox's foreign policy credentials and the fundamental similarity in the two men's thinking
made him serve as Lodge's conscience against infidelity to hallowed
Republican principles of great power nationalism.[53]

The bipartisan conference felt the impact of Lodge's about-face at
once. He immediately dropped a strong hint about where his priorities
lay when, after about fifteen minutes with the Irreconcilables, Lodge
informed the senators at the bipartisan conference that he would be
unable to rejoin them but would meet with them the next day. According to Hitchcock's recollection, when the conferees did assemble then,
Lodge failed to show up and sent word that he had to confer with other
senators. Lodge also told reporters, "There never will be any compromise of principle, of that you may be assured." When the bipartisan
conference met again on January 26, according to news reports, Lodge
issued an ultimatum at the outset. "He [Lodge] regretted to say," Hitchcock related to reporters, "that he found it impossible to resume the
conferences for a compromise except upon the understanding that no
change shall be made in the reservation to Article X, or that on the
Monroe Doctrine." Further attempts to shroud the conference in
secrecy went by the boards. Lodge talked equally freely to reporters. He
deprecated the use of the term "ultimatum," but he did concede that he
had told the conference "what I have already said in public, that there

---

53. Knox's role as a kind of conscience to Lodge is not entirely speculative.
Eleven months later, the Republican lawyer Chandler Anderson recorded in
his diary:

> He [Knox] told me incidentally that Senator Lodge's enormous
> prestige and pride in the defeat of the league was amusing in view
> of the difficulty they had in keeping him in line during the Senate
> debate, and that actually on one occasion he was on the point of
> surrendering to the mild reservationists when several of the bitter
> enders, including Brandegee and himself, had pulled him out of a
> conference with them and got him across the hall into Knox's
> room and read the riot act to him, and thus saved the situation.

Entry, Dec. 16, 1920, Anderson Diary.

can be no compromise of principle, and that it would be impossible to secure, in my judgment, two-thirds of the Senate if any change were attempted in articles [i.e., reservations] II and V, those relating to Article X and the Monroe Doctrine. I said this was a mere statement of the situation." After getting this news from Lodge, the Democrats huddled among themselves to plan for the conference's next meeting.[54]

The bipartisan conference met only twice more, on January 27 and 30. At the first meeting, according to news reports, both sides spent most of the two-hour meeting wrangling over how close they had been to agreement before the Irreconcilables' intervention. After more wrangling about how to proceed, the conferees agreed to meet once more. At that last meeting, on January 30, Hitchcock recounted to reporters that he had begun by reading the text of the reservation to Article X that Taft had proposed. Then he asked Lodge whether he could accept this reservation. "Senator Lodge said definitely he could not accept it," Hitchcock stated. On the Lodge reservations, Hitchcock added, "He said that he could not consent to the slightest modification." In his own statement to the press, Lodge agreed that the Article X reservation "can not permit of change." The same held true for the Monroe Doctrine reservation: "The right to interpret the Monroe Doctrine, pertaining to the United States alone, must never be open to question." In the face of the Republicans' stand, Hitchcock further recounted, "There was no dramatic climax. By common consent, when this point was reached, we adjourned." When a reporter asked Hitchcock whether the conference was through for the day, he replied, "We are through – for good."[55]

The collapse of the bipartisan conference measurably worsened the chances for a constructive outcome to the League fight. This conference embodied the only meaningful effort at compromise during the entire controversy. The attachment of the adjective "bipartisan" – a word not then commonly in use – was telling. This was the one truly bipartisan moment on Capitol Hill during the League fight. It had witnessed the only genuine effort at reconciling differences and working together across party lines. After its failure, Senate consent to the peace treaty could come, as earlier in November, just one way – through surrender. The Democrats and mild reservationists would have to submit to the unaltered Lodge reservations as the price

54. *New York Times*, Jan. 25, 27, 1920. For Hitchcock's later recollection, see *Congressional Record*, 66th Cong., 2nd Sess. (Mar. 5, 1920), 3890. Cf. statement by Walsh, ibid. (Feb. 21, 1920), 3232.

55. *New York Times*, Jan. 28, 31, 1920. The full texts of Hitchcock's and Lodge's statements to the press are also in *Congressional Record*, 66th Cong., 2nd Sess. (Jan. 30, 1920), 2285–2287.

for approval of the treaty and League membership. Some of the mild reservationists, particularly McNary and Kellogg, again made noises about taking matters to the Senate floor and joining the Democrats in trying to pass less-stringent reservations. But others, most notably Colt, privately admitted that they would stick with Lodge if push came to shove. Given the mild reservationists' party loyalty and small numbers, their threats now looked less dangerous to Lodge than the ire of the Irreconcilables and strong reservationists. The best that a coalition between forty Democrats and, at most, ten or twelve mild reservationists could hope to effect was a stalemate that differed only slightly from the one that already existed. At the end of January 1920, the situation in the Senate looked even bleaker than before.[56]

III

The collapse of the bipartisan conference came at a doubly inopportune time because of what was and was not happening elsewhere in Washington. This conference and other efforts at compromise in January 1920 did not lack for advice from the sidelines. Bryan came back to the capital at the middle of the month. He met with several Democratic senators and made more public statements. Taft, despite his disagreements with other LEP leaders about lobbying, spent several days in Washington. He met with such mild reservationists as Kellogg, Colt, and McNary. Taft also planned to see McCumber. The North Dakotan, however, had been away since the November votes tending his sick daughter and would not return to the capital until later. McCumber never would take much part in this round of the League fight. Henry White, who had come back from Paris and taken up residence again in Washington, was seeing Lodge and other Republicans. He also sought to promote a compromise on reservations. Root was likewise in Washington once during the latter half of January, but it is not known whether he talked to Lodge or any other senators about the peace treaty.[57]

By far the most important extrasenatorial move to promote compromise came from the White House, although not from Wilson. Just before

56. On the mild reservationists' threats, see *New York Times,* Jan. 28, 1920; Taft to Mabel T. Boardman, Jan. 28, 1920, Taft Papers, reel 217; Karger to Taft, Jan. 31, 1920, ibid. For Colt's position, see Karger to Taft, Feb. 6, 1920, ibid.

57. On Bryan's visit to Washington, see *New York Times,* Jan. 16, 1920; New York *World,* Jan. 16, 1920. On Taft's visit, see Taft to Karger, Jan. 21, 1920, Taft Papers, reel 217; Taft to Helen H. Taft, Jan. 24, 1920, ibid., reel 27. On McCumber's absence from Washington, see R. M. Farrar to Herbert Parsons, Jan. 27, 1920, Herbert Parsons Papers, Columbia University Library, Series III. On White and Root, see note 37 of this chapter.

the bipartisan conference began, Tumulty initiated a behind-the-scenes campaign to get the president to unbend and insert himself into the negotiations. On January 14, Tumulty drafted a letter for Wilson to send to Hitchcock, and he showed this draft to secretaries Baker, Houston, and Lansing and to Mrs. Wilson. The next day, most likely after he had received Hitchcock's report on the conference's first meeting, Tumulty explained to Mrs. Wilson that the two sides would soon reach "their irreducible minimum. It is at this psychological moment that action must be taken – if it is taken at all – in making clear that the President is not insisting upon an unqualified adoption of the Treaty without the crossing of a 't' or the dotting of an 'i.'" Tumulty thought it "wise to interject at the proper moment, if negotiations have seemed to reach a compromise – our own interpretation of the Treaty. . . . It has in it, the great opportunity of obtaining speedily a ratification of the Treaty."[58]

Secretaries Baker, Houston, and Lansing all endorsed the draft of the letter. The editors of the *Papers of Wilson* believe that Mrs. Wilson also encouraged Tumulty to forward it to the president, which he did on January 15. This letter would have had Wilson declare, "I am glad to summarize what seem to me reasonable interpretations on the points which have been the subject of controversy in the Senate for many months." Next came a numbered list of twelve points, which covered most of the Lodge reservations. On all but three of those points, the letter did not take issue with the intent of a reservation and often used the phrase, "I see no objection." On two of the other points, withdrawal and appointments to the reparations commission, the letter disagreed gently with the reservations. On the remaining, vital point, Article X, the letter stated that the problem was assuring that "the moral influence of the Executive branch of the Government . . . for the preservation of peace shall not be diminished," while also making clear "at all times that whenever the employment of military or naval forces is recommended by the League of Nations the power of the Congress . . . to accept or reject such a recommendation is inviolate." In the closing paragraph, the letter reiterated the hope "that the interpretations which I have set forth will be of use in bringing about an early ratification of the Peace Treaty."[59]

As a piece of rhetoric and a negotiating gambit, Tumulty's draft fell

58. Tumulty to Edith Wilson, Jan. 15, 1920, in Link, ed., *Papers of Wilson,* LXIV, 276–277. See also entries, Lansing Desk Diary, Jan. 14, 15, 1920, ibid., 276, 282; Edith Wilson notes, [ca. Jan. 14, 1920), quoted in ibid., 277 n. 1.

59. Tumulty draft, [Jan. 15, 1920], ibid., 278–282. For Baker's, Houston's, and Lansing's approval and the editors' speculation that Mrs. Wilson also approved the draft, see ibid., 277 n. 1, 278 n. 1.

short of perfection. The attachment of a peroration at the end – "America covets the opportunity to serve humanity and to save the world. She must not be denied the opportunity" – did not make this document sing with Wilson's wonted eloquence. The point about Article X neither answered the critical question about whether an obligation remained nor left a mutually satisfactory ambiguity about the answer. Still, despite those flaws, this letter might have made a profound impact if Wilson had approved and released it in a timely fashion. The cumulative effect of listing numbered points corresponding to the reservation followed by agreeable responses created an impression of reasonableness and accommodation. The point about Article X took the same line as the compromise reservation that would elicit the fleeting agreement in the bipartisan conference on January 22. Tumulty did not exaggerate when he told Mrs. Wilson on January 17, "The psychological moment is approaching when the President could strike with great force along the lines suggested." What would soon happen in that conference, he argued, "will give the President, in my opinion, his great opportunity."[60]

The president did not seize that opportunity. The reason he did not sprang once more from the state of his health following the stroke. It is debatable whether the physical or psychological effects of the stroke hurt Wilson more. On the physical side, he suffered not only from his chronic lack of energy and shortened attention span but also from recurring bouts of influenza. The first illness occurred, unluckily, right at this time. On January 20 or 21, as Grayson reported to Wilson's brother-in-law, Stockton Axson, Wilson came down with "a sharp attack of the 'flu,'" which included severe headaches, vomiting, and a high fever. Talking with Ray Stannard Baker, who visited the White House on January 22, Grayson revealed how physical weakness evidently prevented Wilson from making the move that Tumulty proposed. "Grayson says that he is perfectly calm about everything," Baker recorded in his dairy, "*except* the treaty. That stirs him: makes him restless. He tried some days ago to write out his views in regard to the various reservations proposed but soon gave it up."[61]

Actually, Grayson's remarks spoke more to Wilson's psychological condition. Mrs. Wilson also talked with Baker on January 22. She painted an even starker picture of his mental and emotional state. Baker tried, as he put it in his diary, "as diplomatically as I could," to inform Mrs. Wilson that people were blaming her husband as much as Lodge

---

60. Tumulty draft, [Jan. 15, 1920], ibid., 282; Tumulty to Edith Wilson, Jan. 17, 1920, ibid., 287.
61. Grayson to Axson, Jan. 24, 1920, ibid., 325; entry, Jan. 23, 1920, Baker Diary, ibid., 320.

for the treaty stalemate. Mrs. Wilson responded, "They think him stubborn . . . but the President still has in mind the reception he got in the west, he believes the people are with him." Baker, who was an experienced journalist and a novelist, pounced on that remark. "That was the trouble," he recorded in his diary. "He has been ill since last October & cannot know what is going on." Baker did not grasp the full meaning of his insight. Such a condition of time standing still for Wilson and of his dwelling among the cheering crowds on the western tour stemmed directly from the stroke and from the effects of his continued comparative isolation from outside contacts. Someone who has suffered a stroke like Wilson's often continues to live emotionally and mentally in those last days before the stroke. Those were the last moments when he was still fully himself.[62]

Baker picked up again on both Wilson's psychological condition and its impact on the League fight when he further recorded in his diary:

> It is plain that Grayson cannot move him, and also clear from what Mrs. Wilson says that she can do nothing either. I found her in full accord with my suggestion that the President make some great gesture that would thrust aside the trivialities & demand the united response of the country upon the Senate in getting a League & getting it quickly. He would have everyone with him in such a move. Yet he hardens at any such suggestion: the very moment of yielding anything to the Senate seems to drive him into stubborn immovability.

Baker himself got a taste of Wilson's immovability later that day. The situation troubled him so deeply that he "offered to help in any way I could and made a number of definite suggestions to Mrs. Wilson. Later while I was at dinner with the Graysons she called up & said that it seemed impossible now to do anything."[63]

Wilson underscored how compromise had become psychologically impossible for him when he tried to deal with Tumulty's letter. Before the first bout with influenza he was able to make a deletion, a few annotations, and one unimportant addition of a few words to the draft. The annotations consisted of vertical lines alongside several of the more accommodating statements. The deletion removed the first point, "It is evident that when ratifications have been deposited, the interpretations set forth by the United States therein will become a part of the Treaty of

62. Ibid., 320–321. On the psychological effects of the stroke, Dr. Bert E. Park uses the terms "focal psychosyndrome" and "caricature of himself." See Park, "The Aftermath of Wilson's Stroke," ibid., 525–528. Other neurologists are less categorical in viewing these as inescapable conditions to the aftermath of such a stroke, as divorced from the effects of isolation.

63. Entry, Jan. 23, 1920, Baker Diary, ibid., 321.

Peace, so far as the interests of the United States are concerned." This was Tumulty's face-saving way to concede the sore point about whether reservations would be part of the instrument of ratification. Plainly, Wilson would have none of such a concession or of Tumulty's draft, which he shelved.[64]

After that first onset of the flu, the president finally did toy with making a belated entry into the compromise negotiations. On January 26, he responded to Hitchcock's communication that described the breakthrough at the bipartisan conference and forwarded the revised reservation to Article X. The best that Wilson could do in the way of conciliation was to say about the reservation, "To the substance of it I, of course, adhere." But, he quickly added,

> I think the form of it very unfortunate. Any reservation or resolu-
> tion stating that "the United States assumes no obligation under
> such and such an Article unless or except" would, I am sure, chill
> our relationship with the nations with which we expect to be asso-
> ciated in the great enterprise of maintaining the world's peace. . . .
> It is the more important not to create the impression that we are
> trying to escape obligations.

Wilson did concede that "negative criticism is not all that is called for in so serious a matter." He took up the rest of the letter with a disquisition on the need for including a presidential veto in any reservation about withdrawal from the League and a brief comment accepting the reserva-tion on mandates. Unbending as this letter was, Wilson could not bring himself to release it. When the letter went to Hitchcock, an accompany-ing note from Mrs. Wilson stated, "The President's judgment is that it would not set matters forward to publish this communication of his at this time, but he confidantly [sic] leaves to your own judgment the use to be made of it."[65]

Two weeks later, Hitchcock would finally read this letter to the Sen-ate Democrats and release it to the press. It would ironically bear out Wilson's judgment and worsen relations between the White House and the Capitol. This letter would have worsened the situation still further if the senators could have seen other signs of how bitter and removed from political reality the president was. On January 28, two days after

---

64. Tumulty draft, [Jan. 15, 1920], ibid., 278–279.

65. Wilson to Hitchcock, Jan. 26, 1920, ibid. 329–330; Edith Wilson note, quoted in ibid., 330 n. 1. The editors of the *Papers of Wilson* believe that Tumulty wrote this letter to Hitchcock. See ibid., 328 n. 1. I disagree. Its tone and approach are so different from Tumulty's earlier draft that it seems likely that Wilson himself either dictated or substantially revised this letter.

Wilson forwarded the letter to Hitchcock, Mrs. Wilson wrote to Postmaster General Burleson:

> At the President's request, I am sending you the enclosed list of Senators who hindered or did not assist the ratification of the Treaty. He asks that you be kind enough to go over it for him with Senators Hitchcock and Underwood, and that after you have done so you let him know your joint judgment in answer to these two questions: (1) Is it fair? (2) Is it complete[?]

The list contained the names and states of fifty-four senators, Democrats and Republicans, with unexplained check marks beside five of them, lines drawn through two, and a question mark beside one. The request and the list showed that notions of referendum and revenge still burned in Wilson's brain.[66]

Thankfully, the matter went no further. Burleson's prompt, deadpan reply, after consulting with Hitchcock, may have dampened Wilson's ardor. It seems more likely that his second illness distracted him. Sometime at the end of January or beginning of February, Wilson suffered another, equally bad attack of influenza. On February 3, Grayson assured the press that the president only had a cold and "had a narrow escape from influenza." Privately, the doctor admitted, as Ray Stannard Baker recorded in his diary, "The President has had a severe set back – a case of hard cold or influenza." This second illness appears to have triggered an effort by Grayson to induce the president to resign from office. Wilson suffered from the mood swings and depression that also afflict persons who suffer strokes like his. Even before the earlier illness, he had said to Grayson, as Baker noted in his diary, "It would have been better if I had died last fall." Now, it seems, either the severity of this second illness or its coming so soon after the earlier illness helped to push Wilson to the brink of resignation. Several times during the next few months Grayson would whisper to close friends about his effort to get Wilson to resign. At some point he dictated a note to himself that read, "Look up notes re President Wilson's intention to go before the Senate in a wheeled chair for the purpose of resigning."[67]

In those later, whispered confidences, Grayson blamed Mrs. Wilson

---

66. Edith Wilson to Burleson, with enclosed list, Jan. 28, 1920, ibid., 336–337.
67. *New York Times*, Feb. 4, 1920; entries, Jan. 23, Feb. 3, Baker Diary, in Link, ed., *Papers of Wilson*, LXIV, 321, 359; Grayson note, quoted in ibid., 363 n. 1. For Burleson's reply, see Burleson to Edith Wilson, Jan. 28, 1920, ibid., 338–339. For Grayson's divulgences about the resignation plan, see entry, June 10, 1920, House Diary, ibid., LXV, 384; entry, Sept. 2, 1920, John W. Davis Diary, quoted in ibid., LXIV, 363 n. 1; entry, Nov. 28, 1920, Baker Diary, ibid., LXVI, 436.

for blocking the resignation plan. The editors of the *Papers of Wilson* have speculated, however, that Wilson's own renewed "euphoria" at his recovery from this illness played the biggest part in banishing all thought of quitting and in reinforcing his stance of truculent rigidity. Some months afterward, when Grayson told Baker about this effort to get Wilson to resign, Baker remarked in his diary, "It would have far been better if he had!" Baker again grasped the main point. This attempt to get Wilson to step aside marked the most promising approach to compromise from the White House side. Given Wilson's psychological state, Tumulty and Mrs. Wilson were engaging in an exercise in futility with that detailed, conciliatory draft letter to Hitchcock. Of all the behind-the-scenes efforts in the White House, only Grayson's resignation scheme could really have facilitated a compromise. Sadly, none of these three people closest to Wilson ever tried again to get him to think or act differently. Each one lapsed back into her or his accustomed role of uncritical support. Now nothing stood in the way of Wilson's careening down his path of defiance and obstruction.[68]

Starting at the end of the first week in February, events came in a rush. Even more than before, Wilson was indulging in the euphoric behavior brought on by his partial recovery from the stroke. The end of his second bout with the flu abetted this euphoria. At the same time, a well-intended move backfired and moved Wilson to take action. The deadlock between the president and the Republican senators had sown consternation abroad as well as at home. In London and Paris, government leaders and prominent spokesmen had grown increasingly alarmed at the prospect of American failure to ratify the peace treaty and join the League. Lloyd George and Clemenceau might agree with many of the criticisms of the League, but above all else they wanted an American commitment to maintain the peace settlement. They recognized that as long as Wilson was president, the League was the price they would have to pay for such a commitment. Officially, therefore, the British and French governments had continued to avoid any public comment or behind-the-scenes overtures, out of fear of offending the president.[69]

Official reticence did not prevent a well-meaning outsider from seeking to fill the breach. The person who acted was Lord Grey, the former British foreign secretary, who had just returned from his four-month visit to the United States. Acting on his own initiative and without consulting

68. Ibid.
69. On British and French attitudes and reactions toward the deadlock, see George W. Egerton, *Great Britain and the Creation of the League of Nations* (Chapel Hill, N.C., 1978), 177–198.

his government, Grey wrote a letter that was published in *The Times* of London on January 31, 1920, and was reprinted in American newspapers the following day. Grey admonished his countrymen and the other Allies to be patient and understanding toward the U.S. Senate's objections and to remember that the overriding concern was American participation in the League. "Without the United States," he argued, "it will have neither the overwhelming physical nor moral force behind it that it should have, or if it has the physical force it will not have the same degree of moral force, for it will be predominantly European, and not a world organization, and it will be tainted with all the interracial jealousies of Europe." Therefore, Grey concluded, "If the outcome of the long controversy in the Senate has been to offer co-operation in the League of Nations, it would be the greatest mistake to refuse that co-operation because conditions are attached to it, and when that co-operation is accepted, let it not be accepted in a spirit of pessimism."[70]

A number of League advocates and pro-League newspapers, most notably the *New York Times* and *Springfield Republican,* welcomed Grey's letter and urged Wilson to accept the Lodge reservations. Others, such as the New York *World,* reacted more guardedly. The president's reaction was anything but guarded. Outrage proved to be a powerful stimulant to his newfound mood of potency. On February 5, Wilson dictated a statement to the press from "the Executive Office upon Viscount Grey's extraordinary attempt to influence the action of the President and the Senate." In this statement he declared that if Grey were in Washington as ambassador "his government would have been promptly asked to withdraw him." Stinging as this rebuke was, it understated Wilson's anger and recalcitrance. That same day Baker recorded in his diary that Grayson told him that "the Grey letter had made a great difference & that the President might now defer sending his letter to Senator Hitchcock. It is all in a state of utter confusion heightened by the President's illness & his stubborn temperament. He does not want to hear what is going on apparently."[71]

One thing that Wilson may have heard was that Lansing was pleased with the Grey letter. "He thought it very able & clever," Baker also

70. *New York Times,* Feb. 1, 1920.
71. Wilson statement [Feb. 5, 1920], in Link, ed., *Papers of Wilson,* LXIV, 363–364; entry, Feb. 5, [1920], Baker Diary, ibid., 365. For the editorial reactions, see *New York Times,* Feb. 2, 1920; *New York World,* Feb. 2, 1920; *Springfield Republican,* Feb. 3, 1920. On Wilson's reactions, see also Tumulty to Edith Wilson, [Feb. 3, 1920], in Link, ed., *Papers of Wilson,* LXIV, 355; and entry, Feb. 3, 1920, Raymond Clapper Diary, in Raymond Clapper Papers, Library of Congress, Box 6.

recorded on February 5 after a conversation with the secretary of state, "& hardly concealed his satisfaction in the thought that it might hasten action in the Senate, however it might offend the President." Whether word of Lansing's reaction got back to the White House is not known, but it seems more than a coincidence that Wilson chose this moment to lash out at Lansing. On February 7, the president sent him a harshly worded letter asking, "Is it true, as I have been told, that during my illness you have frequently called the heads of the executive departments of the Government into conference? If it is, I feel it my duty to call your attention to considerations which I do not care to dwell upon until I learn from you yourself that this is the fact." This was the first letter that Lansing had received, as he noted in a memorandum, "actually signed by the President since he was taken ill." Lansing attributed the letter's "brutal and offensive" language to Wilson's illness, which had left him "affected by a species of mania, which seems to approach irrationality." How else, Lansing wondered, could one explain this letter at this time? "It sounded like a spoiled child crying out in rage at an imaginary wrong. It seemed the product of an abnormal vanity."[72]

Lansing seized upon Wilson's letter as an opening to depart on his own terms. In a carefully worded reply, which he showed in draft to at least one cabinet colleague, Lansing pointed out that he had called only informal meetings of the cabinet, strictly for discussion, not action, and solely in the interest of keeping the government running as smoothly as possible. Furthermore, Lansing noted, he had always kept the president fully informed of these meetings. "During these troublous times when many difficult and vexatious questions have arisen," Lansing concluded,

> . . . it has been my constant endeavor to carry out your policies as I understood them and to act in all matters as I believed you would wish me to act. If, however, you think that I have failed in my loy-

72. Entry Feb. 5, [1920], Baker Diary, in Link, ed., *Papers of Wilson,* LXIV, 365; Wilson to Lansing, Feb. 7, 1920, ibid., 383; Lansing memorandum, Feb. 9, 1920, ibid., 385–386. In a memorandum written the day that Wilson accepted his resignation, Lansing further speculated on why Wilson chose this time to provoke a confrontation, inasmuch as their disagreements over the treaty and the League and mutual disaffection were so long-standing. The secretary was perceptive about the influence of Wilson's illness, but he indulged in a bit of prejudice by wondering whether Tumulty, as a Catholic, had not conspired against him because of his being a prominent Protestant layman active in the Inter-Church World Movement. Far-fetched as that seems, if anyone would have passed on a report about Lansing's being pleased with the Grey letter, it would have been Tumulty. See Lansing memorandum, Feb. 13, 1920, ibid., 415–419.

alty to you and if you no longer have confidence in me and prefer to have another conduct our foreign affairs, I am of course ready, Mr. President, to relieve you of any embarrassment by placing my resignation in your hands.

To his credit, the secretary agreed to keep the president's letter and his reply private for the moment. As Lansing recorded the next day in his diary, Frank Polk, the undersecretary of state, went to see Grayson and told him "that if I went it would be a tragedy for the Pres[iden]t, as he would receive all the blame. Grayson said he appreciated the situation & would attempt to do something."[73]

Evidently the doctor did try to stop Wilson from going down this road with Lansing. Both Mrs. Wilson and Tumulty later recalled how they tried to dissuade the president from accepting the proffered resignation. Mrs. Wilson wrote some years later in her memoir that she had told her husband that his "letter as written made him look small." Tumulty, who wrote his memoir only a little over a year later, claimed to have told his chief "that in the present state of public opinion it was the wrong time to do the right thing." To both of them, Wilson made the same reply. Mrs. Wilson recalled him joking, "Well, if I am as big a man as you think me I can well afford to do a generous thing. . . . the disloyalty is a personal act; the calling of meetings of the Cabinet is official insubordination; it is my duty to put a stop to that." Tumulty recalled more pungent phrasing: "Tumulty, it is never the wrong time to spike disloyalty. When Lansing sought to oust me, I was upon my back. I am on my feet now and I will not have disloyalty about me." Both recollections rang true to Wilson's new mood of euphoria. He may have been joking to his wife, but he did feel deceptively strong.[74]

At the same time, contrary to Baker's fears, Wilson finally did agree to release his letter to Hitchcock about reservations. Evidently Hitchcock and Carter Glass, who had now taken his seat as senator from Virginia, convinced him to unbend. Some observers applauded the letter. Oscar Straus of the LEP told Tumulty, "It is a master move," and Baker noted in his diary, "It will do real good." Others disagreed. Glass, for one, urged Wilson to go further and endorse the Taft reservation to Article X that Hitchcock had earlier proposed to Lodge. Glass also warned that if the Democrats "must go to the American people on the issue" then they

---

73. Lansing to Wilson, Feb. 9, 1920, ibid., 388–389; entry, Feb. 10, 1920, Lansing Desk Diary, ibid., 398. For Lansing's passing a draft of the letter by a colleague, Secretary of the Interior Lane, see entry, Feb. 8, 1920, Lansing Desk Diary, ibid., 385.
74. Edith Wilson, *My Memoir*, 417–418; Tumulty, *Woodrow Wilson as I Know Him* (Garden City, N.Y., 1921), 445.

must be "able to convince the average citizen that we had exhausted every possible effort to conciliate the adversaries of the administration short of a virtual nullification of the covenant." As usual, the president would have none of such suggestions. Mrs. Wilson replied to Glass that "his judgment is decidedly against the course Sen. G. proposes. Article 10 is the backbone of the Covenant & Mr. Taft[']s proposed reservation is not drawn in good faith." The president remained adamant, she added, in believing "[t]hat initiative ought in no case to be taken by our side. It ought to be forced upon the Repub[licans]. . . . He attaches little importance to party strategy at this juncture & all importance to a clearly defined position taken on principles."[75]

Wilson also indulged his delusions of mastery by showing that he meant to pursue an all-or-nothing approach with the Allies. For the first time since before his stroke, Wilson took diplomatic matters into his own hands. On February 10, he had a public note sent to the British and French rebuking them for what he regarded as their appeasement of Italy's claims to Fiume and other parts of the Adriatic coast. Wilson restored language that Lansing and Polk had sought to soften. Now, the note spoke "with the utmost frankness" and declared that this dispute "raises the fundamental question as to whether the American Government can on any terms co-operate with the European associates in the great work of maintaining peace by removing the causes of war." To let the Italians have their way would mean, the note claimed, that "the old order of things which brought so many evils on the world is to prevail" and, therefore, "the time is not come when this Government can enter a concert of powers the very existence of which must depend upon a new spirit and a new order." The note further observed that many Americans were "fearful lest they become entangled in international policies and committed to international obligations foreign alike to their ideals and their traditions." To allow Italy to prevail "would be to provide the most solid ground for such fears. This Government can undertake no such grave responsibility."[76]

When the Senate resumed consideration of the treaty, those statements would feed grist to the mills of Wilson's critics and opponents. In the meantime, the predicted repercussions from Lansing's resignation

75. Straus to Tumulty, Feb. 7, 1920, ibid., 384; entry, Feb. 8, 1920, Baker Diary, ibid., 385; Glass to Wilson, Feb. 9, 1920, ibid., 387; Edith Wilson to Glass, [Feb. 11, 1920], ibid., 405. Mrs. Wilson's letter is a handwritten draft; it is evident from Glass's reply that he received a more polished version or something like it. See Glass to Wilson, Feb. 12, 1920, ibid., 410–411.
76. Diplomatic note sent as Lansing to Hugh C. Wallace, Feb. 10, 1920, ibid., 401–402. On Wilson's restoration of harsh language, see ibid., 402 n. 1.

did even greater political damage. On February 11 and 12, the two men exchanged blows through correspondence a final time. The president expressed himself as "very much disappointed" in Lansing's explanation of having called cabinet meetings. Accusing him of a history of disloyalty, Wilson asked Lansing to "relieve me of . . . the embarrassment of feeling your reluctance and divergence of judgment" by resigning. The secretary complied with a letter of resignation in which he denied all charges of disloyalty and usurpation. He cited a series of cases in which he had either been ignored or met with "frequent disapproval of my suggestions," and he stated that he was leaving "with a sense of profound relief." When they saw these letters on February 13, Frank Polk and his fellow Wilson loyalist at the State Department, Assistant Secretary Breckinridge Long, tried to prevent further harm. Long went to the White House to talk with Grayson. The doctor evidently succeeded in getting Wilson to answer with a brief note that simply accepted Lansing's resignation. The secretary had already had copies of the previous correspondence mimeographed, and the State Department released those letters and the president's acceptance to reporters at 7:30 in the evening. "Friday, the 13th!" wrote Lansing in a memorandum to himself that evening. "This is my lucky day for I am free from the intolerable situation in which I have been so long."[77]

For Wilson, this would turn out to be the one of the unluckiest days of his career. These days in February 1920 bore out the old saw about bad luck coming in threes. Besides this self-inflicted wound of Lansing's forced resignation, two other blows hit the president from outside. On February 10, Dr. Young, the urologist from Johns Hopkins who had treated Wilson's urinary blockage, remarked offhandedly to a reporter, "As you know, in October last we diagnosed the President's illness as cerebral thrombosis." Although Young insisted that "at no time was his brain power or the extreme power and lucidity of his mental processes in the slightest degree abated," his statement set off a flurry of remarks

77. Wilson to Lansing, Feb. 11, 13, 1920, ibid., 404, 414; Lansing to Wilson, Feb. 12, 1920, ibid., 409–410; Lansing memorandum, Feb. 13, 1920, ibid., 415. See also entry, Feb. 13, 1920, Lansing Desk Diary, ibid., 414; entry, Feb. 13, 1920, Long Diary, Long Papers, Box 2; entry, Feb. 13, 1920, Anderson Diary. In some respects, the most remarkable aspect of this affair was that Wilson had not fired Lansing much sooner, even before Bullitt's testimony. At the end of 1916, Lansing had tried to torpedo Wilson's peace note to the belligerents, and the president had come close to dismissing him. Lansing did not exaggerate when he privately complained about Wilson's treatment of him. Moreover, at Paris, Lansing had earned a widely disseminated reputation as a dull, plodding diplomat. On the peace note incident in 1916, see Link, *Wilson*, V, 221–225.

grounds that he had called cabinet meetings. "My greatest expectations have been more than satisfied," Lansing wrote in another memorandum to himself a week after he resigned. "I never for a moment dreamed of having the whole country rise to my support." Such popular reactions did not stem from public affection for the secretary. Lansing had always been a removed, formal figure and not particularly well known in the country. Rather, the reactions sprang from disaffection from the president and judgments about what his action and stated reason said about him. "It seems the petulant & irritable act of a sick man," Baker wrote in his diary on February 15. ". . . I do not think the Secretary was ill-advised in calling Cabinet meetings. Was there to be no discussion of public business for 4 months? It is 4 months since the President fell ill, & he has himself been able to transact very little public business."[82]

Lansing's removal served to ignite unease about Wilson's ability to govern that had been simmering since soon after he suffered his stroke. When *Literary Digest* collected newspaper opinion during the third week of February, nearly every statement that it cited linked this affair with sour reflections about Wilson's capacity to occupy the White House. For example, the New York *Globe* commented, "If this judgment in the Lansing case be a specimen of the 'fully restored mental vigor' of which Dr. Young has lately assured us, the country is indeed in sore straits." During the previous four months, as well as can be determined, the public had not been quick to judge Wilson harshly, especially in view of his illness. Surveys by *Literary Digest* and other experienced observers found that blame for the deadlock over the peace treaty fell more or less equally on the president and Republican senators, with Lodge often coming in for special condemnation. That tendency to share the blame for the deadlock did not appear to have changed much. Rather, as observers on both sides had repeatedly found, public interest in the League fight had waned and given way to impatience and boredom with the prolonged debate.[83]

Now, something else, both larger and less sharply focused, was at work in the turn that popular sentiment was taking. Now the issue was becoming the president himself and his fitness to fill his office. Wilson had fallen victim to the worst fate that can afflict a leader. He was being found weak and wanting, not able to handle the manifold problems that confronted America in 1920. Everything that afflicted people – from rampant inflation and soaring unemployment to the strikes in

82. Lansing memorandum, "Public Opinion and My Resignation," Feb. 20, 1920, Lansing Papers; entry Feb. 15, [1920], Baker Diary, in Link, ed., *Papers of Wilson*, LXIV, 434.
83. *Literary Digest*, LXIV (Feb. 28, 1920), 13–15.

major industries and the antiradical hysteria of the Red Scare – was being blamed on Wilson. To some extent the blame was legitimate. Virtually every observer in Washington noted the paralysis of government. "Both the executive & legislative bodies are scarcely functioning," commented Baker in his diary. Even McAdoo, Wilson's son-in-law and former secretary of the treasury, admitted to a Texas Democrat that "a drifting course is the worst possible thing for the party. We have had too much of it. This is due, primarily, I believe to the President's unfortunate illness."[84]

Rumblings of a massive public reaction were already in the air. A week after Lansing's resignation, Antoinette Funk, a treasury department official and Democratic party operative who regularly sampled public opinion for McAdoo, told her former boss, "I want to say to you confidentially that I am appalled at the attitude of the people toward the President, and I believe that this is the time for us to follow in the wake of the storm, and not get in front of it and be swept way." The storm that Funk was predicting would ultimately transform the political landscape and seal the outcome of the League fight. Before that happened, the president and the Senate had to play out this last, deciding round.[85]

84. Entry, Feb. 15, [1920], Baker Diary, in Link, ed., *Papers of Wilson,* LXIV, 434; McAdoo to Zach Lamar Cobb, Feb. 25, 1920, McAdoo Papers, Box 230.
85. Antoinette G. Funk to McAdoo, Feb. 20, 1920, ibid.

8

Defeat

On February 9, 1920, the Senate formally resumed consideration of the Treaty of Versailles. During the next thirty-nine days, the senators would again discuss various aspects of the treaty and League membership, but mostly they would talk about reservations. This debate's shorter duration and narrower focus afforded fewer displays of eloquence and less deep discussion of the nation's role in the world. The senators would also vote slightly fewer times because amendments to the text of the treaty were not proposed. Except for the final roll call on consent, all the votes would concern either procedural matters or reservations. In the end, the same package of reservations as before, with a few slight modifications and one addition, would once more gain approval. With those reservations attached, the Senate would vote a final time on consent to the Treaty of Versailles on March 19, 1920.

I

The decision to resume consideration of the treaty lay in Lodge's hands, and it is not completely clear why he chose to reopen the matter. Various Republicans, particularly Hays, the national chairman, still worried that the continuing stalemate might hurt the party's fortunes in the upcoming elections. The same group of organizations that had gathered a month earlier under the LEP's auspices sent a public letter to the president and the Senate urging speedy ratification. This letter called the differences in proposed reservations "insignificant in comparison to the importance of the treaty and the covenant itself." Its signers included Lowell and Straus, but not Taft. At the same time, a number of Democratic senators reportedly took offense at Wilson's coldness toward the earlier compromise effort. According to the New York *World,* several powerful Democrats were ready to break with the president. In addition, as Taft's agent Gus Karger noted, "some Republicans, who hitherto have stood by Lodge, are tired of playing horse with it [the treaty]." In any event, on February 9, Lodge moved to suspend the rules in order to reconsider the Senate's earlier votes on the treaty. "My purpose, and my sole purpose," he explained, ". . . is to bring the treaty before the Senate in the quickest possible way." And that way was, he added, "by modification of the reservations which the Senate adopted."[1]

Lodge's motion to suspend the rules required approval by two-thirds of the senators present and voting. The roll call on his motion and on a procedural challenge offered an early indication of sentiment in the Senate. The motion to suspend passed with sixty-three in favor and seven announced for, six more than two-thirds of the entire Senate. Only nine senators voted no, all of them Irreconcilables; two other members of their cohort were announced against. One of the Irreconcilables who voted against reconsideration was Norris. He was an astute parliamentarian who had earlier used his skills as a member of the House to humble Speaker Joseph G. Cannon. Now, Norris immediately challenged the legality of this procedure. The vice-president, who was in the chair, ruled against Norris, who thereupon demanded a roll-call vote in an attempt to overturn the ruling. The senators voted to sustain the chair, with sixty-two in favor and two more announced for. Ten senators opposed the ruling, the same nine Irreconcilables now joined by a Republican who had previously supported reconsideration. Norris denounced these actions as having broken the law and given "a good excuse for many an anarchist and many a revolutionist and many a Bolshevist to follow his illegal and inhumane conduct and take the law into his own hands."[2]

The next day, Borah became the first senator to refer to Keynes's *Economic Consequences of the Peace,* which he said should be studied by his colleagues and "read by the people of the United States generally." His extensive quotations from the book moved Knox to second Keynes's analysis of the damage done by the treaty's economic provisions. Borah concluded by heaping scorn on "this dishonest dickering at Versailles," which was deservedly "receiving the condemnation of the

---

1. Public letter, in *Congressional Record,* 66th Cong., 2nd Sess. (Feb. 9, 1920), 2676; New York *World,* Feb. 9, 1920; Karger to Taft, Feb. 5, 1920, Taft Papers, reel 217; *Congressional Record,* 66th Cong., 2nd Sess. (Feb. 9, 1920), 2629. For Hays' concern, see Taft to Karger, Feb. 7, 1920, William Howard Taft Papers, Library of Congress, reel 217; and on Democratic senators' discontent with Wilson, see entry, Feb. 7, 1920, Ashurst Diary, in George F. Sparks, ed., *A Many-Colored Toga: The Diary of Henry Fountain Ashurst* (Tucson, Ariz., 1962), 122–123.
2. *Congressional Record,* 66th Cong., 2nd Sess. (Feb. 9, 1920), 2627–2629, 2636–2637.

intellects of Europe." After that, nearly a week passed before any more senators stepped into the forensic fray.[3]

The lull on the floor belied intense activity elsewhere. The Foreign Relations Committee took only a day to approve eight reservations, as modified along the lines approved earlier in the bipartisan committee. Lodge introduced these in the Senate on February 11. As before, the main subject for discussion and contention remained the reservation to Article X. On February 9, as Karger reported to Taft, Lodge met with a group of mild reservationists that included Lenroot, Nelson, McNary, Colt, and Kellogg. "At this meeting, according to Colt," Karger recounted, "Lodge agreed to accept a change in Article X, which in the opinion of Colt will prove to furnish the solution." The change consisted of adding the words "or by any other means" to the language tentatively approved in the bipartisan committee. That language renounced any American obligation to maintain other nations' independence or territorial integrity "by its military or naval forces, or by the economic boycott." Any hope that those added words would gain broad acceptance died aborning. The *New York Times* editorially condemned the proposal as "A Bad Reservation Made Worse," and Hitchcock and Walsh of Montana called the change a sham. Republicans responded by digging in their heels. Fourteen strong reservationists announced that they opposed any further "dickering" over reservations, and six mild reservationists told reporters that they could not support Democratic suggestions for alternatives to this proposed reservation.[4]

Floor debate about the treaty resumed when Medill McCormick, the Republican Irreconcilable from Illinois, invoked Shakespeare and Daniel Webster, along with lengthy quotations from Keynes, to condemn what he decried as the peace settlement's manifold iniquities. McCumber responded with his single contribution to this debate. He argued once more for compromise and insisted that something worthwhile still remained in adherence to Article X, even with the latest Lodge reservation. Another Irreconcilable, Thomas of Colorado, also excoriated the economic provisions of the peace settlement, though without mentioning Keynes. He found those provisions, together with

3. Ibid. (Feb. 10, 1920), 2692–2699.
4. Karger to Taft, Feb. 11, 1920, Taft Papers, reel 217; *New York Times*, Feb. 13, 15, 1920. The fourteen strong reservationists were Cummins, Kenyon, Capper, Curtis, Watson, New, Harding, Spencer, Calder, Wadsworth, Frelinghuysen, Ball, Sutherland, and Dillingham. The six mild reservationists were not identified. For the eight reservations reported to the Senate, see *Congressional Record*, 66th Cong, 2nd Sess. (Feb. 11, 1920), 2735–2736.

the disposition of Germany's colonies, so bad that they would leave the League "converted into an instrument making for a renewal of universal conflict."[5]

This pattern of intermittent debate on the treaty persisted until the last days of February. At one point, Hitchcock blamed the Republicans for the breakdown of the bipartisan conference, and he denounced Lodge's new reservation on withdrawal as "more obnoxious than the original provision . . . and it is nothing in the nature of compromise." Lenroot responded that Hitchcock had "never evinced the slightest desire to negotiate on a line that would secure a two-thirds vote to ratify the treaty." Regarding Article X, he warned that "there can be no compromise of substance on that reservation. We may as well understand that very plainly." Lenroot also urged Democratic senators to "cut loose from the leading strings of the President." Ashurst seconded that call by imploring his fellow Democrats "to be leaders and Senators worthy of a great Republic by not listening to what the White House says. I am as good a Democrat as ever sat here, but I do not consider that it is a part and province of my Democratic duty to vote for the ratification of a treaty only when the White House says so."[6]

February 21 witnessed the first votes on matters of substance in this round of the League fight. Two amendments to the proposed reservation on withdrawal went down to defeat. The only measure to win approval was the original Lodge reservation. Of the forty-five votes in favor, thirty-seven came from Republicans, with three more announced for. Seven Democrats, including three of the usual reservationists – Gore, Shields, and Smith of Georgia – and four westerners also voted for this reservation. All of the twenty no votes came from Democrats, with one more announced against. The voting alignments on these roll calls sent mixed signals about the possible outcome of this round of the League fight. Sharp partisan division persisted from earlier, but a few more Democrats were kicking over the partisan traces to make common cause with Republican reservationists.[7]

The prospect of Democratic defections loomed larger in the eyes of

5. Ibid. (Feb. 16, 1920), 2946–2959; (Feb. 17, 1920), 2991–3007.
6. Ibid. (Feb. 20, 1920), 3175–3178; (Feb. 21, 1920), 3239–3240 .
7. Ibid. (Feb. 21, 1920), 3241–3242. The fourth reliable reservationist Democrat, Walsh of Massachusetts, was absent, as was one of the two Democratic Irreconcilables, Reed. The other Democratic Irreconcilable, Thomas, remained true to his idiosyncratic stand by voting and announcing with his fellow Democrats on two of the three roll calls and not participating in the third.

both friends and foes of League membership. "There seems to be a feeling and opinion that while some of the Democrats will vote against the reservations they may vote in favor of the ratification," Knox's secretary informed anti-League activist and advocate of the outlawry of war Salmon Levinson. The Irreconcilables were still hoping, he added, that Wilson would get nineteen Democrats to stand with them and block consent. Hitchcock gave a similar assessment the next day when he reported to the president that there was "a strong disposition on the part of many democratic senators to abandon the fight against the Lodge reservations." Hitchcock believed that only between fifteen and eighteen of his colleagues, including himself, would stand firm "unless something can be done to regain some of them." He recommended "a definite and positive statement from you" that consent with the Lodge reservations "does not mean ratification." In the meantime, Hitchcock noted, "Lodge proposes to keep the treaty before the Senate continuously beginning Thursday and I expect things to move rapidly and with little debate."[8]

After February 26, consideration of the peace treaty occupied the Senate with no further lapses for the next three weeks and two days. Lodge began by requesting postponement of the Article X reservation, in order to facilitate adoption of the other reservations. Despite objections from Knox, the senators approved a motion to postpone on a voice vote. Later, at the end of the day, they also voted overwhelmingly to adopt Lodge's third reservation, which forbade acceptance of a League mandate without congressional approval. This reservation passed by the second largest margin of any measure in this round of the League fight. The sixty-eight votes in favor included twenty-eight Democrats. Opposing this reservation were just four diehard administration loyalists.[9]

Predictions of lack of debate went awry, however, as Irreconcilables held forth against the League and the treaty at length. Joseph France introduced a resolution that called for a popular referendum on League membership in the 1920 elections. If membership lost, as France trusted it would, his resolution further authorized the president to convene an international conference in May 1921, "to bring about a concert of

---

8. Warren F. Martin to Levinson, Feb. 23, 1920, Salmon O. Levinson Papers, University of Chicago Library, Box 26, Folder 100; Hitchcock to Wilson, Feb. 24, 1920, in Arthur S. Link, ed., *The Papers of Woodrow Wilson* (Princeton, N.J., 1990), LXIV, 466. Borah offered a similar estimate at this time. See Borah to A. L. Dunn, Feb. 24, 1920, William E. Borah Papers, Library of Congress, Box 767.
9. *Congressional Record*, 66th Cong., 2nd Sess. (Feb. 26, 1920), 3500, 3515.

nations as a substitute for the League of Nations" and replace "this treaty of hate and destruction . . . [with] a new treaty, which will look to the rehabilitation of the world through international cooperation and international concerted action for the spread of civilization and for the elevation, education, and liberation of all men everywhere." Reed denounced the League as a British-dominated "serpent of treason" and sneered at "mild reservationists, who long for a rattlesnake with only two fangs instead of a full set of teeth." Norris condemned Britain's treatment of Egypt and added that this "is not the only sin contained in this treaty. It is only a sample. . . . The world does not yet know the extent of the evil that is tied up with the folds of this ponderous treaty." Brandegee delivered one of his sarcastic slurs on League advocates for possessing "the minds of Don Quixote" and fantasizing about "selfishness and greed having been eliminated by the mere resolution of the Senate ratifying the treaty."[10]

Meanwhile, the pace of voting on reservations slowed. Further behind-the-scenes discussions left many senators uncertain about how to proceed. Among the Republicans, mild reservationists and Irreconcilables were pressing their cases for and against compromise gestures. On February 29, Lodge met at his home with Borah and Brandegee, who renewed their threats to bolt the party if there were any concessions on reservations. On March 1, he met with Kellogg, Lenroot, and New, who wanted to find some way of disposing of the treaty. Private estimates varied about where these efforts might lead. Brandegee told Beveridge on February 27 that "attempts to modify his [Lodge's] reservations will not amount to much." He was confident that consent would fail again. Contrariwise, Straus of the LEP, who visited Washington at the beginning of March, recorded in his diary that the mild reservationist Le Baron Colt "seemed very optimistic that ratification would be secured by a two-thirds vote."[11]

10. Ibid. (Feb. 26, 1920), 3500–3514; (Feb. 27, 1920), 3564–3576; (Feb. 28, 1920), 3619–3624.
11. Ibid. (Mar. 1, 1920), 3692–3701; Brandegee to Beveridge, Feb. 27, 1920, Albert J. Beveridge Papers, Library of Congress, Box 219; entry, ca. Mar. 1, 1920, Straus Diary, Oscar S. Straus Papers, Library of Congress, Box 24. See also New York *World*, Feb. 29, 1920; *New York Times*, Mar. 1, 2, 1920. Among the Irreconcilables, Borah was less optimistic about defeating the consent again, whereas among the mild reservationists, Lenroot was less optimistic about winning. See Borah to James M. Beck, Feb. 28, 1920, Borah Papers, Box 770; William H. Short, "Substance of an Interview with Senator Lenroot," Feb. 29, 1920, copy in A. Lawrence Lowell Papers, Harvard University Archives.

The weightiest behind-the-scenes discussions involved Democratic senators. Many, perhaps most, of them reportedly were ready to vote for the Lodge reservations, even if that meant breaking with their president. Public reactions to Lansing's dismissal and the diplomatic note to Britain and France over the Adriatic controversy had demonstrably weakened Wilson's influence among his party brethren. On February 25, the president lowered his standing still further when he announced the appointment of Lansing's successor as secretary of state. As Grayson recounted in a memorandum at the time, Wilson asked him while he was treating the president for a coughing spell at 3 o'clock in the morning, "Do you know of any reason why I should not appoint Bainbridge Colby Secretary of State?" The doctor noted that he tried to discuss Colby – who was a New York lawyer, member of the War Shipping Board, and former Progressive with no experience in foreign affairs – by observing guardedly, "It would really be an unusual appointment." To that Wilson replied, "All those things are in his favor. We do not want to follow precedents and stagnate. We have to do unusual things in order to progress. I believe he is an able and fine man." Few people agreed with that assessment. Editorial reactions varied between puzzlement and condemnation. Privately, several observers concluded that Colby's appointment gave further proof of Wilson's incapacity.[12]

In view of the president's weakened political position and the sentiment among Democratic senators, some of his closest political advisors made a final stab at getting him to relent in his opposition to the Lodge reservations. On February 27, Tumulty wrote a letter to Wilson reporting that two of the administration's most loyal supporters in the Senate, Glass and Joseph Robinson of Arkansas, had told him that "our forces are rapidly disintegrating" and that "nothing but a statement from you will prevent a complete collapse." Yet Tumulty warned against "taking action now irrevocable in character. There is no doubt that the country

---

12. Grayson memorandum, Feb. 25, 1920, in Link, ed., *Papers of Wilson,* LXIV, 473–473. As an example of private reactions, one former associate in the Progressive party, James Garfield, privately dismissed Colby as "unstable, untrained & untrustworthy." Entry, Feb. 25, 1920, James R. Garfield Diary, James R. Garfield Papers, Library of Congress, Box 12. Senator Lodge agreed. Speaking off the record to a reporter, he called the appointment "Worse [*sic*] I ever saw" and speculated that it was "a political plum handed to a man who is willing to serve as a rubber stamp." Entry, Feb. 25, [1920], Clapper Diary, Raymond Clapper Papers, Library of Congress, Box 6.

is tired of the endless Senate debate. The ordinary man in the street is for ratification with the Lodge reservations. He yearns for peace and an early settlement of the whole situation." Those were hard political facts, and Wilson might suffer terrible embarrassment if a majority of Democratic senators should help supply the necessary two-thirds for consent. "My judgment is," concluded Tumulty, "that we should accept the ratification of the Treaty with the Lodge reservations with an address to the American people showing wherein those reservations weaken the whole Treaty and make it a useless instrument." Still, Tumulty believed that the president should acquiesce in the Senate's action and ratify, so as not "to postpone peace and thus aggravate a world situation which is very serious."[13]

Whether Tumulty actually sent that letter is not known. The only copy is in his papers, not Wilson's, and it seems likely that he shied away from giving this advice to the president. If that was the case, then this was one of three abortive efforts to reach Wilson in order to urge him to compromise. The two other moves began on February 29. In New York, Ray Stannard Baker met with House at the colonel's apartment. House recorded in his diary that he urged Baker to go to Washington, "see Mrs. Wilson . . . and, even at the expence [*sic*] of giving offence [*sic*], to urge her to use influence with the President to have him accept whatever amendments the Senate passes and allow the Treaty to be ratified." According to House, Baker made the trip the following day, but there is no record of his meeting with Mrs. Wilson or of her relating his and House's views to her husband. The most significant of these feelers toward influencing Wilson came out of a conclave of Democratic luminaries that met at the Chevy Chase Club, also on February 29. Homer Cummings, the party's national chairman, noted in his diary that, besides himself, those present included Tumulty, six cabinet members, senators Glass and Hitchcock, Representative John Nance Garner of Texas, and such present and former administration officials as Norman Davis, Edward N. Hurley, and Vance McCormick. Also invited but not present, according to Cummings, were two prominent pro-League newspaper editors, Richard Hooker of the *Springfield Republican* and Frank Cobb of the *World*, who sent a letter stating his views.[14]

The two accounts of what transpired at that meeting indicate that

13. Tumulty to Wilson, Feb. 27, 1920, in Link, ed., *Papers of Wilson*, LXIV, 479–480.
14. Entry, Mar. 2, 1920, House Diary, in ibid., LXV, 41; entry, Feb. 29, 1920, Cummings Diary, in ibid., 24.

those high-ranking Democrats wanted to get Wilson to agree to some kind of compromise. On March 5, Postmaster General Burleson wrote to Tumulty:

> In my opinion if the President will prepare the letter discussed at the conference last Sunday night, differentiating in his masterly way the Lodge Reservation to Article Ten and the Article as it is written in the Treaty, and give publicity to same at once, it may so influence Senatorial action when this reservation is voted upon, as to secure the wording of the Reservation enabling the President to accept it. I believe the psychological moment has arrived for this letter to be written and published.[15]

Burleson's language left some doubt about how far the party nabobs wanted the president to go toward meeting the senators. The other account, which was written six or seven years afterward, stated that everyone there emphatically endorsed the idea of acquiescing to the Lodge reservations. In his memoir published in 1927, *The Bridge to France*, Edward Hurley, who had served during the war as chairman of the War Shipping Board, highlighted Cobb's letter, which was read to the conclave. Hurley recalled that the letter made a strong case for Wilson's accepting the reservations and that Hitchcock had agreed with Cobb's position. "Practically every one present concurred with Senator Hitchcock," Hurley added, "and thought that the best interests of the party would be served if the President were to yield his opposition to the reservations." At that point, Hurley further recounted, Glass observed that they were all agreed. "But," Glass continued, "I would like to know, in the present condition of the President's mind and his state of health, who among us will be willing to go to him and tell him that he should accept the reservations." After Glass spoke, Hurley recalled, "There was a hush. Each one waited for some one else to accept the invitation. There was no volunteer."[16]

Hurley's memory does not seem to have exaggerated how strongly the men at that meeting agreed on the need to swallow the Lodge reservations. Publicly and privately, most of the party's leaders wanted to get the treaty behind them on just about any terms. Back in November, Cobb had recommended ratification with the Lodge reservations as a half loaf worth having. The *World* would soon reiterate that argument editorially several times. The only part of Hurley's recollection that did not ring true was his account of Hitchcock's stand. William Short of the LEP noted that in an interview earlier that day,

15. Burleson to Tumulty, Mar. 5, 1920, ibid., 56–57.
16. Edward N. Hurley, *The Bridge to France* (Philadelphia, 1927), 325–327.

Senator Hitchcock gave me to understand that he regained control
of the Democrats in the Senate only by the following tactics: that he
asked them to imagine that the Democrats in the Senate had agreed
to the Lodge reservations, that the President had rejected those
reservations, and that they were placed on the platform committee
to the National Democratic convention at San Francisco and were
drawing a plank on the Treaty situation. He asked those present to
suggest the kind of a plank they would draw.

Hitchcock did not enjoy a reputation for being a strong character, and
he may have talked out of one side of his mouth to Short during the day
and out of the other side to the party bigwigs at night. In any event,
Glass had put his finger on the crux of the issue: Who would bell this
cat by telling the awful truth to Wilson? Nobody did.[17]

It was just as well that none of these men tried to talk to the president. Sometime around the end of February, he began drafting the statement to the Democratic senators that Hitchcock had requested from
him. Wilson devoted most of his comments about "the so-called Lodge
reservations" to the one to Article X. "In regard to the reservation on
that Article," he declared, "I must say in frankness that if the treaty
should be returned to me with such a reservation on Article X, I would
be obliged to consider it a rejection of the treaty and of the Covenant of

17. Short, "Conference with Senator Hitchcock," Feb. 29, 1920, Lowell
Papers. An example of Hitchcock's reputation in the treaty fight comes
from Henry White, who wrote to his son at this time, "Hitchcock has a
light and airy way of treating the subject every time I talk to him about it,
the last occasion being two or three evenings ago." White to John Campbell White, Mar. 2, 1920, quoted in Allen Nevins, *Henry White: Thirty
Years of American Diplomacy* (New York, 1930), 482. It is not certain that
Wilson ever learned about the February 29 meeting at the Chevy Chase
Club. Tumulty did write a note asking Mrs. Wilson to show Burleson's
March 5 letter to the president, but that note and Burleson's letter also
remained in Tumulty's papers, not Wilson's. See Link, ed., *Papers of Wilson*, LXV, 56–57. There is conflicting evidence as to what role Tumulty was
playing at this point. On the one hand, he did keep a promise to McAdoo
to forward to McAdoo letters from Hamilton Holt and James W. Gerard
urging Wilson to acquiesce in the Lodge reservations. See Tumulty to
McAdoo, Mar. 1, 1920, William Gibbs McAdoo Papers, Library of Congress, Box 230. Those letters to McAdoo are in the Wilson Papers, Library
of Congress. On the other hand, Tumulty was helping to draft the harsh letter rejecting the Lodge reservations that Wilson would send to Hitchcock
on March 8. See Tumulty to Edith Wilson, Mar. 1, 1920, in Link, ed.,
Papers of Wilson, LXIV, 24–25; letter drafts, [ca. Feb. 28, Mar. 1, 1920),
ibid., 11–14, 25–28, 30–35.

the League of Nations. Any reservation seeking to deprive the League of Nations of the virility of Article X cuts at the heart of the Covenant itself." The rest of this draft consisted of an argument that Article X was essential to the establishment of a new, just world order capable of assuring peace and preventing another world war. "Every imperialistic influence in the chancelleries of Europe opposed the embodiment of Article X in the League of Nations," Wilson concluded, "and its defeat now would mark the complete consummation of their efforts to nullify the treaty. The doctrine of Article X is the essence of Americanism, and we cannot repudiate it without at the same time repudiating our own history."[18]

This rejection of compromise also seems to have stemmed from Wilson's newfound illusions of strength. The editors of the *Papers of Wilson* speculate that the president himself, not Tumulty, wrote this draft. As they note, he was able to dictate at length to his stenographer, as he evidently did now. Moreover, they believe that the stress on Article X – about which, as they put it, "Wilson was obviously becoming obsessive" – reflects his authorship. Another sign of the president's partial recovery came on March 3, when he left the White House for the first time in five months. At his insistence, he rode for more than an hour in the presidential limousine along the Potomac and up Pennsylvania Avenue to Capitol Hill. Ironically, one of the people who recognized Wilson when the car passed the Capitol was Senator Borah. According to reporters, the Idaho Irreconcilable flashed a broad smile and waved at the president. Once more, the receding physical effects of the stroke were bringing its psychological impact into play. This draft of a statement to the Senate Democrats offered only a foretaste of the public blast that Wilson was about to deliver.[19]

II

The machinations in and around the White House formed the backdrop to the last spurt of debate and voting on the peace treaty in the Senate. From March 2 until the final votes on March 19, with only one lapse, the senators would vote at least once and usually several times every day that they were in session. This wave of roll calls would crest with nineteen of them on March 18. At the same time, the pace of speaking would remain steady, with at least five or six senators entering into the debate each day. Often, however, they would not deliver set speeches

18. Wilson draft, [ca. Feb. 28, 1920], ibid., LXV, 7–9.
19. Ibid., 7 n. 1. For a report of Wilson's ride, see *New York Times*, Mar. 4, 1920.

but would engage in give-and-take over reservations and particular aspects of the peace settlement.

The talk and action on March 2 laid down the main pattern for this last episode in the Senate. The debate included lengthy speeches by Borah and Reed dismissing the Lodge reservations as inadequate. Reed rationalized his own votes for them "because if my country is going to be pushed into a furnace I desire that it shall be burned as little as possible." During and after those speeches, the senators voted five times. Attempts by Democrats to soften two of the Lodge reservations, on domestic questions and the Monroe Doctrine, failed, and the reservations passed. The domestic question reservation attracted fifty-six in favor, with one additional senator, La Follette, announced for. Of the votes in favor, twelve came from Democrats, including, besides the expected reservationists, several westerners. Democrats cast all twenty-five of the votes against this reservation. The Monroe Doctrine reservation passed by an even larger margin, fifty-eight in favor and two more, La Follette and Fall, announced for. This time, sixteen Democrats, including both westerners and three erstwhile administration stalwarts from the South, crossed over to support the reservation. Only twenty-two opposed it, all Democrats. These votes revealed alignments that would persist through the remainder of this round of the League fight.[20]

Again on March 3 and 4, the senators alternated between debating and voting. At the outset, another particularly inflamed aspect of the peace settlement dominated the debate. A Democrat, William King of Utah, introduced a resolution calling for an independent Armenia under the League's protection. Few events during the world war had aroused greater indignation in the English-speaking world than the massacres of Armenian Christians begun by the Turks in 1915. An international drive for relief and protection of the Armenians had begun during the war, headed by Lord Bryce in Britain and initially attracting support in the United States from such men as Roosevelt and Lodge. Early in the peace conference, soon after the unveiling of the Draft Covenant, various people had floated the idea of a League mandate for Armenia; some had proposed that the United States become the mandatory power. Irreconcilables had quickly denounced those proposals as an example of the faraway commitments that League membership would require. Lodge and other Republicans had quietly dropped their earlier championship of the Armenians. Wilson, too, had taken a hands-off attitude toward the mandate idea. On his speaking tour, despite its obvious emotional appeal, he had alluded to Armenia only twice. Fittingly, he

20. *Congressional Record,* 66th Cong., 2nd Sess. (Mar. 2, 1920), 3737–3738, 3741, 3742–3746, 3748, 3749.

had made one of those allusions when he spoke in Salt Lake City, at the Mormon Tabernacle. The Mormon church, to which Senator King belonged, was among several denominations that strongly backed aid and possible intervention on behalf of the Armenians. Even then, Wilson had not mentioned the mandate idea or the possible use of American troops.[21]

King's resolution moved one of the Irreconcilables, Poindexter, to charge that a mandate would require 250,000 troops and cost the staggering sum of $1 billion. To Poindexter, such an enterprise typified "this Frankenstein monster among the Governments of the world." In response, King recalled the hopes of the "Christian nations everywhere . . . [for] the emancipation of Armenia from the tyranny and cruel oppression of the Turkish empire." Borah jumped in to declare, "Europe is still Europe, with all her racial antipathies and imperialistic appetites, . . . and if we assume the task of effectuating a change, save

21. For Wilson's mentions of Armenia, see speech at Kansas City, Sept. 6, 1919, in Link, ed., *Papers of Wilson,* LXVIII, 71; speech at Salt Lake City, Sept. 23, 1919, ibid., 458. Wilson had implicitly ruled out the use of American troops in Armenia earlier in the Salt Lake City speech when he ridiculed the idea of their being sent to distant trouble spots, asserting, "If you want to put out a fire in Utah, you don't send to Oklahoma for the fire engine. If you want to put out a fire in the Balkans, if you want to stamp out the smoldering flames in some part of Central Europe, you don't send to the United States for troops." Ibid., 453. Roosevelt's and Lodge's wartime championship of the Armenians had stemmed in part from their desire to make wholehearted common cause with the Allies, including having the United States go to war against Turkey, which Wilson declined to do, and in part from a more general desire to embarrass his administration by seizing upon a popular issue. Lodge had additional reasons for championing the Armenians: first, a vocal and well-organized Armenian-American constituency in Massachusetts, and second, the principal denomination with missionaries in Armenia, the Congregationalists, being headquartered in Boston. In April, however, Lodge regretfully confessed to Bryce that the United States was not going to do anything for the Armenians: "The fact is, the protracted debate on the League both inside and outside the Senate has wrought a great change in public opinion and the feeling is growing constantly stronger against the United States involving itself in the quarrels of Europe at all. For this reason it will be impossible to get a mandate accepted by the United States and I doubt very much if we could secure a loan from the Government for any political or military purpose." Lodge to Bryce, Apr. 20, 1920, Henry Cabot Lodge Papers, Massachusetts Historical Society. On American policy toward Armenia, see Suzanne Elizabeth Moranian, "The American Missionaries and the Armenian Question, 1915–1927" (Ph.D. diss., University of Wisconsin–Madison, 1994).

as in the past by whatever power of precept and example we may exert, we will end by becoming Europeanized in our standards and in our conceptions of civilization or we will fall into disintegration and as a Republic die."[22]

On March 4, the senators again voted five times, on matters concerning two reservations. Nearly all of the debate concerned the first of those reservations, the one relating to Shantung. Senators on both sides of the issue vied in protesting their devotion to China and detestation of Japan. When Hitchcock protested that this reservation was no real help to China, Lodge answered, "It relieves the United States from being an active and assenting participant in an infamy and a crime." Borah protested that he was "very anxious to render any service that I can for China, [but] going into the league is too high a price to pay even for that." In opposing the reservation, Williams sounded the sourest note by raising the specter of the yellow peril. Harmony between China and Japan was, he warned, "the last thing in the world that the white race wants. . . . Let sleeping dogs lie; do not wake them up." Also, between votes, Hitchcock, Lenroot, Lodge, and Walsh of Montana sparred over what they had and had not agreed to in the bipartisan committee talks a month earlier.[23]

Only one of the five votes taken on March 4 broke sharply with the patterns set previously. That was the first vote, on an amendment to the Shantung reservation offered by Lodge. This amendment embodied the softening language agreed upon earlier by the bipartisan committee. It passed with the largest number of senators in favor of any measure, substantive or procedural, of the entire League fight – sixty-nine voting and three announced for. The only two no votes came from Reed and Sutherland of West Virginia. On the other votes, the senators stayed largely though not completely within the alignments established on earlier roll calls. The Shantung reservation itself passed with forty-eight in favor – including ten Democrats, westerners as well as reservationists and Irreconcilables – and twenty-one opposed, all Democrats. The other reservation, which asserted Congress' role in appointments to international commissions, then passed, fifty-five to fourteen. Those in favor included fifteen Democrats, fourteen voting and one announced, with several southerners joining the earlier bolters.[24]

On March 5, there was another scrap about what had happened in the bipartisan committee, and the reservation forbidding interference under the treaty by the reparations commission with American trade

22. *Congressional Record,* 66th Cong., 2nd Sess. (Mar. 3, 1920), 3792–3808.
23. Ibid. (Mar. 4, 1920), 3839–3862.
24. Ibid. (Mar. 4, 1920), 3848, 3857, 3863, 3864.

with Germany passed. The forty-one votes in favor included the same four Democrats plus one westerner; the twenty-two votes against all came from Democrats. On March 6, the reservation to restrict American financial obligations to support League activities passed by a vote of forty-six in favor; these included such Democrats as Myers and Pomerene, as well as the usual dissidents; the twenty-five against were all Democrats.[25]

In the midst of these votes and speeches, activity off the Senate floor remained intense. Both the *New York Times* and the *World* carried several stories about dealings among the senators. On March 7, according to the *World*, Lodge gathered a group of senior colleagues at his home, "cold nosed fellows, the actual leaders of the Republicans," including Albert Cummins of Iowa, Charles Curtis of Kansas, Reed Smoot of Utah, and James Watson of Indiana. The *World* further reported that the group authorized Watson to communicate with the Democrats. Meanwhile, among the Democrats, there were reports that Furnifold Simmons of North Carolina was drafting compromise language on Article X and that he was trying to see Wilson and gain his approval. There were also reports that the president refused to see Simmons and that this action caused "much irritation" among Democratic senators. Further, according to Watson's recollection over a decade later, Simmons also approached him. Together, Watson recalled, the two of them worked out language that Watson showed to Lodge and urged Simmons to show to the president. When Wilson refused to see Simmons, Watson recalled, "Of course he was pretty vexed about it and said so to me when I kept pressing him to find out what he had done with reference to the matter."[26]

On March 8, when Senate consideration resumed after a Sunday break, matters appeared to be moving closer to some form of agreement. Lodge introduced a motion at the outset to limit debate on the remaining reservations to twenty minutes each, except for the one to Article X. Hitchcock asked for an exception also to be made for the reservation affecting British Empire voting. Lodge agreed, and the senators gave unanimous consent to the new rule. During the next four hours, the senators voted six times and approved three more reservations. These reservations covered the Covenant's disarmament provisions, relations with governments that broke the Covenant, and the

25. Ibid. (Mar. 5, 1920), 3885–3901; (Mar. 6, 1920), 3939–3955.
26. New York *World*, Mar. 7, 8, 1920; James W. Watson, *As I Knew Them* (Indianapolis, 1936), 195–196. See also *New York Times*, Mar. 5, 7, 8, 1920.

treaty's labor clauses, and the votes on them produced the same alignments as earlier roll calls. Favoring these Lodge reservations were between forty-four and forty-nine senators, mostly Republicans. Joining them were at least five and more often eight or ten Democrats, again the same collection of dissidents, westerners, and one or two southerners. Opposing these reservations were between twenty-seven and thirty-two senators – all Democrats except when one mild reservationist, Nelson, joined them on a single vote. After these votes, the senators spent the rest of the day debating on the British Empire voting reservation.[27]

Any attention to what happened in the Senate on March 8 instantly evaporated in light of what the president did at the end of the day. This was when Wilson released the final version of his statement to Hitchcock. Since dictating the first draft, he had accepted a few suggestions from Tumulty, who had also shown the draft to some Cabinet members. Then Wilson had produced a much longer, more polished statement. He had further revised this version by dictating changes to his stenographer and Mrs. Wilson. In itself, the letter gave a further sign of his recovery from the stroke. It was the most extended piece of writing or speaking that he had done since that last speech at Pueblo in September. Even people who deplored his stand acknowledged that this was an impressive rhetorical performance. Unfortunately from the standpoint of those who wanted the United States to join the League on the best available terms, this fresh burst of flame from the old fire of Wilsonian eloquence burned the last remaining bridges to compromise.[28]

The letter breathed a spirit of righteous defiance almost from the opening words. The only subject that Wilson addressed was Article X. This, he asserted, "has become so singularly beclouded by misapprehensions and misinterpretations of every kind." In his view, Article X embodied "a moral victory over Germany far greater even than the military victory," and he avowed that "I could not look the soldiers of our gallant armies in the face again if I did not do everything in my power to remove every obstacle that lies in the way of this particular Article of the Covenant." As for reservations concerning the Covenant, merely interpretative ones struck him as "a work of supererogation," whereas

27. *Congressional Record,* 66th Cong., 2nd Sess. (Mar. 8, 1920), 4004–4021.
28. On the drafting of the letter, see Tumulty to Edith Wilson, Mar. 5, 7, 1920, in Link, ed., *Papers of Wilson,* LXV, 48, 66; photographed copy of revised draft, [ca. Mar. 5, 1920], ibid., 49–55. House, for example, said that he "disagree[d] wholly with his position" and knew nobody "who approves his action" but admitted "he has seldom written a better letter." Entry, Mar. 10, 1920, House Diary, ibid., 80.

others that he had seen were "in effect virtual nullification of those Articles" to which they were addressed. Worst of all, he declared:

> [a]ny reservation which seeks to deprive the League of Nations of the force of Article X cuts at the very heart and life of the Covenant itself. Any League of Nations which does not guarantee as a matter of incontestable right the political independence and integrity of each of its members might be hardly more than a futile scrap of paper as ineffectual in operation as the agreement between Belgium and Germany which the Germans violated in 1914.

Warming to his argument, Wilson delivered what was, in effect, a campaign speech reminiscent of the ones on the tour. He charged that governments that rejected Article X "will, I think, be guilty of bad faith to their people whom they induced to make the infinite sacrifices of the war by the pledge that they would be fighting to redeem the world from the old order of force and agression [*sic*]." Furthermore, he warned, "[m]ilitaristic ambitions and imperialistic policies are by no means dead even in the counsels of the nations whom we most trust and with whom we now most desire to be associated in the tasks of peace." Wilson recalled how he had fought at Paris against "a militaristic party, under the most influential leadership." That party had recently risen again to support Italy's aggressive designs in the Adriatic. Now, those devotees of the "ideal of imperialism" were striving to nullify Article X because it was "the bulwark, and the only bulwark, of the rising democracy of the world against the forces of imperialism and reaction." For America, the choice lay between entering the League "fearlessly, accepting the responsibility and not fearing the role of leadership which we now enjoy," or else retiring "as gracefully as possible from the great concert of powers by which the world was saved. I am not willing to trust to the counsels of diplomats the working out of any salvation of the world from the things which it has suffered."

Finally – as if this declaration of conscience and recitation of world-shaking stakes had not made his stand painfully clear – Wilson concluded the letter with three stinging sentences:

> I need not say, Senator, that I have given a great deal of thought to the whole matter of reservations proposed in connection with ratification of the treaty, and particularly of that portion of the treaty which contains the Covenant of the League of Nations, and I have been struck by the fact that practically every so-called reservation was in effect a nullification of the terms of the treaty itself. I hear of reservationists and mild reservationsts, but I cannot understand the difference between a nullifier and a mild nullifier. Our responsibility as a nation in this turning point of history is an overwhelming one, and if I had the opportunity I would beg everyone concerned to

consider the matter in light of what is possible to accomplish for humanity rather in the light of special national interests.[29]

Wilson wanted his words to draw blood, and they did. In the press, all but the staunchest Democratic newspapers excoriated his stand. The *Washington Post* labeled Wilson "an affirmative irreconcilable," while the Republican New York *Tribune* deplored his "unreasoning acerbity" and "narrow arrogance." Even the country's leading Democratic journal, the *World,* titled its editorial "Ratify!" and declared, "On the question of expediency, which every statesman is obliged to consider, his [Wilson's] position is weak and untenable." The few senators who spoke to reporters that evening after the letter was released made predictable comments. Among the Irreconcilables, Brandegee called it "a point blank refusal of any compromise. The President has strangled his own child." Borah agreed but commended Wilson for making "the issue a League or no League, which is in the form I would like it." Moses picked up on the slam at "mild nullifiers" to quip that he and Kellogg "have been united in the bonds of political wedlock by the Rev. Woodrow Wilson." Some Democrats affected to believe that the president had not completely closed the door to compromise.[30]

The full fury of senators scorned did not erupt until the next day's session on Capitol Hill. On March 9, three of them lashed back at Wilson. Leading off was Lodge, who had declined to talk to reporters the night before. The Republican leader delivered a measured address that blasted Wilson's position, scored political points, and recapitulated the fundamental issue between his great-power nationalism and the president's internationalism. Lodge regretted the remarks and implications in Wilson's letter about France, for whose sacrifices in the war "a great debt of the civilized world is owed," and Italy, whose sacrifices more than justified taking Fiume and the Adriatic coast. Likewise, toward Britain Lodge claimed that, unlike Wilson, "I have never had the slightest desire to make any attack," notwithstanding his support of the earlier Johnson amendment and the current British Empire voting reservation. In taking issue with the president this way, the senator was countering League advocates' charges that their opponents were siding with Germany. He could maintain, with perfect sincerity, that he was a better friend of the Allies than the president.

Lodge saved his most withering scorn for Wilson's disdain for diplo-

29. Wilson to Hitchcock, Mar. 8, 1920, in Link, ed., *Papers of Wilson,* LXV, 67–71.

30. *Washington Post,* Mar. 9, 1920; New York *Tribune,* Mar. 9, 10, 1920; New York *World,* Mar. 9, 10, 1920. For senatorial comments, see also *New York Times,* Mar. 9, 1920.

mats and his exaltation of Article X. "The whole peace conference," he
declared, ". . . was composed of diplomats; the result of their labors is
an alliance, and every provision in the Covenant of the League of
Nations is left in the hands of diplomats." Lodge found Wilson consistent in rejecting the counsel of diplomats and pinning all his hopes on
Article X because "article 10 is not diplomatic. That is why we so much
object to it; that is why the whole country so much objects to it; it is
naked force for which each nation is made individually responsible. . . .
Article 10 is the one pure force article in the covenant. He discards all
the others and stands on that alone." Lodge mockingly thanked Wilson
for having "justified the position that we on this side, all alike, have
taken, that there must be no obligation imposed on the United States to
carry out the provisions of article 10."[31]

Next, a mild reservationist from Wilson's home state of New Jersey,
Walter Edge, proudly donned the "mild nullifier" label. He avowed
himself and other like-minded Republicans "ready and willing to provide that America, which evaded no responsibility in time of war,
should evade none in time of peace; but we insist that America alone
shall decide each individual case without its honor or integrity being
under the slightest question or review." The last and sharpest rejection
of Wilson's stand came from a Democrat who had worked hard for
compromise. Owen announced himself "in favor of passing the treaty
immediately" without any reservations. "But," he conceded, "to keep
the United States out of the league because of the very small differences
between the President and Senator Lodge would be defeating a very
great end for a very small end." For the sake of passing the treaty, he
was willing "to yield to a majority of my colleagues in the Senate . . .
[and] I will not follow any leader who is leading to its defeat or
delay."[32]

Wilson's letter came too late to stop efforts at compromise. Only two
reservations remained for debate and action, and the drive to complete
consideration of the treaty had gained too much momentum. The senators spent the rest of the session on March 9 voting on the next-to-last
reservation. In contrast to the previously heated exchanges about the
British Empire, now they engaged in only brief arguments about
attempts to change the reservation. On seven roll calls on March 9, the
votes again followed established lines. The only measures to win came
from Lodge. Those were two amendments to strengthen the reservation
and the reservation itself. His two amendments passed forty-nine to
twenty-eight and fifty-five to twenty-two; the reservation carried fifty-

31. *Congressional Record*, 66th Cong., 2nd Sess. (Mar. 9, 1920), 4050–4051.
32. Ibid. (Mar. 9, 1920), 4052–4053, 4054–4055.

seven to twenty-two. All the "no" votes came from Democrats, but the numbers of their party brethren who broke ranks to vote in favor rose from nine to fifteen and seventeen. The Democratic bolters were again a mixture of expected reservationists, westerners, and a few southerners. Those voting for the reservation included Owen and Pomerene. Their defections, together with Owen's speech, sowed doubt about whether enough Democrats would stick with Wilson to defeat consent with these reservations.[33]

Now, just one reservation remained before the senators could take a final vote on the treaty. It was that perennially insuperable barrier, the reservation to Article X. Six days would pass, five of debate and a Sunday break, before measures relating to this reservation came to a vote. The slowdown in voting again reflected behind-the-scenes efforts at compromise, together with recognition of the importance of the subject. Everyone agreed that Article X far outweighed everything else in significance to American membership in the League and participation in the peace settlement. This was one subject on which some senators still wanted to get in last words. Likewise, hope for compromise sprang eternal both inside and outside the Senate, and efforts to influence the outcome continued right down to the final vote on the treaty.

Debate during these final days often resembled what had transpired during the previous round of the League fight in two respects. The senators' speeches usually focused on broader aspects of the peace settlement and League membership rather than on reservations. Wilson's critics and opponents, particularly the Irreconcilables, again did most of the talking. No senator spoke longer or more often during these six days than Brandegee. He consumed an entire day's debate with a diatribe against Wilson and Article X, heaping special scorn on "all this tweedledee and tweedledum" about moral and legal obligations. "It is just juggling with words . . . Janus-faced deceptive quibbling." Far better to keep America "free and untrammeled, to take part in any international crisis as the Government – and by the Government, I mean the whole Government, the President and Congress, both – may, when the emergency arises, think best for the country." Brandegee also held forth against efforts "to contrive a set of 'weasel words'" instead of accepting or rejecting the obligation under Article X "in plain, blunt, Anglo-Saxon, Yankee language."[34]

One of the two Democratic Irreconcilables, Thomas, bared the pain that he felt at breaking with his party and with Wilson, whom he had

33. Ibid., (Mar. 9, 1920) 4061–4062, 4065, 4066–4067.
34. Ibid. (Mar. 11, 1920), 4170–4177; (Mar. 12, 1920), 4217–4218; (Mar. 15, 1920), 4319–4320.

known and supported since 1911. "I read this treaty six times," Thomas confessed, ". . . always with the earnest desire to ratify it. I can not do so." The other Democratic Irreconcilable, Reed, felt no pain at breaking with Wilson or anyone else. He chortled that the president was losing support from "mild repudiationists" among their fellow Democrats, and, referring to the ex-president's newspaper column, he sneered at "[t]he great syndicated patriot of America, Brother Taft." Reed also scoffed at claims to "Americanize" the treaty through reservations: "You can no more Americanize it than you can make a domestic animal out of a rattlesnake."[35]

The last Irreconcilable to speak was Knox. He declared "that this attempt to bind the United States by signatures, seals, covenants, protocols, and understandings in writing after the magnificent record that it has made in the last three years, seems like asking a man who has sold all he has and given it to the poor to give bond to be charitable for the future." Also, for the first time in several months Knox reaffirmed his support for the "Knox doctrine," under which the United States would pledge to act in the event of a threat to the peace of Europe. In response, Brandegee agreed that this was the right way "to show the world that we were not trying to shirk any obligation to maintain peace in the world."[36]

Several mild reservationists and Democrats broke in to argue for compromise. "So long as there is no surrender of substance," maintained Lenroot, ". . . I am willing to change the form of the reservation" to Article X. Among the Democrats, Hoke Smith declared, "I am willing to take a reservation which I hope will gather votes and lead toward ratification." Another Democrat, James Phelan of California, tried to soft-pedal the obligation under Article X. He believed that "the exercise of economic pressure will be quite sufficient" to enforce League decisions. William Kirby of Arkansas likewise protested "that there is not 15 cents difference" between this new Lodge reservation and the ones floated earlier in the bipartisan conference.[37]

Voting halted during these days because the main action again shifted to behind-the-scenes dealings. On March 10, according to the *World,* the Republican leaders granted a "day of grace" for compromise efforts conducted principally by Watson for their side and Simmons, whom the

35. Ibid. (Mar. 12, 1920), 4208–4209; (Mar. 12–13, 1920), 4265–4284.
36. Ibid. (Mar 15, 1920), 4330–4331.
37. Ibid. (Mar. 12, 1920), 4211–4213, 4223; (Mar. 13, 1920), 4262–4263, 4282; (Mar. 15, 1920), 4322.

World dubbed "Grand Marshal of the Democratic compromisers." According the *New York Times,* Simmons and Watson tried to draft language that each side could read as satisfactory on Article X. Their effort stalled when Irreconcilables and several strong reservationists balked at any change in the Lodge reservation. Meanwhile, mild reservationists were reportedly threatening to vote with the Democrats if Lodge did not agree to some modification in the reservation. Also, as Henry Stimson recorded in his diary, several of those Republicans had encountered Root, who was in Washington to argue a case before the Supreme Court. These Republican senators, as Stimson put it, "had pounced on him [Root] and dragged him off into a conference on the subject of the new proposed reservation to Article X (I think this was the so-called Watson-Simmons reservation). He had told them that, in his opinion, he saw no substantial difference between this and the original Lodge reservation on the subject." For their part, compromise-minded Democrats were meeting in Owen's office to weigh their options. Some of them found the situation so discouraging that the *World* called Owen's office the "lodge of sorrow."[38]

It is difficult to determine what really lay behind these reports of what the *World*'s correspondent called "whispering, wheedling, and supposing." The one move of substance evidently came out of meetings that Root had with Kellogg and Watson and separately with Lodge to discuss revised language for the reservation. The next day, Kellogg reported to Root that they had gotten all the Republicans except the Irreconcilables and two strong reservationists to agree to a new version, and "we are assured that there are twenty-nine Democrats who will vote for ratification and possibly thirty." On the other side, Borah was worried enough to telegraph La Follette on March 11 asking him to return to Washington. "Situation serious," he noted in the telegram. Why this so-called compromise resolution aroused so much hope and fear is difficult to fathom. All it did was to shift the clause "by the employment of its military or naval forces, its resources, or any form of economic discrimination" to a different place in the reservation. Editorially, the *New York Times* hailed this reservation as one "to which, it seems to us, no reasonable friend of the Treaty can object." But Underwood, who had thus far stayed

---

38. New York *World,* Mar. 10, 11, 1920; *New York Times,* Mar. 11, 1920; entry, Mar. 18, 1920, Stimson Diary, Henry L. Stimson Papers, Yale University Library. See also Root to Kellogg, Mar. 13, 1920, Elihu Root Papers, Library of Congress, Box 138.

silent in the compromise efforts and said nothing about the treaty since early January, denounced this new reservation as "chicanery." Likewise, Simmons conceded, "I cannot deliver sufficient votes to assist him [Lodge]."[39]

For the Democratic senators, the situation immediately took a further turn for the worse. Lodge insisted that he had not changed the substance of his reservation, but threats by the Irreconcilables and some of the strongest reservations to oppose this version moved him to change it on the Senate floor. On March 13, Lodge accepted an additional phrase proposed by Borah: "including all controversies relating to territorial integrity or political independence." Lenroot agreed to the change on the floor, and Lodge claimed that the other sponsors, who included the mild reservationists, also assented. As Herbert Margulies has pointed out, this was an important concession and one that left the Democrats with no face-saving way out.[40]

At the same time, signals were emanating from the White House that the president would have nothing to do with any kind of compromise. When Hitchcock wrote to tell about one effort, he commented, "I assume that you would not accept it." Across the bottom of the letter, Wilson wrote, "You are quite right." Glass and Burleson also reported to Tumulty that the earlier letter to Hitchcock might not be enough to stem defections among the senators. They urged the president to write a letter to Simmons restating his opposition to the Lodge reservations. Although Tumulty drafted such a letter, the editors of the *Papers of Wilson* do not believe that it was sent. Still, some newspapers stated that Wilson had written to Hitchcock again rejecting the Lodge reservations. Between Lodge's stiffening of the reservation and the reports of Wilson's unbending opposition, the Democratic compromisers threw up their hands in despair. "It looks as if the Republicans were determined from the beginning to kill the treaty by indirect means," Simmons told reporters on March 14. He said that he had been canvassing his col-

39. New York *World*, Mar. 12, 13, 1920; Kellogg to Root, Mar. 12, 1920, Root Papers, Box 138; Borah to La Follette, Mar. 11, 1920, Borah Papers, Box 770; *New York Times*, Mar. 13, 1920. See also Karger to Taft, Mar. 9, 1920, Taft Papers, reel 218. The text of this draft of the reservation is in *Congressional Record*, 66th Cong., 2nd Sess. (Mar. 13, 1920), 4363.

40. Ibid. (Mar. 13, 1920), 4264–4265; Herbert F. Margulies, *Mild Reservationists and the League of Nations Controversy in the Senate* (Columbia, Mo., 1989), 240–242. See also Lodge to Root, Mar. 13, 1920, Root Papers, Box 161.

leagues about the revised reservation. "But before we knew what could be done we were confronted with an amendment that made it worse than the original reservation."[41]

III

Those events formed the backdrop to the resumption of voting in the Senate on March 15, which began the push toward final consideration of the treaty. March 15 witnessed the second highest number of roll calls in this round of the League fight. The senators engaged in only brief discussions and voted eleven times on measures relating to the Article X reservation. These measures fell into three categories. The first consisted of three unsuccessful efforts by Irreconcilables and strong reservationists to strengthen this reservation still further. The second category consisted of six equally unsuccessful efforts by Democrats to soften the reservation slightly. The third category consisted of two roll calls on the reservation itself, one on substituting the new language accepted earlier by Lodge and the other on adoption of the measure in committee of the whole. Each of these last two roll calls produced fifty-six votes in favor. They included sixteen Democrats who voted for the substitution and fouteen for the reservation; both times, between ten and twelve westerners joined the familiar defectors. All but one of the opposing votes, twenty-four and twenty-six, came from Democrats; one Irreconcilable, Norris, also voted against the substitution.[42]

Debate could have ended at this point, and the Senate could have moved directly to a vote on the treaty. The roll calls on the Article X reservation completed approval of a package that contained exactly the same fourteen reservations, with only minor verbal changes, as the Lodge reservations of the previous November. Pro-League forces faced

41. Hitchcock to Wilson, [ca. Mar. 11, 1920], in Link, ed., *Papers of Wilson*, LXV, 80; *New York Times*, Mar. 15, 1920. See also Tumulty to Wilson, Mar. 11, 1920, in Link, ed., *Papers of Wilson*, LXV, 81–82; Tumulty to Edith Wilson, Mar. 11, 1920, ibid., 82 and 82 n. 1.

42. *Congressional Record*, 66th Cong., 2nd Sess. (Mar. 15, 1920), 4324–4333. There were a few other anomalies in voting. Several pro-administration southerners also opposed one of the Democratic amendments, and one of their Irreconcilables, Thomas, was announced against both the substitution and the reservation. One other effort by an Irreconcilable – the addition of a declaration of anticolonial principles proposed by France – also lost on a voice vote. Ibid. (Mar. 15, 1920), 4332.

the identical choice of four months earlier – whether or not to acquiesce in the Lodge reservations and accept the treaty with these restrictions. As the *World*'s editorials had already indicated, nearly every League advocate – now including all the leaders of the LEP and virtually all pro-League newspapers – was advocating ratification on this basis as half a loaf worth taking. It was also clear that a number of Democratic senators were leaning that way. After these votes on March 15, reporters at the Capitol were estimating that just under half the Democrats, twenty-three in all, would break with Wilson. That would make a total of fifty-eight for and thirty-eight against – seven votes short of the necessary two-thirds. Lodge agreed, although he told reporters that the treaty might fall short by as few as four votes. These proved to be accurate predictions of the vote on consent.[43]

The closeness of the likely outcome put a brake on any rush to final judgment. Several senators grasped at possible straws of compromise. One was Lenroot, who had emerged as the most active of the mild reservationists during this round of the League fight. On March 16, he told reporters that he would introduce a further reservation stating, "It shall be the declared policy of this Government that, the freedom and peace of Europe being again threatened by any power or combination of powers, the United States will regard such a situation with grave concern, and will consider what, if any, action it will take in the premises." Lenroot explained that he believed this reservation offered a promising meeting ground for senators of various persuasions. He had drafted it in consultation with several colleagues, and it embodied the language of the Knox doctrine. Meanwhile, such Democrats as Simmons and Smith of Georgia were busy concocting ideas for face-saving modifications to the Article X reservation. Bryan also announced that he was coming to Washington to lobby his party brethren to take the treaty on any terms they could get.[44]

The Senate took no votes on March 16 but gave the day over to speechmaking. A reservation offered by Owen criticizing Britain's protectorate over Egypt touched off a round of denunciations of British imperialism and expressions of sympathy for subject peoples. Shields introduced an amendment to Owen's reservation to include Ireland and then denounced the League as incompatible with "the doctrine of the fathers that the United States should not interfere in the affairs of foreign countries; that we should have no entangling alliances with foreign governments." Borah used Owen's reservation as a pretext to denounce the treaty and the League as "this gigantic autocracy, built upon sheer

43. *New York Times*, Mar. 16, 1920; New York *World*, Mar. 16, 1920.
44. New York *World*, Mar. 17, 1920.

power and dependent for its existence upon sheer force." Again citing Keynes's revelations and surveying the expansion of colonial domains, Borah declared, "There never sat in the history of the world such an imperialistic body as that which convened at Versailles." Walsh of Massachusetts also denounced the treaty for gross betrayals of self-determination and asserted that "Article 10 undertakes to maintain the present conditions of the world, with all its injustices to little nations, for force of arms. Article 10 sounds the death knell for little nations now in bondage."[45]

The next day, March 17, brought a resumption of voting on reservations, with only scattered speechmaking. Of the five roll calls taken that day, four dealt with quixotic reservations such as Owen's on Egypt as amended to include Ireland, all of which failed. The only speeches interspersed among these votes were King's plea to approve the treaty and Lodge's recollection of his last talks with Roosevelt: "We were in entire agreement. The position that I have taken throughout and that I take now had his entire approval."[46]

The fifth reservation and last to come to a vote on March 17 was Lenroot's attempt to attach the Knox doctrine, stating American concern for the peace of Europe, to ratification of the treaty. Lenroot allowed the reservation to be compromised somewhat when he accepted an amendment offered by Borah. The amendment repeated a phrase that Elihu Root had coined in a recent speech: "Reserving the independent and uncontrolled power to throw its [the United States'] influence and its weight, whenever the occasion arises, in favor of what it deems to be right in the affairs of the world." This reservation elicited the most spirited speaking of the day. Lenroot asserted that there was "no obligation, . . . no covenant, to take any action . . . [but] we are free to take such action, as in our judgment, justice and right shall warrant." That assertion moved the Democrats' fiercest Wilsonian loyalist, Williams, to dismiss Lenroot's reservation as "this foolish little amendment" and to charge that these reservations had "extracted the teeth from the League of Nations . . . [and] emasculated the treaty." For himself, Williams avowed, "I would infinitely rather that the United States stayed out of the league than to enter it with such reservations and conditions as emasculated the agreement." This was the closest that the senators came to hearing Wilson's views from his own mouth.[47]

45. *Congressional Record*, 66th Cong., 2nd Sess. (Mar. 16, 1920), 4382–4383, 4392–4393, 4395–4396.
46. Ibid. (Mar. 17, 1920), 4444–4458.
47. Ibid. (Mar. 17, 1920), 4458–4462.

The vote on Lenroot's reservation showed how much weight the president still carried among his party brethren in the Senate. The reservation failed to carry, with twenty-five in favor and thirty-nine against. Of the opponents, thirty-one were Democrats, with three more announced against. Joining them were eight Republicans, all but one of them Irreconcilables, including Borah. Only two Democrats broke ranks to vote for the reservation. The twenty-three Republicans voting in favor spanned the entire spectrum of party opinion on the treaty, from mild reservationists to ultra-strong reservationists, including Lodge. None of the Irreconcilables did – not even the original proponent of this doctrine. Knox was absent and did not announce his stand one way or the other.[48]

A final decision on the treaty was fast approaching. Before the vote on the Lenroot reservation, several senators expressed the hope that the next day's session would be the last. After this vote the Senate agreed by unanimous consent to limit speaking on any further reservations or amendments to fifteen minutes per person. The next day's session turned into a marathon of roll calls, as the Senate took nineteen votes, the second highest number of any day in the entire League fight. There were so many votes in part because of the need to dispose of a few more individual motions and in part because of last-ditch Democratic attempts to modify the Article X reservation. Established alignments held firm on all these votes. But the biggest reason so many votes occurred on March 18 could be stated in one word – Ireland. Without warning or explanation, Peter Gerry of Rhode Island, a freshman Democrat, offered a reservation that affirmed "the principle of self-determination" and reiterated sympathy for "the aspirations of the Irish people for a government of their own choosing." The reservation also urged that an independent Ireland "should promptly be admitted as a member of the League of Nations." This reservation set off furious verbal exchanges and prompted repeated attempts to amend and table it. In all, the Gerry reservation accounted for eleven of the nineteen roll calls taken on March 18.[49]

On the Gerry reservation, expected alignments among the senators went haywire. Hitchcock became the first senator to speak in favor of the reservation. Kellogg was the first to oppose it, voicing the main theme of Republican opposition. He protested his pro-Irish sentiments, but he harked back to the Civil War to reject the declaration of self-determination. He maintained that "to announce the doctrine that we

48. Ibid. (Mar. 17, 1920), 4464.
49. Ibid. (Mar. 18, 1920), 4499.

will at all times place our approval upon the secession of a part of a sovereign nation is something that I do not think we ought to do." Lodge similarly avowed his affection for the Irish but rejected "the general principle that is embodied in the reservation, because I think it is unreal; it does not exist in the treaty at all." The rest of the debate on the reservation consisted of declarations of pro-Irish sentiments by Irreconcilables and Democrats and rejections of self-determination by Republicans. Other Democrats, most notably Williams, also condemned the reservation as not germane to the treaty.[50]

This reservation spawned so many roll-call votes because the Republicans treated it like a snake that they were trying to kill or defang. They repeatedly offered amendments to excise references to self-determination or to narrow its scope. Such efforts notwithstanding, the Gerry reservation passed twice. First, in the committee of the whole, it received thirty-eight votes in favor and thirty-six opposed. Of the Democrats, twenty-two voted and five announced for it, whereas thirteen voted and one announced against it. Those who opposed the reservation were nearly all southerners and Wilsonian loyalists, but so were several who favored it, including Hitchcock. Among the Republicans, sixteen voted in favor and sixteen voted against. Those approving the reservation were mostly but not exclusively Irreconcilables, whereas the opponents included Lodge, Kellogg, Lenroot, and others of all persuasions. The second vote came on final adoption, with forty-five for and thirty-eight against. This time the Democratic division stood at twenty-two voting and one announced in favor and eighteen voting and one announced in opposition. The Republicans split was twenty-three for and twenty against.[51]

Within the parties, only one clear differentiation separated who stood which way on the Gerry reservation. All but one of the Irreconcilables, the ever eccentric Thomas, voted for the reservation. Otherwise, Democrats and Republicans of all persuasions voted on both sides. The leaders of both parties voted both ways. Among the Democratic leaders, Hitchcock favored and Underwood opposed the reservation; among the Republican leaders, Lodge and Cummins opposed and Curtis supported it. Although some observers believed that these party divisions reflected desires to appease Irish Americans, that does not seem to have been a major influence. Rather, the votes on the Gerry reservation reflected fatigue and impatience at this late stage in the debate, confusion over

50. Ibid. (Mar. 18, 1920), 4504–4511, 4513–4520.
51. Ibid. (Mar. 18, 1920), 4503, 4512–4513, 4519–4520, 4522, 4527–4528, 4530–4532.

Table 8.1 *Senatorial Support for Wilson Administration Position on Treaty of Versailles, 66th Congress, 2nd Session**

% support	Senators (Democrat, *Republican*, <u>Irreconcilable</u>)
100	Smith (Ariz.)†
98	Simmons
97	Glass, Robinson
96	Jones (N.M.)
95	Comer†, Dial, Gay
94	Culberson
93	Ransdell, Swanson†, Walsh (Mont.)
92	Smith (Md.)
91	Beckham, Harris, Smith (S.C.), Underwood†
90	Hitchcock
89	Gerry
88	Harrison, King, Overman, Sheppard, Stanley†, Wolcott
87	Kendrick, Williams
85	McKellar
84	Fletcher, Johnson (S.Dak.)
79	Pomerene, Trammell
76	Pittman
73	Myers, Nugent
71	Owen
68	Kirby
67	Phelan
65	Chamberlain
64	Henderson
63	Ashurst
62	*McCumber*†
61	<u>Thomas</u>
56	Smith (Ga.)
50	<u>*Penrose*</u>†
44	*Harding*
33	*Ball, Dillingham, Hale, Kellogg, Newberry,*† *Townsend*
32	*Keyes, Lenroot*
31	*Elkins, Phipps*
30	*Calder, Edge, Sterling*
29	*Colt, Cummins*
28	*Nelson,*† *Watson*
27	*Curtis, Page*
26	*Lodge, New, Wadsworth*
25	*Capper, Spencer, Warren*
24	<u>*Johnson*</u> *(Calif.),*† *McLean, McNary*
21	*Kenyon*
20	<u>*Fall,*</u>† *Gore*
19	<u>*Fernald,*</u> *Jones* (Wash.), *Smoot*

(continued)

Table 8.1   *(continued)*

18	*Sutherland*
17	*Frelinghuysen*
16	Shields, *Brandegee*
14	*Borah, Gronna, La Follette, Norris*
13	*France*
11	*Knox, Moses, Poindexter*
10	Reed, Walsh (Mass.)
9	*Sherman*
8	*McCormick*

*Based upon seventy-six roll calls. Percentages are calculated on number of times senator supported Wilson position on votes cast. Total number of senators is ninety-six, although ninety-seven persons served during this period. Bankhead died on March 1, 1920, without casting any votes; his successor, Comer, took his seat on March 5 and participated in the last two weeks' voting. Senators voting on less than 50 percent of the roll calls are marked with a †.

about Democratic defections. During the previous session, the mean support percentage among non-Irreconcilable Democrats had been 92.5; with the reservationists excluded, it had been 97.2. Moreover, in that earlier session more than half of these senators had backed the president on at least 98 percent of their votes. Now, as noted, 85 percent marked the point on the scale above which half of them registered their support. Still, it remained an open question whether enough Democrats would bolt to supply the necessary two-thirds for consent with the Lodge reservations. This would have required twenty-nine or thirty of them to cross over, reaching up to the 90 percent support level.

On the Republican side, the continuity was even more striking. Once again, the only senator from that side of the aisle who supported the Wilson administration position more than half the time was McCumber. Just two others, Penrose and Harding, supported that position on more than a third of their votes. In fact, these three senators' scores represented something of a statistical fluke, which requires explanation. Of these three, only Harding either voted or announced his stand on more than half of the roll calls, and he was recorded just 55 percent of the time. During the rest of this year and in the next, first as the Republican presidential candidate and then as president, Harding would show how misleading it would have been to think him a friend of the League. Of the other two, McCumber voted or announced only eight times, and Penrose only twice. Ironically, Penrose's 50 percent support level reflected his voting against consent to the treaty, which was in accord with Wilson's wishes. Like Shields, Penrose was now joining the Irreconcilables.[54]

Even with those statistical anomalies noted, the mean level of non-Irreconcilable Republican support for Wilson's position showed only minuscule change from what it had been four months earlier. Now, it stood at 26.4 percent, whereas earlier, it had stood at 27.4 percent. Again, excluding McCumber, the mean level of Republican support was 25.4 percent, as opposed to 26.2 percent during the previous round. Curiously, the mean level of support among the Irreconcilables showed a slight rise to 18.2 percent, up from 14.6 percent the previous session. As before, however, removing their deviant, Thomas, lowered the mean to 15.6 percent. Also removing the extreme statistical fluke, Penrose, lowered it further to 13.2 percent, which compared with 12.4 percent without Thomas in the previous session.

The only noteworthy change among the Republicans involved the mild reservationists, again excluding McCumber. Now, none of them voted or announced for the Wilson administration position more than one-third of the time. This was down from their 41 to 49 percent level of earlier support. Although these senators still tended to cluster at the high end of Republican support, some of them now were interspersed among previously stronger reservationists. Perhaps Wilson's slur about "mild nullifiers" contained a grain of truth. Lodge had also been correct in saying that some of these senators were not really mild in their opposition to obligations under Article X and other parts of the treaty. This greater congruence between the mild reservationists and the rest of the Republicans stemmed in part from Lodge's patience in dealing with all party factions and even more from repugnance at Wilson's intransigence.

IV

The day of reckoning in this round of the League fight arrived on March 19, 1920, exactly four months after the same day in the previous round. These two days were a study in contrasts. This time, debate lasted only a little over six hours – not much longer than on an ordinary day in the Senate. The senators voted only five times: on a last-minute reservation offered by Brandegee, on consent to the treaty with the

54. The eleven senators who participated in less than half the roll calls were, with the percentages of votes cast, Comer (20%), Fall (7%), Johnson (Calif.) (39%), *McCumber* (11%), *Nelson* (39%), *Newberry* (4%), Penrose (3%), Smith (Arizona) (4%), Stanley (47%), Swanson (37%), Underwood (33%). As noted earlier, Comer did not take his seat until March 5 and was unable to particpate in earlier roll calls.

Lodge reservations and Gerry reservation, on a motion to return the treaty to the president, on a motion to reconsider, and on a motion to adjourn. The last three votes represented efforts to keep consideration of the treaty alive. Unlike four months earlier, when the outcome had been foreordained stalemate, now there did seem to be a real chance of a two-thirds vote for consent. As the New York *World* noted, "There was no certainty up to the moment of voting that the treaty would be beaten finally." Visitors filled every seat in the galleries. Although twelve senators were absent, the floor was crowded with members of the House. "It was as exciting a day as has been seen in the Senate since the declaration of war," the *World* also observed.[55]

For so weighty an occasion, debate and voting opened on an almost frivolous note. Brandegee made a last stab at mischief making with his reservation, which would have required an exchange of ratifications with other signatories to the treaty within sixty days. This reservation was intended to force Wilson's hand. The time limit, which Brandegee magnanimously extended to ninety days, would have compelled the president to swallow the reservations and complete the process of ratification, rather than sit on the matter in hopes of favorable developments later. Hitchcock ridiculed "the improbable condition of this treaty going to the President, and . . . the improbable condition of his accepting it." He also twitted Brandegee for setting a deadline instead of making the upcoming election "a referendum." Brandegee responded that he would be glad to hold such a referendum, and he scoffed at those who were "burning up with the ardor of a young lover to . . . become a member of the grand congress of the rough riders and militarists of the world." The reservation failed to pass by just one vote, forty-one for and forty-two against. Three Democrats – Reed, Shields, and Walsh of Massachusetts – joined thirty-eight Republicans in favor; three Republicans – Cummins, Wesley Jones of Washington, and Charles Townsend of Michigan – joined thirty-nine Democrats in opposition.[56]

After that roll call, all of the senators who spoke at any length urged their colleagues to vote for consent with the Lodge and Gerry reservations. Each of them directed his arguments at possibly wavering Democrats. The two Republicans who spoke, both mild reservationists, tried to shame them. "The course followed by President Wilson and his followers commands the admiration of no one," asserted Lenroot, who claimed that "break the heart of the world" was just what Wilson now proposed to do. Lenroot also observed that the "heart of the covenant

55. New York *World*, Mar. 20, 1920. See also *New York Times*, Mar. 20, 1920; *Washington Post*, Mar. 20, 1920.
56. *Congressional Record*, 66th Cong., 2nd Sess. (Mar. 19, 1920), 4569–4574.

changed its place many times on the western trip" but that only since his illness had the president said that without Article X it "would be nothing but a scrap of paper." Edge sarcastically congratulated "the irreconcilables on both sides for their clever alliance" to defeat the treaty. "Let us ratify the treaty," Edge implored, ". . . and let us clear the decks here so that we can assume the responsibilities for which we were elected and try to solve some of the pressing domestic problems the uncertainty of which is holding back every type of home development."[57]

The main speakers on this last day were eight Democrats who cast their lot for consent with these reservations. All but one of these senators took his stand regretfully, strictly out of necessity. Park Trammell of Florida maintained that even with the reservations, "there remains enough of good in the plan of the League of Nations for us to give it a trial." Pomerene preached the virtue of compromise and denied Wilson's "nullification" charge. "My soul rebels," Pomerene concluded, "at the thought that 'I shall do nothing because I can not do all that I feel I ought to do.'" King seconded the contention that "even with the reservation to article 10" the treaty could still "bring peace to a distracted world." Joseph Ransdell of Louisiana likewise argued that the League Covenant, though "in some respects greatly weakened, is a powerful instrument for good and entitled to be called an international charter for peace." Myers maintained, despite his disagreement with provisions of the covenant and some reservations, that American membership in the League would brace up other nations "to stand firmly, stoutly, resolutely, and unwaveringly for the rights of humanity and the enforcement of justice."[58]

The only one of these Democrats who put a positive face on his position was Hoke Smith. He praised the reservations as "essential and right," and he claimed that this Lodge reservation to Article X did not differ in any important way from the substitutes that Simmons had previously offered. Because Smith had long since taken his stand as an outspoken reservationist, his remarks may have had a certain I-told-you-so quality, but they also had a quality of desperation. Unusual for a southern Democrat, Smith faced attacks at home not only from Wilson loyalists but also and more ominously from anti-League activists. Chief among his anti-League attackers in Georgia were Thomas Hardwick, his former Senate colleague, and Tom Watson, the one-time Populist turned virulent racist and anti-Semitic demagogue. Watson would soon be calling him "Straddle-bug Smith" and a "blend of Wilsonism and William Howard Taft." Perhaps because he was already feeling so much political heat, Smith drew a comparison between Wilson's commitment now to the

57. Ibid. (Mar. 19, 1929), 4574–4575, 4581.
58. Ibid. (Mar. 19, 1920), 4574, 4578–4580, 4585–4588.

League and Bryan's commitment two decades earlier to free silver. He predicted that history would repeat itself with another electoral disaster for the Democrats. "I presume I would have to do as I did [then]," Smith sighed. ". . . I voted the ticket, but publicly stated that I hoped I would never live long enough to see such a heresy enacted into legislation."[59]

The best speeches by Democratic senators on this final day were the longest and the last ones. The longest and, according to reporters, most impressive performance came from Thomas Walsh of Montana. He made no bones about facing an alternative that was "in a high degree distasteful," either to reject the treaty or to accept it "with reservations that emasculate, if they do not destroy, features that . . . are in no small degree essential to its successful operation as a means to prevent war." Blame for this predicament fell, in Walsh's view, both on Republican senators who had taken a "hypercritical" and obstructionist stance toward the League and on Wilson for his obduracy. For himself, Walsh stated that he had "no hesitancy whatever" in voting for consent with these reservations because, "qualified as it is, it is the best that can be secured." Trying to make League membership an election issue would not improve the situation, he believed; ". . . it is rare that the result of any national election can be regarded as an unequivocal endorsement of any particular issue."

Notwithstanding his disappointment that "article 10 is destroyed so far as the United States is in any sense obligated," Walsh took heart that it remained in the Covenant for other nations to observe and uphold. Walsh also pronounced himself "satisfied upon mature reflection that I myself attached to it [Article X] undue importance. I believe it can be demonstrated that almost, if not quite all, that is or will be accomplished by article 10 is secured to the world by other provisions of the covenant." He deplored the present reservation to that article "because my pride as an American suffers at proposing to the other leagued nations that we come in entitled to any benefits accruing under the system, but decline to assume our proportionate share of the burdens." But Walsh concluded that those who supported the reservations were "men as high-minded as I can claim to be, no less jealous of the honor of the country. . . . Reluctantly I yield my judgment to theirs on that point, and, having dismissed it, the path of duty is perfectly clear to me – so clear that in my conviction there is 'no variables, neither shadow nor turning.'"[60]

59. Ibid. (Mar. 19, 1920), 4588–4593; Watson quoted in Dewey W. Grantham, Jr., *Hoke Smith and the Politics of the New South* (Baton Rouge, La., 1958), 349. On the anti-League sentiment in Georgia and the political fallout for Smith, see note 80 in Chapter 6 of this book.
60. *Congressional Record*, 66th Cong., 2nd Sess. (Mar. 19, 1920), 4581–4585. For reporters' reactions to Walsh's speech, see New York *World*, Mar. 20, 1920.

The last to speak was Owen, who delivered a characteristically plain-spoken argument. He maintained that all but one of the reservations had "no great harm in any of them." The remaining reservation, the one to Article X, also struck him as essentially the same as the Simmons substitute. Since that was the case, Owen did "not believe there is a single Democratic Senator who would not vote for this resolution of ratification if it were not for the belief of such Senators that the President of the United States desires them to defeat the resolution of ratification now pending and would regard their failure to do so as a refusal to follow his view as party leader." Owen implored his brethren to think and act otherwise: ". . . it is not to the interest of the country; it is not to the interest of the Democratic Party to defeat this ratification." Owen deemed it his "duty to the Senate and to the Constitution of the United States, deeply conscious of my duty to the people of our beloved country," to vote for the treaty. "Those who advise the defeat of the resolution may take their own responsibilities."[61]

The debate ended with Owen's speech. Unexpectedly, no other senators wished to speak. Cries of "Vote" rang out in the chamber. After a quorum call, the standard procedure to allow stragglers to get to the floor, the roll call began at 6 o'clock in an atmosphere of suspense. No one knew which way several Democrats would vote. All afternoon, Hitchcock had been making, as he reported to Wilson, "the most strenuous efforts on my part to prevent a majority of the democratic senators from surrendering to Lodge and his reservations." Those defectors made Hitchcock's task tougher, as he explained to Secretary of State Colby: "Every one of the twenty-three already committed to the Lodge reservations is a committee of one to drag others in. I experienced the greatest difficulty in holding twenty-four democrats and some of them were very dubious." Also at the Capitol lobbying the Democratic senators to stick with the president were Postmaster General Burleson and Secretary of the Navy Daniels.[62]

At the beginning of the vote, the Democrats did appear to be deserting Wilson. Three of the first four to answer the roll call – Ashurst, Joseph Beckham of Kentucky, and George Chamberlain of Oregon – answered "Aye." Next came Charles Culberson of Texas, who had not announced which way he leaned. There were rumors that if he voted in favor there might be a stampede in favor of consent. According to later

61. *Congressional Record*, 66th Cong., 2nd Sess. (Mar. 19, 1920), 4593–4596.
62. Hitchcock to Wilson, Mar. 20, 1920, in Link, ed., *Papers of Wilson*, LXV, 109; Hicthcock to Colby, Mar. 29, 1920, ibid., 150. On the lobbying efforts, see also McKellar to Burleson, Mar. 20, 1920, ibid., 120; *New York Times*, Mar. 20, 1920; New York *World*, Mar. 20, 1920; Lodge to Gillett, July 26, 1920, Lodge Papers.

stories, Culberson looked perplexed and hesitated before he answered "Nay." After that, there were no further surprises. The treaty again failed to gain the necessary two-thirds. This time, however, the margin was much narrower than before. On the roll call, forty-nine senators voted in favor and thirty-five against – seven short of two-thirds. The line-up of the full Senate, with the announced positions of twelve absentees accounted for, stood at fifty-seven for and thirty-nine against – also seven short of two-thirds.[63]

This alignment differed from the one four months earlier in a minor and a major way. The minor difference was that two formerly strong reservationists, Penrose and Shields, now joined the Irreconcilables. The major difference was the division among the Democrats. Hitchcock was only technically correct and a bit disingenuous when he claimed to have held twenty-four Democrats in line behind the president. Three of the Democrats who voted against consent – Reed, Thomas, and now Shields – did so because they were Irreconcilables. A majority of non-Irreconcilable Democrats, twenty-three, voted for consent. It was a stinging rebuke to Wilson.

Table 8.2 shows the division among non-Irreconcilable Democrats on the vote for consent to the treaty. It also shows their states and their overall support for the administration position in this round of the League fight.

As the percentages of support show, this alignment was predictable from the patterns of voting established earlier. The mean level of support among those who voted against consent was 95 percent. Among those who voted for consent, the mean level of support was 77.7 percent.

This table also sheds light on why more Democrats did not vote for consent. Several commentators, such as Taft's man Karger, were quick to blame their failure to bolt on the South. As the table indicates, there was merit in that charge. Of the twenty-five non-Irreconcilable Democrats from the former Confederate states plus Kentucky and Oklahoma, seven favored and eighteen opposed consent. Of these senators, only Williams and Glass, who was personally close to Wilson, appear to have voted against consent out of personal conviction. At least some of these southerners seem to have been more willing than their party brethren to go down with Wilson's ship because they feared reprisals from the president. In fact, three of them would lose their bids for renomination in 1920. Gore and Kirby, who had voted for a number of

---

63. *Congressional Record*, 66th Cong., 2nd Sess., (Mar. 19, 1920), 4598–4599. For accounts of the vote, see also *New York Times*, Mar. 20, 1920; New York *World*, Mar. 20, 1920. The story of Culberson's hesitation is in Thomas A. Bailey, *Woodrow Wilson and the Great Betrayal* (New York, 1945), 267.

Table 8.2   *Voting by Non-Irreconcilable Democratic Senators on Consent to the Treaty of Versailles, March 19, 1920*

Senator	State	% Support of Wilson	Senator	State	% Support of Wilson
For			**Against**		
Ashurst	Ariz.	63	Comer	Ala.	95
Beckham	Ky.	91	Culberson	Tex.	94
Chamberlain	Oreg.	65	Dial	S.C.	95
Fletcher	Fla.	84	Gay	La.	95
Gerry	R.I.	89	Glass	Va.	97
Gore	Okla.	20	Harris	Ga.	91
Henderson	Nev.	64	Harrison	Miss.	88
Jones	N.Mex.	96	Hitchcock	Neb.	90
Kendrick	Wyo.	87	Johnson	S.Dak.	84
King	Utah	88	Kirby	Ark.	68
Myers	Mont.	78	McKellar	Tenn.	85
Nugent	Ida.	73	Overman	N.C.	88
Owen	Okla.	71	Robinson	Ark.	97
Phelan	Calif.	67	Sheppard	Tex.	88
Pittman	Nev.	76	Simmons	N.C.	98
Pomerene	Ohio	79	Smith	Ariz.	100
Ransdell	La.	93	Smith	S.C.	91
Smith	Ga.	56	Stanley	Ky.	88
Smith	Md.	92	Swanson	Va.	93
Trammell	Fla.	79	Underwood	Ala.	91
Walsh	Mass.	10	Williams	Miss.	87
Walsh	Mont.	93			
Wolcott	Del.	88			

reservations but against consent, would fall to challenges by pro-administration candidates. By contrast, Smith would lose to the anti-League candidate, Tom Watson, but in part because a Wilson loyalist would split the pro-League vote with Smith.[64]

The oddest and most disappointing performance by a Democratic

64. See Karger to Taft, Mar. 20, 1920, Taft Papers, reel 218. For another statement of the "southern" interpretation, see Bailey, *Wilson and Great Betrayal,* 272. On Gore's defeat, see Monroe Billington, *Thomas P. Gore: Oklahoma's Blind Senator* (Norman, Okla., 1967), 120–124; on Kirby's, see Robert Johnson, *The Peace Progressives and American Foreign Relations* (Cambridge, Mass., 1995), 68; on Smith's, see Grantham, *Smith,* 356–357.

senator came from Underwood. Lansing's "commander" did not play his expected role. After his earlier effort to promote compromise, Underwood had dropped out of the debate. He had not spoken again on the floor after early January, and he had taken part in less than half of the roll calls. Now he voted against consent without explanation. Why Underwood lay low was not clear. He may have been playing it safe in his race for the party leadership, which he did win a month later. But on March 19, his earlier supporters were almost evenly divided between those who voted for and against consent, whereas nearly two-thirds of Hitchcock's supporters were for consent. Furthermore, Underwood would later prove to be a model of bipartisan cooperation in foreign policy with Lodge and Republican administrations in the 1920s. It was a shame that he did not behave differently in this round of the League fight. There was no one else who could have provided southern Democrats with the political cover that they needed in order to defy Wilson.[65]

Following the vote on consent, the senators spent another hour and a half in procedural wrangling. Lodge moved to return the treaty to the president. Hitchcock objected, asking, ". . . why not take a day or two in which to consider the matter?" Lodge responded that his motion followed the Senate's customary procedure, and he added, "Personally I have gone as far as I think I am justified in going to get the treaty ratified. I think, in justice to the country and to the business of the country, we should officially inform the President of the action of the Senate." Both the mild reservationist Lenroot and the Wilsonian loyalist Williams agreed with Lodge, and the motion passed forty-seven to thirty-seven. Six Democrats, including Williams, joined the Republicans to vote in favor, with all of the opposition coming from Democrats. Another administration stalwart, Robinson, thereupon tried a last-ditch ploy to keep consideration of the treaty alive – a motion to reconsider the vote on consent. Seven mild reservationists joined the Democrats to defeat a Republican effort to table Robinson's motion. According to reporters,

65. Underwood did later partially excuse himself by noting that Wilson had threatened to refuse to ratify if the Senate voted for consent with these reservations. "It is nothing but a political move for us to agree to terms that would be rejected by the President." Underwood to Oscar Straus, Apr. 30, 1920, Oscar W. Underwood Papers, Alabama Department of History and Archives, Box 39. See also Underwood to Le Roy Percy, May 18, 1920, ibid. On Underwood's later cooperation with Lodge and the Republicans, see Evans C. Johnson, *Oscar W. Underwood: A Political Biography* (Baton Rouge, La., 1980), 312–317. Underwood never mentions the League or the treaty fight at all in his memoir, *Drifting Sands of Party Politics* (New York, 1928).

mild reservationists and Democrats were huddling in the cloakrooms to talk about passing the motion and taking a second vote on consent to the treaty. On the floor, Brandegee objected that Robinson's motion was out of order, and Cummins, who was presiding, ruled that it was out of order. Lodge then said that he would not object to a second vote on the treaty "if it can be understood that we may take the vote without debate. I should like, if possible, to finish this business to-night."[66]

The senators did finish that evening, on notes that were both comic and sad. Robinson now made a motion to adjourn, which lost thirty-five to forty-one. Hitchcock continued to urge that "we might have a day or two to cool off, and there might possibly be some adjustment." To that McCormick shot back, "Senators on the other side must be getting pretty cool." They were. Robinson withdrew his motion to reconsider, and that was the end of the senators' consideration of the treaty. Before they could adjourn for the day, however, Knox moved to bring up his proposed joint congressional resolution to end the state of war. Several Democrats immediately objected. On the Republican side, Lenroot agreed, but he added, ". . . I think the Senate should proceed in the very near future to take up the subject which is covered in the Senator's joint resolution." This was a clear sign that the mild reservationists had given up on consent to the treaty. Finally, after the close of business, as Ashurst recorded in his diary, "The Republican leaders searched for Mr. Sanderson, Secretary of the Senate, to send the Treaty to the White House forthwith, but, to their disgust, Mr. Sanderson had gone home. He was soon brought back to the Senate by savage words shouted to him over the telephone." Early the next morning, Sanderson carried the same bound volume of the Treaty of Versailles that President Wilson had presented to the Senate eight months before back to the White House. There it would remain, never to be ratified by the United States.[67]

V

Reactions to the outcome of this round of the League fight were different from those four months earlier. Editorial opinion predictably divided along party lines. Republican newspapers blamed Wilson, and Democratic ones generally claimed that no treaty was better than one with the Lodge

66. *Congressional Record*, 66th Cong., 2nd Sess. (Mar. 19, 1920), 4600–4602. On the huddling between the mild reservationists and the Democrats, see *New York Times*, Mar. 20, 1920; New York *World*, Mar. 20, 1920; and Margulies, *Mild Reservationists*, 254–255.
67. Congressional Record, 66th Cong., 2nd Sess. (Mar. 19, 1920), 4602–4604; entry, Mar. 19, 1920, Ashurst Diary, in Sparks, ed., *Many-Colored Toga*, 125.

reservations. Among independent newspapers, the *New York Times* excoriated the "Senate's prolonged and disgraceful exhibition of mean-spirited partisanship," but it also conceded, "The wreck of the Treaty is so complete that the country may well despair of any salvation." Karger reported to Taft that "the League defeat naturally stirred the public tongue. But here, as elsewhere, the chief interest centers about beer and light wines. There is more talk of that than of anything else." Karger was referring to efforts to mitigate the impact of the Volstead Act, the statute that enforced prohibition under the Eighteenth Amendment. Karger was picking up on both the yearning of politicians and the public to move on to other concerns and the first rumblings of what would become one of the most heated and divisive issues of the coming decade.[68]

Even the principal figures in the League fight reacted curiously to this outcome. The Irreconcilables displayed little jubilation. After this vote, Alice Roosevelt Longworth threw another party for them, but things were not the same. "Everyone was tired," she recalled later in her memoirs, "– the day had been long, exhausting, and confusing. It was an exceptionally stupid party – an anticlimax – not like the amusing, unpremeditated evening four months before." Hiram Johnson wrote three letters to his sons in California during the last days of this round of consideration, and he never mentioned the final vote on the treaty. Still, Alice Longworth remembered one other thing about the Irreconcilables' reactions: "For weeks it was really comic how we missed having the League to fight about."[69]

Lodge also gave conflicting signals as to how he felt about the demise of the treaty. One of his biographers later related a story told by Lodge's friend and Roosevelt's sister, Corinne Robinson, who was at his house when he returned from the Capitol on March 19. The senator, she recalled, "went into his library with a heavy brow" and said to her, "Just as I expected to get my Democrats to vote with my Republicans on going into the League, a hand came out of the White House and prevented our going into the League with reservations." By contrast, Lodge wrote to an anti-League activist three days later:

> I do feel rather like a boy let out of school, for week-days and Sundays, all day and many evenings have been absorbed for nearly a year now in the everlasting discussions about the League, the reser-

68. *New York Times,* Mar. 20, 1920; Karger to Taft, Mar. 20, 1920, Taft Papers, reel 218. For a sampling of editorial opinion, see *New York Times,* Mar. 20, 1920.
69. Alice Roosevelt Longworth, *Crowded Hours* (New York, 1933), 303. See Johnson to Hiram Jr. and Arch M. Johnson, Mar. 18, 19, 20, 1920, in Robert E. Burke, ed., *The Diary Letters of Hiram Johnson* (New York, 1983), III.

vations, the practical question of getting the votes and holding the party together. I think on the whole we have done rather well. We have succeeded twice in creating a situation where Wilson either had to take the treaty or else was obliged to defeat it. He has twice taken the second alternative. His personal selfishness goes beyond what I have ever seen in any human being. It is so extreme that it is entirely unenlightened and stupid.[70]

It is tempting to accept the contemporary statement as the more accurate barometer of Lodge's sentiment and dismiss Mrs. Robinson's later recollection. But that would be a mistake. There are good grounds for believing that Lodge was genuinely disappointed at the outcome on March 19. During this round of the League fight, unlike earlier, he seemed to show a real interest in securing consent with his reservations. Both his initial conduct during the bipartisan talks and his later willingness to let Watson dicker with Simmons indicated receptivity to compromise on some matters, even to offer a face-saving retreat to Democrats on Article X. In 1937, Borah told Thomas Bailey that he thought Lodge had been at heart a "League man." Furthermore, the failure to gain two-thirds for consent was not the best tactical victory from his standpoint. It would have been better still to have gotten even more Democrats to defect – enough to supply the necessary margin for consent – and thereby force Wilson to refuse to ratify. That would have been the sweetest revenge of all.[71]

70. Robinson quoted in Karl Schriftgiesser, *The Gentleman from Massachusetts: Henry Cabot Lodge* (Boston, 1944), 350–351; Lodge to James M. Beck, Mar. 22, 1920, Lodge Papers.
71. Borah quoted in Bailey, *Wilson and Great Betrayal*, 407. William Widenor comes to the same conclusion that Lodge sincerely desired to see consent with his reservations. See William C. Widenor, *Henry Cabot Lodge and the Search for an American Foreign Policy* (Berkeley, Calif., 1980), 332–333, 335. This view argues against the view that Lodge was a closet Irreconcilable who sought to defeat League membership through subterfuge and indirection. In fairness, it should be noted that not only League advocates and Wilsonians took that view. Lodge's biographer, Schriftgiesser, also quotes Lodge's daughter, Constance Lodge Gardner, as saying:

> My father hated and feared the Wilson League and his heart was really with the irreconcilables. But it was uncertain whether this league could be beaten straight out this way, and the object of his reservations was so to emasculate the Wilson league that if it did pass it would be valueless and the United States would be honorably safeguarded. My father never wanted the Wilson league, and when it was finally defeated he was like a man from whom a great burden was lifted.

Gardner quoted in Schriftgiesser, *Gentleman from Massachusetts*, 351.

Still, for Lodge, the failure to gain consent with his reservations had one great advantage: It wiped the foreign policy slate clean for the Republican party. Consent with the Lodge reservations would have put heavy pressure on the Republicans to take a stand for League membership on those terms in the 1920 campaign and election. Then, assuming, as seemed all but dead certain, that the Republican nominee won, as president he would almost certainly have had to complete the ratification of the Treaty of Versailles and take the United States into the League of Nations. Instead, with the treaty defeated in the Senate and in constitutional limbo, the Republicans could do as they pleased. Some of them, such as Taft and the mild reservationists, still hoped for its resurrection with these reservations. Others had different ideas. The Knox resolution presented a tactical alternative for making peace, and the occasionally aired idea of an "association of nations" suggested a possible longer-range strategy. Also, a recent speech by Root, which several senators had mentioned in the debate, had outlined approaches to a Republican foreign policy – one that could reap the fruits of involvement in world politics while avoiding the snares of Wilsonian obligations. This result afforded excellent opportunities to pursue what Lodge regarded as his and his party's correct vision of great-power nationalism.[72]

Wilson did not view the vote on March 19 philosophically, at least not immediately. According to a memorandum that Grayson wrote the next day, the president did not learn about the Senate's action until that morning, when Mrs. Wilson broke the news to him. "The President after hearing this adverse news showed every evidence of being very blue and depressed," Grayson wrote in a memorandum the next day. "He said to me: 'I feel like going to bed and staying there.'" Grayson left other, conflicting accounts of when the president heard the news and how he took it. In that same memorandum, Grayson also said that Wilson had slept soundly through the night. On March 25, however, he wrote another memorandum that stated, "The night of March 19th was a very restless one for the President. He was doing a lot of thinking and worrying and holding his tongue. I was with him in his bedroom several times during the night. At about three o'clock while with him he turned to me and said: 'Doctor, the devil is a very busy man.' This is all he said." Later, in his published memoir, Grayson wove these two accounts together and added that Wilson had asked him to read aloud to him from the Bible, Second Corinthians 4:8 – "We are troubled on every side, yet not distressed; we are perplexed, but not in despair." After Grayson finished reading, Wilson said to him, "If I were not a Christian, I think I should

---

72. Cf. the analysis in Margulies, *Mild Reservationists,* 273, and Widenor, *Lodge and American Foreign Policy,* 341–342.

go mad, but my faith in God holds me to the belief that he is in some way working out His own plans through human perversity and mistakes."[73]

In those later accounts, Grayson almost certainly added apocryphal embellishments and confused Wilson's subsequent reflections with his immediate reaction. If the president felt as depressed as the doctor recorded the next day, it is not completely clear why Wilson felt that way. The defection of so many Democrats to vote for consent with the Lodge reservations was embarrassing, and he later expressed special bitterness at Walsh of Montana. But at this time he probably did not know who had said and done what in the Senate. Besides, enough Democrats had stood by him to spare him the greater embarrassment of having to refuse to ratify. Three days later, Wilson thanked Hitchcock for having held the line. "You did everything possible to secure its [the treaty's] passage," he wrote on March 23, "and to protect us from the injury to our honor and to the peace of the world which has been done by the Republican majority in the Senate."[74]

During the week after the vote, Wilson's reactions bounced around among defiance, fantasy, and resignation. On March 25, Grayson noted in that second memorandum that Wilson had "the first talk . . . with me on the subject of the League of Nations since the defeat of the treaty in the Senate." What precipitated their talk was a letter Tumulty had written to Mrs. Wilson, in which he advised that the president should announce his intention not to run for another term in order to facilitate making the League an issue in the campaign. Wilson not only rejected Tumulty's advice, Grayson recorded, but he also believed that by the time of the Democratic convention

> there may be a demand for someone to lead them out of the wilderness. The members of the Convention may feel that I am the logical one to lead – perhaps the only one to champion this cause. In such circumstances I would feel obliged to accept the nomination even if I thought it would cost me my life. I have given my vitality, almost my life, for the League of Nations, and I would rather lead a fight for the League of Nations and lose both my reputation and my life rather than to shirk a duty of this kind if it is absolutely necessary for me to make the fight and if there is no one else to do it.[75]

73. Grayson memorandum, Mar. 20, 1920, in Link, ed., *Papers of Wilson*, LXV, 108; Grayson memorandum, Mar. 25, 1920, ibid., 125; Cary T. Grayson, *Woodrow Wilson: An Intimate Memoir* (New York, 1960), 109.

74. Wilson to Hitchcock, Mar. 23, 1920, in Link, ed., *Papers of Wilson*, LXV, 116. For Wilson's expression of bitterness toward Walsh, see entry, May 31, 1920, Homer Cummings Diary, ibid., 349.

75. Grayson memorandum, Mar. 25, 1920, in Link, ed., *Papers of Wilson*, LXV, 123. For Tumulty's letter, see Tumulty to Edith Wilson, Mar. 23, 1290, ibid., 117–119.

Such illusions of indispensability have a way of turning into self-ful-filling prophecies. For Wilson, this marked the beginning of the saddest chapter in the saga of his disability, the bid to get another presidential nomination and run for a third term. Secretary of State Colby would become his tool and accomplice. Only the combined and surreptitious exertions of Mrs. Wilson, Grayson, Tumulty, and Secretary of the Navy Daniels would prevent this delusional scheme from seeing the light of day. Even discounting his personal fantasies, Wilson's reaction showed how totally obsessed he had become with the League and how bitter he remained toward his adversaries. Later in March, Grayson recorded his saying that the League "is the birth of the spirit of the times" and that "those who oppose it will be gibbeted and occupy an unenviable position in history alongside Benedict Arnold."[76]

But those were not Wilson's only reactions. On March 26, Grayson also recorded in a memorandum that he said, "It is evident[ly] too soon for the country to accept the League – not ready for it. May have to break the heart of the world and the pocketbook of the world before the League will be accepted and appreciated." This reaction undoubt-edly stemmed in part from the severe mood swings that Wilson was undergoing. Grayson noted several times at the end of March how depressed and emotionally fragile the president could be. Also, at the middle of April Grayson recorded a long conversation in which Wilson talked about resigning and about how he had "had nothing but discour-agement from those who should support me" and how "many have failed me in this crucial time." Yet something else was at work, too. This was the first glimmer of the philosophical acceptance of the defeat of the treaty and the League that Wilson would later privately express several times, much to the surprise of those who heard him. What he would stress later and what he hinted at now was his recognition that he might have reached too far and tried to commit his people and his nation to too much. Even in his stroke-weakened frame of mind, Wilson could grasp that the League fight was over and what had really been at stake in it. Unfortunately, more bitterness and conflict would intervene before he and others would face those facts.[77]

76. Grayson memorandum, Mar. 31, 1920, ibid., 149. See also Grayson memo-randum, Mar. 30, 1920, ibid., 145.
77. Grayson memoranda, Mar. 26, 1920, Apr. 13, 1920, ibid., 125, 179. For Wilson's later expressions of philosophical acceptance of the defeat of the League, see John Milton Cooper, Jr., *The Warrior and the Priest: Woodrow Wilson and Theodore Roosevelt* (Cambridge, Mass., 1983), 345.

9

Parting Shots and Echoes

In 1925, the expatriate American poet Thomas Stearns Eliot published what soon became one of his most famous poems, "The Hollow Men." Its last two lines became the best remembered words that Eliot ever wrote:

> This is the way the world ends
> Not with a bang but a whimper.

This was the way the League fight ended. After the last vote in the Senate on March 19, 1920, the issue of ratification of the Treaty of Versailles and League membership would continue to bang around for a while. But the League fight was over. No branch of the American government at either end of Pennsylvania Avenue would ever again deal with that peace treaty or with joining the League. In a little over a year after that last vote, this great controversy would fade away with just a few barely audible whimpers. Its only revival would occur two decades later in a brief, spectacular, but illusory reenactment and reversal.

I

After the vote in the Senate on March 19, the foreign policy initiative passed to the Republicans. They moved quickly to fill the void left by this second and presumably final defeat of consent to the peace treaty. Knox reintroduced his resolution to end the state of war with Germany on March 19, minutes after the vote on the treaty. But before the senators could act, the Republicans in the other wing of the Capitol beat them to the punch. The House of Representatives had previously remained quiescent. Only a few representative had spoken out, sporadically and strictly along partisan lines. They seem to have been deferring to the Senate's sole role in treaty making. Ending the war by congressional resolution was a different matter. Between March 24 and 26, the chairman of the Foreign Affairs Committee, Stephen Porter of Pennsylvania, conferred several times in person and by letter and telephone with former Secretary of State Lansing about a war-ending resolution. Porter then introduced a joint resolution to end the state of war, and on April 8 the Rules Committee brought the measure to the floor under a rule that allowed no amendments and required a final vote the next day.[1]

The House's foreshortened debate also bore out the saying about history repeating itself as farce. The Republican chairman of the Rules Committee, Philip Campbell of Kansas, jibed at Wilson, "Then, 'he kept us out of war,' now he keeps us out of peace." The committee's ranking Democrat, Edward Pou of North Carolina, shot back that "this so-called peace resolution . . . was introduced for the purpose of embarrassing President Wilson." Party lines held firm during the debate, and the only new issues raised in this debate were the legality and constitutionality of ending the war by congressional resolution instead of a peace treaty. Personalities also entered into the debate. Theodore Roosevelt's son-in-law, Nicholas Longworth of Ohio, publicly damned Wilson the same way that his wife had been doing privately for months. He called for "an American peace, a peace of which . . . Roosevelt would not have been ashamed." Claude Kitchin of North Carolina delivered an impassioned defense of Wilson. He was the former majority leader who had broken party ranks in 1917 to vote against the declaration of war. Toward the end of his speech, Kitchin started to suffer symptoms of a stroke which, like Wilson's, left him partially paralyzed and a invalid for the remaining three years of his life.[2]

The House voted three times on this resolution, and all three votes largely followed party lines. First, the rule to consider the measure passed, 214 to 155. Crossing over to favor it were seven Democrats, three of them from New York and two from Massachusetts. Only one Republican, Alvan Fuller of Massachusetts, opposed the rule. Next, a

1. For Porter's consultations, see Lansing memorandum, Mar. 26, 1920, Lansing Papers, Vol. 52. Another Republican member of the committee, John Jacob Rogers of Massachusetts, also consuslted with Chandler Anderson and Henry White. See White to Rogers, Mar. 26, 1920, Henry White Papers, Library of Congress, Box 23, and entry, Apr. 2, 1920, Anderson Diary. See also *Congressional Record*, 66th Cong., 2nd Sess. (Apr. 18, 1920), 5336b. For a fine account of the House and Senate debates on these resolutions to end the war, see Lloyd E. Ambrosius, *Woodrow Wilson and the American Diplomatic Tradition: The Treaty Fight in Perspective* (New York, 1987), 252–257.

2. *Congressional Record*, 66th Cong., 2nd Sess. (Apr. 8, 1920), 5336–5383; (Apr. 9, 1920), 5408–5479, 9371–9375. Only two representatives crossed party lines in the debate. One Democrat, George Huddleston of Alabama, supported the resolution, and one Republican, Patrick Kelley of Michigan, opposed it. On Kitchin's stroke, see Alex Matthews Arnett, *Claude Kitchin and the Wilson War Policies* (Boston, 1937), 292–295.

Democratic move to recommit and thereby kill the resolution failed, with 171 in favor and 222 opposed. The only party deviants on this vote were two Republicans who supported recommittal, Fuller and Patrick Kelley of Michigan, and two Democrats from Massachusetts who opposed it. Finally, the resolution passed, 242 to 150. The difference in the margin from the previous vote derived from the defection of twenty-two Democrats who favored the resolution. Of these defectors, twelve were from New York and three were from Massachusetts; there was a heavy sprinkling of Irish surnames among them. The same two Republicans, Fuller and Kelley, again joined the opposition.[3]

Gratifying as the House's action was to many Republicans, it raised problems. The main problem, in the opinion of Knox and other senators, was that this resolution said nothing about the rights and powers of the United States as one of the victorious belligerents. Particularly pressing were questions regarding seized German property and compensation for claims against wartime damage and losses. Knox therefore drafted a substitute for the House resolution. This new Knox resolution covered the previously unmentioned areas by asserting that the United States retained all rights and privileges under the Armistice and the Treaty of Versailles. It also declared an end to the state of war with Austria-Hungary. On April 30, the Foreign Relations Committee approved the substitution of this resolution for the House's version, and Lodge reported it to the floor.[4]

Senate debate on this resolution, such as it was, opened on May 5. Knox delivered a lengthy disquisition on the propriety and necessity of ending the war in this way, and he attacked Wilson as both an obstacle to peace and a long-standing usurper of Congress' war powers. Knox closed with a call for a new international conference to draw up "an arrangement providing for the codification of international law, the establishment of a court of international justice, and the outlawry of war. . . . It remains open to us, so long as we are unbound by the proposed discredited covenant, to initiate such an agreement among the nations." Thereafter, debate proceeded in a desultory fashion, which probably reflected the senators' fatigue with the

3. *Congressional Record*, 66th Cong., 2nd Sess. (Apr. 8, 1920), 5345; (Apr. 9, 1920), 5479–5481. See also *New York Times*, Apr. 9, 10, 1920. Fuller later served as governor of Massachusetts and gained a measure of fame for reviewing the trial of Sacco and Vanzetti but refusing to commute their death sentences.

4. On the drafting of this Knox resolution, see Knox to Anderson, Apr. 27, 1920, Chandler P. Anderson Papers, Library of Congress, Box 56; Anderson to George G. Wilson, May 4, 1920, ibid. The *New York Times* reported that the Foreign Relations Committee approved Knox's resolution on a straight party vote, but it also reported that McCumber said he was opposed to it. See *New York Times*, May 1, 1920.

whole question of peacemaking. On May 15, the Senate approved this resolution, forty-three to thirty-eight. Two additional senators, both Republicans, were announced for, and five others were announced against, four Democrats and McCumber. Crossing party lines to vote for the resolution were three predictable Democrats, the Irreconcilables Reed and Shields, along with Walsh of Massachusetts. The only Republicans who crossed over in the opposite direction were the two of the mildest of the mild reservationists – Nelson, who voted against the resolution, and McCumber, who announced his opposition but did not vote because of a pair arrangement.[5]

On May 21, the House approved the Knox resolution in place of its earlier version, 228 to 130. Once more, only the same two Republicans opposed the measure; nineteen Democrats, mostly the same ones as earlier, supported it. Wilson had already issued a public statement urging his party to "proclaim itself the uncompromising champion of the Nation's honor and the advocate of everything that the United States can do in the service of humanity" through ratification of the Treaty of Versailles without reservations. On May 27, he issued a veto message. Passage of the Knox resolution would leave, he declared, "an ineffaceable stain upon the gallantry and honor of the United States" and would require "a complete surrender of the rights of the United States." The following day, the House failed to override the veto, 220 to 152 – twenty-eight votes short of the necessary two-thirds. Seventeen Democrats, largely the same ones as on previous votes, favored the override, and the same two Republicans opposed it. From the Republicans' standpoint, this failure to override Wilson's veto was a delicious outcome. Now, they could denounce him as an obstacle to peace more convincingly than ever.[6]

Before this session of the Sixty-sixth Congress adjourned on June 5, the Senate Republicans made one last move in their diplomatic game. On May 13, Warren Harding introduced a resolution that expressed sympathy for the Armenians' "deplorable conditions of insecurity, starvation, and misery." Harding's resolution also affirmed support for Armenian independence and called for the dispatch of a warship and marines to protect the lives and property of American citizens there. The Senate passed this resolution unanimously by voice vote and without debate. Wilson responded on May 24 with a message to Congress urging the passage of legislation to allow the United States to assume a

---

5. *Congressional Record,* 66th Cong., 2nd Sess. (May 5, 1920), 6556–6566; (May 15, 1920), 7101–7102.
6. Wilson press release, May 10, 1920, in Link, ed., *The Papers of Woodrow Wilson* (Princeton, N.J., 1990), LXV, 263–264; veto message, May 27, 1920, ibid., 328–329; *Congressional Record,* 66th Cong., 2nd Sess. (May 21, 1920), 7429; (May 28, 1920), 7808–7809.

League mandate over Armenia. The Republican senators gave his request the back of their hand. On June 1, they adopted a resolution drafted by Knox that rejected the mandate, by a vote of fifty-two to twenty-three. Not a single Republican favored the mandate, not even McCumber or that erstwhile champion of the Armenians, Lodge. The three Democratic Irreconcilables and ten other Democrats likewise voted for Knox's resolution and against the mandate.[7]

Republicans also seized the foreign policy initiative through their party conventions. Those conventions met in various states during the first half of 1920 and then at the national level in Chicago in June. The leaders in this effort were Root and Lodge, although they did not always work in harmony. Root got into the act early. In a widely publicized speech to the New York State Republican convention in February, Root lauded his party brethren in the Senate for guarding against "the terrible mistake of Article X." Instead, Root maintained, ". . . the sense of justice and independent and uncontrolled power of the United States to throw its weight whenever occasion arises in favor of what it deems to be right in the affairs of the world is the greatest single influence toward that justice among nations which is the essential requisite of peace." If and when the United States did join the League with the Lodge reservations, Root added, the next president, a Republican, "should urge upon the society of nations the reform of the League Covenant, so as to make it establish the rule of public right rather than the rule of mere expediency; so as to make the peace of the world rest primarily upon law, and upon the effectiveness and enforcement of law."[8]

The defeat of the treaty on March 19 opened a new path for the Republicans. Now they could pursue aims like the ones that Root was urging without the fetters and complications of League membership. The prime mover in this direction was Lodge. "The League, of course,

---

7. Ibid. (May 13, 1920), 6973–6979; (June 1, 1920), 8073. Wilson's message is in Link, ed., *Papers of Wilson*, LXV, 320–323. For a bitter description of how the Senate received Wilson's message, see entry, May 24, 1920, Ashurst Diary, ibid., 323–324. The Senate also defeated two amendments offered by Democrats that would have partially or fully allowed the mandate, by votes of thirty-four for and forty-one against, and twenty-eight for and forty-six against. On the first vote, four Democrats broke ranks, as did seven on the second. *Congressional Record*, 66th Cong., 2nd Sess. (June 1, 1920), 8072–8073.

8. Speech to New York State Republican convention, Feb. 19, 1920, in Robert Bacon and James Brown Scott, eds., *Men and Policies: Addresses by Elihu Root* (Cambridge, Mass., 1925), 220–221. For Root's intentions behind the speech, see entry, Feb. 22, 1920, Henry L. Stimson Diary, Yale University Library.

has been my sole occupation for more than a year," he told a friend in April, "and I do not want a mistake made if I can help it at [the Republicans' national convention in] Chicago." Root wanted to avoid such mistakes, too, but he believed that the party's platform must include, as he told Lodge in May, "a perfectly clear and unmistakable" declaration in favor of the treaty with reservations:

> That declaration in the Republican platform is going to determine in the public mind and in history whether the work that you have been doing in the last year has been a great political achievement, a successful struggle for the maintenance of our system of government, or whether it has been a mere subterfuge for the purpose of defeating by indirection a Treaty which the Senate did not dare defeat directly.[9]

That last insinuation stung, but Lodge stood his ground. He replied to Root that he agreed with the Irreconcilables that "the convention [should not] commit itself and narrow the issue for the Democrats to ratification with my reservations. They wish to leave the future free. I confess that I do myself. I do not think that we ought to undertake to bind the party or to bind our President, whom we confidently expect to elect, to a foreign policy question of this magnitude eight months beforehand." Lodge's resolve stiffened as the convention approached. "It seems to me it would be a great mistake," he told George Harvey later in May, "(I personally am not willing to do it) to bind ourselves as to the future. The scene shifts fast in Europe and I am not ready, nor are others, to bind our President – if he comes in, as I hope and believe he will –, or our Administration, or our Congress, to their action on the 4th of March."[10]

Lodge also showed Root a model foreign policy plank that he had just written. At the request of party chairman Hays and in collaboration with Knox and other senators, Lodge drafted this plank early in May for the Republican convention in Hays' home state of Indiana. The plank condemned both Wilson and the League as presented and applauded the Senate for having blocked membership without reservations. Lodge said nothing about joining the League or approving the treaty with reservations. He did state, however, "We favor an association of nations to promote peace

---

9. Lodge to Ellerton James, Apr. 24, 1920, Henry Cabot Lodge Papers, Massachusetts Historical Society; Root to Lodge, May 14, 1920, ibid. For other statements of Lodge's cooling to any kind of League membership, see Lodge to Lord Charnwood, Apr. 16, 1920, ibid.; Lodge to Bryce, Apr. 20, 1920, ibid.; Lodge to William Astor Chanler, Apr. 27, 1920, ibid.
10. Lodge to Root, May 17, 1920, Elihu Root Papers, Library of Congress, Box 161; Lodge to Harvey, May 25, 1920, Lodge Papers.

in the world." He also declared in favor of expansion of arbitration, efforts toward disarmament, and establishment of a world court. In one part that Lodge did not write, Knox resurrected his earlier doctrine:

> The Republican party also believes that it should be the declared policy of our government that [if] the freedom and peace of Europe be again threatened by any power of combination of powers, as was the case in 1914, the United States should regard such a situation with grave concern as a menace to its own peace and freedom. We believe that under such circumstances the United States should consult with other powers affected with a view to devising means for the removal of such a menace and be prepared when the necessity arises to render every service, as we did in 1917, for the defense of civilization.[11]

This plank evidently satisfied Root, and he would soon render invaluable assistance to Lodge's campaign to keep the party uncommitted on League membership. Getting the national convention to adopt a foreign policy plank along Lodge's lines proved to be a hard sell. His chief opponent on the platform committee at the convention was W. Murray Crane, Lodge's former Massachusetts colleague in the Senate. Crane was an LEP activist and a close friend of Taft, and he lobbied energetically for a strong statement in favor of League membership with the Lodge reservations in the foreign policy plank. The Irreconcilables responded by threatening to bolt and by deadlocking the platform committee during two and a half days of stormy meetings. In the end, their threats and obduracy carried the day. Another influence that swayed the committee, Crane believed, was Lodge's attitude. "Senator Lodge was very bitter in his opposition to the [pro-League] plank," he observed, "and stated openly that if it was submitted to the convention he would oppose it from the [convention] platform."[12]

11. Annotated draft of foreign policy plank, enclosed with Lodge to Root, May 17, 1920, Root Papers, Box 161. On the drafting of this plank, see also Lodge to Hays, May 9, 1920, Will H. Hays Papers, Indiana State Library, Box 5. Besides another copy of the plank that Lodge sent to Root, Hays' papers also include with this letter a foreign policy plank given to him by Kellogg and Lenroot on May 10 and an undated one by George Harvey. See ibid.

12. Crane to Lowell, June 17, 1920, Lowell Papers. For an account of Crane's effort, see Crane to Charles D. Hilles, July 3, 1920, William Howard Taft Papers, Library of Congress, reel 219. For two recollections by participants, both of questionable accuracy, see James W. Watson, *As I Knew Them* (Indianapolis, 1936), 214–216, and William Allen White, *Autobiography* (New York, 1946), 585. For a good treatment of these deliberations by a historian, see Herbert F. Margulies, *Mild Reservationists and the League of Nations Controversy in the Senate* (Columbia, Mo., 1989), 265–269.

Once more Root supplied the way out. This time he worked his magic with a draft statement that he had given earlier to another member of the platform committee, Ogden Mills. When his fellow Republicans met in Chicago, Root was on his way to Europe to participate in an international conference to set up a world court. Before leaving, he washed his hands of any effort to commit the party to League membership. "I think we shall have to get another President in office," he told Lowell, "or, at all events, elect him to office before there is any possibility of ratification." Why and when Root drafted his plank and gave it to Mills is not clear, but the old master's words did the trick. The statement read:

> The Republican party stands for agreement among the nations to preserve the peace of the world. We believe that such an international association must be based upon international justice and must provide methods which shall maintain the rule of public right by the development of law and the decision of impartial courts, and which shall secure instant and general international conference whenever peace shall be threatened.[13]

Root's artfully evasive language succeeded in burying the League issue at the Republican convention. Otherwise, their platform's foreign policy plank conformed to the model that Lodge had provided for the Indiana party – with one significant exception. Nowhere was there any mention of the Knox doctrine or any pledge to respond to future threats to peace. The closest that anyone came to making such a statement at the convention occurred when Lodge delivered the keynote speech. He laid a litany of blame on "Mr. Wilson" for all the troubles that currently beset the United States at home and abroad and repeated the

13. Republican platform in Donald Bruce Johnson and Kirk H. Porter, eds., *National Party Platforms, 1840–1972* (Urbana, Ill., 1973), 231. On Root's role in drafting the statement, see Taft to Caspar S. Yost, June 19, 1920, Taft Papers, reel 219; Lodge to Corinne Roosevelt Robinson, June 19, 1920, Lodge Papers. For his biographers' interpretations, see Philip C. Jessup, *Elihu Root* (New York, 1937), II, 410, and Richard L. Leopold, *Elihu Root and the Conservative Tradition* (Boston, 1954), 144. The American ambassador to Britain, John W. Davis, who was a Democrat but also a friend of Root, commented to Lansing, "That plank on foreign affairs is certainly the most Delphic not to say cowardly deliverance ever concocted. I doubt if Root really drew it." Davis to Lansing, June 14, 1920, Robert Lansing Papers, Library of Congress, Vol. 53. Lansing agreed, observing that the whole Republican platform "straddles from beginning to end on the live issues and is very emphatic on the dead ones. It is about as near a void as science permits." Lansing to Davis, June 27, 1920, ibid., Vol. 54.

crack, "He has kept us out of peace." Lodge also rehashed and lauded the Senate's resistance to "an alliance and not a league of peace." But he did avow that America "cannot be isolated" and must "march on and not neglect our duty to the world." If necessary, he promised, Republicans would act again as in 1917: "We threw our great weight into the wavering scale and we were all the more effective because we went in without alliance and of our own free will, as we always go to help humanity." All would be well, Lodge was saying, as soon as the country got back to tried-and-true Republican great-power politics: "We must be now and forever for Americanism and nationalism, and against internationalism. There is no safety for us, no hope that we can be of service to the world, if we do otherwise."[14]

Lodge's role as keynote speaker at the 1920 convention and the Republicans' foreign policy stand bore witness to his stature in the party. He stood at the peak of his power and influence. But Lodge's star was about to wane. Four days after he delivered his keynote address and after two days of bitter balloting, the Republican convention nominated Warren Harding for president. Thereby, Harding became the only person who might disturb the party's silence and evasion toward the League. The main excitement of the 1920 campaign would arise from his handling of that issue.

II

The Democrats entered the 1920 campaign with an albatross around their necks. Their albatross was named Wilson. Leading Democrats knew that the Republicans were mining political pay dirt with their attacks on "Mr. Wilson." People seemed unmistakably to be in a mood to blame everything that they did not like, no matter how contradictory or unfair their grievances, on the president and, by extension, his party. At the Democratic convention in June, in San Francisco, the party managers' main work consisted of trying to distance themselves from Wilson. Both the platform committee and the delegates devoted their time and energy largely to domestic issues. Prohibition proved particularly fractious and offered the first taste of the fratricidal strife that would rend the Democrats for the rest of this decade. Choosing a presidential nominee challenged the party, too. After forty-four ballots, the delegates finally settled on Governor James M. Cox of Ohio. Cox won the nomination because, like Harding, he came from the state that had been essential to the Democratic victory four years earlier. Also, unlike the

14. *New York Times,* June 9, 1920.

major contenders for the nomination, he had no connection with the Wilson administration.[15]

On the League, the Democrats did some dodging of their own. The foreign policy plank in their platform opened with the declaration: "The Democratic party favors the League of Nations as the surest, if not the only, practicable means of maintaining the permanent peace of the world and the termination of the insufferable burden of great military and naval establishments." The document went on to praise Wilson at length and to condemn Lodge and the Senate Republicans. But on the question of League membership with reservations, the plank was less than forthright: "We advocate the immediate ratification of the treaty without reservations which would impair its essential integrity; but do not oppose the acceptance of any reservations making clearer or more specific the obligations of the United States to the league associates." Did that mean ratification with the Lodge reservations? The Democratic platform deliberately said neither yes nor no.[16]

But the Democrats could not cast off their Wilsonian albatross. Fanciful as it might seem, there was a real danger that the convention might nominate him for a third term. At the end of May, the president had

15. For an account of the 1920 Democratic convention, see Wesley M. Bagby, *The Road to Normalcy: The Presidendial Campaign and Election of 1920* (Baltimore, 1962), 102–122. This convention was also the first to use microphones and loudspeakers to carry the speakers' voices throughout the hall. In a wonderfully symbolic gesture, Bryan contemptuously waved this newfangled contraption aside and addressed the throng, as always, with his unaided voice. See Paolo E. Coletta, *William Jennings Bryan* (Lincoln, Neb., 1969), III, 128. Bryan also found Cox, a moderate "wet" on prohibition, so distasteful as the party's nominee that, incorrigible partisan though he was, he came close to not endorsing Cox and refused to campaign for him. See ibid., 131–133. Before the convention, the major contenders had been McAdoo, the former secretary of the treasury and Wilson's son-in-law, and A. Mitchell Palmer, the red-baiting attorney general. McAdoo probably would have gotten the nomination if Wilson had declared himself out of the running. Another contender, though not yet much more than a favorite son, was the recently elected governor of New York, Al Smith. On those candidates, see Bagby, *Road to Normalcy,* 54–78.
16. Johnson and Porter, eds., *National Party Platforms,* 213–214. In adopting this plank, the platform committee rejected Wilson's draft of a much longer, stronger declaration that opened, "We favor the unqualified ratification of the Treaty of Versailles" and closed with a reference to the League, "The United States cannot afford to decline full participation in this great enterprise of emancipating the world from wars of aggression." Wilson statement, [May 24, 1920], in Link, ed., *Papers of Wilson,* LXV, 319.

started to work surreptitiously through Homer Cummings and Secretary of State Colby to stampede the delegates in his favor. Two weeks before the start of the convention, Wilson had granted a three-hour exclusive interview to Louis Seibold of the *World*. Seibold's story quoted extensively from Wilson's comments about the current political scene, in which he remarked on both issues and personalities, and Seibold repeatedly stressed how fit and well he looked. "I saw him transact the most important functions of his office with his old-time decisiveness, method and keenness of intellectual appraisement." By the time the convention met, only persistent, concerted efforts behind Wilson's back by Mrs. Wilson, Grayson, Tumulty, Glass, and Daniels were able to smother this scheme before it got to the floor.[17]

Even with his bid for the nomination squelched, Wilson still dominated the convention. The unveiling of a gigantic, flag-draped portrait of the president behind the platform set off a thunderous demonstration. "Men and women climbed on chairs, yelling and waving, stamping, shouting and whistling," the *New York Times* reported, and when a spotlight was beamed onto the portrait, "[o]nce more the crowd went wild." A conspicuous participant in these demonstrations was Franklin D. Roosevelt. The 38-year-old New York delegate and assistant secretary of the navy scuffled with anti-Wilson Tammany men to snatch away his state's placard and parade with it up and down the aisles. Widespread press attention to Roosevelt's gesture – together with his name, his marriage to Theodore's niece, and his New York residence – helped him receive the party's vice-presidential nomination a week later. Those demonstrations reflected more than momentary enthusiasm. Right after the convention, Postmaster General Burleson told another leading Democrat that only carefully circulated stories about Wilson's physical incapacity had prevented his nomination. "If this impression which was generally prevalent throughout the delegations could have

17. New York *World*, June 18, 19, 1920. The Seibold interview was the result of an effort of Tumulty's to show how incapacitated Wilson was – an effort that backfired. See Blum, *Joe Tumulty and the Wilson Era* (Boston, 1951), 242–244. There are a number of revealing documents about Wilson's scheme for a third nomination in Link, ed., *Papers of Wilson*, LXV. See, esp., entries, May 31, [1920], Cummings Diary, ibid., 344–350, 356–357; Wilson notes, [ca. June 10, 1920], ibid., 382; Glass memoranda, June 10, 12, 16, 19, 1920, ibid., 382, 395, 400, 435–436; Tumulty to Edith Wilson, July 4, 1920, ibid., 493–494. For another account of Grayson's efforts, see Robert Woolley's manuscript memoir, ch. 41, Woolley Papers, Box 44. This effort did not completely escape notice in the press. See *New York Times*, June 19, 20, 1920.

been removed," Burleson believed, "nothing could have kept the Convention, notwithstanding the third term bogey, from giving the President the nomination."[18]

In 1920, both parties' presidential campaigns reached back nearly a quarter of a century to find their models. The Democrats were making a virtue of necessity. Strapped for funds and suffering from widespread disaffection within their party, the Democratic nominees imitated William Jennings Bryan's 1896 practice of whistle stop speaking tours around the country. Cox and Roosevelt tried valiantly to appeal to the domestic reform sentiments that had proven so potent before the war. But, as Hiram Johnson had discovered earlier in his unsuccessful quest for the Republican nomination, those "progressive" issues simply did not catch fire in 1920. Just as Johnson had found himself appealing more and more to his Irreconcilable opposition to the League, Cox and Roosevelt stressed their support for League membership.[19]

A poignant encounter helped to cement the Democratic nominees' reliance on that issue. On July 18, Cox and Roosevelt with the president visited for nearly an hour at the White House. Claude Bowers, a Democratic publicist who was accompanying the visitors, later recalled that the sight of Wilson in his wheelchair with a shawl over his paralyzed left arm moved Cox to say, "He is a very sick man." When Cox shook hands with the president, who thanked him in a weak voice for coming, Bowers noticed that Cox had tears in his eyes. After a bit of conversation, Cox declared, "Mr. President, we are going to be a million per cent with you and your Administration, and that means the League of Nations." Wilson replied feebly, "I am very grateful. I am very grateful." The nominees then met with reporters in Tumulty's office and issued

18. Burleson to Daniel C. Roper, July 12, 1920, quoted in Link, ed., *Papers of Wilson*, LXV, 511 n. 3. On Roosevelt's gesture, see Frank Freidel, *Franklin D. Roosevelt: The Ordeal* (Boston, 1954), 63. His resemblance to TR and possible appeal to his former followers bothered the Republicans enough that they dispatched Theodore Roosevelt, Jr., to trail him and to declare on a western stop, "He is a maverick. He does not have the brand of our family." *New York Times*, Sept. 18, 1920. Privately, Lodge, with whom Roosevelt had been friendly and to whom he had once leaked damaging information about perceived inadequacies in Wilson administration defense spending and policies, likewise dismissed him. "He is a well-meaning, nice young fellow, but light," Lodge wrote to a friend. In Lodge's view, Roosevelt's later coming around to support the administration and his initial campaign utterances showed that "[h]is head evidently turned and the effect upon a not very strong man is obvious." Lodge to C. S. Groves, July 26, 1920, Lodge Papers.
19. On the Democrats' campaign, see Bagby, *Road to Normalcy*, 127–134.

statements in praise of Wilson. "What he promised," Cox avowed, "I shall, if elected, endeavor with all my strength to give."[20]

Keeping that promise to stress the League on the campaign trail soon embroiled Roosevelt in controversy. In August, he answered attacks on British Empire votes in the League Assembly by reviving a claim made earlier by Democratic senators. This was the assertion that the United States would control the votes of such Latin American countries as Cuba, Haiti, the Dominican Republic, and Panama. "We are in a very true sense the big brother of these little republics," Roosevelt declared. He recalled his own role in the navy's occupation of Haiti and the Dominican Republic and boasted, "You know I have had something to do with the running of a couple of little republics. The facts are that I wrote Haiti's Constitution myself, and, if I do say it, I think it is a pretty good constitution." Those boasts allowed Harding to profess shock and steal some of the Democrats' old anti-imperialist thunder. "I will not empower an Assistant Secretary of the Navy to draft a constitution for helpless neighbors in the West Indies," he pledged, "and jam it down their throats at the point of bayonets borne by United States Marines."[21]

Cox stuck up for League membership more discreetly, but his and Roosevelt's advocacy of the League ran up against other obstacles. The public evidently felt as apathetic toward the League as it did toward domestic reform issues. "There is a general lack of interest in the League of Nations," Roosevelt's publicity aide reported to him in August, "and many Democrats openly assert their dissatisfaction that the League was made a big issue." Moreover, the Republicans harped incessantly on Article X, which they continued to claim would commit American troops to faraway wars against the wishes of Congress and the people.[22]

As the campaign wore on, the Democratic candidates began to hedge their commitment to Wilson's program. By October, Cox was stressing

20. *New York Times,* July 13, 19, 1920; Bowers letter quoted in James M. Cox, *Journey through My Years* (New York, 1946), 241–244. For other accounts of the meeting, see Grayson memorandum, July 18, 1920, in Link, ed., *Papers of Wilson,* LXV, 520–521, and entry, [ca. July 18, 1920], ibid., 521.

21. *New York Times,* Aug. 19, 23, 1920.

22. Stephen T. Early to Roosevelt, Aug. 6, 1920, quoted in Freidel, *Roosevelt: The Ordeal,* 79 n. On Parsons' and Fisher's bolt, see Parsons to Charles D. Hilles, Aug. 25, 1920, Herbert Parsons Papers, Columbia University Library; Fisher to Lowell, Sept. 21, 1920, A. Lawrence Lowell Papers, Harvard University Archives. Other pro-League Republicans who bolted included Thomas Lamont and Theodore Marburg. See Lamont to Lowell, Sept. 1, 1920, ibid.; Marburg to Taft, July 20, 1920, Taft Papers, reel 219. On other LEP activists who supported Cox, see Ruhl J. Bartlett, *The League to Enforce Peace* (Chapel Hill, N.C., 1944), 188–189.

his support for reservations, especially toward obligations under Article X. He maintained that he would "not insist upon the Treaty just as Mr. Wilson negotiated it" and would "accept reservations . . . that as a matter of good faith will state to our associates in the League that Congress and Congress alone has the right to declare war, and that our Constitution sets up limits in legislation or treaty-making beyond which we cannot go." Roosevelt likewise declared that he favored reservations spelling out that no provisions of the treaty "[were] in any way superior to our Constitution or in any way interfere with the rights of Congress to declare war or send our soldiers overseas." Those declarations led the *New York Times* to question editorially why Wilson issued a public letter in support of Cox and Roosevelt at the end of October.[23]

For all their backsliding, the Democratic nominees looked like true believers compared with Harding and the Republicans. They, too, were harking back to an 1896 model. Harding and the Republicans deliberately imitated William McKinley's "front porch" campaign. Once more, the nominee received carefully selected delegations at his Ohio home and issued appeals crafted by market research to address the concerns of the groups that those delegations represented. This invocation of the McKinley model went deeper than campaign practices. If any presidential candidate in American history can nonpejoratively be called "reactionary," it was Harding. A month before the 1920 Republican convention, he had stated his political philosophy and coined what became the watchwords of his campaign and his presidency in his most memorable utterance: "America's present need is not heroics, but healing; not nostrums but normalcy; not revolution but restoration; not agitation, but adjustment; not surgery but serenity; not the dramatic, but the dispassionate; not experiment but equipoise; not submergence in internationality, but sustainment in triumphant nationality."[24]

That utterance's last alliterative pairing accurately forecast Harding's handling of the League issue. The entire statement also revealed what made him, fortuitously for his party, their ideal nominee in 1920. No matter whom the Democrats nominated, the Republicans were running against Wilson. For them, Harding embodied, as the historian of this election has put it, "the antithesis of Wilson: modest mediocrity rather than arrogant genius; party government rather than one-man govern-

---

23. *New York Times*, Oct. 12, 24, 30, 1920.
24. Harding speech quoted in Randolph Downes, *The Rise of Warren Harding: 1865–1920* (Columbus, Ohio, 1970), 411. On his campaign, see ibid., and Bagby, *Road to Normalcy*, 123–126. The Republican managers updated the technique to include celebrity endorsements by movie and sports stars, an exhibition game by major league baseball teams, newsreel footage of visits to Harding, and the first presidential campaign speech broadcast on radio.

ment; consultation rather than dictation; warm humanity rather than austere intellectualism; genial realism rather than strenuous idealism."[25]

Harding temporized on the League as he did on all major questions. As soon as he got the nomination, he began to cultivate prominent spokesmen on both sides of the issue. In letters, Harding lavished sweet talk on Hiram Johnson, who had left the convention making ominous noises about bolting. The tactic worked. Johnson grumblingly swallowed what he considered the nominee's standpat conservatism at home and softness toward the League abroad, and he promised to hit the campaign trail for the party ticket. Harding had an easier time at first with pro-League Republicans. Taft had known and liked him for years, despite holding his intelligence and backbone in low regard. In July the ex-president started to argue in his newspaper column that Harding's election would be the surest way to get the United States into the League of Nations. Activists on both sides of the issue also journeyed to the candidate's home, where they were treated to his winning personality and came away convinced that he agreed with them.[26]

25. Bagby, *Road to Normalcy,* 101. Later, as Harding's reputation crumbled amid scandal and ridicule, the idea would take root that the Republicans nominated him because they wanted an undemanding second-rater. That was not true. He got the nomination because he was a widely acceptable compromise candidate. It was true, however, that an antipathy to strong leadership had grown up among Republicans. For example, the governor of Kansas told his friend William Allen White, "I have a feeling that we have had all the superman business the party is likely to want and what the period really needs in my judgment is the man who is a product of our institutions and not the product of a peculiar period." Henry J. Allen to White, Mar. 23, 1920, William Allen White Papers, Library of Congress, Series C, Box 51. Taft's informant Gus Karger used the same words to describe sentiment among western progressives at the convention: ". . . they are tired of supermen of the Roosevelt and Wilson stripe anyhow, men who force their objects on the people, when it is about time for the people to force their objects on the leaders." Karger to Taft, June 25, 1920, Taft Papers, reel 219.

26. For Harding's cultivation of Johnson, see their correspondence in Harding Papers, Box 544; Hiram Johnson Papers, Bancroft Library, University of California at Berkeley, Part III, Box 42; and Johnson to Beveridge, July 27, 1920, Albert J. Beveridge Papers, Library of Congress, Box 221. An indication of how much it cost Johnson to endorse Harding can be seen in his correspondence with his friend and former Progressive comrade-in-arms Harold Ickes, who despite agreeing with Johnson on the League endorsed Cox on domestic issues. At the end of one letter, Johnson wrote by hand, "There's just one thing I'll add: 'You're a better man than I am, gungha Din.'" Johnson to Ickes, August 20, 1920, Harold Ickes Papers, Library of Congress, Box 33. Taft's endorsements are in Philadelphia *Public Ledger,* July 20, 30, Aug. 2, 1920.

Public handling of the League and the peace treaty vexed Harding much more than such private wooing. Beginning with his acceptance speech on July 22, the nominee talked out of both sides of his mouth. In the acceptance speech, Harding pledged to "hold the heritage of American nationalism unimpaired and unsurrendered" and excoriated those who wanted its "surrender, whether with interpretations, apologies, or reluctant reservations – from which our rights are to be omitted." Harding also promised as president to sign a congressional resolution to end the war. In making those statements, he bowed to urgings by Lodge not to commit himself to League membership with reservations. Conversely, he ignored pleas from Taft, Crane, and others to leave the door open to membership. He did throw a bone in their direction by alluding to a separate international organization – "an association of nations, cooperating in sublime accord, to attain and preserve peace through justice rather than force, determined to add to security through international law, so clarified that no misconstruction can be possible without affronting world honor."[27]

This effort to satisfy both sides fell flat. Irreconcilables and League advocates alike grumbled about Harding's vagueness. Nor did his next effort do any better. A month later, Harding asserted that "the League as constituted at Versailles is utterly impotent as a preventive of war," and he dismissed the League as nothing more than an alliance of great powers: "I am opposed to the very thought of our Republic becoming a party to so great an outrage upon other peoples." Yet Harding also reiterated his support for "a society of free nations, animated by right and justice, instead of might and self-interest." He believed that such an organization could "take and combine all that is good and excise all that is bad" in the present League, which perhaps could "be amended and revised" in the right direction. That hint marked the closest that Harding would come to an endorsement of League membership.[28]

Tentative as those words were, they infuriated the Irreconcilables. Borah told reporters that he feared loss of American independence in any "association of nations." He instructed the Republican National Committee to cancel his speaking engagements on behalf of the ticket. Johnson likewise grumbled about the nominee's backsliding, and he dragged his feet about hitting the hustings for Harding. Their signals got through to the nominee. Having left the front porch for the cam-

---

27. *New York Times*, July 23, 1920. For Harding's cultivation of pro-League Republicans, see Karger to Taft, July 28, Aug. 10, 18, 25, 27, 1920, Taft Papers, reels 219 and 220; and Crane to Taft, Aug. 11, 1920, ibid., reel 219.

28. *New York Times*, Aug. 29, 1920.

paign trail, Harding used a speech in Des Moines on October 7 to deliver his strongest attack yet on League membership. "I do not want to clarify those obligations," he avowed; "I want to turn my back on them. It is not interpretation, but rejection, that I am seeking. My position is that the proposed league strikes a deadly blow at our constitutional integrity and surrenders to a dangerous extent our independence of action." Harding did tip his hat toward the other side by promising that "I shall advise with the best minds in the United States . . . to the end that we shall have an association of nations for the promotion of peace." That gesture did not mask the drift of Harding's thinking. Borah immediately praised the "great speech at Des Moines," and Johnson announced that he was "ready to jump into the fight for Harding and remain in it until the campaign ends." For the rest of the campaign Harding stuck to his Des Moines formula – denunciation of the League combined with allusions to an alternative international organization.[29]

League advocates caught his drift, too. Even before the Des Moines speech, LEP activists had grown increasingly unhappy with Harding's foreign policy stands. Such GOP stalwarts as Charles Hilles and George Wickersham were privately complaining about Harding to Taft, as was his brother Henry. The ex-president, who had long since publicly nailed his colors to the party masthead, had a tough time keeping these men on board. Taft also had to demand that the LEP refrain from taking any part in the campaign. Other high-placed pro-League Republicans met in New York to discuss how to counteract Harding's apparent isolationist drift. On October 5 and 7, the "best minds" of the party's foreign policy establishment – including Root, Hughes, Henry Stimson, and Herbert Hoover, who had come out publicly as a Republican earlier in the year – considered how to offset what they saw as the insidious influence of Borah and Johnson and sway Harding in their direction after the election.[30]

29. Ibid., Oct. 8, 1920. For Borah's earlier discontent, see ibid., Oct. 2, 5, 1920.
30. For Wickersham's and Hilles' dissatisfaction with Harding, see Hilles to Taft, July 31, 1920, Taft Papers, reel 219; Hilles to Butler, Aug. 28, 1920, Nicholas Murray Butler Papers, Columbia University Library; Wickersham to Henry Taft, Sept. 7, 1920, Taft Papers, reel 220; Wickersham to Lowell, Sept. 9, 1920, Lowell Papers. For Taft's dictation to the LEP, see Taft to Short, Aug. 7, 1920, Taft Papers, reel 550. For accounts of the Republicans' meetings on October 5 and 7, see Schurman to Lowell, Oct. 5, 1920; Parsons memorandum, Oct. 11, 1920, Parsons Papers, Series III, League of Nations File, and Hughes to Wickersham, Mar. 8, 1923, Charles Evans Hughes Papers, Library of Congress, reel 4.

This conclave of foreign policy nabobs decided to issue a public statement, which they asked Root to draft. Two others who had attended the meeting, the prominent New York lawyer Paul D. Cravath and the president of Cornell University, Jacob Gould Schurman, then went over the statement with party chairman Hays before Schurman released it to the press on October 15. The signatories, who numbered thirty-one, comprised a galaxy of luminaries. Besides Root, Hughes, Stimson, and Hoover, the signers included such university presidents as Lowell, Schurman, Nicholas Murray Butler of Columbia, Frank J. Goodnow of Johns Hopkins, John Grier Hibben of Princeton, and Ray Lyman Wilbur of Stanford. Also among the signers were such leaders of the LEP as Wickersham, Henry Taft, Oscar Straus, and William Allen White.[31]

What came to be called the "Statement of the Thirty-One" bore the expected hallmarks of Root's artful draftsmanship. Affirming that the signatories "desire that the United States shall do her full part in association with other civilized nations to prevent war," the statement argued that the issue in the presidential campaign was not about "whether our country shall join such an association of nations." Rather, it was about unreserved acceptance of what Wilson had brought back from Paris. The statement quoted from Harding's earlier speeches and ignored the one at Des Moines. It also praised Republican senators for having resisted any obligation under Article X. On Article X, the signatories declared, "We cannot regard such a provision as necessary or useful for a league to enforce peace." They also affirmed their conviction that "the true course to bring America into an effective league to preserve peace is not by insisting upon the acceptance of such a provision as Article X, . . . but by

---

31. *New York Times,* Oct. 15, 1920. Of all the prominent persons asked to sign, only the president of Vassar College, Henry Noble MacCracken, publicly refused to add his name, declaring that this statement "will not in my opinion have any influence on Senator Harding's foreign policy." Ibid. The signers included the presidents of all the Ivy League colleges and universities except Yale and Pennsylvania, and also MacCracken's brother, who was president of Lehigh. An ardently pro-League Republican, Herbert Parsons, had been present at one of the earlier meetings, but he had made it clear that he wanted nothing to do with the statement and would not support Harding. See Parsons memorandum, Oct. 11, 1920, Parsons Papers, Series III, League of Nations File. On the discussions with Hays, see Cravath to Root, Oct. 11, 13, 1920, Root Papers, Box 138. There is an edited draft of the statement in the Hays Papers, Box 7. A good account of the evolution of this statement is in Lloyd E. Ambrosius, *Woodrow Wilson and the American Diplomatic Tradition: The Treaty Fight in Perspective* (New York, 1987), 282–285.

frankly calling upon the other nations to agree to changes in the proposed agreement which will obviate this vital objection." For those reasons, the Thirty-One concluded that they could "most effectively
advance the cause of international co-operation to promote peace by
supporting Mr. Harding for election to the Presidency."[32]

In view of Harding's subsequent actions, many critics later dismissed
the Statement of the Thirty-One as an exercise in wishful thinking and
self-deception. At least two of the signatories, Hughes and Stimson, later
betrayed a guilty conscience over their roles in the statement and the
campaign. But it was unlikely that the Thirty-One fooled themselves
about how Harding was leaning. Rather, they seem to have been trying
to maintain a modicum of influence over him and seeking to arrest large-
scale defections by their pro-League party brethren. Their ploy worked
in part. Few prominent Republicans bolted over the League issue.[33]

But the Thirty-One failed in their larger aim. After the election,
Harding went through the motions of listening to advocates on both
sides of the League question. He also asked Schurman to study possibilities for a new international organization that might promote disarmament, set up a world court, extend international law, and call conferences to deal with various problems. Harding maintained his
noncommittal public posture until after he entered the White House. In
his inaugural address on March 4, 1921, he sent mixed signals on foreign policy. On the one hand, he praised America's "inherited policy of
non-involvement in Old World affairs," and he declared, "We do not
mean to be entangled." That policy, Harding asserted, ruled out any
"permanent military alliance" and "political commitments." On the
other hand, he avowed America's readiness to join "with the nations of

32. *New York Times*, Oct. 15, 1920.
33. For Hughes' betrayal of a guilty conscience, see Hughes to Wickersham,
    Mar. 8, 1923, Hughes Papers, reel 4, which is a seventeen-page exercise in
    overprotesting the correctness of his actions and an implicit defense of his
    not having resigned as secretary of state when Harding refused to push for
    League membership with reservations. For Stimson's statement, see his con-
    fession of error and posthumous apology to Parsons in Henry Stimson and
    McGeorge Bundy, *On Active Service in Peace and War* (New York, 1948),
    105–106. White may also have felt guilty over his role because he includes
    a sheepish, garbled account of the campaign in his *Autobiography,* (New
    York, 1948), 596. For the interpretation of the signers' motives, see
    Leopold, *Root,* 147–148; and for the interpretation of the statement's
    effect, see Bartlett, *League to Enforce Peace,* 191–192, and Freidel, *Roo-
    sevelt: The Ordeal,* 89–90.

the world great and small, for counsel, to seek the express views of world opinion, to recommend a way to approximate disarmament, . . . to clarify and write the laws of international relationships and establish a world court." Above all, the new president pledged his nation's participation "in any seemly program to lessen the probability of war."[34]

Harding ended the suspense over which way he would fall on League membership on April 12, 1921, with his first address to Congress. The statement on the League came at the end of the fifty-five-minute speech. "In the existing League of Nations, world-governing with its super-powers," Harding declared, "this Republic will have no part. There can be no misinterpretation, and there will be no betrayal of the deliberate expression of the American people in the recent election; and, settled in our decision ourselves, it is only fair to say to the world in general, and to our associates in war, that the League covenant can have no sanction from us." Also, in renewing his pledge to seek an "[i]nternational association for permanent peace," Harding dismissed the League as "constituted for the dual functions of a political instrument of the conquerors and an agency of peace." In addition, he reiterated his campaign promise to sign a congressional resolution to end the state of war with Germany and the former Austria-Hungary, while reserving victors' rights under the Treaty of Versailles. He repeatedly promised participation in "an association to promote peace," in which Americans would "play our fullest part in joining the peoples of the world in pursuits of peace once more."[35]

That was it. That was the last whimper that ended the League fight. Why Harding acted as he did puzzled some observers. Both diehard Wilsonians and some Irreconcilables claimed that he had really opposed League membership all along but had lacked the courage to come out forthrightly against it. Those claims were incorrect. The scholars who have most carefully examined Harding's public and private utterances throughout the League fight have concluded that he really was what he said he was – a strong reservationist who cared most about keeping the Republican party together and winning the 1920 election.[36]

Some others believed that Harding waffled on League membership down to the last minute. His attorney general, Harry Daugherty, later

34. *New York Times*, Mar. 5, 1921. On Harding's dealings with Schurman, see ibid., Jan. 15, 1921; and Schurman to Harding, Feb. 23, 1921, Jacob Gould Schurman Papers, Cornell University Library, Box 3.
35. *Congressional Record*, 67th Cong., 1st Sess. (Apr. 12, 1921), 172–173.
36. Of all the more recent works on Harding, the one that demonstrates most strongly his position toward the League is Downs, *Rise of Harding*.

recounted that he and Mrs. Harding went over the draft of the April 12 speech the night before and excised anything that might hint at possible League membership. That recollection did not ring true. Harding's declaration against the League was too explicit for last-minute tinkering. Besides, he had told Lodge three months earlier that "the country does not want the Versailles League." Harding meant what he said when he professed to be bowing to the will of the people as expressed in the 1920 election. Others shared that view. Lodge and such Irreconcilables as Borah and Johnson took gleeful delight in interpreting their party's sweeping success as a resounding rejection of League membership. Some historians would later endorse their interpretation and call this election a "referendum for isolation."[37]

This view contains some truth, but not the whole truth. Any American presidential election turns on many factors and circumstances, and that was especially true of the Republican triumph in 1920. Outside the South, the Democrats lost nearly everything there was to lose. Not a single nonsouthern Democratic candidate for the Senate won, not even in such normally safe states as Arizona and Oklahoma. In the House, the Republicans swelled their majority to 303 seats. In gubernatorial races, not a single Democrat beyond the borders of the former Confederacy survived the GOP juggernaut, not even the dynamic Al Smith of New York. Likewise, the party's urban strongholds in the Northeast, including Boston and New York City, went Republican. So did two states of the hitherto solid South, Tennessee and Texas. The result was so overwhelming that Underwood called it "the tidal wave."[38]

Actually, this tidal wave altered the political shoreline less than met the eye in November 1920. The outcome of that election hinged more on negative than positive factors. Turnout fell markedly from previous elections, and for the first time in American history less than half of all eligible voters cast ballots. The Democrats fared so badly not so much

37. Harding to Lodge, Dec. 29, 1920, Harding Papers, Box 544. For the story about Daugherty's and Mrs. Harding's excisions from the speech, see Francis Russell, *The Shadow of Blooming Grove: Warren G. Harding and His Times* (New York, 1968), 455–456. For Lodge's and the Irreconcilables' interpretations of the election results, see, for example, Lodge to William Lawrence, Nov. 6, 1920, Lodge Papers; Lodge to McCormick, Nov. 13, 1920, ibid.; and Henry Cabot Lodge, *The Senate and The League of Nations* (New York, 1925), 210.

38. Underwood to Cordell Hull, Dec. 10, 1920, Cordell Hull Papers, Library of Congress, reel 1. For the best assessment of the election results, see Bagby, *Road to Normalcy*.

because people actively turned against them as because so many people who usually supported the party stayed home. Foreign policy influenced the depressed turnout, especially among voters of Irish, German, and Italian extraction, who resented their homelands' treatment at Wilson's hands during the war and at the peace conference. But this influence should not be exaggerated. Several studies of voting in 1920 have found that those ethnic groups did not desert the Democrats in any greater proportion than the electorate generally. The Republicans' good fortune and the Democrats' travail proved equally evanescent. In both of the off-year elections during the next decade, the Democrats would come close to regaining control of Congress. Similarly, the Republicans would win the next two presidential elections thanks in part to the Democrats' fratricide and disarray, and they would never duplicate their 1920 tidal wave.[39]

In electoral politics, mandates really amount to what the participants, winners and losers alike, choose to make of them. Harding read his victory at the polls as a mandate against League membership because he wanted to read it that way. Of all the advice that he received after the election, what swayed him most strongly came from Lodge. Both in person and in a stream of correspondence, Lodge argued that the best and easiest course was simply to drop League membership. He urged Harding to pursue a purely Republican foreign policy. "Whether or not we use anything in the old league is not important," Lodge urged in December 1920. "The one thing that, in my judgment, would be impossible to do, would be to join the league on the theory of making it over."[40]

Other influential Republicans came to the same conclusion as Lodge, although usually more reluctantly and for different reasons. In March 1921, when he became secretary of state, Hughes quickly learned that

39. An interesting assessment of the lack of impact of the League issue came from one of the Thirty-One, Butler, writing to Lord Bryce. While marveling at the popular repudiation of Wilson, Butler believed that the public "was bored by being talked to about the issues of the campaign. There were no issues except President Wilson. It may be doubted that more than 500,000 of the thirty million voters cast their votes with reference to the League of Nations." Butler to Bryce, Nov. 16, 1920, Butler Papers. Similarly, the woman suffrage leader Carrie Chapman Catt analyzed anti-League sentiment as a coalition of opposites, "the socialists and near-socialists" who found the League "too imperialistic and capitalistic" and conservatives who said " 'let us go back to our former isolation, 'the League plan should have been postponed' " whereas the "masses of our people are wholly befogged by the discussion." Catt to Taft, Dec. 12, 1920, Taft Papers, reel 222.
40. Lodge to Harding, Dec. 23, 1920, Lodge Papers.

seeking League membership would reignite the earlier conflict in all its nastiness, no matter what reservations might be attached. "I was reluctant to accept that view," Hughes later recalled, "and I did so only when my friends in the Senate who were favorable to the League – known as 'mild reservationists' – assured me that there was no hope of obtaining the Senate's approval of membership in the League on any terms." Outside the Senate, erstwhile Republican League advocates were in no mood to kick up a fuss, either. The LEP had withered into a tiny, inert organization, and Taft had now acquired a personal stake in not rocking the boat. Harding had promised to name him chief justice as soon as the incumbent, the ailing seventy-five-year-old Edward D. White, vacated the office, as he did when White died in May.[41]

In other ways, the 1920 election could also be legitimately read as a foreign policy mandate. Apart from the invalided president and his most obdurate supporters, nobody stood up for his program of international enforcement through an essentially political organization. The clearest signs of rejection of that program came in the way that all the candidates, Democrats as well as Republicans, shunned Article X and in the way that the losers as well as the winners chose to read the election results. For most of the next two decades, the Democrats would treat Wilsonian foreign policy like a deadly poison. The ex-president's death early in 1924 would spare him and his party embarrassment over the low-priority, arm's-length treatment and lukewarm lip service that they gave to the League that year and again in 1928. By 1932, even Wilson's staunchest defender among leading Democrats, former Secretary of War Newton Baker, would renounce his advocacy of League membership. The man who won the nomination in 1932, Franklin Roosevelt, would go still further. In order to curry favor with William Randolph Hearst, Roosevelt would humiliatingly recant his previous support for the League and other Wilsonian policies. How deeply Roosevelt had learned lessons from his party's fate in 1920 would become clearer still in the ways that he handled public opinion regarding foreign policy during his twelve years as president.[42]

41. Hughes statement in David J. Danelski and Joseph S. Tulchin, eds., *The Autobiographical Notes of Charles Evans Hughes* (Cambridge, Mass., 1973), 213. On Taft, see Pringle, *The Life and Times of William Howard Taft* (New York, 1939), II, 955–959.

42. On Democratic foreign policy stands in the 1920s, see Robert Johnson, *The Peace Progressives and American Foreign Relations* (Cambridge, Mass., 1995), 236–245, 250–252, 267–268. On Roosevelt's recantation, see Frank Freidel, *Franklin D. Roosevelt: The Triumph* (Boston, 1956), 247–248.

III

Before the future "FDR" banished the Republicans from the White House, they enjoyed a dozen years of their own administrations to pursue their 1920 foreign policy mandate. Later interpreters, with the dubious benefit of hindsight, would deride those policies as futile and illusory, tagging them with such derisive labels as "the parchment peace." Those denigrations would be grossly unfair. The first and last of the three Republican secretaries of state of this era, Hughes and Stimson, engaged in resourceful, creative diplomacy that contributed greatly to international order and stability. Hughes's coups in naval disarmament and Far Eastern affairs at the Washington Conference of 1921, together with his repeated interventions to break the impasse over reparations and war debts in Europe, helped to foster the remarkable improvement in the international climate that prevailed in the latter half of the 1920s. Stimson likewise made important forays into naval disarmament and the war debt–reparations tangle. He enjoyed less success than Hughes mainly because the international climate had begun to deteriorate in Europe and Asia. He also clashed with his president, Hoover, over how far to push the limits on American action. In all, the Republicans did well with their foreign policies during that decade.[43]

Still, things did not work out the way that Lodge, Root, Knox, and other great-power nationalists had wanted. Whether TR or anyone like him could have made much headway in the international environment of the 1920s can only be a matter of speculation. None of the leading Republican great-power restorationists exerted much influence toward strong international leadership. Knox died in the fall of 1921 without playing much part in formulating his party's foreign policy. Lodge soldiered on in the Senate as majority leader and chairman of the Foreign Relations Committee, but before his death late in 1924, he found himself marginalized within the party. Only Root lived on through this decade and into the next. He served as a judge on the World Court, which he helped set up, and he continued to bask in the reverential glow of foreign policy canonization. Yet Root exerted little real influence over his party's policies, thanks to both his advancing age and his coldly detached attitudes, and he went to his grave without seeing the United States join his beloved World Court.

This failure of great-power nationalism sprang from an even deeper

43. For attacks on that foreign policy, see J. Chal Vinson, *The Parchment Peace* (Athens, Ga., 1955), and Betty Glad, *Charles Evans Hughes and the Illusions of Innocence* (Urbana, Ill., 1966).

source than the personal and party fates of yesterday's heroes. As William Widenor has observed about Lodge, he had been "too successful for his own good" in the League fight. In order to beat Wilson's brand of internationalism, he had been "forced to adopt an insular nationalism." That observation applies equally strongly to Knox and almost as strongly to Root and perhaps, before his death, even to TR. All of them at various times consorted with and gave aid and comfort to isolationists. They abetted the growth and development of an approach to foreign policy that would help to stymie any return to traditional great-power nationalism.[44]

In the early 1920s an alternative and competing foreign policy sprang up in the Senate under the leadership of the more idealistic isolationists. They included such veteran Irreconcilables as Borah, Norris, and La Follette before his death in 1925. They gained new Republican recruits such as Robert M. La Follette, Jr., who succeeded his father, and Gerald P. Nye of North Dakota. They also attracted younger Democrats, including Burton K. Wheeler of Montana and Huey Long of Louisiana, as well as third-party men such as Henrik Shipstead of Minnesota, a Farmer–Laborite. The Republicans among them revived their prewar insurgency against their party's conservative domestic policies, which they now extended to include pursuit of an antimilitarist, anti-imperialist foreign policy.[45]

During the 1920s, this senatorial foreign policy and the Republican administrations' foreign policy resembled two of that decade's new automobiles. Sometimes they were widely separated; sometimes they sideswiped each other; sometimes they collided head-on; on two notable occasions they traveled harmoniously in tandem. Unlike the Republican administrations, the senatorial insurgents sympathized with nationalist aspirations in Africa and Asia. Borah in particular became a hero among leaders of independence movements on those continents. For these senators, anti-imperialism began at home. They opposed the interventionism in the Caribbean and Central America that had begun under prewar Republican administrations and continued under Wilson. Their persistent criticisms and harassment gradually influenced the Republican administrations of the 1920s to scale back and withdraw from military involvement in the region and, privately, to move toward a nonin-

44. Widenor, *Henry Cabot Lodge and the Search for an American Foreign Policy* (Berkeley, Calif., 1980), 347–348.
45. On these senators, see Johnson, *Peace Progressives*, esp. ch. 3–6. The younger La Follette later left the Republicans to join his brother and other Wisconsin insurgents and radicals to organize the state's Progressive party.

terventionist stance. It would remain, however, for the Democratic Roosevelt to renounce interventionism publicly and make political hay out of his "good neighbor" policy.[46]

More serious clashes with the Republican administrations occurred when the Irreconcilables compelled Harding and Hughes to shelve the "association of nations" idea and when they resisted Hughes's effort to push membership in the World Court. Despite the court's impeccably Republican parentage, Borah, Johnson, and their cohorts denounced membership as a "back door" into the League. They succeeded in blocking consideration of the World Court protocol under Harding and attached such stringent reservations under his successor, Calvin Coolidge, that the whole project had to be renegotiated. Finally, under Franklin Roosevelt, court membership failed to muster the necessary two-thirds in the Senate amid the isolationist upsurge of the mid-1930s.

These senators' influence on Republican foreign policy in the 1920s was not purely obstructionist. Twice, some of the former Irreconcilables worked together with secretaries of state to produce impressive diplomatic results. Early in the decade, Borah and others strongly supported Hughes's naval disarmament treaty and more guardedly endorsed his multilateral pacts to ease tensions in Asia. Then, at the middle of the decade, the outlawry of war advocate Salmon Levinson enlisted Borah behind his scheme. Borah, in turn, interested Hughes's successor as secretary of state, Frank Kellogg, in the project. This former mild reservationist saw a way to make a name for himself by negotiating an international pact under which signatories renounced war as an instrument of their foreign policy. When the Senate came to consider what came to be called the Kellogg–Briand Pact in 1928, the burden of winning consent to the treaty fell to Borah. This pact perfectly embodied his and other idealistic isolationists' approach to more peaceful and just international affairs through setting an example of

46. On Borah's reputation abroad, see note 37, Chapter 3. Among the Irreconcilables, the most idealistic and anti-imperialistic of them, France, did not get to play much of a role because he was defeated for reelection in 1922. Other Irreconcilables who fell by the wayside were Gronna, who lost in a primary in 1920, and McCormick, who also lost in a primary in 1924 and committed suicide before his term expired. Among the nonidealistic Irreconcilables, Poindexter was also defeated in 1922, although the man who beat him was Clarence C. Dill, who as a congressman had voted against intervention in the war and subsequently joined the peace progressive group. Brandegee did win reelection in 1920, but he also committed suicide, in October 1924. These defeats and deaths, together with the earlier death of Knox and resignation of Fall, meant that by the mid-1920s only half of the Irreconcilables remained in the Senate.

avoidance of militarism, alliances, and imperialism, and it nicely epitomized the optimistic international climate of the late 1920s.[47]

The climate died with the decade. The 1930s witnessed steady erosion of international order. The first in a string of crises exploded in
1931, when the Japanese invaded the Chinese province of Manchuria –
in defiance of the League Covenant, Hughes's Washington treaties, and
the Kellogg–Briand Pact. If ever an international controversy seemed
tailor-made for the kind of peacekeeping organization that Wilson had
envisioned, this was the one. Both the clearcut fact of aggression by the
Japanese and their vulnerability to economic sanctions and naval pressure created a situation in which the League of Nations could have
taken significant action. But the League had not lived up to Wilson's
expectations. Its dominant members, Britain and France, shrank from
even strong diplomatic condemnation. They tried to pass the buck to
the United States on the grounds that no other nation had sufficient
power in that part of the world to deter Japan. Neither side would
make the first move. Meanwhile, within the Hoover administration the
president and the secretary of state fell out over whether to threaten the
Japanese with any American action. Stimson wanted to consider the use
of force, and that collided with Hoover's determination to avoid any
thought of belligerency. The rift between them marked the first break in
the Republicans' hitherto united front on foreign policy. In the end, the
League temporized by appointing an investigative commission, which
belatedly branded Japan the aggressor. The League Council recommended no action, but Japan nevertheless withdrew from the League in
protest. It would be the first in a procession of aggrieved members to
quit the organization in the 1930s.[48]

Franklin Roosevelt's election victories in 1932 and 1936 turned the
responsibility for handling foreign policy during the rest of that decade
over to the Democrats. Shortly after Roosevelt's inauguration in 1933,
Germany, which had joined the League in 1925, also withdrew. The
newly installed chancellor, Adolf Hitler, was keeping a campaign promise.
Hitler had also pledged to undo not only Germany's allegedly unfair
treatment in the Treaty of Versailles but also his nation's defeat in the

47. The classic treatment of the Kellogg–Briand Pact is Robert A. Ferrell's
    Peace in Their Time: The Origins of the Kellogg–Briand Pact (New Haven,
    Conn., 1953). On Borah's role in the 1920s see also Johnson, *Peace Pro-
    gressives*, and Le Roy Ashby, *The Spearless Leader: Senator Borah and the
    Progressive Movement in the 1920s* (Urbana, Ill., 1972).
48. On the split between Hoover and Stimson, see Elting E. Morison, *Turmoil
    and Tradition: A Study of the Life and Times of Henry L. Stimson* (Boston,
    1960), 368–404.

world war. He started almost at once to build up his armed forces in defiance of the limits in the peace treaty, and in 1936 he openly broke the treaty by marching into the demilitarized Rhineland. By that time, the Democrats had gotten a taste of the same medicine that the Republicans had swallowed with Manchuria. In 1935, Italy, under the Fascist dictator Benito Mussolini, invaded the African nation of Ethiopia, which was also a member of the League. The Ethiopian emperor, Haile Selassie, publicly denounced Italy before the League Assembly, and he pleaded for aid to repel the Italian aggression. Once more, the British and French held back, in part because they did not want to alienate Italy over what they regarded as an unimportant bit of Africa. As before, they put out feelers to the United States, which was then the world's biggest oil exporter and could have hampered Italy's war effort with an oil embargo. President Roosevelt brushed those feelers aside, in part because he did not want to offend Italian-American voters, as Wilson had done in 1920. The League never took any action regarding Ethiopia, either, but Italy took offense and became the third nation to withdraw from the organization.[49]

Those events showed how far international order had crumbled by the middle of the 1930s. Worse was to come. Nineteen thirty-six also witnessed the outbreak of the Spanish Civil War, in which Germany and Italy openly aided the right-wing rebels. In 1937 Japan's renewed and expanded invasion of China started a full-scale war in Asia, In 1938 Germany annexed Austria, and a full-fledged European war scare resulted from Hitler's demands to annex ethnically German areas of Czechoslovakia, which had a security pact with Britain and France. The American response to these events was unmistakably and overwhelmingly isolationist. New-style public opinion polls revealed huge majorities in favor of taking steps to keep out of any wars overseas. Those polls also showed that over two-thirds of Americans had come to believe that intervention in World War I had been a mistake. Fittingly, in 1937 Congress commemorated the twentieth anniversary of the declaration of war by honoring the men and woman who had voted against it.[50]

By the same token, Wilson's reputation – which had already begun to suffer in the "debunking" climate of the 1920s fostered by Mencken and others who jeered at "Puritanism" – now plunged into the depths of derision. Various authors, now drawing upon freshly released diaries

49. On Roosevelt's response to the Italian conquest of Ethiopia, see Robert M. Dallek, *Franklin D. Roosevelt and American Foreign Policy* (New York, 1979), 110–119.
50. On the isolationist upsurge, see Robert A. Divine, *The Illusion of Neutrality* (Chicago, 1962), and Manfred Jonas, *Isolationism in America, 1935–1941* (Ithaca, N.Y., 1966).

note in the scale." This statement revealed the basic lesson that FDR had learned from the League fight – that "public psychology" and "human weakness" could not stand too much talk about deep matters. He also lauded Theodore Roosevelt for having succeeded where Wilson had failed "in stirring people to enthusiasm over specific individual events, even though these specific events may have been superficial in comparison with the fundamentals."[55]

This lesson would shape the way that Roosevelt dealt with the issues of foreign policy that dominated his presidency after 1938. More than anything else, he strove first to avoid and then to manipulate public debate about foreign policy. Even before World War II broke out in September 1939, Roosevelt broke with the isolationists and sought to aid Britain and France in Europe and China in Asia against aggression by Germany, Italy, and Japan. Yet he always publicly justified his policies and actions as ways to keep war away from America. He also repeatedly sought to obfuscate issues rather than clarify them. He did that most notoriously in his 1940 election eve assurance, "I have said this before but I shall say it again and again and again: Your boys are not going to be sent into any foreign wars."[56]

Given the persistence of isolationist sentiment and broader public repugnance toward intervention in the war from 1939 through 1941, Roosevelt probably displayed wisdom in his deviousness. In fact, he probably was not consciously being devious but was displaying his amazing capacity for psychological denial. No one in his inner circle grew more frustrated with his persistent refusal to face up to the possi-

---

55. Roosevelt to Baker, in Elliott Roosevelt, ed., *FDR: His Personal Letters* (New York, 1950), III, 466–467. Both Wilson and the League fight were evidently on FDR's mind that day since he also wrote letters to Justice Brandeis and Colonel House and instructed his secretary to invite Senator Borah to come to the White House for lunch. Ibid., 466, 467–468. In fact, FDR was reversing the political models that those two men had embodied. On his use of those models, see John Milton Cooper, Jr., *The Warrior and the Priest: Woodrow Wilson and Theodore Roosevelt* (Cambridge, Mass., 1983), 348–354.

56. Roosevelt speech at Boston, Oct. 30, 1940, in Rosenman, ed., *Public Papers of FDR,* IX, 517. To be fair, it must be remembered that he was responding to a flip-flop by his opponent, the equally pro-Allied Wendell Willkie, to attack him as a "warmonger" – charges that Willkie soon afterward dismissed as "campaign oratory." The best account of this incident is in the memoir of his speechwriter, Robert E. Sherwood, *Roosevelt and Hopkins: An Intimate History* (New York, 1948), 190–191, 200–201. "I burn inwardly," Sherwood wrote, "whenever I think of those words 'again – and again – and again.'" Ibid., 201.

ble need to enter the war than Henry Stimson. In 1940, in an early gesture toward bipartisanship, FDR appointed Stimson secretary of war. Stimson acquiesced during the 1940 campaign in the perceived necessity to avoid offending anti-interventionist sentiment. But once the election was over and throughout the first half of 1941, Stimson prodded the president with suggestions about the need to educate the public about the likelihood that the United States might have to enter the war. Roosevelt responded with evasions and vague comments about continued "aid short of war." In his frustration, Stimson compared FDR unfavorably with the way that TR would have acted. Later, writing about himself in his memoirs in the third person, he concluded, "*The essential difference between Stimson and the President was in the value they set on candor as a political weapon.*"[57]

"Uncle Ted" might or might not have acted the way that Franklin Roosevelt did in those years, but one demonstrable effect of his conduct was to help stifle the kind of debate and discussion that had flourished during the League fight. If there was any time after 1920 when such a great public debate should have taken place, it was during the two years between the outbreak of World War II and Pearl Harbor. Here was the war that Wilson and the League advocates had predicted and sought to prevent. Here was the clash between big foreign powers that the Irreconcilables and their successors had striven to keep away from America. Their debate could have resumed where the League fight had left off.

That did not happen. There were sharp and persistent clashes between pro-Allied and anti-interventionist groups. Veterans of respective sides in the League fight played prominent parts in the two major lobbying organizations on opposite sides in this conflict. Fittingly, a former LEP activist, the Kansas Republican newspaper editor William Allen White, headed the pro-Allied group, the Committee to Defend America by Aiding the Allies – better known, for short, as the "White Committee." Its opposite number, the America First Committee, drew upon precedents from the Independence League, especially in enlisting celebrity spokespersons – most notably the country's greatest popular hero, the aviator Charles A. Lindbergh. In the political arena, despite the bipartisan roles played by Stimson and White, the two parties squared off against each other on foreign policy. Yet all the heat and passion of this conflict mainly spawned mutual misrepresentation. The two sides smeared each other as "pro-Nazis" and "warmongers," and

---

57. Stimson and Bundy, *On Active Service*, 376, italics in original. See also ibid., 364–376. FDR's other big bipartisan gesture in 1940 was to appoint another old TR man and the Republicans' 1936 vice-presidential candidate, Frank Knox, secretary of the navy.

FDR ducked the hard questions about what might ultimately be required to crush the forces of evil and guarantee American security. In the end, the Japanese attack on Pearl Harbor and Hitler's sudden declaration of war in December 1941 made this conflict moot – to the evident relief of even most anti-interventionists.[58]

Following Pearl Harbor, Wilson's reputation rose from its previous denigration and quickly soared to the heights of posthumous popular apotheosis. This Wilsonian revival included an outpouring of adulatory books and magazine articles about him and, most impressive of all, "Wilson," a 1944 movie that was the most expensive production yet done in Hollywood – even more expensive than "Gone with the Wind." Wilson's resurrection also helped to ignite pressures from Congress and the public to requite his memory by carrying out his program. During World War II no organization comparable to the LEP emerged because none was needed. Isolationists and other critics of collective security and international enforcement fell silent and left the field of public discussion almost entirely to neo-Wilsonians.[59]

Meanwhile, FDR aimed many of his policies and actions at avoiding what he regarded as Wilson's mistakes. At home, he let others sell themselves and the country on a new vision of postwar international order. Diplomatically, he delegated work on an international peacekeeping organization to the lone Wilsonian in his cabinet, Secretary of State Cordell Hull. Leaving something to Hull was always a sure sign of its low priority for FDR. In another likely sign of wanting to start afresh and shed Wilsonian baggage, Roosevelt adopted Lodge's 1915 term to call his international organization the "United Nations," rather than the League of Nations, which now bore the stigma of allegedly having failed to prevent World War II. The leading American student of international organization has described the UN "as a revised version of the League," but the

58. On the White Committee, see Walter Johnson, *The Battle against Isolation* (Chicago, 1944), and William M. Tuttle, Jr., "Aid-to-the-Allies-Short-of War versus American Intervention, 1940: A Reappraisal of William Allen White's Leadership," *Journal of American History,* LVI (Mar. 1970), 840–858. White was not the only LEP veteran on his committee. Its chief staff person and organizational sparkplug was Clark M. Eichelberger, who had previously worked for the LEP during its dying days in the 1920s and for its successor, the League of Nations Association. On America First and Lindbergh's role in it, see Wayne S. Cole, *America First: The Battle against Intervention, 1940–1941* (Madison, Wis., 1953), and *Charles A. Lindbergh and the Battle against American Intervention in World War II* (New York, 1974).

59. On this Wilsonian revival, see Robert A. Divine, *Second Chance: The Triumph of Internationalism in America during World War II* (New York, 1967), esp. 167–173, 212–213.

revisions in its Charter (not Covenant) incorporated many of the Lodge reservations of 1919 and 1920 and avoided any commitments like the guarantee of political independence and territorial integrity in Article X.[60]

Bipartisanship flowered during World War II. This occurred in part because Roosevelt and, even more, Hull cultivated sympathetic Republicans on Capitol Hill and elsewhere. But this wartime efflorescence of bipartisanship owed much more to the Republicans' surrendering the initiative in foreign affairs and voluntarily assuming the role of loyal followers. The payoff to this bipartisanship came in July 1945, three months after Roosevelt's death. With only two dissenting votes, the Senate consented to the UN treaty. The two dissenters were William L. Langer of North Dakota, a Republican with a background in his state's agrarian radicalism, and Henrik Shipstead of Minnesota, a Farmer–Laborite and one of the isolationist progressives of the 1920s. They exemplified an irreducible minimum of isolationism. Another veteran isolationist and the only Irreconcilable from the League fight still in the Senate, Hiram Johnson, also would have voted against the UN treaty, but he lay dying in Bethesda Naval Hospital. This World War II–spawned brand of bipartisanship, based upon capitulation by the opposition, would continue with some glitches and strains for another two decades.[61]

The combination of events at the close of World War II – the sweeping victory over Hitler and the Japanese, the popular apotheosis of Wilson, and the easy approval of the UN – fostered the illusion of another

60. Inis L. Claude, Jr., *Swords into Ploughshares: The Problems and Progress of International Organization* (New York, rev. ed., 1962), 66. The name "United Nations" first arose as a term to refer to include China among the wartime Allies. On December 29, 1942, FDR changed the term "Associated Powers" to "United Nations" in a memorandum about military cooperation with China. Whether or not he knew that he was adopting Lodge's term is not clear. See Sherwood, *Roosevelt and Hopkins*, 458.

61. Ironically, Langer held the Senate seat occupied during the League fight by McCumber, and Shipstead had defeated Kellogg to come to the Senate in 1923. Two strong reservationists from the League fight, Capper of Kansas and Walsh of Massachusetts, voted for consent to the UN treaty, as did three Democrats who had been in the Senate during the League fight, Gerry of Rhode Island, Glass of Virginia, and McKellar of Tennessee. Two sons of men prominent in the League fight now serving in the Senate also voted for the treaty. One was Taft's son, Robert, who had been an isolationist before Pearl Harbor and remained a critic of bipartisanship. The other was La Follette's son, Robert Jr., who had remained true to his father's isolationism before Pearl Harbor. One Irreconcilable during the League fight, Norris of Nebraska, had switched over to support Roosevelt's pro-Allied policies after 1938, but he had been defeated in 1942 and died in 1944.

League fight with a happy ending. It was only an illusion. Roosevelt succeeded where Wilson had failed mainly because he was luckier in his circumstances. He enjoyed the benefit of hindsight, and he had an opposition that threw in the towel. FDR also avoided deep discussion, and he
drew freely upon two different grand designs for an active, involved
American role in world politics. One was Wilsonian internationalism,
and the other was his distant kinsman's great power nationalism. Of
those two designs, the Theodore Rooseveltian one held far greater sway
over FDR. He showed this both in his zest for the game of great-power
diplomacy during the war and in his conception of postwar order being
upheld by the "Four Policemen" of the victorious Allies – the United
States, the Soviet Union, Britain, and China. FDR leavened his latter-day
embrace of TR's original conception of a great power directorate with a
commitment to anticolonialism, but otherwise he tipped his hat toward
Wilsonianism only occasionally and strictly for public consumption.[62]

As William Leuchtenburg has remarked, the rest of America's twentieth-century presidents have operated "in the shadow of FDR." Not only
did FDR become the measure of success in the White House, but he also
set the course for his successors, particularly in foreign policy. Wilson's
wartime apotheosis proved short-lived. The scorn for him that had begun
with Keynes, Mencken, and others in the 1920s who drew upon "modernist" sensibilities persisted. Intellectuals still reviled him as the embodiment of Victorian prudery and hypocrisy. Central to that reviling were
distrust and eschewal of "idealism" – attitudes that suffered only momentary eclipse during the Wilson revival. During the heyday of that revival
and soon afterward such critics as Walter Lippmann and George Kennan
rejected Wilson's idealism in favor of "realism" based upon calculation of
national interests. Even over half a century later, "Wilsonian" still serves
as a shorthand epithet for naive pursuit of highfalutin principles or, more
pejoratively, "idealism" in world affairs. Likewise, FDR's model of
manipulation, not Wilson's model of education, has shaped the way that
every president since World War II has approached the task of enlisting
public support for his foreign policies. No great or profound debate over
America's role in the world has occurred since the League fight.[63]

62. On FDR's wartime diplomacy and postwar vision, see Dallek, *FDR and
American Foreign Policy*, esp. Part Four.
63. See Leuchtenburg, *In the Shadow of FDR: From Harry Truman to Bill
Clinton* (Ithaca, N.Y., rev. ed., 1994). On the FDR model, see also John
Milton Cooper, Jr., "Great Expectations and Shadowlands: American Presi-
dents and Their Reputations in the Twentieth Century," *Virginia Quarterly
Review*, LXXII (Summer 1996), 377–391.

The closest approach since 1920 to a great foreign policy debate came during the conflict over the Vietnam War. Better than any other event of the second half of the twentieth century, this war exposed the perils of the lack of broad public education and debate in foreign policy. That was true in the run-up to intervention, in the ways the war was waged, and in the methods of disengagement. The overarching framework of the Cold War – which was really a continuation of World War II models – made it difficult to conceive of any role in the world except a struggle against a powerful enemy that threatened both the nation's security and its deepest values – "the American way of life." Under this dispensation, manipulation and sometimes inflammation of opinion could seem indispensable. The stakes were too high, the dangers were too imminent, the issues were too clear to take time for discussion and reflection about proper roles in world politics.

Or at least so things seemed, although not to everyone. At the end of his long life, Walter Lippmann, who was perhaps the last surviving veteran of the League fight, questioned whether "realism" and great-power nationalism were sufficient guides for foreign policy. Likewise, with the end of the Cold War, questions arose about how the United States could and should pursue a role in the world that drew upon both its political principles and its national interests. Another long-term survivor of earlier events, George Kennan, recanted his previous rejection of Wilson and found new value in Wilson's synthesis of international idealism and measured engagement in world affairs. Among historians and writers about foreign policy, there has been a revival of interest in Wilson and his ideas. Perhaps, then, even the last whimpers and echoes of the League fight had not been in vain.[64]

---

64. On Lippmann's questioning, see Lippmann to Arthur M. Schlesinger, Jr., Sept. 25, 1967, in John M. Blum, ed., *Public Philosopher: Selected Letters of Walter Lippmann* (New York, 1985), 615–616, and Ronald Steel, *Walter Lippmann and the American Century* (Boston, 1980), 592–594. On Kennan's revaluation of Wilson, see Kennan quoted in Daniel Patrick Moynihan, *On the Law of Nations* (Cambridge, Mass., 1990), 151, and Kennan, "Comments on the Paper Entitled '*Kennan versus Wilson*' by Professor Thomas J. Knock," in John Milton Cooper, Jr., and Charles E. Neu, eds., *The Wilson Era: Essays in Honor of Arthur S. Link* (Arlington Heights, Ill., 1991), 327–330. Kennan made his remarks to Senator Moynihan's committee, which Moynihan quotes in his book, around the time that he read the essay by Knock on which he comments.

10

Breaking the Heart of the World

A wall in the Imperial War Museum in London used to display a trio of paintings that were done at the end of World War I. Dominating the display and taking up much of the wall was the expatriate American artist John Singer Sargent's massive "Gassed." It is an outdoor scene that shows British soldiers blinded by mustard gas lying on the ground or standing in a line waiting for medical treatment. On either side of that painting hung two much smaller paintings from the peace conference done by the British artist Sir William Orpen. Each of these paintings depicts an ornate interior scene in which the high-ceilinged room dwarfs the human subjects. One painting is of the Council of Ten in the Hall of Clocks at the Quai d'Orsay, the same room where Woodrow Wilson unveiled the Draft Covenant of the League of Nations. The "Big Four" – Wilson, Lloyd George, Clemenceau, and Orlando – sit in the center, and other prominent figures such as Colonel House and Arthur Balfour are close by. The second painting is of the signing of the peace treaty in the Hall of Mirrors at Versailles. It shows the back of the German delegate slumped in a chair with an aide stooping alongside, under the scrutiny of the virtually the same array of conference leaders.[1]

The message conveyed by these paintings was hard to miss. The disparity in size between Sargent's depiction of the horrors of the war and Orpen's portraits of the would-be peacemakers left little doubt about which enterprise was more potent and which was more likely to prevail. The paintings' message also raised and strongly suggested the answer to the great overriding question about the League fight: What did it all mean? Did the outcome of the League fight do what Wilson said it would do? Did the failure of the United States to join the League "break the heart of the world"? Or were the obstacles to peacemaking so great, were the odds stacked so heavily against the restoration of world order, that it was an exercise in futility? Did those obstacles and odds make it, in the words of Shakespeare's Macbeth, "full of sound and fury, signifying nothing"? These questions define the two poles in the argument that lasted for the first four or five decades after the League fight.

1. The Orpen paintings are reproduced in this volume, pp. 271–273.

Unlike most great historical arguments with lasting relevance, this one has led to broad agreement. Since the middle of the twentieth century, few historians or other analysts have doubted that the second set of answers to the question about what the League fight meant is the right one. The near consensus that has emerged around those answers usually employs a more polite phrasing than "sound and fury." It also includes a bow or two toward marginal differences that American membership in the League might have made. But, at bottom, few writers have challenged the notion that the course of American foreign policy and international relations would have been much the same regardless of the outcome of League fight.[2]

Ironically, Wilson's posthumous apotheosis in the 1940s and the sense of having belatedly heeded his warnings have contributed more than anything else to the prevalence of this view of the meaning of the League fight. As usually stated, the prevailing argument boils down to three interlocking propositions. First, Wilson was ahead of his time. Second, Americans were not ready after World War I to make the full-scale commitment to collective security and international enforcement that Wilson demanded. Third, it took World War II to drive home the lessons that Wilson had tried to teach. These propositions need to be examined both separately and together. Separately, each one reveals different assumptions about why the League fight turned out the way it did and what its lasting repercussions were. Together, they provide answers to the question of whether the outcome of the League fight did indeed break the heart of the world.

Each of these propositions is like the face of a three-sided pyramid. Each one takes its shape from the central question of what the League fight meant, yet at the same time each one presents its own distinctive aspect. The first proposition – that Wilson was ahead of his time – speaks directly to his personal role. That role has long since come to be judged as pivotal. Without Wilson, the League fight almost certainly would not have arisen in the first place. A less bold and visionary leader – one who was not ahead of his or her time – would not have attempted to do so much. Likewise, without Wilson, the League fight would almost certainly have ended in some kind of compromise. His unbending insistence upon joining an essentially political international organization with firm obligations under Article X ruled out any halfway house between that position and rejection of membership. In short, the

2. For a recent expression of this view, see Ninkovich, *Wilsonian Century: U.S. Foreign Policy since 1900* (Chicago, 1999), 76.

correctness of Winston Churchill's early pronouncement about "this man's mind and spirit" seems incontrovertible.

But there is more to the proposition that Wilson was ahead of his time, and this is where controversy persists. At issue are the value and meaning placed upon his being ahead of his time. In one way, any strong leader must have the capacity for anticipating events and forecasting opportunities and dangers. This capacity is what Shakespeare meant by recognizing the "tide in the affairs of men which, taken at the flood, leads on to fortune" and what Bismarck meant by hearing the distant hoofbeat of the horse of history. Conversely, leaders must retain an appreciation of how willing and able their followers are to accompany them in great leaps forward. Most interpreters of Wilson in the League fight have stressed the negative aspect of his being ahead of his time. "Too far ahead" is the prevailing judgment, and the controversy revolves around why this appears to have been the case.

Two broad schools of interpretation have arisen to account for this perceived fault. One school is cultural and psychological; the other is circumstantial and physiological. The key word for the first school is "messianic." That word, in its view, captures Wilson's religiously based affliction with delusions of divine revelation and chosenness. He believed, so this argument goes, that he and he alone had both the capacity and the message to save the world. This is a cultural view of Wilson for two reasons. First, it sees him as a product of his own culture – the Anglo-American Protestant middle-class world that flourished in the second half of the nineteenth century. Second, this view grows out of the culture of those who have held it, the twentieth century "modernist" dispensation that arose in Europe before World War I and took firm hold there and in America starting in the 1920s. As applied to Wilson, this view found earliest expression in Keynes's depiction of him in *The Economic Consequences of the Peace* and was soon followed by similar treatment at the hands of Mencken and other "debunkers" of that decade.

The psychological side of this school also flowered early. Starting with the American literary critic Edmund Wilson in the mid-1920s, various writers have attributed Woodrow Wilson's alleged messianism to psychological deformations. As viewed through their Freudian lenses, Wilson emerged from his childhood with a severely damaged ego and unresolved oedipal conflict. Further, those maladjustments bred in him messianic delusions and compulsions toward figuratively mortal conflicts with father figures. This happened first in his academic career and later in politics, where Lodge in the League fight played the part of the last of these adversaries. In fact, Sigmund Freud himself painted just such a portrait of Wilson, in collaboration with the defector from the

American delegation to the peace conference, William Bullitt. Their contribution did not come to light, however, until the 1960s. In the meantime, this essentially Freudian interpretation had already entered the mainstream of American political interpretation, in general through the writings of Harold Lasswell and in particular application to Wilson through the work of Alexander and Juliette George.[3]

This school of interpretation has several shortcomings. The main defect of the cultural interpretation is – to reverse Mark Twain's celebrated crack about Wagner's music ("It's not as bad as it sounds") – it is not as good as it sounds. This interpretation was present though not greatly developed in Keynes's depiction of Wilson in the *Economic Consequences of the Peace* and found fuller expression in the late 1930s in E. H. Carr's *The Twenty Years' Crisis*. More recently, others have stressed racial, gendered, and ethnocentric biases that supposedly crippled him in dealing with the more diverse and disorderly world of the twentieth century. Wilson, in these views, was the exponent of culture-bound, antiquated, hegemonic notions of order ill suited to the realities of the twentieth century.[4]

The main response to this interpretation is – at the risk of impoliteness – so what? Where else except from his own cultural background was Wilson going to get his ideas about world order? It is blatantly presentist and ahistorical to expect anything else. More important, do the origins and limitations of his ideas necessarily invalidate them? Perhaps so, but perhaps not. The alternatives to his vision of order, "pluralism" and "disorder," entailed ethnic and national conflicts, genocides, and world wars. Viewed in that light, Wilson's time-bound views do not look so bad, especially because his insistence upon flexible application of them and adjustment over time left room for growth and change.

Likewise, the stress on Wilson's psychological flaws has three major flaws of its own. First and most clearly, any reading of what Wilson said at almost any time during the League fight makes it difficult to sus-

---

3. See Sigmund Freud and William Bullitt, *Thomas Woodrow Wilson: A Psychological Study* (Boston, 1967), and Alexander George and Juliette George, *Woodrow Wilson and Colonel House: A Personality Study* (New York, 1956). Appropriately, the Georges were students of Lasswell's at the University of Chicago.
4. See E. H. Carr, *The Twenty Years' Crisis* (London, 1939), esp. 102–112. Two able recent presentations of this view of Wilson are in Lloyd E. Ambrosius, *Woodrow Wilson and the American Diplomatic Tradition: The Treaty Fight in Perspective* (New York, 1987), and David Steigerwald, *Wilsonian Idealism in America* (Ithaca, N.Y., 1994).

tain the allegation of messianism. For example, he never uttered the phrase "war to end all wars." That came from Lloyd George, as did "self-determination" as both a phrase and a general principle. Wilson, by contrast, made a limited and circumspect case for his program, as he had done earlier with the Fourteen Points and as he continued to do throughout the League fight. He stressed that the League marked only the indication of the direction and the beginning of the journey toward a more just and peaceful world. He called the League "a living thing," and he expected and wanted it to evolve over time. He repeatedly claimed that he would welcome a better alternative if his opponents could come up with one. To be sure, that was a rhetorical offer, but at a deeper level Wilson meant it sincerely. In laying stress on the obligation under Article X, he revealed that he cared far less about the particular provisions of the treaty and the Covenant and far more about ensuring his nation's commitment to an active role in preserving peace. The only way to reconcile such sophisticated, self-critical arguments with messianism is to impute fantastic deviousness and insincerity to Wilson. This requires a psychological stretch that only a few of his worst enemies in the League fight were willing to make.

The second flaw in this psychological interpretation is that it resembles the biblical parable of the mote and the beam. It detects and pounces on Wilson's supposed shortcomings while remaining oblivious to its own greater limitations. Its own "modernist" assumptions limit and disable this psychological interpretation. Those assumptions stress the supremacy of unconscious and emotional forces, combined with racial, class, and gendered biases. Thereby, Wilson and figures like him – who drew their assumptions from orthodox religious creeds and believed in disinterestedness and the power of reason – have become literally incomprehensible to this modernist sensibility. In fact, it was Wilson's grounding in that very culture of his time, especially his youthful immersion in some of the most sophisticated religious thinking of that day, that inoculated him against the messianic tendencies that did afflict others in the atmosphere of supercharged idealism and evangelism that suffused much of American political life from 1900 to 1920.[5]

5. Examples of Wilson's contemporaries who can fairly be accused of messianic tendencies include not only that paragon of evangelical and conservative Protestantism, Bryan, but also such apparent religious skeptics as La Follette and Roosevelt. On Wilson's religious upbringing and pre-presidential political thought, see John M. Mulder, *Woodrow Wilson: The Years of Preparation* (Princeton, N.J., 1978), and Niels Aage Thorsen, *The Political Thought of Woodrow Wilson, 1875–1910* (Princeton, N.J., 1988).

The final flaw in this psychological interpretation is its downgrading of physiological factors. The need to see the "real" Wilson in his refusal to compromise during the League fight requires adherents to this school to scoff at suggestions that other circumstances in 1919 and 1920 may also have played an important role. Leaving aside the question of whether anyone's behavior at a particular time can reveal the "real" person, this refusal to give consideration to the major stroke that Wilson suffered appears willful or even perverse. How could such a devastating illness *not* have affected his behavior? How could the worst crisis of presidential disability in American history *not* have affected the outcome of the League fight? These objections become particularly acute when they are set against the events of January and February 1920. Then, virtually every League advocate and every member of the president's inner circle, including Tumulty, Dr. Grayson, and Mrs. Wilson, tried to persuade him to compromise. To imagine that a healthier Wilson would not have tried to bring the League fight to a better, more pleasant, more constructive conclusion requires another psychological stretch. It demands an insistence upon personality-warped messianism that borders on the ludicrous.[6]

The other broad school of interpretation of Wilson's being ahead of his time – the one that stresses circumstantial factors – answers that last, health-based objection to the cultural-psychological interpretation. But this second school of interpretation did not originate as a response to the first one. Rather, it initially stressed not his health, but other circumstances, as part of the Wilsonian position during and right after the League fight. Wilson was ahead of his time, this view holds, chiefly because so many of his contemporaries in the nation's political leadership refused to keep up with him. This view shifts the onus for an unsatisfactory outcome to the League fight over to the Republicans,

6. To be fair to those who downgrade the influence of the stroke in particular, it should be noted that none other than Arthur Link once stated, "It is, therefore, possible, even probable, that Wilson would have acted as he did even had he not suffered his breakdown, for it was not in his nature to compromise away the principles in which he believed." Arthur S. Link, *Wilson the Diplomatist: A Look at His Major Foreign Policies* (Baltimore, 1957), 155. When he wrote those words, Link had evidently not completely discarded the critical, sometimes even harsh, view of Wilson that he expressed in the first volume of his biography, *Wilson: The Road to the White House* (Princeton, N.J., 1947), and in *Woodrow Wilson and the Progressive Era, 1910–1917* (New York, 1954). He later modified most of those criticisms of Wilson and reversed his evaluation of the effect of the stroke on Wilson's refusal to compromise in the League fight.

particularly Lodge and, to a lesser degree, Root. These men stand accused of putting personal dislike of Wilson and pursuit of partisan advantage ahead of the greater good of the nation and the world. By contrast, Taft and others in the LEP stand as paragons of enlightenment and bipartisan harmony.[7]

The flaws in such a circumstantial case are not hard to see. Like the opposing school, this one also imputes hidden and ignoble motives to the actors whom it dislikes. It gives little credence to the sincerity and rationality of Lodge or Root when they raised what they regarded as practical and principled objections to Wilson's program. It also fails to recognize that, given their inconstancy in supporting that program, Taft, Lowell, and the Thirty-One Republicans of October 1920 were not so different from their fellow partisans. Furthermore, to deplore partisanship and exalt bipartisanship, as this school does, is to misunderstand the essentially adversarial nature of the American two-party system. Like this country's legal system, the two-party system demands vigorous conflict between the two sides, whereas bipartisanship usually requires abdication by one of the adversaries. This system has built-in limitations. These limitations become particularly acute in harnessing diverse coalitions within one or the other of only two parties and in processes that require supermajorities in one or both houses of Congress, such as the two-thirds needed for approval of constitutional amendments or consent to treaties. But to blame the outcome of the League fight on partisanship is like blaming the weather. To blame Lodge, Root, and others for acting like partisans is to blame them for doing what they were supposed to do.

The most serious flaw in this circumstantial interpretation is that it does not square with the facts of the League fight. In one way, the more culpable partisans were the Democrats. Many of them bowed to Wilson's dictation against their better judgment. Republican senators were scoring partisan points when they leveled such charges at their colleagues across the aisle before the votes on the treaty, but they were largely correct. On the Republican side, what seems noteworthy is not how staunchly the non-Irreconcilable senators opposed Wilson but how far, by their lights, they went to meet him. After the Round Robin and the Foreign Relations Committee's effort to amend the treaty, the Lodge

7. The stress on the nefarious influence of partisanship is one of the few points on which I disagree with the otherwise estimable and incisive treatment of the League fight in Thomas A. Bailey, *Woodrow Wilson and the Great Betrayal* (New York, 1945).

reservations represented a considerable retreat for many of them. As for Lodge, despite his manifest negativism toward the League and hostile stance toward Wilson, he showed much greater flexibility than most interpreters have given him credit for or than he himself cared to remember. Both his dealings with Stephen Bonsal in November 1919 and even more his conduct in the bipartisan talks in January 1920 revealed a wavering in his total rejection of Article X and some openness toward compromise. Lodge did not come away from the League fight a beloved figure, but he was not at all the wily, underhanded villain of contemporary and later caricature.[8]

What this circumstantial view does stress correctly is that others besides Wilson contributed to his being ahead of his time. This view also correctly calls attention to the excessive heat of partisan conflict in 1919 and 1920. Much of that heat stemmed from the emotions that had been whipped up during the war and had not abated after the abrupt end of the fighting in November 1918. Simultaneously with the League fight, those emotions and other discontents were exploding into race riots and lynchings, massive labor strikes, and the Red Scare of 1919 and 1920. Much of the partisan heat of those years also stemmed from the uneasy position of both parties. Thanks largely to their own earlier internecine conflicts, the once-dominant Republicans had endured banishment from the White House and congressional majorities for the longest period in their party's history. Their victory in the 1918 elections raised their hopes, but they gained control of Congress only by narrow margins, and their best presidential prospect, Roosevelt, died in January 1919. By the same token, the Democrats approached the postwar situation with mingled hope and apprehension, and few of them had any stomach for questioning the leadership of their only president to win reelection since Andrew Jackson. In short, these political circumstances would have taxed the resources of

8. Although I am less sympathetic toward Lodge, I do agree in the main with the assessments of him in William Widenor's excellent *Henry Cabot Lodge and the Search for an American Foreign Policy* (Berkeley, Calif., 1980), especially when he says, "We may reasonably assume that Lodge would have swallowed the League had he seen therein the means of securing a Republican victory" (309) and Lodge "had to be less forthright in expressing his views, had to be all things to all men" (322).

9. Grover Cleveland had won a second term as president in 1892, but only after having been defeated in 1888. He remains the only president to have served nonconsecutive terms in the White House.

even the ablest, healthiest leader who tried to pull off a foreign policy coup like Wilson's.[9]

Clearly, the weightiest circumstance of all was that Wilson was not the healthiest of leaders during the League fight. Whether he was the ablest leader available is a different question and one that cannot be answered apart from considerations of his health. With the exception of Thomas A. Bailey, those who developed the circumstantial interpretation of Wilson's performance did not pay much attention to his health. Only with the work of Edwin Weinstein, a trained neurologist, in the 1970s did anyone confront head-on the question of what impact illness in general and the 1919 stroke in particular had on Wilson's behavior. The leading Wilson scholar and editor of *The Papers of Woodrow Wilson*, Arthur Link, soon joined Weinstein in promoting a more physiological interpretation of his life and career. Several of the published volumes of this series came to include extensive notes and appendixes both by Link and his fellow editors and by medical experts about the likely influences of his physical condition at different times but most significantly during the peace conference and the League fight.[10]

Such attention was long overdue in interpreting why Wilson behaved as he did in 1919 and 1920. Moreover, the emphasis on his health throughout his life broadened the inquiry beyond the narrow question of whether the stroke was responsible for his failure to compromise. Unfortunately, in their zeal to pursue their medical interpretation, Weinstein and Link gratuitously attacked the psychological school and provoked a series of furious rejoinders by the Georges, who enlisted a medical expert of their own. The ensuing melee showed neither side at its best, but when the dust had settled some agreement did emerge about the likely influences of Wilson's cardiovascular and neurological condition in 1919 and 1920. The most important area of agreement lay in examining his condition prior to as well as following the stroke. "Cerebrovascular accidents," especially ones such as Wilson suffered, have an antecedent pathology, which often includes "small strokes" and which, even without those, often affects the vic-

10. See Edwin Weinstein, "Woodrow Wilson's Neurological Illness," *Journal of American History*, LVII (Sept. 1970), 324–351, and *Woodrow Wilson: A Medical and Psychological Biography* (Princeton, N.J., 1981). Relevant notes and appendixes to the *Papers of Wilson* are cited above in the notes relating to Wilson's behavior in the summer of 1919 and the impact of the stroke.

tim's personality and behavior. That pathology, together with the impact of age and fatigue, underscores the conclusion that Wilson was operating at a level far below his best standard of performance in the White House.[11]

Unfortunately, this stress on his health and the controversy with the psychological school created the impression that Link and Weinstein were putting all their interpretative eggs in one basket and that they were seeking to exculpate Wilson. That was not the case. Weinstein, in particular, mixed his medical interpretations with a psychological portrait of Wilson that differed in tone but not much in content from earlier views. This was a surpassingly important point that went unnoticed in the scholarly fracas. Whatever the impact of Wilson's stroke, its antecedent pathology, and its subsequent effects, that impact could only have occurred in conjunction with his psychological makeup. Put another way, a different person would have reacted differently to an illness like this.

It might seem tempting to try to reconcile the psychological and physiological interpretations by claiming that the stroke and its surrounding neurological condition simply accentuated his personality deformations and exacerbated his messianic tendencies. But such an attempt at reconciliation would only make a bad interpretation worse. The one sound element in that blending of views is the neurologists' finding that such strokes often exaggerate their victims' personality traits. Clearly, this was true with Wilson. Combined with the ill effects of his isolation from outside contacts, his stroke appears to have destroyed previously exercised compensations for tendencies toward

11. On the controversy, see Edwin Weinstein, James William Anderson, and Arthur S. Link, "Woodrow Wilson's Political Personality: A Reappraisal," *Political Science Quarterly*, XCIII (Winter 1978–79), 585–598; George and George, "*Woodrow Wilson and Colonel House:* A Reply to Weinstein, Anderson, and Link," ibid., XCVI (Winter 1981–82), 641–643; George and George, "Issues in Wilson Scholarship: References to Early Strokes in the Papers of Woodrow Wilson," *Journal of American History*, LXX (Mar. 1984), 845–853; Arthur S. Link, David W. Hirst, John Wells Davidson, and John E. Little, "Communication," ibid., 945–955; Alexander George, Michael T. Marmor, and Juliette George, "Communication," ibid., 955–956. For an appraisal of Weinstein's book and the first two items in this battle of the articles, see Dorothy Ross, "Woodrow Wilson and the Case for Psychohistory," ibid., LXIX (Dec. 1982), 659–668, and Lloyd E. Ambrosius, "Woodrow Wilson's Health and the Treaty Fight," *International History Review*, IX (Feb. 1987), 73–84.

proposition about his being ahead of his time. This second proposition shifts attention from leaders to followers. Of these three propositions, this one has stirred the least controversy. Few interpreters have doubted that, indeed, the American people in 1919 and 1920 were unwilling to take up the burden that Wilson wanted to thrust upon them.

Perhaps the chief reason this proposition has gone relatively unchallenged is that it originated with Wilson himself. His bitter outburst to Grayson after the defeat of the treaty in March 1920 about people not supporting his program and having to break the heart of the world was more than a passing fancy. After he left the White House, Wilson's bitterness subsided, but his thinking remained the same. During the last year of his life, according to the recollection of his brother-in-law, Stockton Axson, Wilson said that it would have been "a mere personal victory" if he had prevailed in the League fight. Likewise, his daughter Margaret recalled that around the same time he said to her, "I think it was best after all that the United States did not join the League of Nations." Reiterating his eschewal of "only a personal victory," he explained to her, "Now, when the American people join the League it will be because they are convinced it is the right thing to do, and then will be the *only right* time for them to do it." Finally, she recalled, he added with a smile, "Perhaps God knew better than I did after all."[13]

It is hard to dispute the assessment of the person who should have known best. Still, the question needs to be asked: Is this proposition correct? Were people during and immediately following the League fight unwilling to follow Wilson? One answer is that not everyone was unwilling. A substantial minority of indeterminate size stood strongly behind him and his conception of obligations under the League. Where the majority stood is more difficult to assess. Public opinion polling based upon interviews and sampling did not begin until a decade and a half after the League fight. In the meantime, the best available indicators remain the *Literary Digest*'s regular canvasses of newspaper editors and those occasional straw polls conducted among such groups as college students. Partisan ties consistently swayed the editors. More than two-thirds of Republicans favored the Lodge reservations, and over three-quarters of the Democrats supported Wilson's call for unreserved League membership. The college students showed a strong plurality for unreserved membership and a substantial minority for the Lodge reser-

13. Ray Stannard Baker interview with Axson, Aug. 28, 1931, R. S. Baker Papers, Box 99; Margaret Wilson recollection quoted in Edith Giddings Reid, *Woodrow Wilson: The Caricature, the Myth and the Man* (New York, 1934), 236.

vations. None of these surveys registered much outright opposition to the League. The chief pro-Irreconcilable newspapers were the ones in William Randolph Hearst's ostensibly Democratic chain and the *Boston Transcript*. No major Republican organ, not even the New York *Tribune* or the *Chicago Tribune*, advocated complete rejection, and some, such as the St. Louis *Globe-Democrat* and *Los Angeles Times*, echoed the views of Taft and the LEP.

Those indicators showed several things about public opinion in 1919 and 1920. Clearly, views on the League and Article X covered a spectrum that ranged from diehard Wilsonianism to staunch isolationism. Not surprisingly, the majority occupied a broad middle ground that stretched from critical support of Wilson's position through several degrees of reservationism toward obligations under the Covenant, especially Article X. Most strikingly, isolationism does not appear to have attracted a big following. That limited appeal may seem surprising in view of the isolationists' invocation of such sacred political texts as Washington's Farewell Address and the Monroe Doctrine. It may also seem surprising because for several generations foreign policy leaders and analysts have assumed that the American public will naturally lapse into isolationism without careful manipulation and frequent exhortations against enemies and dangers. Incomplete and unscientific as it is, the evidence from the League fight does not indicate widespread or natural tendencies toward isolationism among the mass of Americans.

Another indicator of public opinion toward League membership and its obligations comes from the Senate, in both voting and speaking. Six-year terms and election from states rather than apportioned districts do insulate senators to some extent from public opinion, and the men who dealt with the peace treaty in 1919 and 1920 repeatedly touted their independence of judgment and their fidelity to conscience. Still, despite those factors, alignments in the Senate accorded nicely with the other indicators of public opinion. In their votes on the treaty itself, 80 percent favored League membership in one form or another, whereas only 20 percent rejected it altogether. In their speeches, both mild reservationist Republicans and others who were not so mild affirmed their conviction that America had an obligation to maintain the peace. Interestingly, too, not every Irreconcilable was an isolationist. Knox rejected League membership and criticized other parts of the treaty because he found them unwarranted and unjust, but he repeatedly offered as an alternative his "Knox doctrine," which was a security pledge to Britain, France, and possibly other Allies. Outside the Senate, such anti-League activists as George Harvey also favored security commitments to Britain and France.

Additional support for the proposition that Americans were not ready to heed Wilson's call comes from the 1920 election. Harding's "tidal wave" victory convinced many participants then and interpreters later that this was a mandate against League membership – a "referendum for isolation." In fact, the election became such a mandate and referendum only because some leaders, especially Harding and Lodge, chose to read it that way. The evidence does not accord with such a reading. Both sides trimmed their sails on the League issue. Despite their promise to Wilson, the Democratic nominees effectively endorsed the Lodge reservations and abandoned Article X. Harding perfected the technique of talking out of both sides of his mouth on a hot foreign policy issue – the technique that Franklin Roosevelt would adopt in similar circumstances twenty years later. For all his quasi-Irreconcilable talk during the campaign, Harding also tipped his hat toward the popular desire to promote international peace when he stressed an "association of nations." He could legitimately have read his triumph at the polls as a mandate for League membership with the Lodge reservations instead of reading that victory as permission to stay out.

In sum, the indicators from both the people and their political representatives in 1919 and 1920 show mixed and unclear attitudes on the critical issue of an obligation to maintain world order. Wilson's program unquestionably enjoyed only minority support, as did the isolationists' position. Majority opinion does not yield to a clearcut reading either for or against international commitments. That is most likely because the largest numbers of American and their leaders did not hold sharply defined views. Subsequently, in the mid-1930s, the views of a large majority did shift strongly over to isolationism. But what is most remarkable about that later isolationist upsurge is how fleeting it was. Warily as he trod, Franklin Roosevelt had a much easier time after 1938 in pursuing pro-Allied and quasi-interventionist policies than anyone could have predicted. Even taking into account the changed circumstances at the end of the 1930s – especially the greatly heightened sense of clear and present danger after the fall of France in 1940 – the brevity of the isolationists' heyday and the ease with which FDR and others finally combated them was remarkable. This later experience also raises questions about how unready Americans really were to assume commitments like the ones that Wilson had urged. Perhaps Wilson reconciled himself too soon and too cheerfully to seeing the hand of God at work in his defeat.

Consideration of where the public stood during the League fight leads logically to the third proposition about its meaning – that it took World War II to get Americans to heed the Wilsonian message. This third proposition requires acceptance of the preceding one, and it strikes closest to the central question of what the League fight really meant. Agreeing with these two propositions requires believing that the League fight meant comparatively little. This belief assumes further that American membership in the League and greater participation in world politics would not have done much to forestall the breakdown of international order in the 1930s. A different outcome to the League fight, so this answer holds, would not have prevented World War II. Failure to follow Wilson did not "break the heart of the world." Here is the heart of the matter. The basic question remains: Is this so?

The strongest argument in support of this third proposition is the observation that things did happen that way. World War II evidently did induce near universal and lasting support for Wilsonian commitments to maintain international order and peace. Two questions immediately arise about this proposition. First, could anything else have induced such support? Second, what were the nature and consequences of the support that World War II did induce?

The first question requires contemplation of alternatives. The critical consideration here is not so much League membership or Article X in itself but, as Wilson insisted, the American public's frame of mind toward a commitment to uphold world order. The critical time for creating the proper frame of mind was during and just after the League fight. Three possible alternative outcomes and aftermaths might have made a major difference.

One alternative is that Wilson might have won the League fight more or less on his own terms. The essential element for this outcome was a healthy Wilson. This Wilson might have made more speaking tours to educate the public further about what his program entailed. He might have bargained successfully with the Republican senators to achieve a mutually face-saving compromise about the obligation under Article X. He might have run for and won a third term, or he might have picked a successor, such as Newton Baker, who was firmly committed to pursuing his foreign policies. Those circumstances could have gotten American diplomacy in the 1920s and the League of Nations off to a much different start than they did get, and they could have helped to foster an effective structure of collective security. This alternative raises two objections. It requires a huge stretch of the imagination, and it downplays the influences besides Wilson's health that kept him from winning the League fight.

The second alternative also requires an imaginative stretch, but it envisions almost no difference in the outcome of the League fight itself. This alternative is that Theodore Roosevelt might have been elected president in 1920. The essential element here was a living Roosevelt. This Roosevelt might have resumed and expanded his earlier pursuit of great-power nationalism. Whether or not he chose to take the country into the League, he might have made strong commitments, formally or informally, toward maintaining world order. Granted that the international scene had changed greatly since Roosevelt's imperialist heyday, he might still have relished brandishing his big stick more openly as the world's greatest single power instead of as one of several great powers. Those circumstances could also have gotten American diplomacy in the 1920s off to a different start, and they could likewise have helped to foster an effective collective security system. Still, this alternative may also require too much of an imaginative stretch.

The last alternative does not require much of a stretch at all, and it also contemplates almost no difference in the League fight itself. This alternative is that General Leonard Wood might have won the Republican nomination and been elected president in 1920. Wood was the strongest contender going into the convention, and only his principled but unwise refusal to make deals kept him from winning the nomination. On the League, he stood firmly committed to membership with reservations. More generally, especially through his invocation of the Roosevelt mantle, Wood promised to be a strong, activist president. As a career military man who had been kept out of the world war, Wood might have paid a lot more attention to security concerns and might have used leadership of the League as a way to compensate for the wartime supreme command that he had craved. Inasmuch as Hughes was almost fated to be the first Republican secretary of state in the 1920s, he might have accomplished even more than he did under the constraint that Harding imposed on him. These circumstances could also have set a far more activist course for American diplomacy in that decade and could have contributed to greater concern for collective security.

Still, even this last, most plausible alternative can only remain speculative. Like the other alternatives, it remains open to the objection that things did not happen that way, or, as Mencken once jibed at democracy as a theory of government, "all the known facts lie against it." Those known facts include the performance of the Allied powers in the League and elsewhere in the 1920s. Even with matters left to themselves and unhampered by reservations to Article X, the British and French failed to erect a strong collective security system. Between their limited vision and their unreconstructed pursuit of short-term advantages at each others' and their defeated foes' expense, the European powers did little to build any world order, much less a new world order. It is hard to imagine that a greater American presence could have compensated completely for the weakness and wariness that characterized postwar European diplomacy. Likewise, the simultaneous impact in the 1930s of the depression and the breakdown of international order cannot be imagined away. Disillusionment with World War I had set in earlier in Europe than in America, but people in both places succumbed to the sentiments that spawned appeasement and isolationism. In the face of such known facts, these alternatives lose much of their plausibility.

Or do they? Do all the known facts lie against these alternatives? Other known facts are that appeasement faded rapidly after 1938 and that the Allies, minus Italy and Japan, did go to war for a second time in 1939. Other known facts are that FDR did successfully challenge isolationism, however deviously and imperfectly, and that America did intervene in this second world war. Whether things might have gone better with a strong collective security system present from the early 1920s onward is worth asking again. The real flaw in "the peace that failed" after World War I did not lie in its specific provisions or its general slant but, rather, in the subsequent lack of will to maintain it. Such will could have ensured firm responses to aggression by Japan in 1931, Italy in 1935, and Germany in 1936 and 1938. Such will could also have encompassed more generous attitudes toward the treaty's financial terms and willingness to consider revisions in territorial boundaries under conditions that did not involve threat and coercion. An essential element in instilling a firm but constructive will to maintain the peace settlement of 1919 could have been the commitment that Wilson and others wanted to instill in the American people. Perhaps these alternatives were not so implausible after all.

The other question that needs to be asked about this third proposition about the meaning of the League fight is what it amounts to. How did World War II convert Americans to Wilsonian commitments? What were the consequences of the way in which this conversion took place? World War II did shock Americans into an appreciation of the interdependence of the world and the stake that they had in the maintenance of international order. But, despite the popular apotheosis of Wilson, this was not really a conversion to his ideas and approaches. FDR's obfuscation of the differences between great-power nationalist and Wilsonian visions of international commitment, coupled with the collapse of nearly all opposition, isolationist or otherwise, smothered popular reflection on America's proper role in the world. For the great majority, this was a foxhole-style conversion. Americans came to believe that they needed to maintain commitments in the world because they were fighting a powerful and implacable enemy. This was true both during World War II against the Nazis and later in the Cold War against the Communists. This war-borne dispensation would form the only basis on which the United States has thus far been able to sustain a great-power role in the world. Small wonder, then, that American foreign policy seemed adrift after the end of the Cold War.[14]

Except for the basic fact of international commitment, this was not the way that Wilson wanted things to turn out. The critical Wilsonian element that has been missing since World War II has been education of the public through informed discussion and debate. In the 1950s and 1960s, realists such as George Kennan and Walter Lippmann would decry sloppiness, moralism, emotional outbursts, and lack of proportion in American foreign policy, and they would blame those shortcomings in part on "Wilsonian" idealism. Those realists put their finger on significant, often dangerous, flaws, but they were completely off-base in their ascription of blame. Wilson had desired above all to make the public constantly aware of and reflective about foreign policy in order to avoid exactly the flaws that those realists deplored. He wanted Americans to think about their role in the world in many different circumstances and over the long haul, not to be in a state of perpetual fear and trigger-happiness about real or imagined enemies. He wanted his country to gain experience in world leadership over time in noncrisis situations, not to lurch along with a permanent wartime mentality. An America guided by those Wilsonian lights after 1945 might have gone in many of the same directions as it did anyway, but it would have gone with a different spirit and attitudes.

Why the World War II–style conversion to international commitment took a non-Wilsonian form is a critical question. The responsibility, or blame, lies in several quarters. Wilson himself sometimes betrayed his own convictions about educating the public. During World War I, he allowed popular hatreds and repressions – "the beast of patriotism," as Frank Ninkovich has called such things – to be stirred up. On his speaking tour he occasionally appealed to revenge toward Germany and anti-Red sentiments. Wilson also neglected to do necessary preparatory work in sharing his ideas with the public and with other political leaders. It is interesting to speculate what might have happened if Wilson had taken the steps in the summer of 1918 that he did a year later. What if he had

14. Here I am disagreeing with Frank Ninkovich's contention in his brilliantly argued book, *The Wilsonian Century,* in which he maintains that Americans during and after World War II became Wilsonians without Wilson. See, esp., 144, 223–226. What I argue in this paragraph and the next is that this is a contradiction in terms, that the critical Wilsonian elements of education of the public and enlightened pursuit of an international role were missing.

held meetings with individual senators or small groups of them? What if he had made a speaking tour? In fact, he did contemplate such a tour then but let the opportunity pass because of the press of war-related business. Also, Allied victory remained in doubt until the end of the summer of 1918, and Wilson could not tell how much leverage he would have over the peace settlement until he went to Europe at the end of the year. Still, this modern Prometheus would have done well to prepare his fellow mortals better for the gift that he wanted to bring them.[15]

There was another element of defiance of fate in this attempt to educate the public. As Robert Kraig has shown, Wilson represented a latter-day flowering of the golden age of American oratory. That oratory, which drew upon the classical models of Demosthenes and Cicero, had seen its brightest hours during the decades between 1810 and 1880, particularly before and during the Civil War. After 1896, domestic reform issues had helped to spawn a revival of that kind of oratory by such figures as Bryan, Roosevelt, La Follette, Beveridge, Borah, and Hiram Johnson, as well as Wilson. Like Wilson, those men redirected their oratorical firepower to foreign policy during World War I. The prominence of most of those other men in the League fight ensured that Wilson's major opponents were using the same oratorical approach as he was, aimed at educating the public. That was what made the League fight such a great public debate.[16]

But the sun was setting on this type of politics. Two-party competition had always featured manipulation and heated emotional appeals. Starting in the 1880s, marketing and advertising techniques began to infect politics. The use of those techniques culminated in the Republicans' carefully crafted campaign behind McKinley in 1896, which Harding's 1920 effort copied and refined. At the same time, a different oratorical approach, borrowed from Protestant evangelism, was coming into fashion. Both Bryan and TR, who coined the term "bully pulpit" for the presidency, drew upon this evangelical model, as they blended emotional and symbolic appeals with their educational expositions. Even Wilson was not immune to touches of evangelism, as he showed in some of his speeches on the tour in 1919. Also, as his encounter with the microphone and the amplifier in San Diego demonstrated, still more changes were in the offing. First radio, then newsreels, and finally television would vastly enlarge politicians' ability to reach the public. But that gain would come at the expense of shorter exposures with less

15. Ibid., 224.
16. Robert A. Kraig, "Woodrow Wilson and the Lost World of the Oratorical Statesman," Ph.D. diss., University of Wisconsin–Madison, 1999.

opportunity for education and more for manipulation. Heavy as his responsibility was, that greatest student of the League fight, Franklin Roosevelt, did not act alone in setting a pattern that precluded further great debates like this one.[17]

The lack of such debate would serve America and the world badly not only during the years immediately following World War I but also for the rest of the twentieth century. Lack of such debate formed one of the major sources of the foreign policy flaws that Kennan, Lippmann, and other like-minded critics deplored during the Cold War. It may be unseemly to carp at success in a good cause, such as World War II or the Cold War, but too often in those conflicts the United States did behave like a clumsy, ignorant giant that inflicted excessive anguish and harm on others and itself. What went wrong in the outcome of the League fight was that a chance had been lost – a chance to ground this nation's foreign policy more soundly and gain precious experience earlier, before having to take up the burdens of singular world leadership.

Both that missed opportunity and the possible alternatives should call into question the prevailing answer to the question of what the League fight meant. Was it really just an interesting and heated conflict but at bottom an exercise in "sound and fury"? Or did it mean something different? Was it truly a great missed opportunity? Did its outcome "break the heart of the world" after all?

One last consideration needs to be noted in answering the overriding question of what the League meant. This is the matter of what was at stake.

The stakes that Wilson strove to win in the League fight were nothing less than to prevent a recurrence of the carnage that had raged from 1914 through 1918. Even without seeing with his own eyes, he grasped how truly death-dealing and calamitous modern industrial-technological warfare had become. He also recognized that death and wounding and destruction did not comprise the sum of this kind of war's evil effects. He saw that order had broken down not only among nations but also within them, releasing terrible passions that might feed into lurid ideologies.

Wilson does not need to be exalted to the status of a secular prophet in order to appreciate his vision. He understood Communism only

17. The end product of these developments would be the universally condemned "sound bite" of the 1990s. In fact, this kind of shortening of messages and the public attention span antedated the major intrusion of nonprint media. During World War I, the Committee on Public Information had distributed prepackaged messages for speakers, which lasted four minutes. The volunteer speakers, who numbered in the thousands, were called "Four Minute Men" and "Four Minute Women."

dimly, although he recoiled from the Bolsheviks' revolutionary violence. He did not foresee Fascism and Nazism, although he feared the nationalist passions that he saw unleashed in Europe and elsewhere. He did not foresee nuclear weapons, although he did envision how conventional warfare could become even more terribly destructive, as it did in World War II, Korea, and Vietnam. Wilson did not need to be a prophet. It was enough for him to be a sensitive man who had glanced into the abyss that yawned ahead if people and nations did not mend their ways. He never claimed to be a messiah or to have surefire solutions. As he said repeatedly on his speaking tour for the League, he was offering only some insurance against a repetition of what had just ravaged the world. But, he insisted, any insurance, even limited, partial insurance, was better than none. This was the same man who had cried out to Frank Cobb of the New York *World* in March 1917, as he agonized over whether to intervene in the war, "If there is any alternative, for God's sake let's take it."[18]

Did the outcome of the League fight "break the heart of the world"? Of course it did. It is not necessary to claim that a different outcome would have prevented the rise of Hitler, the Holocaust, World War II, or the dropping of the atomic bomb. Just to list those events and to remember other things that have occurred between the end of World War I and the last decade of the twentieth century is to gain an appreciation of what the stakes in the League fight really were. Just to recall those events is to see that Wilson was absolutely right to grasp at any insurance against such things happening. Decent and reasonable people disagreed with him. They did not see the stakes the way Wilson did, and they believed that what he was asking was excessive and dangerous. Wilson failed to be as flexible and persuasive as he should have been, and his illness turned him into the biggest obstacle to a more-constructive outcome. But two facts remain incontrovertible. For all their decency and intelligence, Wilson's opponents were wrong. For all his flaws and missteps, Wilson was right. He should have won the League fight. His defeat did break the heart of the world.

18. J. L. Heaton, ed., *Cobb of the "World": A Leader in Liberalism* (New York, 1924), 270. Some controversy later arose about when Wilson talked with Cobb and what he said, but even the leading skeptic about the interview conceded that Wilson's reluctance to enter the war and concerns about the effects of American intervention on international order were accurately depicted. See John Milton Cooper, Jr., *The Vanity of Power: American Isolationism and the First World War* (Westport, Conn., 1969), 211 n. 43.

A Note on Sources

Historians like to display their research. They usually have two motives for doing this. One is a laudable wish to smooth the path for others who labor in the same vineyard. The other is a less commendable compulsion to prove how diligent, industrious, and thorough they have been. By displaying those virtues, many historians hope to forestall criticism and disagreement with how they have rendered and interpreted their subject.

I can offer no exception to the second motive, as I show by the list of manuscript collections below. But I would also like to do something to help those who work in this field. In particular, I want to make clear that the most valuable research that has gone into this book can be done by anyone who enjoys two advantages. One is access to a well-stocked research library or a library that can readily borrow material. The other is a few weeks to spend at the Library of Congress and at one or two other repositories in the Northeast and one in the Midwest.

Any respectable research library will have two of the most overweeningly important sources for studying this subject. One is Arthur Link's monumental, comprehensive, unfailingly informative edition of *The Papers of Woodrow Wilson*; the other is the *Congressional Record*. Such a research library should also have a microfilm edition of the *New York Times* – which is also available on-line. Some research libraries will also have microfilms of the New York *World* and the *Washington Post*. These can also be readily borrowed, as can microfilms of other newspapers. These sources go a long way toward supplying the essential story of the League fight and its principal actors.

Manuscript collections available on microfilm can supply much of the rest of the story. These include the papers of such major figures as William Howard Taft, Robert Lansing, Charles Evans Hughes, and Henry Stimson. The papers of Woodrow Wilson are also available on microfilm and need to be consulted occasionally, but the Link edition of the *Papers of Woodrow Wilson* renders the necessity for such consultations few and far between.

There are two indispensable research trips. These are to repositories in Washington and Boston. In Washington, the Library of Congress houses an array of papers of actors who figured large on all sides in the League fight. The value of the collections is usually self-evident from the names of the figures involved, such as Elihu Root, Philander C. Knox, and William E. Borah. Two of the most valuable collections represent less-prominent figures. One is the papers of Chandler P. Anderson, which includes his diary and illuminates the inner workings of the Republican opposition to the League. The other is the papers of Albert J. Beveridge, which is the best single source on the Irreconcilables and other diehard foes of the League and their relations with mainstream Republicans.

In Boston, the Massachusetts Historical Society houses the papers of Henry Cabot Lodge. These make up by far the most revealing collection of anyone in the Senate or the Republican party. A short distance away in Cambridge, the Harvard University Archives hold the papers of A. Lawrence Lowell. This collection ranks a close second behind the papers of William Howard Taft in illuminating the affairs and thinking of pro-League Republicans and the League to Enforce Peace. Next door at Harvard, in the Houghton Library, there is a small but valuable collection of papers of the League to Enforce Peace.

Two other helpful, though not strictly indispensable, research trips are to New York and Chicago. In New York, the Columbia University Library holds the papers of Nicholas Murray Butler, which also illuminate much about Republican reactions to the League, and Herbert Parsons, a passionately pro-League Republican. In Chicago, the library of the University of Chicago houses the papers of Salmon Levinson, the proponent of the outlawry of war and a fellow traveler with the Irreconcilables. Next to the Beveridge Papers, this is the most revealing collection about the anti-League forces.

Secondary sources have likewise been important to me in this study. Let me just mention a few works that have proven truly invaluable. Thomas A. Bailey's two volumes, *Woodrow Wilson and the Lost Peace* (1944) and *Woodrow Wilson and the Great Betrayal* (1945), are over fifty years old, but their interpretations stand the test of time. Again and again, I marveled at how often Bailey "got it right." Similarly, both the information and intepretative stance in Ruhl J. Bartlett, *The League of Enforce Peace* (1944), remain sound and informative.

Among more recent works, several have struck me as truly outstanding. On groups of senators, Ralph A. Stone's, *The Irreconcilables: The Fight against the League of Nations* (1970), Herbert F. Margulies, *The Mild Reservationists and the League of Nations Controversy in the Senate* (1989), and Robert Johnson's, *The Peace Progressives and American*

Foreign Relations (1995) are based upon exhaustive research and convey insightful interpretations. For command of the subject and richness of thought and analysis on any individual figure in the League fight, nothing surpasses William C. Widenor, *Henry Cabot Lodge and the Search for an American Foreign Policy* (1980).

On aspects of foreign policy and the League fight centering on Wilson, two excellent works are Lloyd E. Ambrosius, *Woodrow Wilson and American Diplomatic Tradition: The Treaty Fight in Perspective* (1987), and Thomas J. Knock, *To End All Wars: Woodrow Wilson and the Quest for a New World Order* (1992). Also, the extensive editorial notes and medical commentary in the relevant volumes of the *Papers of Woodrow Wilson* contain important and incisive interpretations of his role at several critical junctures in the League Fight.

Helpful guidance to primary and secondary materials can be found in Karen Dawley Paul, ed., *Guide to Research Collections of Former United States Senators, 1789–1995* (1995); Jo Anne McCormick Quatannes, *Senators of the United States: A Historical Bibliography* (1995); and John M. Mulder, Ernest M. White, and Ethel S. White, eds., *Woodrow Wilson: A Bibliography* (1997).

I. Manuscript Collections

This list takes its cue from the *Michelin Guide*. **Bold-face** entries are meant to be the equivalent of the *Michelin*'s three and two stars, "worth a journey" and "worth a detour." I have made these recommendations sparingly in cases where there is only one collection in the repository.

My recommendations are more generous where there are several collections of value in the repository, especially in the Library of Congress. Some good collections, such as the Ray Stannard Baker and Edward M. House papers, have not been boldfaced because most of their important material is reproduced in Arthur S. Link, ed., *The Papers of Woodrow Wilson*. The Wilson Papers at the Library of Congress are boldfaced because there are occasional items of value that are not in the Link edition and because they are available on microfilm. An * indicates availability on microfilm.

Chandler P. Anderson Papers, Library of Congress
Hamilton Fish Armstrong Papers, Seeley Mudd Library, Princeton University
Thomas A. Bailey Papers, Stanford University Library
Newton D. Baker Papers, Library of Congress
Ray Stannard Baker Papers, Library of Congress
Roger Baldwin Papers, Seeley Mudd Library, Princeton University
John H. Bankhead Papers, Alabama Department of Archives and History

Albert J. Beveridge Papers, Library of Congress
Tasker H. Bliss Papers, Library of Congress
Stephen Bonsal Papers, Library of Congress
William E. Borah Papers, Library of Congress
Charles H. Brough Papers, University of Arkansas Library
William Jennings Bryan Papers, Library of Congress
Albert S. Burleson Papers, Library of Congress
Nicholas Murray Butler Papers, Columbia University Library
Arthur Capper Papers, Kansas Historical Society
Arthur Capper Papers, Governor's Office Files, Kansas Historical Society
Raymond Clapper Papers, Library of Congress
Bainbridge Colby Papers, Library of Congress
George Creel Papers, Library of Congress
Homer S. Cummings Papers, Alderman Library, University of Virginia
Frances Denton Papers, Yale University Library
Walter E. Edge Papers, Seeley Mudd Library, Princeton University
Albert B. Fall Papers, Huntington Library
Albert B. Fall Papers, New Mexico State University Library
Albert B. Fall Papers, University of New Mexico Library
David R. Francis Papers, Missouri Historical Society
Joseph S. Frelinghuysen Papers, Rutgers University Library
Moreton Frewen Papers, Library of Congress
Harry Garfield Papers, Library of Congress
Gay Family Papers, Louisiana State University Library
Carter Glass Papers, Alderman Library, University of Virginia
Edwin F. Goltra Papers, Missouri Historical Society
Thomas P. Gore Papers, Carl Albert Center, University of Oklahoma
Hanna-McCormick Family Papers, Library of Congress
Warren G. Harding Papers, Ohio Historical Society*
Will H. Hays Papers, Indiana State Library
Gilbert M. Hitchcock Papers, Library of Congress
Gilbert M. Hitchcock Papers, Nebraska Historical Society
Hamilton Holt Papers, Rollins College Archives
Herbert Hoover Papers, Hoover Presidential Library
Irwin H. Hoover Papers, Library of Congress
Edward M. House Diary and Papers, Yale University Library
Charles Evans Hughes Papers, Library of Congress*
Cordell Hull Papers, Library of Congress
Harold L. Ickes Papers, Library of Congress
Hiram Johnson Papers, Bancroft Library, University of California–Berkeley
Wesley M. Jones Papers, University of Washington Library
Frank B. Kellogg Papers, Minnesota Historical Society
John B. Kendrick Papers, American Heritage Center, University of
    Wyoming
Philander C. Knox Papers, Library of Congress
Robert M. La Follette Papers, Library of Congress
Robert Lansing Papers, Library of Congress*

League to Enforce Peace Papers, Houghton Library, Harvard University
Irvine L. Lenroot Papers, Library of Congress
Salmon O. Levinson Papers, University of Chicago Library
Isaac H. Lionberger Papers, Missouri Historical Society
Walter Lippmann Papers, Yale University Library
Henry Cabot Lodge Papers, Massachusetts Historical Society
Breckinridge Long Papers, Library of Congress
A. Lawrence Lowell Papers, Harvard University Archives
William Gibbs McAdoo Papers, Library of Congress
Kenneth D. McKellar Papers, Shelby County Archives, Memphis, Tennessee
Charles L. McNary Papers, Library of Congress
Ogden L. Mills Papers, Library of Congress
John Bassett Moore Papers, Library of Congress
Victor Murdock Papers, Library of Congress
William Starr Myers Papers, Seeley Mudd Library, Princeton University
Knute Nelson Papers, Minnesota Historical Society
George W. Norris Papers, Library of Congress
George W. Norris Papers, Nebraska Historical Society
John Callan O'Laughlin Papers, Library of Congress
Robert L. Owen Papers, Carl Albert Center, University of Oklahoma
Herbert Parsons Papers, Columbia University Library
George Wharton Pepper Papers, University of Pennsylvania Archives
Amos Pinchot Papers, Library of Congress
Gifford Pinchot Papers, Library of Congress
Key Pittman Papers, Library of Congress
Frank L. Polk Papers, Yale University Library
Atlee Pomerene Papers, Kent State University Library
Joseph E. Ransdell Papers, Louisiana State University Library
James A. Reed Papers, Missouri Historical Society
James A. Reed Papers, University of Missouri–Kansas City Library
Edgar Eugene Robinson Papers, Stanford University Library
Joseph T. Robinson Papers, University of Arkansas Library
Theodore Roosevelt Papers, Library of Congress*
Elihu Root Papers, Library of Congress
Chester Rowell Papers, Bancroft Library, University of California–Berkeley
Charles Seymour Papers, Yale University Library
Lawrence Y. Sherman Papers, Illinois Historical Society
William H. Short Papers, Rollins College Archives
Furnifold M. Simmons Papers, Duke University Library
Hoke Smith Papers, University of Georgia Library
Henry L. Stimson Diary and Papers, Yale University Library*
Oscar Straus Papers, Library of Congress
Robert A. Taft Papers, Library of Congress
William Howard Taft Papers, Library of Congress*
Charles S. Thomas Papers, Colorado Historical Society
Park Trammell Papers, University of Florida Library
Joseph P. Tumulty Papers, Library of Congress

Oscar W. Underwood Papers, Alabama Department of Archives and History
Henry van Dyke Papers, Firestone Library, Princeton University
James W. Wadsworth Papers, Library of Congress
David I. Walsh Papers, Holy Cross University Library, Worcester,
    Massachusetts
Thomas J. Walsh Papers, Library of Congress
Francis Warren Papers, American Heritage Center, University of Wyoming
Henry White Papers, Columbia University Library
Henry White Papers, Library of Congress
William Allen White Papers, Library of Congress
John Sharp Williams Papers, Library of Congress
Woodrow Wilson Papers, Library of Congress*
Leonard Wood Papers, Library of Congress
Robert W. Woolley Papers, Library of Congress
John D. Works Papers, Stanford University Library

II. Published Letters and Diaries

As above, **boldface** indicates "worth a journey." *The Intimate Papers of Colonel House* do not receive this designation because they have been superseded in nearly all cases by the Link edition of the *Papers of Woodrow Wilson.*

Bacon, Robert, and James Brown Scott, eds., *Men and Policies: Addresses by Elihu Root.* Cambridge, Mass.: Harvard University Press, 1925.
Bonsal, Stephen, *Unfinished Business.* Garden City, N.Y.: Doubleday, Doran and Co., 1944.
Burke, Robert E., ed., *The Diary Letters of Hiram Johnson.* Seven volumes. New York: Garland Publishing, Inc., 1983
Heath, Harvard, ed., *Into the World: The Diary of Reed Smoot.* Salt Lake City: Signature Books, 1997
Latane, John H., ed., *Development of the League of Nations Idea: Documents and Correspondence of Theodore Marburg.* Two volumes. New York: Macmillian Co., 1932.
Link, Arthur S., ed., *The Papers of Woodrow Wilson.* Sixty-nine volumes. Princeton, N. J.: Princeton University Press, 1966–1994.
Marburg, Theodore, and Horace Flack, eds., *Taft Papers on the League of Nations.* New York: Macmillan Co., 1920.
Seymour, Charles, ed., *The Intimate Papers of Colonel House.* Four volumes. Boston: Houghton, Mifflin Co., 1926–1928.
Sparks, George F., ed., *A Many-Colored Toga: The Diary of Henry Fountain Ashurst.* Tucson: University of Arizona Press, 1962.

Index

Illustrations are indicated in **bold**.